Second Witness

Analytical and Contextual Commentary on the Book of Mormon

Volume 3

Enos–Mosiah

Second Witness

Analytical and Contextual Commentary on the Book of Mormon

Volume 3

Enos–Mosiah

Brant A. Gardner

GREG KOFFORD BOOKS
SALT LAKE CITY, 2007

In the interests of internal stylistic consistency and clarity for the reader, I have standardized abbreviations of books of scriptures in parenthetical citations, including in quotations, lowercased words that are in all capitals in the King James Version (e.g., "Lord"), and removed the italics that appear in the King James Version passages. I have also routinely added periods to "A.D./B.C." in quotations. To distinguish among the various persons with the same name in the Book of Mormon, their order of appearance will be indicated by a subscript number. Thus Mosiah_1 is the grandfather of Mosiah_2.

Published in the USA

Jacket design by John Hamer based on the "Anthon Charactors Transcript" (upper panel) and glyphs from Izapa Stela 1 (lower panel). The archaeological site of Izapa was occupied during Book of Mormon times, but is of no known connection to the Book of Mormon.

2011 5 4 3

Greg Kofford Books, Inc.
P.O. Box 1362
Draper, UT 84020

www.koffordbooks.com

Library of Congress Cataloging-in-Publication Data

Gardner, Brant.
Second witness : analytical and contextual commentary on the Book of Mormon / Brant A. Gardner.
p. cm.
Includes bibliographical references and index.
ISBN 978-1-58958-047-3 (6 volume set) -- ISBN 978-1-58958-041-1 (v. 1) -- ISBN 978-1-58958-042-8 (v. 2) -- ISBN 978-1-58958-043-5 (v. 3) -- ISBN 978-1-58958-044-2 (v. 4) -- ISBN 978-1-58958-045-9 (v. 5) -- ISBN 978-1-58958-046-6 (v. 6) 1. Book of Mormon--Criticism, interpretation, etc. I. Title.
BX8627.G36 2007
289.3'22--dc22

2007029312

Contents

Sorenson's correlation of Book of Mormon geography with the Mesomaerican map, reproduced here from Volume 1, p. 333, for ease of reference.[1]

---

[1]John L. Sorenson, *An Ancient American Setting for the Book of Mormon* (Salt Lake City: Deseret Book/Provo, Utah: Foundation for Ancient Research and Mormon Studies, 1985), 37. Used by permission.

Enos: Commentary

Enos 1

Enos 1:1

> 1 Behold, it came to pass that I, Enos, knowing my father that he was a just man—for he taught me in his language, and also in the nurture and admonition of the Lord—and blessed be the name of my God for it—

Our initial information about Enos comes from Jacob' s declaration that Enos is his son and heir, designated to receive, preserve, and write on the plates according to Nephi's desires (Jacob 7:27). Neither this declaration nor Enos's short personal introduction tells us much about him. We do not know when he was born, how old he was when he received the plates, nor when Jacob died.

Chronology: The next specific date is just prior to Enos's death where he notes that 179 years have passed since Lehi's departure from Jerusalem (Enos 1:25). In other words, from the time of Nephi's death until Enos's death (presuming it came soon after his closing message), only two writers on the small plates encompassed 124 years between them. This span of time requires advanced ages for both Jacob and Enos, perhaps eighty-seven years apiece. That is a venerable age for the ancient world, but Nephi lived into his seventies; these ages would not be impossible, though remarkable. (Of course, moving Jacob's probable date of birth to a later year shortens this span; see commentary accompanying 1 Nephi 18:7.)

It seems, given the chronological problems, that Enos may have been fairly young at his father's death. He heard and accepted Jacob's instructions about writing on the plates, but these instructions did not acquire urgency until later in Enos's life—hence the transformational experience he describes in this chapter.

Culture: It is curious that Enos explains that his father taught him in the language of his father *and* in the ways of the Lord. We can readily understand the second idea, for we also strive to teach our children the ways of the Lord. What is less clear is why Jacob would have to teach Enos his "language." Nephi stated that he has been "taught somewhat in all the learning of my father. . . . The language of my father . . . consists of the learning of the Jews and the language of the Egyptians" (1 Ne. 1:1–2). While this seems to be a parallel statement, the difference is that Enos specifically mentions being taught the language where Nephi writes in the "language of my father."

I suggest that Enos is literally speaking about learning Jacob's language. Obviously, he is not talking simply about the unconscious way in which all toddlers absorb grammar and vocabulary from their parents. One possible reason for this statement is to indicate that Jacob taught him the language of the Old World (Hebrew) because the Nephites are now speaking a different language. This interpretation is appropriate, even likely, given the Nephites' linguistic adaptation to a new location. But a second and more likely meaning is that Jacob taught Enos the writing system (Egyptian) that he would need for his record on the plates.[1] Regardless of the spoken language, the plates require a specific script and vocabulary, modeled after the brass plates.

Variant: For this variant it is best to quote Skousen directly: "The typesetter for the 1911 LDS edition accidentally set 'he was just a man' [instead of "he was a just man"], one of the more amusing typos in the history of the text—and obviously wrong. This error in the 1911 LDS edition was corrected in the subsequent LDS edition (1920)."[2]

Enos 1:2

> 2 And I will tell you of the wrestle which I had before God, before I received a remission of my sins.

Enos jumps into his story after the briefest of introductions. Unlike Jacob's writings, which focused on his mission to his people, Enos tells an intensely personal story, a return to the narrative that characterized much of 1 Nephi.

Culture: The book of Enos is an important departure from the books of Nephi and Jacob. But what is significant is what is missing: any reference to an official position among the people. There are no recorded public ceremonies or recognition of status. Nephi was made king, and Jacob was declared a priest. Enos is a prophet, but it seems to be much more similar to the role of a prophet in ancient Israel rather than the personal/institutional role filled by a modern Mormon prophet. Enos is *a* prophet (v. 19), but there were many prophets (v. 22).

Although I have argued that Jacob was reinstated to a position of formal—or at least recognized—authority as a result of his encounter with Sherem, this position apparently was not passed on to Enos. He does not appear to hold the position of chief priest, perform any formal priestly functions, mentions no public function at all (except for possibly participating in the Nephite military campaigns, v. 24), and apparently continues to be marginalized, as Jacob was during part of his ministry. This pattern seems the more likely for Enos because it becomes painfully obvious in subsequent small plate writers—Enos's descendants.

What can we reconstruct of Nephite society at this point? Certainly the chief ruler would have been a king and likely there was a chief priest, as the size of the community would warrant a religious specialist. However, the religious position was

---

[1]Mosiah 1:4 notes that Egyptian is required for reading the brass plates: "For it were not possible that our father, Lehi, could have remembered all these things, to have taught them to his children, except it were for the help of these plates; for he having been taught in the language of the Egyptians therefore he could read these engravings, and teach them to his children."

It is probable that Nephi writes in "Egyptian," which Mormon describes as "reformed Egyptian" nearly a thousand years later (Morm. 9:32). As a record keeper, Enos would have needed to know this language of the records.

[2]Royal Skousen, *Analysis of Textual Variants of the Book of Mormon*, THE CRITICAL TEXT OF THE BOOK OF MORMON (Provo, Utah: The Foundation for Ancient Research and Mormon Studies, 2005), Vol. 4, Part 2, 1072.

not hereditary through Jacob. If it were hereditary, it probably reverted to the descendants of Nephi, or possibly to a newly appointed priestly line.

Enos 1:3

> 3 Behold, I went to hunt beasts in the forests; and the words which I had often heard my father speak concerning eternal life, and the joy of the saints, sunk deep into my heart.

The fact that Enos is hunting alone suggests that he was considered experienced enough to hunt without a companion. We may consider him of an age to be reflective but cannot guess an age. Almost certainly, a youth in this society would have been viewed as adult much earlier than his modern counterpart. I hypothesize that Enos was no younger than early to mid-teens, but he could also have been older. Nothing in the narrative gives us a clue. What *is* certain is that Jacob taught him and that Enos is remembering his teachings in the past, not the present. Jacob's words have worked into Enos's heart over time, a situation that many modern parents can understand and perhaps take comfort in.

Enos tells us explicitly that he has learned about Yahweh from his father. For some reason, at this particular time those teachings acquire urgency. Enos feels the need to have a personal experience of the things his father has taught him.

Enos 1:4

> 4 And my soul hungered; and I kneeled down before my Maker, and I cried unto him in mighty prayer and supplication for mine own soul; and all the day long did I cry unto him; yea, and when the night came I did still raise my voice high that it reached the heavens.

The key to Enos's experience is the hunger in his soul. Enos does not have his transformational experience because he thought it might be nice. His "wrestle" before Yahweh (v. 2) was a real effort, not a tossed-off prayer. This desire from the core of his spiritual being must fight through the limitations of his natural man to his spiritual self. His hunger of the spirit was greater than his hunger for food, for he indicates that he prays throughout a day and a night.

Enos does not say what topics engaged him in prayer, but we may assume from his subsequent statements that it was a time of self-revelation, a realization of his standing before Yahweh. It certainly became a time of sincere repentance for the sins of which he became aware.

Enos 1:5–6

> 5 And there came a voice unto me, saying: Enos, thy sins are forgiven thee, and thou shalt be blessed.
> 6 And I, Enos, knew that God could not lie; wherefore, my guilt was swept away.

Because Yahweh's voice declared that Enos's sins had been forgiven, we can assume that at least some of his long prayer was spent in recognizing and repenting of those sins. But that is not all. Many are forgiven of their sins without also hearing the voice of the Lord. Therefore, Enos was not only repenting but being called as a prophet. It is to bestow this high calling upon him that Yahweh spoke directly to him. Indeed, a prophetic calling, by definition, demands direct communication.

It is also interesting that Enos does not *feel* his sins swept away until he recognizes that he *believes* Yahweh's declaration. This is an important aspect of repentance, for while the actual removal of sin happens through the power of God (and the miracle of the Atonement), we nevertheless are not truly forgiven until we are able to forgive ourselves. Enos's sins were already gone from Yahweh's accounting; but until they were gone from his own, they remained with him as painful remembrances and perhaps even spiritual shame. Enos was able to let them go, however, because of Yahweh's declaration, and his understanding that Yahweh would not lie.

Enos 1:7–8

> 7 And I said: Lord, how is it done?
> 8 And he said unto me: Because of thy faith in Christ, whom thou hast never before heard nor seen. And many years pass away before he shall manifest himself in the flesh; wherefore, go to, thy faith hath made thee whole.

Enos could feel the weight of sin lifted from him. This was not an ephemeral experience, but one with tremendous power. The removal of sin was dramatic and conclusive. Enos did not wonder if perhaps he had been forgiven. Enos could *feel* that the burden of sin was gone, a change so dramatic that he immediately asked how it could have happened.

The answer is that the atonement comes through the Messiah. This is the crowning message of Nephi and Jacob, and now Enos has his foundational prophetic experience grounded in that very knowledge. Enos will also be a prophet who declares the Atoning Messiah for he has had personal experience with salvation through the coming Messiah. This is the key of the Nephite religion. It is not simply Messianic. Rather, it focuses on the Messiah's atoning mission over his eschatological mission—the most important distinction made about Nephite Messianic beliefs. This small community of displaced Jews was not unique in their belief in the Messiah, but they were unique in retaining the earlier Israelite understanding of the atoning mission of the Messiah. (See 1 Nephi, Part 1: Context, Chapter 1, "The Historical Setting of 1 Nephi.")

Enos 1:9

> 9 Now, it came to pass that when I had heard these words I began to feel a desire for the welfare of my brethren, the Nephites; wherefore, I did pour out my whole soul unto God for them.

The Nephites, after hearing Sherem's confession and repenting, immediately wanted to share that message. So does Enos. It is this turning of interest from self to others that may mark the prophetic calling. All prophets would have had experiences similar to Enos's in experiencing tangibly the forgiveness of sins. What makes them prophets is their ability to turn outward for the benefit of others. A prophet is no prophet if he keeps his knowledge to himself. The calling absolutely requires that one care deeply for others.

Enos 1:10–11

> 10 And while I was thus struggling in the spirit, behold, the voice of the Lord came into my mind again, saying: I will visit thy brethren according to their diligence in keeping my commandments. I have given unto them this land, and it is a holy land; and I curse it not save it be for the cause of iniquity; wherefore, I will visit thy brethren according as I have said; and their transgressions will I bring down with sorrow upon their own heads.
> 11 And after I, Enos, had heard these words, my faith began to be unshaken in the Lord; and I prayed unto him with many long strugglings for my brethren, the Lamanites.

Verses 10 and 11 provide an interesting contrast. The events in verse 10 cause those in verse 11. That is, Enos's faith which begins "to be unshaken" comes as a result of the "voice of the Lord" in Enos's mind. Presented this simply, there is no question but that hearing Yahweh's voice might increase one's faith. In this case, however, it appears that it really was *hearing* the voice rather than the *message* of the voice that had this effect.

Yahweh speaks to Enos, responding to his query about the Nephites. We might expect the Lord to give him some promise about the future of his people or about their current needs. Instead, Yahweh responds with the promise of the land, not the people.

The land's promise is that it is chosen, a holy place. The people benefit from it to the degree of their righteousness. This was the covenant with Lehi (2 Ne. 1:9), and it becomes Yahweh's covenant with Enos. The only promise for the Nephites is contingent upon their righteousness. Indeed, Yahweh's final promise is that he will visit the Nephites' wickedness upon their own heads. When Yahweh says that he "will visit thy brethren according as I have said," he appears to be making a conceptual division between Enos and his brethren. I suspect that this is due to the continued separation of the believers in the true Nephite religion from those who are in power and who appear to be espousing an apostate religion (likely similar to the one Sherem preached). Enos seems to have no trouble understanding this fairly bleak picture of the future (v. 13).

Enos 1:12–13

> 12 And it came to pass that after I had prayed and labored with all diligence, the Lord said unto me: I will grant unto thee according to thy desires, because of thy faith.
> 13 And now behold, this was the desire which I desired of him—that if it should so be, that my people, the Nephites, should fall into transgression, and by any means be destroyed, and the Lamanites should not be destroyed, that the Lord God would preserve a record of my people, the Nephites; even if it so

> be by the power of his holy arm, that it might be brought forth at some future day unto the Lamanites, that, perhaps, they might be brought unto salvation—

Enos's increase in faith moves him to continue in supplication until he receives the desired promise.

Culture: What Enos desires is that, should the Nephites be destroyed, a record will be preserved to bring the gospel to the Lamanites. We need to understand this great subtext in Enos's plea.

When Enos first begins to pray, he prays for the Nephites. This is normal, for they are his own people, the society in which he lives. However, his supplications for his people results in only a minimal assurance: Yahweh will visit the Nephites' acts upon their heads. In other words, Yahweh will reward or punish them as they deserve through their actions. Clearly, Yahweh is cautious about making commitments where the future history of the Nephites is concerned.

Another interesting point is that Enos so fully accepts this response and, in his greater supplication, focuses not on the Nephites but on the preservation of their records should they be destroyed. He rather pessimistically accepts the future failure of Nephite society to follow Yahweh and thus to be preserved. Enos has certainly greatly abbreviated his day-long conversation with Yahweh and has probably received the same prophetic vision of the future that Nephi had seen (and which Jacob surely understood whether he had seen or read it). Enos may well understand that there will be a great destruction of the Nephites within a few generations, for such is recorded in the book of Omni (Omni 1:5–7).

From a sociological perspective, what allowed Enos to so easily accept such a gloomy future for his people? Perhaps it was because he had witnessed the Nephite apostasy that was apparently only temporarily reversed with the Sherem incident. Perhaps even after Jacob's reinstatement in a social position commensurate with his status as Yahweh's prophet, Enos saw trends that made him accept that the struggle of the Nephites to remain faithful was not over. Indeed, the later evidence in Omni suggests a rather widespread continuation of some apostate practices that eventually led to their destruction.

History: While it is only an inference, it appears that Enos had been taught sufficiently to keep a record on the plates but had not necessarily read them. Enos's understanding of the future history of the Nephites appears to come exclusively through this epiphanal experience, not through Nephi's record. When Enos begins to pray, he is pondering on Jacob's words, not on the written text.

Another inference, but probably a significant one, is that Enos pondered his father's *words* rather than *text*. In many early literate societies, the text itself becomes sacred. Dutch biblical scholar Karel van der Toorn has suggested that the Torah came to stand in the place of icons in other religions. That is, the veneration that other religions might have given their iconic representations of deity were refocused in Israel on the Torah as representation of deity.[3]

Notice how the tradition accompanying the ceremonial Torah scroll highlights its special and sacred nature:

> Sefer Torah (in Hebrew: "Book [of] Torah") (plural: sifrei Torah) is a specially hand-written copy of the Torah or Pentateuch, which is the holiest book within Judaism and venerated by Jews. It must meet extremely strict standards of production. In its completed state it is stored in the holiest spot within a synagogue called the Aron ("Ark") usually built along the wall that most closely faces Jerusalem, the direction faced by Jews when engaged in prayer. . . .
>
> According to Jewish law, a sefer Torah is hand-written on *gevil* [parchment traditionally prepared] by using a quill (or other writing utensil) dipped in ink. . . . Written entirely in Hebrew, a sefer Torah contains 304,805 letters, all of which must be duplicated precisely by a trained *sofer* ("scribe"), an effort which may take as long as approximately one and a half years. Any error during inscription renders the sefer Torah pasul ("invalid"). According to the Talmud (the oral law of the Jewish People), all scrolls must also be written on *gevil* parchment that is treated with salt, flour and *m'afatsim* (a residual of wasp enzyme and tree bark) in order to be valid. Scrolls not processed in this way are considered invalid.
>
> During cantillation, following the often dense text is aided by a *yad* ("hand"), a metal or wooden hand-shaped pointer that protects the scrolls by avoiding unnecessary contact of the skin with the parchment.[4]

Later in the Book of Mormon, the brass plates are transferred with Laban's sword and the Liahona as ceremonial objects denoting sacred rulership (Mosiah 1:16). Certainly at that point, the text itself is considered sacred. Joyce Marcus described this principle:

> Among those societies in which access to books was restricted to a special class, writing was considered sacred, and often said to have been a "gift from the gods." In the case of ancient Egypt, for example, the baboon-headed deity Thoth was considered the inventor of writing. In ancient China, either Fu His (the inventor of commerce) or Ts'ang Chieh (the four-eyed dragon) was considered the inventor of writing. Writing was thus *given* to man by supernatural or divine beings.[5]

It is therefore reasonable to assume that the record was at least sacred in purpose, if not in its physical form, for Enos. As such, if Enos had received his knowledge from the text, it seems likely that he would have noted the sacred origin of his information. Indeed, both Nephi and Jacob cited text (including whole passages) to support their preaching. Enos does not. Is it because he has not yet read the small plates?

---

[3]Karel van der Toorn, "The Iconic Book: Analogies between the Babylonian Cult of Images and the Veneration of the Torah," quoted in William G. Dever, *Did God Have a Wife?: Archaeology and Folk Religion in Ancient Israel* (Grand Rapids, Mich.: William B. Eerdmans Publishing, 2005), 49.

[4]"Sefer Torah," *Wikipedia: The Free Encyclopedia*, http://en.wikipedia.org/wiki/Torah_scroll (accessed August 2005).

[5]Joyce Marcus, *Mesoamerican Writing Systems: Propaganda, Myth, and History in Four Ancient Civilizations* (Princeton, N.J.: Princeton University Press, 1992), 28.

Almost certainly, after Enos's experience, his sensitivity to things of the Spirit would increase, increasing his desire to know the contents of the sacred records he is preserving. What Enos has unquestionably learned from his father is the importance of the plates. Thus, when he does pray for a great blessing from the Lord, it concerns these records.

Enos 1:14

> 14 For at the present our strugglings were vain in restoring them to the true faith. And they swore in their wrath that, if it were possible, they would destroy our records and us, and also all the traditions of our fathers.

From a Nephite perspective, the two objects of Lamanite hatred are the "traditions of our fathers" and "our records." In later restatements of this conflict, only the traditions remain. For all intents and purposes, however, traditions and records are the same issue.

What are the "traditions of our fathers"? It is possible, but not likely, that these traditions are the inherited religious beliefs—their Jewish traditions out of Jerusalem. Laman and Lemuel may not have been very religious, but their rebellion was not against God (in their eyes) as much as it was against the oppression of their younger brother who had usurped the right of leadership for the family.

Rather, it is the tradition that Nephites are morally superior that galled the Lamanites and would continue to be a source of conflict. The very existence of the Nephites was a reminder, according to their traditions, that they had precedence over the Lamanites. The lesson of later Mesoamerica is instructive here. When the young city of Tenochtitlan began to flex its military and political muscle, it made moves to claim a Toltec heritage. This tradition established the city as legitimate.[6]

In the earlier times of the Lamanites, we may also assume that they also made appeals to legitimacy. Whereas the Lamanites probably mixed with other communities (as did the Nephites), their claim to inherent rights of leadership was diminished by the Nephites' countering claims, handed down through the traditions established by Lehi's blessings and Nephi's acts of leadership within the family. In addition, the records of the Nephites established and probably sacralized those claims.

In later Mesoamerican society, written maps, or *lienzos*, established the land rights of certain groups.[7] Mesoamericans held documents in esteem as legal, moral, and religious proof of claims upon land or leadership, as evidenced by how rapidly the Nahuas (Aztecs) adopted the written documents required by the Spanish courts.[8] Thus, when the Lamanites threatened the records of the Nephites, they were threatening the legitimacy of the Nephite claims to rulership.

---

[6]Susan D. Gillespie, *The Aztec Kings* (Tucson: University of Arizona Press, 1989), 25.

[7]Marcus, *Mesoamerican Writing Systems*, 153–89.

[8]Arthur J. O. Anderson, Frances Berdan, and James Lockhart, *Beyond the Codices: The Nahua View of Colonial Mexico* (Berkeley: University of California Press, 1976), 44–219, presents translations of a number of documents created for Spanish legal purposes. The authors note that this is a small sampling (p. 4).

Enos 1:15

> 15 Wherefore, I knowing that the Lord God was able to preserve our records, I cried unto him continually, for he had said unto me: Whatsoever thing ye shall ask in faith, believing that ye shall receive in the name of Christ, ye shall receive it.

Enos's desire to preserve the records now has multiple contexts. He is preserving them for a beneficial purpose, but the urgency of the preservation itself is based on explicit Lamanite threats against them.

Enos 1:16–17

> 16 And I had faith, and I did cry unto God that he would preserve the records; and he covenanted with me that he would bring them forth unto the Lamanites in his own due time.
> 17 And I, Enos, knew it would be according to the covenant which he had made; wherefore my soul did rest.

Yahweh covenants to preserve the plates. Yahweh had shown Nephi that his words would be preserved and would play a major role in the redemption of Israel. Enos apparently did not know this prophecy—hence his urgency to assure the records' preservation. Therefore, he requires it of Yahweh. The difference in Enos's case is the covenant. Where Nephi was shown the future, with Enos Yahweh makes his intention to preserve official.

Enos 1:18

> 18 And the Lord said unto me: Thy fathers have also required of me this thing; and it shall be done unto them according to their faith; for their faith was like unto thine.

Could this wording contain a hint that Enos should become more familiar with the records now in his charge? Enos's request is not new, and Yahweh lets him know that his fathers (at least Jacob and Nephi) have made the same request. Yahweh nevertheless renews the promise of preservation.

Vocabulary: Royal Skousen notes that the phrase "thy fathers have also *required* . . . " probably uses the word *require* in the more obsolete meaning of *request*.[9]

Enos 1:19

> 19 And now it came to pass that I, Enos, went about among the people of Nephi, prophesying of things to come, and testifying of the things which I had heard and seen.

Enos's account is not sufficiently specific to identify exactly what he preached. He prophesied of "things to come" but does not say what those "things" were. When we

---

[9]Skousen, *Analysis of Textual Variants*, 2:1083, provides examples from the Oxford English Dictionary where *require* has the meaning of *request*.

see a similar phrase "that which is to come" in King Benjamin's speech,[10] it is in the context of the coming mission of the Atoning Messiah. As the quintessential message of the Nephite gospel, it is very possible that this is the meaning in Enos as well.

Enos 1:20–21

> 20 And I bear record that the people of Nephi did seek diligently to restore the Lamanites unto the true faith in God. But our labors were vain; their hatred was fixed, and they were led by their evil nature that they became wild, and ferocious, and a blood-thirsty people, full of idolatry and filthiness; feeding upon beasts of prey; dwelling in tents, and wandering about in the wilderness with a short skin girdle about their loins and their heads shaven; and their skill was in the bow, and in the cimeter, and the ax. And many of them did eat nothing save it was raw meat; and they were continually seeking to destroy us.
> 21 And it came to pass that the people of Nephi did till the land, and raise all manner of grain, and of fruit, and flocks of herds, and flocks of all manner of cattle of every kind, and goats, and wild goats, and also many horses.

Culture: These two verses are packed with information, and it is tempting to treat them separately. However, doing so would obscure the dramatic contrast between Lamanite and Nephite. In addition to the distinction in name, their lifestyles are described as having diverged tremendously, with the Lamanites being depicted as more nomadic as hunter-gatherers, while the agrarian Nephites assume both a reasonable permanence of location and a more complex social organization.

Above and beyond these specifics are the values differences between Lamanite and Nephite. While hunting and gathering is a viable lifestyle (particularly in food-rich Mesoamerica) it is diametrically opposed in all facets to the more structured and localized life of the Nephites. It is normal to assume that our own customs are good and that different customs are unusual (at best) or terrible (typically). Thus, it is quite understandable that Enos characterized the Lamanites in the worst possible terms. When combined with their obvious enmity, discussing Lamanites in pejorative terms is only to be expected, and we should read those comments with great caution.

The Lamanite cultural catalog most likely began as an accurate description of the differences in the two communities. The pejorative descriptions persist throughout the Book of Mormon,[11] however, even when it becomes obvious that they no longer accurately describe the Lamanites. This discrepancy between description and reality occurs because the Nephites are viewing the world in a way similar to the people of the ancient Near East. Malina and Rohrbaugh describe that worldview:

---

[10]Mosiah 3:1, 3:18, 4:11, 5:3, 18:2. The same meaning appears in Alma 5:48, 7:6, 30:13, 58:40; Hel. 8:22–23.

[11]While the entire catalog is not repeated, elements are used in various descriptions of the Lamanites: Mosiah 9:2, 9:12, 10:12, Alma 17:14, 47:36 (apostates are more "Lamanite" than Lamanites), Hel. 3:16. As the Book of Mormon progresses, a new stereotype is added. A characteristic of non-Nephite behavior becomes characterized by the paired set of "murder" and "plunder": Mosiah 2:3, 10:7, Alma 23:3, Hel. 6:23, 7:21, 11:25, 3 Ne. 4:5, Ether 8:16.

> The dyadic, collectivist orientation of Mediterranean societies results in the typical Mediterranean habit of stereotyping. People were not known by their psychologically unique personalities or unique character traits, but rather by general social categories such as place of origin, residence, family, gender, age, and the qualities of other groups to which they might belong. One's identity was always the stereotyped identity of the group. This meant that social information considered important was encoded in labels such groups acquired. Thus, "Cretans are always liars, vicious brutes, lazy gluttons" (Titus 1:1). "Judeans have no dealings with Samaritans" (John 4:9). Jesus was a disreputable "Samaritan" (8:48) or "Galilean" (7:52). "Can anything good come out of Nazareth?" (John 1:46).[12]

The longer the time from the original landing, the less accurate the stereotype becomes as a statement of historical conditions, if it ever was completely accurate historically. The catalogue of cultural stereotyping should be read not only for the specific description, but for the contrast it creates between Lamanite and Nephite.

"They became wild, and ferocious": This information is more a value judgment than a cultural description. It is intended to contrast the uncivilized Lamanite with the civilized Nephite. Lamanite and Nephite are not just enemies, they are opposites. The Nephites are not just religiously superior, they are culturally superior.

The evidence for Lamanite "wildness" and "ferocity" is that they "fed . . . upon beasts of prey. . . . And many of them did eat nothing save it was raw meat." The terminology "beasts of prey" suggests that the Lamanites were hunting animals rather than keeping them. One does not refer to domesticated animals as "beasts of prey." Enos is therefore describing people who hunt wild animals for a living rather than tending domesticated or semi-domesticated flocks.

Enos's apparent condemnation of a hunting lifestyle is an interesting contrast to his own experience where his great epiphany occurred while hunting. This is not a condemnation of hunting but a description of a lifestyle that is opposite of the Nephites. The Lamanite beasts of prey contrast with the Nephite "flocks of herds, and flocks of all manner of cattle of every kind, and goats, and wild goats." Enos is therefore contrasting the way in which the two peoples obtain their meat. The Lamanites are "wild and ferocious" because they hunt and eat animals that are also "wild and ferocious" (beasts of prey). Lamanites are wild. Nephites are civilized. It is questionable whether the Lamanites actually ate raw meat, but it is certainly significant in the wild/cultured opposition that Enos is creating. Of course wild men would eat raw meat like wild animals.

"dwelling in tents, and wandering about in the wilderness": These details describe a nomadic people. This contrasts to the Nephites who live in buildings and cities. It is the next logical contrast after their food. Uncivilized Lamanites eat raw food and dwell in tents. Civilized Nephites have domesticated animals (and cooked food) and live in buildings in cities.

This description of nomadic Lamanites contrasts directly with some of the later descriptions of Lamanites which identifies cities and, even more importantly, a

---

[12]Bruce J. Malina and Richard L. Rohrbaugh, *Social-Science Commentary on the Gospel of John* (Minneapolis, Minn.: Fortress Press, 1998), 149–50.

large army. The hunter-gatherer lifestyle is suited to small groups, not large ones. The greater food needs represented by cities and armies require that the community be engaged in careful tending of the food, such as farming or the apparently purposeful "flocks of herds" Enos speaks about. We may be confident that those armies are supported by towns and farms, and not by the hunter-gatherer lifestyle.

"full of idolatry": Enos gives no examples, but certainly we can understand that his idea of idolatry would resemble that in Jewish theology. Unless this statement is an exaggeration, the "Lamanites" would have begun worshipping idols as divine and altering their religious practices to accommodate them. However, because Jacob uses the term "Lamanite" as a collective for all non-Nephites (Jacob 1:14), it is also very likely that the idol-worshipping Lamanites are those native populations who have become Lamanites by designation rather than the direct descendants of Jacob's brother.

"filthiness": The Book of Mormon uses the term "filthiness" (in all forms) to describe spiritual distance from God, not hygiene.[13] This should be read in conjunction with idolatry and not as a description of their lifestyle. It is probably a reference to the cultural definition of the Lamanite mark. (See commentary accompanying 2 Nephi 5:21.)

"with a short skin girdle about their loins and their heads shaven": This is surely descriptive of at least some of the Lamanites. It is most likely descriptive of the earliest groups who would have stayed along the coastal regions of the Guatemalan coast. Sorenson suggests:

> What can we tell about living conditions in the land of first inheritance? The coastal plain where the landing of Lehi would have occurred was uncomfortably hot and humid. That climate favored rapid crop growth, but the weather would be unpleasant for colonizers. The Nephites soon fled up to the land of Nephi, where the elevation permitted living in greater comfort. As Nephi tells the story, the Lamanites down in the hot lowlands were nomadic hunters, bloodthirsty, near naked, and lazy (2 Ne. 5:24, Enos 1:20). The circumstances of life in that environment could account for some of those characteristics. Many centuries later the Spaniards spoke in like terms of natives in the same area. The Tomas Medel manuscript, dating about A.D. 1550, just a generation after the first Spaniards arrived in the area, reported that the Indian men on the Pacific coast of Guatemala "spent their entire lives as naked as when they were born." That practice may have seemed a sensible response to the oppressive climate. In the late seventeenth century Catholic priest Fuentes y Guzman contrasted the "lassitude and laziness" of the same lowlanders with the energy of the highland inhabitants. As for getting a living, the tangle of forest and swamp along the coast itself may have been too hard for the Lamanite newcomers to farm effectively, since they wouldn't immediately get the knack of cultivation in that locale. (They, or their fathers, might not even have been farmers in Palestine.) It may have been economically smart for them to hunt and gather the abundant natural food from the estuaries, while again the damp heat would make their lack of energy understandable.[14]

---

[13]1 Ne. 5:27, 15:33–34; 2 Ne. 9:16; Jacob 3:3, 5, 9–10; Mosiah 7:30–31; Alma 5:22, 7:21, 32:3; Morm. 9:4, 14.

[14]John L. Sorenson, *An Ancient American Setting for the Book of Mormon* (Salt Lake City: Deseret Book/Provo, Utah: Foundation for Ancient Research and Mormon Studies, 1985), 140.

We should remember, however, that this is a description based (at best) upon the early experience of the Nephites and Lamanites, which became a codified or stereotyped description. We find similar references to minimal clothing for the Lamanites in Mosiah 10:8, Alma 3:5, 43:20, and 49:6. However, each of these citations places the clothing in a military context, and probably says more about battle attire than daily attire. To the extent that we find larger Lamanite populations later in the Book of Mormon, we may assume that those urban Lamanites would have had the same taste for fine clothes as the Nephites of Jacob's time. As with other items in this cultural catalog, the intent is to contrast naked Lamanites with clothed Nephites.

"a blood-thirsty people": The warlike Lamanites are implicitly contrasted with the peaceful Nephites. Later, this phrase becomes descriptive of Lamanite politics. Rather than "blood-thirsty," the Lamanites (and the Gadiantons) are said to love murder and plunder (Mosiah 2:3, 10:7; Alma 23:3; Hel. 6:23, 7:21, 11:25; 3 Ne. 4:5; Ether 8:16).

"their skill was in the bow, and in the cimeter, and the ax": The bow, the first weapon on this list, is rather controversial in Mesoamerica, as there is no positive proof of its existence at this period. However, recent research has shed more light on the subject. William Hamblin concludes:

> There is no inscriptional evidence relating to the use of bows in Mesoamerica. However, there are limited artistic representations of the use of the bow by at least the second century A.D. Furthermore, there are numerous stone projectile points that can be classified as arrowheads, and the current trend in scholarship is to reclassify such projectile points as arrowheads, thereby dating the use of the bow by Mesoamericans to at least the first millennium. It is also possible that some Mesoamericans used arrows with non-stone projectile points. Thus there is no reason to maintain that the mention of the bow in the Book of Mormon is incompatible with the archaeological evidence from Mesoamerica.
>
> I should emphasize one last point. The fact that the bow was known in Mesoamerica does not mean that all cultures in that region would have used the weapon or would have used it extensively in warfare. As Christian Feest puts it: "Since the bow undoubtedly represents the highest development of arms technology in the tribal world, it seems strange that it is not always employed as a weapon of war. In Polynesia bows and arrows were restricted to hunting; in parts of Melanesia the spear replaced the bow, and even the civilizations of Mexico and Peru preferred the spearthrower. Since there are no technical reasons for this, it is likely that the bow was less suited to the particular war tactics of these regions." One could add that, although the bow was known throughout Africa, some African tribes preferred not to use it in warfare.[15]

The second weapon listed is the cimeter, "scimitar" to give its modern spelling. In modern literature, it always refers to the sickle-shaped sword associated with the Middle East. In Mesoamerica no swords of this shape are known. However, in the Book of Mormon we are also dealing with a conflation of vocabularies that

---

[15]William J. Hamblin, "The Bow and Arrow in the Book of Mormon," in *Warfare in the Book of Mormon*, edited by Stephen D. Ricks and William J. Hamblin (Salt Lake City: Deseret Book/Provo, Utah: Foundation for Ancient Research and Mormon Studies, 1990), 386.

can make some identifications imprecise. The Nephites would have applied Old World vocabulary to New World artifacts (including plants, animals, and weapons). Another disjuncture would have been Joseph Smith as a translator, who might have used his modern vocabulary on cultural items with no exact modern counterpart.

William Hamblin and Brent Merrill find a Mesoamerican weapon that may have been the Book of Mormon "cimeter":

> One of the earliest Mesoamerican candidates for the Book of Mormon scimitar is found in a Late Preclassic sculpture that shows a warrior holding in one hand a macuahuitl and in the other a strange curved weapon. . . . It is impossible to say for certain what this item is supposed to represent. However, a similar weapon is known in India—the haladi. Note that this warrior holds both a macuahuitl sword and a curved weapon just as Zerahemnah is described in the Book of Mormon as being armed with.
>
> In our opinion, however, the Book of Mormon cimeter should probably be identified with a curved, ax-like weapon held by many of the figures in the Temple of the Warriors at Chichen Itza. It appears to be a curved piece of wood in the end of which was inserted obsidian or flint blades. . . . Although in appearance it is somewhat like an ax, it is structurally different, in that an ax has a straight shaft of wood with a blade mounted on the shaft, while this weapon has a curved shaft of wood with a blade mounted at the tip of the wood.[16]

Karl Taube describes another scimitar-like weapon: "The Early Classic stucco façade at Acanceh, Yucatan, portrays a star-marked War Serpent coiled around a sickle-shaped weapon, a type of obsidian sacrificial knife known for Teotihuacán. The blade handle is bound with fibrous material."[17]

The mention of an "ax" is much less controversial, as several types of weapons easily fit the general concept of this weapon designed for striking with a chopping motion.

The reason for describing the Lamanites is so that the Nephites may be favorably contrasted with them. Therefore, Enos gives us the positive Nephite stereotype.

"[They] . . . till the land, and raise all manner of grain, and of fruit . . . ": Grain and fruit communicate that the Nephite have farms and live a settled, not nomadic, life. Once a society discovers crops that will reliably support an agricultural strategy for their survival, the ties to the land get stronger, and "wandering about in the wilderness" like the Lamanites becomes unacceptable and socially irresponsible.

"flocks of herds, and flocks of all manner of cattle of every kind, and goats, and wild goats, and also many horses": One important aspect in this catalogue of animals is the contrast between tending "flocks" as opposed to hunting "beasts of prey." Enos is directly contrasting Nephite and Lamanite strategies for obtaining meat: husbandry versus hunting, civilized animals versus wild animals.

---

[16]William J. Hamblin and A. Brent Merrill, "Notes on the Cimeter Scimitar in the Book of Mormon," in ibid., 361. Their Fig. 3, chap. 15, p. 339, includes a drawing of this curved implement.

[17]Karl Taube, "The Turquoise Hearth: Fire, Self Sacrifice, and the Central Mexican Cult of War," in *Mesoamerica's Classic Heritage*, edited by David Carrasco, Lindsay Jones, and Scott Sessions (Boulder: University Press of Colorado, 2000), 301.

Also important are the particular animals. As noted in the discussion of 2 Nephi 5:11, "flocks" is a somewhat problematic term, particularly "flocks *of* herds." Assuming that it is not a translator or transcription error,[18] some linguistic shift has occurred, allowing Enos to conflate two terms that we would use for separate collective descriptions. Archaic English contains specific collectives for specific types of animals: "a pride of lions," "a murder of crows," etc. In English, "flocks" refer to fowls and "herds" refer to cattle, sheep, goats, or horses. "Flocks of herds," at least in English, is nonsense because it implies two different types of animals in the same phrase.

In short, "flocks of herds" is a mistake, and the question is why. Certainly Joseph Smith, a farm boy, understood the standard vocabulary of both agriculture and husbandry. It seems much more likely that the terms used to describe the semi-domesticated collectives of Mesoamerican animals have shifted in some way by Enos's time.

John L. Sorenson discusses the concepts of domestication attached to "flocks" and "herds" without noting Enos's unusual usage. His comments are instructive for the possible linguistic disjuncture that might explain why the Book of Mormon names animals not known to be present in Mesoamerica:

> The late Dennis Puleston of the University of Minnesota concluded a few years ago that the Maya ate the flesh of "semi-domesticated animals" far more often than had been thought. I have accumulated additional evidence to support Puleston's point. Considering all we now know about animal use in Mesoamerican cultures, it is fair to state that most of what the Book of Mormon says about animals is plausible. Some of the book's statements remain hard to square with present knowledge, but the picture is considerably more acceptable to scientists than a few years ago.
>
> The terms flocks and herds are easy to account for. Deer and pigs (peccary) could have fallen under those terms. Fowls in flocks were common. The turkey (Meleagris sp. and Agriocharis sp.) was, after all, an American native. Other domesticated, tamed, or at least caged fowls included the Muscovy duck, Tinamou duck, quail, "pheasant," "partridge," "dove," curassow, cotinga, roseate spoonbill, macaw, chachalaca, and parrot. The term flocks could have included such smaller animals much used by native peoples in Mesoamerica as hares, rabbits, and the paca and agouti (both rodents the size of small pigs).
>
> Dogs are mentioned at five places in the Book of Mormon, but nothing is said of their use. Two types (perhaps two species) were common in Mesoamerica. The large, white, humped mastiff (Nahuatl *itzcuintepotzotli*) was the creature whose noisy descendants plague Mexican villages today. A smaller, hairless sort (Nahuatl *xoloitzcuintli*) was fattened and eaten as a delicacy. The Spaniards relished the flesh of these animals at the time of the conquest, although they would have been offended, as most of us would be, at being offered the flesh of the bigger dog. Perhaps Nephite "flocks" included fattened dogs.[19]

---

[18]Skousen, *Analysis of Textual Variants*, 2:1089–91, does not list this as a variant, only a difficult reading. After analysis of the various terms, Skousen is no closer to a solution than I. He suggests: "Interpreting *herds* as referring to sheep (in distinction to cattle) seems to work better than introducing the excessive redundancy of the proposed emendation 'flocks **and** herds and flocks of all manner of cattle of every kind.'"

[19]Sorenson, *An Ancient American Setting for the Book of Mormon*, 292–93.

What about the horse? Again, Sorenson notes:

> I recently summarized evidence suggesting that the issue is not settled. Actual horse bones have been found in a number of archaeological sites on the Yucatan Peninsula, in one case with artifacts six feet beneath the surface under circumstances that rule out their coming from Spanish horses. Still, other large animals might have functioned or looked enough like a horse that one of them was what was referred to by horse. A prehispanic figure modeled on the cover of an incense burner from Poptun, Guatemala, shows a man sitting on the back of a deer holding its ears or horns, and a stone monument dating to around A.D. 700 represents a woman astride the neck of a deer, grasping its horns. Then there is another figurine of a person riding an animal, this one from central Mexico. Possibly, then, the deer served as a sort of "horse" for riding. (That was a practice in Siberia until recently, so the idea is not as odd as moderns might think. Besides, in the Quiche languages of highland Guatemala we have expressions like *keh*, deer or horse, *keheh*, mount or ride, and so on).[20]

The linguistic evidence from the Quiché is particularly interesting, and *keh* for "deer" can be reconstructed to proto-Quichean, placing the term firmly in pre-Hispanic times.[21] Thus, the Quiché, when faced with an animal without a name in their language, applied their "deer" to the horse. Of course Sorenson's suggestion about *keheh* for "mount or ride" may or may not refer to the riding of deer (likely to have been a ritual/shamanistic function) as this term could easily be derived from regular grammatical rules after the association of *keh* with "horse." "Hippopotamus" is Latin for a "river horse," even though it does not look like or function in any way similar to a horse. The practice of using a familiar name for an unfamiliar animal is amply attested.

The process of assigning familiar labels to unfamiliar animals is not only well known in cultures in contact with new conditions but also an acceptable translating strategy. Thus, we can explain the Book of Mormon "horse" by three possibilities. Science may yet determine that horses did exist pre-Hispanically in the Mesoamerican region. At the moment, that is only a possibility. Second, in documents dealing with inter-cultural data, the linguistic labeling of a new animal with the term for an old one is well known. In the case of shifting linguistic labels, this process could have occurred with the Nephites and then been accurately translated by Joseph Smith. Alternatively, Joseph could be the source of "horse" since he would have been unfamiliar with the animal named on the plates. Evidence of the translation process throughout the Book of Mormon suggests to me that this latter possibility is more likely, though Sorenson clearly favors the second option.

It is significant that the Book of Mormon never describes a "horse" that is acting as we would expect a horse to act. It is never ridden. It is never described doing any work (though it is associated with a "chariot" in Alma 18:9). Even if science confirms the presence of true horses during Book of Mormon times, there is no textual evidence that they were used in the way most cultures used the horse. In fact, one of the contexts in which the word "horse" appears is that of food animals:

---

[20]Ibid., 295.

[21]Lyle Campbell, *Quichean Linguistic Prehistory* (Berkeley: University of California Press, 1977), 48.

> Therefore, there was no chance for the robbers to plunder and to obtain food, save it were to come up in open battle against the Nephites; and the Nephites being in one body, and having so great a number, and having reserved for themselves provisions, and horses and cattle, and flocks of every kind, that they might subsist for the space of seven years, in the which time they did hope to destroy the robbers from off the face of the land; and thus the eighteenth year did pass away. (3 Ne. 4:4)
>
> And now it came to pass that the people of the Nephites did all return to their own lands in the twenty and sixth year, every man, with his family, his flocks and his herds, his horses and his cattle, and all things whatsoever did belong unto them. (3 Ne. 6:1)

Of course this is only suggestive and not conclusive. However, these verses continue to highlight the lack of horse-like use in the Book of Mormon. (See commentary accompanying Alma 18:8–9.)

Enos 1:22

> 22 And there were exceedingly many prophets among us. And the people were a stiffnecked people, hard to understand.

The modern LDS model of church organization assumes a single prophet at the head of a unified organization. This is not the model of the Old Testament nor certainly of the early Nephite society. During Nephi's lifetime the community had both Nephi and Jacob as "prophets," although Jacob was officially the priest while Nephi acted as ruler. Enos summarizes his post-epiphany life by saying he preaches and prophesies (v. 19). Thus, Enos is a prophet, yet speaks of "exceedingly many prophets." This description fits the Old World model of the prophet who calls for social and religious repentance, rather than the contemporary model of a person who leads a community of religious adherents.

Although I have posited a general repentance after Jacob's encounter with Sherem, it was not complete or long-lasting. If the proposed scenario is correct in hypothesizing that much of the social unrest resulted directly from trading with powerful non-Nephite communities, we may assume that such contact continued and that the pressures to conform to the larger Mesoamerican ideology/culture continued. Thus the people would have continued to be "stiffnecked."

"hard to understand": The Nephites had a hard time understanding Yahweh's way. They did not find it difficult to comprehend what a Nephite said.[22]

Enos 1:23–24

> 23 And there was nothing save it was exceeding harshness, preaching and prophesying of wars, and contentions, and destructions, and continually reminding them of death, and the duration of eternity, and the judgments and the power of God, and all these things—stirring them up continually to keep them in the fear of the Lord. I say there was nothing short of these things, and exceedingly great plainness of speech, would keep them from going down speedily to destruction. And after this manner do I write concerning them.

---

[22]Skousen, *Analysis of Textual Variants*, 2:1093, agrees with this reading.

24 And I saw wars between the Nephites and Lamanites in the course of my days.

The wars explain why Enos lists "prophesying of wars, and contentions, and destructions, and continually reminding them of death." The prophets' preaching focuses on the same topics as all other prophets (the return to righteousness) but the message is intensified by the danger of death in war, which highlights the urgency not to delay repentance. It is possible, particularly in a generation only once removed from the fathers who had come from Jerusalem, that Enos saw multiple prophets preaching of coming war as a parallel to the conditions in Jerusalem which led to the Lehite exodus. At that time there were also wars and rumors of wars and many prophets warning the people of the coming tribulations.

Enos emphasizes in his preaching the Nephites' persistent tendency to move away from Yahweh's path. The call to return was harsh because only the harshness of the penalties kept "them from going down speedily to destruction."

Enos would have understood, after his epiphany, that speedy destruction awaited his people if they continued along the path they had begun during his father's lifetime. That path was "speedy" because it was so tempting. It tempted them away from their religious/cultural heritage, snaring them in a new culture containing new religious ideas which could supplanted those they had received from Nephi, Jacob, and all the other prophets Enos mentions.

Chronology: Enos's brevity contrasts with his longevity. He must have lived into his nineties and had charge of the plates perhaps as long as eighty years. (See discussion accompanying Enos 1:1.) His personal record-keeping consists of one specific event (his epiphany) and a brief synopsis. Perhaps to Enos near the close of his life, all events but one blended into the two generalizations of preaching and wars.

Enos 1:25

25 And it came to pass that I began to be old, and an hundred and seventy and nine years had passed away from the time that our father Lehi left Jerusalem.

Allowing for about eight years of travel through the wilderness to Bountiful, the Nephites had been about 170 years in the New World. At that point, they were no longer a transplanted Old World colony. From this point on (though probably from much, much earlier), the Nephites were surely a New World culture that had adapted to the climate and foodstuffs and had worked out relationships with the other towns/cultures around them.

While the presence of other established cultures is not described explicitly, the Nephite assimilation or borrowing of physical and perhaps ideological culture from those other peoples runs under the text of the Book of Mormon, just as the religion of Canaan runs faintly but traceably under the Old Testament. (See 1 Nephi, Part 1: Chapter 2, "Introduction to 1 Nephi.")

Chronology: Enos's death occurred somewhere in 407 B.C. using January 586 B.C. as the date of the departure from Jerusalem.

Enos 1:26

> 26 And I saw that I must soon go down to my grave, having been wrought upon by the power of God that I must preach and prophesy unto this people, and declare the word according to the truth which is in Christ. And I have declared it in all my days, and have rejoiced in it above that of the world.

At the end of his life, Enos's foundational event was still his initial encounter with Yahweh in the forest. Indeed, how could it not be? Whatever revelations Enos received thereafter, that first experience was transcendent, both in the great effort which accomplished it and the power of the experience itself.

Like Jacob, Enos testifies of the coming Messiah. The potential conflict between the law and the preaching of the Messiah that Sherem proposed is certainly not present in Enos's understanding. He understands the coming atoning Messiah and preached that understanding.

Enos 1:27

> 27 And I soon go to the place of my rest, which is with my Redeemer; for I know that in him I shall rest. And I rejoice in the day when my mortal shall put on immortality, and shall stand before him; then shall I see his face with pleasure, and he will say unto me: Come unto me, ye blessed, there is a place prepared for you in the mansions of my Father. Amen.

Reference: Enos concludes with a final testimony that emphasizes both the redemptive aspect of the Messiah's mission and the resurrection. His language echoes two King James texts: "My mortal shall put on immortality" is certainly patterned after 1 Corinthians 15:53–54:[23] "For this corruptible must put on incorruption, and this mortal must put on immortality. So when this corruptible shall have put on incorruption, and this mortal shall have put on immortality, then shall be brought to pass the saying that is written, Death is swallowed up in victory." Similarly, Job 19:26 is the source of the phrase "see his face": "And though after my skin worms destroy this body, yet in my flesh shall I see God."

Like similar allusions to King James English in the Book of Mormon, these parallels simply indicate the presence of those phrases in Joseph's mind as ways for translating the meaning. Enos understood and attested to the reality of the resurrection of the body. Joseph Smith couched Enos's meaning in phrases of similar meaning; their familiarity indicates nothing more than the well-known fact that the literary cadences of the Book of Mormon are intentionally patterned after the King James Version.

---

[23]These verses appear to have strongly impacted Joseph Smith's vocabulary. We see echoes of them in 2 Ne. 2:11, 9:7; Mosiah 16:10; Alma 5:15, 40:2, 41:4; Morm. 6:21.

Jarom: Commentary

Jarom 1

Jarom 1:1

> 1 Now behold, I, Jarom, write a few words according to the commandment of my father, Enos, that our genealogy may be kept.

Both Nephi and Jacob charged their successors with maintaining objects sacred to the people. Enos, however, simply instructs his son to maintain the family genealogy. A similar charge marks the transition between Jarom and his son Omni (Omni 1:1). Yet neither Jarom nor Omni (nor Jacob and only tangentially Nephi) record a genealogy. The only genealogical information is Jarom's identification of his father's name. Why is the one thing that the authors understood as the primary reason for keeping the record in the first place missing?

They do include genealogy insofar as they indicate their connection to the lineage that is caring for the small plates. From the rest of what they include, they clearly believe that the indication of their relationship to the transmission line is all that is specifically required. The concept of genealogy includes beginnings (and therefore begettings) as well as the linking of such information through time. Certainly the chronological ordering of a genealogy fits with the concept of a history, and the probable sacred nature attached to particular kin might be the link by which these ideas were melded.

Jarom 1:2

> 2 And as these plates are small, and as these things are written for the intent of the benefit of our brethren the Lamanites, wherefore, it must needs be that I write a little; but I shall not write the things of my prophesying, nor of my revelations. For what could I write more than my fathers have written? For have not they revealed the plan of salvation? I say unto you, Yea; and this sufficeth me.

History: Jarom gives us little personal information aside from affirming, though without explication, that he has prophecies and revelations. It is reasonable to assume that Jarom is a righteous man attempting to follow Yahweh's way. John S. Tanner extracts some historical information about Jarom:

> Jarom may not have done any public teaching or preaching at all. Although he referred to "my prophesying" and "my revelations," he spoke in the third person of "the prophets, and the priests, and the teachers [who] labor diligently, exhorting . . . the people to diligence; teaching the law of Moses" (Jarom 1:11)—as if he were not one of them. Also he wrote, "Our kings and our leaders were mighty men in the faith of the Lord; and they taught the people the ways of the Lord" (1:7), sounding like a bystander outside the loop of government power and official church responsibility.

> On the other hand, Jarom referred to Nephite warfare and trade in the first person: "We withstood the Lamanites. . . . And we . . . became exceedingly rich in gold . . . in buildings, and in machinery, and also in iron and copper, and brass and steel, making all manner of tools of every kind to till the ground, and weapons of war" (Jarom 1:7–8). Jarom sounds as if he was a soldier and artisan.[1]

Text: Jarom's reason for his scanty record is not that he lacks revelations, but rather that "these plates are small" and that his prophecies confirm those already written. The fact that earlier prophets have spoken and written on the same themes as a contemporary prophet does not lessen the value of the contemporary prophets, so we may take his concern about the size of the plates at face value. Supporting evidence is Amaleki's final statement that the "plates are full" (Omni 1:30).

As discussed in the commentary accompanying 1 Nephi 6:1–3 (see also Behind the Text: Chapter 6, "The Physical Plates"), Nephi probably made the plates, including many more leaves than he personally used. All of the other writers on the small plates wrote on the appended blank leaves, not creating new ones. Indeed, given the increasing marginalization of Jacob's lineage from that of the rulers and Jacob's polemics against the rich, it seems probable that Jacob's descendants lacked resources to create new plates. By the time of Jarom there are few sheets left. Amaleki fills the last blank (described in Omni 1:30).

Jarom 1:3

> 3 Behold, it is expedient that much should be done among this people, because of the hardness of their hearts, and the deafness of their ears, and the blindness of their minds, and the stiffness of their necks; nevertheless, God is exceedingly merciful unto them, and has not as yet swept them off from the face of the land.

This verse suggests a state of general apostasy, but this view is inaccurate (vv. 6–8). Rather, it is more accurate to see a prophet who recognizes that there is still work to be done and still hard-hearted people in his flock. Jarom qualifies his first statement in the next verse.

Jarom 1:4

> 4 And there are many among us who have many revelations, for they are not all stiffnecked. And as many as are not stiffnecked and have faith, have communion with the Holy Spirit, which maketh manifest unto the children of men, according to their faith.

There are two types of Nephites: those who are stiffnecked and those who have faith. Jarom understands that those who have faith will follow the commandments, including the Nephite version of the Mosaic law that Nephi taught at the end of his reign, and which Jacob and Enos continued.

---

[1]John S. Tanner, "Jacob and His Descendants as Authors," in *Rediscovering the Book of Mormon*, edited by John L. Sorenson and Melvin J. Thorne (Provo, Utah: Foundation for Ancient Research and Mormon Studies, 1991), 56.

Jarom 1:5

> 5 And now, behold, two hundred years had passed away, and the people of Nephi had waxed strong in the land. They observed to keep the law of Moses and the sabbath day holy unto the Lord. And they profaned not; neither did they blaspheme. And the laws of the land were exceedingly strict.

Jarom turns from the stiffnecked people who were likely his particular audience to what appears to be the majority of Nephites. On the whole, Nephite society at this point is one founded upon and ruled by Mosaic law, augmented by the teachings of their prophets concerning the Atoning Messiah. Jarom highlights the general righteousness because he sees that, as a direct fulfillment of the prophecies, they will remain in the land in accordance with their righteousness.

In particular, Jarom mentions that they "profaned not; neither did they blaspheme." A modern interpretation might be that they did not swear or take the Lord's name in vain. This would be too simple a reading for an ancient people. These terms indicate the people's relationship to their God. Blasphemy would be a denial of Yahweh, and profaning Yahweh would be a diminishing of Yahweh's value. Seen in the context of competing religions, these are indications that the Nephites remained faithful to Yahweh as their one God and did not follow after any other God. If the seeds had been sown for what would later be labeled as the order of the Nehors (see "Excursus: Religion of the Nehors," following Alma 1), then one of the interpretations of "not profane" would be that they did not deny Yahweh's atoning mission. (See "Excursus: The Nephite Understanding of God," following 1 Nephi 11.)

Chronology: Two hundred years from what I accept as Lehi's departure date (January 586 B.C.) places this next dated event at 392 B.C.

Jarom 1:6

> 6 And they were scattered upon much of the face of the land, and the Lamanites also. And they were exceedingly more numerous than were they of the Nephites; and they loved murder and would drink the blood of beasts.

Culture: This brief description of the Lamanites and the Nephites describes the Nephites as "scattered upon much of the face of the land." It is the description of a large population inhabiting a sizeable geographical region. Since the Nephites are city dwellers, with dependent agricultural sites, the description suggests numerous towns and villages that are allied with the Nephites and who therefore fit Jacob's definition of "Nephite." In other words, Nephite economic and political power has been sufficiently strong to motivate other towns in the general geographic area to consider themselves Nephites.

The Lamanites are likewise "scattered" but, interestingly, have become more numerous than the Nephites. Jarom's father, Enos, had caricaturized the Lamanites as nomadic hunter-gatherers (see commentary accompanying Enos 1:20). Hunter-gatherer societies cannot grow very large because large groups would soon outstrip the carrying capacity of their territory. While population growth might explain why the

Lamanites were "scattered" over a large region, it does not explain their numerical superiority to the Nephites. Such an imbalance, historically, predicts the adoption of agriculture and husbandry. Thus, whatever the Nephite clichés in describing them, the Lamanites have, in reality, become just as urbanized as the Nephites.

In the Mesoamerican context, the definition of "Lamanite" would include anyone not "friendly" to the Nephites. Archaeological evidence from this period supports a picture of many towns and villages in Mesoamerica.[2] From the Nephite perspective, any community who was not "friendly" to the Nephites would qualify as "Lamanite," even if it did not contain a single lineal Lamanite. (See "Excursus: Anthropology and the Book of Mormon," following 1 Nephi 18.) As Armand L. Mauss, professor emeritus of sociology at Washington State University notes: "The Lamanites are often described in the Book of Mormon as a fallen and degenerate people, especially in comparisons with the righteous Nephites. Of course, as the putative authors of the record in question, the Nephites were free to characterize their antagonists as they wished, and demonizing of the "other" has been a recurrent process in all of human history."[3]

Jarom also says the Lamanites "loved murder and would drink the blood of beasts." On the basis of the frequent wars alone, it is possible to see why he would describe them as loving murder. However, it is also possible to read it as a description of Lamanite religious practices. Murder is conceptually different from deaths that occur in battle, so it may be a reference to the Mesoamerican practice of killing (or sacrificing) captives. Jacob 2:19 suggested that a legitimate use of wealth was to ransom captives; thus, the "love of murder" could be read as the traditional Mesoamerican fate of unredeemed captives.[4] The connection between human sacrifice as an aspect of the Lamanite religion and the various events in the Book of Mormon will recur. (See, for example, commentary accompanying Alma 24:9–11.)

Jarom's specific denunciation about drinking animal blood may have been to point out that the Lamanites were violating the Mosaic law, which prohibited the eating of the blood of meat animals: "Notwithstanding thou mayest kill and eat flesh in all thy gates, whatsoever thy soul lusteth after, according to the blessing of the Lord thy God which he hath given thee: the unclean and the clean may eat thereof, as of the roebuck, and as of the hart. Only ye shall not eat the blood; ye shall pour it upon the earth as water" (Deut. 12:15–16). This impious behavior

---

[2]Susan Toby Evans, *Ancient Mexico and Central America: Archaeology and Culture History* (London: Thames & Hudson, 2004), 185, "The period from about 600 to 300 B.C. covers the transition from a time when Mesoamerica had one strong cultural influence over a huge region—a cultural horizon—to a period of widespread regional developments."

The largest city in the area suggested for the Nephites during this time period was Kaminaljuyú (Sorenson's candidate for the city of Nephi). Evans, ibid., 202, notes: "In the Verbena phase (400–300 B.C.), Kaminaljuyú's affiliations were directed toward the Pacific Coast and the Motagua Valley that extended east toward the Caribbean Sea, while interaction with groups to the northwest withered."

[3]Armand L. Mauss, *All Abraham's Children: Changing Mormon Conceptions of Race and Lineage* (Urbana: University of Illinois Press, 2003), 116.

[4]Linda Schele and David Freidel, *A Forest of Kings: The Untold Story of the Ancient Maya* (New York: William Morrow and Company, 1990), 148.

would have been seen as a further indication of Lamanite baseness, a continuation of the cultural clichés Jacob and Enos had employed earlier. It was "accurate" in contrast to the "civilized" Nephites but may not have been historically correct. It is best seen as a stereotype.

Geography: The emerging Nephite/Lamanite conflicts should be seen in the context of Mesoamerican culture in general. While Schele and Freidel are describing specifics of the much later institution of Maya kingship, it seems reasonable that the general relationship of ruler/subject would be present in Book of Mormon times, establishing the trends that would result in the Maya kings of the Classic period (A.D. 250–800).[5] They note:

> The political geography of the Maya consisted of island cities of royal power in a sea of townspeople and village folk. Kings worked hard to establish firm control over the countryside and to expand their authority as far as possible in the direction of other polities. From the beginning of the institution of kingship, military confrontation was not only a fact of life but a necessary and inevitable royal responsibility. With the proliferation of polities, the civilized territories expanded at the expense of the freeholders.[6]

This general description also fits the ongoing tensions between Nephite and Lamanite, punctuated by frequent wars waged to consolidate their respective territories. We may picture the Nephites as towns surrounding and beholden to the village/city of Nephi, with similar towns and villages beholden to similar Lamanite power centers. The wealth and technological prowess of the Nephites would make them prime targets of rivalry and objects of conquest by war.

Jarom 1:7

> 7 And it came to pass that they came many times against us, the Nephites, to battle. But our kings and our leaders were mighty men in the faith of the Lord; and they taught the people the ways of the Lord; wherefore, we withstood the Lamanites and swept them away out of our lands, and began to fortify our cities, or whatsoever place of our inheritance.

Culture: Significantly, Jarom's description of Nephites and Lamanites "scattered over the face of the land" turns immediately into military conflict. Given political alliances traditional in the Maya region, such conflict is a direct result of the population expansion. Also significantly, Jarom does not refer to Nephite armies but rather to "our kings and our leaders." Kings were military leaders, not just strategists. Schele and Freidel note: "Kings did not take their captives easily, but in aggressive hand-to-hand combat."[7] Jarom is accurately portraying both the social conditions and the military actions known to have prevailed among the Maya, the

---

[5]Ibid., 424, "These major features of kingship . . . succeeded in the Classic period lowlands because they were grafted onto a Late Preclassic [500 B.C.–A.D. 250] institution of kingship that appealed more to the principle of personal charismatic power endowed in the role of the shaman than to the principles of lineage and genealogy."

[6]Ibid., 60.

[7]Ibid., 143.

culture region of the Nephites, according to John Sorenson's well-accepted geographical hypothesis.[8] While at least four centuries separate Jarom's time from the Classic Maya, I do not consider the time period to be an obstacle to this hypothesis. The Classic Maya developed from political precursors that may date to at least 800 B.C.[9] In preindustrial ancient society, change did not run at nearly the modern pace, and it was common for social institutions to last for centuries.

Archaeology: For many years, the prevailing scholarly opinion visualized Mesoamericans as peaceful star-gazers, with little or no military activity. The Book of Mormon's description of fortifications seemed out of place against that peaceful assumption. Subsequent research has revealed a war-torn Mesoamerica complete with fortifications from early times.

Archaeologist David Webster notes: "A sizable Late Preclassic [500 B.C.–A.D. 250] community existed at Punta de Chimino, and some archaeologists believe that the impressive earthwork fortifications that defended the Punta de Chimino peninsula were first built at that time. If so, warfare had very deep roots in the region."[10]

Sorenson, in surveying the archaeological literature on the military evidences at Mesoamerican sites, notes:

> [This table] gives the site counts according to ten chronological periods. Keep in mind again that the numbers are not comprehensive or inflexible since they depend on the accidents of discovery. Because the periods I am using here are purely chronological, they may differ slightly from phase or period attributions in the original sources, for the authors of those use divergent systems of terminology. The numbers reflect the fact that a single site was often used through more than one period.[11]

Fortified and Defensive Sites by Period

Period	Definite	Possible
Early Preclassic (pre-1000 B.C.)	0	1
Early Middle Preclassic (1000–600 B.C.)	0	2
Late Middle Preclassic (600–400 B.C.)	5	1
Late Preclassic (400–50 B.C.)	30	2
Protoclassic (50 B.C.–A.D. 200)	26	8
Early Classic (A.D. 200–400)	14	8
Middle Classic (A.D. 400–650)	11	13
Late Classic (A.D. 650–850)	27	11
Epiclassic (A.D. 850–1000)	12	10
Postclassic (A.D. 1000–Conquest)	177	16

Sorenson's chart identifies fortifications both for Jarom's time period and for later periods. Jarom's period, 386 B.C., falls into the general end of the Late Middle

[8]John L. Sorenson, *An Ancient American Setting for the Book of Mormon* (Salt Lake City: Deseret Book/Provo, Utah: Foundation for Ancient Research and Mormon Studies, 1985), see chapter 1.

[9]David Drew, *The Lost Chronicles of the Maya Kings* (Berkeley: University of California Press, 1999), 129–30.

[10]David Webster, *The Fall of the Ancient Maya: Solving the Mystery of the Maya Collapse* (London: Thames & Hudson, 2002), 275.

[11]John L. Sorenson, "Fortifications in the Book of Mormon Account Compared with Mesoamerican Fortifications," in *Warfare in the Book of Mormon*, edited by Stephen D. Ricks and William J. Hamblin (Salt Lake City: Deseret Book/Provo, Utah: Foundation for Ancient Research and Mormon Studies, 1990), 429.

Preclassic and the Late Preclassic on the above chart. Fortifications become increasingly frequent, particularly between the earlier time periods and approximately 400 B.C. when Jarom notes the beginnings of Nephite fortifications.

It is highly probable, as Sorenson notes, that these numbers understate the actual frequency. He explains:

> After all, it is not easy to identify some sites as fortified. In some cases, archaeologists doing field reconnaissance have reported only hillside "terraces," although further examination has convinced others that these had defensive intent. Nor is it easy to spot moats or ditches that subsequent natural or human actions have obscured, particularly when the features may lie at a considerable distance—even miles—from built-up sites. Walls can be especially hard to detect where the materials from which they were constructed have been carried off for various nonmilitary purposes by ancient or modern peoples. (The potentially ephemeral nature of walls is demonstrated by one built at a comparatively recent date: the Spanish in colonial days forced the Indians to erect a great stone wall enclosing a huge area of the Valley of Mexico to contain the Europeans' cattle. Over two million people worked for four months on the vast project, yet today no traces of it seem to have been identified.)[12]

Sorenson has suggested the Guatemalan site of Kaminaljuyú as a candidate for the city of Nephi.[13] At Jarom's time period, interesting correspondences to the Book of Mormon account exist in archaeological discoveries at Kaminaljuyú, as described by Muriel Porter Weaver: "During the Middle and Late Preclassic years (600 B.C. to 300 A.D.) religious architecture got off to a good start. Temple-pyramids, which in some cases served also as burial mounds were arranged along both sides of a long rectangular plaza or avenue. Religion was the driving motivation, and all nearby peoples must have contributed heavily, in time and muscle, to the necessary labor force."[14]

So far the picture fits with the image that the city of Nephi flourished in the early time period, yet required outside help. As the city grew and prospered, it would be able to command an increasing contribution of labor from surrounding areas, and its architectural development would manifest that growth. Muriel Porter Weaver continues: "The glory and luxury evident at Kaminaljuyú can only signify a high degree of social stratification with wealth, power, and prestige in the hands of an elite few. The trend toward standardization of ritual material and the exclusion of certain artifacts such as figurines from the rich tombs suggests that religion was becoming formalized and rigidly patterned."[15]

This picture also agrees with types of social evolution hinted at in Jacob's record, even though the codification of religion Weaver suggests for Kaminaljuyú probably postdates the Nephite presence there and stems from the later Lamanite possession of the site.

In spite of the general agreement, there may be some difference between the archaeology and the Book of Mormon account on one point. Weaver notes:

---

[12]Ibid., 428.

[13]Sorenson, *An Ancient American Setting for the Book of Mormon*, 47.

[14]Muriel Porter Weaver, *The Aztecs, Maya, and Their Predecessors: Archaeology of Mesoamerica* (New York: Seminar Press, 1972), 81.

[15]Ibid., 83.

"Apparently there was no fear of outsiders since the sacred or civic centers were located on open valley floors without visible means of protection."[16]

While this description contradicts Jarom's statements about the fortifications, he mentions them only after the city has been in existence for at least 150–70 years. Such fortifications may have been removed when the Lamanites took over the site 120 years later. Furthermore, evidences of such fortifications may be hard to find, and finally, up to this point, the city has relied on its warrior-kings rather than its fortifications. While such archaeological evidences must be acknowledged, they certainly do not exclude Kaminaljuyú as the plausible site for the city of Nephi. Mesoamerican fortifications consisted of some permanent features as well as temporary defenses built for particular occasions.[17]

Sorenson summarizes the archaeological evidence for Jarom's period:

> The centuries after Nephi and his brother Jacob died are barely described in the Book of Mormon. Neither the scriptural record nor archaeology tells us much about how life went on at that time, but Pennsylvania State University in the late 1960s investigated some remains of the occupation of Kaminaljuyú dating from the third to sixth centuries B.C., the period the books of Enos and Omni represent so briefly. The settlement then was already good sized. The excavators interpret it as having been occupied by several kin groups or lineages (notice Jacob 1:13), each living in a certain sector of the site. The central sacred area at that time seems to have consisted of rows of large burial mounds. These were probably where the elders of the kin groups were buried and honored. This custom basically agrees with the treatment of honored leaders of Israelite kin groups in Palestine when they died. Perhaps during the centuries of warfare and "stiff-neckedness" after Nephi and Jacob died (Enos 1:22–24), the original temple fell into disuse as a center for religious practices, while burial rites for the group's patriarchs were emphasized. At least we hear nothing about the temple between Jacob's day and the time when the Zeniffites reoccupied the land, over 400 years later (Jacob 1:17; Mosiah 11:10, 12; compare Alma 10:2).[18]

Jarom 1:8

> 8 And we multiplied exceedingly, and spread upon the face of the land, and became exceedingly rich in gold, and in silver, and in precious things, and in fine workmanship of wood, in buildings, and in machinery, and also in iron and copper, and brass and steel, making all manner of tools of every kind to till the ground, and weapons of war—yea, the sharp pointed arrow, and the quiver, and the dart, and the javelin, and all preparations for war.

Jarom's evidence of Nephite prosperity is their accumulation of valuable items and their "fine workmanship of wood, in buildings. . . . " Mesoamerican climate precludes the possibility that "fine workmanship of wood" would be preserved very often, but it is certain that any wealthy city in Mesoamerica would display its wealth in its public architecture, just as Jarom indicates.

His weapons catalog includes those most common in Mesoamerica but does not mention swords, scimitars, or bows. (See commentary accompanying Enos 1:20.) Since those items do show up later in the Book of Mormon, we cannot

---

16Ibid., 81.

17Webster, *The Fall of the Ancient Maya*, 98.

18Sorenson, *An Ancient American Setting for the Book of Mormon*, 145.

presume that they were not present here but simply that Jarom, for some unknown reason, did not think them important enough to list. Possibly, though speculatively, Jarom's list of the Nephite wealth-items focuses on items of value to other Mesoamericans. Therefore, he mentions the more typical armaments as evidence of their acculturation, even in warfare.

This is the last reference to metallurgy involving "iron, copper, brass, and steel, . . . scarcely 200 years after Nephi arrived in the New World. About 250 years later, however, King Noah taxed all people who possessed these metals (Mosiah 11:3)."[19]

Jarom 1:9

> 9 And thus being prepared to meet the Lamanites, they did not prosper against us. But the word of the Lord was verified, which he spake unto our fathers, saying that: Inasmuch as ye will keep my commandments ye shall prosper in the land.

Jarom first notes the Nephites' successful preparations and only second the promise of preservation, which comes into effect conditioned upon their righteousness. Jarom correctly notes that their preparation is as important as the promise. This is an application of the Nephite foundational promise (2 Ne. 1:9).

Jarom 1:10–12

> 10 And it came to pass that the prophets of the Lord did threaten the people of Nephi, according to the word of God, that if they did not keep the commandments, but should fall into transgression, they should be destroyed from off the face of the land.
> 11 Wherefore, the prophets, and the priests, and the teachers, did labor diligently, exhorting with all long-suffering the people to diligence; teaching the law of Moses, and the intent for which it was given; persuading them to look forward unto the Messiah, and believe in him to come as though he already was. And after this manner did they teach them.
> 12 And it came to pass that by so doing they kept them from being destroyed upon the face of the land; for they did prick their hearts with the word, continually stirring them up unto repentance.

In these three verses, Jarom summarizes the role and success of the prophets. His use of the word "threatened" indicates how clearly they preached the consequences of falling away from the Lord's way. Only righteousness would activate Yahweh's promise. Thanks only to the prophets' diligence in reminding the people of their obligation did the people keep the law.

Victor L. Ludlow notes the significance of Jarom's statement that the prophets "taught them to believe in the coming Messiah 'as though he already was.' This mental association of anticipating something in the future as though it were already

---

[19]Wm. Revell Phillips, "Metals of the Book of Mormon," *Journal of Book of Mormon Studies* 9, no. 2 (2000): 43.

present helped the people remember their weaknesses and repent of their sins. . . . If society today could anticipate Christ's second coming and the reality of the judgment day and resurrection as though they were all happening now, perhaps more people would return to the gospel paths and avoid further divine punishments."[20]

Jarom 1:13

> 13 And it came to pass that two hundred and thirty and eight years had passed away—after the manner of wars, and contentions, and dissensions, for the space of much of the time.

Chronology: Jarom gives a date of 238 years after the departure from Jerusalem, corresponding to approximately 355 B.C. Presumably Jarom is now approaching death. His mention of years does not date the specific events he mentions, for he says only that they occurred in the thirty-eight years since his last entry. Jarom has apparently been in charge of the plates for fifty-nine years. Assuming that he was at least ten when he received them from Enos, he was at least sixty-nine and probably older. His longevity thus resembles the long lives of Jacob and Enos.

Jarom 1:14

> 14 And I, Jarom, do not write more, for the plates are small. But behold, my brethren, ye can go to the other plates of Nephi; for behold, upon them the records of our wars are engraven, according to the writings of the kings, or those which they caused to be written.

The constraints of space that Jarom notes are corroborated by the very short entries of the next several writers. However, the last writer has a more extended entry, so Jarom presumably could have written at greater length. Apparently, however, the dominant feature of Nephite society was its wars with the Lamanites, records of which are available on the "kingly" records.

Culture: Jarom's observation that the other plates are "according to the writings of the kings, *or those which they caused to be written*" describes a change in record-keeping from Nephi, who kept the records personally. By Jarom's time, Nephite society had become sufficiently complex and stratified that the kings delegate the record-keeping function.[21] The increasing complexity and stratification of society was a theme against which Jacob had preached.

---

[20]Victor L. Ludlow, "Scribes and Scriptures," in *1 Nephi to Alma 29*, edited by Kent P. Jackson, STUDIES IN SCRIPTURE (Salt Lake City: Deseret Book, 1987), Vol. 7, 200.

[21]Dorie Reents-Budet, *Painting the Maya Universe: Royal Ceramics of the Classic Period* (Durham, N.C.: Duke University Press, 1994), 55:

> In some cases . . . the master pottery painters were sons of the nobility who seemingly were not in direct line for the throne. To convey these regal connections, the master artists placed their signatures on the vessels next to the depicted rulers. In a few rare instances, the artists' nominal phrases include their elite titles and royal parentage. This same situation is reported from sixteenth-century Utatlán, Guatemala: specialized artists came from within the royal lineages, where the younger sons and other close relatives of the lords who held the highest sociopolitical offices, and were not in direct line to inherit the throne.

Jarom 1:15

> 15 And I deliver these plates into the hands of my son Omni, that they may be kept according to the commandments of my fathers.

By passing the plates to his son, Jarom fulfills, though very sketchily, the genealogical aspect of his charge (Jarom 1:1).

Reents-Budet notes that while this was clearly a male-dominated profession, there is at least one instance of an inscription by a woman with the title "Lady Scribe." Ibid., 48

Omni: Commentary

Omni 1

Omni 1:1

1 Behold, it came to pass that I, Omni, being commanded by my father, Jarom, that I should write somewhat upon these plates, to preserve our genealogy—

Literature: Omni begins as Jarom did, with a formal declaration that he will preserve his genealogy but gives no genealogical details except to confirm that Jarom is his father. Almost certainly, he copied this opening phrase from his father's record. It should therefore be considered formulaic rather than descriptive.

Omni 1:2

2 Wherefore, in my days, I would that ye should know that I fought much with the sword to preserve my people, the Nephites, from falling into the hands of their enemies, the Lamanites. But behold, I of myself am a wicked man, and I have not kept the statutes and the commandments of the Lord as I ought to have done.

Culture: Omni describes himself as a Nephite, a warrior, and a wicked man. Obviously, armed conflict has intensified in frequency. Also obviously, Omni's use of *Nephite* is absolutely political. Omni is a Nephite in contrast to the enemy Lamanites. He is a Nephite because of his allegiance to his community, not because of his religion. However, he is also a Nephite due to lineage traced through his fathers back to Jacob and Lehi. Jacob 1:13 indicates a continuation of clan designations, so those are available to Omni.

Omni 1:3

3 And it came to pass that two hundred and seventy and six years had passed away, and we had many seasons of peace; and we had many seasons of serious war and bloodshed. Yea, and in fine, two hundred and eighty and two years had passed away, and I had kept these plates according to the commandments of my fathers; and I conferred them upon my son Amaron. And I make an end.

Chronology: Omni's first date is 276 years after the departure from Jerusalem. This would be 318 B.C. according to the lunar calendar.

Redaction: Omni clearly made entries at least twice, and perhaps three times. The first entry (vv. 1–2) may have concluded with the 276 year date or, perhaps, the beginning of the next entry. The last entry is clearly the one beginning with the final date, as there is no reason in the text for the two dates to have been given at the same writing.

It seems likely, however, that he wrote only twice, once 276 years after the departure from Jerusalem and again six years later just before he gives the plates to his son. Thus, he apparently had the plates for forty-five years before he made his first entry. This would not be unusual, given the performance of his ancestors from Enos on, and especially since Omni obviously did not consider himself an expert on spiritual matters.

To speculate, he may have decided to make his first entry after being seriously wounded (since he declares himself a warrior), but he would have been older than forty-five by perhaps ten years—surely an advanced age for a man to still be engaged in warfare. When he makes his final entry six years later, he is presumably near death and considers that he has fulfilled his charge to "keep the plates"—not necessarily to record, but to preserve.

History: Using the 586 B.C. departure date, Omni writes between 318–312 B.C. In highland Guatemala, this period corresponds to the Middle Preclassic (or "Miraflores") period when religious architecture flourished in Kaminaljuyú. This architecture is Mesoamerican, however, not Israelite. Instead of menorahs and horned altars, archaeologists find world trees and effigy altars. However, the process of iconic assimilation would have occurred much earlier in Nephite history, I suspect within a decade after arrival.

How then should we see the people of Nephi in this context? The Nephites are now acculturated and have adopted the artistic traditions of the host culture's architecture and pottery. With the posited increase of trade and the resulting influence of external ideas, Jacob's warning speech makes sense, given the social and archaeological context in highland Guatemala for this time.

Accommodation to the physical culture need not preclude the continuation of Israelite religion.[1] Modern Latter-day Saints adorn their homes with Christmas trees that originated with pagan rites and have no trouble recontextualizing them as an acceptable part of Mormonism. Indeed, given the absence of the typical Christian crucifix, it might be difficult to identify LDS homes in an archaeological record from those of neighbors of other religions. Photographs of temples and the presence of scriptures and Church magazines would probably not survive long enough for archaeologists of the future to identify a Mormon sub-strand in the larger culture.

Omni 1:4

> 4 And now I, Amaron, write the things whatsoever I write, which are few, in the book of my father.

Redaction: Amaron dispenses with the formulaic introduction and simply declares his authorship, specifying that it will be brief. Both this declaration and his actual text indicate that he wrote it all at a single sitting. His successor, Chemish, states

---

[1]Lawrence H. Schiffman, *From Text to Tradition: A History of Second Temple and Rabbinic Judaism* (Hoboken, N.J.: KTAV Publishing House, 1991), 89.

that he produced his entry at a single sitting (v. 9), providing circumstantial evidence that Amaron did as well.

Omni 1:5

> 5 Behold, it came to pass that three hundred and twenty years had passed away, and the more wicked part of the Nephites were destroyed.

Chronology: This date locates the destruction at 276 B.C. Thirty-eight years have passed since Amaron received the plates from Omni. In this period, the Nephites' political situation has worsened, obviously because of increased warfare. In 276 B.C., some event occurred which selectively destroyed "the more wicked part of the Nephites." What might have happened? The only evidence comes in the following verses.

Omni 1:6–7

> 6 For the Lord would not suffer, after he had led them out of the land of Jerusalem and kept and preserved them from falling into the hands of their enemies, yea, he would not suffer that the words should not be verified, which he spake unto our fathers, saying that: Inasmuch as ye will not keep my commandments ye shall not prosper in the land.
> 7 Wherefore, the Lord did visit them in great judgment; nevertheless, he did spare the righteous that they should not perish, but did deliver them out of the hands of their enemies.

Ammaron declares the same thing that Jarom did (Jarom 1:9–12). There have been conflicts with the Lamanites and the promise of the land applies. The significant difference is that Jarom declares that the Nephites were sufficiently righteous to prevail due to the constant preaching of the prophets, priests, and teachers (Jarom 1:11–12). In Ammaron's account, the negative promise has been applied: "the Lord did visit them in great judgment." The final result is the preservation of the Nephites, but the contrast to Jarom indicates that along with the increasing warfare there are more times when the conflict is unfavorable to the Nephites.

History: The report is cryptic: The enemies of the Nephites (the Lamanites) destroyed the more wicked among the Nephites, but the righteous were preserved and the city was "deliver[ed]." It seems likely that a major Lamanite offensive attacked the city of Nephi, not just the surrounding territory and villages. Apparently they succeeded in penetrating into the city, killing a large number—more than the amount of casualties expected from an engagement between armed warriors alone.

No military action could have been precise enough to have singled out all of the "wicked" and spared the "righteous." Casualties are inevitable, even among the righteous. If we return to the scenario constructed around Jacob's discourse, he was addressing the city's wealthy and probably politically powerful elite. While the religious pendulum had swung to righteousness at the end of Jacob's life, social pressures away from righteousness were great. The typical integration of religion and politics makes it probable that the wealthy and powerful were espousing some other version of religion than that preached by Jacob, Enos, and the other prophets.

The true gospel's disciples, however, were apparently not among the rich and powerful. Assuming that the elites occupied one section of the city while the poor occupied another suggests an explanation for the differential destruction visited upon them. First, it is unlikely that the wealthy would have been personally engaged in the fighting, which reinforces the idea that the Lamanite army had penetrated the city itself. Second, the target of Mesoamerican warfare was not destruction, but dominance—capturing community leaders and, if they were not held for ransom, subjecting them to public humiliation and ritual sacrifice. Killing or carrying away these leaders for sacrifice could legitimately be described as "destruction," since they were no longer present, much as the removal of the leadership of Judah to Babylon "destroyed" Jerusalem, even though it still stood and people still lived there. Similarly, any booty taken from the city would more likely come from the wealthier sections. The inferior economic/political status of the "righteous" would have made them undesirable objects of capture. Thus, the social/religious distinction in the city of Nephi led to the divergent fates of the "wicked" and the "righteous" that Amaron recorded.

Predictably, after this devastation, the surviving "righteous" would naturally have recognized their salvation and increased in religious fervor while even nonbelieving survivors would have been strongly motivated to repent as part of recovering from the invasion.

Although this scenario is necessarily speculative, it seems that the Lamanites did not establish a permanent presence in the land or city of Nephi, but they would have reduced or broken the Nephite alliance with surrounding dependent towns. The Nephite political region would have moved into the Lamanite political sphere of influence. Combined with the fact that the Nephite population became significantly poorer and less powerful, the increasing numerical and political superiority of the surrounding Lamanite populations would have accelerated.

This hypothetical reconstruction will become even more important later in the book of Omni when Amaleki records the exodus of $Mosiah_1$ and the righteous from that city.

Omni 1:8

8 And it came to pass that I did deliver the plates unto my brother Chemish.

Other than Nephi himself, Amaron is the only writer on the small plates to pass them horizontally to a brother rather than vertically to a son, presumably because he had no eligible son. Although this is the only occasion on the small plates, we will see both plate transmission and leadership transmission to brothers in Mormon's text, as well as in Mesoamerican political tradition. (See commentary accompanying Alma 52:3–4 and Mormon 1:2.)

Chronology: The next date appears in Mosiah 6:4 at the coronation of $Mosiah_2$. At that point, 476 years had passed since Lehi left Jerusalem, making the date 124

B.C. In the 156 intervening years—about thirty years longer than the time between Jacob and Enos—seven people are involved in the narrative: Amaron, Chemish, Abinadom, Amaleki, $Mosiah_1$, Benjamin, and $Mosiah_2$. Amaron and Chemish are brothers, suggesting a relatively brief stewardship for Chemish. Amaleki's life begins in the "days" of $Mosiah_1$, and he dies during the reign of Benjamin, before 124 B.C.

The plate tradition for this period includes five people, and four generations: Amaron/Chemish, Abinadom, Amaleki, and $Mosiah_2$. If each generation were the same length, the plates would be in the hands of each writer thirty-nine years (including the time to $Mosiah_2$'s coronation). This cannot be the correct distribution of years, however, as Amaleki has the plates through much of the life of $Mosiah_1$ and sees the coronation of Benjamin, which would have occurred only after Benjamin had reached an appropriate age—perhaps, to hypothesize on the youthful side, twenty.

Since Amaleki uses the phrase "began to be old" (v. 25), a phrase that meant their seventies or later for Nephi, Jacob, and Enos (Jacob 1:9, 7:26; Enos 1:25; see commentary accompanying Jacob 1:9), we can reasonably assume that Amaleki was about seventy when he died. This figure, however, leaves about eighty-six years when the plates were in Chemish's and Abinadom's possession and further assumes that $Mosiah_2$'s coronation happened immediately after Amaleki gave the plates to Benjamin, which is unlikely.

Benjamin was old when he transferred the kingdom to $Mosiah_2$; he died three years later (Mosiah 6:5). If we assume that Benjamin had the plates at least twenty years before effecting the transfer, then Benjamin and Mosiah possessed the records jointly for sixty-six years or perhaps thirty-three years apiece. This span is much shorter than that of the other recordkeepers. Perhaps the frequent wars had something to do with short lives.

Omni 1:9

> 9 Now I, Chemish, write what few things I write, in the same book with my brother; for behold, I saw the last which he wrote, that he wrote it with his own hand; and he wrote it in the day that he delivered them unto me. And after this manner we keep the records, for it is according to the commandments of our fathers. And I make an end.

Since Chemish witnesses Amaron's entry, it suggests that Amaron made it on his deathbed. Perhaps he was fatally wounded during the war, lingering only long enough to complete his entry and transmit the record.

Redaction: Perhaps Chemish wrote his brief account in two sittings, the first very soon after receiving the plates. The phrase "and after this manner we keep the records" apparently belongs with the charge to keep the plates but with no mention of "genealogy."

After this introductory paragraph, however, Chemish apparently had nothing to say. When he was ready to pass the plates on, he simply ended his entry. There is no indication of how long he kept them, but presumably not long, since he was of the same generation as Amaron who had them for thirty-eight years. Obviously Chemish was Amaron's younger brother, since possession of the plates was the right of the firstborn.

Omni 1:10

> 10 Behold, I, Abinadom, am the son of Chemish. Behold, it came to pass that I saw much war and contention between my people, the Nephites, and the Lamanites; and I, with my own sword, have taken the lives of many of the Lamanites in the defence of my brethren.

Redaction: In contrast to his father, Abinadom apparently wrote some time after receiving the plates. The brevity of his text and the brusqueness of the conclusion suggest that he is writing near the end of his life, possibly at a single sitting, immediately before turning the plates over to his son.

History: Abinadom notes that he has seen "much war and contention" between Nephites and Lamanites. Significantly, "much war" and "much contention" suggest more than two or three incidents. In addition, Abinadom feels it important to describe himself as a warrior who has killed Lamanites "in the defense of my brethren." While "in the defense" might be formulaic, it seems more probable that he means it literally and that the wars are defensive rather than offensive.

Assuming the correctness of the social model I have described, it seems that the Lamanites made a significant incursion into the land of Nephi in 276 B.C., although the city survived and could be rebuilt as defensible. However, its relations with the surrounding towns diminished, making it more vulnerable to attack.

The wars Abinadom describes do not sound like large-scale military actions. Furthermore, if the Lamanites with their numerical superiority had been so motivated, they could have organized a large army and overwhelmed the Nephites. Instead, the Nephites' defensive strategies succeeded, suggesting small-scale military actions, probably targeting specific surrounding towns. As already noted, any enemy of the Nephites was a Lamanite (Jacob 1:14), and there is no evidence, at this point, of a "Lamanite" nation. More likely are smaller towns or cities who act against the Nephites. A single town or city might not keep up a multiple-year action in which it is repeatedly repelled, but a number of towns might try for the same prize sequentially, retreating to lick their wounds while the next one takes its chances. The Nephites, however, would have seen near-continuous warfare. That the Nephites were able to fend off the multiple attacks suggests a fairly large population, even after the destruction of the "more wicked part" of the people.

Omni 1:11

> 11 And behold, the record of this people is engraven upon plates which is had by the kings, according to the generations; and I know of no revelation save that which has been written, neither prophecy; wherefore, that which is sufficient is written. And I make an end.

Abinadom's record is short for two reasons: the kings keep the official record and he has no new revelations to record. As a man of war, he apparently concentrated on physical rather than spiritual survival. However, his clear knowledge of the kings' records, coupled with the isolation of Jacob's lineage from political power indicates that the existence of this record was common knowledge. Perhaps it was read from on public occasions or otherwise mentioned at public events.

Chronological: Abinadom does not specifically record passing the plates on to his son, Amaleki; but Amaleki begins his own account in Zarahemla rather than in the city of Nephi as did his father. It seems unlikely that Abinadom would have nothing to say if he had journeyed from Nephi to Zarahemla. Since only Amaleki mentions that journey, Abinadom probably died in Nephi.

Abinadom's failure to mention the recipient of the plates—which has been a consistent feature of even the briefest of his successors' record—suggests that Amaleki was too young at his father's death to receive them directly and that they were held in trust by an unnamed steward, possibly Abinadom's brother since the plates were, at times, entrusted to brothers.

Omni 1:12

> 12 Behold, I am Amaleki, the son of Abinadom. Behold, I will speak unto you somewhat concerning Mosiah, who was made king over the land of Zarahemla; for behold, he being warned of the Lord that he should flee out of the land of Nephi, and as many as would hearken unto the voice of the Lord should also depart out of the land with him, into the wilderness—

Because Amaleki states that he was "born in the days of Mosiah" (Omni 1:23), it implies that he had already begun his reign. However, it may simply be a synonym for Mosiah$_1$'s general lifetime.

Redaction: After so many writers who have had nothing to say, Amaleki has very important information, but he compresses it to a tight summary, not a running narrative as the events occurred. If my hypothesis is correct that Amaleki was very young when the exodus occurred, it would explain why his account is retrospective.

The fact that none of Amaleki's record recounts present events and the general brevity of the account suggest that he followed the example of his forebears in creating his account at a single sitting near the end of his life. There are no breaks in style or narrative that would suggest he left the material and returned to it. It also reads as though he composed as he wrote, rather than first composing, then writing. He doesn't relate how he came to witness these events, and the book's ending in particular has the feeling of someone who is wandering through his own narrative rather than closing with a purposeful and powerful message, as Nephi, for instance, had done.

Nevertheless, Amaleki does echo Nephi's separation from his brothers. Yahweh warned both Nephi and Mosiah$_1$. Both flee to a new location with "as many as would hearken unto the voice of the Lord" in Mosiah$_1$'s case and "and all those who would go with me. And all those who would go with me were those who believed in the warnings and the revelations of God" in Nephi's case (2 Ne. 5:6). Did Amaleki also see a parallel in Mosiah$_1$'s flight to a new territory that was already occupied and an unrecorded similarity in Nephi's journey?

History: One of the most significant events in Nephite history is recorded tersely in the second half of verse 12, and once again, we must draw on reasoned speculation to fill in the gaps. Amaleki states that the Lord commanded Mosiah$_1$ to take his people away from the land of Nephi. First, Mosiah$_1$ is obviously a prophet. Equally important, Mosiah$_1$ does not appear to be of Jacob's lineage. Prophets are called by Yahweh and are not consigned to a particular lineage.

Second, Mosiah$_1$ became king over Zarahemla. Amaleki does not describe Mosiah$_1$'s status in the city of Nephi. We might assume that he was also king in Nephi, but I argue that he was not. Jacob 1:11 explains that the kings of Nephi "were called by the people, second Nephi, third Nephi, and so forth, according to the reigns of the kings." It seems unlikely that, once adopting a regnal name, a ruler would revert to his birth name. Mosiah$_1$'s name is obviously his personal name. Furthermore, the tradition of referring to the ruler as "Nephi the ____th" completely disappears from the Book of Mormon after this point. Perhaps the throne name had disappeared earlier—no ruler is identified by any name between Jacob and Amaleki—but there seems to have been no reason to change the tradition before Amaleki unless the Lamanite destruction of the "more wicked part" (Omni 1:5) occasioned a change in the nature of Nephite kingship.

The most reasonable explanation is that Mosiah$_1$ was a prophet, but not the king. The command to flee came to him as prophet, as it had come to Lehi in Jerusalem and to Nephi in the land of their first inheritance. Those who follow Mosiah$_1$ are, like Nephi's followers, "as many as would hearken unto the voice of the Lord."

Obviously some chose to stay behind in a city continually under siege from various Lamanite groups. This relentless, hostile pressure suggests two reasons for the Lord's command at this point: (1) The Lamanites were planning an attack that would have overwhelmed the city. The Lord therefore instructed the righteous (those who would obey the prophet) to flee to save their lives, or (2) The Nephites decided to relieve the Lamanite pressure by making concessions to the Lamanite culture, notably, an official capitulation by the rulers. Given the conflation of politics and religion in the ancient world, the environment would have been untenable for the righteous.

While the first hypothesis is more straightforward, the second better explains why the king does not lead the exodus. Had the king of the Nephites gone with Mosiah$_1$, Amaleki would almost certainly have recorded it and the right of kingship would have continued with that King Nephi upon entering Zarahemla. Assuming that this analysis is correct, then the king's absence must be explained. Either he is dead, or he chooses to remain behind. It would be unusual to have a king endangered when his preservation was possible, so we may reasonably assume that the king chose not to leave.

When we return to the undercurrent of acculturation that flows through Nephite history and the tension between the righteous and the wealthy, a break between the religious (those who heed Yahweh's call and follow $Mosiah_1$) and the worldly/wealthy (who follow the king) is quite understandable. The tension finally erupted into division. Unlike the event that precipitated the break between Nephi and his brothers (the death of Lehi), no single event is identified to which we can ascribe this particular division. However, the increased warfare suggests that the cause is Lamanite pressure: a pressure that is resolved in victory, defeat, or accommodation. As I read the evidence, it was accommodation. A possible confirmation of this hypothesis comes from Zeniff, a Nephite who returns to the land of Nephi. His record indicates some of the reasons he wants to return: "I, Zeniff, having been taught in all the language of the Nephites, and having had a knowledge of the land of Nephi, or of the land of our fathers' first inheritance. . . . " (Mosiah 9:1). Zeniff is selected as a spy because he speaks the language of the Nephites, a requirement that would hardly be important unless that remained the language of the people in the land of Nephi. This suggests that a people into whom Zeniff could easily blend were in possession of the city of Nephi.

Archaeology: Why did $Mosiah_1$ choose to go in the direction he did? Yes, Yahweh was leading him, but it was also a natural direction. As Sorenson notes, the Book of Mormon never mentions traveling south out of Nephi.[2]

The more northerly direction (through the wilderness area) was a known trade route. Trade routes are difficult to trace archaeologically, but they may be presumed when an identifiable trade good moves from one location to another. In the case of Kaminaljuyú (Sorenson's city of Nephi), a major export was obsidian, which had a nearby source and was even worked in Kaminaljuyú.[3]

The volcanic processes that produce obsidian are so distinctive that pieces can be accurately traced to their source, even from many miles away. The Kaminaljuyú obsidian is known as El Chayal. El Chayal obsidian was traded down the coast during the early years of the Book of Mormon period; but at $Mosiah_1$'s time period, a distribution channel had been developed that traded El Chayal obsidian into Veracruz, northwest of Kaminaljuyú.[4] Thus, an established route and the assurance of friendly town(s) to the northwest help explain $Mosiah_1$'s flight in that direction.

Omni 1:13

> 13 And it came to pass that he did according as the Lord had commanded him. And they departed out of the land into the wilderness, as many as would hearken unto the voice of the Lord; and they were led by many preachings and prophesyings. And they were admonished continually by the word of God; and they were led by the power of his arm, through the wilderness until they came down into the land which is called the land of Zarahemla.

---

[2]John L. Sorenson, *An Ancient American Setting for the Book of Mormon* (Salt Lake City: Deseret Book/Provo, Utah: Foundation for Ancient Research and Mormon Studies, 1985), 12.

[3]Jane W. Pires-Ferreira, "Obsidian Exchange in Formative Mesoamerica," in *The Early American Village*, edited by Kent V. Flannery (New York: Academic Press, 1976), 302–3.

[4]Ibid.

Geography: As Joseph Allen notes, "The term 'wilderness' in the Book of Mormon apparently refers to mountainlands or forests as well as dense jungles. The term 'wilderness' means uninhabited areas."[5] While there are many "wildernesses" in the Book of Mormon, one stretch of "wilderness" is consistently described as a buffer between the land of Zarahemla and the land of Nephi. Sorenson summarizes:

> In late B.C. times a continuous wilderness strip separated Nephite Zarahemla from Lamanite territory. Furthermore, at least during the events recorded in the books of Mosiah and Alma, the city of Nephi (also called Lehi-Nephi) was some distance from the "narrow strip of wilderness" proper. On the Lamanite side of the border zone considerable wilderness space seems to have separated the city of Nephi from the transition strip. A good deal of searching for lost lands, marchings and countermarchings of foes, and wilderness travel went on in that extensive space. (See, for example, Mosiah 19:9–11, 18, 23, 28; 23:1–4, 25–31, 35; Alma 17:8–9, 13; 23:14, in light of verses 9–12; 24:1.)[6]

Sorenson suggests as this "wilderness" the mountain range along the north/northwest border of the valley of Guatemala that separates that area from the Grijalva River Valley, his candidate location for Sidon.[7] (See Map, "Plausible Locations in Mesoamerica for Book of Mormon Places," p. 4.) Thus, Mosiah$_1$ leads his people out of the land of Nephi, moving generally toward Zarahemla and passing through the "wilderness" which, in this case, is a mountainous strip.

Coming out of the "wilderness," the people of Mosiah go "down" to Zarahemla. Sorenson further points out that, in the ancient world, "up and down" refer to elevation, not cardinal direction.[8] Zarahemla is consistently "down" from the land of Nephi.[9] This makes sense as Zarahemla is located along a river, and the river necessarily is in the lower elevations of its valley. Even so, highland Guatemala is yet a higher elevation than the Grijalva River basin. The real-world topography fits the consistent references to it in the Book of Mormon.

History: We do not know how long the journey from Nephi to Zarahemla took, but it was not necessarily short. Ammon's journey between Zarahemla and the land of Nephi lasts forty days (Mosiah 7:4), and Alma's people traveled in the opposite direction for twenty-one days according to Sorenson's reconstruction from textual hints, though over a somewhat lesser distance.[10] The discrepancy between the two journeys appears to be related to the geography of the area, where the headwaters of two rivers are close together. (See commentary accompanying Mosiah 8:8.)

There is no easy way to calculate the time Mosiah$_1$'s people required to travel the 180 miles that Sorenson estimates for Mosiah's journey. The description of the journey, particularly that the people were "admonished continually," suggests that the journey was long enough that the people's patience

---

[5]Joseph L. Allen, *Exploring the Lands of the Book of Mormon* (Orem, Utah: SA Publishers, 1989), 287.
[6]Sorenson, *An Ancient American Setting for the Book of Mormon*, 12.
[7]Ibid., 153.
[8]Ibid., 23.
[9]Allen, *Exploring the Lands of the Book of Mormon*, 289.
[10]Sorenson, *An Ancient American Setting for the Book of Mormon*, 8.

was tried to the point where Yahweh needed to "admonish" them. They were guided through the wilderness, but we must remember that Israel was also guided and supported by Yahweh's arm in their "wilderness," and their journey lasted forty years. Furthermore, there is no indication that Yahweh guided them by the most direct route. Rather, it sounds as if the Lord pointed them in the right direction but that they had to find their own way there. It would not be unreasonable to assume that the journey took at least the forty days Ammon's group required (Mosiah 7:4–5), perhaps longer, given the large group of Mosiah$_1$'s people. However, the number forty should not necessarily be taken literally. It had long been a generic number in the Old World, a tradition that may have survived in the New World. Even without that influence, it is culturally significant in Mesoamerica, where the number systems are built on base twenty. The number appears frequently in Mesoamerican descriptions, indicating that it is also likely to be some type of generic number.[11]

During their trek through the wilderness, they would have had to subsist on the land as they probably left in some haste ("flee"), and could not completely provision themselves for travel. Although they were city dwellers, it seems likely that they also regularly supplemented their diet by hunting and would have increased their amount of hunting on the march. No doubt they also gathered wild plants and fruits en route.

Omni 1:14

> 15 And they discovered a people, who were called the people of Zarahemla. Now, there was great rejoicing among the people of Zarahemla; and also Zarahemla did rejoice exceedingly, because the Lord had sent the people of Mosiah with the plates of brass which contained the record of the Jews.

Geography: Sorenson suggests the site of Santa Rosa along the Grijalva River as his candidate for the location of Zarahemla, listing the following reasons:

> The largest archaeological site on the upper Grijalva in an appropriate position to qualify as Zarahemla is Santa Rosa. . . . By 1974 the site had been inundated by waters backed up nearly 70 miles behind Angostura Dam. . . .
>
> Linguistic research tells us that the upper Grijalva lay at the juncture of two major areas where long-established peoples and their languages existed. A couple of thousand years ago the Mayan languages probably extended throughout much of Guatemala to about the mountainous wilderness strip that separates the highlands of that nation from the Grijalva River valley. Downstream, from near Chiapa de Corzo and extending north and westward, were speakers of Zoque dialects; in the isthmus proper was the closely related Mixe language. Both blocs, the Mayan speakers on the Guatemalan and groups using tongues of the Mixe-Zoquean family on the isthmian side of Santa Rosa, had been there a long time. Ancestral Mixe-Zoquean has been shown to be the probable language of the Olmecs of the Gulf Coast, while Mayan speakers likely had been in the Cuchumatanes Mountains of Guatemala since well before 1000 B.C. (Evidence is uncertain, however,

---

[11]Alonzo L. Gaskill, *The Lost Language of Symbolism: An Essential Guide for Recognizing and Interpreting Symbols of the Gospel* (Salt Lake City: Deseret Book, 2003), 137–38.

whether Mayan languages were spoken until post-Book of Mormon times in the actual areas of the southern Guatemalan highlands where the Nephite and Lamanite settlements are best placed.) But neither major language group seems to have been established on the upper Grijalva, at least not until well into A.D. times. That intermediate zone seems to have been a linguistic frontier. Zarahemla's people had moved into the area from the Gulf Coast through lands occupied by Zoque speakers for centuries. His local followers in Mosiah's day likely spoke a language like Zoquean. Mosiah and his party, coming from the opposite direction, were among the first of a long series of groups who drifted down out of Guatemala into this valley over the next thousand years.

The archaeological sequence at Santa Rosa is interesting in terms of the Book of Mormon, although the findings will always remain incomplete because the site is now underwater. Major public construction in the form of what seem to have been "temple" or "palace" foundation mounds started on a modest scale at approximately 300 B.C. That coincided with growth in population, which produced the "city" of Zarahemla that Mosiah's party encountered a couple of generations later. The place remained no larger than a modest town, as we think of size, during the time when Mosiah, Benjamin his son, and Mosiah II reigned. Around 100 B.C. a spurt in the city's prosperity is evident, and a large number of major public structures were erected. That condition continued for around a century. Except for the site of Chiapa de Corzo far downstream, Santa Rosa became the largest, most significant "city" in the Grijalva basin just at the time when Zarahemla is reported by the Book of Mormon as becoming a regional center.[12]

As Sorenson points out, an interesting combination of factors reinforces Santa Rosa as the potential site for Zarahemla. The archaeological indication of a population explosion in Santa Rosa soon after Mosiah$_1$ and his people entered Zarahemla is quite suggestive. While the linguistic data do not tell us much at the moment, the position of Zarahemla along a linguistic and probably cultural frontier will certainly impact our understanding of some of the events later discussed for Zarahemla. (See commentary accompanying Alma 2:8–9, 22–30.)

Culture: Most fascinating is the reception given to Mosiah$_1$'s people: They are met with rejoicing. Since Mosiah's people have been struggling through the wilderness for forty days or more, they certainly would not have been able to present themselves as a royal procession. Rather, they would have been bedraggled and hungry refugees, in need of food and rest.

Rather than envisioning a spontaneous welcoming celebration, I suggest that Amaleki is conflating details of the story that actually occurred in a different sequence. The cause of the rejoicing comes from an explication of their genealogy, but this detail does not actually occur until later (v. 18). At that point, the Zarahemlaites rejoiced. I conjecture that Amaleki has restructured his story to create a socially and spiritually accurate history rather than one more faithful to the actual sequence of events.

Furthermore, the standard processes of two strange groups meeting in the ancient world would dictate a different scenario. First, the Zarahemlaites would have had to determine that Mosiah$_1$ and his people were not a military patrol and, on Mosiah$_1$'s side, that the Zarahemlaites would not immediately attack them. The

---

[12]Ibid., 153–55.

next stage would have been welcoming the strangers and offering them hospitality. Perhaps it was during the process of exchanging information so that they might know how to treat each other that the rejoicing began. From the brief text, it seems that the brass plates played a key role. Amaleki states that the Zarahemlaites "did rejoice exceedingly, because the Lord had sent the people of Mosiah$_1$ with the plates of brass which contained the record of the Jews."

Why would the plates have had this effect? I suggest that possession of the record—rare in itself, but also on the distinctive brass plates—served a talismanic function identifying Mosiah$_1$ as an important man. Since the Nephites' acceptance based on genealogy occurred after the initial reception, apparently it was the very fact of possessing such an important item as the plates that prompted the Zarahemlaites' acceptance of the Nephite refugees.

Conferring on the content of the plates must have occurred later. At that point, the common genealogy of the two groups would have been established, making their incorporation into a single people less improbable than one might imagine. It would not be the political union of two groups of strangers but the reunion of long-lost relatives.

History: I have already argued that Mosiah$_1$ was not the king in Nephi. (See commentary accompanying Omni 1:12.) Nevertheless, he must have been of Nephi's lineage both because he later becomes king and because he had the brass plates, which would have remained with the kingly line. (Jacob and his descendants never mention transmitting the brass plates, only the small plates of Nephi.)[13] Thus, Mosiah$_1$ had to have a genealogical right to the plates. Furthermore, he also took with him the Liahona and the sword of Laban. (Benjamin gives them to Mosiah$_2$ [Mosiah 1:16], hence, they had to have come with Mosiah$_1$.)

The Book of Mormon is entirely silent about the people who remained in Nephi or from whom Mosiah$_1$ and the believers fled. Was it a new invading army of Lamanites? Or were the Nephite leaders becoming so wicked that they turned on the righteous? Either possibility is plausible, but the outcome of either would be that the city of Nephi became a Lamanite holding, using as the definition of "Lamanite" those unfriendly to the Nephites.

The only information Amaleki gives about Zarahemla is that both the land and city are named the same as the current ruler. It is likely that Zarahemla founded this city, giving it his name. While he founded the city, he certainly did not begin the lineage. Just as the Nephites continued to trace their origins to the Old World

---

[13]Donald Arthur Cazier, "A Study of Nephite, Lamanite, and Jaredite Governmental Institutions and Policies as Portrayed in the Book of Mormon" (Master's thesis, Brigham Young University, 1972), 72. "If Mosiah was not the king when he left the land of Nephi, the question arises as to how he happened to get the large plates of Nephi, which obviously accompanied him to Zarahemla (W of M 3). The fact that no account is given of a reenactment of the Nephi-Laban episode suggests that Mosiah may have had easy access to the records. If he was not the king, it is possible that Mosiah, as a descendant of Nephi (Mosiah 25:13), was a member of the royal household, and as such had access to the royal treasury."

after sojourns in both Nephi and Zarahemla, the people of Zarahemla are named for a more recent king but traced their history to Mulek, who had come from Jerusalem. According to Amaleki, God had led the people of Zarahemla "into the land where Mosiah$_1$ discovered them; and they had dwelt there from that time forth" (Omni 1:16). No date is given for this migration from the location where the original Mulekites landed to this place where Mosiah$_1$'s people meet with Zarahemla's people.

Sorenson suggests:

> The people of Zarahemla seem to have been named after their leader, who reported to Mosiah that his ancestors had arrived from the Mediterranean area by boat and that he was a descendant of "Mulek," a son of Zedekiah, the last of the Jewish kings before the Exile. The voyage arrived first in the land northward, then moved south. Probably they first settled at the east-coast site known later as "the city of Mulek" (note Alma 8:7). "And they came from there up into the south wilderness" (Alma 22:31), where Mosiah later encountered them. Factions had warred among themselves; Zarahemla was now chief over one group (Omni 1:17). If the city of Zarahemla was named after him (or his father), then his group would not have been in that spot for very long, although they might have lived in the general locale for some time.[14]

It is a fairly common practice in the Book of Mormon to name a city after its founder. Since we have a man named Zarahemla at the head of the city named Zarahemla, Sorenson's suggestion that they had not been in that area very long appears to be correct. The people's identity was modified by the lifetime of the man Zarahemla. This would mean that Zarahemla's ancestors had been in the north for over four hundred years before traveling south up the Sidon River valley, though the migration up the valley may have been incremental.

Omni 1:15

> 15 Behold, it came to pass that Mosiah discovered that the people of Zarahemla came out from Jerusalem at the time that Zedekiah, king of Judah, was carried away captive into Babylon.

Culture: These two peoples could learn about each other's genealogy so quickly because kinship was the chief identifier for individuals. Sorenson discusses the principle of kin interactions for a later Book of Mormon event:

> When Alma had approached him, Amulek identified himself as a "Nephite" (Alma 8:20). "I am Amulek . . . a descendant of Nephi," Alma 10:2–3 reports him saying. Mosiah 17:2 gives Alma's descent in identical language. We understand, then, that the two were establishing that they belonged to the same lineage. A Mayan practice at the time of the Spanish conquest shows the same principle governing how to get along in strange territory: "When anyone finds himself in a strange region and in need, he has recourse to those of his name [kin group]; and if there are any, they receive him and treat him with all kindness."[15]

---

[14]Ibid., 148.

[15]Ibid., 212, citing William A. Haviland, "Principles of Descent in Sixteenth Century Yucatan," *Katunob* 8, no. 2 (December 1972): 64.

Understandably, therefore, one of the acts in dealing with the newcomers emerging from the wilderness would be to examine genealogies to ascertain possible kinship obligations. What they found was a supremely important kinship—one which placed the origins of both groups in Jerusalem, which by now must have nearly become the stuff of legend.

Having thus established an important bond linking them both to a common sacred origin, the Zarahemlaites welcomed their new kin appropriately: with rejoicing.

Omni 1:16

> 16 And they journeyed in the wilderness, and were brought by the hand of the Lord across the great waters, into the land where Mosiah discovered them; and they had dwelt there from that time forth.

History: The story of the Mulekites up to this point begins in the same place as that of the Lehites and at roughly the same time. During Zedekiah's reign, the Lord instructed Lehi to leave Jerusalem, and the Mulekites took shape as a group when Zedekiah, a Babylonian client king, was dethroned.[16]

---

[16]Orson Scott Card, *The Book of Mormon: Artifact or Artifice?* Adapted from a speech given at the BYU Symposium on Life, the Universe, and Everything, February 1993, http://www.nauvoo.com/library/card-bookofmormon.html (accessed June 2004), provides an interesting alternative reading of the Zarahemlaite background:

> Let me offer an aside on the matter of Zarahemla and the Mulekites. Much has been made of the statement by King Zarahemla that his people were descended from the youngest son of King Zedekiah. Extraordinary and completely unconvincing efforts have been made to find such a son, overlooked by the Babylonian captors of Jerusalem; just as much effort has been devoted to explaining how a good Jaredite name like Mulek could show up in the family of an Israelite king. But is this really necessary?
>
> In Meso-American culture, every ruling class had to assert an ancient ancestor who was a god or, at the very least, a king in an admired culture. Whoever ruled in the Valley of Mexico always had to claim to be descended from or heirs of the Toltecs. Rival Mayan cities would play at ancestral one-upmanship. Imagine, now, the vigorous and dangerous Nephites, coming down the valley of the Sidon River from the highlands of Guatemala. King Zarahemla is negotiating with King Mosiah. Mosiah tells him of his ancestry, of course, and the story of how God led Lehi and Nephi out of Jerusalem at the time when Zedekiah was king of Israel.
>
> To Mosiah, what he is doing is bearing his testimony and asserting the divine guidance that he receives as the legitimate king of a chosen people. To Zarahemla, what he is doing is claiming that his lineage gives him the right to rule over the people of Zarahemla and displace him from the kingship. So what does Zarahemla do? Well, Mosiah admits that his ancestors were not kings in Israel. So Zarahemla picks his most noble ancestor, Mulek, and then declares him to be the son of that last king of Israel. Thus if anybody has the right to rule over anybody, it's Zarahemla who has the right to rule over Mosiah and his people. But Mosiah kindly points out that if Zarahemla and his people are descended from Israelites, they certainly seem to have forgotten the language and writing, and therefore have obviously degenerated from the high culture of Israel. The Nephites, on the other hand, have preserved a writing system that no one else uses, and which Zarahemla can't read. They have a history accounting for every year since they arrived in America, which Zarahemla of course cannot produce.
>
> In the end, whatever negotiation there was ended up with Zarahemla bowing out of the kingship and his people becoming subject to rule by the Nephites. But the story of Mulek served a very useful purpose even so—it allowed the people to merge, not with the hostility of conquerors over the conquered, though in fact that is what the relationship fundamentally was, but rather with the idea of brotherhood. They were all Israelites.

Siegfried H. Horn, professor emeritus of archaeology at Andrews University, provides the following historical background on Zedekiah:

> When Nebuchadnezzar put Zedekiah, Jehoiachin's uncle, on the throne of Judah, the Babylonian king changed his name from Mattaniah, "Gift of Yahweh" to Zedekiah, "Righteousness of Yahweh." He probably did this so that the new name would serve as a continual reminder of his solemn oath of loyalty to Nebuchadnezzar, by his own God Yahweh who was considered to have acted as a just witness (2 Kgs. 24:17, 2 Chr. 36:13, Ezek. 17:15–19). Zedekiah, however, was a weak character, and although he was sometimes inclined to do right, he allowed himself to be swayed from the path of loyalty and fidelity by popular demands, as the history of his reign clearly shows.
>
> For a number of years—according to Josephus, for eight years—Zedekiah remained loyal to Babylonia. Once he sent an embassy to Nebuchadnezzar to assure the Babylonian monarch of his fidelity (Jer. 29:3–7). In Zedekiah's fourth year (594/593 B.C.), he himself made a journey to Babylon (Jer. 51:59), perhaps having been summoned to renew his oath of loyalty. Later, however, under the constant pressure of his subjects, particularly the nobility, who urged him to seek the aid of Egypt against Babylon, Zedekiah made an alliance with the Egyptians (Jer. 37:6–10, 38:14–28). In doing so, he disregarded the strong warnings of the prophet Jeremiah. This Egyptian alliance was probably made after Pharaoh Psamtik II had personally appeared in Judah in 591 B.C. and had given Zedekiah all kinds of assurances and promises of help.
>
> Nebuchadnezzar had prudently refrained from attacking Egypt, in order to avoid the trap that the Assyrians had earlier fallen into. Nevertheless, he was unwilling to lose any of his western possessions to Egypt; he therefore marched against Judah as soon as Zedekiah's Egyptian alliance became apparent. Nebuchadnezzar systematically devastated the land, practically repeating what Sennacherib had done a century earlier.[17]

Zedekiah reigned from 597 B.C.E. to 586 B.C.E. Lehi was called as a prophet in the first year of his reign (1 Ne. 1:4), and Mulek left shortly after his reign ended. In vengeance for Zedekiah's treachery, Nebuchadnezzar killed his sons before his eyes, then blinded Zedekiah and carried him off to Babylon (2 Kgs. 25:7). The Bible reports no other details, but the Book of Mormon makes it clear that a son named Mulek avoided the fate of his brothers and crossed the ocean as part of the group that eventually becomes the people of Zarahemla (Mosiah 25:2, Hel. 8:21).

Of the name "Mulek" and this enigmatic son of Zedekiah, Sorenson notes:

> "Mulek" appears as "Muloch" in the printer's manuscript of the Book of Mormon and as "Mulok" in printed editions from 1830 to 1852; the name then became "Mulek." However it was pronounced, the name comes to us of course as Nephite ears heard it from the people of Zarahemla, and their pronunciation could have changed it somewhat from the Old World Hebrew familiar to us. What is clear throughout these variations in the spelling of the name is that we have here a reflex of the Hebrew root *mlk*, as in Hebrew melek, "king."
>
> Nowhere in the Bible are the children of Zedekiah enumerated, let alone named, although we are told that he had daughters as well as sons (Jer. 43:6, 52:10). He was twenty-one on his accession to the throne. Being a noble, he already had the economic resources to have possessed a wife and child(ren) at that time. After his accession, he took multiple wives in the manner of the kings of Judah before him (Jer. 38:22–23 refers to

[17]Siegfried H. Horn, "The Divided Monarchy: The Kingdoms of Judah and Israel," in *Ancient Israel*, edited by Hershel Shanks (Washington, D.C.: Biblical Archaeology Society, 1998), 146–47.

Zedekiah's "wives") so that when he was captured at age thirty-two, he might have had a considerable progeny.

Robert F. Smith has mustered evidence that a son of Zedekiah with a name recalling Mulek may actually be referred to in the Bible. Jeremiah 38:6 in the King James translation speaks of Jeremiah's being cast into "the dungeon [literally, "pit"] of Malchiah the son of Hammelech." The last five words should be rendered more accurately, "Malkiyahti, the son of the king." This personal name could have been abbreviated to something like "Mulek." Thus Jeremiah might have been put into "the [very] dungeon of Mulek[?], the son of the king [Zedekiah]" referred to in the Hebrew text of Jeremiah 38:6.[18]

Robert F. Smith's suggestion has been controversial, even among LDS scholars.[19] Nevertheless, as archaeologist Jeffrey R. Chadwick recounts Smith's argument:

> Smith also suggested that the Book of Mormon name Mulek might be a shortened form of the biblical Hebrew Malkiyahu. In support of this possibility, he noted that while Jeremiah's scribe is called Baruch . . . in Jeremiah 36:4, a longer form of his name— . . . (Berekhyahu)—appears on an ancient stamp seal impression published by Israeli archaeologist Nahman Avigad. Since the Hebrew long-form name Berekhyahu could apparently be expressed in a hypocoristic (short form) version like Barukh, Smith reasoned that perhaps the long form Malkiyahu could have a short form like Mulek. In that event, the "Malkiyahu son of the king" in Jeremiah 38:6 could well have been the Book of Mormon's Mulek, son of King Zedekiah (see Hel. 8:21).[20]

This suggestion has been strengthened by archaeological evidence:

> Recently, an ancient Judean stamp seal has been identified as bearing the Hebrew form of the name "Malchiah son of Hammelech." Does this mean that an actual archaeological relic that belonged to an ancient Book of Mormon personality has been located? Has the seal of Mulek been found?
>
> To answer this question requires us to explore a number of different but related issues. First, a word of explanation. The reading of Jeremiah 38:6 in the King James Version is somewhat misleading. The Hebrew Bible . . . [text is] pronounced Malkiyahu ben hamelek. The name Malkiyahu was reasonably rendered into English as "Malchiah" by the King James scholars, and the word ben was accurately translated as "son." But the King James term Hammelech . . . is not really a name; it is a transliteration. In Hebrew, hamelek means "the king" (ha is the definite article "the," and melek is the word for "king"). Thus, accurately translated, Jeremiah 38:6 refers to "Malkiyahu son of the king." Noted biblical scholar John Bright translates the phrase as "Prince Malkiah" (the term prince referring to a royal son) in his Anchor Bible commentary on Jeremiah.[21]

Of course this is the most promising connection between Mulek and Zedekiah. However, another alternative is possible. What relationship did Mulek have to the throne of Israel? Although identified as Zedekiah's son, he is not numbered among them. Possibly, "son" is used metaphorically rather than literally. Hershel Shanks,

---

[18]John L. Sorenson, *Nephite Culture and Society: Collected Papers*, edited by Matthew R. Sorenson (Salt Lake City: New Sage Press, 1997), 110–11.

[19]Jeffrey R. Chadwick, "Has the Seal of Mulek Been Found?" *Journal of Book of Mormon Studies* 12, no. 2 (2003): 73.

[20]Ibid, 74.

[21]Ibid.

editor of the *Biblical Archaeology Review*, provides three possible ways that "son" was used in connection with royalty: "(1) the word means what it says; (2) 'son' refers to a royal official unrelated by blood to the king; [or] (3) 'son' refers to any male scion [descendant] of the royal family."[22] The non-kin connection is supported by a bulla, or clay seal, identified as the official seal of the "son" of King Jehoiakim. This "son" is named Yerame'el, but Shanks finds it doubtful that he is King Jehoiakim.[23] By this reading, Mulek would be an important functionary rather than a legitimate son, all of whom where killed, according to the Bible text.

If Mulek was a literal son, then how did he survive? Joseph L. Allen suggests four hypotheses:

> 1. Some Book of Mormon readers suggest that Mulek was only a baby and that those who were charged with his care literally carried him away from Jerusalem and saw to it that he was brought to the New World.
>
> 2. Other readers propose that perhaps Mulek was disguised as a daughter and was taken into Egypt prior to coming to the Promised Land.
>
> 3. A further possibility is that the mother of Mulek may have been pregnant at the time and that she was the one escaped the wrath of the Babylonians. This proposal would explain, as do the above two proposals, the reason for this group's not having any records with them. The group had no time to collect records, as they were fleeing. The mother's major concern probably was the protection of her unborn [child] and, as such, she played the role of other great women in history who were inspired by the Lord that their children had very significant missions to fill.
>
> 4. A fourth proposal reflects the possibility that Mulek was not even born at the time his older brothers were killed. This proposal suggests that Zedekiah/Mattaniah, who was blind, had children while in captivity among the Babylon. Thirty years later, when the Jews were released from Babylon would then be the time that Mulek, now a young man, was led by the Lord to the "Land North." These proposed events are then in line with the commentary of Archaeologist [Bruce] Warren, who identified the date of the Mulekites' arrival to Mesoamerica at about 536 B.C., which matches a significant date in the Nuttall Codex.[24]

Allen appears to prefer the fourth proposal based upon the date correspondence in the Nuttall Codex and his interpretation of the *danzante* figures at Monte Albán. Contrary to Allen's preference, this is probably the least viable of the alternatives. The Nuttall Codex is a Mixtec document probably dating to the fifteenth century. The Mixtecs are a Central Mexican culture group who are distant in language and culture from the area where the majority of the Book of Mormon took place. On these grounds alone the connection between a date in the Nuttall and anything in the Book of Mormon is questionable. The Mixtec calendar used the same general system as most Mesoamerican calendars. They combine day, month, and year signs into sets that recur every fifty-two years.[25] In all of the Mesoamerican calendars,

---

[22]Hershel Shanks, *Jerusalem: An Archaeological Biography* (1995), 107–8, quoted in John L. Sorenson, "Was Mulek a 'Blood Son' of King Zedekiah?" *Insights: A Window on the Ancient World*, February 1999, 2.

[23]Ibid.

[24]Allen, *Exploring the Lands of the Book of Mormon*, 272.

[25]Arthur G. Miller, "Introduction to the Dover Edition," *Codex Nuttall*, edited by Zelia Nuttall (New York: Dover Publications, 1975), xiv.

only the Maya Long Count used a fixed date in history in addition to the fifty-two-year cycle. Therefore, while it is relatively easy to know when a Maya Long Count date correlates to the Western calendar, most Mesoamerican dates recur every fifty-two years and we cannot tell from that date alone in which fifty-two-year cycle it occurred. It is rather like having a month/day calendar, but no year date. We might know, for instance, that April 6 is an important date, but seeing the date alone does not tell us the particular year in which April 6 occurs.

Allen prefers this reading because he accepts Monte Albán as the probable site for the city of Mulek and reads the *danzante* figures as reminiscences of the Babylonian captivity. Monte Albán was an important Zapotec center in Oaxaca that began its history around 500 B.C. Archaeologist Susan Toby Evans describes the *danzantes:* "One monumental construction that may possibly have been established in Monte Albán Early I phase [500–300 B.C.] is a collection of bas-relief portraits, the *danzantes*, called "dancers" because of their unusual postures. To date, over 300 danzante sculptures have been recovered, many of them reused as steps in later buildings. Many scholars believe that these are portraits of sacrificial victims . . . but an alternative view presents them as figures undergoing age-set rituals."[26] The sacrificial reading might correlate with Allen's reading only in that it was captives who were sacrificed. However, even in that case, the iconography appears to emphasize the sacrifice, not the captivity. Equally certainly, these sacrifices did not survive their captivity, which is required for Allen's "born in Babylon" hypothesis.

I follow Sorenson's hypothesis which locates the city of Mulek at La Venta rather than Monte Albán. The internal distances in Sorenson's correlation appear to fit the data better and suggest that Allen may have been over-influenced by the *danzante* figures to accept Monte Albán.

As a final issue with the "born in Babylon" hypothesis, Omni 1:15 notes: "The people of Zarahemla came out from Jerusalem at the time that Zedekiah, king of Judah, was carried away captive into Babylon." "At the time" does not seem to allow time for a child to be born in the Babylonian captivity.

In any case, the political unrest was sufficient reason for Mulek and his associates to flee from Jerusalem. It also seems reasonable, if Mulek was Zedekiah's actual son, that he escaped death with his brothers by being a young child or an infant, even an unborn infant. His status as a nominal prince (or, if not Zedekiah's son, his possible important court position) would explain why the city was named for him.[27]

Like the Lehites, the Mulekites fled through the "wilderness" (Omni 1:16); but without more details, their route is impossible to trace. Since it was not unusual for the people of Israel to see their history in terms of sacred models, having any

---

[26]Susan Toby Evans, *Ancient Mexico and Central America: Archaeology and Culture History* (London: Thames & Hudson, 2004), 192. Evans notes that the evidence for sacrifice is similar to that garnered for a San José Mogote's Monument 3 which "depicts a figure with a puffy, slitted eye, lips drawn back in a grimace, overall posture of vulnerability , the stylized bloom of rounded elements on the chest and abdomen suggesting the guts after disembowelment" (188).

[27]J. N. Washburn, *Book of Mormon Guidebook and Certain Problems in the Book of Mormon*, bound in one volume (Self-published, 1968), 25.

journey begin "in the wilderness" has symbolic associations with the exodus from Egypt, regardless of the specifics of geography. We also have no details about the vessel in which they crossed the ocean or the ocean route they took. However, they landed in the "north" compared to Lehi's landing (Hel. 6:10). This landing was apparently in the Jaredite territory that the Nephites later called "Desolation" because of the evidence of the devastating genocidal battles there (Alma 22:29–30). Furthermore, the city of Mulek was on the east coast.[28] From that original location, the Mulekites moved (again, no details are given) to Zarahemla, a location "south" of Desolation and "north" of the land of Nephi.

Archaeology: This discussion must begin with an acknowledgment of archaeology's limitations in elucidating history and particularly our inability to identify any archaeological artifact as "Mulekite." There is no better archaeological evidence for the Mulekites than for the Lamanites and Nephites. (See "Excursus: Archaeology and the Book of Mormon," following 1 Nephi 18.) There is also no worse evidence for the Mulekites than for the Lamanites and Nephites. For all Book of Mormon peoples, the archaeological goal cannot be one of firm identification, but rather of the plausible context of a known time period and culture. With the union of Nephites and Mulekites, the Book of Mormon story becomes more culturally diverse, thus justifying a discussion about a hypothetical but plausible relationship between the Mulekites and Mesoamerican archaeology.

The oldest major Mesoamerican civilization is called the Olmec, a name assigned to the residents of the southern Gulf lowlands in the southern part of the modern state of Veracruz. The name they called themselves is not known. This culture provided the foundation of many later architectural and artistic forms, including writing with glyphs (though few of the early forms have been found and have disputed translations). The Olmec are generally considered to date from 1500 to 600 B.C. and were at their most influential between 1200 and 600 B.C., with fading influence lasting to A.D. 1.[29] They are considered to be Mesoamerica's most advanced and influential culture during the time of their florescence.[30] (See Ether, Part 1: Context, Chapter 1, "Historical Background of the book of Ether.")

The Mulekites arrived in this Olmec culture region during the final years of Olmec influence. Obviously, the Mulekites were able to survive as a distinct cultural group, and perhaps their ability to do so can be attributed to their arrival at a time when the Olmec political hegemony had been disrupted and when it would no longer swallow a new group whole into the larger society.

Sorenson has suggested the Olmec site of La Venta as a plausible location for the city of Mulek. In particular, he notes of La Venta Stela 3: "This massive monument dating about the sixth century B.C. seems to show the meeting of leaders

---

[28]David Palmer, *In Search of Cumorah* (Bountiful, Utah: Horizon Publishers, 1981), 147.

[29]Richard A. Diehl and Michael D. Coe, "Olmec Archaeology," in *The Olmec World: Ritual and Rulership*, edited by Michael D. Coe (Princeton, N.J.: Princeton University Art Museum, 1996), 11–13.

[30] Ibid., 22.

of two ethnic groups. The man on the right looks very much like a Jew of that time."[31]

The stela is suggestive, but Sorenson's interpretation is heavily based on the interpretation of the man's facial features, including the beard. Sorenson himself describes the wide variety of facial types in Mesoamerican populations.[32] The suggestion that a beard is necessarily a marker of a foreign population oversimplifies a complex relationship between the physiology of the population and the artistic record. Beards are not uncommon in Mesoamerican art and not conclusively markers of foreignness. Nevertheless, Sorenson's suggestion is important. Describing the move of the Zarahemlaites from the city of Mulek, Sorenson further suggests:

> One gets the impression reading about chief Zarahemla's people in the Book of Omni that they were localized and unsophisticated (for example, they were not literate). Those characteristics ring true for what was going on at the same period in Mesoamerica. Reference to warfare in their background in the centuries before 200 B.C. (Omni 1:17) fits too. In light of these agreements it is not unreasonable that the descendants of the shipload constituting Mulek's party were able to find a niche for themselves in the land, incorporating and ruling over some remnant of the people left in the land southward after the abandonment of Olmec La Venta.[33]

The reasons are unclear, but both the Olmec sites of San Lorenzo and La Venta were abandoned around 400 B.C. although they were near the end of their dominance around 600 B.C. It is absolutely certain that the Mulekites would have adapted to the Olmec cultural ways during the three hundred years between their landing in the Olmec culture region and their encounter with Mosiah$_1$'s at Zarahemla, which is located on the periphery of Olmec influence. Like the Nephites, the Mulekites would have adopted the material culture of their powerful neighbors. They would have become Mesoamericanized. A significant difference between Sorenson's position and mine is the nature and direction of rule. Sorenson sees the Mulekites as ruling in La Venta. I see them as absorbing Olmec culture but lacking political dominance until they moved to Zarahemla where they either founded the city and, hence, automatically become politically dominant by default or took over an existing city, including, naturally, its political system.

By moving to Zarahemla, the Mulekites (at least the remnant that were the people of Zarahemla) were removing themselves to the periphery of Olmec influence. This move may have resulted from the political upheavals following the disintegration of the Olmec power structures. The ancient Olmec lived in an area currently home to two linguistic-cultural groups, the Mixe and the Zoque. The linguistic reconstruction of the languages indicates that during the time of the

---

[31]Sorenson, *An Ancient American Setting for the Book of Mormon*, 121.

[32]John L. Sorenson, *Images of Ancient America: Visualizing the Book of Mormon* (Provo, Utah: Foundation for Ancient Research and Mormon Studies, 1998), 18–23.

[33]Ibid., 120.

Olmec the two daughter languages were a single language called Mixe-Zoque.[34] The later split in the languages also represents a separation of peoples and politics.

Archaeologist Susan Toby Evans describes population movements that are very similar to the Book of Mormon's description of a cultural confluence in this area:

> A few centers of interior Chiapas survived what appears to have been major population restructuring in the period 400–200 B.C., when La Venta's important influence on this region was dead, and Maya centers in the Petén were growing powerful. In fact, Maya peoples began to push into the northern part of the interior of Chiapas, and Zoque-culture communities that survived, such as Santa Rosa [Sorenson's Zarahemla], Chiapa de Corzo [Sorenson's Sidom], and Mirador [Sorenson's Ammonihah], show a strong presence of Maya trade wares and architectural styles. Yet continued elite ties with other Mixe-Zoque peoples of the Isthmian region are indicated by the very early calendric monument, Chiapa de Corzo's Stela 2, dated to 36 B.C. Chiapa de Corzo is one of Mesoamerica's oldest continuously occupied communities, and in the Late Formative period [300 B.C.–A.D. 1] it had one of Mesoamerica's earliest true palaces.[35]

When the people of Zarahemla and the righteous refugees from Nephi met, two separate material and intellectual cultures joined. Even though both began in Jerusalem, the intervening three hundred years meant that they absorbed much of the surrounding material and intellectual cultures, leading to some similarities but also to differences. From this point on, the Book of Mormon shows a discernible Jaredite influence (brought into Zarahemla as part of the Mulekites' Mesoamerican experience) as well as the necessity of cultural accommodation, as indicated by the problem of language (vv. 17–18).

Omni 1:17

> 17 And at the time that Mosiah discovered them, they had become exceedingly numerous. Nevertheless, they had had many wars and serious contentions, and had fallen by the sword from time to time; and their language had become corrupted; and they had brought no records with them; and they denied the being of their Creator; and Mosiah, nor the people of Mosiah, could understand them.

Culture: What does it mean that the people of Zarahemla are "exceedingly numerous"? As I read it, they greatly outnumbered the Nephites (Mosiah 25:2), but still inhabited only a single land surrounding a single main city. Their influence is, therefore, not all that great. Later texts will indicate that Zarahemla had a regional influence, but that is not apparent at this early time.

Like the Nephites, they have had "wars and serious contentions" although Amaleki does not explain who their enemies were. The Zarahemlaites would not have typified their opponents as "Lamanites" because they would not have known the term. Furthermore, if the Nephites did not find the Zarahemlaites for three hundred years, then it is logical that the "true" Lamanites would not have found

---

[34]Lyle Campbell and Terrence Kaufman, "A Linguistic Look at the Olmecs," *American Antiquity* 41, no. 1 (January 1976): 80–88.

[35]Evans, *Ancient Mexico and Central America*, 222, 223. Internal quotation marks silently removed. Text skips an inserted page on calendrics.

them either. This verse makes it incontestably clear that the Book of Mormon is speaking of, but not naming, indigenous peoples. In the context of Mesoamerican archaeology, this picture of war and political unrest fits what is known as the readjustment that must have accompanied the decline of the Olmec hegemony. The Zarahemlaites would be a group moving out of the homeland to a safer area.

Amaleki also states that the Zarahemlaite language has been corrupted, they brought no records with them, and they deny the Creator. First, we should understand the issue of language. Mormon later indicates that "the Hebrew hath been altered by us also" (Morm. 9:33) so that by the end of the record, at least, the Nephites are no longer speaking the language they left Jerusalem with. It is subtle but significant that Mormon uses the term "altered" while $Mosiah_1$ says that the Zarahemlaites' language has been "corrupted." The connotations suggest an insider/outsider perspective. For the insider, changes are simply alterations. For the outsider who must confront "alterations"—particularly alterations of such magnitude that the other group cannot be understood—it is a case of "corruption." The implication is not merely the development of a different dialect but a language. For instance, Appalachian English in the United States preserves older forms of British English and has done so since the seventeenth century. Even given the fact of constant communication between the two groups (greatly accelerated in the twentieth century by radio, television, and ease of travel), it does not seem unlikely that British and American English would remain mutually intelligible, with only dialectical differences. The Nephite and Zarahemlaite languages are not just different dialects. They are mutually unintelligible. At least one of the two is no longer speaking Hebrew, and possibly neither is.

The Mulekite lack of records is significant. Gary R. Whiting, an elder in the Community of Christ Church (formerly RLDS), suggests: "The lack of records had been a stumbling block for the Mulekites, in that without them to stabilize their language it had become corrupt."[36] Although this explanation is commonly accepted, it does not seem reasonable that possession of texts would have stopped or even necessarily slowed the pace of linguistic change. More probably, it is simply that, without records, there was no reason to preserve a language whose speakers could communicate only with a group of others that shrank with every generation. There was no reason not to adopt the language of the people among whom the Mulekites found themselves.

Assuming that they acquired the language of the Olmec area, they would have learned common Zoquean or common Mixean.[37] If Sorenson's candidate location of Zarahemla in the Grijalva River Basin is correct, the Zarahemlaites would have

---

[36]Gary R. Whiting, "The Testimony of Amaleki," in *The Book of Mormon: Jacob through Words of Mormon. To Learn with Joy*, edited by Monte S. Nyman and Charles D. Tate Jr. (Provo, Utah: BYU Religious Studies Center, 1990), 300.

[37]Lyle Campbell, "Mesoamerican Linguistics," mimeograph, April 1976, section giving language groupings from 600 B.C.E. to 1 C.E. These are the daughter languages of the putative Olmec language, termed Mixe-Zoque.

been in territory historically associated with Zoque speakers.[38] I hypothesize that the Zarahemlaites/Mulekites were part of the historical movement of Zoquean speakers from the Oaxacan area up the Grijalva River Valley. It is perhaps because of their linguistic affinity with Zoquean speakers in the area that Amaleki described the Zarahemlaites as "exceedingly numerous"; he meant the speakers of the *lingua franca* of Zarahemla were exceeding numerous, not specifically those in residence in Zarahemla.

As already noted, one effect of the absence of records would have allowed the very rapid disappearance, possibly within three generations, of Hebrew speakers. The second effect, however, was the loss of their religion. Without scriptures, the Zarahemlaites lacked conceptual anchors to their ancestral religion and would have been more susceptible to the influence of local religions. Naturally, Amaleki describes this religious change as apostasy, which is, predictably, the Nephite perspective. Both the Nephites and Zarahemlaites began with the same God in Jerusalem. The Nephites have kept the God of the brass plates. Without the anchor of those plates, the Zarahemlaites have gradually adopted the deities of their new land.

When the Nephites arrived in Zarahemla, they were a smaller group merging into a larger body of people. Despite the merging, their language, material culture, and religion were all different. The inevitable tensions will help explain some of the future religious changes among the Nephites, in particular, the rise of churches during the time of $Alma_1$.

Omni 1:18

> 18 But it came to pass that Mosiah caused that they should be taught in his language. And it came to pass that after they were taught in the language of Mosiah, Zarahemla gave a genealogy of his fathers, according to his memory; and they are written, but not in these plates.

In describing the merger of the Nephites and the Zarahemlaites, J. N. Washburn suggests that "the lamb ate the lion,"[39] meaning that the smaller population dominated the larger. The evidence is the choice of $Mosiah_1$ as ruler of the combined population and the Zarahemlaites learning the Nephite language, rather than the other way around. Still, it would have been unusual if Nephite became the dominant language of the area. Correlating language to geography suggests that the Nephites brought perhaps a Hebrew and/or Maya heritage to the merger, while the Zarahemlaites contributed a Zoquean linguistic and Epi-Olmec cultural background. The persistence of Zoque in that geography throughout discernable history[40] suggests that Nephite (whatever that exact language may have been) did not become the dominant language of the Zarahemlaites and therefore of the future Nephites. If anything, Zoque probably became the Nephites' daily language soon

---

[38]Søren Wichmann, *The Relationship Among the Mixe-Zoquean Languages of Mexico* (Salt Lake City: University of Utah Press, 1995), xx.

[39]Washburn, *Book of Mormon Guidebook*, 26.

[40]Evans, *Ancient Mexico and Central America*, 222, 239.

after their arrival in Zarahemla. (See Ether, Part 1: Chapter 1, "Historical Background of the Book of Ether.")

Text: Amaleki also notes that other records are being kept—almost certainly the large plates in $Mosiah_1$'s possession. When Mormon abridges the record, he would have had a fuller account of the Nephite/Zarahemlaite merger than that offered by Amaleki. Mormon's account of this incident must have been in the lost 116 pages.

Omni 1:19

> 19 And it came to pass that the people of Zarahemla, and of Mosiah, did unite together; and Mosiah was appointed to be their king.

Culture: Amaleki's bald narrative conceals a fascinating conundrum. How is it possible for $Mosiah_1$, the leader of a smaller group of refugees who have been wandering in the wilderness, to become the king over a larger population in an established, and presumably more prosperous, city?

Although my reconstruction is in the realm of speculation, the combination of factors that place Zarahemla in a Mesoamerican milieu at this particular time and place provide some interesting clues. As background, we must return to Sorenson's location of Zarahemla at the archaeological site of Santa Rosa. Its history of occupation in one form or another dates back to 1000 B.C.E.[41] Thus, the Mulekites had earlier moved into an area that already had some organization and structure.

Santa Rosa's marked development during the late Preclassic (500 B.C.–A.D. 250) covers both the Zarahemlaites and the Nephites. During this period, the site is characterized by advanced architecture, known to be of imposing dimensions in at least a few instances. Typical are "stone walls and sloping batters (*talud*) covering earthen fills, and floors of tamped, sometimes burned, clay."[42] The florescence of the site occurs during the Protoclassic (A.D. 250–600),[43] which was during the time it was under Lamanite control after the Nephite center had moved northward to Bountiful. This is consonant with my hypothesis that the Nephite holdings were typically less imposing and archaeologically important than those of their enemies, called Lamanites in the Book of Mormon but likely including multiple cities and cultural groups in modern terms.

Santa Rosa has distinctive ceramic styles that change over time, producing a rough dating system that corresponds to the pottery types that were popular during certain times. In addition, the ceramics show some correlations to styles from other sites. In the time period which would have included the Nephite arrival, certain pieces of pottery show a relationship to ceramics of Kaminaljuyú (Sorenson's candidate for the city of Nephi), a relationship strong enough that archaeologist

---

[41] Agustin Delgado, *Archaeological Research at Santa Rosa, Chiapas and in the Region of Tehuantepec* (Provo, Utah: New World Archaeological Foundation, Brigham Young University, 1965), 79.

[42] Ibid.

[43] Ibid.

William T. Sanders termed it "perhaps the closest linkage of our material to other regions."[44]

While the Book of Mormon story that residents of Nephi (Kaminaljuyú) moved to Zarahemla (Santa Rosa) is not the only possible explanation for the presence of Kaminaljuyú-style pottery in Zarahemla, it is a plausible one. The Book of Mormon description finds potential confirmation, and, significantly, no contradiction, in the archaeology of the proposed site of Zarahemla. (From this point, for the sake of simplicity, I will no longer add qualifiers like "proposed site" or "hypothesized scenario," although the reader should certainly be aware that this reconstruction remains speculative.)

At this period, Kaminaljuyú (Nephi) was both larger and wealthier than Santa Rosa (Zarahemla). Santa Rosa's dramatically more ambitious architecture corresponds in time to the arrival of the Nephites, strongly suggests that Mosiah$_1$'s people would have arrived at a town that, while populous, was not nearly as well built nor elegant as Kaminaljuyú. Delgado notes that while Santa Rosa might have been grander than its nearer competitors, it was "rather poor when compared with Chiapa de Corzo,"[45] a contemporary site downriver on the Grijalva/Sidon. (Sorenson hypothesizes that Chiapa de Corzo may have been the site of Sidom.[46])

To summarize, the city of Nephi became increasingly wealthy and prosperous in ancient Mesoamerica. That wealth caused Jacob great distress because of its social consequences and its fostering of unrighteous principles. Probably the righteous in Nephi continued to feel antipathy toward the accumulation of worldly wealth, and they, presumably, were those who willingly followed the Lord's commandment to Mosiah$_1$ to leave the city. Certainly Mosiah$_1$ and other leaders would have been among the well-educated social elite of Nephi, even if their followers were not. After wandering, but simultaneously being "led," in the wilderness, the Nephites reach Zarahemla/Santa Rosa, an established city but one of less wealth and fewer fine buildings. Socially, they moved from an opulent city to one of relative poverty (though it is doubtful that many of the Nephites who went with Mosiah$_1$ were part of the elite in Nephi).

Another indication is that Zarahemla is not called a king, even though he is clearly the town's leader. This distinction in rulership may indicate that Zarahemla was not yet sufficiently independent and powerful to adopt hereditary kingship as a mode of government. Mosiah$_1$, however, came from a tradition of kingship and was related to Nephi's kings (or he could not have taken possession of the plates and other symbols). Mosiah$_1$'s arrival from a more powerful location, his close connection to a regnal line, and his demonstrable ties to ancestral right of rulership as evidenced by the plates are all factors that would make his selection as king logical, even in the face of a larger population of people with a foreign language and customs.

---

[44]William T. Sanders, *Ceramic Stratigraphy at Santa Cruz, Chiapas, Mexico* (Provo, Utah: New World Archaeological Foundation, 1961), 53.

[45]Delgado, *Archaeological Research at Santa Rosa*, 79.

[46] Sorenson, *An Ancient American Setting for the Book of Mormon*, 205.

Omni 1:20

> 20 And it came to pass in the days of Mosiah, there was a large stone brought unto him with engravings on it; and he did interpret the engravings by the gift and power of God.

Archaeology: Mesoamerica is unique in the Western hemisphere for its writing systems. While the best-known is that of the Maya, the roots of literacy are much earlier, probably extending to the Olmec.[47] Part of that tradition includes inscriptions on stelae, or large stones. The fact that Mosiah$_1$ viewed an engraved stone is unusual only in Amaleki's description that it was "brought" to Mosiah$_1$. It must have required some effort to transport the stone. Perhaps it was a smaller stela.

Most of the stelae with hieroglyphs discovered to date have been in the Maya area, but earlier texts exist in early forms of Mixe and Zoque. The most complete text (Stela 1 of La Mojarra, from a village of that name on the Acula River in Veracruz, Mexico) has Zoque as the underlying language.[48] Only eleven texts in this Epi-Olmec script are currently known,[49] but surely many more were created in antiquity.

Interestingly, the Zarahemlaites moved from an area with tradition of literacy in the language they were likely speaking, yet they were unable to read this stone. Either they were illiterate[50] or the stone was written in an earlier form of the language. The second explanation is possible since it recounts the story of Coriantumr$_1$, a Jaredite survivor, who might have spoken a different language.[51] However, Zoque is a daughter language of the earlier Mixe-Zoquean. It seems probable that a literate population would have been able to make some sense of it since the glyphs are generally phonetic. Sorenson's suggestion that they were illiterate therefore seems more likely.[52] If the Zarahemlaites were illiterate, it confirms their relative poverty and lower status compared to the immigrating Nephites.

Omni 1:21–22

> 21 And they gave an account of one Coriantumr, and the slain of his people. And Coriantumr was discovered by the people of Zarahemla; and he dwelt with them for the space of nine moons.

---

[47]Lyle Campbell, *The Linguistics of Southeast Chiapas, Mexico* (Provo, Utah: New World Archaeological Foundation, Brigham Young University, 1988), 19. Other writing systems also exist in the area, several of them in such small samples as to resist translation.

[48]John Justeson Terrence Kaufman, "Un descriframiento de la escritura jeroglifica epi-olmeca: metodos y resultados," *Archaeologia* (July–December 1992): 15, 20.

[49]Ibid., 16. It should be noted that this translation has become controversial after a find which produced a text that does not appear amenable to translation with the interpretation presented by Justeson and Kaufman. See "Mesoamerican Relic Provides New Clues to Mysterious Ancient Writing System," a press release from Brigham Young University, http://byunews.byu.edu/release.aspx?story=archive04/Jan/Isthmian (accessed July 2005).

[50]Sorenson, *An Ancient American Setting for the Book of Mormon*, 120.

[51]Not to be confused with Coriantumr$_2$, a Lamanite general whose story begins in Helaman 1:15.

[52]Sorenson, *An Ancient American Setting for the Book of Mormon*, 120.

22 It also spake a few words concerning his fathers. And his first parents came out from the tower, at the time the Lord confounded the language of the people; and the severity of the Lord fell upon them according to his judgments, which are just; and their bones lay scattered in the land northward.

Coriantumr is the same man identified as the last Jaredite in the book of Ether. The Zarahemlaites "discovered" him, but it is not clear whether they did so in the land of Zarahemla or earlier in their history. The brief explanation of the events depicted on the stela all have counterparts on the various stelae from the later Classic period (A.D. 250–800) among the Maya, though the correspondence is not precise. The presence of ancestors attest to the main figure's right of rulership.[53] Based on known stelae dealing with kings and history, it is certain that Coriantumr would have been the central figure of that stela.[54]

Victory over another people is also frequently commemorated with an engraving on a stela, but the putative "stela of Coriantumr" does not seem to fit this model. Not only is it virtually unheard of to create a monument to the defeat of one's people, but such a topic leaves unanswered the question about the carver, if Coriantumr's people have been vanquished. Carving a stela takes time and resources to support the carvers. Without a kingdom, Coriantumr would have had no means of providing support, would not likely have been himself a carver, and almost certainly would not have wanted to memorialize his defeat.

There are two possibilities. Since the information on Coriantumr comes through Mosiah$_1$'s inspired (but perhaps not literal?) reading of the stone, the explanation may be a prophetic/seeric "reading" of the stone, supplying information that does not appear in its inscription. Mosiah$_1$ would be using the stone as a base text but expanding it with information about the Jaredite destruction. The other option is that the stone was truly unique in the type of information it recorded.

The discussion of the Jaredites is reserved for the volume of commentary on the book of Ether. However, it is important to recall that the Jaredites match Olmec geography and history for Mesoamerica. This does not mean that the Olmec were the Jaredites or that the Jaredites were the Olmec. Rather, it means that the Jaredites would have participated in the Olmec culture and that Olmec culture is an acceptable backdrop for understanding the Jaredite cultural milieu.

Omni 1:23

23 Behold, I, Amaleki, was born in the days of Mosiah; and I have lived to see his death; and Benjamin, his son, reigneth in his stead.

Amaleki is younger than Mosiah$_1$, but older than Benjamin. This notation makes it certain that Amaleki is writing in Zarahemla.

---

[53]Linda Schele and David Freidel, *A Forest of Kings: The Untold Story of the Ancient Maya* (New York: William Morrow and Company, 1990), 141.

[54]Ibid. See index entries s.v. "stela." Sixteen different nobles are depicted as the central characters of their individual stela.

Omni 1:24

> 24 And behold, I have seen, in the days of king Benjamin, a serious war and much bloodshed between the Nephites and the Lamanites. But behold, the Nephites did obtain much advantage over them; yea, insomuch that king Benjamin did drive them out of the land of Zarahemla.

By now, the mention of wars is no surprise. It is, however, important to remember that "Lamanite" is a political, not a genealogical, definition. "Lamanite" is a collective term for anyone who opposes the Nephites (Jacob 1:14).

Almost certainly, these particular Lamanites are not those who had been vexing the city of Nephi. Those Lamanites would have had to come 180 miles from their own region to find Zarahemla. It is much more likely that these opponents are is close proximity to the land of Zarahemla, perhaps continuing hostilities that had begun years before the arrival of the Nephites. (See commentary accompanying Omni 1:17.)

Master's candidate Donald Arthur Cazier suggests that "the reign of Mosiah I seems to have been singularly free from wars and contentions, but more than once Benjamin, during his reign, was forced to defend his people against a Lamanite invasion."[55] In addition to the Lamanite invasions, which had no discernible connection to the change of power from Mosiah$_1$ to Benjamin, the eruption of the internal religious contentions during Benjamin's reign (W of M 1:14–16) suggests that it was this very change in rulership that offered the opportunity for the rise of the contentions. Mosiah$_1$ would have had a honeymoon period where the importance of the new union quelled possible dissent. The death of a king is often a dangerous time in monarchies, and in Zarahemla, coming so freshly from a tradition completely different from that of the Nephites, it is likely that the internal convulsions were ignited by the possibilities offered by the transition from one king to another.

Omni 1:25–26

> 25 And it came to pass that I began to be old; and, having no seed, and knowing king Benjamin to be a just man before the Lord, wherefore, I shall deliver up these plates unto him, exhorting all men to come unto God, the Holy One of Israel, and believe in prophesying, and in revelations, and in the ministering of angels, and in the gift of speaking with tongues, and in the gift of interpreting languages, and in all things which are good; for there is nothing which is good save it comes from the Lord; and that which is evil cometh from the devil.
>
> 26 And now, my beloved brethren, I would that ye should come unto Christ, who is the Holy One of Israel, and partake of his salvation, and the power of his redemption. Yea, come unto him, and offer your whole souls as an offering unto him, and continue in fasting and praying, and endure to the end; and as the Lord liveth ye will be saved.

---

[55]Cazier, "A Study of Nephite, Lamanite, and Jaredite Governmental Institutions and Policies," 83.

Unlike his father and grandfather, Amaleki is a man of demonstrable faith, and he bears his final testimony of the Messiah as he prepares to close his record.

Text: Amaleki has "no seed," which may mean that he has no children at all, although there is a slight possibility that he means he has no sons, as transmission of the plates is always through the male line. In any case, Amaleki's conclusion terminates the transmission line that began when Nephi gave the small plates to his brother Jacob. The small plates are reunited with Nephi's other plates, to be transmitted with them.

Omni 1:27–30

> 27 And now I would speak somewhat concerning a certain number who went up into the wilderness to return to the land of Nephi; for there was a large number who were desirous to possess the land of their inheritance.
> 28 Wherefore, they went up into the wilderness. And their leader being a strong and mighty man, and a stiffnecked man, wherefore he caused a contention among them; and they were all slain, save fifty, in the wilderness, and they returned again to the land of Zarahemla.
> 29 And it came to pass that they also took others to a considerable number, and took their journey again into the wilderness.
> 30 And I, Amaleki, had a brother, who also went with them; and I have not since known concerning them. And I am about to lie down in my grave; and these plates are full. And I make an end of my speaking.

Redaction: These four verses are an obvious afterthought. Amaleki has correctly declared the future transmission line and borne personal testimony. It should be the end of his record. Yet despite that clear conclusion, he tacks on another bit of history. It is tempting to assume that the triggering event was his brother's departure (v. 30), but that does not seem likely. Amaleki is now near death. Even though his brother could be younger, he would still be relatively old for such a speculative adventure at this time in Amaleki's life. Furthermore, Amaleki has not heard again from his brother. Had the brother left only days before, this statement would be odd. More likely, these events occurred years earlier. I note in the commentary accompanying Mosiah 7:1 that these verses create a small chronological issue that is best resolved by having the departure of the group including his brother occur prior to Benjamin's coronation. (See commentary in the section on chronology following Mosiah 7:1 for an analysis of these issues.)

History: Amaleki is summarizing the history of Zeniff, a story told more fully later (Mosiah 9–22).

Culture: Zeniff was one of the Nephites who accompanied Mosiah$_1$ from the city of Nephi (Mosiah 9:1). Amaleki's brother joined Zeniff's expedition (v. 30). Both men had to have been young enough to be interested in returning and physically able to withstand the journey's rigors. Therefore, this backtrailing occurred relatively soon after the arrival of the Nephites in Zarahemla, say, perhaps no more than ten years. Considering that the Nephites fled for their lives from the city of Nephi, why were there not one, but two separate backtrailing expeditions? Zeniff apparently participated in both expeditions. His record clarifies that the purpose of the first was military conquest, while the second was more peaceful. After being forced out, the Nephites might feel strongly about military reprisal, but why would they mount a military expedition that had to travel about 180 miles through the "wilderness" before they could actually find their enemies? A reasonable hypothesis is the comparative wealth of the city of Nephi (Kaminaljuyú) compared to Zarahemla's (Santa Rosa's) poverty. Zeniff's expedition may have indulged in nostalgia for the lost "good life," something like Laman's and Lemuel's longing for their comfortable life.

While this expedition will be discussed later (see commentary accompanying Mosiah 9:1–7), Zeniff's introduction offers an intriguing hypothesis: "I, Zeniff, having been taught in all the language of the Nephites, and having had a knowledge of the land of Nephi, or of the land of our fathers' first inheritance, and having been sent as a spy among the Lamanites that I might spy out their forces, that our army might come upon them and destroy them—but when I saw that which was good among them I was desirous that they should not be destroyed" (Mosiah 9:1). Zeniff is part of a reconnaissance party that scouts out the city of Nephi prior to bringing up the army (Mosiah 9:2). He has two qualifications as a spy. First, he is familiar with the land of Nephi, and second, he knows "the language of the Nephites." This statement virtually announces that some members of the army are Zarahemlaites who therefore do not speak Nephite. Furthermore, Nephite, not Lamanite, is apparently still the language of the land of Nephi. Apparently the city has not been overwhelmed by invading Lamanites, or they speak the same language as the former Nephites. Rather, Mosiah$_1$'s people fled from Nephites who no longer believed in the God of Israel (or at least in his living prophets), and who evidently included not only wealthy Nephites but also the reigning king. Thus, Zeniff's ability to speak "Nephite" confirms that Nephites still occupy the land and city of Nephi.

Text: Amaleki tells us that "these plates are full," confirming that the physical plates, undoubtedly the originals made by Nephi, had blank sheets that had been used by his successors, beginning with Jacob and continuing with Jacob's successors. The large-plate tradition continued with the king-line and therefore had access to the resources and labor to create new plates. It appears that Jacob's descendants did not have access to similar resources to create new plates to be added to the originals that Nephi made.

Words of Mormon: Commentary

Words of Mormon 1

Words of Mormon 1:1–2

1 And now I, Mormon, being about to deliver up the record which I have
been making into the hands of my son Moroni, behold I have witnessed
almost all the destruction of my people, the Nephites.
2 And it is many hundred years after the coming of Christ that I deliver these
records into the hands of my son; and it supposeth me that he will witness the
entire destruction of my people. But may God grant that he may survive them,
that he may write somewhat concerning them, and somewhat concerning
Christ, that perhaps some day it may profit them.

Text: The most important fact about this text is an omission. This verse is our introduction to the man for whom the book is named. It is not surprising that Mormon's name does not appear in the text between 1 Nephi and Omni because Mormon inserted those records without any abridging or editing. He is named on the title page, but Moroni wrote that page at the end of the process. At this point, just after the close of Omni, the Nephites have been in the New World about three hundred years and this is the first time the text tells us about the man who is creating the record we are reading.

Mormon begins with a simple declaration of who he is and when he is writing. This is essential since he is inserting this text into a record created much earlier. He must make a significant break to help the reader clearly understand the transition from the small plates to his abridgment of the large plates. Nevertheless, he says nothing more besides his name and the time of writing.

Words of Mormon 1:3

3 And now, I speak somewhat concerning that which I have written; for after I had made an abridgment from the plates of Nephi, down to the reign of this king Benjamin, of whom Amaleki spake, I searched among the records which had been delivered into my hands, and I found these plates, which contained this small account of the prophets, from Jacob down to the reign of this king Benjamin, and also many of the words of Nephi.

The modern LDS readership of the Book of Mormon is familiar with Mormon and the large and small plates. We know that Mormon is the abridger/editor of our Book of Mormon and that he took most of his account from what we call the large plates of Nephi. In this verse Mormon refers to "that which I have written." The antecedent for that statement is all Mormon has written to that point. Mormon did not write any of the material we have as 1 Nephi through Omni. Nevertheless, he makes this statement in the context of linking the small plate material to his own abridgment. He assumes the understanding that we know of our experience with the text, but this is not information that is available in the text itself as it exists in the printed edition.

Clearly, Mormon must have explained at the beginning of his record (the lost 116 pages, or book of Lehi) who he is and what he is doing. He assumes that his relationship with the reader is so clear that he sometimes does not even identify himself in his continued editorial explanations. For example, in Mosiah 8:1, he states: "And it came to pass that after king Limhi had made an end of speaking to his people, for he spake many things unto them and only a few of them have I written in this book, he told his people all the things concerning their brethren who were in the land of Zarahemla." He does not explain who "I" is or provide any information about his creation of the book.

As another example:

> Now this account did cause the people of Mosiah to mourn exceedingly, yea, they were filled with sorrow; nevertheless it gave them much knowledge, in the which they did rejoice.
>
> And this account shall be written hereafter; for behold, it is expedient that all people should know the things which are written in this account.
>
> And now, as I said unto you, that after king Mosiah had done these things, he took the plates of brass, and all the things which he had kept, and conferred them upon Alma, who was the son of Alma; yea, all the records, and also the interpreters, and conferred them upon him, and commanded him that he should keep and preserve them, and also keep a record of the people, handing them down from one generation to another, even as they had been handed down from the time that Lehi left Jerusalem. (Mosiah 28:18–20)

Mormon's editorial insertion here indicates a foreknowledge of what will come later in the book, assuming that the reader will know that Mormon will record it. And again, he does not identify who "I," is, his typical pattern.[1]

One exception comes at 4 Nephi 1:23, a transition from Mormon's abridgment to his own holographic record: "And now I, Mormon, would that ye should know that the people had multiplied, insomuch that they were spread upon all the face of the land, and that they had become exceedingly rich, because of their prosperity in Christ."

Another exception, and the most interesting one, is 3 Nephi 5:12–19:

> And behold, I am called Mormon, being called after the land of Mormon, the land in which Alma did establish the church among the people, yea, the first church which was established among them after their transgression.
>
> Behold, I am a disciple of Jesus Christ, the Son of God. I have been called of him to declare his word among his people, that they might have everlasting life.

---

[1]See Alma 3:17–19; 6:2–3, 5; 23:6; 48:19–21; 49:2–3; 53:10; Hel. 2:13–14; 3:16–17; 12:25 [All of chap. 12 is an intercalation]; 3 Ne. 7:3, 23–24; 28:36–37; 30:1.

> And it hath become expedient that I, according to the will of God, that the prayers of those who have gone hence, who were the holy ones, should be fulfilled according to their faith, should make a record of these things which have been done—
>
> Yea, a small record of that which hath taken place from the time that Lehi left Jerusalem, even down until the present time.
>
> Therefore I do make my record from the accounts which have been given by those who were before me, until the commencement of my day;
>
> And then I do make a record of the things which I have seen with mine own eyes.
>
> And I know the record which I make to be a just and a true record; nevertheless there are many things which, according to our language, we are not able to write.
>
> And now I make an end of my saying, which is of myself, and proceed to give my account of the things which have been before me.

To this point, Mormon has simply assumed that we know who he is. In fact, even Words of Mormon was likely written after this statement in 3 Nephi. (See Words of Mormon 1:2.) Thus, at this very late point in the abridgment comes the most complete introduction to the man, Mormon. I argue that this may not have been Mormon's first introduction but simply the first that has been preserved. Obviously, he assumes that the reader knows who he is and what he is doing, which logically suggests that he made an initial introductory statement that was lost with the 116 pages. All of the writers on the small plates began by identifying themselves. It seems logical that Mormon would have followed this convention, especially since he would have had to clarify his role and simultaneously explain that the record was an abridgment.

As the Words of Mormon show, when Mormon needed to make a textual transition, he attempted to smooth it out by providing linking and explanatory material. Mormon probably used a similar technique when he began his record in the initial 116 pages. Mormon could not assume that the reader would understand who he was and how he produced the text (especially when he made editorial comments without further self-identifications) unless he had previously introduced himself, describing his divine call to abridge the records and his purpose in so doing.

Given this requirement, then, 3 Nephi 12:19 seems somewhat aberrant. If Mormon had previously introduced himself, why does he do it again? As I read the text, it is governed by the unusual text that comes next: the record of the Atoning Messiah's appearance to his people. By its very content, this was Mormon's most sacred text. Not only that, but "I am a disciple of Jesus Christ, the Son of God. I have been called of him to declare his word among his people, that they might have everlasting life" (3 Ne. 5:13).

Mormon prefaces this section by declaring himself as an apostle, a witness for the Savior. Mormon is not introducing himself as an editor but as an apostle, a special witness to the Messiah.

Redaction: Words of Mormon concludes the small plates and provides a transition to the abridgment of the large plates. As Mormon explains, he has already seen the near-destruction of his people, which occurred soon before Mormon's death (Morm. 6), and is about to give the record to his son (W of M 1:2). Clearly, he does not anticipate writing much more on the plates.

His statement, "I speak somewhat concerning that which I have written" (v. 3), raises the question: what has he written? This must be his abridgment of the large-plate material: "After I had made an abridgment from the plates of Nephi, down to the reign of . . . Benjamin, . . . I searched among the records which had been delivered into my hands, and I found these plates" (v. 3). This surprisingly vivid little description tells us that Mormon did not work with a single set of records in chronological order. Even if each ruler produced only a single set of plates, they were not compiled into a single group. If Mormon had been looking only for the very next record, he would have simply moved to the next volume on the shelf (or whatever the Nephite storage system was). The fact that he had to search tells us that there were numerous sets of records, and they were not in chronological order. Mormon had to impose physical as well as literary order on them as he extracted their most salient facts.

Individual books were named for specific dynasties, a designation system that Mormon retains, but the entire set of records had a collective name: "the plates of Nephi." The use of this consistent designation for what was demonstrably multiple sets of records indicates that, regardless of the specific content of any single record, they all were part of the "plates of Nephi." (See Behind the Text: Chapter 3, "Mormon's Sources.")

Mormon found the small plates when he was searching for the next set of the large plates to abridge. Mormon did not know about these small plates, was not looking for them, and was surprised when he found them. Probably he interrupted his larger task to read them and determine what he had discovered. Finding that they were actually in the hand of the original Nephi would have been irresistible for any man with a historical interest, and abridging the plates surely gave Mormon such an interest even if it were not natural to him. This distinctive version of the story Mormon had already abridged would be as interesting to him as reading Mormon's account of that time period would be to us today.

Mormon labels this a "small account." Jacob 1:1 calls them "small plates" (see also Jarom 1:2, 14), thus leading to the LDS tradition of calling them the "small plates of Nephi." As already discussed in Behind the Text: Chapter 6, "The Physical Plates," Nephi probably used the brass plates as his model in determining the physical size and shape of his two sets of plates: the "small" and the "large." Almost certainly all of the individual sheets were the same size. The "small" plates were fewer in quantity and the "large" plates were more numerous.

Incidentally, the term "large plates" never appears in the Book of Mormon. Nephi himself says that he made "a full account of my people" on "the plates of Nephi" but that "these plates"—meaning what we would call the "small plates"—also are called the plates of Nephi (1 Ne. 9:2). This distinction may be momentarily confusing for modern readers, but it was certainly clear to Nephi.

It also seems reasonable that Mormon made a new set of plates for his abridgment with sheets of the same size as Nephi's. Modern descriptions of the plates describe them as held together with rings, but no one mentions that a group of them were smaller in shape. Since Mormon included these holographic plates in the abridged set, then Mormon's own plates resembled Nephi's in size and shape, just as sheets of store-bought paper are of a standard size today. In addition to the convenience and logic of following an existing size and shape, the sacred nature of the records would also encourage conformity. (See Behind the Text: Chapter 3, "Mormon's Sources.")

Another interesting fact is that Mormon apparently had no difficulty reading what Nephi wrote. True, there was enough difference that what had once been "Egyptian" is now "reformed Egyptian" (Morm. 9:32). But aside from this mention, Mormon could obviously read Nephi's record and assumed that anyone able to read his record could also read Nephi's. This is probably an indication of his training as a scribe.

Text: Because the Book of Mormon itself makes no distinction between what we call the "large plates" (political record) and the "small plates" kept by Nephi through Amaleki, the internal reference to both sets and their relationships between the various source materials is important to understand.

First, the internal references to sources are typically to the "plates of Nephi," without any other modifier. When Mormon refers to both sets, he uses "plates of Nephi" to mean what we would term the large plates.[2] He gives no name to the "small plates." In verse 4, he simply refers to "these plates" (v. 4) and contrasts them to the better known set, the "plates of Nephi."

Two specific references to the (large) "plates of Nephi" merit particular examination:

> And now, the city of Jashon was near the land where Ammaron had deposited the records unto the Lord, that they might not be destroyed. And behold I had gone according to the word of Ammaron, and taken the plates of Nephi, and did make a record according to the words of Ammaron.
>
> And upon the plates of Nephi I did make a full account of all the wickedness and abominations; but upon these plates I did forbear to make a full account of their wickedness and abominations, for behold, a continual scene of wickedness and abominations has been before mine eyes ever since I have been sufficient to behold the ways of man. (Morm. 2:17–18)

Mormon, like Nephi, has made two records, the first, more complete account, written directly on the "plates of Nephi" and the second, his abridgment, on "these plates."

> And it came to pass that when we had gathered in all our people in one to the land of Cumorah, behold I, Mormon, began to be old; and knowing it to be the last struggle of my people, and having been commanded of the Lord that I should not suffer the records which had

---

[2]Mosiah 1:6, 16; 28:11; Alma 37:2; 44:24; 3 Ne. 5:10; 26:6, 11; 4 Ne. 1:19; Morm. 1:4.

> been handed down by our fathers, which were sacred, to fall into the hands of the Lamanites, (for the Lamanites would destroy them) therefore I made this record out of the plates of Nephi, and hid up in the hill Cumorah all the records which had been entrusted to me by the hand of the Lord, save it were these few plates which I gave unto my son Moroni. (Morm. 6:6)

Mormon specifies that his source material for the abridgment was the "plates of Nephi," the political and social history begun by Nephi and called by that name by the generations of writers who continued the record. However, the plates of Nephi were not Mormon's only primary source material. The Nephite records included, at the very least, the brass plates, the twenty-four plates that contained Ether's record (Mosiah 8:9), and what we call the "small plates of Nephi." In 3 Nephi 5:9–11, Mormon describes other records: "But behold there are records which do contain all the proceedings of this people; and a shorter but true account was given by Nephi. Therefore I have made my record of these things according to the record of Nephi, which was engraven on the plates which were called the plates of Nephi. And behold, I do make the record on plates which I have made with mine own hands."

Mormon's description of "a shorter but true account . . . given by Nephi" (this Nephi is Nephi$_3$, who was contemporary with Christ's visit) contrasts with "records which do contain all the proceedings of this people" (3 Ne. 5:9). For his abridgment, Mormon, no doubt after reviewing the lengthier record, decided that Nephi$_3$'s shorter record would better serve his purposes and therefore abridged this "book of Nephi" which is found on "the plates which were called the plates of Nephi" to produce his own record. The large-plate tradition is not an edited record such as the one that Mormon produces, but one that may contain not only the official record but subsidiary records. Not only do we find this smaller account of Nephi$_3$ but also the record of Zeniff (preserved in Mosiah 9–10) and the record of imputed records of the people of Alma, the sons of Mosiah, and Ammon.

As Mormon indicates, he is writing on plates "which I have made with mine own hands" (v. 11). This note reminds us that producing plates was a prerequisite to writing on them. One reason that the record on the small plates ended was because all of the sheets were full of writing (Omni 1:30) and that Amaleki either could not or did not choose to make more (most likely could not).

In summary, then, the context of Mormon's records makes it clear that the "plates of Nephi" were not a single continuously "bound" set of plates. The collected set of records that constituted the "plates of Nephi" included multiple records from multiple writers. There were likely separate records such as the official records of Zeniff's people. It is also probable that some perishable records such as the letters Mormon includes in the book of Alma had been copied onto the non-perishable plates. The entire set was collectively called the "plates of Nephi."

Words of Mormon 1:4

> 4 And the things which are upon these plates pleasing me, because of the prophecies of the coming of Christ; and my fathers knowing that many of

> them have been fulfilled; yea, and I also know that as many things as have been prophesied concerning us down to this day have been fulfilled, and as many as go beyond this day must surely come to pass—

Mormon explains that he has a personal attachment to these records. He has certainly read them and appreciates their prophecies of Christ. While the writers had only anticipated the coming of the Christ, Mormon knows that he came and fulfilled the prophecies.

Words of Mormon 1:5

> 5 Wherefore, I chose these things, to finish my record upon them, which remainder of my record I shall take from the plates of Nephi; and I cannot write the hundredth part of the things of my people.

Redaction: Mormon provides additional information about how he structured his writing but unfortunately also complicates the picture. Part of the problem is verb tenses. Mormon will "finish [his] record upon" the small plates but "shall take" the remainder of his record from the plates of Nephi. In connection with that larger collective name of "plates of Nephi," he indicates that he "cannot write the hundredth part of the things of my people."

The problem is the juxtaposition of "finishing" on the small plates, but continuing to write most of our current Book of Mormon starting at Mosiah. If Mormon is near death when he is writing this interlude (W of M 1:1), he does not have enough time to abridge the records between Benjamin's reign and his own time. Daniel H. Ludlow summarizes the problem:

> In verse 5, Mormon mentions that he is going to finish his record upon "these things" and that he will take the remainder of his record "from the plates of Nephi." Several questions have been raised concerning this brief verse by Mormon: (1) First of all, to what is he referring when he states he is going to finish his record? (2) To what plates is he referring when he says he will finish his record upon these things? (3) To what section of his writings is he referring when he talks of the remainder of his record?
>
> Most Book of Mormon scholars have assumed that when Mormon refers to finishing "his record" he had in mind the rest of his writings in the small section entitled The Words of Mormon. Most scholars also assume that "these things" refer to the small plates of Nephi. If this interpretation is correct, then the section entitled The Words of Mormon was written at the end of the small plates of Nephi. According to these scholars, the fact that Amaleki says the small plates of Nephi are already full (Omni 30) does not necessarily rule out the possibility of adding the brief notes that make up The Words of Mormon.
>
> Mormon's reference to the "remainder" of his record is a little more confusing. Some scholars believe that here Mormon is referring to the rest of his writings in The Words of Mormon, the ideas of which he obtained from the large plates of Nephi. Other scholars, however, believe that Mormon is referring to that portion of his abridgment from the large plates of Nephi which he has not yet written on his plates of Mormon. Unfortunately, the pronoun reference in verse 5 does not make it possible to determine Mormon's meaning exactly.[3]

---

[3]Daniel H. Ludlow, *A Companion to Your Study of the Book of Mormon* (Salt Lake City: Deseret Book, 1976), 171–72.

Mormon's record is obviously the abridgment he is creating from the plates of Nephi. The most interesting suggestion is that the Words of Mormon are inscribed on the small plates, a very literal application of "upon." However, it is not a necessary addition, as Mormon is just as clearly adding these plates before giving the set to Moroni. Hence, this act of inclusion is equally a "finishing upon" as writing on the physical plates would be. The suggestion that Mormon must still write the history covering from Mosiah to 4 Nephi contradicts the intent of verse 1 and thus does not appear to be a reasonable interpretation.[4]

Words of Mormon 1:6

> 6 But behold, I shall take these plates, which contain these prophesyings and revelations, and put them with the remainder of my record, for they are choice unto me; and I know they will be choice unto my brethren.

Redaction: Once again, Mormon tells us what he will do, namely, "put them with the remainder of my record." We now have sufficient information to suggest a solution to the textual process of receiving both the small plates and the Words of Mormon.

Mormon found the small plates when he was looking for more source material among "the plates of Nephi" for his abridgment. This source material consisted of many sets of plates, titled according to the political or religious dynasty that each dealt with. The most logical interpretation is that Mormon read though the small plates of Nephi, then set them aside and continued the narration from Benjamin to 4 Nephi. When he was almost finished, the Lord reminded him of these small plates before he gave the plates to Moroni and that he should include them with his abridged record "for a wise purpose" (v. 7).[5]

Mormon inserted the small plates in correct chronological order, then added Words of Mormon as a transitional chapter, tying the inserted plates to the following abridgment. This scenario resolves the problem of assuming that he inserted the small plates in his record as soon as he found them.

A separate issue is how Joseph Smith encountered the material when he was translating. The evidence suggests that, when the translation resumed after the loss of the 116 manuscript pages, Joseph continued with Mosiah and the small plate material was translated last. (See commentary accompanying Jacob 4:7.) If Mormon inserted the small plates into the text, where did he place them? If we assume that Joseph Smith translated by a continuous examination of the plates, it would seem unusual that he would skip these plates. However, since the translation method

---

[4]Eldin Ricks, "The Small Plates of Nephi and the Words of Mormon," in *The Book of Mormon: Jacob through Words of Mormon, To Learn with Joy*, edited by Monte S. Nyman and Charles D. Tate Jr. (Provo, Utah: BYU Religious Studies Center, 1990), 216, appears to hold this position.

[5]I suspect that he made the addition after finishing 4 Nephi but prior to writing his eponymous book. Once embarked on the process of abridging, there was no reason to stop to consider adding the small plates until that abridgment had been completed. Since Moroni completes his father's book (Morm. 8:1) it would not appear that Mormon had time to consider the addition and write Words of Mormon at that time.

often did not require the examination of the plates, there is no reason to suppose that their physical location had any specific relationship to the time when they were translated.

Words of Mormon 1:7

> 7 And I do this for a wise purpose; for thus it whispereth me, according to the workings of the Spirit of the Lord which is in me. And now, I do not know all things; but the Lord knoweth all things which are to come; wherefore, he worketh in me to do according to his will.

Mormon did not know the "wise purpose," but the Lord did. That purpose became plain when the first 116 pages of the translated abridgment were lost. The Lord explains to Joseph Smith during this episode:

> And now, verily I say unto you, that an account of those things that you have written, which have gone out of your hands, is engraven upon the plates of Nephi;
>
> Yea, and you remember it was said in those writings that a more particular account was given of these things upon the plates of Nephi.
>
> And now, because the account which is engraven upon the plates of Nephi is more particular concerning the things which, in my wisdom, I would bring to the knowledge of the people in this account—
>
> Therefore, you shall translate the engravings which are on the plates of Nephi, down even till you come to the reign of king Benjamin, or until you come to that which you have translated, which you have retained;
>
> And behold, you shall publish it as the record of Nephi; and thus I will confound those who have altered my words.
>
> I will not suffer that they shall destroy my work; yea, I will show unto them that my wisdom is greater than the cunning of the devil.
>
> Behold, they have only got a part, or an abridgment of the account of Nephi.
>
> Behold, there are many things engraven upon the plates of Nephi which do throw greater views upon my gospel; therefore, it is wisdom in me that you should translate this first part of the engravings of Nephi, and send forth in this work. (D&C 10:38–45)

In this revelation, the Lord makes no clear differentiation between the large and small plates. Just as Nephi gave them the same name, so does the Lord. Nevertheless, the two sets of plates *must* be what he means in verses 38 and 39: "And now, verily I say unto you, that an account of those things that you have written, which have gone out of your hands, is engraven upon the plates of Nephi; Yea, and you remember it was said in those writings that a more particular account was given of these things upon the plates of Nephi" (D&C 10:38–39).

Verse 38 clearly refers to the large plates—the source of the 116 manuscript pages "which have gone out of your hands." Verse 39, however, shifts the emphasis. In the text of "those writings" (meaning the large plates alluded to in verse 38), the Lord notes that "it was said . . . that a more particular account was given of these things upon the plates of Nephi." If we read "plates of Nephi" in *this* verse to be the same as the "plates of Nephi" in the previous verse, the document contradicts itself, stating that a more particular account was written in that same document—simultaneously a separate document, but the same. This would make no sense except that the small plates were also called by the same name and that they were physically included in the large-plate abridgment.

We may speculate, therefore, that at the end of the material immediately prior to the inclusion of the small plates, Mormon would have written a transition between the abridgment and the small plates similar to that in Words of Mormon. In that missing transition, the plates would have been named and described as a "more particular" account. Joseph Smith would have already read this transition and would remember it at the Lord's reminder. It may be, however, that the Lord did not have him translate it at that time, again for the "wise purpose" of foiling a possible attempt to discredit the translation by altering the 116 manuscript pages.

Words of Mormon 1:8–9

> 8 And my prayer to God is concerning my brethren, that they may once again come to the knowledge of God, yea, the redemption of Christ; that they may once again be a delightsome people.
> 9 And now I, Mormon, proceed to finish out my record, which I take from the plates of Nephi; and I make it according to the knowledge and the understanding which God has given me.

Mormon concludes his discussion of organizing the record by reiterating his purpose: to convince his brethren of the Messiah's mission.

Redaction: Here Mormon means that he will return to his already-abridged text, not that he would begin Benjamin's story. Consistent with his terminology, he indicates that the source of the abridgment is the "plates of Nephi," an allusion to the fact that he has added the small plates in their chronological order but that the reader will now be returning to the abridgment. Mormon's testimony about his personal relationship to the plates is understandable from Mormon the editor, to whom all of these historical records were in the "present tense"—that is, present before him. While the documents deal with various narrative layers, Mormon's "present" spans the whole work, and his frequent editorial insertions all indicate this type of "present" consciousness while he works with the historical material.

Words of Mormon 1:10

> 10 Wherefore, it came to pass that after Amaleki had delivered up these plates into the hands of king Benjamin, he took them and put them with the other plates, which contained records which had been handed down by the kings, from generation to generation until the days of king Benjamin.

Text: When Amaleki delivers the plates to Benjamin, they become part of the royal collection of records. In his preface to the 1830 edition of the Book of Mormon, Joseph Smith indicates: "I would inform you that I translated, by the gift and power of God, and caused to be written, one hundred and sixteen pages, the which I took from the Book of Lehi, which was an account abridged from the plates of Lehi, by the hand of Mormon. . . . "[6] This preface was removed in the 1837 and subsequent editions of the Book of Mormon.[7]

Quinn Brewster, professor of mechanical engineering, University of Illinois, has analyzed the Book of Mormon's structure and suggests that Joseph Smith may not have been completely aware of the interrelationships among the source plates as he dictated the text.[8] While Brewster's analysis depends upon a very different reading of the hints in Words of Mormon,[9] he is apparently correct about Joseph's understanding of the plates' composition. The best evidence is the preface's indication that the book of Lehi was taken from the plates of Lehi. This is not correct, according to the internal evidence from the translation we have received.

Without dispute, the lost 116 pages constituted a "Book of Lehi." Nevertheless, the translation that picks up immediately in Mosiah comes from the plates of Nephi, according to the consistent references Mormon makes in the Mosiah-Mormon section of our current Book of Mormon. It is also certain that there was a record of Lehi's deeds, probably created early in the family exodus, from which Nephi quoted Lehi in Nephi's record (1 and 2 Nephi).[10] There was a difference, however, between the record of Lehi and the book of Lehi. The record of Lehi would have been the source material Nephi consulted when writing his account in the large plate and small plate tradition. The necessity of carrying Lehi's record when they already had the heavy brass plates suggests that it was probably written on a perishable material.[11] When Nephi fled from his brothers, he took the brass plates and the Liahona but does not mention any other plates (2 Ne. 5:12), although later in that same chapter, Nephi speaks of "other plates" on which he has a more particular history (2 Ne. 5:29). Nephi abridged the record of Lehi, at least on the small plates, but also made and kept a more complete record on the large plates. While a record of Lehi certainly existed, it probably was not originally engraved on metal plates. It is possible that Nephi copied it into his large plates in its entirety. In any case, the book of Lehi was Nephi's composition that included information from the record of Lehi.

The suggested resolution to this excursion into the Book of Mormon "plate tectonics" is that Joseph simply assumed that "plates of Lehi" existed because of the physical plates in front of him, Mormon's mention of plates as source material, and the existence of the book of Lehi. The book of Lehi, as translated, continued to the beginning of our Book of Mosiah, both of which were on the large plates of Nephi.

---

[6]Preface, *Book of Mormon* (1830 Facsimile Edition. Rpt., Independence, Mo.: Herald House, 1970).

[7]Quinn Brewster, "The Structure of the Book of Mormon: A Theory of Evolutionary Development," *Dialogue: A Journal of Mormon Thought* 29, no. 2 (Summer 1996): 130.

[8]Ibid.

[9]For instance, Brewster hypothesizes that Mormon wrote the Mosiah–Mormon section *after* Words of Mormon. Ibid., 132.

[10]S. Kent Brown, "Nephi's Use of Lehi's Record," in *Rediscovering the Book of Mormon*, edited by John L. Sorenson and Melvin J. Thorne (Provo, Utah: Foundation for Ancient Research and Mormon Studies, 1991), 3–14.

[11]Ibid., 5, for perishable material argument.

Words of Mormon 1:11

> 11 And they were handed down from king Benjamin, from generation to generation until they have fallen into my hands. And I, Mormon, pray to God that they may be preserved from this time henceforth. And I know that they will be preserved; for there are great things written upon them, out of which my people and their brethren shall be judged at the great and last day, according to the word of God which is written.

Mormon is speaking of the small plates. It is somewhat curious that he prays for their preservation, since he has included them in his own set of plates, for which he also prays preservation. However, this petition may be formulaic rather than specific. His desire is for the words of the plates to come to future generations, and perhaps Mormon foresaw that including them in his set of plates might have resulting in their being skipped—which actually seems to have happened, if the book of Mosiah immediately followed the book of Lehi in the translation sequence. Mormon is therefore praying that future generations would have the words of the small plates, not that he is concerned for the physical preservation of the plates themselves. This seems to suggest that Mormon believed that the small-plate material would be part of the record that the future translator produced.

Words of Mormon 1:12

> 12 And now, concerning this king Benjamin—he had somewhat of contentions among his own people.

Mormon does not describe these contentions, but the union of two people with different languages and cultures, whatever their common roots, could not have been easy. No difficulties are mentioned in the reign of King Mosiah$_1$, either because the new arrangement was still in its "honeymoon" period or simply because they were not reported.

However, Mormon's source material surely included more details, so we can safely assume that Mormon applied a heavy editorial hand, preserving the fact without discussing the specifics. It is quite probable that these contentions were discussed more fully in the lost 116 pages. Mosiah 1:1 begins with the statement that "and now there was no more contention in all the land of Zarahemla, among all the people who belonged to king Benjamin." That statement is irrelevant unless it refers to significant contentions that came before. Mormon's brief statement here stands in place of what would have been a more complete accounting (given Mormon's editorial habits).

Words of Mormon 1:13

> 13 And it came to pass also that the armies of the Lamanites came down out of the land of Nephi, to battle against his people. But behold, king Benjamin gathered together his armies, and he did stand against them; and he did fight with the strength of his own arm, with the sword of Laban.

There seems to be no connection between the internal contentions and the battle with the Lamanites except, possibly, the inference that internal contentions were temporarily resolved by the need to meet the greater external threat. (See commentary accompanying Jacob 3:13 for the conceptual difference between contentions and wars.) It is significant that Benjamin participated in the actual fighting and also that he used Laban's sword. This sword, now more than three hundred years old, was a sacred/political relic. Even with care, three centuries of maintaining an edge would have diminished the blade's strength, since sharpening and filing removes tiny amounts of metal. Although Nephi had also wielded it in battle—and no doubt his successors had as well—it is possible to read this reference as a ceremonial function more than a military one, a visual symbol of union, and a reminder of the Lord's promises and watch-care.

Words of Mormon 1:14

> 14 And in the strength of the Lord they did contend against their enemies, until they had slain many thousands of the Lamanites. And it came to pass that they did contend against the Lamanites until they had driven them out of all the lands of their inheritance.

The expansive phrase, "all the lands of their inheritance," must refer to lands surrounding Zarahemla. "Land of inheritance" had described the land of Nephi before Mosiah$_1$'s exodus; but it cannot possibly be included in this reference. Lamanites inhabited the land of Nephi during the entire reigns of Zeniff, Noah, and Limhi. Since Limhi and his people have not rejoined the Nephites in Zarahemla, and since this battle apparently came after Zeniff's departure, the land of first inheritance remained firmly in Lamanite hands at this point. From this point on, the land of Nephi is designated as the "land of first inheritance."[12]

Words of Mormon 1:15

> 15 And it came to pass that after there had been false Christs, and their mouths had been shut, and they punished according to their crimes;

The placement of this verse immediately after expelling the Lamanites by force from the lands of Zarahemla and soon after the "contentions" suggests that these false Christs are arising among the Zarahemlaites and represent significant apostate tendencies among Benjamin's people. Verse 16 will again mention contentions and describe Benjamin as cooperating with the prophets to establish peace.

It is expected that the Nephite religion would generate controversy. The Mulekites were no longer observing the tenets of the religion they had brought from Jerusalem. Conversion to the Nephite Messianic religion therefore required the abandonment of their known deities and observance.

---

[12]Mosiah 9:1, 10:13; Alma 22:28, 54:12–13. The exception is Ether 7:16 which refers to an earlier Jaredite land.

It is interesting that Mormon describes the problem as false *Christs*. When Sherem challenged Jacob, modern interpreters (though not the record itself) labeled him an anti-Christ, not a false Christ.[13] Mormon, writing ca. A.D. 400, may be using different wording than that on Benjamin's plates. What might he have meant?

A false prophet is one who teaches falsehoods. While a "false Christ" would also teach falsehoods, the person himself is "false." To be a false Christ, the person must claim to *be* Christ. Sherem denied the future Christ entirely, so it seems unlikely that Sherem would have attempted to claim this future Messiah's identity. Furthermore, only adherents to the Nephite religion would have known enough to present themselves as a "Christ," but such a claim seems unlikely given the religious cohesiveness of $Mosiah_1$'s followers. Nor does it seem likely that the Zarahemlaites, who had lost their Jewishness and had had only a generation of instruction in the Messianic religion would have made such a claim. Mormon seems to be capturing something else in this phrase of "false Christs."

A possible explanation comes from the Nahua concept of *teixiptla*, even though this hypothesis is speculative and even though both term and culture postdate the Book of Mormon era: "The Aztecs appear to have been a people compelled to insist on the visible presences of their gods," explains ethnohistorian Burr Cartwright Brundage. "In the conceptualization of these presences they went to extremes of detail. . . . But the Aztecs had a special type of idol which differed radically in that it was animate and incarnate. This was the *teixiptla*, 'image' or 'representative,' a person who wore the regalia, acted out the part of the god, and then was sacrificed."[14] Some aspects of the Aztec *teixiptla* probably did not pertain to Benjamin's time, such as the final sacrifice of the incarnate deity. However, the custom of representing a god by donning its masks appears very early in Mesoamerican history. The site of Chalcatzingo was abandoned in 500 B.C. and contains impressive art in the Olmec style. On Monument 2 are found "four persons. . . . At the right is a seated personage who faces two central figures walking towards him and a third who walks away on the left. The standing figures wear their 'bird-serpent' masks so their faces cannot be seen. The seated individual has turned his mask to the back of his head, revealing his face and pointed beard. All the masks seem to cover the entire face instead of simply the mouth area."[15] The masks indicate the presence of the extra-human in the scene. That the seated personage wears a mask turned to the rear highlights that these are men in costume, or men imitating gods, just like the later Aztec *teixiptla*.

---

[13]For example: Daniel H. Ludlow, *A Companion to Your Study of the Book of Mormon* (Salt Lake City: Deseret Book, 1976), 161; Joseph Fielding McConkie and Robert L. Millet, *Doctrinal Commentary on the Book of Mormon* (Salt Lake City: Bookcraft, 1987–92), 2:85; George Reynolds and Janne M. Sjodahl, *Commentary on the Book of Mormon*, edited and arranged by Philip C. Reynolds (Salt Lake City: Deseret Book, 1955–61), 1:489–90.

[14]Burr Cartwright Brundage, *The Fifth Sun* (Austin: University of Texas Press, 1979), 57.

[15]David C. Grove, *Chalcatzingo: Excavations on the Olmec Frontier* (London: Thames & Hudson, 1984), 119.

Perhaps "false Christs" was an appropriate term because these individuals were impersonating deities from the displaced competitor religions. If this speculative scenario is, in fact, what Mormon meant, then it is obvious why this practice would have caused "contention" in Zarahemla along both ethnic and religious lines.

Words of Mormon 1:16

> 16 And after there had been false prophets, and false preachers and teachers among the people, and all these having been punished according to their crimes; and after there having been much contention and many dissensions away unto the Lamanites, behold, it came to pass that king Benjamin, with the assistance of the holy prophets who were among his people—

Perhaps the false prophets, preachers, and teachers simply expand the category of "false Christs" or perhaps they represent others who were championing competing religions. In any case, Mormon's terse account reveals that their presence caused tremendous discord in Zarahemla. First, the contentions led to "crimes" which required formal punishment. Of course, in the ancient world with its overlapping categories of rulership and religion, the presence of a competing religious structure probably also threatened the political structure—hence, the "crimes."

The situation was serious enough that, in Mormon's odd phrase, there were "many dissensions away unto the Lamanites." In other words, the dissenters resolved their resistance to the newly imposed religious/political regime by defecting to the Lamanites. In Book of Mormon terms, the "Lamanites" would have been a non-Nephite group, but not necessarily the very enemies who had just been defeated by Benjamin's armies. Nevertheless, they did go to some "Lamanite" (read non-Nephite) group. Presumably, they retreated toward the old Jaredite (Olmec) homeland, where their linguistic, cultural, and religious heritage was still viable.

Words of Mormon 1:17–18

> 17 For behold, king Benjamin was a holy man, and he did reign over his people in righteousness; and there were many holy men in the land, and they did speak the word of God with power and with authority; and they did use much sharpness because of the stiffneckedness of the people—
> 18 Wherefore, with the help of these, king Benjamin, by laboring with all the might of his body and the faculty of his whole soul, and also the prophets, did once more establish peace in the land.

Note that peace follows both powerful preaching and military success. Benjamin dealt effectively with the external military threat from the Lamanites with a military response and with the internal threat of apostasy and religious disunion by "sharp" preaching that either produced repentance on the part of the dissidents or their departure.

Text: This is the end of a chapter and book.

Mosiah

Part 1: Context

1

Historical Background of the Book of Mosiah

The first fixed date mentioned in the book of Mosiah occurs 476 years after the departure from Jerusalem, a date that correlates to 124 B.C. (See commentary accompanying 1 Nephi 10:4 for information on how this commentary calculates Nephite years.) That date is for the coronation of Mosiah$_2$. Therefore, this date is necessarily not only later than the arrival of the Nephites in the land of Zarahemla but also after the entire reign of Benjamin and the death of Mosiah$_1$. A plausible time frame for the arrival of the Nephites in Zarahemla is 162 B.C. (See section on chronology following Mosiah 7:1.) This time frame places the book of Mosiah during the Preclassic period of Mesoamerica (500 B.C.–A.D. 250), sometimes also called the Protoclassic and therefore tells us the time depth at which we must look at Mesoamerican civilization for our cultural context.

The next important information for the book of Mosiah is that we have a shift in the location of the action. The book of Omni tells us that Mosiah$_1$ escaped from the land of Nephi with those who believed the Nephite religion and would follow him. They left the land in which all of the action had taken place up to that point and entered a new land where the people of Zarahemla had a different language and had forgotten their Jerusalem religion (Omni 1:17).

John Sorenson geographically correlates the land of Nephi to highland Guatemala, historically part of the Maya culture area. When the Nephites left the land of Nephi (highland Guatemala), they went to Zarahemla (the Grijalva Valley, according to Sorenson), a distance of perhaps 180 miles and part of the greater Olmec culture region.[1] The center of the Olmec culture was in the north near the mouth of the Grijalva. At this point in history, Olmec culture was fading, but its society and culture were long-lived and had, arguably, influenced the Jaredites from

[1]Probably Zoque speakers at this point in time. Zoque is a daughter language (along with Mixe). The language assumed to be that spoken by the Olmec is the ancestor of the two daughter languages, called Mixe-Zoque. See commentary accompanying Omni 1:16 and Ether, Part 1: Context, Chapter 1, "Historical Background of the Book of Ether."

at least 1300 B.C. down to its last survivor, whose life overlapped with that of the Nephite newcomers. Zarahemla was certainly exchanging information with the emerging Maya world, but it was on the periphery of the Maya cultural sphere and still retained connections to the ancestral Olmec lands northward. (See Ether, Part 1: Context, Chapter 1, "Historical Background of the Book of Ether" for more information on the Olmec.)

From this point on in the Book of Mormon, it is essential to understand the general trend of cultural development in the Maya area, since it has a tremendous effect on the narrative that unfolds in the Nephite world. While the rising culture of the Maya has unique aspects, much of it follows general Mesoamerican themes that had been present in the earlier Olmec culture. According to archaeologist John Henderson:

> Few Maya centers had densely populated residential zones; most people lived dispersed in the surrounding territory. Procurement of jade and other luxury goods, as well as utilitarian items, was an important function of Classic Maya political economic organization. Enclaves of Mayas living far beyond their home territories reflect a basic pattern of Maya territoriality, representing a strategy of ecological diversification. Such enclaves expanded access to valuable raw materials and to varied environments for crop cultivation. They also facilitated communication and interaction. All of these patterns are found, at least in embryonic form, in Olmec civilization.[2]

The ways in which people interacted with land did not necessarily change, but it seems likely that significant social variations developed. The Preclassic period saw the development of three social trends that had a marked impact on Book of Mormon history. The first was the concept of the Maya king. Maya kingship was not simply the establishment of a mode of rule but also a set of religious concepts and social distinctions that flowed from that ideology. It is of particular importance to note the type of society that produced the Maya king. David A. Freidel, professor of archaeology at Southern Methodist University, and Linda Schele, an epigrapher and professor of art at the University of Texas, suggest: "We propose that the institution of *ahaw* [Maya term roughly translated as "king" or "lord"] originated in the first century B.C.; that it was invented to accommodate severe contradictions in Maya society between and ethos of egalitarianism and an actual condition of flourishing elitism brought on by successful trade and interaction between the Lowland Maya and their hierarchically organized neighbors over the course of the Preclassic era."[3]

For Book of Mormon studies, Schele's and Freidel's proposition has two immensely important points. The first is the date. The first century B.C. places this development squarely in the time frame of the book of Mosiah—indeed extending

---

[2]John S. Henderson, *The World of the Ancient Maya* (Ithaca, N.Y.: Cornell University Press, 1997), 84.

[3]David A. Freidel and Linda Schele, "Kingship in the Late Preclassic Maya Lowlands," in *The Ancient Civilizations of Mesoamerica*, edited by Michael E. Smith and Marilyn A. Masson (Malden, Mass.: Blackwell Publishers, 2000), 423.

through the book of Alma and most of 3 Nephi.[4] This is the most important time period for Mormon, who dedicates more pages to this century and a half (Mosiah$_1$ entered Zarahemla about 162 B.C.) than any other comparable period of time. In a word, the times of greatest social upheaval in the Book of Mormon directly correspond to a time period when the Maya world is also undergoing a tremendous shift in political/religious ideology.

The second critical aspect of their proposition is that the institution of kingship was a way to resolve increasing social pressure against a previous egalitarianism. (See 2 Nephi, Part 1: Context, Chapter 2, "Overview of 2 Nephi.") We have seen that Nephi himself established the charter of Nephite society on Isaiah's social egalitarianism, a principle that King Benjamin reiterated in his great discourse. (See commentary accompanying Mosiah 2:12.) Indeed, Nephite society reasserted this principle of egalitarianism as a fundamental principle throughout their history. However, it was a principle under constant attack from those very pressures that Schele and Freidel have identified as influencing the rise of the Maya kings. This pressure toward increased social stratification becomes significant in the last hundred years before Christ in the archaeological record and increases in importance from that time on.[5]

In addition to the change in Maya social structure that positioned the king at the apex, another development in the Maya world also became important during this time period. Like the development of the kingship concept and the rise of social hierarchies, it became an important pressure within Nephite society. During this period, the evidence becomes clearer for the formation and spread of the Mesoamerican cult of war.[6]

The "cult" of war was an intertwined set of political and religious themes that manifested themselves in Mesoamerican warfare. Wars were fought, not simply as political strategies, but also for religious reasons. Men demonstrated and increased their personal valor through successful battles, and the cult of human sacrifice became an essential element of the seating of Maya kings. Some of the earliest artistic evidence for this practice comes from this pivotal century before Christ. According to epigrapher Linda Schele and Mary Ellen Miller, professor of art history at Yale University:

---

[4]The Book of Mormon would suggest that the development of kingship in this region was earlier than the first century B.C. This would not be surprising since the dating is dependent upon discovering architectural/iconographic remnants of the trappings of kingship. The institution certainly began prior to the time it was immortalized in stone.

[5]William A. Haviland and Hattula Moholy-Nagy, "Distinguishing the High and Mighty from the Hoi Polloi at Tikal, Guatemala," in *The Ancient Civilizations of Mesoamerica*, edited by Michael E. Smith and Marilyn A. Masson (Malden, Mass.: Blackwell Publishers, 2000), 42–43.

[6]Simon Martin, "Under a Deadly Star: Warfare Among the Classic Maya," in *Maya: Divine Kings of the Rain Forest*, edited by Nikolai Grube (Cologne, Ger.: Könemann, 2001), 176.

> The image on the Leiden Plaque [late Preclassic, 500 B.C.–A.D. 250[7]] refers to a second event that is vital to the process of accession. A captive, who is to be sacrificed as a blood offering sanctifying the transformation of the new king, lies bound and prostrate at his feet. The captive, marked as a noble by an ahau glyph on his head, was taken in battle specifically to serve in this ritual. Unhappy with his fate, he lifts his bound wrists and kicks his feet, twisting his body to look back across his shoulder, perhaps hoping for a reprieve. Other representations of accession ceremonies confirm that ritual sacrifice was a regular and necessary part of the process sanctifying the new ruler. At Piedras Negras, victims are shown stretched across an altar, their hearts excised. The heir designation rites recorded in the Bonampak murals were followed by sacrificial rituals that lasted for over a year. The battle to take the victims, their torture, and eventually their sacrifice are all depicted graphically.[8]

When the Nephites began a new life in a new location, they did so at a pivotal point in Mesoamerican history. Pressures were building all around them that reshaped the cultures of the Preclassic period. Those developmental pressures may have been greatest in the areas occupied by the Lamanites, but the people of Nephi were not immune to them. In many ways, it is precisely those developmental pressures that explain the direction of Nephite history from here to the end of Mormon's text.

---

[7]For the relationship between the Book of Mormon and Mesoamerican kingship rituals, it is important to note that, in addition to being from the right time period, the Leiden Plaque is also written in Epi-Olmec characters, rather than Maya. The plausible location of the land of Zarahemla lies in the region characterized by Epi-Olmec writing rather than Maya glyphs.

[8]Linda Schele and Mary Ellen Miller, *The Blood of Kings: Dynasty and Ritual in Maya Art* (New York: George Braziller, 1986), 110.

2

Mormon's Structural Editing: Books and Chapters

Mormon was a very careful editor and historian. He appears to have worked from an outline, evidenced by references to what might be included in the future (such as Helaman 2:12–13) and he certainly worked with an overall plan of how the work he created would serve the purpose of "convincing . . . the Jew and Gentile that Jesus is the Christ, the Eternal God" (Title Page). Mormon's work constitutes the longest and most complex scriptural writing preserved. No writer of either the Old or New Testament has written so much material that focused on demonstrating a particular religious point.[1] No other writer in all of scripture has described a thousand years of history in such a way to tie that history to the will and work of God. With so much care and forethought, it is both sad and ironic that we do not have the work that Mormon wrote.

The loss of the 116 manuscript pages that Martin Harris took to show to his wife effectively removed Mormon's entire opening text. In its place we have the material we know as 1 Nephi–Omni, but those works are neither written by nor edited by Mormon. Mormon's first book would have been the book of Lehi, and we are missing it entirely. While the book of Lehi certainly contained many of the same events, Nephi retold his story in 1 Nephi with an emphasis on the spiritual message that was unlikely to have been presented in the same way in the original book of Lehi. We do not know how Mormon would have edited Nephi's story. The time period from Enos to Mosiah_1 might well have contained more details than the very sketchy information we currently have for that time period. It is virtually certain that Mormon's book of Lehi did not begin with the now famous "I Nephi, being born of goodly parents . . . " (1 Nephi 1:1) as that is an indicator of first-person text. It is not characteristic of the edited text that we have from Mormon.[2]

[1]Only the Deuteronomists, as conceived in the documentary hypothesis, have had as much impact on the preserved tradition.

[2]Mormon does use texts with the "I, [name]" formula, such as the inserted record of Zeniff in Mosiah 9. However, these are clearly inserted texts and Mormon typically has some introductory material to give context to the inserted texts. Therefore I suggest that Mormon would have been the first writer

In addition to the textual information contained in the 116 pages, their loss also prevents us from discussing how Mormon worked as an editor until we begin with the material in Mosiah. The material from 1 Nephi to Omni can tell us about other authors, but they cannot tell us much about Mormon save that he put those plates together with his work according to the Lord's instruction (W of M 1:3–7). Beginning with the book of Mosiah, however, we have access to the text that Mormon edited and we can ask questions of that material that teach us about the kinds of editorial decisions that Mormon was making.

Before examining structural elements that represents Mormon's decisions, I should note that there is a type of structural information in the Book of Mormon that cannot be ascribed to Mormon. John H. Gilbert, who set type in E. B. Grandin's shop for the first edition of the Book of Mormon, later described the manuscript: "Every chapter, if I remember correctly, was one solid paragraph, without a punctuation mark, from beginning to end."[3] This information does require an important caveat as we analyze the Book of Mormon for doctrinal information. Since all of the paragraphing and punctuation was done by the compositor it goes beyond available evidence if any argument is based upon paragraphs, sentences, or the punctuation in sentences. If ever our interpretation of the text relies upon those pieces of information, we are making an analysis based on what a competent reader worked out in the text but not what was placed there by Mormon or by Joseph Smith during translation. There are two structural elements that are original to Mormon's text. Mormon preserved the divisions into books and created the chapter divisions. I will examine those units to try to understand the principles Mormon used to know when to change from book to book and chapter to chapter.

Book Names

Unlike sentences and paragraphs, the names of books were clearly part of the dictated text. The best evidence for the presence of these book changes comes from the original manuscript as that is the closest to the plate text we can get. Unfortunately, the original manuscript is poorly and incompletely preserved. Nevertheless, there are a number of cases where the book name changes are indicated in the text. When the original manuscript marks the change from Alma to Helaman, there is no change in the page. Oliver Cowdery continued to

---

rather than begin with an inserted text. It is also probable that the beginning of his text would introduce himself as the editor and explain his purpose in writing. See commentary accompanying Words of Mormon 1:3.

[3]Thomas W. Mackay, "Mormon as Editor: A Study in Colophons, Headers, and Source Indicators," in *Journal of Book of Mormon Studies* 2, no. 1 (Fall 1993): 90–109. The lack of paragraphs and punctuation has been faithfully reproduced in the typescript of the original manuscript. Royal Skousen, ed., *The Original Manuscript of the Book of Mormon*, THE CRITICAL TEXT OF THE BOOK OF MORMON, Vol. 1 (Provo, Utah: Foundation for Ancient Research and Mormon Studies, 2001), 104; *Book of Mormon Critical Text: A Tool for Scholarly Reference*, 3 vols. (Provo, Utah: Foundation for Ancient Research and Mormon Studies, 1987).

write on the same page. However, he drew a horizontal line covering most of the page following the end of Alma and just prior to beginning Helaman. Below this solid ink line is a slightly indented title "The Book of Helaman." The next line has a roughly centered "Chapter I" and the following line begins the chapter synopsis.[4]

The use of the solid line to make a book separation does not appear to be original to the text but rather a device used in that particular instance. While there are no other chapter breaks preserved in the original manuscript for Mormon's text, there are two more examples in the 1 Nephi to Omni section. The extant manuscript preserves the change from 1 Nephi to 2 Nephi and a damaged page where Jacob changes to Enos. Neither of those two book breaks employs the horizontal line divider.

The manuscript marking the division between 1 Nephi and 2 Nephi has only a space and then "The Book of Nephi An account of the death of Lehi. . . . " This particular book break is interesting in that the modern conventions of 1 Nephi and 2 Nephi are absent. The word "second" is written above the line and in between the words "The ^second^ Book" (where the ^ indicates the word being written above the line in the manuscript). Skousen notes that the word "second" is in Oliver's hand and has a heavier ink flow.[5]

It is reasonably clear that some indication on the plates allowed Joseph to dictate that a change was coming. The name of the book was dictated from the plates. Since we are now examining Mormon's editorial work we must understand which books were original to his conceived text.

Joseph Smith indicated that the lost 116 pages comprised the book of Lehi.[6] No other book is indicated. This suggests that the original text of Mormon's work as originally conceived would have been:

- Lehi
- Mosiah
- Alma
- Helaman
- Nephi (our 3 Nephi)[7]
- Nephi (our 4 Nephi)
- Mormon

Mormon tells us that the material we have from 1 Nephi to Omni was all contained on a different set of plates that we call the small plates of Nephi and that

---

[4]Skousen, ed., *The Original Manuscript of the Book of Mormon*, 487.

[5]Ibid., 164.

[6]*Book of Mormon* (1830; rpt., Independence, Mo.: Herald House, 1970), 1.

[7]Mormon certainly would not have named this "3 Nephi" simply because our books of 1 and 2 Nephi were not included. What we have as the third book of Nephi would have been the first to appear in Mormon's text. The evidence from the 1830 edition tells us that none of the Nephis were identified by a number. In Mormon's work, they are identified by genealogy: "The book of Nephi, the son of Nephi which was the son of Helaman," and "The book of Nephi, which is the son of Nephi, one of the disciples of Jesus Christ."

he added these upon being prompted by the Spirit (W of M 1:7). They were not part of his original plan. Mormon did indicate that the book of Ether should be available: "And this account shall be written hereafter; for behold, it is expedient that all people should know the things which are written in this account" (Mosiah 28:19). In spite of this promise, Mormon himself does not include it, nor is there any indication of where he would have added it. There is nothing in Ether that is required to understand Mormon's work save the historical information about secret combinations among the Jaredites. Even this information is simply background as Mormon had already made his point. Perhaps the book of Ether was intended to be an appendix in the same way that the small-plate material was included, but was not part of Mormon's conceived text.

Mormon's originally conceived work contained seven different books. He claims that his source material is the "plates of Nephi," which we understand as the large plates of Nephi and represented the more official records of the Nephite people. We now turn to the question of why the names of the books change.

Based upon our experience with the small plates, it is not uncommon to assume that the book names change when a new person writes on them. This easily explains Nephi, Jacob, Enos, and Jarom. It works for the first writer in Omni, but then that book contains a large number of writers who do not create new book names. Of course many of them hardly create new paragraphs, so we can understand that they might not have wanted to highlight their meager contribution with a change in book name. All of this is a fine explanation for the small-plate material, but it doesn't work for the books in Mormon's work which were taken from the large-plate tradition. Virtually all of those books have more than one writer.

- Book of Lehi: Lehi, $Nephi_1$, and unknown authors until the reign of Mosiah. This covers a period of nearly 400 years.
- Book of Mosiah: $Mosiah_1$, Benjamin, $Mosiah_2$, $Alma_1$
- Book of Alma: $Alma_2$, $Helaman_1$
- Book of Helaman: Helaman, $Nephi_2$

Clearly the book names do not change based on the writer or prophet associated with the book. On what principle do they change? Important pieces of information come from the transition between the book of Alma and the book of Helaman. The book of Alma contains the writings of $Alma_2$ (but not $Alma_1$) and $Helaman_1$ the son of $Alma_2$. The book of Helaman starts with $Helaman_2$ the son of $Helaman_1$. In Alma 63:11 we learn that the plates have been given to $Helaman_2$ the son of $Helaman_1$. In Helaman 2:2 we learn that $Helaman_2$ is appointed to sit as chief judge. His father was not a sitting chief judge, although his grandfather ($Alma_2$) had been. $Alma_2$ had relinquished the judge seat to devote his efforts to preaching the gospel. He had records and took them with him. When $Helaman_1$ the son of $Alma_2$ received the plates, they were outside of the political line. When the new book begins with Helaman the son of Helaman, it is a new book in the hands of a new lineage of sitting judges. This change allows us to hypothesize that the change in book names is related to the shift in the ruling dynasties and the passage of the plates in and out of those dynasties. Does the theory hold up?

The first book of the large plates and therefore Mormon's work was the book of Lehi. Nephi indicated that those plates contained "an account of the reign of the kings" (1 Ne. 9:4). After Nephi there were other kings who received the throne name of "Nephi" (Jacob 1:11), so we must suppose that the large plates contained the records of these "Nephies." We do not have another book name change for about 400 years when we have a new book of Mosiah. What happens between the book of Lehi and Mosiah? While the specifics are lost in the 116 pages, we do know that Mosiah$_1$ flees the city of Nephi with the plates and becomes king in Zarahemla. Had Mosiah$_1$ been one of the "Nephi" kings we might expect that he too would continue the book of Lehi. However, he is a new king in a new place. He is the founder of a new dynasty and therefore may legitimately begin a new book.

The transition from the book of Mosiah to the book of Alma is another change in political dynasty. Mosiah$_2$'s sons refused the kingship and the monarchy is replaced by a system of judges. The book of Alma begins not with Alma$_1$, but with the first of the new dynasty of rulers when Alma$_2$ became the chief judge. Alma$_2$ takes the record with him when he leaves to preach and his son continues to write in the book of his father. I have already noted that the change from the book of Alma to the book of Helaman occurs with the change of ruling dynasty. The plates of Nephi move back to the ruling line and are part of the ruling dynasty.

In the book of Helaman the Gadianton robbers seize the government and Nephi$_2$, the son of Helaman$_2$, takes the record with him. As with Alma$_2$ and Helaman$_1$, the record has moved out of the political line. By the time we arrive at 4 Nephi, the record and the rulership have been reunited in the person of Nephi$_4$, son of Nephi$_3$ and similarly one of the twelve.[8] This is a change from both location and dynasty after the Gadianton usurpation and therefore represents a new book.

Mormon receives the records after a period of political discord sufficiently severe that the last record keeper hid the plates until such time as Mormon was ready for them (4 Ne. 1:48–49). The shift from 4 Nephi to Mormon may also be seen as a significant shift in the transmission line of the plates.

This leaves us with the shift from Helaman to 3 Nephi. The record is already out of the hands of ruling line and Nephi$_2$ (son of Helaman$_2$). There is no indication that Nephi$_2$'s position in the government changes at the beginning of this record. This book change appears to be the sole exception to the rule of changing dynasties. Nevertheless, it should not follow the same rules as the rest of the books, as it comes from a completely different source (3 Ne. 5:8–10). (See 3 Nephi, Part 1: Context, Chapter 2, "The Name of the Book of [3] Nephi.")

Changing Chapters

[8]Clyde James Williams, "Nephi^4," in *Book of Mormon Reference Companion*, edited by Dennis L. Largey (Salt Lake City: Deseret Book, 2003), 589.

In the same way that the changes in book names were marked in the plate text, the changes from one chapter to another were also part of the original plate text. Royal Skousen, a professor of linguistics and English language at Brigham Young University, has studied the manuscripts of the Book of Mormon and tells us: "Evidence suggests that as Joseph Smith was translating, he apparently saw some mark (or perhaps extra spacing) whenever a section ended, but was unable to see the text that followed. At such junctures, Joseph decided to refer to these endings as chapter breaks and told the scribe to write the word "chapter" at these places, but without specifying any number for the chapter since Joseph saw neither a number nor the word 'chapter.'"[9] Mormon (and the authors of the small plates) used some type of convention that separated their ideas into units that we understand as chapters. Because we have only the dictated manuscript and not the original plates, it is unclear what the marker was that signaled a change. As Skousen indicates, it may have been some spacing that made it clear that something new was beginning. It is also possible that there was little difference in the signal for the end of a chapter and the signal for the end of a book. "'Chapter' appears in the original manuscript at the very beginning of a section, even before the title of a new book. Thus 'Chapter' was originally incorrectly written at the end of 1 Nephi and before the beginning of 2 Nephi. Only later was this chapter specification crossed out by Oliver Cowdery and placed after the title of the book ('The Book of Nephi')."[10] Even small books that have no internal divisions, such as Enos, Jarom, and Omni, originally had the word "chapter" at the beginning. In books with multiple chapters, the chapter numbers were added later.[11]

Because some indication of a break between units was present on the plates, we can examine those divisions to attempt to understand what textual events triggered a conceptual break in the Mormon's mind. Of course, one of the important caveats of researching Mormon's textual breaks is that we must return to the original 1830 chapter breaks which represent those present on the plates. The 1879–1981 editions of the Book of Mormon follow new chapters assigned by Orson Pratt and do not represent Mormon's original construction.[12]

Examining the chapter breaks leads to a typology of the kinds of changes that initialized a chapter break. Of course, the typology is not particularly clean, because

---

[9]Royal Skousen, "Critical Methodology and the Text of the Book of Mormon," in *Review of Books on the Book of Mormon* 6, no. 1 (1994): 137.

[10]Ibid. "The Book of Nephi" is the plate designation for what we know as 2 Nephi. Oliver Cowdery later added "The ^second^ book of Nephi ^Chapter 1^."

[11]Ibid., 138. Skousen also notes that at times the inserted chapter numbers were incorrect. Oliver Cowdery inadvertently skipped a number when numbering the chapters in Mosiah, an error that was corrected by the compositor.

[12]Pratt used very different criteria in assigning his chapters. In cases where the text followed scriptures from the King James Version of the Bible, Pratt attempted to construct chapter and verse designations that followed that scripture as it appeared in the King James Version. While Pratt usually left chapter ending in the places Mormon had created them, there are cases where Pratt pulled in material from the next chapter and made the break later. For this reason the analysis in this book is based solely on the chapter breaks as found in the 1830 edition.

chapters include different types of material. For instance, one of the most common chapter breaks occurs between the end of an embedded discourse and the resumption of the framing narration. However, chapters are not always created when this kind of transition occurs. Thus, we can say that this type of change was used as a probable, but not rigid, signal of a chapter break. Examining the types of boundary topics or texts can shed light on Mormon's editorial process.

Five types of chapter breaks can be identified from the 1830 edition of the Book of Mormon.

1. *Transitions from inserted speech to narrative.* The shift from the two types of material is an important dividing line that became a chapter break. At times the break comes at the end of the inserted discourse (typically marked with "Amen"). In other cases, the narrative ends the chapter and the inserted speech begins the next chapter.[13] (See commentary accompanying Alma 8:1–2 for a suggestion of the reason that Mormon tends to preserve inserted sermons as a whole unit.)

2. *Breaks between speakers or between two speeches by the same speaker.*[14] Reports of the Savior's discourses in 3 Nephi represent a special case. Chapter breaks occur when Christ begins to address a new theme. In our versified copies of the Book of Mormon the chapter breaks for text that follows the King James Version (either Matthew or other cited texts such as Isaiah or Malachi) also follow the chapter breaks (and versification) of the King James Version. These are not original to the manuscript, however. Even in the long citations from Isaiah, Mormon's chapter breaks are thematic and correspond to the text rather than to the chapters as they appear in the King James Version.[15]

3. *Breaks at year designations.* Very common examples are " . . . therefore, there was much peace among the people of Nephi until the fifth year of the reign of the judges" (Alma 1:33) or "And thus ended the eighty and fifth year" (Hel. 11:38). The frequency of these markers suggests that Mormon wrote his account from his sources that were probably compiled annually, featuring significant highlights. Although the break occurs at a year marker, it does not break at every year, nor at predictable years. Mormon appears to have used this method of creating a new chapter when it was convenient to a

---

[13]In the following set of data, the indication of the chapter break is given by listing the two chapters in-between which the break has occurred. In each example there will be two sets of numbers. The first two numbers are from the 1830 edition, and the numbers in parentheses are the modern chapter breaks that correspond to the original divisions (following the excellent chart found in Mackay, "Mormon as Editor," 104–9).

Mosiah 1/2 (3/4); Mosiah 2/3 (4/5); Mosiah 3/4 (5/6); Mosiah 6/7 (10/11); Mosiah 8/9 (16/17); Alma 2/3 (4/5); Alma 3/4 (5/6); Alma 4/5 (6/7); Alma 5/6 (7/8); Alma 6/7 (8/9); Alma 8/9 (11/12); Alma 14/15 (26/27); Alma 15/16 (29/30); Alma 19/20 (42/43); Alma 26/27 (58/59); Helaman 2/3 (6/7); 3 Nephi 2/3 (5/6); 3 Nephi 4/5 (10/11) [End of Mormon's interjection, resuming the account]; 3 Nephi 11/12 (26:5/26:6); 3 Nephi 12/13 (27:22/27:23); Mormon 3/4 (7/8) [shift between Mormon's testimony, closed with Amen, and the return to narrative]; Ether 1/2 (4/5); Ether 2/3 (5/6); Ether 3/4 (8/9) [Moroni's interjection closes 3, narrative returns in 4]; Moroni 1/2 (1/2); Moroni 6/7 (6/7); Moroni 9/10 (9/10).

[14]Alma 7/8 (9/10); Alma 9/10 (13:9/13:10); Alma 17/18 (37/38) [addressing a different son]; Alma 18/19 (38/39) [addressing a different son]; Alma 27/28 (60/61); Alma 28/29 (61/62); Helaman 4/5 (12/13).

[15]3 Nephi 5/6 (13:24/13:25); 3 Nephi 6/7 (14/15); 3 Nephi 7/8 (16/17); 3 Nephi 8/9 (18/19); 3 Nephi 10/11 (23:13/23/14); 3 Nephi 13/14 (29/30); Moroni 7/8 (7/8); Moroni 8/9 (8/9).

narrative history, but it depended more on the conclusion of one narration and the beginning of the next than it did on the simple fact of a year change.[16]

4. Transitions between major record groups in the source material. This type of transition is closely akin to the breaks between books but instead reflects Mormon's taking up a new record within the same book, for example, inserting Zeniff's account into his larger narrative of Mosiah.[17]

5. Transitions between subject changes. These are the least obvious of the chapter divisions.[18]

The Case of Mosiah Chapter 1

Mosiah 1 lacks a synopsis as an introduction, a departure from Mormon's invariable practice with every other book he edited (and excluding the small book of Mormon which he wrote, not edited). This omission strongly suggests that Mosiah 1 was not the beginning of the book of Mosiah. Skousen's examination of the printer's manuscript indicates that Mosiah 1 originally appeared as the third chapter. The text that constituted the first two chapters of Mormon's version of Mosiah was apparently copied onto the 116 pages that were lost. Our current copy of Mosiah is therefore missing text that Mormon intended us to have.[19]

---

[16]Alma 1/2 (3/4); Alma 10/11 (15/16); Alma 22/23 (50/51); Alma 23/24 (51/52); Alma 24/25 (53/54); Alma 25/26 (55/56); Alma 29/30 (62/63); Helaman 1/2 (2/3); Helaman 3/4 (10/11); 3 Nephi 1/2 (2/3); 3 Nephi 3/4 (10/11); Mormon 1/2 (3/4).

[17]Mosiah 5/6 (8/9) [insertion of the record of Zeniff]; Mosiah 10/11 (22/23); Mosiah 11/12 (28:19/28:20); Alma 11/12 (16/17); Alma 12/13 (20/21); Alma 13/14 (22/23) [in this case, the transition marks the end if Mormon's editorial remarks and a return to the original source]; Alma 16/17 (35/36); Alma 20/21 (44/45).

[18]Mosiah 4/5 (6/7); Mosiah 7/8 (13:24/13:25); Mosiah 9/10 (21/22); Mosiah 12/13 (28:19/28:20); Alma 21/22 (49/50); 3 Nephi 9/10 (21:21/21:22); 3 Nephi 12/13 (27:22/27:23); Mormon 2/3 (5/6); Ether 4/5 (11/12); Moroni 2/3 (2/3); Moroni 3/4 (3/4); Moroni 4/5 (4/5); Moroni 5/6 (5/6).

[19]Skousen, "Critical Methodology and the Text of the Book of Mormon," 138, discusses the chapter numbering against a statement Brent Metcalfe made suggesting that there was only a single missing chapter:

> Here Oliver Cowdery originally wrote "Chapter III," then changed this to "Chapter I" by deleting the last two numbers. This is characteristic of how Oliver corrected mistakes. Contrary to Metcalfe's interpretation, Oliver Cowdery definitely did not first write "Chapter II" and then cross out the whole number and insert a I before the crossed-out II. All three I's have the same ink flow and spacing. Based on Oliver's scribal practice, I would argue that if Oliver had written II and wanted to change it to I, he would have either crossed out the second I or crossed out both I's and followed it with a single I with an intervening space.

This information comes from the printer's manuscript and not the original. The cross-out of the chapter number is easily understood on the original; but when the printer's manuscript was copied, the end of Words of Mormon and the beginning of Mosiah are on the same page. Royal Skousen, ed., *The Printer's Manuscript of the Book of Mormon*, THE CRITICAL TEXT OF THE BOOK OF MORMON (Provo, Utah: Foundation for Ancient Research and Mormon Studies, 2001), Vol. 2, Part 1, 284. Clearly the small-plate material was copied first even though it was translated later. That transition would have been apparent on the original but is blurred by the copying process that gives us the printer's manuscript. Nevertheless, this cross-out suggests that when Oliver Cowdery finished copying the small plate material he began with the older text from the original and simply copied what he found there. The correction to the chapter number was made later. I proposed this scenario to Royal Skousen in an

The manuscripts also indicate that while our current Mosiah 1 did not begin a new book, it did in fact begin a new chapter. Does the pattern of chapter breaks provide any suggestions about what is missing? Mosiah 1:1 reads more like a conclusion than an introduction: "And now there was no more contention in all the land of Zarahemla, among all the people who belonged to king Benjamin, so that king Benjamin had continual peace all the remainder of his days." While modern editing would suggest the conclusion at the end of a previous chapter, Mormon frequently places concluding material at the beginning of the subsequent chapter, if there was some other reason for the break. Mosiah 7 begins with a similar statement but does not refer to obviously previous events. There are two reasonable possibilities for the content of the missing chapter II. Either it contained an inserted sermon which gave Mormon a reason to end or it contained a major historical shift as we have between our current chapters 6 and 7. Because the beginning of our Mosiah 1 summarizes important information about conflict and Words of Mormon reiterated that conflict, I suggest that the missing chapter covered the civil war during Benjamin's reign. Perhaps the missing chapter I contained the information about Mosiah$_1$'s flight from the city of Nephi and installation as king in Zarahemla and chapter II covered the political conflicts that broke into civil war in his son's reign. This hypothesis is strengthened by the fact that this is the record of Mosiah and of not Benjamin. The double change of ruler and location would be sufficient reason to begin a new dynastic record.

Skousen suggests:

> All of this leads me to believe that the lost 116 pages included not only all of Lehi, but also part of Chapter I of the original Mosiah. Joseph Smith retained from the summer of 1828 some small portion of the translation (D&C 10:41) and may have added a few additional pages in March 1829 (D&C 5:30), just prior to Oliver Cowdery's arrival in the following month. In all, these pages probably included the following portions from the beginning of the original Mosiah; the rest of chapter I, all of chapter II, and perhaps the beginning of chapter III. In fact, these few pages could have been part of the original manuscript that was placed in the cornerstone of the Nauvoo House in 1841. If so, they could well have been crossed out so as not to repeat the end of Amaleki's account (from the book of Omni in the small plates) and the material Mormon covered in his transitional "The Words of Mormon."[20]

---

email. His personal response confirmed that this was likely. Royal Skousen, email to Brant Gardner, December 2004.

[20]Skousen, ed., *The Printer's Manuscript of the Book of Mormon*, 1:139. This way of beginning a chapter is not atypical of Mormon's style. It is more likely that we have the entire chapter preserved.

Mosiah

Part 2: Commentary

Mosiah 1

Mosiah 1:1

> 1 And now there was no more contention in all the land of Zarahemla, among all the people who belonged to king Benjamin, so that king Benjamin had continual peace all the remainder of his days.

Vocabulary: "Continual peace" refers to the quality and depth of the peace, not necessarily the duration. This phrase is applied to a period as short as a single year (Alma 3:32) and to another as long as twenty-two years (Mosiah 10:5). This expression is not found in the standard works outside of the Book of Mormon.[1]

Variant: The printer's manuscript has the heading "Chapter III," rather than our current chapter 1.[2] Words of Mormon is a transition between the text of the small plates and the text of the large plates. What we are missing is the material from the large plates dealing with King $Mosiah_1$, for whom this book should be named. It is therefore probable that this section would have been Mosiah chapter 2, which must have been lost with the 116 manuscript pages. (See Mosiah, Part 1: Context, Chapter 2, "Mormon's Structural Editing: Chapters and Books.")

Text: One of the curious aspects of the book of Mosiah is what *isn't* here. In all of the books that Mormon abridged from the large plates of Nephi (Alma, Helaman, 3 Nephi, and 4 Nephi) there is a preface that explains the contents of each book. There isn't one for Mosiah. Mosiah is very much the same kind of book as the others, so logic tells us that it should have been present. The best explanation for its absence is that it was written on the plates, but was part of the lost 116 pages, along with what appears to have been Mosiah chapter 1 and perhaps 2.

Mosiah 1:2–3

> 2 And it came to pass that he had three sons; and he called their names Mosiah, and Helorum, and Helaman. And he caused that they should be taught in all the language of his fathers, that thereby they might become men of understanding; and that they might know concerning the prophecies which had been spoken by the mouths of their fathers, which were delivered them by the hand of the Lord.
>
> 3 And he also taught them concerning the records which were engraven on the plates of brass, saying: My sons, I would that ye should remember that were

---

[1]See Mosiah 7:1; 19:29; 29:43; Alma 1:12; 4:5; 30:2, 5; Helaman 3:23; 3 Nephi 6:9. Alison V. P. Coutts et al., "Complete Text of Benjamin's Speech with Notes and Comments," in *King Benjamin's Speech*, edited by John W. Welch and Stephen D. Ricks (Provo, Utah: FARMS, 1998), 481.

[2]*Book of Mormon Critical Text: A Tool for Scholarly Reference*, 3 vols. (Provo, Utah: FARMS, 1987), 2:356.

> it not for these plates, which contain these records and these commandments, we must have suffered in ignorance, even at this present time, not knowing the mysteries of God.

Culture: These verses provide some tremendously important information but so matter of factly that it is easy to miss their significance. Benjamin was obviously a good father who taught his children. Certainly he taught them the gospel. Significantly, however, he is teaching his sons the words of two different record traditions. The second is actually named (the brass plates), which identifies the first by elimination as the large plates. "The prophecies which had been spoken by the mouths of their fathers, which were delivered them by the hand of the Lord" are obviously not on the brass plates but were the prophets in their own Nephite tradition. The plates of Nephi are part of the items transferred upon the bestowal of kingship, as we will see later, so they are quite literally "delivered" (Mosiah 1:16). The phrase "by the hand of the Lord" recognizes the sanctity of the charge to preserve the plates. Mosiah had obeyed this charge by bringing the plates with him during the exodus from the land of Nephi.

Second, Mormon summarizes that Benjamin "caused that they should be taught in all the language of his fathers." Language in the Book of Mormon can mean both linguistics and also the larger category of culture. (See commentary accompanying 1 Nephi 1:2–3.) Here, it probably has its linguistic sense, for such instruction was to assure "that thereby they might become men of understanding; and that they might know concerning the prophecies which had been spoken by the mouths of their fathers."

The cultural meaning might still explain "men of understanding," but the final phrase ties the teaching of "language" to the words of the large plates. Benjamin's sons learn the language specifically for the purpose of knowing "the prophecies which had been spoken by the mouths of their fathers." The minimum possible interpretation is that they were taught to read. However, the meaning of "language" meant more than literacy alone; it also means a specific language as the next verse clarifies.

At this point, however, it is enough to note that literacy was sufficiently unusual that it was mentioned even in Mormon's abridgment. There is, naturally, no mention of the fact that a child learns the spoken language of his or her parents. That is expected. Clearly, these sons are learning a second language.

Redaction: Verses 1–2 are wholly Mormon's words. They are based, certainly, upon the data on his source plates, but these verses summarize what was surely more detailed data from the plates of Nephi. Mormon's editorializing continues until the middle of verse 3 where he cites Benjamin's discourse to his sons. Mormon explains that he has selected this discourse because in it Benjamin describes why the information on the plates is valuable. Mormon would be very sensitive to this explanation, for his task in abridging the record was to preserve that value for future generations. He therefore saw this discourse as directly relevant to his purposes in creating his plates.

Mormon's contexting for this embedded discourse is a quick sketch of the necessary historical background to explain the discourse, but his purpose is to preserve the discourse, not to recount history. That we may extract historical/anthropological data from his introduction is felicitous, but Mormon was not consciously attempting to communicate these items of information. Indeed, virtually all of Mormon's choices are governed by spiritual rather than historical criteria, as we would understand these terms.

Mosiah 1:4

> 4 For it were not possible that our father, Lehi, could have remembered all these things, to have taught them to his children, except it were for the help of these plates; for he having been taught in the language of the Egyptians therefore he could read these engravings, and teach them to his children, that thereby they could teach them to their children, and so fulfilling the commandments of God, even down to this present time.

Redaction: This statement is a quotation from Benjamin, a source text embedded in Mormon's abridgment. While we cannot be certain that there is no abridgment of the discourse itself (neither here nor in future examples), it seems reasonable to assume that the embedded discourse tends to remain intact and that Mormon's interjections will be fairly clearly identified as his own. In this passage, for instance, changes in subject and or verb tense signal a switch to the speaker from Mormon's source document.

Culture: Verse 4 is directly tied to the conception of language and learning the words of the fathers. In particular, Benjamin highlights the importance of the brass plates but ties the importance of the plates to the importance of learning "language." Lehi was "taught in the language of the Egyptians[;] therefore he could read these engravings [brass plates]."

Benjamin's discourse to his sons explains the gravity of learning their contents. To pass this information on, Lehi had to learn the "language of the Egyptians." What Mormon must have omitted in its abbreviation is that the material preceding Benjamin's discourse must have constituted a fuller explanation of why it was necessary to learn a particular language to retain literate access to the brass plates and also to the large plates produced by their own ancestor. This instruction comes after nearly four hundred years in the New World and after the Nephites have relocated among a more numerous people who did not speak the same language (Omni 1:17). Therefore, Mormon's explanation about learning language is necessary background—not a child's normal learning of his parents' language but rather a specific educational effort to provide him with command of a language he would not otherwise know.

Concerning the language itself, we need to distinguish "language" from "script." There is some possibility that the two are not the same—that the language is Hebrew but the script is Egyptian. Of course it is also possible that both language and script are "Egyptian." The substitution of one script for another to represent a known language is not a particularly difficult task. Both Japanese and Chinese are able to use the same script. Examples of Hebrew language written with Egyptian script are attested. Hamblin cites the example of the Byblos Syllabic texts:

> The earliest known example of mixing a Semitic language with modified Egyptian hieroglyphic characters is the Byblos Syllabic inscriptions (eighteenth century B.C.), from the city of Byblos on the Phoenician coast. This script is described as a "syllabary [that] is clearly inspired by the Egyptian hieroglyphic system, and in fact is the most important link known between the hieroglyphs and the Canaanite alphabet." Interestingly enough, most Byblos Syllabic texts were written on copper plates. Thus, it would not be unreasonable to describe the Byblos Syllabic texts as a Semitic language written on metal plates in "reformed Egyptian characters," which is precisely what the Book of Mormon describes.[3]

Representing a language with a different script is not difficult. Learning a different language with a different script for that language is much more difficult. I suggest that the emphasis on language was on the language proper and not just the script, so I lean to the explanation that both Egyptian language and script were necessary to read the brass plates. Regardless of the language that Benjamin's sons were speaking, the written language (and/or script) was different, requiring a focused educational effort. The result of the education was to make them both "men of understanding" and literate in the brass plates and, by extension, the large plates.

Because Lehi and Nephi had to go through the same process of learning the language of the brass plates, presumably this is why Nephi created his plates on that model. Nephi must have not only been familiar with them but attached both emotional and spiritual significance to the language/script itself. Whatever the origin of the language on the brass plates, it was sacralized for him. The experience of obtaining the brass plates had been a watershed event in young Nephi's life, and it is not unreasonable to suppose that the physical presence of the plates would have had even greater import for him than for Lehi. We may conjecture that, in addition to replicating the medium (metal plates) and the language, Nephi may even have borrowed the physical dimensions of his plates from the brass plates. (See Behind the Text: Chapter 3, "Mormon's Sources.")

Mosiah 1:5

> 5 I say unto you, my sons, were it not for these things, which have been kept and preserved by the hand of God, that we might read and understand of his mysteries, and have his commandments always before our eyes, that even our fathers would have dwindled in unbelief, and we should have been like unto our brethren, the Lamanites, who know nothing concerning these things, or even do not believe them when they are taught them, because of the traditions of their fathers, which are not correct.

Culture: Benjamin provides important information in this explanation. First, the ability to read the prophetic record has been a prerequisite to the existence of

---

[3]William J. Hamblin, "Sacred Writings on Bronze Plates in the Ancient Mediterranean," Working Paper (Provo, Utah: Foundation for Ancient Research and Mormon Studies, 1994), 8.

continued belief, in contrast to "our brethren, the Lamanites." In this particular case, however generalized "Lamanite" has become, Benjamin obviously refers to the original Lamanites, the brothers of Nephi. He thus positions the Nephites and Lamanites of his time far apart with respect to religion, a positioning that he attributes directly to Nephite possession of the sacred records—both the brass plates and whatever record Lehi had made.

By not having access to the brass plates, the Lamanites would be deprived of much of what we consider to be the Old Testament. They would probably have had no copies of Lehi's records, and they would have had no access whatever to Nephi's writings, simply because Nephi did not begin his record until after the separation between the two groups. Benjamin assumes that, whatever the religious beliefs of the Lamanites in his day, they do not reflect the true religion. He attributes this condition to their inability to read the accounts, which is not a statement about their literacy but a statement about their lack of a text. As a second problem, Benjamin notes that not only have they lost their religion, but that they "even do not believe them when they are taught them, because of the traditions of their fathers, which are not correct." This tells us that there have been unrecorded missions to the Lamanites.

Benjamin's argument to his sons emphasizes the necessity of reading the plates (learning Egyptian), since the alternative is becoming like the Lamanites and losing their religion. What he fails to explain is why reading the plates should be so essential. Obviously, the Lamanites would not have originally been illiterate and they could have copied (or written) their own scriptures. Further, the original Lamanites could have maintained their religion through oral means. The achievement of other nonliterate peoples in reciting foundational myths, memorizing lengthy and complex genealogies, and linking the observance of certain laws and practices with specific principles and commandments is both well known and stunningly impressive to Western observers who rely on printed texts instead of trained memories.

Linking action to belief—a strong component of any religious ritual—would only impress each more firmly in the memory. Indeed, as Benjamin makes clear, the Lamanites of his day do in fact have an active oral tradition, but this tradition is so powerful in its worldview that it prevents them from adopting Nephite ways (including the true religion), even when they learn them.

Societies all change over time, and the literate ones simply have better records of those changes. Some variation in the traditions between Nephite and Lamanite might be attributable to written versus oral recollections of the Old World religion, but clearly the Lamanites had made deliberate choices to remember differently from the Nephites. Almost certainly it was cultural change more than a lack of a particular written record that caused the divergence between the two. The best explanation of the wide divergence, as I see it, was that the Lamanites adopted native culture so completely that the Nephites appropriated the name "Lamanite" as a generic label for all non-Nephite peoples. For their part, they mightily resisted that native influence, returning repeatedly to their sacred texts to provide sanction for such efforts. The people of Zarahemla occupied a transitional zone between the Epi-Olmec cultures and the Maya. Obviously, they, too, had succumbed to the native influence; but because they could be recalled to their Israelite origins by hearing the true religion (and "true culture") preached to them, they were numbered among the Nephites.

Mosiah 1:6

> 6 O my sons, I would that ye should remember that these sayings are true, and also that these records are true. And behold, also the plates of Nephi, which contain the records and the sayings of our fathers from the time they left Jerusalem until now, and they are true; and we can know of their surety because we have them before our eyes.

Benjamin's first emphasis is on the brass plates and only secondarily on the plates of Nephi. One reason for this emphasis, despite the absence of brass-plate material except for quotations from Isaiah, is that Benjamin is highlighting the distinction between the Nephites' preservation of the Old World religion and the Lamanites' loss of it. As the direct tie to that Old World, the brass plates both contain the literal and symbolic ties to the God of Abraham, Isaac, and Jacob.

Mosiah 1:7

> 7 And now, my sons, I would that ye should remember to search them diligently, that ye may profit thereby; and I would that ye should keep the commandments of God, that ye may prosper in the land according to the promises which the Lord made unto our fathers.

Scripture: Benjamin concludes this part of his discourse with a summary of his reason for teaching language and the brass plates to his sons. Mormon's interjection in the next verse makes it clear that this is not the last of Benjamin's teachings. The reason for learning to read the brass plates is to keep the commandments, which are in turn directly related to the promise from the Lord to the Nephites that this land would be theirs and that they would prosper if they did keep those commandments (1 Ne. 4:14, 2 Ne. 1:20).

Mosiah 1:8–9

> 8 And many more things did king Benjamin teach his sons, which are not written in this book.
> 9 And it came to pass that after king Benjamin had made an end of teaching his sons, that he waxed old, and he saw that he must very soon go the way of all the earth; therefore, he thought it expedient that he should confer the kingdom upon one of his sons.

Redaction: Mormon indicates that he has reached the end of his quotation from the source material. He also indicates that he had selected this material from a larger quantity of Benjamin's teachings to his sons. Since the next event of importance is the conferral of the kingdom, perhaps Benjamin continued by giving a formal discourse on governance to these princes of the kingdom. Arguably, Benjamin gave this discourse rather late in life; thus, the embedded quotation about the records may be an explanation of the learning they have already received, rather than an explanation of why they will learn this language.

We may also presume that Benjamin's teachings to his sons have contained moral lessons that Mormon must have weighed for their value to the reader, comparable to Lehi's discourses to his sons or those of $Alma_2$ to his sons. Nevertheless, Mormon selected only this one section from Benjamin's discourse. His reason was to quote an ancestral prophet's emphasis on the significance of the record, a point with which he would particularly resonate as he was charged with abridging and preserving them, a holy task.

Vocabulary: According to Alison V. P. Coutts and her colleagues: "Benjamin uses the word 'expedient' here and in Mosiah 4:27; 5:3; 6:1. Webster's 1828 dictionary defines 'expedient' as 'tending to promote the object proposed; fit or suitable for the purpose; proper under the circumstances.' Benjamin's usage does not convey the sense of a practical shortcut, as in the modern meaning of the word, but more of being suitably necessary for reconciliation."[4]

Mosiah 1:10

> 10 Therefore, he had Mosiah brought before him; and these are the words which he spake unto him, saying: My son, I would that ye should make a proclamation throughout all this land among all this people, or the people of Zarahemla, and the people of Mosiah who dwell in the land, that thereby they may be gathered together; for on the morrow I shall proclaim unto this my people out of mine own mouth that thou art a king and a ruler over this people, whom the Lord our God hath given us.

Culture: Mosiah is the first in this list of sons. That primacy of position and his confirmation as the next king allow us to assume that he is Benjamin's first-born son. While we have no such information about Benjamin, we may conjecture that he was the first-born son of $Mosiah_1$ who followed this general principle as he established his new dynasty. While Nephi was certainly not the oldest son, neither was his father a king. Except for the beginning of Nephite society, the kings and later the judges follow a father-to-oldest-son pattern in all but exceptional cases.

It is perhaps important at this historical point that Benjamin makes a distinction between the people of Zarahemla and the people of Mosiah. We might expect to find considerable separation between the two groups until two or three generations of intermarriage had had their effect; but as Benjamin makes quite clear, their peoplehood is not a matter of kin groups but of political allegiance. The people of Zarahemla retain the name of their last ruler, who has surely died by this

---

[4]Coutts et al., "Complete Text of Benjamin's Speech," 495. I have changed the original italics to quotation marks for stylistic consistency in this volume.

time, while the lineal Nephites are designated as the "people of Mosiah." This term refers to $Mosiah_1$, as Benjamin has not yet appointed $Mosiah_2$ as his successor.

A close reading of the text discloses that Benjamin is currently experiencing peace (v. 1), strongly suggesting that controversy and conflict have marked earlier periods of his reign. Given the typical lifespan in the Book of Mormon and the overlap between $Mosiah_1$ and Benjamin, at least sixty years have passed since the arrival of the Nephites in the land of Zarahemla, yet two identifiable political factions still exist, one retaining the identity of Zarahemla and the other that of Mosiah. This division becomes the background against which Benjamin's coming proclamation must be understood (v. 11), while potential (or past) divisions between the two groups may also explain why Benjamin needs to declare $Mosiah_2$'s kingship "from mine own mouth." The clear pronouncement in a public forum would decrease potential disagreements about succession—at least to the extent that Benjamin's kingship is recognized as valid.

Redaction: Mormon moves from one embedded speech to another with no interstitial text. The speech stands on its own. So far in Mosiah, our best deduction from its form back to the original plates of Nephi is that they tend toward the first person. While this is a predictable form for speeches, they had to be recorded, and it is therefore not likely that we have exact transcriptions, especially given the inevitable lack of polish in oral speech. It is more likely that first person is a literary device to reflect the importance of the focal character, the king. No doubt those recording the discourses followed the original, but we have no reason to believe that they were not condensed, polished, and otherwise edited. In short, these clean first-person discourses signal quotations from the plates of Nephi, but we should be cautious in assuming that we have word-for-word dialogue from any of the speakers.

Mosiah 1:11–12

> 11 And moreover, I shall give this people a name, that thereby they may be distinguished above all the people which the Lord God hath brought out of the land of Jerusalem; and this I do because they have been a diligent people in keeping the commandments of the Lord.
>
> 12 And I give unto them a name that never shall be blotted out, except it be through transgression.

Culture: What is Benjamin's reason for giving the two peoples a new name? The answer lies in his explanation that this new name will let them "be distinguished above all the people which the Lord God hath brought out of the land of Jerusalem." Only three groups are known to have come from the land of Jerusalem: the Lamanites, the Nephites, and the people of Mulek who are now the Zarahemlaites. (The Jaredites do not come from Jerusalem.) It is quite unlikely that Benjamin is referring to the Lamanites, because the Zarahemlaites have no kinship to the Lamanites and would lump them with all of the "others"—as outsiders and potential enemies or perhaps trading partners. Even the Nephites would have no need of a name to distinguish them "above" the Lamanites, as they have considered themselves superior from the beginning, with remnants of their low opinions showing in Enos 1:20 and Jarom 1:6. Rather, Benjamin is giving a new name to the combined people of Zarahemla and the people of Mosiah so that this new people will be greater than "all the people which the Lord God hath brought out of the land of Jerusalem"—a new whole that is greater than the sum of its parts. Benjamin is making a bold political move designed to preserve the internal peace he has created, perpetuating it by restructuring the political world within the city of Zarahemla. While kin divisions will certainly remain, Benjamin intends to erase political divisions and unify the people.

This new naming is clearly tied to religious principles. Benjamin specifically states that he can confer a new name upon them because "they have been a diligent people in keeping the commandments of the Lord." In the context of Words of Mormon 1:16–18, Benjamin sees this political move as specifically related to the resolution of the internal religious conflicts that Mormon summarized. Although such a combination of political and religious motives is unusual to our modern world, it is characteristic of the ancient world. In that culture, reality was defined through religion, and the validation of a political reality was the leader's persuasive claim or demonstration of Yahweh's sanction.

Mosiah 1:13

> 13 Yea, and moreover I say unto you, that if this highly favored people of the Lord should fall into transgression, and become a wicked and an adulterous people, that the Lord will deliver them up, that thereby they become weak like unto their brethren; and he will no more preserve them by his matchless and marvelous power, as he has hitherto preserved our fathers.

The new name is concomitant with a new covenant, a close paraphrase of Yahweh's covenant to the Nephites (1 Ne. 4:14, 2 Ne. 1:20). Lehi's statement of that covenant is: "And he hath said that: Inasmuch as ye shall keep my commandments ye shall prosper in the land; but inasmuch as ye will not keep my commandments ye shall be cut off from my presence." (2 Ne. 1:20) For his part, Benjamin proclaims that although he is creating a new people "above" the old peoples who emigrated from Jerusalem, Yahweh's promise follows righteousness and can therefore be renewed for this new people—new in their political identity but continuing their status as Yahweh's people.

Mosiah 1:14

> 14 For I say unto you, that if he had not extended his arm in the preservation of our fathers they must have fallen into the hands of the Lamanites, and become victims to their hatred.

Benjamin's final statement is an argument from history supporting the covenant's continuation; both peoples have survived the "hatred" of the Lamanites (which I read here to mean, generically, the outsider/enemy), because of Yahweh's favor.

Mosiah 1:15–17

15 And it came to pass that after king Benjamin had made an end of these sayings to his son, that he gave him charge concerning all the affairs of the kingdom.

16 And moreover, he also gave him charge concerning the records which were engraven on the plates of brass; and also the plates of Nephi; and also, the sword of Laban, and the ball or director, which led our fathers through the wilderness, which was prepared by the hand of the Lord that thereby they might be led, every one according to the heed and diligence which they gave unto him.

17 Therefore, as they were unfaithful they did not prosper nor progress in their journey, but were driven back, and incurred the displeasure of God upon them; and therefore they were smitten with famine and sore afflictions, to stir them up in remembrance of their duty.

Redaction: At the end of Benjamin's embedded discourse, Mormon returns to condensed narrative. In the next verse, he describes the official bestowal of authority on Mosiah but simply gives Benjamin's instructions on the nature of the coming meeting. Why did Mormon quote that passage but condense the ceremonial transfer of the kingly symbols? The answer must lie in the importance of the new covenant, which unifies these two remnants of Israel into a new single people, represented under a refreshed covenant carried over from the previous peoples.

Culture: The transition from verse 16 to 17 is critical to understanding verse 17. When Benjamin gives Mosiah "charge concerning the affairs of the kingdom," we are seeing him transfer political power to Mosiah. Part of that ceremonial transferal of title and authority includes some specific items: "the records which were engraven on the plates of brass; and also the plates of Nephi; and also, the sword of Laban, and the ball or director."

Each of these items originated in or near Jerusalem. They are physical proofs that Yahweh has preserved this people. They have great interest as historical relics, but their true value is that they are highly charged with religious meaning. For Benjamin, the religious meaning is most important, as underscored by his definition of the director. Benjamin highlights its religious meaning, not its historical one. In the combined world of religious politics, these sacred relics serve as physical reminders of the covenant between the people and Yahweh. They are physical witnesses of Yahweh's fulfillment of that promise.[5]

---

[5]Thomas W. Murphy, "Laban's Ghost: On Writing and Transgression," *Dialogue: A Journal of Mormon Thought* 30, no. 2 (Summer 1997): 105, relates a situation described by anthropologist Claude Lévi-Strauss from his *Triste Tropiques*. Lévi-Strauss had introduced writing to the Nambikwara tribe in Brazil. He was surprised to see a chief authoritatively "reading" lines on the paper "as through they were instructions for the appropriate allocation of the goods." Murphy quotes Lévi-Strauss: "Writing had, on that occasion, made its appearance among the Nambikwara but not, as one might have imagined, as a result of long and laborious training. It had been borrowed as a symbol, and for a sociological rather than an intellectual purpose, while its reality remained unknown. It had not been a

Mosiah 1:18

18 And now, it came to pass that Mosiah went and did as his father had commanded him, and proclaimed unto all the people who were in the land of Zarahemla that thereby they might gather themselves together, to go up to the temple to hear the words which his father should speak unto them.

Text: The break between our current Mosiah 1 and 2 is not part of the 1830 text. When Mormon edited this section, he did not consider it finished until the end of our chapter 3, where Benjamin concludes one of his formal discourses. However, though not a chapter break, it is still clearly a textual break. The next verse is Mosiah 2:1: "And it came to pass that after Mosiah had done as his father had commanded him, and had made a proclamation throughout all the land, that the people gathered themselves together throughout all the land, that they might go up to the temple to hear the words which king Benjamin should speak unto them." Note the repetition between verse 1:18 and verse 2:1. In 1:18 Mosiah "went and did as his father had commanded him" and in 2:1 ". . . after Mosiah had done as his father had commanded him." Additionally, both verses first record Benjamin's intent to have the people gather, and their gathering. These dual themes, both repeated, suggest that it is not Mormon's transition, but rather one from the plates. The entire section concerns Benjamin, not $Mosiah_2$, and the original preserves $Mosiah_2$'s actions primarily as his faithful fulfillment of Benjamin's order. Even though there is no first person, the structure of these two verses strongly suggests a formulaic expression that is not necessarily a hallmark of Mormon's editorial interjections. These verses are likely part of the original, just as the embedded speech is. (From this point on I will discontinue the subscript indication of Mosiah unless it is required to differentiate him from his grandfather.)

---

question of acquiring knowledge, or remembering or understanding, but rather of increasing the authority and prestige of one individual—or function—at the expense of others."

Murphy's article analyzes the Book of Mormon as a modern text and those arguments are not relevant here. What is relevant, however, is the concept of writing as a political force. In the transferral of written plates they become a symbol as much if not more than a purveyor of information. The symbolic function is most clearly seen in the Liahona that accompanied the plates as symbols of regnal power. The Liahona apparently no longer worked but maintained its associative power because of its past meaning, not its current function.

Mosiah 2

Mosiah 2:1

1 And it came to pass that after Mosiah had done as his father had commanded him, and had made a proclamation throughout all the land, that the people gathered themselves together throughout all the land, that they might go up to the temple to hear the words which king Benjamin should speak unto them.

History: Because the introduction to this occasion is explicitly connected with the law of Moses (Mosiah 2:3), we may legitimately look to the scriptures for an explanation of this type of gathering. Terrence Szink and John Welch link Benjamin's speech to the complex of autumn festivals of ancient Israel:

> Of the three annual festival times in ancient Israel, the autumn festival complex was the most important and certainly the most popular in ancient Israel. In early times it apparently was called the Feast of Ingathering. According to many scholars, the various components of the autumn festival were celebrated as a single season of celebration in the earliest periods of Israelite history. Its many elements were not sharply differentiated until later times, when the first day of the seventh month became Rosh ha-Shanah (New Year), followed by eight days of penitence, then followed on the tenth day of the month by Yom Kippur (Day of Atonement) and on the fifteenth day by Sukkot (Festival of the Tabernacles), concluding with a full holy week.[1]

Although the authors discuss the important correlations they see between Benjamin speech and these Israelite festivities, the differences, which they do not analyze, are also important. This discussion will deal with both. Given the 476 years that have passed since the departure from Jerusalem (Mosiah 6:5), it is reasonable to expect at least some evolution, particularly in adaptations that would accommodate traditional festivals of the New World. It seems reasonable that the Zarahemlaites, who had lost other Israelite beliefs, had engaged in these local practices prior to their union with the Nephites.

One point of conjunction between the Israelite and New World practices occurs in the New Year celebration. Allen Christenson, an assistant professor of humanities and classics at Brigham Young University who is conversant in Quiché Maya, has examined the correlation between the Maya November harvest festival and rituals of coronation and kingly renewal: "Throughout the history of the Maya,

[1]Terrence L. Szink and John W. Welch, "King Benjamin's Speech in the Context of Ancient Israelite Festivals," in *King Benjamin's Speech*, edited by John W. Welch and Stephen D. Ricks (Provo, Utah: FARMS, 1998), 159.

who dominated southern Mesoamerica, the most important public festival of the year was timed to coincide with the main corn harvest in mid-November. For the most part, this also served as the New Year's day of the solar calendar, when kingship was renewed."[2]

As noted, the Hebrew autumn festivals included the New Year celebration. Indeed, we will also examine this particular speech in the context of a special type of New Year celebration from an Old World context. Prior to that, however, we should also note the Mesoamerican background for New Year's celebrations.[3] A new year was also heralded with great ceremony. However, another very important type of New Year celebration may enter into Benjamin's New World accounting. Understanding this possible Mesoamerican influence requires a brief discussion of the Mesoamerican calendar, with which the Zarahemlaites were most certainly familiar and which the Nephites would have had difficulty avoiding. According to archaeologist Muriel Weaver Porter:

> The 260-day cycle, already in use during Preclassic times, formed a basic part of all Mesoamerican calculations. Among the Mexica, this cycle was known as the Tonalpohualli . . . ; the Maya called it the Tzolkin. This cycle was composed of 20 day signs, which ran consecutively, combined with a number from 1 to 13 as a prefix. A day would be designated, for example, as 5 Atl (water) or 8 Tochtli (rabbit) in the Tonalpohualli. In order for the exact day 5 Atl to come around again, 260 days would have to elapse (or 20 x 13, since there is no common denominator). This 260-day cycle is not based on any natural phenomenon and we do not know how to account for its invention. In addition to the Tonalpohualli or Tzolkin, another cycle ran concurrently, resembling our solar year of 365 days. This was made up of 18 months of 20 days each (18 x 20 = 360), plus 5 additional days of apprehension and bad luck at the end of the year. Days were numbered from 0 to 19. The Mexica called the 360-day year the Xihuitl, and the 5-day period of bad luck the Nemontemi. The equivalent Maya periods were named the Haab (360 days) and Uayeb (5 days).[4]

These two independent but concurrent calendars both began again every 260 and 360+5 days. However, every 52 years, their beginning dates coincided:

> The Tzolkin and the Haab ran concurrently, like intermeshed cog-wheels, and to return to any given date, 52 years, or 18,980 days, would have to elapse (because both 365 x 52 and 260 x 73 = 18,980). In other words, the Tzolkin would make 73 revolutions and the Haab 52, so that every 52 calendar years of 365 days one would return to the same date. A complete date in this 52-year cycle might be, for example, 2 1k 0 Pop (2 1k being the

---

[2]Allen J. Christenson, "Maya Harvest Festivals and the Book of Mormon," *Review of Books on the Book of Mormon* 3 (1991): 1.

[3]The possible correspondence of this festival with a New Year's celebration is compelling, but the timing of the new year may have been different in the New World. Randall Spackman places the new year in the New World with the new moon on February 25 in the twenty-sixth year of the judges. Randall P. Spackman, "Introduction to Book of Mormon Chronology," FARMS Reprint Series (Provo, Utah: Foundation for Ancient Research and Mormon Studies, 1993), 30. This conflicts with the idea of an autumn harvest festival. However, with the passage of time in the New World, perhaps the new year correlation was stronger than the harvest festival connection.

[4]Muriel Porter Weaver, *The Aztecs, Maya, and their Predecessors: Archaeology of Mesoamerica* (New York: Seminar Press, 1972), 103.

position of the day in the Tzolkin, 0 Pop the position in the Haab). Fifty-two years would pass before another 2 Ik 0 Pop date returned.

> One cannot overemphasize the significance of this 52-year cycle for Mesoamerican peoples. It is called the Calendar Round or Sacred Round. Aside from the Maya and Mexica we know it was in use by the Mixtecs, Otomis, Huastecs, Totonacs, Matlazinca, Tarascans, and many other groups. The cycles of time are believed to have been primarily divinatory in purpose. When these coincided, it was an event of great importance, marked by special ceremonies and perhaps by the enlargement of architectural structures.
>
> It was expected that the world would end at the completion of a 52-year cycle. At this time, among the Mexica in the Valley of Mexico, all fires were extinguished, pregnant women were locked up lest they be turned into wild animals, children were pinched to keep them awake so that they would not turn into mice, and all pottery was broken in preparation for the end of the world. In the event the gods decided to grant man another 52 years of life on earth, however, a nighttime ceremony was held in which the populace followed the priests through the darkness over a causeway to the top of an old extinct volcano that rises abruptly from the floor of the basin of Mexico, known today as the Hill of the Star, the hill above Ixtapalapa. There, with all eyes on the stars, they awaited the passage of the Pleiades across the center of the heavens, which would announce the continuation of the world for another 52 years. When the precise moment came, a victim was quickly sacrificed by making a single gash in his chest and extracting the still palpitating heart. In the gory cavity the priests, with a fire drill, kindled a new flame that was quickly carried by torches across the lake to the temple in Tenochititlan, and from there to all temples and villages around the lake. This was known as the New Fire Ceremony among the Mexica, and in some way this same completion and renewal of each 52-year cycle was recognized by all Mesoamericans. It was probably rare for a person to witness more than one of these celebrations in his lifetime, so undoubtedly it was an event approached with great anticipation and relived many times after its passing.[5]

For our purposes, we note that the fifty-two-year cycle is not only extremely significant but is also marked at times by the "enlargement of architectural structures."[6] This accompanying feature will become particularly important as we analyze the gathering of Benjamin's people at the temple in Zarahemla.

An alternative parallel for this special occasion is the Old Testament jubilee year. Every seven years was a sabbatical, and every seven sabbaticals was the jubilee. Szink and Welch describe the relevant context for seeing this particular festival as a jubilee year:

> The jubilee text of Leviticus 25 compares closely with two sections of Benjamin's speech. Leviticus 25 reflects the words and phrases associated with the jubilee in ancient times. A considerable density of phrases and ideas from these chapters can be found in the latter portions of Mosiah 2 and 4, sufficient to indicate a textual dependency of Benjamin's words on these or similar jubilee texts. The main parallels between these passages and Benjamin's speech can be outlined as follows:
>
> - Benjamin's "return the thing" (Mosiah 4:28) recalls "return every man unto his possession" (Leviticus 25:10).
> - His injunction "Ye will not have a mind to injure one another" (Mosiah 4:13) echoes "Ye shall not oppress one another" (Lev. 25:14, 17).

---

[5]Ibid., 103–4.
[6]Ibid., 103.

- At the jubilee, it was required: "He shall reckon with him" (Lev. 25:50; compare 15–16). Similarly. Benjamin said: "Render to every man according to that which is his due" (Mosiah 4:13).
- "And if thy brother be waxen poor, and fallen in decay with thee; then thou shalt relieve him: yea though he be a stranger or a sojourner; that he may live with thee" (Lev. 25:35) has the same import as "Ye . . . will succor those that stand in need, . . . ye will not . . . turn him out to perish" (Mosiah 4:16).
- "I am the Lord your God, which brought you forth" (Lev. 25:38) implies the same conclusion as "Do we not all depend upon the same Being, even God, for all the substance which we have" (Mosiah 4:19).
- The promise in Leviticus reads: "Wherefore ye shall do my statutes and keep my judgments, and do them; and ye shall dwell in the land in safety. And the land shall yield her fruit" (Lev. 25:18–19); and in Benjamin, "If ye would keep his commandments ye should prosper in the land" (Mosiah 2:22).

These relatively specific parallels, coupled with similarities in the overall tone and concerns of the jubilee texts and Benjamin's speech, indicate Benjamin's intense feelings about helping the poor, establishing God's covenant among his people, being conscientious in walking in the paths of righteousness, and realizing man's utter dependence on God for life and sustenance. These may well be attributable to the heightened sense of these principles felt by the ancient Israelites during the jubilee season.

A further parallel, expressing the spirit behind all sabbatical and jubilee laws, is found in Deuteronomy 15:9: "Beware that there be not a thought in thy wicked heart, saying, The seventh year, the year of release, is at hand; and thine eye be evil against thy poor brother, and thou givest him nought; and he cry unto the Lord against thee, and it be sin unto thee." This compares closely with Benjamin's injunctions to his people to impart freely of their substance to the poor without grudging (see Mosiah 4:22–25).[7]

We now have two parallels for the background of Benjamin's speech. The Israelite context may be a jubilee year, while the Mesoamerican context may be the beginning of a "century." Which was it? It is possible that the true answer is "both." Jubilee years occur every fiftieth year (after the seventh set of seven years). The Mesoamerican "century" occurred every fifty-two years. With the close proximity of the cycles, it would not be unreasonable to find the two merging into a single ceremony. This process of religious adaptation is called syncretism, and most religions which come into close contact with other religions (particularly dominant ones) will exhibit some form of syncretism, whether mild or extensive.

Modern Christian practice shows any number of cases of syncretism, particularly where a symbol is borrowed from another context. An early example is the Christian appropriation of the figure of the youth with a ram on his shoulders, a pagan figure representing humanity.[8] In Christian hands, this symbol for humanity became a symbol for Christ. Later (and more current) examples would be the yule log and the Christmas tree, both appropriations from paganism. The point is not the borrowing, which is normal, but rather the importance of realizing that the borrowing can occur within the context of continued faith. The modern Christian

---

[7]Szink and Welch, "King Benjamin's Speech in the Context of Ancient Israelite Festivals," 195–96.

[8]John Dominic Crossan, *The Essential Jesus: What Jesus Really Taught* (San Francisco: HarperSanFrancisco, 1995), 13.

is fully capable of enjoying an Easter that includes bunnies and colored eggs (in addition to a celebration of the resurrection, of course), without understanding the borrowing of rabbits and eggs from ancient pagan spring fertility symbols. Those religions have not survived, but their symbols have.

We may suppose that, in the same way, Nephite/Zarahemlaite culture also borrowed elements of the surrounding cultures (as would be quite evident in their architecture). Thus, I hypothesize that Benjamin had the unique opportunity of living at the important juncture of a New Year/New "Century" that also coincided with an actual or assimilated jubilee year. This auspicious combination of events provides the background for the specific ceremonies, for the details of the speech, and for the temple's building/renewal that Benjamin proposes. It also helps explain why King Benjamin chose to crown Mosiah three years before his own death (Mosiah 6:4–5). Although Benjamin describes himself as old (Mosiah 2:30), he was obviously not on the verge of death. Rather, he saw this time as appropriate for naming a new king and renaming his people because the year itself as a moment of renewal, the beginning of a new "century."

Mosiah 2:2

> 2 And there were a great number, even so many that they did not number them; for they had multiplied exceedingly and waxed great in the land.

Culture: Either this verse is simple hyperbole, or something more is going on. It is important that these are Mormon's words, a conclusion drawn from the text in front of him. He states that the population was great—"even so many that they did not number them." At issue may not be the quantity, but the very act of numbering. As Alison V. P. Coutts and her collaborators have noted: "Censuses were often taken in the Old Testament (Ex. 30:12; Num. 1:1–4, 26; 2 Sam. 24; 1 Chr. 21). Generally the purpose was to prepare for war, but censuses were also taken as preparation to serve God (Num. 4:1–3, 21–23). In 1 Chronicles 23, some kind of census appears to have been associated with David making his son Solomon the king, a situation somewhat analogous to Benjamin's coronation of Mosiah."[9]

Mormon may be saying that a census was usually associated with this festival but that the enumeration was not done at this time. This hypothesis is strengthened by the fact that Benjamin, at the end of his discourse, "take[s] the names of all those who had entered into a covenant with God to keep his commandments" (Mosiah 6:1). Apparently, the traditional census was taken, not at the beginning of the festival, but at the end of Benjamin's call to the new name and new unity.

Mormon's description also suggests that this gathering is exceptional. The size of the crowd is emphasized both here and in Benjamin's realization that he must build a tower. No doubt there would have been numerous public gatherings in

---

[9]Alison V. P. Coutts et al., "Complete Text of Benjamin's Speech with Notes and Comments," in *King Benjamin's Speech*, edited by John W. Welch and Stephen D. Ricks (Provo, Utah: FARMS, 1998), 506.

earlier years, but this one drew a crowd that was unexpectedly large. I suggest that a plausible constellation of reasons was the coronation of a new king, the new name which represented Benjamin's effort in forging a new society from the conflicts experienced between the Nephite and Zarahemlaites, the jubilee/new year (new "century"), and Benjamin's proclamation at the temple site. I hypothesize that the people have already begun to work on this temple and that their collective labor will be required to complete it.

Variant: The printer's manuscript has "that *thereby* they might rejoice" for verse 4. This was an accidental omission by the 1830 typesetter.[10]

Mosiah 2:3–4

> 3 And they also took of the firstlings of their flocks, that they might offer sacrifice and burnt offerings according to the law of Moses;
> 4 And also that they might give thanks to the Lord their God, who had brought them out of the land of Jerusalem, and who had delivered them out of the hands of their enemies, and had appointed just men to be their teachers, and also a just man to be their king, who had established peace in the land of Zarahemla, and who had taught them to keep the commandments of God, that they might rejoice and be filled with love towards God and all men.

In addition to coming together for a speech, the people are coming for a communal religious rite. The law of Moses provides not only for individual worship but also for community worship. Community acts not only reinforce the purpose of the religious event but also help to cement the people through their mutual participation. Szink and Welch observe that the typical New Year, like most festivals" prescribed in the Old Testament, "evidently began with burnt offerings of animals of 'the first year.' 'In the seventh month, in the first day of the month . . . ye shall offer an offering made by fire unto the Lord (Lev. 23:24–25).'"[11]

Such sacrifices not only strengthen the supposition that this is a New Year ceremony, but also give us information about the scale of this communal rite: "And they also took of the firstlings of their flocks, that they might offer sacrifice and burnt offerings." Whom does Mormon mean by "they"? This verse directly follows the discussion of those who are coming to the ceremony, not the priests who are in the town. Thus, the people themselves are apparently bringing animals to sacrifice. While only one animal would be sacrificed for each family group at most, still the number must have been very large. Probably most of the meat would provide the feast which followed. Thus, the sacrifices would not only reinforce the religious aspect of the ceremonies but also solve the pragmatic problem of feeding such a large assemblage.

---

[10]Royal Skousen, *Analysis of Textual Variants of the Book of Mormon*, THE CRITICAL TEXT OF THE BOOK OF MORMON (Provo, Utah: Foundation for Ancient Research and Mormon Studies, 2005) , Vol. 4, Part 2, 1143.

[11]Szink and Welch. "King Benjamin's Speech in the Context of Ancient Israelite Festivals," 164.

Mosiah 2:5

> 5 And it came to pass that when they came up to the temple, they pitched their tents round about, every man according to his family, consisting of his wife, and his sons, and his daughters, and their sons, and their daughters, from the eldest down to the youngest, every family being separate one from another.

Culture: (I will examine the subject of the tents after the next verse.) This verse provides important organizational information about Benjamin's people, first that the people come as kin groups—the official unit of recognition for a politically and religiously important ceremony. In contrast, for example, we would not expect the entire family to come to market. Second, this event is one which requires the participation of even the youngest and oldest members of the family. Further, this verse establishes that the basic organizational unit of Nephite society was the kin group.

Third, Nephite society was clearly patriarchal, as evidenced by the emphasis on male leadership. Both the unit and its members are defined in relationship to "every man": his family, his wife, his sons, his daughters. This arrangement is no surprise, for Hebrew society is also patriarchal. However, this text confirms the practice's continuation in the New World. It also seems likely that they continued the practice of primogeniture, or the inheritance of the eldest son. The fact that the children are ranked from oldest to youngest suggests that age order is significant in their society. It also provides corroboration for the supposition that Mosiah is Benjamin's eldest son.

History: The gathering by families echoes the Feast of Tabernacles, as Szink and Welch have observed: "The Mosaic Law specified that "all . . . males shall appear before the Lord God" (Ex. 23:17), and in Deuteronomy the entire family was expected to participate: "And thou shalt rejoice in thy feast, thou, and thy son, and thy daughter, and thy manservant, and thy maidservant, and the Levite, the stranger, and the fatherless, and the widow, that are within thy gates (Deut. 16:14; compare 31:10–12)."[12]

Mosiah 2:6

> 6 And they pitched their tents round about the temple, every man having his tent with the door thereof towards the temple, that thereby they might remain in their tents and hear the words which king Benjamin should speak unto them;

Culture: Queries anthropologist John Sorenson:

> What was a Nephite "tent"? Would the crowd have been seated in sprawling shelters like Arabs? The term tent is used some 64 times in the Book of Mormon, so the question may deserve attention.
>
> Biblical translators have usually rendered the Hebrew root 'hl to English as "tent"; however, it has a rather wide range of possible meanings. Sometimes it referred to full-fledged tents on the pattern of those used by desert nomads of southwestern Asia; but to

---

[12]Ibid., 184.

semi-nomads like Abraham, Isaac, and Jacob the term could also mean "hut" as well as "tent." In later usage, as the Israelites became sedentary village or city dwellers, its meanings were extended further. For example, in Psalm 132:3 and Proverbs 7:17 the related word *'ohel* means "canopy (over a bed)," while in the New Testament, John 1:14 says literally "he pitched his tent among us" to communicate the thought "he lived among us." A Hittite account has the god Elkunirsha living in a "tent" made of wood. In writings from South Arabia in Lehi's day and also in classical Arabic, languages closely related to Hebrew, the root stood for "family" or "tribe" as well as tent. In the related Semitic language of the Babylonians, a word from the same root meant "city," "village," "estate," or "social unit," and even formed part of the word for bed. An Egyptian equivalent could be read as "hut, camel's hair tent, camp." Furthermore, Dr. Hugh Nibley reminds us: "throughout the ancient world . . . the people must spend the time of the great national festival of the New Year living in tents." But for this occasion Israelites came to use makeshift booths made of branches, as fewer and fewer of their town-dwelling numbers owned genuine tents. The Nephites, of course, routinely lived in permanent buildings (see, for example, Mosiah 6:3). Alma's people "pitched their tents" after fleeing to Helam, but then they "began to build buildings" (Mosiah 23:5). Military forces on the move are said to have used tents (Alma 51:32, 34; 58:25), but it is nearly unbelievable that the entire Lamanite army referred to in Alma 51 lugged collapsible tents on their backs through tropical country hundreds of miles from the land of Nephi. Far more likely they erected shelters of brush or whatever other materials could be found in the vicinity, referring to those or any other temporary shelters by the traditional word for tent. Farmers in parts of Mesoamerica still throw together simple brush shelters when they stay overnight at their fields in the busiest work season, and at the time of the Spanish conquest, Bernal Diaz reported that the soldiers of their Indian allies "erect their huts" as they move on campaign. So when we read that Benjamin's subjects sat in their tents listening to his sermon, we should understand that they might have been under shelter a good deal different from what comes to mind when we hear "tent."[13]

Why did this large assemblage need shelter? Did they want privacy for sleeping arrangements, or possibly shelter against rain? A more compelling reason is that the people need shelter against the sun. Ceremonial plazas large enough to hold the size of the crowd described here are, perforce, cleared land. If this plaza were paved with worked stone, as is typical of many Classical Mesoamerican urban sites, direct sunlight could become unbearably hot. A "tent" or lean-to would provide shade, yet allow the breeze to pass through the loosely assembled sides.

As another detail, the description that the "door" faces toward the temple so that the people can hear Benjamin's speech suggests that they are used during the day, not simply at night.

Native homes in this area are typically built of sticks fixed firmly in the ground and rising vertically. They typically have doors but no windows. The homes have thatched roofs, and no filler in the spaces between the vertically placed sticks. These homes are remarkably pleasant, with sun and breeze coming through the openings. While the "tents" would not be permanent, a temporary shelter on the same principles would provide the same benefits.

---

[13]John L. Sorenson, *An Ancient American Setting for the Book of Mormon* (Salt Lake City: Deseret Book/Provo, Utah: Foundation for Ancient Research and Mormon Studies, 1985), 160.

It is also possible, as Szink and Welsh suggest, that the "tents" are part of the observance of the Feast of Tabernacles. They point out that the people "remained in their tents during the speech, surely for ceremonial reasons. If it had not been religiously and ritually important for them to stay in their tents, the crowd would have stood much closer to Benjamin and been able to hear him [better]."[14]

Mosiah 2:7

> 7 For the multitude being so great that king Benjamin could not teach them all within the walls of the temple, therefore he caused a tower to be erected, that thereby his people might hear the words which he should speak unto them.

This description has two interesting aspects. First, Benjamin apparently builds the tower because he is surprised by the large attendance. The tower is a response to the crowd, not planned as part of the occasion. Second, he should not have had to build it in the first place. Why? The tower elevates Benjamin so that he can see over the crowd and so that his voice will carry over the hum of the crowd. However, temples in Mesoamerica were used for that precise purpose, with some excellent acoustics in some of the ceremonial centers. A person speaking from the steps of the temple could be heard at other temples in the complex or within the ceremonial courtyard.[15] In the Mesoamerican context, then, the temple should have already provided the benefits of a tower. Yet Benjamin built a tower. At this point, Mesoamerican culture may provide a persuasive explanation. If, as I have hypothesized, Benjamin's speech was occurring as part of a new year/jubilee/new century festival, and if part of Benjamin's effort to unite the people and build or rebuild temples as part of the renewal of the new century, then Benjamin is standing on the temple site but not in front of a finished temple. It had not yet been built. Benjamin thus constructs a tower because the permanent "tower," or temple, is not there.

A corroborating detail is that Benjamin's son, Mosiah, also calls a gathering of all of the people, yet has no need to build a similar tower (Mosiah 25:1–4). By that time, the temple had been finished, and Mosiah no doubt addressed the people from its steps.

Archaeology: The best analysis of the text suggests that Benjamin's speech took place at a major festival and symbolized a new beginning for the combined Zarahemlaite and Nephite peoples. The best candidate for Zarahemla, according to John L. Sorenson, is the archaeological site known as Santa Rosa.[16] This location is located on the west side of the Grijalva River in Chiapas, Mexico. Sorenson notes:

---

[14]Szink and Welch, "King Benjamin's Speech in the Context of Ancient Israelite Festivals," 184.

[15]A number of anecdotal descriptions of the acoustics of various sites has been collected in "The Acoustics of Maya Temples," http://www.luckymojo.com/esoteric/interdisciplinary/architecture/ecclesiastical/mayanacoustics.html (accessed March 2007).

[16]Sorenson, *An Ancient American Setting for the Book of Mormon*, 49.

> The archaeological sequence at Santa Rosa is interesting in terms of the Book of Mormon, although the findings will always remain incomplete because the site is now underwater. Major public construction in the form of what seem to have been "temple" or "palace" foundation mounds started on a modest scale at approximately 300 B.C. That coincided with growth in population, which produced the "city" of Zarahemla that Mosiah's party encountered a couple of generations later. The place remained no larger than a modest town, as we think of size, during the time when Mosiah, Benjamin his son, and Mosiah II reigned. Around 100 B.C. a spurt in the city's prosperity is evident, and a large number of major public structures were erected. That condition continued for around a century. Except for the site of Chiapa de Corzo far downstream, Santa Rosa became the largest, most significant "city" in the Grijalva basin just at the time when Zarahemla is reported by the Book of Mormon as becoming a regional center.[17]

Even more intriguing for the story of Benjamin is a particular archaeological feature of one of the temples that appears to have been constructed about this time. Santa Rosa was excavated and documented by the New World Archaeological Foundation. As part of the excavation into one of the pyramid mounds the archaeologists discovered an unusual feature. There was a plaster floor over the foundation layer that was intentionally laid and smooth. This, in itself, is unusual because Mesoamerican pyramids are built to demonstrate external volume, not usable interior space. The plaster floor is a location that was intended to be covered over and never seen again. The plaster itself, while interesting, was much more interesting for what it covered. In the words of the excavating archaeologist, Augustín Delgado: "The plaster floor continued in both trench extensions. In contact with it, both above and below, was a thin layer of gravel. That below was of different natures to either side of the medial line of the temple. To the north it was composed of larger fragments of broken stone, while to the south it was natural gravel. The difference was probably due to the source of the material."[18] Normal construction techniques indicate that labor may have been divided along kinship lines, with differing groups responsible for different parts of the construction. Art historian Linda Schele and archaeologist Peter Mathews describe the probable procedure:

> No tax or labor records have survived to identify the workmen who labored on the great public buildings. However, we have other hints about how construction projects worked. Archaeologists consistently find thin walls creating "construction pens" inside pyramids, and often neighboring pens have different fill materials. These pens have been found under courts and plazas, so that they may have served as much to organize labor as to provide containing walls inside a construction. A likely system would have been to assign a certain number of pens to different lineages, who would then be responsible for finding the fill and bringing it to the pens. Each lineage would have fed its own people and perhaps contributed additional food and materials to the main construction project.[19]

---

[17]Ibid., 155.

[18]Agustín Delgado, *Archaeological Research at Santa Rosa, Chiapas and in the Region of Tehuantepec* (Provo, Utah: New World Archaeological Foundation, Brigham Young University, 1965), 9.

[19]Linda Schele and Peter Mathews, *The Code of Kings: The Language of Seven Sacred Maya Temples and Tombs* (New York: Scribner, 1998), 28.

What sets the Santa Rosa gravel apart from the construction pens in other temples is not a method of construction, but a methodically constructed feature—one that was intended to be unseen at the bottom of a major temple. The two fill types were carefully separated with the division line running an astrologically significant east to west. Another archaeologist working at Santa Rosa, Donald Brockington, discusses how this particular feature might expand on the normal lineage connections to construction sites: "To the north the gravel was broken and to the south it was rounded. I supervised that excavation and, upon noting the difference, carefully searched the gravel, finding no mixture whatever. Not only does the difference suggest two sources of materials but it may be taken to imply two separate groups, each working on its section. Further, the medial line runs roughly east-west."[20] The east-west medial line suggests that it represents the path of the sun, symbolically tying this feature to the greater world. These are not multiple lineages represented by multiple construction pits, but two precise layers of gravel, carefully gathered, carefully separated, and carefully plastered over. Brockington also noted that the general settlement pattern "might be interpreted to suggest a clustered village divided into moieties and oriented in relationship to a ceremonial construction."[21] The social picture that may be extracted from the data suggest two major divisions in Santa Rosa. The east-west median dividing the carefully separated gravel types also suggests the presence of two major groups in the city. In addition, the construction of this particular temple appears to date to around the time of Benjamin's speech.[22]

This archaeological evidence suggests a very tempting, albeit speculative, scenario. Benjamin's discourse was given at the temple site where Benjamin built a temporary tower. As part of Benjamin's coronation of his son, he reidentified his people, making of two a single people. As part of this ceremony, the people symbolized their new unity physically by laying a ceremonial flooring consisting of two different gravels. This representation of division was then plastered over as a representation of unity. The separation was no longer visible. It was symbolically buried in the temple and conceptually buried in the new sacred space. The new temple became the physical embodiment of the covenant.

History: Stephen D. Ricks suggests that the tower is related to the Israelite practices of coronation: "A society's most sacred spot is the location where the holy act of royal coronation takes place. For Israel, the temple was that site. So we read that during his

---

[20]Donald L. Brockington, *The Ceramic History of Santa Rosa, Chiapas, Mexico* (Provo, Utah: New World Archaeological Foundation, Brigham Young University, 1967), 60–61.

[21]Ibid., 60.

[22]Of course archaeological dating cannot be precise, but the strata suggest that this floor was constructed in the right general period. Delgado indicated that the structures above that floor date to the Classic, with the substructures being earlier. This at least leaves open the probability that the floor is also Preclassic (or the time period of the Book of Mormon). Caches of later pottery found under the floor were located in pits dug through the floor. Thus the flooring already existed when the later pottery was cached. Delgado, *Archaeological Research at Santa Rosa, Chiapas and in the Region of Tehuantepec*, 29.

coronation Joash stood 'by a pillar [of the temple], as the manner was' (2 Kings 11:14)."[23]

Ricks then suggests that Benjamin's tower might correspond to a dais, specifically relying upon a particular understanding of the "pillar" by which Joash stood: "De Vaux connects these pillars with the 'brasen scaffold' that Solomon built (2 Chr. 6:13), upon which he stands and kneels 'before all the congregation of Israel,' and from which he offers the dedicatory prayer for the temple; further, de Vaux suggests that the phrase near the pillar be translated 'on the dais.'"[24]

While this possibility is interesting, the text in Mosiah suggests that the tower was for communication, that the structure was temporary, and that it was created after the crowd had assembled. This scenario makes it less likely that the tower acted as a dais. In the context of a Mesoamerican town with an existing temple, the temple itself would be sufficient to serve as such a "tower-dais." But for Benjamin's speech, the tower existed as a communications device, not as sacred space. The sacred space was the temple around which they gathered.

Demography: The people of Zarahemla would have come both from the city itself and from the outlying land called Zarahemla. Consequently, the population would have been larger than the number who typically lived inside a Mesoamerican ceremonial center. We have little idea how many would have been present, since the census was not taken. Sorenson suggests 25,000, based on the ability of John Wesley to preach to "20,000 people in the open in England, which suggests that the size of the assembly in Zarahemla was perhaps a little larger."[25] The larger number is suggested by the next verses' record that many of the assembled could not hear, suggesting more than those who were able to hear Wesley.

Mosiah 2:8

> 8 And it came to pass that he began to speak to his people from the tower; and they could not all hear his words because of the greatness of the multitude; therefore he caused that the words which he spake should be written and sent forth among those that were not under the sound of his voice, that they might also receive his words.

Culture: Even with the addition of the tower, all the gathered people were unable to hear Benjamin's word. Therefore he ordered that a written text be circulated. Why would the people remain at the site if they could not hear (and perhaps not see) the person they came to hear and see? The answer is that the people had multiple reasons for coming. For many of them, the celebration, visiting with friends, and the feasting would be reason enough to linger.

A second important piece of information is that the speech was written down expressly so that the people could have his words. Clearly some portion of the

---

[23]Stephen D. Ricks, "Kingship, Coronation, and Covenant in Mosiah 1–6," in *King Benjamin's Speech*, edited by John W. Welch and Stephen D. Ricks (Provo, Utah: FARMS, 1998), 244.

[24]Ibid., 246.

[25]Sorenson, *An Ancient American Setting for the Book of Mormon*, 157.

Nephites was literate, but we do not know the extent of that literacy. It would be very unusual for any ancient society to have a very high literacy rate, particularly among its farmers. It seems unlikely that the written speech existed in sufficient copies so that even a fraction of them could have their own copies. The time, writing materials, and personnel required to make hundreds (let alone tens of thousands) of copies would be prohibitive. It seems more likely that a limited number of copies was created. Benjamin's emissaries read the speech to the more distant of the crowd and probably to gatherings in hamlets throughout the land.

Mosiah 2:9

> 9 And these are the words which he spake and caused to be written, saying: My brethren, all ye that have assembled yourselves together, you that can hear my words which I shall speak unto you this day; for I have not commanded you to come up hither to trifle with the words which I shall speak, but that you should hearken unto me, and open your ears that ye may hear, and your hearts that ye may understand, and your minds that the mysteries of God may be unfolded to your view.

Redaction: Mormon gives a direct introduction to the text he is copying. It is very clearly a copy from the plates and very clearly the text that Benjamin "spake and caused to be written." Since official copies of the speech were created, it seems reasonable that Mormon copied it without editing, its language subject only to Joseph Smith's translation. We may also presume that, because this is an official written text, Benjamin took pains in its construction and that we might here find evidence of literary techniques not normally seen in spontaneous oral discourse. Indeed "a stunning array of literary structures appears in Benjamin's speech, purposefully and skillfully organized. Benjamin's use of chiasmus, all types of parallelisms, and many other forms of repeating patterns add focus and emphasis to the main messages and the persuasive qualities of this text."[26] The structured art of the text applies to the first part of Benjamin's sermon. I read the second phase as a spontaneous discourse. (See commentary accompanying Mosiah 4:4.)

Rhetoric: Benjamin begins his speech by declaring that the people will be hearing divine words, for the "mysteries of God will be unfolded." This statement tells his audience that he is speaking Yahweh's behalf and that, through Benjamin, Yahweh's will is to be proclaimed.

Scripture: Benjamin unfolds "mysteries of God" in the sense that this is information that is either new to the people or which is being reinforced afresh. Because God is different from us, we realize that we do not understand all that God does or intends (Isa. 55:8–9). Whenever a prophet explains the will of the Lord, the "mysteries" are being

---

[26]John W. Welch, "Parallelism and Chiasmus in Benjamin's Speech," in *King Benjamin's Speech*, edited by John W. Welch and Stephen D. Ricks (Provo, Utah: FARMS, 1998), 315.

unfolded. They are "mysteries" by definition because they come from a God whose thoughts are not our thoughts and whose ways are not our ways (Isa. 55:8).[27]

Vocabulary: John W. Welch, Donald W. Parry, and Stephen D. Ricks provide the following insight about the phrase "this day."

> The phrase "this day" may be very significant in the scriptures. This solemn and emphatic concept appears, for example, in the famous covenantal text at the end of the book of Joshua: "Choose you this day whom ye will serve. Ye are witnesses against yourselves that ye have chosen you the Lord, to serve him. And they said, We are witnesses. So Joshua made a covenant with the people that day (Josh. 24:15–25). It seems that words of this nature were especially used in antiquity in reference to religious or ceremonial holy days.
>
> The words "this day" appear eighteen times in the Book of Mormon. Six occurrences are regular expressions meaning "at this time," and one in Alma 30:8 quotes Joshua 24:15. But the remaining eleven all appear in conjunction with holy Nephite gatherings at their temples.
>
> King Benjamin uses the phrase "this day" five times in his monumental speech, and each time it occurs at ritual and covenantal highpoints in the text: He enjoins the people to give heed to "my words which I shall speak unto you this day" (Mosiah 2:9). He calls the people as "witnesses this day" that he has discharged his duties as king according to the law and has a pure conscience before God "this day" (Mosiah 2:14–15; compare Deut. 17:14–20). He declares "this day" that his son Mosiah is their new king (Mosiah 2:30). He affirms that "this day [Christ] hath spiritually begotten you" (Mosiah 5:7). These usages are

---

[27]It is not unusual to assume that the "mysteries" of God are something quite beyond our understanding. We tend to believe that they must be some of the difficult questions of religion or theology. This idea, although popular, is not necessarily scriptural. The scriptures assume that the "mysteries" are entirely knowable and are accessible through prayer and the scriptures.

Nephi tells us: "For he that diligently seeketh shall find; and the mysteries of God shall be unfolded unto them, by the power of the Holy Ghost, as well in these times as in times of old, and as well in times of old as in times to come; wherefore, the course of the Lord is one eternal round" (1 Nephi 10:19). Access to the mysteries comes from diligently seeking. He specifically notes that this has always been so.

Benjamin provides an interesting context for the "mysteries" when he suggests that the Nephites already understand the mysteries of God because of the brass plates: "And he also taught them concerning the records which were engraven on the plates of brass, saying: My sons, I would that ye should remember that were it not for these plates, which contain these records and these commandments, we must have suffered in ignorance, even at this present time, not knowing the mysteries of God" (Mosiah 1:3).

When Alma is preaching with Amulek in Ammonihah he presents the opposite process. He describes what happens when people decide not to believe: "And they that will harden their hearts, to them is given the lesser portion of the word until they know nothing concerning his mysteries" (Alma 12:11). For Alma, the word of God is the "mysteries." When they receive less and less of the word of God, they receive less and less of the mysteries.

As a final example, the ability to translate the Book of Mormon becomes one of the "mysteries" that will be revealed: "Ask that you may know the mysteries of God, and that you may translate and receive knowledge from all those ancient records which have been hid up, that are sacred; and according to your faith shall it be done unto you" (D&C 8:11).

Any revelation of God's will, any understanding that we have of God's ways or thoughts, becomes to us a revelation of mystery. Mysteries are things that we do not normally understand, and without revelation we would understand nothing of God. It is the entire purpose of the gospel to open those mysteries to us.

important covenantal markers. It seems likely that Benjamin is using this phrase not as a mere literary embellishment, but as a term with legal and religious import.

. . . Further corroboration for these pointed uses of "this day" in the Book of Mormon can be found in Hebrew literature. In Hebrew the word *etzem* is significant. It appears, for example, in Exodus 12:17, "Ye shall observe the feast of unleavened bread; for in this selfsame day [b'etzem hayom hazeh] have I brought your armies out of the land of Egypt." Abraham Bloch has recently concluded that "this descriptive word was not a mere literary flourish" but a technical term of art with some unknown special significance.

For further insight, Bloch turns to the medieval Jewish jurist Nahmanides, who "noted with great amazement that *etzem* ['self-same'] was used only in connection with the observance of Yom Kippur [the Israelite festival of the Day of Atonement] and Shavuot [the biblical festival of the Firstfruits, or Pentecost]." The implication is that this term was used to indicate that these high holy days in and of themselves produced a binding legal effect or holy religious status.

Evidently, in Nephite language and rhetoric, the phrase "this day" often indicated the covenantal and legal status of a holy day, much as "this day," "today," or "this selfsame day" did in Hebrew."[28]

Mosiah 2:10

10 I have not commanded you to come up hither that ye should fear me, or that ye should think that I of myself am more than a mortal man.

This verse can be read in connection with Mormon's brief statement that there had been false Christs with whom Benjamin had contended. As already noted, the Mesoamerican context suggests that men would have impersonated and represented the native gods. (See commentary accompanying Words of Mormon 1:15.) Benjamin had to work hard to remove those contentions from his people, and he is here reminding them of that fact. He very specifically references those "false Christs" when he declares that "ye should [not] fear me, [n]or that ye think that I of myself am more than a mortal man." The declaration of his mortal state is an important aspect of Benjamin's address because it places him in direct contrast to the "false Christs" or the god-impersonators. Although a king and a prophet who speaks for Yahweh (as he has just declared), Benjamin declares himself human and therefore qualitatively different from the pagan religion he has recently overthrown among his people and lands.

The second context for this statement relies on the same deification of person. Rather than specifically relating to the "false Christs," Benjamin may also be referring to the nature of Mesoamerican kingship. The best evidence for kingship among the Maya shows the distinct necessity of connecting not only to a royal but also to a divine lineage.[29]

---

[28]John W. Welch, Donald W. Parry, and Stephen D. Ricks, "This Day," in *Reexploring the Book of Mormon*, edited by John W. Welch (Provo, Utah: FARMS, 1992), 117–19.

[29]Linda Schele and Mary Ellen Miller, *The Blood of Kings* (New York: George Braziller, 1986), 103. This implied comparison is strengthened by similar implied comparisons to other kings as the speech progresses. See verses 12–14 with accompanying commentary.

Mosiah 2:11

> 11 But I am like as yourselves, subject to all manner of infirmities in body and mind; yet I have been chosen by this people, and consecrated by my father, and was suffered by the hand of the Lord that I should be a ruler and a king over this people; and have been kept and preserved by his matchless power, to serve you with all the might, mind and strength which the Lord hath granted unto me.

Benjamin draws lines around the nature of the Nephite king. He is human even though rightfully consecrated. He rules through his lineage, but also through Yahweh's power. While Yahweh is declared to be behind the throne, he is not declared to sit on the throne.

Culture: Benjamin notes that he rules because "I have been chosen by this people." Of course, he also notes that he rules by lineal right ("consecrated by my father") and as with all things, by Yahweh's grace. We see in this statement the presence of what will be known as the "voice of the people," a mechanism of rule that becomes more formally established in the reign of the judges that Benjamin's son will institute. (See "Excursus: The Voice of the People," following Mosiah 29.)

This revelation of Benjamin's dependence upon his subjects for the right to rule fits with general anthropological understandings of many ancient or less complex civilizations. Most societies have rules, but each society must also devise ways of enforcing those rules. Anthropologist A. R. Radcliffe-Brown, describes the most common options: (1) a moral sanction in which each person would express displeasure with the offender; (2) a ritual sanction in which religious forces are brought to bear upon the guilty, making them "unclean" or otherwise unfit for participating in the community, or (3) a penal sanction, in which persons empowered by the society inflict punishment under law.[30]

King Benjamin has no standing army. His successors do not have standing armies. There is no mention of a police force or any other body specifically entitled to preserve law. The larger the society the more some kind of enforcement will be required, but during our entire record of Nephite society we do not see specific social mechanisms of control. It is probable that the larger the society became the more the king's guards become the enforcement mechanism; for instance, Gideon is the king's "captain" (Mosiah 20:17), suggesting some standing body that could have been used for enforcement as well as for the protection of the king.

Mosiah 2:12

> 12 I say unto you that as I have been suffered to spend my days in your service, even up to this time, and have not sought gold nor silver nor any manner of riches of you;

---

[30]A. R. Radcliffe-Brown, *Structure and Function in a Primitive Society* (New York: The Free Press, 1968), 214–15.

Culture: Verses 12–14 create implicit comparisons between Benjamin as a king and other available models of how a king should act. Only in the context of comparisons to other kings can we understand Benjamin's declaration of the kind of king he was not. In this case the comparison is the socio-economic position of the Nephite king. Benjamin has not "sought gold nor silver nor any manner of riches" of his people. This stands as a clear implication that the people would be aware that there were other kings who had done so. Indeed, the institution of kings and the accompanying social hierarchies embodied in that type of government will continue to be one of the leitmotifs of Nephite apostasy throughout the Book of Mormon.

While we can take Benjamin at his word that he has not sought wealth at the expense of this people and that he has not levied taxes (v. 14), it is also clear that he must have required something from the people, since a central government cannot exist without goods in some form flowing from the people. And in fact, the town's ceremonial architecture suggests the form that support took: the temple with its walls. Such building projects require large amounts of labor that perforce remove people from other pursuits. Almost certainly some of this effort was governed by the season, with food production taking precedence. Benjamin's point is not that they have not contributed to the support of government, but that they have not contributed to enriching Benjamin. Benjamin is reminding them that the requirements have not been burdensome. In verse 14 Benjamin notes his desire "that there should nothing come upon you which was grievous to be borne."

This relationship establishes the possibility of a political hierarchy that does not engender a social hierarchy. Because a persistent source of downfall in Nephite society is the evil that comes when one person elevates himself above another, is here emphasizing social egalitarianism as the foundation of Nephite society. (See 2 Nephi, Part 1: Context, Chapter 2, "Overview of 2 Nephi.")

Mosiah 2:13

> 13 Neither have I suffered that ye should be confined in dungeons, nor that ye should make slaves one of another, nor that ye should murder, or plunder, or steal, or commit adultery; nor even have I suffered that ye should commit any manner of wickedness, and have taught you that ye should keep the commandments of the Lord, in all things which he hath commanded you—

Culture: In verses 10–11 Benjamin differentiates himself from the kings who declared themselves divine; in verses 12–13, Benjamin contrasts his administration with that of the other kings with which the people would be familiar. John Welch points out that Benjamin is stressing that Nephite society is unique in opposing these common elements: "The use of dungeons or prisons was apparently tolerated in Israel (Jer. 37:15, 1 Ne. 7:14), generally in the land of Nephi (Mosiah 17:5), in the land of Ammonihah (Alma 14:18, 23), and among the Lamanites (Hel. 5:21);

but by special dispensation, the use of prisons was not allowed in Zarahemla under King Benjamin or in other lands by special royal decrees (Alma 23:2)."[31]

This decree against prisons in Alma 23:2 was a special protection for sons of Mosiah and other missionaries in Lamanite lands. That such a special decree was needed suggests that Lamanites more commonly used prisons or dungeons than the Nephites. There does not appear to be any significant difference in the usage of "dungeon" or "prison," since both terms are applied to the same site (Alma 8:30).

In his speech at this point, Benjamin is reminding his people—who obviously know what prisons are without any explanation being needed—that he has spared them this form of punishment. Since we know that Benjamin's reign has not always been peaceful, he had some other way of dealing with lawbreakers, most likely banishment. Words of Mormon 1:16 refers to defections to the Lamanites. While many of the defections to the Lamanites are voluntary, it would not be surprising if there were also involuntary banishments of certain individuals. Nevertheless, the nature of Benjamin's speech will indicate that there remain in Zarahemla some who might still sympathize with the old government and religion, so any involuntary banishments were not the equivalent of a purge.

Likewise, enslavement had to be a real threat or Benjamin's prohibition of it would carry not weight. In point of fact, both the Maya and the Aztec practiced slavery. For the Maya, slavery may have been practiced in both the Classic and Postclassic periods, depending on the interpretation of certain iconography. Archaeologist Sylvanus Morley writes:

> Slavery seems to have been practiced in both the Classic [A.D. 250–800] and Postclassic stages, despite Bishop Landa's [born 1524, died 1579] assertion that it was introduced in late Postclassic times by one of the Cocom rulers of Mayapan. This is difficult to believe in view of the frequent representations of the so-called "captive figures" on Classic Maya monuments. These "captive figures" are very likely representations of enslaved prisoners of war. . . .
>
> In Postclassic times, when we have documentary evidence for slavery, the condition would seem to have arisen in one of five different ways: (1) by having been born a slave; (2) by having been made a slave in punishment for stealing; (30) by having been made a prisoner of war; (4) by having become an orphan; and (5) by having been acquired by purchase or trade. Provision was made by law and custom for the redemption of children born into slavery. . . Prisoners of war were always enslaved. Those of high degree were sacrificed immediately, but those of lower rank became the property of the soldier who had captured them.[32]

However, Norman Hammond, professor of archaeology at Boston University, warns against reading more modern practices back into ancient Mesoamerican society: "[Slavery] is evocative, and it may well be that Maya slavery was less exploitative, and more like the villeinage of medieval England, or the patron-client relationship with mutual obligations that Tambiah notes for medieval Southeast

---

[31]Welch, "Benjamin, the Man: His Place in Nephite History," in *King Benjamin's Speech*, edited by John W. Welch and Stephen D. Ricks (Provo, Utah: FARMS, 1998), 40.

[32]Sylvanus G. Morley, *The Ancient Maya* (Stanford, Calif.: Stanford University Press, 1956), 159.

Asia."[33] Whatever the exact details of the practice, it is clear from Benjamin's lumping it with prisons that slavery was clearly negative and that its absence from Zarahemla was a politically enlightened act.

The prohibitions against murder and plunder come as a set, most probably because Benjamin intended them to refer to the same context of political achievement. Although most societies have prohibitions against murder (as distinct from execution, war, or religious ritual), Benjamin may here be using the term to include—and therefore to disapprove of—Mesoamerican human sacrifice. Plunder, the acquisition of goods through acts of war, or raids, is both a motive and a reward for armed action, which was unquestionably very common in Mesoamerica. Both murder and plunder will recur again as a set in the Book of Mormon text.[34] It seems reasonable to see Benjamin setting himself apart from the other kings in disassociating himself also from the Mesoamerican cult of war, which was becoming dominant in this Maya culture region. Benjamin's prohibition of adultery may contain an echo to Jacob's denunciations of marital infidelity and multiple wives, suggesting that Benjamin had continued the norm of "one man, one woman," again a contrast with neighboring cultures.

In summary, Benjamin states that he has not suffered his people to "commit any manner of wickedness," again, in suggested contrast between Nephite society and neighboring societies who do commit all "manner of wickedness." In the tradition of ancient societies, the self-definition of King Benjamin's people included their understanding that they are different from the "others," a practice that we have seen as early as Enos (see commentary accompanying Enos 1:20) and which probably carried over from his own father.

Text: A possible confirmation that these specific legal prohibitions began in contrast to Lamanite (broadly defined) society appears in the Lamanite king's proclamation after his conversion by the sons of Mosiah: ". . . that they ought not to murder, nor to plunder, nor to steal, nor to commit adultery, nor to commit any manner of wickedness" (Alma 23:3). The very order of the prohibited acts, which repeats Benjamin's list, and the presence of the sons of Mosiah suggests that both kings are reciting the Nephite law code.[35]

This probability is underscored by the repetition of nearly the same list of legal prohibitions in three other places (Mosiah 29:36, Alma 30:10, Hel. 6:23). Significantly, Mosiah 29 also attributes transgression of these legal/moral norms to the iniquity of unnamed kings:

> For behold I say unto you, the sins of many people have been caused by the iniquities of their kings; therefore their iniquities are answered upon the heads of their kings. . . .

---

[33]Norman Hammond, "Inside the Black Box: Defining Maya Polity," in *Classic Maya Political History*, edited by T. Patrick Culbert (Cambridge, Eng.: Cambridge University Press, 1991), 265.

[34]Mosiah 10:17; Alma 23:3; Hel. 6:23, 7:21, 11:25; 3 Ne. 4:5; Ether 8:16.

[35]John W. Welch, "Benjamin's Speech: A Masterful Oration," in *King Benjamin's Speech*, edited by John W. Welch and Stephen D. Ricks (Provo, Utah: FARMS, 1998), 61, notes this repetition and sees in it a measure of the importance assigned to Benjamin's text.

> And he also unfolded unto them all the disadvantages they labored under, by having an unrighteous king to rule over them;
>
> Yea, all his iniquities and abominations, and all the wars, and contentions, and bloodshed, and the stealing, and the plundering, and the committing of whoredoms, and all manner of iniquities which cannot be enumerated—telling them that these things ought not to be, that they were expressly repugnant to the commandments of God. (Mosiah 29:31, 35–36)

Perhaps even more important than their function as Nephite law is this relationship to the traits of foreign kings. These are not empty proscriptions against unusual circumstances but rather define the nature of the threat of outside cultures. These phrases become virtual code words to describe the characteristics of the outside cultural influences against which the Nephite prophets continue to fight throughout the Book of Mormon.

Mosiah 2:14

> 14 And even I, myself, have labored with mine own hands that I might serve you, and that ye should not be laden with taxes, and that there should nothing come upon you which was grievous to be borne—and of all these things which I have spoken, ye yourselves are witnesses this day.

Culture: There is a direct correlation between Benjamin's statement that he has "labored with mine own hands" and "that ye should not be laden with taxes." The operation of government has correlated expenses, even in a nonmonetized economy like the Nephite/Zarahemlaite community. Benjamin was able both to rule and also to raise his own food, a clear suggestion of a political organization much simpler than that which prevailed within the generation of Mosiah's reign.[36]

Benjamin began his discourse by defining his reign, first in contrast to cultural expectations, and second, by the benefits to his people. Now he concludes this section by declaring that the congregation is witnesses of the truthfulness of what he has said.

Mosiah 2:15

> 15 Yet, my brethren, I have not done these things that I might boast, neither do I tell these things that thereby I might accuse you; but I tell you these things that ye may know that I can answer a clear conscience before God this day.

Literature/History: There are three independent clauses in this sentence. The first two are negatives, and the third a positive. First, Benjamin indicates that he has not described his reign's political/legal legacy as a boast. Certainly his achievements are benefits of his rule and foundational elements in his definition of Nephite law. He is justly proud of them, but he did not list them to elicit public accolades.

The next clause is the most fascinating. Benjamin states that this list of achievements is not presented as an accusation. In what sense could these

---

[36]Sorenson, *An Ancient American Setting for the Book of Mormon*, 192.

apparently good features accuse his people? I hypothesize that Benjamin is here reminding his people of the past "contentions," against which he has had to fight mightily. One result of these contentions resulted in many defections to the Lamanites (Words of Mormon 1:16). It seems plausible that Benjamin survived a near-civil war, of words if not of armed conflict, with some of the battle lines being drawn between the Lamanite religious/political system (indicated by the false Christs and false prophets) and the Nephites' traditional religion. It is a reasonable assumption that many in Benjamin's audience felt at least some sympathies for the losing side. In this emotionally charged context, Benjamin is giving a message of forgiveness and acceptance to the ambivalent, reassuring them that while he stands affirmatively for one type of political/religious system, he does not actively reproach them for being less affirmative in their own choice. It is a generous statement of peace and love.

In the third clause, Benjamin proffers his main motive: He wants a clear conscience before Yahweh, to whom he is ultimately accountable. It is a summary statement at the end of his career, an assertion that he has done his best. This clause not only describes his purpose but also announces that he will be relinquishing rule.

Mosiah 2:16–17

> 16 Behold, I say unto you that because I said unto you that I had spent my days in your service, I do not desire to boast, for I have only been in the service of God.
> 17 And behold, I tell you these things that ye may learn wisdom; that ye may learn that when ye are in the service of your fellow beings ye are only in the service of your God.

Rhetoric: Benjamin again asserts that his catalog of achievements is not a boast. Rather, he shifts the focus back to Yahweh, a skilled rhetorical movement that acknowledges but moves beyond his possible "accusation." Benjamin reminds his people that his efforts in their behalf have not come from a desire for personal gain, but rather from a relationship with Yahweh.

He then extends this relationship with Yahweh to his people. This sentence is an important transition to the rest of his sermon, because he will ask his people to rename themselves as part of a new covenant. The Nephites always declare their relationship to Israel and hence see themselves as people of the covenant. Benjamin is not dismissing that covenant, but presenting a new social covenant that includes a renewal of the covenant with Yahweh. They will still be Israelites, but a newly formed body of Israelites with new communal bonds and a renewed declaration of their client/patron relationship with Yahweh. He establishes their ability to enter into a personal relationship with Yahweh, just as Benjamin has and just as they have with Benjamin.

In ancient Mesoamerican society, the people were culturally primed to accept a special relationship between king and God, even to accept the king as God. The culture of Zarahemla assumed such a relationship. Thus, many, if not most, of Benjamin's audience would have been culturally inclined to believe that lineage and rank created that relationship; but Benjamin removes these exclusive elements by assuring them that the special relationship stems from actions that anyone can perform, regardless of lineage or rank, regardless of poverty or wealth. For this reason, he tells them that he is teaching them "wisdom," clarifying their understanding of the truth. This teaching, by implication, also stands in contrast to what they would learn from the surrounding kings. Benjamin, through the use of his personal example, becomes a tangible manifestation of how the assumed exclusive relationship of king and God may be expanded, enjoyed by all.

Scripture: How is it possible that "when ye are in the service of your fellow beings, you are only in the service of your God"? The first implication is that of a servant-master relationship, with benefits to each party. It is the master's responsibility to provide appropriately for the servant, and the servant's responsibility to fulfill the master's will. While the servant is certainly bound to obey, he benefits by the right to and responsibility for goods and actions that might otherwise be unavailable to him.

In the divine relationship, we become the Lord's servants when we enter his service. With the Lord as our master, we also have access to abilities and possibilities that are otherwise unavailable. We willingly yield him our obedience in exchange for greater blessings. Our modern world places such an emphasis on freedom that we can easily miss how we benefit. As analogy, an employee of a large firm willingly exchanges his "freedom" to be elsewhere than the office for the rewards and compensations that the firm offers its employees. In accomplishing the company's goals, the employee gains experience and increases his talents in ways not previously available. While exploitive employers, like wicked masters, are certainly a risk of such relationships, it is not a danger in a relationship with the Lord. Rather, the relationship offers only benefits.

Benjamin here invites all of his people to enter into the same kind of personal servant/master relationship with Yahweh that he has. The key element of establishing this relationship is to serve—in this case, to serve one's fellow beings. This interesting formulation is echoed in two different teachings of Jesus. First, Jesus also condensed the essential relationship with God into a single concept, that of love: "Jesus said unto him, Thou shalt love the Lord thy God with all thy heart, and with all thy soul, and with all thy mind. This is the first and great commandment. And the second is like unto it, Thou shalt love thy neighbour as thyself. On these two commandments hang all the law and the prophets" (Matt. 22:37–40).

Second, Jesus also commanded his followers to serve their fellow beings: "And the King shall answer and say unto them, Verily I say unto you, Inasmuch as ye have done it unto one of the least of these my brethren, ye have done it unto me" (Matt. 25:40).

Understanding such Godlike love can be the entire basis for one's relationship to God (the purpose of the law and the prophets) because such a love will govern one's actions as though it were God. Service emerges from such love. Because Benjamin's people have been schooled in the law of Moses (Mosiah 2:3), Benjamin is refocusing them much as Jesus did—away from the particulars of the law and into the heart of it.

Mosiah 2:18–19

> 18 Behold, ye have called me your king; and if I, whom ye call your king, do labor to serve you, then ought not ye to labor to serve one another?
> 19 And behold also, if I, whom ye call your king, who has spent his days in your service, and yet has been in the service of God, do merit any thanks from you, O how you ought to thank your heavenly King!

Rhetoric: Benjamin is building a logical case. Beginning with the incontrovertible evidence of his work in service of his people, Benjamin is creating an analogy between that known past and the new covenant he will propose, moving from the physical to the spiritual, from the tangible earthly king to the spiritual celestial king. In that covenant, the people must accept a new or renewed relationship with Yahweh. Verse 18 expands the theme of service introduced in verse 17, stressing that it is an achievable goal. If Benjamin can serve them, surely they can serve one another. Benjamin is not asking them to do anything that he has not already done, a fact they themselves have witnessed (v. 14).

Benjamin has begun by describing the master's perspective—specifying what is required of the servant. Now he examines how the servant should view the master. The people are grateful to Benjamin for his services and also for his freeing them from burdens "grievous to be born." Yet Benjamin is the servant of the heavenly king. Thus, the people should in reality be expressing thanks to the heavenly king—Benjamin's master. Rather than building a society in which the earthly king is the master, Benjamin is focusing the people's gratitude and service on the heavenly king.

Mosiah 2:20–21

> 20 I say unto you, my brethren, that if you should render all the thanks and praise which your whole soul has power to possess, to that God who has created you, and has kept and preserved you, and has caused that ye should rejoice, and has granted that ye should live in peace one with another—
> 21 I say unto you that if ye should serve him who has created you from the beginning, and is preserving you from day to day, by lending you breath, that ye may live and move and do according to your own will, and even supporting you from one moment to another—I say, if ye should serve him with all your whole souls yet ye would be unprofitable servants.

Rhetoric: The main point of Benjamin's argument is in the first and last clauses of this single sentence spanning two verses. Even if they were to give Yahweh all thanks and praise, they would still be "unprofitable servants." Why is Benjamin presenting the relationship as an impossible one, despite their (presumed) best efforts? Why tell them that they can never be considered "profitable" servants?

In the master/servant relationship, actions and benefits flow both ways through the relationship. A master may have a servant so talented or so specialized that he becomes indispensable. In a modern sports analogy, a "franchise player" may be so valuable to the team that he must be treated with special rules. He or she is thus a "profitable" servant because he or she contributes tremendously to the financial benefits of the team owners. In contrast, Benjamin is simply proclaiming that Yahweh's benefits to his people are so great that no servant's contributions begin to equal the benefits from the master. Benjamin is teaching the principle of grace, couched in terms of the servant/master relationship.

In Luke 17:5–10, the Savior uses the identical term of profitability to teach his apostles:

> And the apostles said unto the Lord, Increase our faith.
>
> And the Lord said, If ye had faith as a grain of mustard seed, ye might say unto this sycamine tree, Be thou plucked up by the root, and be thou planted in the sea; and it should obey you.
>
> But which of you, having a servant plowing or feeding cattle, will say unto him by and by, when he is come from the field, Go and sit down to meat?
>
> And will not rather say unto him, Make ready wherewith I may sup, and gird thyself, and serve me, till I have eaten and drunken; and afterward thou shalt eat and drink?
>
> Doth he thank that servant because he did the things that were commanded him? I trow not.
>
> So likewise ye, when ye shall have done all those things which are commanded you, say, We are unprofitable servants: we have done that which was our duty to do.

In other words, our faith increases when we realize the true extent of the servant/master relationship. While modern readers, who accept an employer/employee relationship but see demeaning elements in a master/servant relationship, may wince at this parable, Jesus simply accepts this dynamic of his culture and uses its commonness to teach a point. And obviously, the disciples understood: A servant receives benefits for fulfilling his obligations, but fulfilling those obligations is one's duty, it is not exceptional.

These two parables of unprofitable servants and masters have complementary meanings in the two scriptures. Jesus is teaching his apostles how to increase their faith. Benjamin is teaching his people about the abundant grace of the eternal master. In both cases, it is the nature of the depicted relationship that models our relationship with God.

Mosiah 2:22

> 22 And behold, all that he requires of you is to keep his commandments; and he has promised you that if ye would keep his commandments ye should prosper in the land; and he never doth vary from that which he hath said; therefore, if ye do keep his commandments he doth bless you and prosper you.

Benjamin now explains why his listeners are unprofitable servants in a passage that extends through verse 25. First, Benjamin describes what the master requires of his servant(s). This great Yahweh, this heavenly master and king, only "requires of you . . . to keep his commandments." Clearly, Benjamin's people already know these commandments. Benjamin is not instructing them about the commandments but rather about the central behavior—obedience to the commandments—in establishing their personal relationship to Yahweh.

In exchange for their obedience, this great master promises that "ye should prosper in the land," a benefit that they know their Master can grant. Benjamin emphasizes Yahweh's immutability. Yahweh does not change or renege on his promises. Since Yahweh has promised that they will prosper if they keep the commandments, then they assuredly will prosper if they obey, for Yahweh will keep his word (his covenant).

Mosiah 2:23

> 23 And now, in the first place, he hath created you, and granted unto you your lives, for which ye are indebted unto him.

Although Yahweh requires little of us, he provides us with great blessings. Not only does he promise prosperity in this land, but he has "granted unto you your lives, for which ye are indebted unto him." Far more foundational than prosperity, we owe our very existence to this eternal master.

Mosiah 2:24

> 24 And secondly, he doth require that ye should do as he hath commanded you; for which if ye do, he doth immediately bless you; and therefore he hath paid you. And ye are still indebted unto him, and are, and will be, forever and ever; therefore, of what have ye to boast?

Benjamin attempts here to explain the problem of grace and works without casting it as a theological question. We begin mortality in debt to God for our very lives; but when we attempt to repay him for our lives by obedience to his commandments, he immediately blesses us, leaving the original debt untouched. By the very nature of God and by the nature of mortality, we are unable to "catch up" to God's blessings. While some blessings might seem to be "earned," the overall set of blessings can never be earned.

This principle of Benjamin's is more clearly stated in the Doctrine and Covenants 130:20–21: "There is a law, irrevocably decreed in heaven before the foundations of this world, upon which all blessings are predicated—And when we obtain any blessing from God, it is by obedience to that law upon which it is predicated." This scripture describes the same principle as Benjamin: When we obey, we are immediately blessed.

What do we do with those very real and frequently painful situations in which a desired blessing does not appear to be "immediate" at all? Benjamin combines this principle of human obedience with Yahweh's overarching grace, making it a close match with Nephi's understanding: "It is by grace that we are saved, after all we can do" (2 Ne. 25:23).

Mosiah 2:25

> 25 And now I ask, can ye say aught of yourselves? I answer you, Nay. Ye cannot say that ye are even as much as the dust of the earth; yet ye were created of the dust of the earth; but behold, it belongeth to him who created you.

Rhetoric: Benjamin's crowning argument in his analogy of the unprofitable servant is the obvious fact that we cannot compete with Yahweh as a purveyor of blessings. Rather, humankind is ultimately and irrevocably dependent on Yahweh. We are not even as much as the "dust of the earth"—not because we are valueless but because we cannot create even something so common. Yahweh, however, has created both the dust and humanity from the dust. Benjamin is not making a statement about the absolute value of human beings; rather, he is commenting on our position as servants in relationship to Yahweh.

Mosiah 2:26

> 26 And I, even I, whom ye call your king, am no better than ye yourselves are; for I am also of the dust. And ye behold that I am old, and am about to yield up this mortal frame to its mother earth.

Rhetoric: Benjamin neatly ties up his argument by returning to his introduction, again using himself as a focus. Although he has strongly argued that everyone can have the same relationship with Yahweh that he himself has had, here he underscores the social difference between the king and the people. Even though he is superior in privilege and rank, yet he also is "of the dust." He is as much Yahweh's creation as they, just as much an unprofitable servant as they. Benjamin has thus explored both sides of the servant/master relationship with his people, assured them that they are capable of entering into this relationship, described some of its blessings, and indicated that they will always be bound to Yahweh (their master) in gratitude because of his abounding grace. He seals this description by including himself in it.

Our modern assumptions may make us miss the significance of Benjamin's words. An ancient audience would assume that their king was infinitely superior to them, sacred, and taboo. Many societies forbade ordinary persons to touch the king and, in some cases, even to look at him. This reverence for the king's person obviously had implications for religious sanction as a tool for governance. It would not be unusual for Benjamin's people, particularly the Zarahemlaites who were apparently more Mesoamericanized than the Nephites, to see Benjamin as more than a man, despite his strong affirmation that he was only a man. In this context, Benjamin's placing himself on the same level as his people before Yahweh is a startling declaration, one that certainly would have impressed his audience.

Mosiah 2:27

> 27 Therefore, as I said unto you that I had served you, walking with a clear conscience before God, even so I at this time have caused that ye should

> assemble yourselves together, that I might be found blameless, and that your blood should not come upon me, when I shall stand to be judged of God of the things whereof he hath commanded me concerning you.

The concluding sentence of verse 26 (Benjamin describes himself as nearing death) should be read with verse 28, where he returns to the purpose of his assembly—to fulfill his final obligation as Yahweh's servant (v. 15) and transmit Yahweh's commands to his people.

Scripture: Benjamin acknowledges that being the leader (or Yahweh's servant) carries with it the responsibility to faithfully carry out Yahweh's will for those over whom Benjamin has stewardship. All leaders have similar obligations. Like any servant, we will be judged (at least in part) on how we fulfill the responsibilities God has given us for others.

Mosiah 2:28–29

> 28 I say unto you that I have caused that ye should assemble yourselves together that I might rid my garments of your blood, at this period of time when I am about to go down to my grave, that I might go down in peace, and my immortal spirit may join the choirs above in singing the praises of a just God.
> 29 And moreover, I say unto you that I have caused that ye should assemble yourselves together, that I might declare unto you that I can no longer be your teacher, nor your king;

Benjamin declares two reasons for the assembly. First, he must discharge his duty to Yahweh, and second, he will abdicate both his throne and his position as "teacher." The abdication of the throne is an important event in this discourse but Benjamin devotes much less time and effort to it than to his spiritual goal of discharging his responsibilities before Yahweh. Before Benjamin can relinquish his title of "teacher," he has one final great lesson to communicate in this sermon.

Mosiah 2:30

> 30 For even at this time, my whole frame doth tremble exceedingly while attempting to speak unto you; but the Lord God doth support me, and hath suffered me that I should speak unto you, and hath commanded me that I should declare unto you this day, that my son Mosiah is a king and a ruler over you.

The passing of the kingship is accomplished with this simple declarative statement; but Benjamin now dwells on the teaching and discharge of his obligations. It is tempting to read "my whole frame doth tremble exceedingly" as a consequence of Benjamin's age (v. 26), but he lives three years beyond this point. Rather, it seems more significant that he is in the process of delivering a powerful sermon as Yahweh's messenger. Thus, he trembles because of the effects of the Spirit on his physical body. Later, the Spirit also descends upon his people with such power that they are unable to speak the joy they felt (Mosiah 4:20). Benjamin is trembling in spiritual anticipation of his people's great transformation.

Mosiah 2:31

> 31 And now, my brethren, I would that ye should do as ye have hitherto done. As ye have kept my commandments, and also the commandments of my father, and have prospered, and have been kept from falling into the hands of your enemies, even so if ye shall keep the commandments of my son, or the commandments of God which shall be delivered unto you by him, ye shall prosper in the land, and your enemies shall have no power over you.

Having fulfilled the first of his purposes by naming Mosiah as his successor, Benjamin now turns to his major purpose in assembling the people.[37] He will be giving them a new covenant, creating a new and formal relationship between the people and their God. He begins by discussing their relationship to their new king. His very first commandment is: "I would that ye should do as ye have hitherto done." These are people who have elected to remain with Benjamin rather than defect to the Lamanites. Almost certainly, for the most part they agreed with Benjamin's rule and followed his laws. Benjamin invokes that same willingness to follow his son as the appropriate response.

Benjamin uses history to teach the importance of following his commands. He reminds them of the temporal prosperity they have enjoyed under Mosiah$_1$ and himself. It is interesting that the major evidence of prosperity is that they have not fallen into the hands of their enemies. What is the link between victory in battle and prosperity? Aside from the obvious "prosperity" of retaining one's independence, in Mesoamerica there was a very close economic tie between losing a war and experiencing privation. The conquered people were required to pay tribute of their goods, therefore having less for themselves. This problem will play a major role in the story of Zeniff and his followers (whose story begins in Mosiah 9).

Returning to his theme of Yahweh as a heavenly king, Benjamin links the prosperity under his father's rule and his own to Yahweh's promise of prosperity if the people would obey. (For the Nephite foundational promise, see commentary accompanying 2 Nephi 1:9.) Thus, he has declared the continuation of the dynasty, required his people to continue their support, and turned their ultimate allegiance to the eternal king—Yahweh.

Mosiah 2:32

> 32 But, O my people, beware lest there shall arise contentions among you, and ye list to obey the evil spirit, which was spoken of by my father Mosiah.

---

[37]Benjamin is obviously speaking to the entire assembled congregation which includes men, women, and children. Nevertheless, he specifically addresses "my brethren." I suspect that in a patriarchal society this term was used as a collective that might appropriately include women and children even though they are not specifically mentioned. There is certainly no indication that anyone was excluded from the new covenant.

After instructing his people to follow in their current path, Benjamin reminds them to take care lest the contentions rise again. We are not told specifically what those contentions were, but since Benjamin links the contentions to the "evil spirit" we may assume that they dealt with religion (and since religion was intimately associated with rulership, they dealt also with politics).

Even though Benjamin mentions his father's teachings about the "evil spirit," we do not have those teachings in our current Book of Mormon. We cannot tell if Mormon included it in the lost sections of Mosiah (see chapter 2) or if he elected not to discuss it at all. While we do not have the specific teachings of $Mosiah_1$, Benjamin obviously assumed that his people remembered them.

The phrasing suggests, not a generalized attitude of negligence or disobedience, but the actual influence of an evil being. I hypothesize that $Mosiah_1$ found himself a faithful Nephite king in a recently pagan Zarahemla. It was a Zarahemla that had lost the Old Testament religion of its founding fathers and had probably lapsed into practices adopted freely from their Mesoamerican neighbors.

Having lost their Israelite religion, $Mosiah_1$ may have needed to teach them the concept of the "evil spirit" as one of the elements of the Israelite religion they had lost. There is no reason to believe that this "evil spirit" equates with the personage of Satan. In fact, it would be rather anachronous were it to refer to the person we understand as the devil. (See commentary accompanying 2 Nephi 2:17.) Rather, it embodies a concept that stands in juxtaposition to God and his righteousness. In the context of $Mosiah_1$ and Zarahemla, it is most likely that the "evil spirit" was a collective designation for any and all of the Mesoamerican deities.

Vocabulary: The term "list" should be read as "incline toward" rather than "listen."[38]

Mosiah 2:33

> 33 For behold, there is a wo pronounced upon him who listeth to obey that spirit; for if he listeth to obey him, and remaineth and dieth in his sins, the same drinketh damnation to his own soul; for he receiveth for his wages an everlasting punishment, having transgressed the law of God contrary to his own knowledge.

Benjamin sets up a contrast between the "wo" attached to obeying the evil spirit and the "prosperity" attached to obeying Yahweh. In each case, the human action has an accompanying response from the extra-human (Yahweh or the evil spirit). Benjamin then goes into detail about the nature of that woe. It occurs when the sinner has not repented and thus "dieth in his sins," inevitably to reap the "reward" of "damnation to his own soul." This warning is tailored to Benjamin's people, for they understand Yahweh's will. Will they choose to go against it, especially when their behavior is currently acceptable (v. 31: "Continue to do as ye have hitherto done")?

---

[38]Coutts et al., "Complete Text of Benjamin's Speech," 535.

Mosiah 2:34–35

> 34 I say unto you, that there are not any among you, except it be your little children that have not been taught concerning these things, but what knoweth that ye are eternally indebted to your heavenly Father, to render to him all that you have and are; and also have been taught concerning the records which contain the prophecies which have been spoken by the holy prophets, even down to the time our father, Lehi, left Jerusalem;
> 35 And also, all that has been spoken by our fathers until now. And behold, also, they spake that which was commanded them of the Lord; therefore, they are just and true.

Benjamin reminds the people that he is not teaching them new doctrine but rather reviewing material they have already been taught and renewing their existing commitment. Significantly, he conscientiously notes that perhaps the little children have not been taught these things, meaning that these instructions have been repeatedly taught since the time of $Mosiah_1$. Nevertheless, Benjamin develops an argument that creates literary tension between grown men, who might follow evil, and the "young children" who do not. This is his first mention of this important theme.

Benjamin reviews not only the general doctrine, but also its sources: the "fathers" and the "records." Both sources teach Yahweh's commandments.

Mosiah 2:36

> 36 And now, I say unto you, my brethren, that after ye have known and have been taught all these things, if ye should transgress and go contrary to that which has been spoken, that ye do withdraw yourselves from the Spirit of the Lord, that it may have no place in you to guide you in wisdom's paths that ye may be blessed, prospered, and preserved—

Benjamin explains further why his people are under the potential penalty of damnation should they follow the evil spirit. The first requirement is that they should know Yahweh's commandments, and he lays before them the evidence that they do. Knowing these things, but choosing to act contrary to them, is a choice to "withdraw yourselves from the Spirit of the Lord."

Probably Benjamin very purposefully uses the phrase "Spirit of the Lord" in this context as a contrast to "evil spirit." He is creating an easily understood polarity between "the good spirit" (Yahweh) and the evil spirit.

Mosiah 2:37

> 37 I say unto you, that the man that doeth this, the same cometh out in open rebellion against God; therefore he listeth to obey the evil spirit, and becometh an enemy to all righteousness; therefore, the Lord has no place in him, for he dwelleth not in unholy temples.

The "man that doeth this" is one who has received the gospel (v. 36), the all-important prerequisite. If we receive, understand, and believe in the gospel, but still elect to follow the evil one, that choice brings us "out in open rebellion against God." We rebel because, by definition, we were once on God's side and have chosen the opposite course. When we are in such a state of rebellion, the spirit of God necessarily withdraws from us. God has no place in us, not by his choice but because we make no room for him, having chosen another "god" instead.

Vocabulary: We are familiar with the image of the body as a temple, an image also used in the New Testament (John 2:21, 1 Cor. 6:19). The image is appropriate in ancient Israel because of the sanctity of the temple, and that imagery certainly carried over to the Nephite temples in the New World. In the New World, however, the imagery may have had extended meaning. The "contentions" against which Benjamin has fought would have been religious rebellions with competing temples devoted to the worship of the "evil spirit." Thus, the "unholy temple" for Benjamin would have a dual meaning—not only the physical body of the person who has turned away, but the competing temple to which that person likely has turned.

Mosiah 2:38–39

> 38 Therefore if that man repenteth not, and remaineth and dieth an enemy to God, the demands of divine justice do awaken his immortal soul to a lively sense of his own guilt, which doth cause him to shrink from the presence of the Lord, and doth fill his breast with guilt, and pain, and anguish, which is like an unquenchable fire, whose flame ascendeth up forever and ever.
> 39 And now I say unto you, that mercy hath no claim on that man; therefore his final doom is to endure a never-ending torment.

Reference: The imagery of a never-ending fire was available to Benjamin from the small plates of Nephi (2 Ne. 9:16, Jacob 6:10). The closest match to Benjamin's statement is Jacob 6:10: "And according to the power of justice, for justice cannot be denied, ye must go away into that lake of fire and brimstone, whose flames are unquenchable, and whose smoke ascendeth up forever and ever, which lake of fire and brimstone is endless torment." (See also 2 Nephi 9:16.) "Never-ending torment/endless torment" and "unquenchable" fire are so close in meaning that it seems likely that this phrases had struck Benjamin, who almost certainly read these phrases on the small plates after receiving them from Amaleki.

Benjamin concludes that "mercy hath no claim on that man; therefore his final doom is to endure a never-ending torment." First, Benjamin warns in strong terms that the consequence of choosing to rebel against Yahweh is a "never-ending torment," likened to being burned by fire. While that is certainly a dreadful image, Benjamin is not trying to frighten people into obedience by describing the result but rather to describe the type of person to whom such a torment would apply. This punishment will fall on the unrepentant individual who dies "an enemy to God." These are not necessarily the same condition. One may fail to repent of many sins but not necessarily be an "enemy to God." Rather, the "enemy to God" is an open rebel, someone who has known the gospel yet has chosen to turn against Yahweh and has voluntarily become an enemy to Yahweh.

Significantly, Benjamin also notes that this eternal torment is reserved for those who die in the state of enmity to Yahweh. Thus, Benjamin is discussing a grievous sin, but one from which a person can choose to repent—and can be forgiven—before death.

The next fascinating aspect of Benjamin's instruction is how this torment occurs. We might expect that God would assign the torment as the just deserts of one who dies as an enemy to God. However, that is not what Benjamin describes, Rather, it is "a lively sense of his own guilt" that produces the firelike "guilt, and pain, and anguish." The torment is internal, not external. It is self-imposed, not levied by a vengeful and wrathful Yahweh. The pain and anguish are not literal fires of a geographical hell but are rather like an unquenchable fire. Benjamin is placing the blame for this penalty squarely on the shoulders of the sinner. This doctrinal understanding presages the Doctrine and Covenants that also describes the individual's role in his or her final judgment:

> For he who is not able to abide the law of a celestial kingdom cannot abide a celestial glory.
>
> And he who cannot abide the law of a terrestrial kingdom cannot abide a terrestrial glory.
>
> And he who cannot abide the law of a telestial kingdom cannot abide a telestial glory; therefore he is not meet for a kingdom of glory. Therefore he must abide a kingdom which is not a kingdom of glory. (D&C 88:22–24)

Not only does each person "abide" the kingdom for whose law he or she is fitted, but he or she could have been a candidate for full celestial rewards:

> And also they who are quickened by a portion of the telestial glory shall then receive of the same, even a fulness.
>
> And they who remain shall also be quickened; nevertheless, they shall return again to their own place, to enjoy that which they are willing to receive, because they were not willing to enjoy that which they might have received. (D&C 88:31–32)

As Benjamin stresses, the punishment results from one's own choices, especially the choice not to repent.

Mosiah 2:40

> 40 O, all ye old men, and also ye young men, and you little children who can understand my words, for I have spoken plainly unto you that ye might understand, I pray that ye should awake to a remembrance of the awful situation of those that have fallen into transgression.

Rhetoric: Note that Benjamin here addresses "those that have fallen into transgression" without actually accusing any specific portion of his congregation. Adding this mild reprimand to the contentions that have already been noted, we have a new perspective on his vocative "O, all ye old men." Benjamin uses a sequence of descriptions for those he is accusing. He begins by addressing "all ye old men." To the old men he adds the young men, and ends with "you little children who can understand."[39] This rhetorical technique artfully includes everyone in the congregation but allows Benjamin to emphasize the "old men" as the first and most important category. Adding the other age groups softens the effect of the direct accusation.

Why would Benjamin have a particular interest in the "old men"? If my hypothesis is correct that the contentions had centered between the "old religion" of Zarahemla and the "new religion" of a true knowledge of Yahweh, then that old religion would have been the natal faith of the oldest men. No doubt, they were more likely to continue in it than the younger men. Thus, Benjamin is continuing to attack the roots of the religious contention, declaring those who would support the old religion to be enemies to Yahweh and subject to the penalties he has just described—penalties coming from their own choices, and therefore avoidable by their own choices.

Nevertheless, as I read this passage, Benjamin does not want to be accusatory in singling out a part of his people. He thus manages to be both direct and indirect, both specific and generally cautionary.

Mosiah 2:41

> 41 And moreover, I would desire that ye should consider on the blessed and happy state of those that keep the commandments of God. For behold, they are blessed in all things, both temporal and spiritual; and if they hold out faithful to the end they are received into heaven, that thereby they may dwell with God in a state of never-ending happiness. O remember, remember that these things are true; for the Lord God hath spoken it.

Rhetoric: This verse is a transition from the fate of Yahweh's enemies to the next, and more important, theme, the spiritual application of these principles.

Text: Although the current text places a chapter break at this point, the 1830 edition does not. It is important to consider this discourse as a whole, for our current chapter 3 contains the real message of Benjamin's discourse. Up to this point, he has explained and interpreted his audience's own past so that he can now present them with their future.

---

[39]In a patriarchal society such as the Nephites', I assume that the address to men was not intended to be exclusively for the men, but rather was directed to the men as representing their families.

Mosiah 3

Mosiah 2:41–3:1

> 41 And moreover, I would desire that ye should consider on the blessed and happy state of those that keep the commandments of God. For behold, they are blessed in all things, both temporal and spiritual; and if they hold out faithful to the end they are received into heaven, that thereby they may dwell with God in a state of never-ending happiness. O remember, remember that these things are true; for the Lord God hath spoken it.
> 1 And again my brethren, I would call your attention, for I have somewhat more to speak unto you; for behold, I have things to tell you concerning that which is to come.

I have repeated the last verse from chapter 2 to make Benjamin's transition clearer. To recapitulate, Benjamin has just finished describing the eternal punishment that will befall the unrepentant who choose to follow the "evil spirit" rather than Yahweh till the ends of their lives. He now turns to a more positive theme—the one for which the assembly has been convened.

The transition thus reinforces the theme he has already introduced—the opposition of good and bad in the next life. Having concluded his discussion about the awful state of the wicked, Benjamin now invites his people to "consider on the blessed and happy state of those that keep the commandments." Yet this is not the theme upon which he dwells in 3:1. Instead he seems to introduce a new topic: "that which is to come." This phrase is used to indicate the coming Messiah. (See commentary accompanying Enos 1:19. The phrase is repeated in Mosiah 5:3.)

Benjamin begins by recalling their attention.[1] As I envision the situation, most of the audience has not been surprised by the announcement that Mosiah will succeed Benjamin and, similarly, would consider most of the remaining information a review, rather than new instruction. Most of those who really wanted to follow the "evil spirit" had already defected to the Lamanites. Benjamin has already been speaking for some time. It is probably in the fall after the harvest. They have eaten well. It is warm and no doubt sunny. The crowd is dense. The children are restless. Even though the people listened as Benjamin continued, there is probably much ambient noise—the sound of cloth as weary people shift their positions, whispered

---

[1]Royal Skousen, *Analysis of Textual Variants of the Book of Mormon*, THE CRITICAL TEXT OF THE BOOK OF MORMON (Provo, Utah: Foundation for Ancient Research and Mormon Studies, 2005) , Vol. 4, Part 2, 1163, notes that we expect the phrase "call one's attention **to something.**" He suggests that the meaning of the phrase is probably "I would have you pay attention."

admonitions to the children, perhaps the rustle of leaves as the breeze blows through their shelters. Thus, I read this verse as Benjamin's call for attentiveness as he approaches the most important part of his sermon.

Mosiah 3:2–3

> 2 And the things which I shall tell you are made known unto me by an angel from God. And he said unto me: Awake; and I awoke, and behold he stood before me.
> 3 And he said unto me: Awake, and hear the words which I shall tell thee; for behold, I am come to declare unto you the glad tidings of great joy.

Culture: Mesoamerican culture would have impressed upon Benjamin's people the need for a close link between the king and the supernatural world. This same element would be an expectation in the Nephite culture as well. Thus, Benjamin's audience would have been intensely interested in his announcement that he had seen an angel and received a message from him. I suggest, however, that the unusual doubling of the command "awake" with the repetitious "I awoke" may be Benjamin's attempt to clearly differentiate his experience from that of the Mesoamerican king-shaman, whose communion with the other world occurred in a trance or dreamlike state.

According to Schele (an epigrapher) and Freidel (an archaeologist), "Shamans are specialists in ecstasy, a state of grace that allows them to move freely beyond the ordinary world—beyond death itself—to deal directly with the gods, demons, ancestors, and other unseen but potent beings. Shamanic ecstasy can last moments, hours, or even days, but the amount of time spent in trance is less important than the knowledge of its existence."[2] This trance can be induced by deliberate action on the shaman's part, often involving blood sacrifice, as they explain:

> If the Pre-Columbian Maya practiced bloodletting and sacrifice to sustain the cycle of the soul, they also did it to enter trance and commune with the gods. Recall that the Vision Serpents conjured up by the ancients in trance rituals have names. Some, like the great War Serpent, the Waxaklahun-Ubah-Kan, have special roles in Maya cosmology that we can identify. When the Vision Serpents open their jaws, they convey the gods and the ancestors into the land of the living. One of the most masterful representations of this rite to have survived from Classic times is the beautiful Lintel 25 (Fig. 4:23), commissioned by Shield-Jaguar of Yaxchilan. The scene depicts the principal wife of this king conjuring up the founder of her husband's lineage during his accession rites. Wearing the costume of a Tlaloc warrior, this ancestor emerges from the jaws of a frightening, double-headed beastie with a half-flayed body decorated with feather fans. He is Waxaklahun-Ubah-Kan, the Maya War Serpent.[3]

While the concept of the induced trance and the serpent's role as a spiritual conduit may be very foreign to us, Mesoamerican people would have found them

---

[2]David Freidel, Linda Schele, and Joy Parker, *Maya Cosmos: Three Thousand Years on the Shaman's Path* (New York: William Morrow and Company, 1993), 33.

[3]Ibid., 207–8.

familiar modes of spiritual communication. However, Benjamin makes it clear that, although he is the king and therefore has the expected contact with the "other" world, it is qualitatively different from the Mesoamerican norm.

Benjamin reports that the angel twice told him to "awake." Why would a prophet of Benjamin's caliber need to be told twice? And why did he feel it necessary to report this detail? Perhaps, given the Mesoamerican expectations of a vision trance, Benjamin was emphasizing that the vision may have begun in a dream but the communication occurred while he was awake, not in a trance or in a trance-like sleep.

Reference: The angel brings a message of "glad tidings of great joy," a phrase that echoes Luke 2:10: "And the angel said unto them, Fear not: for, behold, I bring you good tidings of great joy, which shall be to all people." The Book of Mormon change of "good" to "glad" retains the corresponding emotional content. The Book of Mormon is consistent in using "glad tidings of great joy" (Alma 13:22, Hel. 16:14), but "glad tidings" is also a King James (KJV) phrase (Luke 1:19, 8:1; Acts 13:32; Rom. 10:15). In addition to suggesting that an angelic messenger has a typical way of putting at ease the person to whom he appears, it seems reasonable that the close resemblance in wording stems from the similarity of the message and Joseph's familiarity with KJV wording.

Mosiah 3:4

> 4 For the Lord hath heard thy prayers, and hath judged of thy righteousness, and hath sent me to declare unto thee that thou mayest rejoice; and that thou mayest declare unto thy people, that they may also be filled with joy.

Benjamin continues in his service to his people. Not only has he labored physically, but he has also labored spiritually, and this communication has come in response to his prayers.

Literature: The angel announces tidings of great joy; Benjamin may rejoice and may also declare this message to his people so that can rejoice. "Joy" or a form of it appears three times in two verses, expanding the meaning of the word. In the first declaration, the message itself is "tidings of great joy." The message's contents contain "joy." Next, the joy is transferred and focused to Benjamin, and third, to his people. (See commentary accompanying 2 Nephi 2:25 for an analysis of "joy.")

Mosiah 3:5

> 5 For behold, the time cometh, and is not far distant, that with power, the Lord Omnipotent who reigneth, who was, and is from all eternity to all eternity, shall come down from heaven among the children of men, and shall dwell in a tabernacle of clay, and shall go forth amongst men, working mighty miracles, such as healing the sick, raising the dead, causing the lame to walk, the blind to receive their sight, and the deaf to hear, and curing all manner of diseases.

Just as the good tidings to Mary concerned the advent of the Savior, so they do for Benjamin. Of course, the timing is significantly different. For Mary, the event was imminent—a matter of months. For Benjamin, this event lay over a century in the future. Why, given such a difference, would this particular piece of news come to Benjamin now? I suggest that the reason is associated with the larger timing of the new king and the new covenant.

It does not seem likely that the Messiah's mission was itself new to the people. Although Mosiah 3:5–11 is a catalog of Jesus's earthly ministry and his atonement, much of the substance of this revelation had been available for generations through the small plates of Nephi; and surely the believing descendants of Nephi who came to Zarahemla would have shared these crucially important teachings with the people of Zarahemla, since they had lost the knowledge of their creator (Omni 1:17). Therefore, in the two generations that had passed, the congregation assembled before Benjamin would have repeatedly heard the substance of Benjamin's declaration about the Messiah's mission. We know that they observe the law of Moses (Mosiah 2:3), which, in the New World, has included the hope of the Messiah since the days of Nephi (2 Ne. 25:24).

The numerous small differences in detail indicate that Benjamin received a vision of Jesus' ministry and is reporting his own experience, rather than citing scripture. Even where there is thematic overlap, Benjamin is giving the information in a fresh way. Certainly his prophetic vision would dominate his recollection, despite his familiarity with the scriptures left by earlier prophets who had similar experiences. For example, Nephi had a similar vision, but it came in response to a personal question. Benjamin receives this information, not only as a result of his personal righteousness (although no mention is made of seeking more information on this point), but "that thou mayest declare unto thy people, that they may also be filled with joy" (Mosiah 3:4). In contrast to Nephi's personal experience, Benjamin's is explicitly public.

Benjamin explains why this knowledge is the core of his sermon: Salvation comes through the name of Yahweh-Messiah (v. 17). This theological point, combined with Benjamin's desire to give a new name to his people, explains the timing of the message. Benjamin is setting up his covenant with a powerful reminder of the importance of the name that they will bear.

Internal Reference: Even though Benjamin is citing his personal revelation of the Savior, many details were already available about Jesus's ministry from the small plates of Nephi. For example, 1 Nephi 11:31 also notes Jesus's healing of the sick: "And he spake unto me again, saying: Look! And I looked, and I beheld the Lamb of God going forth among the children of men. And I beheld multitudes of people who were sick, and who were afflicted with all manner of diseases, and with devils and unclean spirits; and the angel spake and showed all these things unto me. And they were healed by the power of the Lamb of God; and the devils and the unclean spirits were cast out."

Significantly, despite the similarities, Benjamin adds new information: Jesus will raise the dead, give sight to the blind, and restore hearing to the deaf.

Although Nephi certainly saw these acts of healing in vision, he does not list them among the recorded acts that he saw Jesus perform. Benjamin must be referring to his own revelation and not to Nephi's revelation, at least not the version recorded on the small plates.

External Reference: One of the fragments from the Dead Sea Scrolls discusses a Messiah who will redeem and resurrect (4Q521). Note that one of the aspects of this redeemer is healing.

> [. . . For the hea]vens and the earth shall listen to His Messiah [and all w]hich is in them shall not turn away form the commandments of the holy ones. Strengthen yourselves, O you who seek the Lord, in His service.
>
> Will you not find the Lord in this, all those who hope in their heart? For the Lord seeks the pious and calls the righteous by name. Over the humble His spirit hovers, and He renews the faithful in His strength. For He will honor the pious upon the th[ro]ne of His eternal kingdom, setting prisoners free, opening the eyes of the blind, raising up those who are bo[wed down]. And for [ev]er(?) I (?) shall hold fast [to] the [ho]peful and pious [. . .]
>
> [. . .] shall not be delayed [. . .] and the Lord shall do glorious things which have not been done, just as He said. For He shall heal the critically wounded, He shall revive the dead, He shall send good news to the afflicted, He shall [. . . the . . .], He shall lead the [. . .] and the hungry He shall enrich (?).[4]

John Tvedtnes references this fragment in his discussion of the Messiah in the Book of Mormon and in the Dead Sea Scrolls. He notes that: "Most of the elements found in this text are found in the messianic passage in Isaiah 61:1–3." He also notes that the elements of the Messiah's mission from both Isaiah and the Dead Sea Scrolls fragment appear in the Book of Mormon, though not all in the same place as they do in Isaiah or the Dead Sea Scrolls.[5]

Mosiah 3:6

> 6 And he shall cast out devils, or the evil spirits which dwell in the hearts of the children of men.

While most of the catalog of Jesus's ministry is unsurprising, this statement shows that Benjamin continues to adapt the angel's message to his people's needs. Nephi had also recorded that Jesus would cast out devils (1 Ne. 11:31); but Benjamin has added a definition. While Old World "devils" are particular spirit entities that enter a person to cause physical, mental, and emotional distress, Benjamin expands "devils" to include "evil spirits." He is thus reminding his listeners of "the evil spirit" he earlier applied to those who followed the local religion (Mosiah 2:32, 37). In other words, Benjamin is

---

[4]Michael Wise, Martin Abegg, Jr. and Edward Cook, *The Dead Sea Scrolls: A New Translation* (San Francisco: HarperSanFrancisco, 1996), 421.

[5]John A. Tvedtnes, *The Most Correct Book: Insights from a Book of Mormon Scholar* (Salt Lake City: Cornerstone, 1999), 334. The same fragment is quoted in Alison V. P. Coutts et al., "Complete Text of Benjamin's Speech with Notes and Comments," in *King Benjamin's Speech*, edited by John W. Welch and Stephen D. Ricks (Provo, Utah: FARMS, 1998), 546–47, however, it is incorrectly identified as 4Q251 rather than the correct 4Q521. It is obviously a typographical error that transposed two numbers. My thanks to John Tvedtnes who tracked down the correct reference for me, email, January 18, 2005.

stressing the function of the "devils/evil spirits" in causing spiritual illness, rather than physical ailments, making this function of Jesus' mission directly relevant to his people. The name of the Messiah will have power to cast that "evil spirit" out from among them. The contentions over alternate religions will be cast from their midst.

Mosiah 3:7

> 7 And lo, he shall suffer temptations, and pain of body, hunger, thirst, and fatigue, even more than man can suffer, except it be unto death; for behold, blood cometh from every pore, so great shall be his anguish for the wickedness and the abominations of his people.

Internal Reference: 1 Nephi 12:10–11 records Nephi's vision of garments being made white in Christ's blood. This redemptive theme clearly links the Savior's blood to his function as Atoner—a different meaning than the other common theme of ridding one's own garments of the blood of others (meaning the discharge of one's spiritual duty).[6] Benjamin then adds the additional detail that Jesus will bleed from every pore, an item that Nephi had not mentioned earlier. (See commentary accompanying verse 11.)

Mosiah 3:8

> 8 And he shall be called Jesus Christ, the Son of God, the Father of heaven and earth, the Creator of all things from the beginning; and his mother shall be called Mary.

Internal Reference: The name of Jesus's mother is another of Benjamin's contributions. Nephi saw her but did not name her (1 Ne. 11:18). According to Coutts et al.: "The name Mary was a common Jewish name. In Hebrew it is spelled Miriam, notably also the name of the sister of Moses (Num. 26:59). The name in Hebrew means 'one who is exalted.' In other words, the mother of the Savior would be called 'one who is exalted.'"[7]

Earlier prophets (e.g., 2 Ne. 25:19) have explicitly associated the Messiah and Jesus. As with the earlier passage in Nephi, the use of "Jesus Christ" as a name is problematic, because "Christ" is a title. (See commentary accompanying 2 Ne. 25:19.)

Vocabulary: Benjamin gives the Messiah a title that is unique to the Book of Mormon. The Messiah is "the Father of heaven and earth." 2 Nephi 25:12 is the first use of this title: "When the day cometh that the Only Begotten of the Father, yea, even the Father of heaven and of earth, shall manifest himself unto them in the flesh, behold, they will reject him. . . . " The same title also appears in Alma 11:39 ("And Amulek said unto him: Yea, he is the very Eternal Father of heaven and earth. . . . ") and in Helaman 14:12 (" . . . Jesus Christ, the Son of God, the Father of heaven and of earth . . . ").

---

[6] 2 Nephi 9:44, Mosiah 2:28, Mormon 9:35
[7] Ibid., 549–50.

Although unique to the Book of Mormon, this title resembles some also used in the Bible: "And I will make thee swear by the Lord, the God of heaven, and the God of the earth, that thou shalt not take a wife unto my son of the daughters of the Canaanites, among whom I dwell" (Gen. 24:3). This verse uses "Lord" instead of "Father" but is the same in emphasizing the creative role, which is assigned to the Lord rather than being an explicit function of the Messiah. However, the Genesis term is not nearly as formulaic as the Book of Mormon title.

Matthew 11:25 comes closest to the Book of Mormon title: "At that time Jesus answered and said, I thank thee, O Father, Lord of heaven and earth, because thou hast hid these things from the wise and prudent, and hast revealed them unto babes." In this verse, the Old Testament form of "Lord of heaven and earth" is a speech of Jesus directed explicitly to God the father. The Book of Mormon, in contrast, consistently refers to Yahweh-Messiah rather than his Father (the Most High God). In both 2 Nephi 25:12 and Mosiah 3:8, "Father of heaven and of earth" follows "only begotten son" or "son of God." Thus, the Book of Mormon presents the very interesting problem that terminology of the Father and the Son refer to the same individual. I am not suggesting that God the Father and Jesus are the same nor that this is what the Book of Mormon intends, but only that the epithets appropriate to Yahweh-Messiah included both. The titles refer to the conceptual realm referenced by our position in relation to the Messiah. When Yahweh-Messiah is in the heavens, he is the Father. When he is in the role of Messiah on earth, he is the Son. (See "Excursus: The Nephite Understanding of God," following 1 Nephi 11.)

The Book of Mormon statements about the Messiah emphasize two aspects—his mission and his divinity. He is proclaimed as divine and termed the creator. Thus, for Nephites, the Messiah is proclaimed as Yahweh. This is a conceptual difference from the way post-exilic Israel viewed the Messiah. The Old World expected a king to reign. In the Davidic tradition, that king was conceptually differentiated from the Lord. For example, in Psalms 2:7, the Lord anoints/establishes the king.[8] In the Book of Mormon, the Messiah is himself the heavenly king. From Nephi on, therefore, Messianic expectations in the Book of Mormon are different from those of the Old World Israelites. Nephi's vision established the person of Jesus as the mortal incarnation of Yahweh and, with that connection, shifted the Messianic expectations from ruler to deity. The Book of Mormon is replete with Messianic expectations, but they are salvific, not regnal. The Book of Mormon expects an Atoning Messiah, not a military conqueror.

Culture: The Maya are the only culture of the New World that has left us writing that can now be deciphered. One of the set descriptions of a god was *ch'ul chaan ch'ul kab*, or

---

[8]"I will declare the decree: the Lord hath said unto me, Thou art my Son; this day have I begotten thee" (Ps. 2:7). Frank Moore Cross, *Canaanite Myth and Hebrew Epic* (Cambridge, Mass.: Harvard University Press, 1973), 257, notes: "Central in these fragments of liturgy is the Canaanite formula of divine sonship of the king which marked the 'high theology' of the Jerusalem court. The formula appears specifically in 2 Samuel 7:14a, Psalms 89:27f, Isaiah 9:5, and in Psalms 2:7."

heavenly god, earthly god.[9] While this is not precisely the father/child image of the Book of Mormon text, it is nevertheless interesting that a divine descriptor would expressly include the two elements of heaven and earth, just as we see in the Book of Mormon phrase. This does not suggest that there is a genetic relationship between the Maya phrase and that of the Book of Mormon. It is simply interesting that this conceptual reference to a deity for both realms would also exist among the Maya whose gods are most typically associated with a single realm of operation.

Variant: The 1830 typesetter inadvertently left off the word *of* in the title for Christ. The title here should read "father of heaven and *of* earth," which conforms to other instances of the same title (2 Ne. 25:12; Hel. 14:12, 16:18).[10]

The glyphs read *ch'ul chaan, ch'ul kab'* or "divine/sacred [one] of heaven, divine/sacred [one] of earth" (my translation).

Mosiah 3:9

> 9 And lo, he cometh unto his own, that salvation might come unto the children of men even through faith on his name; and even after all this they shall consider him a man, and say that he hath a devil, and shall scourge him, and shall crucify him.

Internal Reference: Nephi also wrote of Jesus's crucifixion (1 Ne. 11:33; 2 Ne. 10:3, citing Jacob).

Mosiah 3:10

> 10 And he shall rise the third day from the dead; and behold, he standeth to judge the world; and behold, all these things are done that a righteous judgment might come upon the children of men.

Internal Reference: The detail that Jesus would rise on the third day is new in Benjamin's speech although both Jesus's resurrection (2 Ne. 26:1) and his role as a judge were already known (1 Ne. 13:33, 22:21; 2 Ne. 9:15; etc).

Mosiah 3:11

> 11 For behold, and also his blood atoneth for the sins of those who have fallen by the transgression of Adam, who have died not knowing the will of God concerning them, or who have ignorantly sinned.

Culture: Verse 7's mention of Jesus bleeding at every pore provides the framework for verse 11, in which blood is the agent of atonement. From our modern perspective, such an association underscores the significance of Christ's suffering in

[9]The translation John Montgomery gives is "heavenly god, earthly god." The word *ch'ul* is "sacred, god." *Chaan* means "the heavens" and *kab'* is "the earth." The appearance of the two together is eerily similar to the Book of Mormon's title "Lord of heaven and earth." John Montgomery, *Dictionary of Maya Hieroglyphs* (New York: Hippocrene Books, 2002), 83.

[10]Skousen, *Analysis of Textual Variants*, 2:1167–68.

Gethsemane. For Benjamin's audience, however, a powerful cultural meaning linked blood and efficacy. According to Maya scholars Schele and Miller:

> Blood was the mortar of ancient Maya ritual life. The Maya let blood on every important occasion in the life of the individual and in the life of the community. It was the substance offered by kings and other nobility to seal ceremonial events. . . . After the birth of an heir, the king performed a blood sacrifice, drawing his own substance as a[n] offering to his ancestors. Human sacrifice, offered to sanctify the installation of a king in office, was in some cases recorded as a vital part of accession imagery. . . . At death, Maya kings were placed in richly furnished tombs that often displayed the imagery of the watery Underworld, their walls painted the color of blood or in blood symbols. In the Maya view, none of these behaviors was bizarre or exotic but necessary to sustain the world.[11]

While they are here discussing the evidence from the post-Book of Mormon period, evidence for the conceptual power of blood dates back to Olmec time (at least to 900 B.C.).[12] We have already seen what seem to be the beginning of many practices that are articulated more fully in later Maya culture, and we will see more. The Mesoamerican concept of auto-sacrifice required that blood drawn from different and specific parts of the body, depending on the ritual. For Mesoamericans, the Messiah's bleeding from every pore would indicate the measure of his self-sacrifice, involving, as it was, his entire body. The Messiah was the self-sacrifice for his people.

Benjamin stresses the atoning power of the Messiah's blood. While his people would have been culturally disposed to attribute other-worldly power to blood, atonement was not part of their understanding. Thus, Benjamin is singling out this aspect of the Messiah's mission from other possible associations with blood. It would be easy for his people to assume that the Messiah's sacrifice was simply another of the kingly blood sacrifices they were already familiar with; but that would be a grave mistake. Benjamin articulates the theology of the Messiah's atoning power in association with his blood—the medium that made the atonement effective.

Scripture: Benjamin notes that the Messiah's sacrifice is universal. It covers even those who know nothing of it—those who might be described as "without law." They sin in ignorance, committing acts that are violations of the law, but they may be forgiven such transgressions because they do not know the law. While some sins may be so heinous as to be universally accepted as sin, Benjamin is here not talking about that category of behavior but rather about sin as related to the will of the person who commits the act. Where the law is known, not making the correct choice is sin. Where the law is not known, an individual who makes an incorrect choice may not be considered as sinning. Therefore, according to Benjamin, the nature of sin cannot deal with the action alone

---

[11] Linda Schele and Mary Ellen Miller, *The Blood of Kings* (New York: George Braziller, 1986), 14–15.

[12] David A. Freidel, "Preparing the Way," in *The Olmec World: Ritual and Rulership* (Princeton, N.J.: Princeton University Art Museum, 1996), 6–7; Karl A. Taube, "The Rainmakers: The Olmec and Their Contribution to Mesoamerican Belief and Ritual," in ibid., 99–100.

but rather with the intent and will of the actor. This emphasis on intent is the focus of the Savior's discourse on the Sermon on the Mount (Matt. 5, 3 Ne. 12).

Mosiah 3:12

> 12 But wo, wo unto him who knoweth that he rebelleth against God! For salvation cometh to none such except it be through repentance and faith on the Lord Jesus Christ.

Rhetoric: Here Benjamin reprises the earlier theme (Mosiah 2:37) that those who chose to follow the "evil spirit" were rebels against Yahweh. Now Benjamin proclaims woe upon those rebels. Why does this curse appear in the middle of "glad tidings" of the atonement?

Benjamin has just taught that Yahweh-Messiah performs an atoning sacrifice (v. 12), the only means to salvation. Between establishing the need for an atonement and assuring his listeners that only Yahweh-Messiah can perform the atonement, Benjamin describes the power of blood and warns against rebellion. In this context, it seems likely that Benjamin is warning those in the assembly who might still feel allegiance to the other religion—one which emphasizes blood but without any power to atone. It is the cultural context that links blood with rebellion and, hence, explains Benjamin's condemnation. Such an association seems missing from any other context.

Another explanation is that this interpolated curse could be simply an aside that occurred to Benjamin as he spoke. The speech is so carefully crafted, however, that positing a hasty insertion contradicts the rest of the carefully argued text.

Mosiah 3:13

> 13 And the Lord God hath sent his holy prophets among all the children of men, to declare these things to every kindred, nation, and tongue, that thereby whosoever should believe that Christ should come, the same might receive remission of their sins, and rejoice with exceedingly great joy, even as though he had already come among them.

Rhetoric: Benjamin is clearly moving toward the new covenant he wishes to establish among his people: to follow the Atoning Messiah. Now, however, he must help his people understand how the new covenant is related to the covenant they have already made to obey the law of Moses. Thus, this verse is a transition to achieve two tasks. First, he establishes that the covenant with Yahweh-Messiah is available to all people. This point is critical because the covenant must include the blood-line Gentiles in the group, not only the Zarahemlaites who have intermarried with the surrounding people for the past 500 years, but the lineal Gentiles who constituted a significant fraction of the population of the city of Nephi. (See 2 Nephi, Part 1: Context, Chapter 1, "The Historical Setting of 2 Nephi.") Considering the exclusivity of the law of Moses in the Old World, the uncharacteristic religious inclusiveness is itself another indicator of the presence of Gentiles among the Nephites. Universal inclusivity was important in the religious/

political life of the New World long before Peter's vision of the gospel net began missionary efforts among Gentiles in the Old World. Benjamin stresses to his listeners that the prophets' mission was "[to] all the children of men, to declare these things to every kindred, nation, and tongue."

Second, Benjamin highlights the Messiah's importance, even before his mortal mission. When an act that will take place a hundred years in the future is declared as the only means of salvation, what is one to do today? Benjamin's response is that his people (the believers) "might receive remission of their sins, and rejoice with exceedingly great joy, even as though he had already come among them." Although future, the atonement has current validity. The sacred promise of the atonement from the beginning of the world allows those who live prior to the physical event to experience its full benefit.

Although we have relatively few specifics about the nature of the religious contentions Benjamin has countered, Sherem had used the far distant Messiah as one of his arguments against Jacob (Jacob 7:2). It is not an unreasonable argument, after all. How can next year's rain benefit this year's corn? How could a distant Messiah benefit people in the here and now? It seems entirely possible that this argument continued to be used against Benjamin's religion.

Mosiah 3:14–15

> 14 Yet the Lord God saw that his people were a stiffnecked people, and he appointed unto them a law, even the law of Moses.
> 15 And many signs, and wonders, and types, and shadows showed he unto them, concerning his coming; and also holy prophets spake unto them concerning his coming; and yet they hardened their hearts, and understood not that the law of Moses availeth nothing except it were through the atonement of his blood.

These two verses must be read together for the logical impact Benjamin desired. To establish a new covenant with the Messiah, Benjamin must justify superseding the Mosaic law but without invalidating it. To do this, he notes that the law of Moses is from Yahweh but that Yahweh gave it because of the people's "stiffneckedness." The unstated but clear conclusion is that this is a lesser law, one suited to a lesser people, while a people prepared for a greater covenant could go beyond the law of Moses. In this verse, Benjamin not only posits the possibility of the new covenant, but also relates it to the people's ability to accept it. This connection echoes his earlier emphasis that his audience consists of people who have chosen to follow him and Yahweh, and to cast out the contentious.

Benjamin explains the limitations of the law of Moses. While the Mosaic covenant is important, even that covenant depends on the atonement of Yahweh-Messiah. Benjamin purposefully invokes the image of the Messiah's atoning blood, not only setting up associations with the Mesoamerican conceptions of blood sacrifice but also with the blood sacrifices of the Mosaic law.

It seems reasonable to posit the people's familiarity with the Israelite Day of Atonement. Biblical scholar William Smith describes it as "the great day of national humiliation, and the only one commanded in the Mosaic Law. The mode of its observance is described in Leviticus 16."[13] In addition to the well-known practice of transferring sin to goats (the origin of the term "scapegoat") the ceremonies of atonement prominently feature blood sacrifice. Smith continues:

> [The priest] next sacrificed the young bullock as a sin-offering for himself and his family. Taking with him some of the blood of the bullock, he filled a censer with burning coals from the brazen altar, took a handful of incense, and entered into the most holy place. He then threw the incense upon the coals and enveloped the mercy-seat in a cloud of smoke. Then, dipping his finger into the blood, he sprinkled it seven times before the mercy-seat eastward. The goat upon which the lot "For Jehovah" had fallen was then slain and the high priest sprinkled its blood before the mercy-seat in the same manner as he had done that of the bullock. Going out from the Holy of Holies he purified the holy place, sprinkling some of the blood of both the victims on the altar of incense.[14]

Hebrews 13:10–13 clearly equates the sin offering of Exodus 29:10–14 with Jesus's atonement—including the casting out of the "scapegoat."[15] Since the Day of Atonement occurred five days before the Feast of Tabernacles, if Benjamin's speech is occurring during a Feast of Tabernacles as suggested (see commentary accompanying Mosiah 2:1), the people would have had a fresh reminder of the link between blood and atonement. Their ceremony differed somewhat in time and location and had to differ because of the difficulty of coming up with bulls and goats (which are not attested for Mesoamerica). The point, however, for Benjamin's discourse is that blood is associated with atonement, both in the law of Moses and through the Messiah.

What Benjamin has done, in a deft and swift stroke, is to equate the blood of the sacrifice on the Day of Atonement under the law of Moses with the future atoning blood of the Messiah. For Benjamin, they are the same blood, and it is the Messiah's future blood that makes efficacious the ritual blood of the sacrificial animal under the law of Moses. Thus, the Atoning Messiah not only supersedes the law of Moses, but is the foundation from which the law of Moses draws its own atoning power.

Mosiah 3:16

> 16 And even if it were possible that little children could sin they could not be saved; but I say unto you they are blessed; for behold, as in Adam, or by nature, they fall, even so the blood of Christ atoneth for their sins.

This interjection of the salvation status of little children can, I believe, best be explained as an undercurrent in the religious controversy that had plagued his people. Certainly, his teaching presumes some controversy on the subject.

---

[13]William Smith, *Smith's Bible Dictionary* (Old Tappan, N.J.: Fleming H. Revell, 1970), 61.
[14]Ibid.
[15]Coutts et al., "Complete Text of Benjamin's Speech," 554.

Benjamin opens with a hypothetical: "if it were possible that little children could sin." He thus reminds the people of their understanding that little children are incapable of sin. Benjamin is not explaining this principle but simply using it as part of his example. He also takes for granted the people's understanding that the ability of the children to sin depends on their age. There is a point where the same act changes from not being a sin to becoming a sin for that person. That point depends on some concept of the child's no longer being "little."

He next significantly comments that the Messiah's blood atones for children's sins—meaning things they do that would be sin were they capable of sinning. Other than simply stating that the Messiah atones for children, why is Benjamin bringing this up? It is critical to remember that this statement follows his declaration that Yahweh-Messiah makes efficacious even the atonement available through the law of Moses. He is contrasting the law of Moses to the future Messiah. His apparently unrelated comment about the children is part of that same carefully crafted contrast, one which he expects his audience to understand without his making it explicit.

Nephi's teachings on baptism emphasize the choices that one must make to enter the baptismal covenant:

> And he commandeth all men that they must repent, and be baptized in his name, having perfect faith in the Holy One of Israel, or they cannot be saved in the kingdom of God.
>
> And if they will not repent and believe in his name, and be baptized in his name, and endure to the end, they must be damned; for the Lord God, the Holy One of Israel, has spoken it. (2 Ne. 9:23–24)

> And now, if the Lamb of God, he being holy, should have need to be baptized by water, to fulfil all righteousness, O then, how much more need have we, being unholy, to be baptized, yea, even by water! (2 Ne. 31:5)

> And he said unto the children of men: Follow thou me. Wherefore, my beloved brethren, can we follow Jesus save we shall be willing to keep the commandments of the Father? (2 Ne. 31:10)

In each statement, Nephi stresses that being baptized requires a purposive action—recognizing the need to repent, then repenting. Jesus was baptized as a man. Therefore, we follow his example. When we follow Jesus, we must keep commandments, which assumes our ability both to understand what a commandment requires and the ability to actually perform the action. In short, baptism requires the ability to make responsible choices. Modern Saints take such a requirement for granted, but would Benjamin's people have done so?

Because Benjamin's people followed the law of Moses, they believed that salvation came through the covenant, which was part of their birthright and was physically symbolized in males by circumcision at the age of eight days. Thus, according to the law of Moses, salvation begins with infants; yet according to the Messiah's gospel, it must come later, when the person making the covenant is capable of responsible choices. For Benjamin's people, the dissonance between the law of Moses and the hope in the Messiah concerning children was apparently a point of discussion, even of controversy. Benjamin is here bringing the Messiah's atonement into an arena that dissenters would have claimed as the exclusive domain of the law of Moses—the salvation of children. While the atonement saves us from sin, it also saves us before sin. Just as the Messiah's blood is the effective aspect of Mosaic atonement, so too is the Messiah's blood the effective aspect of the salvation of children—not the blood of the circumcision.[16]

The rest of Benjamin's argument is important for understanding verse 19 below. Even though children are not capable of sin, they are still "fallen," for "as in Adam, or by nature, they fall." We expect the association of Adam and the fall, but the concept of "by nature" is unique to Benjamin. Benjamin equates "nature" with the fall. Because it occurs in children who cannot sin, the "fall/nature" is an inheritance of Adam, not a personal defect in the child. This definition is critical to understanding Benjamin's discussion of the "natural man" (v. 19).

Mosiah 3:17

> 17 And moreover, I say unto you, that there shall be no other name given nor any other way nor means whereby salvation can come unto the children of men, only in and through the name of Christ, the Lord Omnipotent.

This verse is a transition from the previously significant "blood" to "name," the concept he first introduced in verse 9. This transition is critical to his task in this sermon, which is to persuade his people to take upon them the name of Yahweh-Messiah to symbolize their unified covenant. In the ancient world, a name itself had power, a fact of which Benjamin shows himself aware. Margaret Barker, a former president of the Society for Old Testament Study, suggests that one of the Deuteronomic reforms involved a shift in the religious conception of the name of Yahweh.[17] She suggests:

> Older texts suggest that before the reform the Name had been simply a synonym for the presence of Yahweh, and not a substitute. There are several examples of this:
>
> Behold the Name of Yahweh comes from far,
> Burning with his anger and in thick rising smoke;
> His lips are full of indignation
> And his tongue is like a devouring fire. (Isa. 30:27)
>
> This is a fire theophany in anthropomorphic terms. Similarly we find in the Hebrew of Ps. 75:5 "Your Name draws near." In Ps. 20:1–2 Yahweh, the Name, dwells in the sanctuary:

---

[16]The physical representation of the Mosaic covenant is clearly inscribed in male flesh. Nevertheless, women were part of the covenant. While our modern society is much more cognizant of the need for equal recognition, the Israelite patriarchal society was not so understanding. I suggest that women were part of the covenant because they belonged to a man. They were wives or daughters and participated in their husband's or father's covenant.

[17]Margaret Barker, *The Great Angel: A Study of Israel's Second God* (Louisville, Ky.: Westminster/John Knox Press, 1992), 97.

> Yahweh answer you in the day of trouble!
> The Name of the God of Jacob protect you!
> May he send you help from the sanctuary,
> And give you support from Zion.
>
> With this we might compare "the dwelling place of thy name" (Ps. 74:7); or "Go now to my place that was in Shiloh, where I made my Name dwell at first" (Jer. 7:12).[18]

As I have suggested (see 1 Nephi, Part 1: Context, Chapter 1, "The Historical Setting of 1 Nephi"), Lehi was more strongly affiliated with the older aspects of Israel's religion. Along with the emphasis on the Atoning Messiah, it is reasonable that this older conception of Yahweh's name would also be part of the Nephite religious inheritance. When Benjamin asks that they take upon themselves the name, he was asking for more than a casual identification with a religious group.

Benjamin also deftly uses the phrase "children of men" as a transition between the salvation effected on behalf of children, his earlier idea, and the concept that salvation is available to all human beings.

Internal Reference: Nephi also taught that Yahweh-Messiah's name has salvific power: "And now, behold, my beloved brethren, this is the way; and there is none other way nor name given under heaven whereby man can be saved in the kingdom of God. And now, behold, this is the doctrine of Christ, and the only and true doctrine of the Father, and of the Son, and of the Holy Ghost, which is one God, without end. Amen" (2 Ne. 31:21).

Vocabulary: The construction of **no . . . only** in this verse should be read as **no . . . except**. "No other way nor means whereby salvation can come unto the children of men **only [except]** in and through the name of Christ.[19]

Mosiah 3:18

> 18 For behold he judgeth, and his judgment is just; and the infant perisheth not that dieth in his infancy; but men drink damnation to their own souls except they humble themselves and become as little children, and believe that salvation was, and is, and is to come, in and through the atoning blood of Christ, the Lord Omnipotent.

Now the themes of salvation/damnation come together. The gospel of Christ requires conscious decisions. The child who dies in infancy will not perish spiritually because the atonement suffices for any actions that would otherwise be sin in one capable of responsible choice. However, for adults who make their own choices, sin is possible, and those men will "drink damnation to their own souls." Benjamin emphasizes that, while the infant is saved automatically, men are not. The difference lies in their accountability. While the same actions in men spell sin

---

[18]Ibid., 97–98.

[19]Royal Skousen, *Analysis of Textual Variants of the Book of Mormon*, THE CRITICAL TEXT OF THE BOOK OF MORMON (Provo, Utah: Foundation for Ancient Research and Mormon Studies, 2005), Vol. 4, Part 3, 3:1847.

and damnation, the infant is free from sin because of the atoning power of the future Messiah.

The damnation of the men is significant for two reasons. First, it mildly refers to the "old men, young men" that we saw in Mosiah 2:40. Once again, Benjamin is noting that their willful choices ("willful rebellion") can lead to damnation. Second, Benjamin dangles before them an all-important "unless," which serves two rhetorical purposes.

On one level, it forms a transition between the themes of damnation and salvation. On the other, it instructs his hearers in the characteristics required for salvation. Fittingly, he stresses the automatic salvation of infants by telling his audience that they must "become as little children." He reemphasizes the salvation of the infants and extends the power that saves them (the Messianic atonement) to the men, adding to the image the humility of children. Nevertheless, this mention of "blood" may hint that the salvation of the men lies in the Messiah's blood and not in their circumcision, just as the salvation of the infants lay also in the Messiah's blood (and not in their circumcision).

Mosiah 3:19

> 19 For the natural man is an enemy to God, and has been from the fall of Adam, and will be, forever and ever, unless he yields to the enticings of the Holy Spirit, and putteth off the natural man and becometh a saint through the atonement of Christ the Lord, and becometh as a child, submissive, meek, humble, patient, full of love, willing to submit to all things which the Lord seeth fit to inflict upon him, even as a child doth submit to his father.

The rhetorical function of this verse is to explain the "unless" introduced in the previous verse. Why should there be a difference between infants and men? Because of the condition that includes both the infants and the men—the fall that means both of them are in a "natural" state. (According to v. 16, "natural" is equivalent to "fallen.") In verse 16 the infant was fallen, yet saved. In verse 19, men are fallen (natural), yet condemned. Why?

The natural man is condemned because of his fallen nature and because of his sins. Because men make the willful decision to sin, in contrast to infants who cannot make such decisions, such men are enemies to Yahweh. This injunction echoes Benjamin's earlier preaching against those who willfully rebel against Yahweh—a good definition of an enemy. Thus, Benjamin is consistent: Those who choose to follow the "evil spirit" by choosing to sin are enemies to Yahweh. Once again, however, there is an "unless," which is couched in the language of transformation: "*unless* [italics mine] he yields to the enticings of the Holy Spirit, and putteth off the natural man and becometh a saint through the atonement of Christ the Lord, and becometh as a child, submissive, meek, humble, patient, full of love, willing to submit to all things." The language Benjamin uses is very descriptive and instructive.

First, while we become "natural man" because of the fall, we are not left alone. The Holy Spirit entices us. The choice to follow God is not distasteful, but rather a recognition of the joyous taste of the gospel and the choice to acquire more. Next, to yield to those enticings requires that we transform our natures: to put off the natural man and to become a "saintly" child. Benjamin then describes the attributes of that "child."

When we remember that the ancient world made no distinction between religion and politics (see commentary accompanying 2 Nephi 32:1), the quality of "submissiveness" takes on added meaning beyond the spiritual realm in which we could see its applications. In the context of Benjamin's times, submissiveness should be understood as enjoining upon his hearers support for their new identity as a people and for the new government, while rejecting any lingering sympathies toward the old religion.

Mosiah 3:20–21

> 20 And moreover, I say unto you, that the time shall come when the knowledge of a Savior shall spread throughout every nation, kindred, tongue, and people.
> 21 And behold, when that time cometh, none shall be found blameless before God, except it be little children, only through repentance and faith on the name of the Lord God Omnipotent.

Benjamin concludes this section of the discourse by declaring that "the time shall come when the knowledge of a Savior shall spread throughout every nation, kindred, tongue, and people." Why does he select this theme as his conclusion?

He has been talking directly to and about his own people, yet he now broadens his message to include others as recipients of the gospel message. Modern Saints would hear this message in the context of universal missionary work and think, "Of course," but the essence of Benjamin's message is not the spread of the gospel (v. 20) but rather the application of gospel requirements to all people (v. 21). Benjamin contrasts "natural" yet "saved" infants with "natural" yet "condemned" men. What is the difference? It is the knowledge of the gospel. With it, men either choose to obey it ("yield to the enticings of the Holy Spirit," v. 19) or live contrary to it ("come out in open rebellion against God," 2:37). What does this mean for those who, like children, do not know the law, yet, as men, are capable of choosing? Benjamin assures his listeners that they may yet be saved (Mosiah 3:11).

The New World contained more people who did not know the law than those who did. Benjamin's people might have felt that they were being held to a higher standard and, hence, were vulnerable to greater condemnation than their Lamanite brethren. To combat this possible misconception, Benjamin stresses that eventually all will be accountable to gospel standards. His listeners are accountable right now; but eventually "none shall be found blameless before God, except it be little children, only through repentance and faith on the name of the Lord God Omnipotent."

Mosiah 3:22

> 22 And even at this time, when thou shalt have taught thy people the things which the Lord thy God hath commanded thee, even then are they found no more blameless in the sight of God, only according to the words which I have spoken unto thee.

Benjamin's conclusion places his people among those who know of the Atoning Messiah and are therefore responsible for their actions under the Messiah's law. The fact that they are "no more blameless" may indicate that some, through their Zarahemlaite heritage, might have considered themselves as people who were without law and therefore were saved along with the children. Benjamin closes this loophole. Everyone in the congregation is "no more blameless."

Benjamin is quoting the angel, which suggests that he also derived the preceding part of the discourse from that source as well. However, the structure and delivery of the message are Benjamin's, adapted to his people's specific needs at that moment. It is a great tribute to the power and art of Benjamin's discourse that it can still move audiences worlds away in time and culture from the original setting.

Vocabulary: "Only according to the words which I have spoken," should be read "**except** according to the words. . . "[20]

Mosiah 3:23–24

> 23 And now I have spoken the words which the Lord God hath commanded me.
> 24 And thus saith the Lord: They shall stand as a bright testimony against this people, at the judgment day; whereof they shall be judged, every man according to his works, whether they be good, or whether they be evil.

Benjamin here reiterates the sacred nature of the text he has delivered. Verse 22 has indicated that the people are "no more blameless," and now assures them that this occasion, this sermon, this angelic text, has changed their status so that "they shall be judged, every man according to his works, whether they be good, or whether they be evil." The hearing of the word has placed them under the power of the Word.

Mosiah 3:25–27

> 25 And if they be evil they are consigned to an awful view of their own guilt and abominations, which doth cause them to shrink from the presence of the Lord into a state of misery and endless torment, from whence they can no more return; therefore they have drunk damnation to their own souls.
> 26 Therefore, they have drunk out of the cup of the wrath of God, which justice could no more deny unto them than it could deny that Adam should fall because of his partaking of the forbidden fruit; therefore, mercy could have claim on them no more forever.

---

[20] Skousen, *Analysis of Textual Variants*, 3:1847.

27 And their torment is as a lake of fire and brimstone, whose flames are unquenchable, and whose smoke ascendeth up forever and ever. Thus hath the Lord commanded me. Amen.

Benjamin reprises his earlier discussion of the fate of the enemy to Yahweh. He had earlier stated in Mosiah 2:38–39:

> Therefore if that man repenteth not, and remaineth and dieth an enemy to God, the demands of divine justice do awaken his immortal soul to a lively sense of his own guilt, which doth cause him to shrink from the presence of the Lord, and doth fill his breast with guilt, and pain, and anguish, which is like an unquenchable fire, whose flame ascendeth up forever and ever.
>
> And now I say unto you, that mercy hath no claim on that man; therefore his final doom is to endure a never-ending torment.

Benjamin stresses the "awful view of their own guilt" (3:25) and "lively sense of his own guilt" (2:38). "Shrink from the presence of the Lord" also appears twice (2:38, 3:25). The anguish of the damned is "like an unquenchable fire, whose flame ascendeth up forever and ever," "whose flames are unquenchable, and whose smoke ascendeth up forever and ever" (2:38, 3:27). Both passages describe the demands of justice, under which "mercy hath no claim" (2:38, 3:26). In short, Benjamin is intentionally reprising that earlier text. Why?

Benjamin is concluding a speech unit that began with Mosiah 2:31. The unit is divided into two sections, each dealing with a particular type of spiritual culpability. The first discusses the religio-political "contentions" among his people that he has quelled. While they are a believing people ("I would that ye should do as ye have hitherto done," 2:31), they might still be enticed by the "evil spirit" (2:33). He who yields to this evil spirit is willfully rebelling against Yahweh and "drinketh damnation to his own soul" (2:33), a phrase repeated in Mosiah 3:25. Benjamin pronounces this religio-political culpability on all "except it be your little children that have not been taught concerning these things" (Mosiah 2:34), a corollary to the innocence of little children in the second part.

The two sections are quite tightly correlated, with the first emphasizing the current political situation, and the second emphasizing the spiritual expansion of that same principle. The first half of the discourse addresses the temporal *now* while the second half addresses the spiritual *forever*. The parallelism between the two sections reemphasizes the general principles, while the differences highlight the different temporal and spiritual arenas to which the principles are applied.

Text: This verse ends a chapter in the 1830. The chapter break concludes the first set discourse, which began in our current Mosiah 2.

Mosiah 4

Mosiah 4:1

1 And now, it came to pass that when king Benjamin had made an end of speaking the words which had been delivered unto him by the angel of the Lord, that he cast his eyes round about on the multitude, and behold they had fallen to the earth, for the fear of the Lord had come upon them.

History: Benjamin has concluded a specific section of his discourse and now observes the effect of his words on the assembled population. He could easily see that they had "fallen to the earth" and could readily interpret their response.

It is also possible that some of this process was part of a public pageant, one also known in the Old World:

> On the theme of eternity, the closing sound of every royal *acclamatio*, King Benjamin ended his address, which so overpowered the people that they "had fallen to the earth, for the fear of the Lord had come upon them" (Mosiah 4:1). This was the kind of proskynesis at which Benjamin aimed! The proskynesis was the falling to the earth (literally, "kissing the ground") in the presence of the king by which all the human race on the day of the coronation demonstrated its submission to divine authority; it was an unfailing part of the Old World New Year's rites as of any royal audience.[1]

Whether this rite would endure unchanged for more than 500 years and in two widely separated cultures is an unanswerable question. Nevertheless, it seems anthropologically sound that lowering oneself to the ground before a monarch communicates respect and humility in many cultures and contexts, whether it is specifically derived from the Old World or not.

If the event were purely spontaneous, a few of the most susceptible may have first fallen, then their neighbors, recognizing the appropriateness of the gesture, would have followed the example of those who began the posture. If the event were orchestrated, then the people would have expected the ceremony to include a particular point at which this action was required. Which scenario best fits Benjamin's speech?

As I read Benjamin's address, it seems more likely to me that the action was a spontaneous response to the power of the speech itself. Although Nibley suggests that the theme of eternity marked the end of a coronation declaration, the coronation event is buried in the text, a simple declaration many verses earlier. Benjamin has not yet reached his climax—giving his people their new name. Therefore, the people seemed overcome by the realization of these principles to

---

[1]Hugh Nibley, *An Approach to the Book of Mormon* (Salt Lake City: Church of Jesus Christ of Latter-day Saints, 1957), 264.

them. He has pointedly addressed their recent difficulties, warned of the potential for continued contention, and spelled out the implications for both political prosperity/poverty and religious salvation/damnation. This was indeed a very personal speech, which they understood on a very personal level.

Text: This verse, a new chapter in the 1830 edition of the Book of Mormon, presumably was also marked by as the beginning of a new section on the plates themselves. Mormon saw something in Benjamin's discourse as concluding one part and beginning something new. It could have been as simple as the end of quoted material, since chapters frequently end at such a point.

Yet even though Benjamin's discourse has reached a conclusion and we return to the narrative of the event itself, the event is not over. Mormon provides a transition at this point in a synopsis that occupies verses 1–3 and the very beginning of verse 4. It seems unlikely that he is simply copying the record on the plate because the text is clearly past tense and descriptive.

Mosiah 4:2

> 2 And they had viewed themselves in their own carnal state, even less than the dust of the earth. And they all cried aloud with one voice, saying: O have mercy, and apply the atoning blood of Christ that we may receive forgiveness of our sins, and our hearts may be purified; for we believe in Jesus Christ, the Son of God, who created heaven and earth, and all things; who shall come down among the children of men.

History: As with the proskynesis event, the "one voice" declaration also might have been a familiar ritual from the pageant. Nibley has observed:

> In the ancient world, the *hazzan*, the *praecentor*, or the *stasiarch*, would be handed a piece of paper. . . . Then the emperor . . . or someone else would tell him what he wanted the people to chant. . . . The whole thing is directed by the man on the tower. The old man, the *praecentor*, comes down, they ask questions, the king interprets the law to them, and they all answer together. . . . It isn't as if they all spontaneously recited this whole thing in one voice. It says it was in one voice, but that's the way it was done.[2]

Mormon's synopsis of the event is not the original text. "And they had viewed themselves in their own carnal state, even less than the dust of the earth" (v. 2). This sentence is the motive of the proskynesis, but it requires being inside the mind of the entire population. The address certainly had an effect upon the people. It is quite possible that these were the precise feelings of every member of the prostrate population. However, it is much more likely that it is an interpretation of the event than an exact record. The language is taken from Benjamin's address and presages the beginning of Benjamin's next discourse, thus continuing to suggest that Mormon is creating a summary by drawing on information from both the previous and subsequent portions of the address. It seems likely to me that the cry of the

---

[2]Hugh Nibley, quoted in Alison V. P. Coutts et al., "Complete Text of Benjamin's Speech with Notes and Comments," in *King Benjamin's Speech*, edited by John W. Welch and Stephen D. Ricks (Provo, Utah: FARMS, 1998), 571.

people may be reported as Mormon's summary-interpretation, or that of the original writer's.

Whether this response to Benjamin's discourse is spontaneous or scripted, however, the people's reaction was the same. They were so profoundly humbled that the Spirit visited them (v. 3).

Mosiah 4:3

> 3 And it came to pass that after they had spoken these words the Spirit of the Lord came upon them, and they were filled with joy, having received a remission of their sins, and having peace of conscience, because of the exceeding faith which they had in Jesus Christ who should come, according to the words which king Benjamin had spoken unto them.

Scripture: The people have asked for the effects of the atonement to come upon them, and the Spirit responds by assuring them of the remission of their sins. They are filled with the joy that Benjamin had described in his "tidings." Significantly, joy in the Book of Mormon is often related to experiences with the Spirit. (See comments on 2 Nephi 2:25.)

History: According to contemporary LDS theology, the remission of sins requires baptism. Perhaps we may assume that all of the people were already baptized. While this may have been the case, the text does not say so, and the historical context suggests that baptism may not have been a universal event in Nephite/Zarahemlaite life.

As noted in the comments on 2 Nephi 31 where baptism is introduced to Nephi's people, baptism performs a cleansing function, not the modern triple function of cleansing, accepting Christ by covenant, and becoming a member of his church. Baptism's covenantal declaration of belief in Yahweh-Messiah does not become an explicit theme in the Book of Mormon until Alma$_1$ begins baptizing in the Waters of Mormon.

Would all of the assembled people have been baptized? Certainly it is possible, but Mosiah$_1$ (Benjamin's father) would have had to institute it and require it of the entire people. The Zarahemlaites had forgotten Yahweh and lost most of the Mosaic law, but baptism prior to Christ's earthly mission was known in the Old World only as a cleansing ritual. Only the Nephites, before Christ, associated that cleansing with the Messiah's mission. Thus, the Zarahemlaites would have had no tradition of baptism connected with the Messiah, if they had any such rite at all. Mosiah might have imposed it upon the people through his authority as king, but this action would have violated the very nature of the ordinance, which requires repentance and a willing change of heart as prerequisites to accepting the Messiah. This process is inconsistent with a mandated ritual, although the Old World certainly saw later examples of politically imposed baptisms.

The political and religious difficulties stemming from the clash of cultures that continued into Benjamin's reign suggest that his people felt no universal agreement about the need for baptism as a signal of accepting Yahweh-Messiah. Although the message about the Messiah was not new to them, as we have seen, the Messianic focus of Benjamin's speech and the particulars of their covenant suggest that this aspect is new to the people, at least on such a scale.

Nephi's introduction of baptism reveals it as a new covenant, then, and one that had an ambiguous fit into known ritual. (See commentary on 2 Nephi 32:1.) When Benjamin declares the Messiah's atonement, he says nothing about baptism as a requirement. Rather, he emphasizes the atonement itself and Christ as its provider. He implies that his people still understand the law of Moses as the means of atonement for sin. This information, combined with Alma's new emphasis on baptism, suggests that, at this point in Nephite history, baptism is not widely practiced.

When the Spirit descended upon the assembled population of the land of Zarahemla, the collective people's sins were cleansed. Probably many among them were not baptized, yet their faith made the atonement efficacious. In this pre-Christian environment where the forward-looking rites mixed with the current law of Moses, it appears that the communal function of the Day of Atonement sacrifice prevailed over the association between the individual acceptance of Christian baptism. For Benjamin's people, their communal acceptance stood in place of the individual baptism. Speaking from their understanding about the remission of sin through the application of sacrificial blood, they plead with Yahweh to "apply the atoning blood of Christ that we may receive forgiveness of our sins" (Mosiah 4:2).

Mosiah 4:4

> 4 And king Benjamin again opened his mouth and began to speak unto them, saying: My friends and my brethren, my kindred and my people, I would again call your attention, that ye may hear and understand the remainder of my words which I shall speak unto you.

Text: Mormon is again quoting the original document, not summarizing it.

Culture: Benjamin addresses himself to four groups: (1) friends, (2) brethren, (3) kindred, and (4) people. It is easy to understand "friends," "kindred," and "people." "Friends" was a category that both included and surpassed kin, which clearly denotes a genealogical relationship. In Nephite society, "kindred" would be a tribal designation, while "people" refers to the entire assembly, not just the Nephites.

But "brethren" is an oddity. In its strictest sense, it means male siblings. However, Benjamin cannot mean this definition, since "kindred," which would include brothers, is another category. I argue that, just as we modern Latter-day Saints use the kin terms "brother" and "sister" to mean a gospel relationship, not a genetic one, so Benjamin was probably likewise referring to male cobelievers. The later Nahuatl language also used kin terms for social purposes.[3] Inside the overall "people" there were believers and those who did not yet believe, even though they were part of the community. Under these circumstances, where there were both

---

[3]Brant A. Gardner, "A Structural and Semantic Analysis of Classical Nahuatl Kinship Terminology," in *Estudios de Cultura Nahuatl* 15 (1982): 89–124.

believers and nonbelievers in the same community, the term "brethren" becomes an appropriate address to that portion of the community who were already believers. Only this division between believers and nonbelievers in the same community appears to adequately explain the four terms of address.

Rhetoric: Benjamin here again "call[s] your attention." As earlier, (Mosiah 3:1), he refocuses the people's attention with this appellation from the distraction occasioned by their outcry, falling to earth, and descent of the Spirit. The phrase acts as a reconvening, once the congregation has savored the joyous effects of the Spirit. Obviously time has passed, although there is no indication of how much.

Mosiah 4:5

> 5 For behold, if the knowledge of the goodness of God at this time has awakened you to a sense of your nothingness, and your worthless and fallen state—

Text: Probably this verse influenced Mormon's choice of words in his synoptic remarks (v. 2).

Scripture: Benjamin is referring to the people's humility before Yahweh, a quality which precedes repentance and forgiveness. Clearly the people had experienced both, and Benjamin knew it by the Spirit.

Rhetoric: Verses 5–8 form a logical set in that they progress naturally from one theme to another. However, verse 10 reiterates the concept begun in verse 5. Benjamin is a sufficiently talented speaker that this second iteration is not a mere repetition. Nevertheless, the sequence is rather like an aside, a reminder to Benjamin's listeners that they have already heard this discussion. Such a characteristic is more typical of oral discourse than a written text. I believe that there is considerable evidence that Benjamin's first discourse was very tightly crafted and probably written, or at least composed mentally prior to delivery, while this speech may have been delivered impromptu.

The context also suggests spontaneity, because, although Benjamin hoped for a certain outcome, he could not have written his speech presupposing it. Even if Nibley is correct in suggesting that the entire pageant was scripted, Benjamin could not have scripted the power of the Spirit's impact. The more spontaneous feeling in this second discourse suggests that the written texts Mormon describes (Mosiah 2:8) were not scripts handed out ahead of time but reports on the words and covenants Benjamin had declared.

Mosiah 4:6–7

> 6 I say unto you, if ye have come to a knowledge of the goodness of God, and his matchless power, and his wisdom, and his patience, and his long-suffering towards the children of men; and also, the atonement which has been prepared from the foundation of the world, that thereby salvation might come to him that should put his trust in the Lord, and should be diligent in keeping

> his commandments, and continue in the faith even unto the end of his life, I mean the life of the mortal body—
> 7 I say, that this is the man who receiveth salvation, through the atonement which was prepared from the foundation of the world for all humankind, which ever were since the fall of Adam, or who are, or who ever shall be, even unto the end of the world.

Verses 5 and 6 set up a series of conditions with verse 7 as the conclusion. Benjamin's argument presents five conditions following by a blessing. The conditions are:

- You have come to humble yourselves (his imagery of "nothingness").
- You have come to a knowledge of the goodness of God (and other qualities).
- You have come to a knowledge of the atonement.
- You will be diligent in keeping God's commandments.
- You will continue to do so throughout this life.

He concluded that "this is the man" (who does all of these things) who will therefore receive salvation.

Rhetoric: Another indication that this discourse is spontaneous is the explanation Benjamin adds at the end of verse 6. A man must continue in faith "even unto the end of his life"—a correct statement, but to clarify any possible conflation of physical life (which ends at death) with spiritual life (which does not), Benjamin clarifies: "I mean the life of the mortal body." We would not expect such clarifying asides in a written text, but rather in oral discourse (or written transcripts of oral discourse).

Mosiah 4:8

> 8 And this is the means whereby salvation cometh. And there is none other salvation save this which hath been spoken of; neither are there any conditions whereby man can be saved except the conditions which I have told you.

Benjamin has changed the theme of his discourse at this point. His earlier focus was on atonement and sin, which yielded a communal repentance/forgiveness. Repentance and forgiveness clear the slate, but they provide only the ability to progress. They are not progression in and of themselves. Benjamin is now teaching (or reminding) his people of the difference between accepting the atonement and ultimate salvation. He uses the Messiah's atonement as the transition.

Throughout his discourse, Benjamin has emphasized the Messiah. In the first speech, he emphasized the Messiah's atoning blood—the aspect of the atonement that yields a remission of sins. Now he stresses that the name of Yahweh-Messiah is the only name by which salvation may be achieved. Although he does not make a formal theological division between the two, Benjamin uses blood as the image of atonement, and name as the image of salvation. (See commentary accompanying Mosiah 3:17 for more information on the Name.) The conditions for salvation are those Benjamin recited in verses 5 and 6.

Mosiah 4:9

9 Believe in God; believe that he is, and that he created all things, both in heaven and in earth; believe that he has all wisdom, and all power, both in heaven and in earth; believe that man doth not comprehend all the things which the Lord can comprehend.

Rhetoric: In what way does this injunction to believe in *Yahweh* constitute a conceptual transition from the *Messiah* as future redeemer to anything else? The question arises because most of Benjamin's transitions have been purposeful and clear, yet this apparent transition neither concludes the previous material nor introduces the next section, which seems to return to the topic of verse 5. I believe that the explanation lies in the fact that the Book of Mormon associates Yahweh and the Messiah more closely than we would do in our modern theology. The injunction to believe in God (Yahweh) is therefore a punctuation of the discussion of the Messiah (Yahweh). (See "Excursus: The Nephite Understanding of God," following 1 Nephi 11.)

Nevertheless, Benjamin here lists a different set of circumstances and different items about which one must have faith. It is possible that this reference is to the Messiah and his Father, the Most High God, rather than to the Messiah and Yahweh (considered as the same being).

Reference: Benjamin repeats the phrase "both in heaven and in earth." This is probably a reference to a Book of Mormon title for Yahweh. (See commentary accompanying Mosiah 3:8.)

Mosiah 4:10

10 And again, believe that ye must repent of your sins and forsake them, and humble yourselves before God; and ask in sincerity of heart that he would forgive you; and now, if you believe all these things see that ye do them.

The language of verses 5 and 10 is different, but the intent is the same. Verse 5 emphasizes descriptions of humility ("a sense of your nothingness, and your worthless and fallen state"); yet while Benjamin explicitly invokes humility in verse 10, it is a true transition. After the partial aside of verse 5–9, Benjamin returns to the starting point of humility from which he will discuss the relationship of forgiveness and salvation, moving from the humility of prostration to the glory of gospel living. He makes the transition by reminding them of their recent experience with repentance and forgiveness. Knowing that they have powerfully felt the joy of the Atonement he encourages them to take the next step in the process of progress: "if you believe all these things see that ye do them." "Doing" forms the conceptual theme for the next part of his discourse. Benjamin builds from the foundation of communal repentance to structure communal gospel action.

Mosiah 4:11

11 And again I say unto you as I have said before, that as ye have come to the knowledge of the glory of God, or if ye have known of his goodness and have

tasted of his love, and have received a remission of your sins, which causeth such exceedingly great joy in your souls, even so I would that ye should remember, and always retain in remembrance, the greatness of God, and your own nothingness, and his goodness and long-suffering towards you, unworthy creatures, and humble yourselves even in the depths of humility, calling on the name of the Lord daily, and standing steadfastly in the faith of that which is to come, which was spoken by the mouth of the angel.

Rhetoric: Verse 11 is an obvious repetition and Benjamin labels it as such: "I say unto you as I have said before. . . . " Again he is using a device of oral narrative. The message is powerful, but its structure is not as streamlined as the first discourse.

Mosiah 4:12

12 And behold, I say unto you that if ye do this ye shall always rejoice, and be filled with the love of God, and always retain a remission of your sins; and ye shall grow in the knowledge of the glory of him that created you, or in the knowledge of that which is just and true.

Now Benjamin takes up fully the theme of "doing." He uses his people's experience with the Spirit to help them understand reasons for obeying the gospel. Their experience has filled them with joy: "ye have come to the knowledge of the glory of God . . . and have received a remission of your sins, which causeth such exceedingly great *joy* [italics mine] in your souls." Benjamin promises that they can always have that precious feeling ("ye shall always *rejoice*"). If they continue in humility and faith, they will grow in their knowledge. Benjamin probably does not make the distinction between faith and knowledge that modern Saints would. Rather, growing in faith and growing in knowledge would both lead to continued joy.

Mosiah 4:13

13 And ye will not have a mind to injure one another, but to live peaceably, and to render to every man according to that which is his due.

Benjamin begins to describe a series of attributes of one who continues in humility and faith. While all of these actions are taken by individuals, they all occur in social arenas. The communal nature of the experience underscores the communal nature of the covenant they will make. Benjamin's main purpose is still to heal and restore the community. While he talks about these traits as individual duties, the similar collective actions of individuals creates a type of community and a type of communal interaction.

In this context, the first communal benefit, significantly, is that "ye will not have a mind to injure one another, but to live peaceably." The fruit of accepting Yahweh-Messiah as a community is that they will no longer desire "to injure one another." Both by their removing the source of contentions and by infusing a new spirit, the old antagonisms disappear. They will "live peaceably" among themselves.

They will also "render to every man according to that which is his due." Under what circumstances had men *not* received their due? This point will become clearer as we examine the rest of the communal actions on Benjamin's list, but we may suspect that some men are not receiving their due because wealth is concentrated in a limited number of hands. Such economic inequality was the downfall of the city of Nephi. Those who fled from it had seen the destructiveness of class divisions—and indeed, were likely fleeing from them. Thus, they would be highly sensitive to issues of the redistribution of wealth. Just as social egalitarianism was an underpinning of Nephite religio-political culture in the land of Nephi, it becomes foundational for the combined Nephite-Zarahemlaite nation.

Mosiah 4:14

> 14 And ye will not suffer your children that they go hungry, or naked; neither will ye suffer that they transgress the laws of God, and fight and quarrel one with another, and serve the devil, who is the master of sin, or who is the evil spirit which hath been spoken of by our fathers, he being an enemy to all righteousness.

This verse may be read in two different ways, depending on whether the context is modern or ancient.

Modern Context: According to the modern context, with which we are well familiar, parents are responsible to teach their children gospel principles, care for them, and provide the necessities of life (food and clothing, but, by extension, education, medical care, etc.). We should also teach them to avoid quarrels—not small spats that inevitably accompany family life but serious quarrels that divide families and lead to hatred and vengeance.

Ancient Context: Benjamin conceptually divided his people into the "infants" and the "men" (Mosiah 3:18). In this section of the discourse, he echoes that division, speaking of children in this verse and of adults in verse 16 ("ye yourselves"). One of Benjamin's themes has been to reinforce the Nephite principle of social and economic egalitarianism. (See commentary accompanying Mosiah 2:12 and Mosiah 3:13.) In this light, it is significant to note how he approaches this particular instruction. He does not tell parents to feed and clothe their children. He says: "Ye will not suffer your children that they go hungry, or naked."

At the end of verse 13 Benjamin suggested that this new society would "render to every man according to that which is his due." As his first example, Benjamin offers the obvious. No parent would deny their children food or clothing. Those necessities are their due, and a good parent will provide them. What Benjamin is suggesting is that this natural provision for one's children will be extended to the community. The young children of the community who were Benjamin's examples of those who will be raised with the new gospel will be raised in a society that provides all their "due" in social and economic needs.

This analogy of the obvious responsibilities of the parent being extended to the entire community continues when Benjamin enjoins parents to teach their children Yahweh's laws. These parents give their children their due by teaching them the correct gospel. Whereas food and clothing emphasize social and economic egalitarianism, this injunction emphasizes the contrast between the true Nephite religion and the old religion that was previously taught. Social unity depends on religious unity. Everyone must teach the same laws. The ancient world did not differentiate politics from religion.[4] Yahweh's laws are the people's laws. Any other laws teach division, not unity.

In this context, quarreling cannot be permitted because it is specifically connected with the evil spirit, that same "evil spirit" against which Benjamin has already preached (Mosiah 2:32). These fights are not family squabbles, but conflicts that have ripped the people apart, with some physically removing themselves to join the Lamanites. Benjamin has earlier declared that those who follow the "evil spirit" are in rebellion against Yahweh. Now Benjamin forbids teaching these contentious concepts to the children to prevent them from being passed on to another generation.

Mosiah 4:15

> 15 But ye will teach them to walk in the ways of truth and soberness; ye will teach them to love one another, and to serve one another.

Verses 13 and 14 gave commands about what not to do. The people of this new covenant were not to do things that would create social strife. Now Benjamin turns to the positive instructions. Just as the negative instruction proscribed social strife, the positive instructions enhance social cohesiveness. In addition to giving others their due, this new society should embrace all members as a family and love and serve each other. The negative instruction highlighted the minimum standards. The positive instruction teaches the people the ideal.

Mosiah 4:16

> 16 And also, ye yourselves will succor those that stand in need of your succor; ye will administer of your substance unto him that standeth in need; and ye will not suffer that the beggar putteth up his petition to you in vain, and turn him out to perish.

Again, it is useful to read this verse in a dual context, both ancient and modern.

Ancient Context: Here the emphasis shifts from children to adults. The "men" must teach the "children" and act for the good of the community. Just as the "children" require food and clothing, so do the needy. Benjamin is creating a direct parallel between nurturing infants and nurturing needy adults. These verses should be read as conceptual parallels. Compassionate aid to the needy dismantles the pride in social divisions that leads to contention. Withholding substance from the needy creates an intensifying spiral of divisiveness: the needy remain in need, and the wealthy become

---

[4]Saburo Sugiyama, "Teotihuacan as an Origin for Postclassic Feathered Serpent Symbolism," in *Mesoamerica's Classic Heritage: From Teotihuacan to the Aztecs*, edited by David Carrasco, Lindsay Jones, and Scott Sessions (Boulder: University Press of Colorado, 2000): 117, "In Mesoamerica, relgiion and politics were so tightly interwoven that it is often difficult to separate them into their distinct strands."

hoarders. Benjamin is here describing how the community must heal past wounds. His clearness and directness tell us that he is addressing the people's real experiences prior to this time.

Modern Context: How should we read this verse in our modern context? Benjamin's people were primarily agricultural and rural. Their economy was not monetary but exchange. Thus, a needy person had probably been displaced from his land (hence, had become unable to grow his own food) or was prevented from doing so by other conditions: youth, old age, or illness, for example. Their needs were for sustenance in hard times.

In our monetary society, need is now much more complex. The beggars who put up their petitions to us may or may not be in need of food but still have genuine needs. However, in a monetary society, the nature of our charity is also different. Where the ancient beggar could only request assistance from his neighbors, modern needy have access to governmental programs that can assist with a larger range of needs. Where the ancient emphasis was on personal contact with the needy, the modern emphasis is on supporting social structures that have been developed for that purpose. As the next verse clarifies, the real problem is the giver's pride. When we give freely and generously, we dismantle pride, the source of many social ills, and the needy will be taken care of.

Mosiah 4:17–18

> 17 Perhaps thou shalt say: The man has brought upon himself his misery; therefore I will stay my hand, and will not give unto him of my food, nor impart unto him of my substance that he may not suffer, for his punishments are just—
> 18 But I say unto you, O man, whosoever doeth this the same hath great cause to repent; and except he repenteth of that which he hath done he perisheth forever, and hath no interest in the kingdom of God.

Benjamin is describing social divisions along economic lines. This argument assumes first that the needy are truly in need of food and that there are those in the society with abundant resources who could relieve that need. Furthermore, how people react to this socio-economic situation has spiritual implications. The example he gives is of self-justification—a person who is unwilling to share his substance and who invents reasons to justify his selfishness. Yahweh knows those motives and, as indicated in verse 18, attributes them as sin to the person who withholds assistance citing them.

Once again, we must assume that Benjamin is describing real conditions in Zarahemla and instructing his people in strong terms that those who perpetuate such economic divisions have no place in Yahweh's kingdom. Because Benjamin is intent on creating Yahweh's kingdom in Zarahemla, this warning is a very thinly veiled threat against the selfish. If they have no place in Yahweh's kingdom, they have no place in Benjamin's kingdom.

Mosiah 4:19

> 19 For behold, are we not all beggars? Do we not all depend upon the same Being, even God, for all the substance which we have, for both food and raiment, and for gold, and for silver, and for all the riches which we have of every kind?

This is a masterful argument. Benjamin has just stated that one of the effects of truly living the gospel will be generosity to the needy. He has also reminded his people of their excuses for withholding that substance. We need to remember that:

- Benjamin has previously invoked the master/servant concept to describe the people's relationship to God (Mosiah 3:14–25).
- Benjamin has used that relationship as a model for current social interactions (Mosiah 2:18).
- The "substance" that the needy lack is food and raiment.
- The wealthy, whom Benjamin sees as perpetuating economic disparities among the people have a different kind of "substance": gold, silver, and "all the riches."
- "Beggar" is a word with powerful connotations, including both economic and social subservience to a higher class/power.

Thus, Benjamin adroitly blends multiple concepts to make an important point. First, he has described a wealthier class who is reluctant to share with the lower class and who justifies their withholding by blaming the needy for causing their own problems—hence, being unworthy of assistance. In other words, two problems overlap: class and need. The "beggars" are those of the lower class who "beg" food and raiment from the higher class who has "all the riches."

To combat this socio-economic division among his people, Benjamin invokes another hierarchy of higher and lower status, with Yahweh possessing the higher status. Benjamin places Yahweh, the source of the wealth, above the wealthy, who thereby become beggars before Yahweh: "Do we not all depend upon the same Being, even God, for all the substance which we have, for both food and raiment, and for gold, and for silver, and for all the riches which we have of every kind?" The wealthy therefore also occupy a dependent position; they also need charity, and those needs have been met by a merciful God. Thus, a group so blessed should show the same charity to a lower class that Yahweh has shown them.

Mosiah 4:20

> 20 And behold, even at this time, ye have been calling on his name, and begging for a remission of your sins. And has he suffered that ye have begged in vain? Nay; he has poured out his Spirit upon you, and has caused that your hearts should be filled with joy, and has caused that your mouths should be stopped that ye could not find utterance, so exceedingly great was your joy.

Benjamin reinforces the status of the wealthy as beggars by reminding them of an example that is not even a day old. They have literally begged Yahweh for mercy, a petition he immediately and bountifully filled in such a great measure that "your mouths should be stopped that ye could not find utterance, so exceedingly great was your joy."

Mosiah 4:21

> 21 And now, if God, who has created you, on whom you are dependent for your lives and for all that ye have and are, doth grant unto you whatsoever ye ask that is right, in faith, believing that ye shall receive, O then, how ye ought to impart of the substance that ye have one to another.

Benjamin now makes the example explicit. Yahweh, who is clearly of higher status, grants tremendous blessings to those of lower status. Therefore, those among Benjamin's people who also have comparatively higher status should likewise generously bless those of lower status.

An unstated assumption of Benjamin's argument is that these are communal laws that the newly united people of Zarahemla should obey. The people of Zarahemla would have understood that these laws apply internally, but not necessarily externally—to enemies. In much the same way, modern Latter-day Saints can discharge our obligations for charity through fast offerings, an internal opportunity for alms-giving.

Mosiah 4:22

> 22 And if ye judge the man who putteth up his petition to you for your substance that he perish not, and condemn him, how much more just will be your condemnation for withholding your substance, which doth not belong to you but to God, to whom also your life belongeth; and yet ye put up no petition, nor repent of the thing which thou hast done.

Culture: Benjamin's conclusion focuses simultaneously on the selfish withholding of substance and also on the attitude that creates the social division. While Benjamin does not apparently see the economic disparity per se as a problem, he is obviously concerned with the judgmental attitudes that result. It is the social division into "betters" and "lessers" on the basis of substance against which he preaches.

Thus, if Benjamin's people judge someone to be of lower status and therefore unworthy of assistance, so will Yahweh, who is of much higher status, judge them as unworthy. This is precisely the sentiment expressed in Matthew 7:2: "For with what judgment ye judge, ye shall be judged: and with what measure ye mete, it shall be measured to you again."

Mosiah 4:23

> 23 I say unto you, wo be unto that man, for his substance shall perish with him; and now, I say these things unto those who are rich as pertaining to the things of this world.

The condemnation for withholding substance in the face of need is that Yahweh, the ultimate source of the wealthy man's substance, will similarly withhold his bounty. Therefore, the wealthy in attempting to safeguard their status, will lose it. Benjamin's explanation that he is speaking of those who are "rich as pertaining to the things of this world" makes it clear that he understands that there are spiritual riches as well. Those spiritual riches actually obey the same rules, but that is not Benjamin's current concern. His immediate purpose is to describe a more desirable social order, which has strong spiritual implications.

Mosiah 4:24

> 24 And again, I say unto the poor, ye who have not and yet have sufficient, that ye remain from day to day; I mean all you who deny the beggar, because ye have not; I would that ye say in your hearts that: I give not because I have not, but if I had I would give.

Just as the wealthy are subservient to Yahweh, so too are the "poor without sufficient means" subservient to the "poor with sufficient means." Even a small differentiation in substance is sufficient to create social divisions. Those who lack gold and silver but who have food and raiment are also under an obligation to avoid creating social distinctions. They may not have surplus to give, but they must be willing to give if they could.

History: Benjamin's division between two types of poor follows a conceptual division seen in the Bible. John Dominic Crossan, chair of the Historical Jesus section of the Society of Biblical Literature, describes the social distinctions among the poor in the Bible:

> The most common words for the needy in the Hebrew Bible are *ani* and *ebyon*. "The difference . . . was in the immediacy of need. Whereas the *ani* was pressed by debts and dependent upon the good grace of an employer creditor, the *ebyon* needed to be helped at once if he was to survive." [citing Gildas Hamel] Those terms, however, often appear as a tandem set—as they do, for example, in these representative cases:
>
> You shall not withhold the wages of the poor [*ani*] and needy [*ebyon*] laborers, whether other Israelites or aliens who reside in your land in one of your towns. (Deut. 24:14)
>
> Hear this, you that trample on the needy [*ebyon*], and bring to ruin the poor [*ani*] of the land. (Amos 8:4)
>
> The murderer rises at dusk to kill the poor [*ani*] and needy [*ebyon*], and in the night is like a thief. (Job 24:14)[5]

While it may be too convenient to see the "poor without sufficient means" as a translation for *ebyon* and the "poor with sufficient means" as a translation for *ani*, the Book of Mormon usage certainly replicates the essential meaning and distinction, regardless of the actual word on the plates.

---

[5] John Dominic Crossan, *The Birth of Christianity: Discovering What Happened in the Years Immediately after the Execution of Jesus* (San Francisco: HarperSanFrancisco, 1998), 320.

Mosiah 4:25

> 25 And now, if ye say this in your hearts ye remain guiltless, otherwise ye are condemned; and your condemnation is just for ye covet that which ye have not received.

In other words, the problem is not the absolute possession of goods, but one's attitude toward one's possessions. Even the poor may fall under condemnation if they lack generosity and egalitarian acceptance of others. This principle is a fundamental aspect of the type of society that Benjamin is attempting to create. Ekkehard W. Stegemann, professor of New Testament at the University of Basel, Switzerland, and Wolfgang Stegemann, professor of New Testament at the Augustana Hochschule in Neuendettelsau, Germany, describe the social implications of an economic system based on equality of exchange:

> The most elementary form of the exchange of goods is *reciprocity*, the exchange of gifts between individual persons, households (families), or clans (relatives). This network of mutual production among persons and social groups with comparable status rests ultimately on the reciprocity (quid pro quo) and is not oriented toward profit (*balanced reciprocity*). Thus, in principle reciprocity presupposes symmetry or balance of exchange and is connected with a careful calculation of exchanged goods and services. Equivalents do not always have to correspond with each other directly but can also be granted the giver (on a delayed basis) through prestige or loyalty (say, in the relationship of patron and client). This form of exchange is called *general reciprocity*. If we can perceive a certain element of delay in the balance of quid pro quo in general reciprocity, balance is lacking altogether in *negative reciprocity*, which is ruled not by the ethic of the golden rule but by an interest in doing to another what one does *not* want done to oneself. This is the ethnic of hostility against enemies and all groups of people with whom one is not in a reciprocal relationship. Thus, for example, the form of balanced reciprocity within a small circle—the family, household, clan, and even neighbors—is not granted to strangers. Hence, relations with strangers are dominated by the *negative* form of reciprocity, in which self-interest and profit are permitted to dominate. . . .
>
> Thus, if we may generalize, reciprocity rules above all in rural areas; and beyond village and kinship solidarity, negative reciprocity with unrelated people and strangers makes possible a modest amount of profit.[6]

In terms of an economic model for society, Benjamin is clearly including the entire city as part of the in-group deserving of balanced reciprocity. Those who attempt to create social distinctions are treating members of the same city as though they were outsiders. They are giving them the same social treatment as they would an enemy, and Benjamin's purpose in establishing the new covenant is to create of those who might have been considered socially segregated (or "enemies" in the social sense) a single in-group or clan that depends on egalitarian treatment (balanced reciprocity).

---

[6]Ekkehard W. Stegemann and Wolfgang Stegemann, *The Jesus Movement: A Social History of its First Century*, translated by O. C. Dean, Jr. (Minneapolis, Minn.: Fortress Press, 1999), 35.

Mosiah 4:26

> 26 And now, for the sake of these things which I have spoken unto you—that is, for the sake of retaining a remission of your sins from day to day, that ye may walk guiltless before God—I would that ye should impart of your substance to the poor, every man according to that which he hath, such as feeding the hungry, clothing the naked, visiting the sick and administering to their relief, both spiritually and temporally, according to their wants.

Benjamin summarizes his intent. His people have received a remission of sin through the Spirit; but to "retain" that remission "from day to day," they must relieve the needy by sharing their substance. It is difficult to understand the connection between a remission of sins and "impart[ing] of your substance to the poor." We understand our sins individually and therefore the cures for sin are also individual. We receive a remission of sins through personal repentance and a change of behavior. The Nephites received a communal remission of sins by communal repentance and a communal change of behavior. The communal understanding of sin from the law of Moses was still applicable in Nephite society and therefore communal actions were entirely appropriate and necessary to that communal remission of sins. In the case of Benjamin's people, one of the major sins they were developing was precisely the communal sin of social hierarchies that did not impart of their substance to others as though they were family. (See commentary accompanying Mosiah 4:25 above.) That social sin could lead to social discord and the future of Zarahemla will attest that it leads to social fission. Under these circumstances it is obvious why the Nephites would have their remission of sins tied to their ability to impart of their substance to the needy.

Mosiah 4:27

> 27 And see that all these things are done in wisdom and order; for it is not requisite that a man should run faster than he has strength. And again, it is expedient that he should be diligent, that thereby he might win the prize; therefore, all things must be done in order.

Benjamin teaches an important spiritual lesson. There are so many things to do in gaining exaltation that we might become discouraged at the magnitude of the effort required. But Benjamin assures us that, although the task is not less, the time pressures are. We may achieve our goals within our individual capacities. None of us will be required to "run faster than [we have] strength."

Rhetoric: While this concept is tremendously important, why does Benjamin position it here? His immediate context has been the importance of caring for the needy. What is the connection between that concept and the need to do "all these things . . . in wisdom and order"? I suggest that Benjamin is here addressing, not the problems of individuals, but the larger problem of the community. While an individual might easily decide to share, it isn't the movement of substance that is Benjamin's concern, but rather the elimination of social stratification on the basis of substance. Because the ultimate problem is social, stemming from engrained concepts of rank and wealth, such attitudes cannot be changed overnight. Benjamin is proposing a radical social reorganization, which cannot succeed without the application of wisdom and order over time. Nevertheless, the people must "be diligent, that thereby [they] might win the prize." They must keep their eyes on the ultimate goal even while dealing patiently and wisely with the prickly realities of unlearning the old social/economic order.

Mosiah 4:28

> 28 And I would that ye should remember, that whosoever among you borroweth of his neighbor should return the thing that he borroweth, according as he doth agree, or else thou shalt commit sin; and perhaps thou shalt cause thy neighbor to commit sin also.

Here is another example of how possessions may cause social divisions. Borrowing an object is accompanied by the social obligation of returning it. Not doing so can also create strife and division. This is true to a small extent even within a family, but when the borrowing occurs across greater social distance, the potential danger to the community is greater. A borrowed but unreturned item can polarize two clans if the borrowing occurred between them. Each clan is obligated to support its own kin against outsiders, and the individual act of borrowing can escalate to a communal issue.

Benjamin therefore teaches that the one who borrows but does not return has committed a sin. However, he also notes that "perhaps *thou shalt cause* thy neighbor to commit sin" (italics mine). How is it that the lender causes the borrower to sin? The answer comes in the way we see social obligations. If we lend something to a spouse or a sibling, our fear of losing the item is diminished. Both by perhaps physical and certainly social proximity the item is not "lost" to us. However, the more distant the loan, the fewer social ties ameliorate any possible problems. If we loan to a stranger we not only encounter a greater physical separation, we have a greater social separation. Therefore, if we loan in cases where we have more emotional attachment to that which is loaned than we do to the borrower, we have created a situation that may easily escalate into social conflict (which is what Benjamin is trying to prevent).

It is in this context that we should see the command not to borrow in Deuteronomy: "The Lord shall open unto thee his good treasure, the heaven to give the rain unto thy land in his season, and to bless all the work of thine hand: and thou shalt lend unto many nations, and thou shalt not borrow" (Deut. 28:12). In the case of Israel, they are allowed to create relationships of obligation where other nations are obliged to Israel, but should not create a situation where they are obliged to another nation. The social distance between nations is among the greatest known in the ancient world, and was certainly a point of great contention. Contrast this, however, with the instruction from Matthew: "And whosoever shall compel thee to go a mile, go with him twain. Give to him that asketh thee, and from him that would borrow of thee turn not thou away. Ye have heard that it hath been said, Thou shalt love thy neighbour, and hate thine enemy. But I say unto you, Love your enemies, bless them that curse you, do good to them that hate you, and pray for them which despitefully use you, and persecute you" (Matt. 5:41–44).

The instruction on borrowing occurs in verse 42. I have included the surrounding context to make the social situation more visible. The Lord is teaching a way for the people to deal with their particular society, and that it is to treat their enemies as families. He specifically reverses the normal expectation that one would "love thy neighbour, and hate thine enemy" with "love thy enemies." In other words, treat the enemies as though they were neighbors and subject to the same internal rules. Hence, one would allow someone to borrow if they were family or close, but typically one would not treat an enemy in this way. Just as Benjamin was creating a new society, the Lord was attempting to create a new social reality. For both Benjamin and the Lord, that society was one that extended the boundaries of family outward to encompass larger and larger numbers of people.

Mosiah 4:29–30

> 29 And finally, I cannot tell you all the things whereby ye may commit sin; for there are divers ways and means, even so many that I cannot number them.
> 30 But this much I can tell you, that if ye do not watch yourselves, and your thoughts, and your words, and your deeds, and observe the commandments of God, and continue in the faith of what ye have heard concerning the coming of our Lord, even unto the end of your lives, ye must perish. And now, O man, remember, and perish not.

Benjamin has described two specific communal "sins": the social stratification caused by selfish withholding of substance and the social tensions created when substance is loaned (rather than given, as in the first case) but not returned. In both cases, the effect is social division. In both cases, their causes are declared sin.

Benjamin realizes that these two examples do not exhaust the catalog of possible sins, even of possible social sins. He therefore specifies that his people can sin in many other unspecified ways. The solution is to conform one's thoughts, words, and deeds to Yahweh's commandments. If Benjamin's people, and we modern readers, follow this principle and continue steadfastly in that effort, then we may achieve salvation—then we will not perish.

Benjamin's final statement is his plea that his people follow these commandments so that they will "remember, and perish not."

Text: This injunction concludes another portion of Benjamin's discourse, and occasions a chapter break in the 1830 edition. The next chapter begins with Mormon's introduction to another portion of copied text.

Mosiah 5

Mosiah 5:1

> 1 And now, it came to pass that when king Benjamin had thus spoken to his people, he sent among them, desiring to know of his people if they believed the words which he had spoken unto them.

Text: Because a chapter begins here in the 1830 edition, Mormon probably marked it in some way as a division on the plates. Such breaks between the end of a copied speech and before another begins commonly correspond to chapter breaks in the English versions. Mormon presents a summary of what happens next. The text switches from discourse to narrative, as Benjamin sends messengers among the people to get their reply.

Culture: Unlike their earlier outcry and falling to the earth, which Benjamin had observed personally from his tower, he now requires a more extensive canvassing. Perhaps this break was also an opportune time for Benjamin to rest, for the people to talk among themselves, and perhaps also time to cook and eat a meal. Other sermons from Nephi and Jacob appear to have been delivered over two days. Perhaps this one was similarly divided between two days.

Benjamin's messengers were asking a particular question: Were the people willing to enter into a new covenant, accept a new name, and become a new people? (v. 6). This issue is, for Benjamin, much more important than the coronation of the next king. Because the covenant is communal, not individual, he seeks a communal response. Benjamin cannot be satisfied with a vague impression of a positive response. Rather, he needs to know that the whole community is ready to undertake this change.

Mosiah 5:2

> 2 And they all cried with one voice, saying: Yea, we believe all the words which thou hast spoken unto us; and also, we know of their surety and truth, because of the Spirit of the Lord Omnipotent, which has wrought a mighty change in us, or in our hearts, that we have no more disposition to do evil, but to do good continually.

Redaction: Verses 2–5 comprise the congregation's declaration of willingness to enter into a covenant. The precision of the words, as well as the descriptive introduction that "they all cried with one voice," indicates that Mormon is quoting his source plates at this point. While the precision of the words indicates copying from the plates, it would have been literally impossible for the entire people to utter this lengthy speech in unison. Therefore, Mormon (or his original source) is also giving a polished, literary version of what was almost certainly less polished and unified. The very fact that Benjamin sent out messengers means that they reached different clans at different times. Unless the messengers were simultaneously passing out written instructions about a choral response to be given at a later point (which would require near universal literacy—which is unlikely), it was physically impossible for the large crowd to respond in this way.

An orchestrated, ritual response seems to greatly diminish the spiritual power of the occasion. The rest of the text, as I read it, suggests a spontaneous and emotional response, not one controlled by a script from past events. The people's declaration of faith in the words of their king (v. 4), while certainly reflecting their feelings, seems an unlikely speech for Benjamin to put in their mouths, given his humility. If he had written a choral response, it seems more likely that he would have had the people express faith in the words of the angel through the king. For these reasons, I see as the most likely scenario that the people genuinely had one intent in their hearts which they communicated in "one voice"; the written account of that occasion reflects a more polished version of those unified expressions.

Culture: In the context of Benjamin's emphasis on his people's social unity and particularly his characterization of the "evil spirit" as the temptation that leads to contention, it is possible to interpret their declaration as their intention to change their social interactions and that they no longer felt the prejudices and selfishness for which Benjamin had chastised them. Their sudden freedom from a desire to do evil may express their resolve to no more follow the evil spirit of contention between the old ways and the new covenant.

Scripture: Regardless of how this particular passage would have impacted Benjamin's people, it is a powerful statement to modern readers. The process of repentance is indeed one of a "mighty change." The old man must be removed, and we must be renewed in Christ. Just as Benjamin describes their experience in terms of a transformation (they are now children of Yahweh-Messiah, v. 7) we too must be transformed.

Mosiah 5:3

> 3 And we, ourselves, also, through the infinite goodness of God, and the manifestations of his Spirit, have great views of that which is to come; and were it expedient, we could prophesy of all things.

The people declare that they are so filled with the Spirit that they "have great views of that which is to come." By this they mean the future Messiah. When Benjamin began to speak of the Messiah, he used the same language: "I have things to tell you concerning that which is to come" (Mosiah 3:1). Therefore the people are declaring that they understand the Messiah's atoning mission as Benjamin has explained it. The Spirit is so strong that they could prophesy.

Even though this statement is a literary account that was probably not a completely accurate representation of the spiritual state of each and every person, it is a true depiction of the strength of feeling experienced by the community.

Mosiah 5:4

> 4 And it is the faith which we have had on the things which our king has spoken unto us that has brought us to this great knowledge, whereby we do rejoice with such exceedingly great joy.

This simple description captures the process that has brought the people to this point. Their years of experience with Benjamin, their good king, have given them faith in him. That initial willingness to believe has made it possible for them to receive the greater revelation of the Spirit. Both through Benjamin's words and through the outpouring of the Spirit, they have received "great knowledge" which fills them with spiritual joy.

Mosiah 5:5

> 5 And we are willing to enter into a covenant with our God to do his will, and to be obedient to his commandments in all things that he shall command us, all the remainder of our days, that we may not bring upon ourselves a never-ending torment, as has been spoken by the angel, that we may not drink out of the cup of the wrath of God.

This is the high point of the entire day's address. Benjamin has brought them together to give them a new name (Mosiah 1:11), which springs from the covenant that his people now express their willingness to make. Such a covenant has no power unless it is voluntary. Benjamin realizes at this point that he has achieved his goal. The new covenant/new name will result in a unified community. Its internal divisions will be dissolved "in wisdom and order" (Mosiah 4:27). They themselves will dismantle the socio-economic disparities that separate them from each other.

Mosiah 5:6

> 6 And now, these are the words which king Benjamin desired of them; and therefore he said unto them: Ye have spoken the words that I desired; and the covenant which ye have made is a righteous covenant.

Redaction: This is certainly the recorded speech of Benjamin. Unlike the stylized response of the people, these are likely Benjamin's words or very close to them. Benjamin declares that this is precisely the response he had hoped for. The people's willingness to covenant lets him make the formal announcement of the covenant, symbolized by his bestowal of a new name.

Mosiah 5:7

> 7 And now, because of the covenant which ye have made ye shall be called the children of Christ, his sons, and his daughters; for behold, this day he hath spiritually begotten you; for ye say that your hearts are changed through faith

> on his name; therefore, ye are born of him and have become his sons and his daughters.

Benjamin prepares his people for their new name with a brilliantly multi-layered description of the change that has come over them, a description which evokes multiple themes simultaneously. The first and most obvious is relationship of the son/daughter to the father. In all societies, this relationship is charged with expectations of mutual obligations. Thus, Benjamin simultaneously creates a loving relationship and invokes the obligations it presents.

Defining the Messiah as the father in this transformation comes from the nature of the relationship of humans to the divine. Yahweh-Messiah is father to Benjamin's people because he is the instrument of their new birth. This special definition does not confuse the relationship of Yahweh to his Father (the Most High God) in the heavens. (See "Excursus: The Nephite Understanding of God," following 1 Nephi 11.)

Benjamin uses birth as a metaphor of transformation, suggesting that his people may have understood the life of the spirit as separate from the body with the spirit becoming the physical body at birth. That transformation from spiritual to physical is now reversed, with a spiritual birth occurring even as the individual remains in the physical world. His connection of transformation with children recalls his earlier evocation of children as the righteous. The "old men" and others whom he cautioned for their affiliation with past contentions are now transformed into children. They are no longer rebels but fully embraced by the Messiah's atoning sacrifice.

Mosiah 5:8

> 8 And under this head ye are made free, and there is no other head whereby ye can be made free. There is no other name given whereby salvation cometh; therefore, I would that ye should take upon you the name of Christ, all you that have entered into the covenant with God that ye should be obedient unto the end of your lives.

Vocabulary: The term "head" here refers to the person.[1] I am not sure why "head" is used here, unless English lacks a better term. The usual connotation of "head" is "firstmost" or "principal." I see this word as attempt to designate both the person and the position of the Messiah, with whom Benjamin's people (and we) have entered into a relationship. That relationship places him above us. Thus, this term denotes both the Messiah as a person and his position of being our leader/ruler/master.

Culture: The significance of accepting a new name as a people is underscored by a commentary from Sir James George Frazer's *The Golden Bough* which, even in

---

[1]An argument could also be made for "head" as in a division or change—such as a headline. However, that definition was apparently not part of Joseph's vocabulary. Noah Webster, *An American Dictionary of the English Language* (1828, electronic edition, Deseret Book, 1998).

abridgment, is monumental. Although Frazer's language is somewhat condescending (e.g., "savage"), he nevertheless shows illuminates the importance attached to naming for many ancient peoples:

> Unable to discriminate clearly between words and things, the savage commonly fancies that the link between a name and the person or thing denominated by it is not a mere arbitrary and ideal association, but a real and substantial bond which unites the two in such a way that magic may be wrought on a man just as easily through his name as through his hair, his nails, or any other material part of his person. In fact, primitive man regards his name as a vital portion of himself and takes care of it accordingly. Thus, for example, the North American Indian "regards his name, not as a mere label, but as a distinct part of his personality, just as much as are his eyes or his teeth, and believes that injury will result as surely from the malicious handling of his name as from a wound inflicted on any part of his physical organism. This belief was found among the various tribes from the Atlantic to the Pacific, and has occasioned a number of curious regulations in regard to the concealment and change of names." Some Esquimaux take new names when they are old, hoping thereby to get a new lease of life. The Tolampoos of Celebes believe that if you write a man's name down you can carry off his soul along with it. Many savages at the present day regard their names as vital parts of themselves, and therefore take great pains to conceal their real names, lest these should give to evil-disposed persons a handle by which to injure their owners.[2]

The reality of the name-person connection was also an important part of Near Eastern culture. Bruce H. Porter of the LDS Institute of Religion in San Marcos, California, and Stephen D. Ricks of Brigham Young University note:

> In the cultures of the ancient Near East, existence was thought to be dependent upon an identifying word, that word being a "name." The name of someone (or something) was perceived not as a mere abstraction, but as a real entity, "the audible and spoken image of the person, which was taken to be his spiritual essence." [citing W. Brede Kristensen.] According to Philo of Alexandria, the name "is like a shadow which accompanies the body." Similarly, Origen viewed the name as the designation of the individual's essence.[3]

While the naming of Benjamin's people exhibits none of Frazer's taboos, this event obviously carried symbolic significance. (See commentary accompanying Mosiah 3:17.) Benjamin expects this new name to represent the transformation of his previously divided people into a united people. That Benjamin considers the name itself to have power is evident in how he caps the covenant with it. There is no other name by which salvation may be had (Mosiah 3:17, 5:8). Taking upon them the name of Yahweh-Messiah is not nearly so passive as a modern designation of Christian—nor even of "Latter-day Saint." The name included all of the covenants subsumed under that name and identified the person who bore it as one

---

[2]James George Frazer, *The Golden Bough: A Study in Magic and Religion*, one-volume abridged edition (New York: Macmillan, 1963), 284–85. Internal references undocumented.

[3]Bruce H. Porter and Stephen D. Ricks, "Names in Antiquity: Old, New, and Hidden," in *By Study and Also by Faith: Essays in Honor of Hugh W. Nibley on the Occasion of His Eightieth Birthday, 27 March 1990*, edited by John M. Lundquist and Stephen D. Ricks, 2 vols. (Salt Lake City: Deseret Book/ Provo, Utah: FARMS, 1990), 1:501. See also Truman G. Madsen, "'Putting on the Names': A Jewish-Christian Legacy," in ibid., 1:458.

of the covenant. The name of Yahweh-Messiah had the same meaning for Benjamin's people as circumcision did for the Old World Hebrews.

Mosiah 5:9

> 9 And it shall come to pass that whosoever doeth this shall be found at the right hand of God, for he shall know the name by which he is called; for he shall be called by the name of Christ.

Benjamin has linked the name of Yahweh-Messiah with future salvation (and has implied a temporal salvation—at least from contention). Here that promise is made explicit. Benjamin realizes that this is a voluntary covenant and that the individual making the covenant is the most important focal point; the communal covenant is the collective manifestation of the individual covenants. Thus, when the individual abides by the covenant, he occupies a place on Yahweh's right hand.

Significantly, he is on the right hand because "he shall be called by the name of Christ." This name carries with it a genuine identity. In Benjamin's world, one may not be called by that name unless he fulfills the covenant. The two cannot be separated. For Benjamin, living a Christian life was taken for granted with the bearing of the name.

Mosiah 5:10

> 10 And now it shall come to pass, that whosoever shall not take upon him the name of Christ must be called by some other name; therefore, he findeth himself on the left hand of God

Because the covenant is voluntary, some might choose to reject it. Benjamin clearly declares the choice to be either/or. There is no blending of options, no middle ground. Since the only name through which salvation comes is Yahweh-Messiah, if one refuses to be called by that name, one cannot be saved. Thus, one is called by Yahweh-Messiah's name and sits on Yahweh's right hand (and is one of the covenant people), or one is called by some other name—a name which has no power to save—and therefore will be on Yahweh's left hand (symbolically out of the covenant).

Vocabulary: The symbolism of the left and right hand is ancient and widespread. Given the statistical predominance of right-handedness, the right hand has long been associated with truth, good, and "right." The left hand symbolizes the opposite. The word "sinister" comes from the Latin *sinistra,* meaning "left hand."[4] Thus, sitting on the right hand of God is very good, while being on the left hand of God is equivalent to being excluded from his presence entirely.

Literature: Verses 10–12 form a very nice chiasm, as John W. Welch has noted:

---

[4]Richard Lederer, *The Miracle of Language* (New York: Pocket Books, 1991), 52.

a And now it shall come to pass that whosoever shall not take upon him the *name* of Christ
  b must be *called* by some other name
    c therefore he findeth himself on the *left hand of* God
      d and I would that ye should *remember* also that this is the name that I said I should give unto you
        e that never should be *blotted out*
          f except it be through *transgression*
          f therefore take heed that ye do not *transgress*
        e that the name be not *blotted out* of your hearts
      d I say unto you, I would that ye should *remember* to retain the name written always in your hearts
    c that ye are not found on the *left hand of God*
  b but that he hear and know the voice by which ye shall be *called*
a and also the *name* by which he shall call you.[5]

This particular chiasm clearly exhibits a reversal of elements. Nevertheless, it does not readily exhibit all of the characteristics attributed to classical chiasmus. Welch explains: "Chiasmus is the literary technique of creating double structures in which the second half of a composition mirrors and balances the first half, but in reverse order. In general, the device is useful for several literary purposes, especially for concentrating attention on the main point of the passage by placing it at the central turning point rather than in a topic sentence at the beginning of a paragraph, as is the trend with modern writers."[6]

In this particular example of reversed parallelism, the central point is *transgression* in which the passage's clear intent is to focus on the power of the name. We have a reversal of elements that does not emphasize the theme in the classical way. In this case, Benjamin is creating a logical progression and reverses the order so that, in this particular case, the emphasis rests on the first and last element rather than the center elements. This structure does not deny the chiasmus but simply warns against assuming that all chiastic structures should be interpreted in precisely the same way.

Welch analyzes the entire structure of Benjamin's discourse as chiastic, suggesting an organizational framework that had been previously constructed for the oral discourse. The use of chiasms to order an oral discourse shows forethought, not spontaneity. In Benjamin's discourse, finding overarching chiastic structures requires accepting that the entire discourse was outlined before its presentation; yet this finding is contradicted by the evidences of orality in the second half of the sermon. Its spontaneity and dependence on the audience's reaction suggest, rather, the absence of an outlined chiastic structure.

Furthermore, Welch's chiastic arrangement includes conceptual structures that he has placed in chiastic relationship to each other that contradict the contextual

---

[5]John W. Welch, "Parallelism and Chiasmus in Benjamin's Speech," in *King Benjamin's Speech*, edited by John W. Welch and Stephen D. Ricks (Provo, Utah: FARMS, 1998), 370.

[6]Ibid., 320.

interpretation in this commentary. For instance, the "what is man" category covers elements that might be read into that category for a modern man but which do not harmonize with the contextual meaning of the passages. Welch positions Mosiah 2:10–11 as part of the "what is man" theme,[7] while I see it as part of a set of contrasts to external rulers.

Authentic chiasms definitely appear as literary structures in the Book of Mormon, but others may be artificially created. Those that cast the widest net by dealing with conceptual categories are the most difficult to sustain; identifying themes is subject more to modern than ancient interpretation. The reader should read Welch's full article about the chiastic elements he has identified in Benjamin's speech and evaluate the evidence personally.

Mosiah 5:11

> 11 And I would that ye should remember also, that this is the name that I said I should give unto you that never should be blotted out, except it be through transgression; therefore, take heed that ye do not transgress, that the name be not blotted out of your hearts.

Like all of Yahweh's covenants, this one can be broken only on the human end. The covenant stands forever, as long as we fulfill our part of its obligations.

Mosiah 5:12–13

> 12 I say unto you, I would that ye should remember to retain the name written always in your hearts, that ye are not found on the left hand of God, but that ye hear and know the voice by which ye shall be called, and also, the name by which he shall call you.
> 13 For how knoweth a man the master whom he has not served, and who is a stranger unto him, and is far from the thoughts and intents of his heart?
> Benjamin here returns to his theme of the master/servant relationship but now with the purpose of illuminating the nature of the covenant with the image.

Because the Messiah's name is written in the people's hearts, they will "know the voice by which ye shall be called." This "calling" represents the obligations due the servant of the master. The master "calls" and the servant responds (Mosiah 26:24). Although the relationship is that of master and servant, it is not a relationship of distance, but of intimacy. The servant's duties bring him into contact with the master, allowing him to come to know the master intimately, earning the right to sit on master's right.

It is also important that Benjamin continues to stress the dualism of the left/right hand, not only here but also in the next verse.

Mosiah 5:14

> 14 And again, doth a man take an ass which belongeth to his neighbor, and keep him? I say unto you, Nay; he will not even suffer that he shall feed among

---

[7]Ibid., 330.

> his flocks, but will drive him away, and cast him out. I say unto you, that even so shall it be among you if ye know not the name by which ye are called.

This verse is particularly difficult to fully understand, because Benjamin assumes a level of information among his listeners that is not part of our modern context. These elements include:

- This verse describes someone who does not know the name "by which ye are called," a contrast with the servant in the previous verse who does know the name by which he is called.
- The ass was considered unclean.[8]
- On the literal level, Benjamin is saying that an unclean animal would be driven away from one's "clean" flocks.
- The action one would take in expelling the unclean animal is related to those who do not know the name by which they are called.

I see two possible readings for this verse. Likely Benjamin intended to evoke both meanings for his listeners. The first is the clear separation between good and evil. The good may remain with Yahweh, but the evil cannot. The second implication is that action must be taken to drive the unclean animal (individual) from the clean flock (congregation of the righteous). Because Benjamin has no police force, he is indicating a spiritual rejection by the heavenly king and possibly a physical banishment by the earthly king.

Mosiah 5:15

> 15 Therefore, I would that ye should be steadfast and immovable, always abounding in good works, that Christ, the Lord God Omnipotent, may seal you his, that you may be brought to heaven, that ye may have everlasting salvation and eternal life, through the wisdom, and power, and justice, and mercy of him who created all things, in heaven and in earth, who is God above all. Amen.

Benjamin seals the new covenant upon the people. Their half of the covenant is to "be steadfast and immovable, always abounding in good works." As they honor their obligations, Yahweh-Messiah—their spiritual father—will seal them up as his. They will bear his name and assume his attributes. Upon them he will bestow everlasting salvation and eternal life.

Text: This is the end of the quotation from Benjamin, and Mormon again ends a chapter. Although the sermon is over, the ceremonies are not, for the coronation has yet to follow. Mormon omits any description of this event. For his purposes, the really important actions have been recorded; the rest are merely historical details necessary to move the story along to the spiritually significant event.

---

[8]See Lev. 11:1–8, Deut. 14:3–8, Alison V. P. Coutts et al., "Complete Text of Benjamin's Speech with Notes and Comments," in *King Benjamin's Speech*, edited by John W. Welch and Stephen D. Ricks (Provo, Utah: FARMS, 1998), 607.

Mosiah 6

Mosiah 6:1–2

> 1 And now, king Benjamin thought it was expedient, after having finished speaking to the people, that he should take the names of all those who had entered into a covenant with God to keep his commandments.
> 2 And it came to pass that there was not one soul, except it were little children, but who had entered into the covenant and had taken upon them the name of Christ.

Benjamin orders a census that not only lists the people but records their decision about the covenant. How young are the "little" children? Presumably they are too young to articulate in so many words the content of the covenant, meaning that they cannot be accountable for it; furthermore, they are also already covered by Christ's atonement (Mosiah 3:16).

But beyond the practical purpose of the census are two unusual implications. First, even though this is a complete census, it contradicts the statement in Mosiah 2:2 that a census was not taken because there were so many people. This difference may simply reflect that both the time and purpose are now different. The census at the beginning of the gathering may have been a typical facet of the recurring ceremony; therefore, its omission would have been noteworthy, needing explanation. When Benjamin enumerates the people, however, its purpose is less that of a census than to record the covenantal declarations. Such declarations, taken person by person, allowed each person to state his or her intention before witnesses, thus physically and individually responding to what had earlier been a communal activity. Furthermore, because their names were listed, all of the power associated with naming was invoked. The name of Yahweh-Messiah had been given to the people; here they reciprocate, and the name of the individual covenanter is given to Yahweh-Messiah (through the king's messenger).

The second implication of this census is its timing. It would have been a time-consuming activity, even with all of the people in one place. Just as the delivery of Benjamin's text required literate servants, so would recording the names. It seems unlikely that the Zarahemlaites were universally literate, since almost all ancient societies that kept records had a specialized literate class in both the Old and New World, but particularly the New World.[1] Even if we assume a higher literacy rate

[1] Dennis Baron, "From Pencils to Pixels: The Stages of Literacy Technology," http://www2.english.uiuc.edu/baron/pencils%20to%20pixels.htm (accessed January 2005):

than might be expected, the scribes still had to take up scattered stations with writing instruments. If the name-taking had to be completed before the coronation could begin, the next event described in the text, it would have caused a significant delay. It seems reasonable that the original record maker, motivated by the strong connection between bestowing the name on the people and recording the names of the people who made the covenant, simply recorded the two events in sequence but that, because of logistical considerations, the name-recording may have been spread out over the rest of the festival.

Text: Although we have no way of knowing, it seems probable that Mormon recorded the events in the same sequence as his source document. The spiritual significance of recording the names would have been very important to the original historian, but Mormon's brief summary suggests that he saw it as less significant. Additionally, to this point we see little evidence that Mormon reworks his material extensively. His abridging efforts are mostly narrative ties between quoted speeches. If this perception is accurate, then coming up with a different order from that of the original scribe would have been unusual for him.

Apologetics: If we approach these verses with the hypothesis that Joseph Smith alone was responsible for the text, this disjunction between in-context and later-context importance becomes even more problematic. It is one thing to say that he would not have understood the importance of the name exchange in ancient civilizations but quite another to suppose that he understood it well enough to leave the tracks—then pushed it into the background of the text. Such a technique would have been either surprisingly inconsistent or surprisingly subtle.

Mosiah 6:3

> 3 And again, it came to pass that when king Benjamin had made an end of all these things, and had consecrated his son Mosiah to be a ruler and a king over his people, and had given him all the charges concerning the kingdom, and also had appointed priests to teach the people, that thereby they might hear and know the commandments of God, and to stir them up in remembrance of the oath which they had made, he dismissed the multitude, and they returned, every one, according to their families, to their own houses.

> Of course writing never spread very greatly in the ancient world. William Harris (1989) argues convincingly that no more that ten percent of the classical Greek or Roman populations could have been literate. One reason for this must be that writing technology remained both cumbersome and expensive: writing instruments, paints, and inks had to be hand made, and writing surfaces like clay tablets, wax tablets, and papyrus had to be laboriously prepared. Writing therefore remained exclusive, until cheap paper became available, and the printing press made mass production of written texts more affordable and less labor-intensive.

Linda Schele and David Freidel, *A Forest of Kings: The Untold Story of the Ancient Maya* (New York: William Morrow and Company, 1990), 58, note: "An ahau ["lord"] achieved fame as a scribe—not a political office, yet a highly valued specialist rank." They also note that a lineage of scribes had its own compound and temple at Copán. Ibid., 316.

Redaction: Mormon quickly summarizes the end of the festival in this single verse. His Mormon's purpose in including Benjamin's sermons is spiritual, not historical, focused exclusively on the spiritual transformation of the people into a new covenant society united under the name of Yahweh-Messiah. Thus, in a single sentence he rushes through what must have been the elaborate coronation ceremonies, the appointment (and probably the ordination) of priests, and other significant and time-consuming events, including the census.

Culture: As the multitude assembled by families, so they return home "according to their families." Once again this statement reminds us that the kin group was the primary organizational unit. The association of the kin groups and their "homes" confirms that Benjamin's people followed the typical Mesoamerican pattern of kin-based housing clusters. When each individual returns to his own house according to his family, the implication is that housing and families are geographically linked.

In Mesoamerica, this pattern continues to the present in more traditional communities and can be seen archaeologically in the types of shelter/temple groupings in many sites.[2]

Mosiah 6:4

> 4 And Mosiah began to reign in his father's stead. And he began to reign in the thirtieth year of his age, making in the whole, about four hundred and seventy-six years from the time that Lehi left Jerusalem.

Chronology: This verse contains two important pieces of historical information: first, that Mosiah begins his reign at the age of thirty, and second, that his reign begins 476 years after the departure from Jerusalem. In the dating system being used in this commentary, Mosiah's anointing would have occurred about 124 B.C. (See commentary accompanying 1 Nephi 10:4 for information on how this commentary calculates years.)

Mosiah 6:5

> 5 And king Benjamin lived three years and he died.

This short sentence records the end of one of the greatest figures of the Book of Mormon, a man who took two separate nations enmeshed in external and internal turmoil, and united them into a new religious community. His reward was that, for the rest of his life, "there was no contention among all his people for the space of three years" (v. 7).

Mosiah 6:6

> 6 And it came to pass that king Mosiah did walk in the ways of the Lord, and did observe his judgments and his statutes, and did keep his commandments in all things whatsoever he commanded him.

---

[2]Kent V. Flannery, "Two Possible Village Subdivisions: The Courtyard Group and the Residential Ward," in *The Early Mesoamerican Village*, edited by Kent V. Flannery (New York: Academic Press, 1976), 73 and Linda Schele and Peter Mathews, *The Code of Kings: The Language of Seven Sacred Maya Temples and Tombs* (New York: Scribner, 1998), 299.

Redaction: It seems likely that this verse is not only Mormon's synopsis of Mosiah's reign but also his evaluation of him. Mormon uses history to highlight the spiritual. I hypothesize that Mormon's source would not have contained such a simple summary. Although declarations of kingly piety are well known, they usually come in the context of actions. In this verse, then, we see Mormon as editor, extracting from his source the essential information he wants to communicate.

Mosiah 6:7

> 7 And king Mosiah did cause his people that they should till the earth. And he also, himself, did till the earth, that thereby he might not become burdensome to his people, that he might do according to that which his father had done in all things. And there was no contention among all his people for the space of three years.

Culture/Redaction: This verse is also most likely a synopsis of Mormon's source material, and it provides significant information about his editorial procedures. First, the coronation and reign of a new king would have been the most important political event of the period, no doubt reflected as such in the source document. Mormon does not omit it, but he almost certainly assigns it diminished importance. With due caution, we can work forward from Benjamin's address and backward from Mormon's summary to conjecture about Nephite/Zarahemlaite society at this point.

From Benjamin's sermon, we know that he labored with his own hands to be sure that his people would not be oppressed. He was also very concerned about the social stratification created by wealth and instituted the new covenant, at least in part, to eliminate strife resulting from such stratification. No doubt, the historians who recorded events in after Benjamin's sermon and during Mosiah's early reign were keenly conscious of the social dimensions of the covenant. Thus, it seemed to have been important for them to record that the people, including Mosiah, tilled the soil. Since this society was an agricultural one, the information seems completely unremarkable. The Book of Mormon seldom mentions farming, harvests, or weather unless there was some kind of famine-causing disaster or to differentiate the Nephites from the "uncivilized" culture of the Lamanites (Enos 1:20-21). Why, then, would the original historians have recorded these events at all, and why, in particular, would they have impressed Mormon enough to include them?

It seems reasonable to me that the original writers were spelling out the social consequences of the social covenant. It is unlikely that every merchant or trader took up farming as an exclusive occupation; rather, farming symbolizes the social leveling that occurred when even the king would till the ground. Thus, while the three years of peace may have spelled, to the war-weary Mormon, a lack of armed conflict with their neighbors, the mention of tilling seems to describe a social reorganization that eliminated class stratification. If there is no social distance between the king and the peasant, then there is no distinction throughout the society. Thus, the political peace from armed conflict against the Lamanites is matched by internal peace as the people accept and implement the spiritual and social covenant.

Text: This verse closes a chapter in the 1830 edition, but the chapter break fits in a different organizational category than those Mormon created for Benjamin's address. In this case, he is clearly beginning a new story: the expedition undertaken to find those who had returned to the land of Nephi years earlier.

This break may signal Mormon's awareness that one major story has ended and another has begun, rather than the organization of his source. That material seems to have been organized year by year, rather than event by event, a known feature of at least later Mesoamerican documents. Many of the extant codices use year markers to separate scenes and actions. Perhaps the most interesting example is the "Anales de Cuauhtitlan" (Annals of Cuauhtitlan), translated into Spanish from a circa 1570 Nahuatl document. It is organized, as its name suggests, by the passage of time, covering hundreds of years. Typically, it announces a year, then summarizes events that occurred in that year. Several years are listed without any events.[3] It would appear that the author of the "Annals of Cuauhtitlan" is copying the overall structure from a pre-Columbian document, else there would be no reason for the empty years. It suggests that structuring by years was a native literary tradition.

Such annual structure is less clear in the Book of Mormon, but the similarities are suggestive and become particularly marked during the reign of the judges. Apparently Mormon felt free to change the organizational structure of his source to meet his own literary needs.

---

[3]"Anales de Cuauhtitlan," in *Codice Chimalpopoca*, edited by Primo Feliciano Velázquez (Mexico City: Universidad Nacional Autónoma de México, 1975), 5.

Mosiah 7

Mosiah 7:1

> 1 And now, it came to pass that after king Mosiah had had continual peace for the space of three years, he was desirous to know concerning the people who went up to dwell in the land of Lehi-Nephi, or in the city of Lehi-Nephi; for his people had heard nothing from them from the time they left the land of Zarahemla; therefore, they wearied him with their teasings.

Text: The 1830 edition begins a new chapter here. Mormon sees the experiences of those who returned to the land of Nephi as a major event in the people's spiritual history. Finding them and leading them back is a pivotal event, triggering several other significant stories, including a major conversion among the Lamanites and the emergence of Alma$_1$ as a spiritual leader.

This incident is first mentioned in Omni 1:27–30:

> And now I would speak somewhat concerning a certain number who went up into the wilderness to return to the land of Nephi; for there was a large number who were desirous to possess the land of their inheritance.
>
> Wherefore, they went up into the wilderness. And their leader being a strong and mighty man, and a stiffnecked man, wherefore he caused a contention among them; and they were all slain, save fifty, in the wilderness, and they returned again to the land of Zarahemla.
>
> And it came to pass that they also took others to a considerable number, and took their journey again into the wilderness.
>
> And I, Amaleki, had a brother, who also went with them; and I have not since known concerning them.

In verse 1 Mosiah is referring to the second of these expeditions. We have a little more information about the first expedition in Mosiah 9:1–2, in which Zeniff tells his story, explaining the first expedition briefly as background. He does not mention the number of survivors as Omni does. This second expedition was also quite numerous, apparently enough for a small village, according to Zeniff. They seem to have been motivated by a desire for their ancestral land and perhaps remembrances of an easier life there. According to Omni's description of the departure, they left during the reign of Benjamin (or perhaps Mosiah$_1$), not during the reign of Mosiah$_2$. The story of their rediscovery begins three years after the coronation, the same year during which Benjamin died. The mission to find them could have left either before or after this event; but given his stress on unity, they may have felt that it would have grieved him if they left before his death.

Geography: While this passage contains no specific geographic information, it implies that the land of Nephi was not within easy reach of Zarahemla, either because of forbidding terrain or because of simple distance.

Chronology: Deciphering the chronology from Mosiah$_1$ to the Zeniffite/Nephite reunion is a complex task. The first relevant fixed date is 320 years after Lehi left Jerusalem (approximately 276 B.C.); in this year, the "more wicked part of the Nephites (Omni 1:5) were destroyed. The next firm date is Mosiah$_2$'s coronation 476 years after Lehi left Jerusalem (approximately 124 B.C., Mosiah 6:4). A rough chronology can be approximately calculated from other data in the text.

The next important date following the coronation of Mosiah$_2$ is 509 years after Lehi left Jerusalem, and 33 years after the coronation (92 B.C., Mosiah 29:46). In this year three important things occur:

- King Mosiah$_2$ dies (Mosiah 29:46)
- Alma$_1$ dies (Mosiah 29:45)
- The reign of the judges begins (Mosiah 29:44).

The reign of the judges signals a change in some dating practices in the Book of Mormon, but the other two pieces of information illuminate this particular chronology. Mosiah dies at age sixty-three (Mosiah 29:46) and Alma at eighty-two (Mosiah 29:45). Thus, Mosiah$_2$ was born in 155 B.C., and Alma in 174 B.C.

Ammon left in search of the Zeniffites in 121 B.C., three years after the coronation. There is no indication of how much time elapsed between Ammon's departure from Zarahemla and the arrival of Limhi and Alma's people, but these events apparently occurred quite rapidly—certainly after 121 B.C. and probably no later than 120–119 B.C. (Alma would have been about fifty-three at this point.)

But when did Zeniff and his people leave Zarahemla? Zeniff unfortunately uses his own calendar, dating events from the beginning of his own reign. We know a precise count of years, but it is not easy to integrate them into the larger calendar that began with Lehi's leaving Jerusalem. Zeniff mentions one event that occurred twelve years after his reign, another in the thirteenth year, and the last (Laman's death) twenty-two years after the beginning his reign (Mosiah 9:11, 14; 10:3). Laman's death apparently triggered conflict between the Lamanites and the Zeniffites, resulting in a war which the Zeniffites won. At some unspecified point, Zeniff died.

Noah succeeded him. At another unspecified point—but after Noah had indulged in a conspicuous building spree—Abinadi began his prophetic mission among Noah's people and was put to death two years later (Mosiah 12:1). Noah's own death occurred almost immediately. Limhi, Noah's successor, had peace for two years (Mosiah 19:29).

These events give us some time frames to work with. The first is an absolute minimum number of years from the time Zeniff left to the time until his descendants returned: twenty-two years for Zeniff's reign, two years between the time of Abinadi's first visit and his death, and two years of peace under Limhi. Therefore, the Zeniffites were in the land of Lehi-Nephi for no fewer than twenty-six years.

While this figure is the absolute minimum, the actual number of years must have been larger. The chronology becomes particularly fuzzy between (1) the Zeniffite victory and Abinadi's first mission, and (2) the end of Limhi's period of peace and Ammon's arrival. Here conjecture must substitute for firmer information. How long, for instance, did it take to subjugate Limhi's people? Obviously it did not happen in a matter of a few days, but a year was probably ample. Was there more than a year of semi-slavery before Ammon's arrival? This calculation yields the probable minimum of twenty-seven years in Lehi-Nephi.

How much time elapsed between the Zeniffite victory and Abinadi's first visit? Two major events occurred in that time period: Zeniff's death and Noah's coronation. Because the text appears to move quickly between those events, perhaps only months separated the two. Indeed, the stress of the battle may have precipitated Zeniff's death, for he notes that he is "in my old age" (Mosiah 10:10). I see no compelling reason to add a lengthy period of time here.

How much time elapsed between Noah's coronation and Abinadi's first visit? The text suggests that Noah constructed many elaborate buildings, a project that, given the nature of manual labor, had to have taken considerable time (Mosiah 11:8–13). I also hypothesize that most of these projects were completed before Abinadi's second visit, since Noah's reign terminated so quickly afterward. Given the numbers of buildings, the materials, and their widespread locations (Shilom, as well as Lehi-Nephi, Mosiah 11:13), a period of about ten years seems reasonable. This time span increases the Zeniffite stay to thirty-seven years.

Now let's integrate the two calendars. We have no information on how much time passed between the arrival of Mosiah's people in Zarahemla and Zeniff's desire to return to the land of inheritance. Was it a case of instant homesickness, or did nostalgia build gradually, blurring the more unpleasant aspects of life in Nephi and making it seem more appealing? If the latter, perhaps five years might be seen as the maximum. This would date Mosiah$_1$'s arrival in Zarahemla as no earlier than 162 B.C. The Zeniffites left Zarahemla in approximately 157 B.C. Zeniff died in approximately 137 B.C. He almost certainly accompanied Mosiah$_1$ from Nephi to Zarahemla, since he claims a special knowledge of the land of Nephi (Mosiah 9:1). He was thus probably more or less of an age with Mosiah$_1$. The fact that he died "in my old age" helps us formulate an estimate of how long Mosiah$_1$ and Benjamin reigned. Zeniff would have died approximately thirteen years before the anointing of Mosiah$_2$. If Mosiah$_1$ and Zeniff died in the same year, Mosiah$_1$ would have been king for twenty-seven years, and Benjamin for thirteen. Amaleki apparently also left the city of Nephi, since he was born "in the days of Mosiah" and lived to see Benjamin become king (Omni 1:23). Since Amaleki considered himself to be old (Omni 1:25), he was presumably at least fifty when he died. Mosiah$_1$ would naturally have been older, so that Amaleki could be "born in the days of Mosiah."

Verses 27–30 present something of a chronological problem as they follow the anointing of Benjamin. This would place the death of Mosiah$_1$ very early in the chronology, within the estimated five years prior to the departure of the Zeniffites. While this is possible, lengthening Benjamin's reign to thirty-five years, it is also possible that these returnees left before Benjamin's coronation and Omni simply noted the information as an aside. As such, the events it records may or may not be in chronological order.

Perhaps the strongest argument for seeing the departure after Benjamin's coronation lies in a problematic textual variant. In Mosiah 21:28, the 1830 edition references Benjamin as though he were the sitting king in Zarahemla during Ammon's rescue mission. Clearly, Mosiah$_2$ was the king when Ammon left. The plausible explanation for that variant would argue for Benjamin being the king when the Zeniffites left Zarahemla. (See commentary accompanying Mosiah 21:28.)

Vocabulary: The word *teasings* is likely used with the more archaic meaning of "to worry or irritate by persistent action which vexes or annoys."[1]

Mosiah 7:2

> 2 And it came to pass that king Mosiah granted that sixteen of their strong men might go up to the land of Lehi-Nephi, to inquire concerning their brethren.

This expedition is a modest one—sixteen is large enough for self-defense, small enough for rapid movement, but far too small to be a settlement.

Is the number sixteen significant? If there had been twelve, we would immediately know that it also had symbolic significance. Just as the numbers three, seven, twelve, and forty have special meaning in our Old World scriptures, Mesoamerica also attached significance to numbers, particularly four, which represents completion or wholeness. This number appears in many creation accounts (e.g., four world trees, four deities assigned to the four directions, and four ages of creation).[2] As four fours, sixteen would seem like an emininently satisfying number to a native Mesoamerican.

Mosiah 7:3

> 3 And it came to pass that on the morrow they started to go up, having with them one Ammon, he being a strong and mighty man, and a descendant of Zarahemla; and he was also their leader.

---

[1]Royal Skousen, *Analysis of Textual Variants of the Book of Mormon*, THE CRITICAL TEXT OF THE BOOK OF MORMON, Vol. 4, Part 2 (Provo, Utah: Foundation for Ancient Research and Mormon Studies, 2005), 2:1208, quoting the Oxford English Dictionary.

[2]The Mexica five-age, or five-sun system is probably a later elaboration of the more basic Mesoamerican four-sun myth. See Brant A. Gardner, "Reconstructing the Ethnohistory of Myth: A Structural Study of the Aztec 'Legend of the Suns,' in *Symbol and Meaning beyond the Closed Community*, edited by Gary Gossen (Albany: Institute for Mesoamerican Studies, State University of New York at Albany, 1986), 19–34.

Text: Mormon begins the story with a synopsis. His source may have been either the "official" royal history kept by Mosiah's historian or the record kept by the party of sixteen. It will soon become apparent, however, that the latter is correct. Either Mormon was using it directly or it was later copied into the "official" record. Given the varied nature of the other sources Mormon uses (letters, missionary accounts, and secondary records such as that behind 3 Nephi) it would be most logical that these various sources had been copied into the plates of Nephi rather than being stored as separate records.

Literature: There is a slight possibility that this verse camouflages a Mesoamerican literary style. Several Mesoamerican languages allow a single "word" to incorporate pronouns, verbs, and direct and indirect objects. This linguistic ability to contain what we would consider short sentences in a single word or couple of words led to a structural parallelism that was not built on twos, which is common in English (repetition of an element so that there are two representations of it) but rather on a set of three in which each element was a different adjectival or adverbial description of the main subject.

For example, Ammon is characterized by three descriptions: he is a "strong and mighty man," "a descendent of Zarahemla," and "also their leader." If we assume that Joseph Smith is translating meaning more than words (as evidence throughout this commentary suggests) and attempting to make the English meanings clearer than the original text (which the relative smooth reading of the English text suggests) then we might "untranslate" this verse back into a Mesoamerican language model that yields a stripped-down triple modifier of Ammon, with the English required to make better sense of the verse removed: "[they had with them] Ammon; Strong-and-mighty-man-he-was, Zarahemla-descendant-he-was, leader-he-was."

An interesting aspect of this hypothetical reconstruction is that it focuses on Ammon's leadership as the most prominent idea, rather than leaving it as a near-afterthought, which it seems to be in English. The Mesoamerican literary device positions the most important item last because the triplet moves the mind to follow and emphasize the sequence.

This comment is a possibility only. It should not be construed as proof that a Mesoamerican language was involved. It is completely possible that this feature appears coincidentally, just as constructions characteristic of Hebrew might also occur coincidentally. Nevertheless, since the reconstruction provides a better reason for the word order than the English translation, it is at least worth noting.

Mosiah 7:4

> 4 And now, they knew not the course they should travel in the wilderness to go up to the land of Lehi-Nephi; therefore they wandered many days in the wilderness, even forty days did they wander.

Geography: Distances in the Book of Mormon are measured by time. Thus, Ammon's journey from Zarahemla to Nephi took forty days. However, this route was obviously not the most direct, since Alma and his converts made essentially the same journey in reverse, accompanied by women, children, and flocks, in only twenty-one days (Mosiah 18:1–7; 23:1–3; 24:20, 25).[3]

History: The journey of Mosiah$_1$ and his people began from the land of Nephi in haste and apparent danger. While they may have had a general idea of which direction to go, they had no specific destination in mind. They did not map their route and almost certainly did not travel directly to Zarahemla. Similarly, we can conclude that Ammon's group did not have a map or knowledge of a trade route. Apparently, there had been no attempts to communicate directly, either for personal or commercial reasons. The people of Zarahemla know nothing of Zeniff's group and have no relations with the Lamanites in the land of Nephi.

The forty days may either be a literal record, meaning that they had to spend approximately half of their time searching for the land, or it may be a symbolic number indicating a long time—perhaps the forty years' wandering of the children of Israel or a tenfold multiplication of four in the Mesoamerican system. However, it may also be an approximation, a figure rounded off for convenience. Certainly Ammon's group would have gathered all available information about landmarks that Mosiah$_1$'s people passed and how long their journey took. The length of time required could not have been a precise distance, but knowing the approximate time required would tell Ammon when they might have traveled too far.

Mosiah 7:5

5 And when they had wandered forty days they came to a hill, which is north of the land of Shilom, and there they pitched their tents.

Culture: Because pitching tents seems to be the equivalent of creating temporary shelters, these "tents" may have been lean-to or booths, like the temporary structures erected at the time of Benjamin's sermon. (See commentary accompanying Mosiah 2:6 for more information on tents.) The fact that they selected a hill suggests that they chose high ground for better range of vision and better potential defense. Although they do not mention military preparations, it seems reasonable that they would have exercised caution when entering the land of the Lamanites.

Mosiah 7:6–7

6 And Ammon took three of his brethren, and their names were Amaleki, Helem, and Hem, and they went down into the land of Nephi.
7 And behold, they met the king of the people who were in the land of Nephi, and in the land of Shilom; and they were surrounded by the king's guard, and were taken, and were bound, and were committed to prison.

This group of four is a small scouting party, carrying out a quick reconnoiter. The fact that they were willing to approach a royal excursion, which would have been armed,

---

[3]John L. Sorenson, *An Ancient American Setting for the Book of Mormon* (Salt Lake City: Deseret Book/Provo, Utah: Foundation for Ancient Research and Mormon Studies, 1985), 7.

suggests that they had some way of recognizing that they had reached the people they sought. But if they did not know where they were going (v. 4), then how did they know that they had found the correct people? Mormon does not tell us.

The first possibility is that Nephites were so distinctive they could recognize each other on sight, suggesting the contrast between the Lamanite "skin of darkness" and Nephite fairness. Limhi's guards mistook Ammon's party for the outlaw former priests of King Noah,[4] so Ammon and his party were not immediately classified as Lamanite. Nevertheless, the evidence of the text does not support an obvious difference in pigmentation that would allow for immediate distinction between Nephite and Lamanite. (See commentary accompanying 2 Nephi 5:21.)

The second, and more probable, way that Ammon recognized Limhi was that they had been directed to Limhi's city by local peoples they had questioned. Ammon and his three companions were obviously outnumbered. They would not have approached a well-armed contingent in the open without some belief that they had found the people for whom they searched. Furthermore, because Ammon didn't really know where he was going, it would be absolutely amazing if the very first people he happened to meet were the people he hoped to find. It seems more plausible that Ammon's party asked about the people of Zeniff when they began to encounter small villages after they emerged from the wilderness. The smaller villages would not have standing armies, and it seems likely that rules of hospitality typical of rural populations would require them to assist needy travelers. In such a scenario, Ammon would have led a small party, not the whole group, into a village. The villagers would have not been alarmed by weapons for hunting; but if Ammon's group were carrying military weapons (assuming a culturally known difference between the two types), the scouting party would have left them with the larger party. Since the people of Zeniff were tributaries to the Lamanites, the villagers wouldn't see a small party searching for them as a threat to the Lamanite city that dominated the area. There would be no reason to prevent Ammon's party from finding Zeniff's people.

Culture: Though the discussion of Limhi's rule is still in the future, it is worth noting that Limhi is considered not only a king but and a king over two lands: the land of Lehi-Nephi and the land of Shilom, south and slightly east of Nephi. Both of these lands were part of the original grant from the Lamanite king to Zeniff (Mosiah 9:6), retained through Noah to Limhi, in spite of the contentions and wars with the Lamanites. The implications of this grant will be examined later in the story of Zeniff. (See commentary accompanying Mosiah 9:7.)

Mosiah 7:8

8 And it came to pass when they had been in prison two days they were again brought before the king, and their bands were loosed; and they stood before

---

[4]We learn in Mosiah 21:23–24 that they were considered to be the renegade priests of Noah. Mormon does not give us that information at this time because his readers do not have the necessary background to know who the priests are nor why they should be considered enemies.

the king, and were permitted, or rather commanded, that they should answer the questions which he should ask them.

Redaction: This verse presents the interesting textual phrase: "were permitted, or rather commanded." The second phrase, "or rather commanded," interprets the first, "were permitted." The connotations of the two phrases are sufficiently different that they make unlikely companions—nor are they literary parallels. I suggest that the second phrase was added by someone commenting on the ironic possibilities of the first.

The two candidates for the person who added that phrase are Mormon and Joseph Smith. While an argument might be made for either, Mormon seems more likely to me. This verse is description, rather than quotation; it is the kind of text that Mormon has digested from the source documents before him. As one familiar with the prerogatives of kings, Mormon would also be in a better position than Joseph to understand the irony of the official version—"permitted." As I have already pointed out, Mormon tends to quote dialogue but create descriptive summaries. Because this particular word appears in Limhi's opening statement (v. 11), Mormon almost certainly quotes it but could not resist the editorial insertion.

As a side note, this entry also provides confirmation of what we have probably already assumed: that even in his abridgment, Mormon is faithful to his sources. Because we cannot compare his version with the original, such details as this are our best indicator of Mormon's close reliance on the texts he is abridging.

Mosiah 7:9

9 And he said unto them: Behold, I am Limhi, the son of Noah, who was the son of Zeniff, who came up out of the land of Zarahemla to inherit this land, which was the land of their fathers, who was made a king by the voice of the people.

It is typical for a king to declare himself formally. In this case, Limhi identifies himself by citing his lineage. He makes an explicit connection with the land of Zarahemla, because that is most likely the source of ultimate authority. Limhi does not, apparently, know that his captives are also from Zarahemla, so his statement to Ammon is not one of recognition of commonality but rather his assertion of authority.

This practice is also known from later Mesoamerican records. Those who moved from one area to another recapitulated their link to a remote but established lineage. The Cakchiquel specifically received their authority from Nacxit, the ruler in Tollan: "The Lord Nacxit said: 'Climb up to these columns of stone, enter into my house. I will give you sovereignty.'"[5] Neither the "Popol Vuh" nor the "Title of the Lords of Totonicapan" for the Quiché mentions sovereignty directly, but both

---

[5]*Annals of the Cakchiquels and Title of the Lords of Totonicapán*, translated by Dionisio José Chonay and Delia Goetz (Norman: University of Oklahoma Press, 1974), 65.

trace their foundational lineages to events in Tollan.[6] Tollan is "the place of cattail reeds" and is either a mythical place of origin or a designation for a particular people and place (Tula, Hidalgo) that was populated from around 700 A.D. to 1200 A.D. during which time it grew to become the dominant power in Central Mexico and influenced much of Mesoamerica. In spite of the similarity in name, all Mesoamerican descriptions of Tollan do not refer to the later city of Tula (Hispanicized version of the Nahuatl *Tollan*). Even before the references cited for the Cakchiquel and Quiché, Maya cultures would invoke Tollan as the source of their authority. In the earlier times, the reference was not Tula but Teotihuacan. However, the reference to authority was the same. David Stuart, an epigrapher from the Peabody Museum of Harvard University noted: "I . . . argue that Maya rulers kept open a claim to this earlier history, evoking Teotihuacan as both a place and an idea of political origin. This discussion [is] based in large part on my earlier decipherment of the Classic Maya name for Teotihuacan, 'Place of Cattails,' (equivalent to Nahuatl *Tollan*)."[7]

Reference: See "Excursus: "The Voice of the People," following Mosiah 29.

Mosiah 7:10–11

10 And now, I desire to know the cause whereby ye were so bold as to come near the walls of the city, when I, myself, was with my guards without the gate?

11 And now, for this cause have I suffered that ye should be preserved, that I might inquire of you, or else I should have caused that my guards should have put you to death. Ye are permitted to speak.

Redaction: Possibly, this speech is a direct quotation; however, it seems more likely that the text is approximate but conveys the meaning accurately. Presumably, Limhi's court would have included a recorder who could have preserved the exact text, if necessary. But even a partial paraphrase would have been created by a trained, official scribe. Mormon again seems to be quoting his source.

Mosiah 7:12–13

12 And now, when Ammon saw that he was permitted to speak, he went forth and bowed himself before the king; and rising again he said: O king, I am very thankful before God this day that I am yet alive, and am permitted to speak; and I will endeavor to speak with boldness;

13 For I am assured that if ye had known me ye would not have suffered that I should have worn these bands. For I am Ammon, and am a descendant of

---

[6]"Title of the Lords of Totonicapan," in ibid., 169–171; *Popol Vuh: The Definitive Edition of the Mayan Book of the Dawn of Life and the Glories of Gods and Kings*, translated by Dennis Tedlock (New York: Simon and Schuster, 1985), 171–76; *Popol Vuh*, translated by Dennis Tedlock (New York: Simon and Schuster, 1985), 171–76.

[7]David Stuart, "The Arrival of Strangers': Teotihuacan and Tollan in Classic Maya History," in *Mesoamerica's Classic Heritage: From Teotihuacan to the Aztecs*, edited by David Carrasco, Lindsay Jones, and Scott Sessions (Boulder: University Press of Colorado, 2000), 466.

Zarahemla, and have come up out of the land of Zarahemla to inquire concerning our brethren, whom Zeniff brought up out of that land.

Culture: In Ammon's half of this formal exchange, he repeats the basic genealogical formula. Limhi had declared his lineage through the founder of the dynasty and identified its ultimate authority in Zarahemla. Ammon is no king, but his lineage likewise links him to Zarahemla, both the king (his ancestor) and the land (the current political regime). Ammon, a lineal Zarahemlaite, was entrusted with the mission of finding a dynasty founded by a lineal/cultural Nephite from the original city of Nephi. Such an assignment suggests that the Zarahemlaites were thoroughly accepted as participants in Benjamin's new covenant. Had there been any continuing animosity between the descendants of Nephi and the descendants of Zarahemla, then almost certainly, the mission would have been given to a descendant of Nephi.

Mosiah 7:14

14 And now, it came to pass that after Limhi had heard the words of Ammon, he was exceedingly glad, and said: Now, I know of a surety that my brethren who were in the land of Zarahemla are yet alive. And now, I will rejoice; and on the morrow I will cause that my people shall rejoice also.

Just as Zoram's oath (1 Ne. 4:37) altered a hostile relationship, Ammon's simple declaration frees him and his companions from their chains and signals the beginning of a celebration. No longer a danger, they are kinsmen and welcome guests. This rapid shift of position is precisely the kind of social relationship that kinship creates. The declaration of genealogy serves this very purpose of distinguishing friend from foe.

Limhi declares a day of rejoicing not simply because Ammon has arrived, but because he now "know[s] of a surety that my brethren who were in the land of Zarahemla are yet alive." It seems like an odd statement. Why would he ever doubt it? Zeniff's party was small compared to the Nephites who remained in Zarahemla. This statement of uncertainty, carried across three generations, suggests the level of conflict in the union of the Nephites and Zarahemlaites. It must have seemed at least possible to Limhi that the contentions had increased to the point of armed conflict, conflict in which the more numerous Zarahemlaites easily had numerical superiority and might have exterminated or exiled the lineal/cultural Nephites, who were Limhi's "brethren."

Mosiah 7:15

15 For behold, we are in bondage to the Lamanites, and are taxed with a tax which is grievous to be borne. And now, behold, our brethren will deliver us out of our bondage, or out of the hands of the Lamanites, and we will be their slaves; for it is better that we be slaves to the Nephites than to pay tribute to the king of the Lamanites.

Culture: Limhi succinctly summarizes their social/economic situation. In addition to his genuine joy at restoring the contact with their own people, Limhi immediately feels an upsurge of hope that Zarahemla will provide a powerful ally who will free them from Lamanite oppression. How could Limhi assume in one sentence that the Nephites in Zarahemla were dead and, in the next, assume that they were sufficiently numerous and powerful to prevail against the Lamanites? This transition occurs so quickly that it suggests omitted parts in the exchange between Ammon and Limhi. Either Ammon told Limhi more about the situation in Zarahemla, or Limhi assumed that Zarahemla was reasonably powerful if it were able to spare and outfit the search party.

Limhi's assertion that it is better to be slaves to the Nephites than tributaries of the Lamanites is probably hyperbole. For the statement to be literally true, Limhi would have to have a knowledge of Nephite slavery, which Benjamin has made clear does not exist among his people. Indeed, it is difficult to imagine the level of destitution required for kinsmen to become slaves. More likely, Limhi is rhetorically exaggerating their pain to elicit the assistance in a fight about which Ammon, as yet, knows nothing.

Mosiah 7:16

> 16 And now, king Limhi commanded his guards that they should no more bind Ammon nor his brethren, but caused that they should go to the hill which was north of Shilom, and bring their brethren into the city, that thereby they might eat, and drink, and rest themselves from the labors of their journey; for they had suffered many things; they had suffered hunger, thirst, and fatigue.

Redaction: Obviously, Ammon did not divulge the existence of his party until he knew they would be favorably received. Because the text of his exchange with Limhi does not include the revelation of his party, it must have been on the plates but Mormon chose to report only the result. Mormon is condensing the account before him.

Mosiah 7:17

> 17 And now, it came to pass on the morrow that king Limhi sent a proclamation among all his people, that thereby they might gather themselves together to the temple, to hear the words which he should speak unto them.

As promised, Limhi declared a day of public rejoicing, sending out messengers for his people to leave their fields. Like other Mesoamerican settlements, including Zarahemla, most of the people live outside the town on their land. The proclamation is both a necessary and the most effective way of communicating with the scattered population.

The very fact of gathering generates rejoicing. Usually only two events would draw the people from their fields: war or festival. Since the proclamation did not announce war, this gathering was obviously the second—a festival. They would remain together for at least a day, bringing their provisions with them to form the basis for a communal exchange of food. This sharing was as important a factor in maintaining social connections in an agricultural society as is gossip on the periodic market days.

The temple in Limhi's city probably followed the same pattern as other Mesoamerican temples. It would be built in a large enclosure, which served as a public gathering space. A stepped pyramid, the temple itself would focus attention on the king and allow him to address the people conveniently.

Mosiah 7:18

> 18 And it came to pass that when they had gathered themselves together that he spake unto them in this wise, saying: O ye, my people, lift up your heads and be comforted; for behold, the time is at hand, or is not far distant, when we shall no longer be in subjection to our enemies, notwithstanding our many strugglings, which have been in vain; yet I trust there remaineth an effectual struggle to be made.

Redaction: Although Mormon gives us Limhi's opening speech, he skips Ammon's address (Mosiah 8:2–3). Limhi begins by declaring that his people's deliverance is at hand. This liberation, we know (v. 15), is keyed to Ammon's arrival. But despite this strong connection, Limhi does not introduce Ammon and his brethren. He does not even mention them! Most likely, this was not an oversight. It simply wasn't necessary. No doubt such momentous news had already spread throughout the land. Limhi's people know that it was one of the reasons they were gathering for this special festival. Strangers, especially friendly strangers from that other homeland, was not the kind of news that anyone would forget to pass along.

Why, since Mormon abbreviates Ammon's discourse, does he quote Limhi's? I believe there are two reasons. Limhi reviews his people's history and also stresses their faith. Both of those topics are significant to Mormon, especially the second. When Ammon begins, he explains Benjamin's new covenant. This topic would have been tremendously important to his Limhi's people but too thoroughly discussed in Mormon's text to need more than a cursory review.

Mosiah 7:19–20

> 19 Therefore, lift up your heads, and rejoice, and put your trust in God, in that God who was the God of Abraham, and Isaac, and Jacob; and also, that God who brought the children of Israel out of the land of Egypt, and caused that they should walk through the Red Sea on dry ground, and fed them with manna that they might not perish in the wilderness; and many more things did he do for them.
>
> 20 And again, that same God has brought our fathers out of the land of Jerusalem, and has kept and preserved his people even until now; and behold, it is because of our iniquities and abominations that he has brought us into bondage.

Limhi began his discourse with a promise of salvation, expressing confidence and hope even though "our many strugglings . . . have been in vain." How can Limhi speak with such assurance of the "effectual struggle to be made"? I believe that the answer again is connected to Ammon—not only a reconnection to Zarahemla, but a reconnection with Yahweh's people. The hope that he holds out for his people are two mighty interventions by Yahweh for his people in the form of a life-saving exodus: first, the flight of Israel from Egypt, and second, the flight of Lehi's family from the doomed Jerusalem. Limhi seems to be using these examples to suggest that their salvation will come, not in a rescuing invasion by the Zarahemlaites, but in his people's exodus to Zarahemla.

Their previous ineffectual struggles had been military attempts to allow them to remain free in the land of Nephi. These futile attempts make it clear that the next effort has to be different. Confirmation that Zarahemla still exists opens up the possibility of salvation by escape—a flight to refuge.

But why hadn't the Limhites thought of this solution earlier? Why couldn't they have left whether Zarahemla existed or not? I hypothesize that they may not have known a direction to go where they would not have found the land already occupied by people who would have resisted their incursion. We must remember that their attempt to find Zarahemla had failed. Without kin to go to, any other people would be non-kin and therefore strangers and enemies. Under those conditions they would have been trading a military difficulty with the known Lamanites for a military difficulty with unknown Lamanites. Zarahemla, however, offers refuge, not only through lineage, but through the welcome represented by Zarahemla's representatives.

Mosiah 7:21

> 21 And ye all are witnesses this day, that Zeniff, who was made king over this people, he being over-zealous to inherit the land of his fathers, therefore being deceived by the cunning and craftiness of king Laman, who having entered into a treaty with king Zeniff, and having yielded up into his hands the possessions of a part of the land, or even the city of Lehi-Nephi, and the city of Shilom; and the land round about—

Rhetoric: Limhi begins to recount his people's history. This is not because they do not know it, but because that history frames current events. When Limhi recounts the arrival of his people in the land of Nephi, he describes Zeniff as "over-zealous" and "deceived." Zeniff called himself over-zealous (Mosiah 9:3) and likely came to feel that they had been deceived (Mosiah 9:14–15). Limhi is explaining their current situation by pointing to the sins of their fathers.

The contrast between this bondage-producing past and his people's current righteousness lets Limhi encourage an increase of faith that they can be liberated. I suspect that, by recounting the tale of Lamanite deception, he is preparing his people psychologically to abandon their homes for the eventual move to Zarahemla.

Geography: Sorenson assumes that the city of Nephi (pre-Zarahemla) and the city of Lehi-Nephi are the same; he suggests the archaeological site of Kaminaljuyú (outside modern Guatemala City, Guatemala) as a logical location.[8] While he makes a geographical case for this assignment, it is also possible that there is a difference between Lehi-Nephi and Nephi. For example, when Zeniff returns to the land of his fathers, he does not return specifically to the *city* of his fathers. While nearly every city was surrounded by "lands" as dependent areas, the Book of Mormon also uses "land" more generically as a region. Sorenson suggests that Zeniff's chief motive for moving back to Lehi-Nephi might have been arable land.[9] Therefore, he may not have been primarily motivated by the reacquiring the buildings of the urban site. The possibility of Lehi-Nephi and Nephi as separate sites helps us visualize a more logical scenario for Mosiah$_1$'s exodus and Zeniff's return. Mosiah$_1$ did not bring all of the Nephites with him, nor does it seem likely that all of the lineal Nephites would have vanished from the area. However, Zeniff did not, apparently, meet any kinfolk. He negotiated with a Lamanite king, who ruled over the city of Nephi (to which the city of Lehi-Nephi would have been dependent, if, in fact, it was a separate city).

Kaminaljuyú was both relatively important and rich at this time. Susan Toby Evans, professor of anthropology at Pennsylvania State University, describes the city during this time period: "In the highlands above the coast, Kaminaljuyú during the Arenal phase (300 B.C.–A.D. 100) continued to direct more of its attention toward the coastal plain rather than toward the Chiapas highlands. During this period, the later part of Miraflores culture, population densities were greatest and the site underwent its most expansive program of monumental building and production of sculptures."[10] It seems odd that, right at the time of greatest population expansion, the residents of the city of Nephi (if it were Kaminaljuyú) would voluntarily abandon it for Zeniff's small group, especially since they would have been seen as outsiders. For these reasons, it seems more reasonable to envision a smaller village of Lehi-Nephi in the land of Nephi than to assume that Lehi-Nephi and the city of Nephi are identical locales.

Mosiah 7:22

> 22 And all this he did, for the sole purpose of bringing this people into subjection or into bondage. And behold, we at this time do pay tribute to the king of the Lamanites, to the amount of one half of our corn, and our barley, and even all our grain of every kind, and one half of the increase of our flocks and our herds; and even one half of all we have or possess the king of the Lamanites doth exact of us, or our lives.

History: Limhi's mention of "tribute" as the mechanism of transferring goods to the Lamanite overlord follows the general model of Mesoamerican political conflicts. Military actions and political alliances created dependencies between villages and the more powerful cities. The tribute exacted flowed into the city, increasing its wealth. The Codex Mendoza is a document created around twenty years after the Spanish

---

[8]Sorenson, *An Ancient American Setting for the Book of Mormon*, 169.

[9]Ibid., 161.

[10]Susan Toby Evans, *Ancient Mexico and Central America: Archaeology and Culture History* (London: Thames & Hudson, 2004), 227.

conquest, between 1541 and 1553, at the request of the Spanish king and created with the assistance of native scribes. Among other things, it records the tributes paid to Tenochtitlan (the site of modern Mexico City), the capital of the Mexica (Aztecs).[11]

The Codex Mendoza lists the tribute from various cities. The items required varied slightly from city to city, likely based on the resources available. Common were blankets and military uniforms. In addition, other natural resources were required such as corn, amaranth, beans salt, maguey syrup, and even wooden beams. Some were required to provide luxury items such as jade, copper, or gold.[12] For the Limhites, clearly, their series of lost battles had forced the economy to a subsistence level that contrasted with the luxury goods King Noah could manufacture. The need to turn over half of their production to their Lamanite masters would have reduced even further the margin upon which nonessentials could be produced.

The level of tribute exacted may have been punitive, rather than a standard amount, especially since not paying the tribute was a capital crime.[13] In other words, this oppressive level of tribute, backed up by military might, was designed to keep Limhi's people in such subjection that another uprising was not possible.

Mosiah 7:23–24

> 23 And now, is not this grievous to be borne? And is not this, our affliction, great? Now behold, how great reason we have to mourn.
> 24 Yea, I say unto you, great are the reasons which we have to mourn; for behold how many of our brethren have been slain, and their blood has been spilt in vain, and all because of iniquity.

Rhetoric: Limhi began his address by encouraging his people's faith (vv. 19–20), implying that he expects their faith to save them from current distress. But if their faith is so strong, why then are they in such dire straits? The explanation lies not in their current faith, but the sins of their fathers. Limhi's questions are rhetorical: "is not this grievous to be borne? And is not this, our affliction, great?" He answers his own question: "Yea . . . great are the reasons which we have to mourn." He does not need to persuade anyone that their afflictions are real. What he must do is differentiate between the causes of their afflictions and their faith.

Limhi's first point is that Yahweh did not cause these afflictions. Iniquity did. As a result, the people forfeited the Lord's protection, leading to their current distress. Limhi recounts these iniquities to denounce them and to disassociate them his current people's faith.

Mosiah 7:25

> 25 For if this people had not fallen into transgression the Lord would not have suffered that this great evil should come upon them. But behold, they would

---

[11]Frances F. Berdan Patricia Rieff Anawalt, eds. and trans., *The Essential Codex Mendoza,* volumes 2 and 4 of the full edition, bound together (Berkeley: University of California Press, 1997), xii.

[12]Ibid., 4:43–115.

[13]In Mosiah 11:3, King Noah extracts a tribute that is only one fifth of the production of his people, a figure Mormon includes with the intent of making Noah appear excessive.

> not hearken unto his words; but there arose contentions among them, even so much that they did shed blood among themselves.

History: By speaking of the unrepentant transgressors as "they," Limhi differentiates them from his current audience, even though "this people" must include them. We will see below his reasons for making this subtle distinction. He also clearly refers to a specific transgressive incident, which led to shedding each other's blood. The people's history provides two possibilities. The first is in quarreling among the original party of which Zeniff was a member. The group that dissolved into internal feuding that led to armed strife. However, this event happened before the colony was established. The second death is Abinadi's. That is the next story and the execution of a prophet could rightly been seen as the cause of the "great evil [that] should come upon them."

Mosiah 7:26–28

> 26 And a prophet of the Lord have they slain; yea, a chosen man of God, who told them of their wickedness and abominations, and prophesied of many things which are to come, yea, even the coming of Christ.
> 27 And because he said unto them that Christ was the God, the Father of all things, and said that he should take upon him the image of man, and it should be the image after which man was created in the beginning; or in other words, he said that man was created after the image of God, and that God should come down among the children of men, and take upon him flesh and blood, and go forth upon the face of the earth—
> 28 And now, because he said this, they did put him to death; and many more things did they do which brought down the wrath of God upon them. Therefore, who wondereth that they are in bondage, and that they are smitten with sore afflictions?

Rhetoric: Even though "this people" (Limhi's current listeners) are in bondage because of iniquity and Yahweh is just in exacting punishment for murdering a prophet, those who committed the sin are not "you" (the listeners) but "they" (Noah and his chief priests). Therefore, his people may still hope for deliverance.

Mosiah 7:29

> 29 For behold, the Lord hath said: I will not succor my people in the day of their transgression; but I will hedge up their ways that they prosper not; and their doings shall be as a stumbling block before them.

Reference: Limhi quotes Yahweh directly. The fact that he does not provide a reference shows that his people could identify the source. But this quotation does not appear in any of our scriptures. Logically, this "unknown" scripture may have been either the brass plates and the large plates of Nephi, which Mormon abridged. A somewhat similar concept appears in Job 4:7–8: "Remember, I pray thee, who ever perished, being innocent? or where were the righteous cut off? Even as I have seen, they that plow iniquity, and sow wickedness, reap the same." Righteousness provides access to Yahweh's blessings; unrighteousness produces punishing results. Limhi's quotation uses the term "stumbling block" where Job's image is of "reaping." This does not mean that the Lord places obstacles in our way, but rather that our own actions yield consequences that make life more difficult for us.

Mosiah 7:30–32

> 30 And again, he saith: If my people shall sow filthiness they shall reap the chaff thereof in the whirlwind; and the effect thereof is poison.
> 31 And again he saith: If my people shall sow filthiness they shall reap the east wind, which bringeth immediate destruction.
> 32 And now, behold, the promise of the Lord is fulfilled, and ye are smitten and afflicted.

Reference: The imagery of sowing and reaping more closely resembles the wording in Job; still there seems to be no direct connection between the two sources. Reynolds and Sjodahl suggest:

> The reference to "the east wind" [v. 31] as an agent of destruction shows that the author of these texts was influenced by a mode of thinking that obtained in ancient Palestine. In that country the east wind then as now was harmful to vegetation. In the winter it is dry and cold, and in the summer it is dry and hot. It carries off the moisture on the leaves rapidly causing them to wither and die. On the Mediterranean this east wind is known as a *levanter*, and is regarded as dangerous to sailors. It was in such a storm that Paul was shipwrecked, and, with all the crew and passengers, stranded on the island of Malta. (See Acts 27:14–44).[14]

In the Mediterranean climate, each of the four winds assigned to the four cardinal directions had differing effects. Biblical scholar William Smith describes the both the winds and their culturally assumed traits:

> That the Hebrews recognized the existence of four prevailing winds as issuing, broadly speaking, from the four cardinal points, north, south, east and west, may be inferred from their custom of using the expression "four winds" as equivalent to the "four quarters" of the hemisphere. (Ezek. 37:9, Dan. 8:8, Zech. 2:6, Matt. 24:31) The north wind, or, as it was usually called "the north," was naturally the coldest of the four (Eccl. 43:20), and its presence is hence invoked as favorable to vegetation. . . . It is described in Proverbs 25:23 as bringing rain. . . . The east wind crosses the sandy wastes of Arabia Deserts before reaching Palestine and was hence termed "the wind of the wilderness." (Job 1:19, Jer. 13:14) It blows with violence, and is hence supposed to be used generally for any violent wind (Job 27:21, 38:24; Ps. 48:7; Isa. 27:8; Ezek. 27:26). In Palestine the east wind prevails from February to June. The south wind, which traverses the Arabian Peninsula before reaching Palestine, must necessarily be extremely hot (Job 37:17, Luke 12:55). The west and southwest winds reach Palestine loaded with moisture gathered from the Mediterranean, and are hence expressly termed by the Arabs "the fathers of the rain." Westerly winds prevail in Palestine from November to February.[15]

---

[14]George Reynolds and Janne M. Sjodahl, *Commentary on the Book of Mormon*, edited and arranged by Philip C. Reynolds, 7 vols. (Salt Lake City: Deseret Book, 1955–61), 2:94.

[15]William Smith, *Smith's Bible Dictionary* (Old Tappan, N.J.: Fleming H. Revell, 1970), 746.

Limhi's quotation of the "east wind" has its Old Testament connotations of destruction. It seems unlikely that winds in the New World would have exactly the same effects as those in the Old World. Therefore, we can be reasonably safe in assuming that this verse was recorded on the brass plates. Furthermore, it means that the Zeniffites must have copied the scriptures that were on the brass plates and brought them to the land of Nephi. This detail corroborates the fact that Noah's priests knew the prophecies of Isaiah. This copy must have been written on a less permanent (and more portable) material.

This quotation also corroborates the fact that the brass plates contained material not in our current Old Testament. At least two prophets of the Old Testament period, Zenock and Zenos, appear only in the record of the Book of Mormon. These two prophets seemed to stress either the coming of Christ or the future of Israel (Zenos's allegory of the olive tree). Because Limhi's quotation urges repentance, possibly they were part of the context in which Zenos gave his allegory. However, a quotation from Zenock also shows him chastising his audience: "For it is not written that Zenos alone spake of these things, but Zenock also spake of these things—For behold, he said: Thou art angry, O Lord, with this people, because they will not understand thy mercies which thou hast bestowed upon them because of thy Son" (Alma 33:15–16).

Although such a conclusion is highly speculative, I have the feeling that, based on these short quotations, Limhi's quotation may be from Zenock's prophecies as recorded on the brass plates.

Rhetoric: Limhi is still developing the contrast between his faithful people and their desperate circumstances. Limhi explains that consequences follow transgression; previous transgressions led to current sufferings. Nevertheless, because those consequences are linked to past unrighteousness, they may hope to remove them by righteousness (in the near future).

Mosiah 7:33

> 33 But if ye will turn to the Lord with full purpose of heart, and put your trust in him, and serve him with all diligence of mind, if ye do this, he will, according to his own will and pleasure, deliver you out of bondage.

Rhetoric: This is the point toward which Limhi has been working. Here he makes his implicit promise explicit. Faith can erase their sufferings caused by past transgression.

Text: Although a chapter break occurs here in the 1879 edition, there is no break in the 1830 edition (which breaks between modern chapters 8 and 9). Even though the remainder of the chapter is an abridgment of the rest of Limhi's presentation, not a quotation, the modern chapters 7–8 (following the 1879 chapter divisions) should be read together, as dealing with a single event.

Mosiah 8

Mosiah 8:1

1 And it came to pass that after king Limhi had made an end of speaking to his people, for he spake many things unto them and only a few of them have I written in this book, he told his people all the things concerning their brethren who were in the land of Zarahemla.

Text: This is a continuation of Limhi's discourse, and there is no chapter break in the 1830 edition. Indeed, this should not be seen as a separate chapter from the previous, as both comprise Limhi's discourse.

Mormon steps into the narrative frame here, to tell us that "I" have written only a few of Limhi's statements. We do not, of course, know what he omitted; but why has he chosen to quote the passages that he did? As already noted, he did not quote Ammon's description of Benjamin's new covenant because he has just given an extensive quotation from it and his audience is not the Limhites but modern readers. Instead, he quotes Limhi's sketch of his people's "iniquities" and Abinadi's death. These events will appear in greater detail when Mormon copies Zeniff's record. I hypothesize that Mormon began his physically arduous task of engraving the plates only after he had thought through carefully what to include and what to abridge. Therefore, he knew that he would include Zeniff's detailed record. Why, then did he include Limhi's brief discourse? This is the kind of material (events and backgrounds) that he has previously excluded in favor of quoting sermons—and even then he did not quote every sermon. For instance, at this point, he begins abbreviating Limhi's discourse.

What prompted his editorial decision at this point? The simple answer is that the historical material in Limhi's discourse is important. However, history is not the point of the discourse. Rather, its point is the important principles of faith, sin, repentance, and hope. That discussion is the reason Mormon includes the speech.

It is not completely clear if what he omits are the descriptions/information about their brethren in Zarahemla or whether that information followed the formal discourse. The description suggests the latter. I see Limhi's declaration as having great formal significance: He is transforming an expression of communal culpability into communal hope. Even though the information about Zarahemla would be very interesting to Limhi's audience, it seems to be a less formal subject. Possibly there was a recess of some sort between Limhi's formal discourse (the quotation) and the presentation about Zarahemla (the summary).

Mosiah 8:2

2 And he caused that Ammon should stand up before the multitude, and rehearse unto them all that had happened unto their brethren from the time that Zeniff went up out of the land even until the time that he himself came up out of the land.

While Limhi may have given some information about Zarahemla, he is wise to yield the floor to Ammon at this point. It is more than the simple courtesy of allowing a visitor to speak. Ammon constitutes the "proof" of both Zarahemla's existence and their hope of deliverance. In addition to being that fascinating person—a stranger in the community—Ammon was also connected with their ancestral land and could tell them about another faithful people. All of these factors made him tremendously interesting and exciting.

Mosiah 8:3

3 And he also rehearsed unto them the last words which king Benjamin had taught them, and explained them to the people of king Limhi, so that they might understand all the words which he spake.

Redaction: As noted, Mormon elects to describe the explanation of Benjamin's teachings rather than repeat them. Though they were important for Limhi's people, Mormon knew that he had already presented them in full. It is important to know that Limhi's people received the instruction about the new covenant but not important for Mormon's readers to see it again.

Mosiah 8:4

4 And it came to pass that after he had done all this, that king Limhi dismissed the multitude, and caused that they should return every one unto his own house.

Culture: Although it may be making too much of too little, this passage shows an interesting contrast with Benjamin's dismissal of his people. Mormon described the earlier event:

> And again, it came to pass that when king Benjamin had made an end of all these things, and had consecrated his son Mosiah to be a ruler and a king over his people, and had given him all the charges concerning the kingdom, and also had appointed priests to teach the people, that thereby they might hear and know the commandments of God, and to stir them up in remembrance of the oath which they had made, he dismissed the multitude, and they returned, every one, according to their families, to their own houses. (Mosiah 6:3)

In both cases, the king dismisses the assembly, appropriately so since a formal assembly requires a clearly marked conclusion. In both, the people return to their homes. Once again, this is logical, as many, if not most, of the people would live at some distance from the town's ceremonial center. However, Benjamin's people, but not Limhi's, return home "according to their families." As already noted,

Mesoamerican kin groups typically lived near each other, creating family compounds. Why, then, do Limhi's people simply go home without families being specified?

It is impossible to know whether this apparent omission reflects a truly different social structure and, even if does, whether it is significant or not. Certainly kinfolk continued to be important for Limhi's people, but the people who came with Zeniff were not necessarily entire kin groups. The original settlers probably cut across family boundaries, giving them less well-defined kin structures. Additionally, the Limhites had reorganized after the assassination of their king and the collapse of his political/religious structure. Such restructuring may also have altered some kin organizations by removing or demoting some of them. In short, the Limhites may not have had strong extended kin-based compounds. They would certainly have had households for the nuclear family and near kin, but likely not the larger kin-group compounds that were more likely in the older Zarahemla.

Mosiah 8:5

> 5 And it came to pass that he caused that the plates which contained the record of his people from the time that they left the land of Zarahemla, should be brought before Ammon, that he might read them.

Redaction: Mormon is presenting a severely edited version here. He has omitted, for instance, any mention of where or when this event took place; but it could not have been a continuation of Limhi's discourse. Naturally the plates would have been heavier than paper and stored in a safe place—probably the palace of the king. In Mesoamerican public architecture, the residence of the king was often near the main temple in the smaller cities, where the public assembly would have been held. Perhaps this is why Mormon makes no mention of a new location.

Because Mormon is abbreviating so severely, why does he even include this reference to Zeniff's history, which he will quote more fully in the next chapter? I hypothesize that this particular verse has no intrinsic importance except to explain the question Limhi asks Ammon in the next verse. Verse 6 is a transition to the next important subject (seers and prophets), and it is this topic, not Zeniff's history, that is important to Mormon.

History: Zeniff apparently brought with him the Nephite custom of recording official dynastic history on plates (e.g., the large plates of Nephi). He probably did not bring blank plates with him from Zarahemla but had them made in the land of Nephi after they had met their first requirement of assuring adequate food and shelter. While the Lamanite king may have simply moved some of his people out of a village, letting Zeniff's people move into an intact village, probably some adaptation (and certainly annual maintenance) of the home would have been required. It seems less likely that the Lamanite king would have dispossessed his own people of fields under production. Rather, the Zeniffites may have been assigned adjacent but uncultivated lands. In either scenario, they would have had to give agriculture their first attention. Making metal plates would have been considerably lower on the priority list.

Mosiah 8:6

6 Now, as soon as Ammon had read the record, the king inquired of him to know if he could interpret languages, and Ammon told him that he could not.

Redaction: This verse explains why Mormon reported that Ammon read Zeniff's record: it introduces the question of interpreting other written documents. Zeniff's plates bridge the action between Ammon's interest in Zeniff/Limhi and this revelation of new records.

It is possible to reconstruct some of Mormon's source. After the public meeting, Ammon and Limhi go to the king's residence, and Limhi gives him the history of his city's founders to read. Because this history is on plates, Limhi remembers another set of plates that his people found but which they cannot read. He asks Ammon whether he can interpret languages. Although we can deduce Limhi's mental association from what happens next, it must have been an unexpected question for Ammon. This suggests that Mormon's source is reporting a conversation with reasonable accuracy. Therefore, Mormon, despite his abridgment, is preserving the sequence of events in the original.

Mosiah 8:7

7 And the king said unto him: Being grieved for the afflictions of my people, I caused that forty and three of my people should take a journey into the wilderness, that thereby they might find the land of Zarahemla, that we might appeal unto our brethren to deliver us out of bondage.

History: Limhi's explanation provides not only more history of his people but also some geographical details. Even before Ammon's arrival, Limhi had hoped for political deliverance from Zarahemla. The fact that these hopes were dashed once explains why Limhi immediately rejoiced when actual representatives from Zarahemla arrived.

Mosiah 8:8

8 And they were lost in the wilderness for the space of many days, yet they were diligent, and found not the land of Zarahemla but returned to this land, having traveled in a land among many waters, having discovered a land which was covered with bones of men, and of beasts, and was also covered with ruins of buildings of every kind, having discovered a land which had been peopled with a people who were as numerous as the hosts of Israel.

Geography: The geographical correlation suggested by Sorenson[1] has the Mulekites landing in Olmec-dominated territory on the Gulf of Mexico. Their split-off colony moved south along the Grijalva River to found Zarahemla. Zeniff's emigrants would have followed the Grijalva to its headwater and then down the

---

[1]John L. Sorenson, *An Ancient American Setting for the Book of Mormon* (Salt Lake City: Deseret Book/Provo, Utah: Foundation for Ancient Research and Mormon Studies, 1985). See also John L. Sorenson, *Mormon's Map* (Provo, Utah: FARMS, 2000).

other side of the mountains into the Guatemalan highlands. How did Limhi's people possibly miss Zarahemla when they went the other direction?

Lawrence Poulsen, a research biochemist retired from the University of Texas, examined three-dimensional maps of the Book of Mormon regions. He noted that, while the land of Zarahemla is plausibly located along the Grijalva River, there is a roughly parallel Usumacinta River valley to the east. Most interesting is that the headwaters of the two rivers are within perhaps ten miles of each other. How then did Limhi's search party miss Zarahemla? They followed the wrong river. Coming from the opposite direction they found the headwaters of the Usumacinta rather than the Grijalva.[2]

Mosiah 8:9–11

> 9 And for a testimony that the things that they had said are true they have brought twenty-four plates which are filled with engravings, and they are of pure gold.
> 10 And behold, also, they have brought breastplates, which are large, and they are of brass and of copper, and are perfectly sound.
> 11 And again, they have brought swords, the hilts thereof have perished, and the blades thereof were cankered with rust; and there is no one in the land that is able to interpret the language or the engravings that are on the plates. Therefore I said unto thee: Canst thou translate?

First, the explorers, who had been gone a sufficiently long time to cause concern, knew they would need to explain their protracted absence, especially their inability to find Zarahemla. Bringing back such exotic items as the golden plates and the clearly foreign weapons would verify the truth of their tale.

Limhi's list of the artifacts begins and ends with the plates, indicating that they were the items that most interested him. However, the other trophies support the explorers' description that they had found a great battlefield. Except for the plates, all of their trophies are battle related—both the defensive armor (breastplates) and offensive weapons (swords). Historian William J. Hamblin notes of these breastplates:

> The single Book of Mormon reference to the use of metal armor comes from a very ambiguous passage in Mosiah 8:10. . . .
>
> [W]e might ask what these Jaredite breastplates looked like. We have no explicit evidence from the text, but I will suggest below that the Nephite breastplate can be equated with Maya pectoral breastplates, which were hung around the neck and covered the middle chest. If this is true, then a Jaredite breastplate of metal could be thought of as a medallion or disk hung around the neck either entirely or partially composed of metal. Indeed, we have archaeological evidence of precisely such breastplates from the Olmec civilization, which is generally equated with the Jaredites.[3]

---

[2]Lawrence Poulsen, "Tale of Two Rivers," http://bomgeography.poulsenll.org/two_rivers.html (accessed January 2005). The river bed for the Grijalva has changed from more ancient times. The map depicts the more modern course. The locations for the headwaters were not changed.

[3]William J. Hamblin, "Armor in the Book of Mormon," in *Warfare in the Book of Mormon*, edited by Stephen D. Ricks and William J. Hamblin (Salt Lake City: Deseret Book/Provo, Utah: Foundation for

Hamblin's suggestion of the nature and possible shape of the Jaredite breastplates is quite likely correct. Our assumption of a medieval armor when we hear the work "breastplate" is the result of our modern conditioning and should not be imposed on a different time and people. The sole difficulty in associating the Olmec breastplates with those listed in the text is the metal itself. The Olmec typically used iron rather than copper and brass. It is not known whether the presence of those terms in our English text is representative of the authentic Jaredite metal or perhaps a mistranslation based upon Joseph's assumptions of the type of metal that would have been used.

The swords are obviously iron, since they have rusted: the blades are "cankered" and the hilts have "perished." There is no archaeological evidence of iron swords in Mesoamerica.

As for the plates, it is unclear where the explorers found them. It seems very unlikely that they would have been left on or brought to the battlefield. It seems more likely that they would have been housed in one of the ruined buildings that the explorers also found. The only Mesoamerican codex found *in situ* was in a temple. Therefore, a temple, or the enclosure on top of a stepped pyramid, was one place where such records might be found, but the king's residence, as we can see from our reconstruction of Ammon's reading Zeniff's record, is another.

The fact that the records were there to be found suggests either complete annihilation of the residents or a flight so rapid that the sacred records were abandoned without even taking the time to hide them in a secure location as the keepers of the Qumran records did.

Mosiah 8:12

> 12 And I say unto thee again: Knowest thou of any one that can translate? For I am desirous that these records should be translated into our language; for, perhaps, they will give us a knowledge of a remnant of the people who have been destroyed, from whence these records came; or, perhaps, they will give us a knowledge of this very people who have been destroyed; and I am desirous to know the cause of their destruction.

Limhi's curiosity about the record is quite understandable. It could have been only the dynastic record of an unrelated Mesoamerican people. Instead, they were what we know as the book of Ether, a history that fit into the sacred records that the Nephite already had. Possibly, since the prophet Ether witnesses, but was not involved in, the final battles, he may have brought his record to the building where he knew it would be found, a location directed by the Spirit so that Limhi's explorers *could* find it.

Mosiah 8:13–14

> 13 Now Ammon said unto him: I can assuredly tell thee, O king, of a man that can translate the records; for he has wherewith that he can look, and translate

---

Ancient Research and Mormon Studies, 1990), 405, 406. I have removed several paragraphs analyzing the idea of metal breastplates.

all records that are of ancient date; and it is a gift from God. And the things are called interpreters, and no man can look in them except he be commanded, lest he should look for that he ought not and he should perish. And whosoever is commanded to look in them, the same is called seer.
14 And behold, the king of the people who are in the land of Zarahemla is the man that is commanded to do these things, and who has this high gift from God.

History: When Moroni entrusted the plates to Joseph Smith, he also gave him "two stones in silver bows—and these stones, fastened to a breastplate, constituted what is called the Urim and Thummim—deposited with the plates; and the possession and use of these stones were what constituted "seers" in ancient or former times; and that God had prepared them for the purpose of translating the book" (JS—H 1:35).

"Urim and Thummim" refers to sacred stones in the Old Testament (Ex. 28:30, Lev. 8:8, Deut. 33:8). The Book of Mormon itself does not use this term. The Book of Mormon's "interpreters" were identified with the Urim and Thummim only later, after an article in the 1833 *Evening and Morning Star*. References that appear to be earlier, such as the reference from Doctrine and Covenants 10:1 (a revelation from 1828), are a later insertion into the text and were not part of the earlier revelation.[4] (See commentary accompanying Alma 37:22–23.)

The interpreters have functional similarities to the Old Testament Urim and Thummim. Hendrik C. Spykerboer, professor of Old Testament studies at Trinity Theological College in Brisbane, Australia, describes the biblical objects:

> Although both [Urim and Thummim] are plural in form, they seem to refer to single objects that functioned as sacred lots and may have had the form of dice, pebbles, or sticks. Another possibility is that they were two stones, one white and the other black. According to the texts in Exodus and Leviticus Moses put the Urim and Thummim into Aaron's breastpiece, a small square pocket attached to the ephod, an outer covering.... What is clear is that they were associated with the priestly office and were used when people came to seek divine consultation....
>
> The contexts where the Urim and Thummim are mentioned seem to indicate that these lots fell into disuse when the monarchy was established. The parallel texts in Ezra 2:63, Neh. 7:65, and 1 Esdras 5:40 may imply that a return to the use of the Urim and Thummim was not expected.[5]

The Book of Mormon interpreters certainly share the oracular function. They are mentioned during Jaredite times (approximately 1500 B.C. to perhaps 200 B.C.) so they would not be the very same instruments used by Aaron and later priests.[6] Yahweh comments to the brother of Jared on them and their function:

---

[4]Richard Van Wagoner and Steve Walker, "Joseph Smith: 'The Gift of Seeing'," *Dialogue: A Journal of Mormon Thought* 15, no. 2 (Summer 1982): 61.

[5]Hendrik C. Spykerboer, "Urim and Thummim," in *The Oxford Companion to the Bible*, edited by Bruce M. Metzger and Michael D. Coogan (New York: Oxford University Press, 1993), 786–87.

[6]Joseph Fielding Smith, "Your Question," *Improvement Era* 57, no. 6 (June 1954). Retrieved from *GospeLink 2001/*, CD-ROM (Salt Lake City: Deseret Book, 2000), "The Lord gave to the brother of

> And behold, when ye shall come unto me, ye shall write them and shall seal them up, that no one can interpret them; for ye shall write them in a language that they cannot be read.
>
> And behold, these two stones will I give unto thee, and ye shall seal them up also with the things which ye shall write.
>
> For behold, the language which ye shall write I have confounded; wherefore I will cause in my own due time that these stones shall magnify to the eyes of men these things which ye shall write. (Ether 3:22–24)

Ether's stones are clearly meant to help interpret the writings (the twenty-four gold plates) that Ether is sealing up. Alma 37:21–35 gives additional history about these plates. During this discussion about the twenty-four gold plates, Ammon tells Limhi that Mosiah possesses the interpreters with which such things may be read. It is clear from the description that these interpreters are the two stones that Joseph Smith later received, since the description corresponds so precisely: "And now he [Mosiah] translated them [the twenty-four gold plates] by the means of those two stones which were fastened into the two rims of a bow"[7] (Mosiah 28:13).

Mosiah's interpretation fulfills Ether's prophecy that the two stones (interpreters) would be used to translate the twenty-four plates. But where did Mosiah get them? Limhi does not list them as part of the objects that his explorers brought back from the land of the Jaredites, and Mosiah already had them, or else Ammon would not have known about them. John Tvedtnes, examining the question of the two stones' provenance, concludes: "The Lord could have retrieved the interpreters from their hiding place and given them to Mosiah. The Nephites of Zarahemla may have found the hiding place of the stones. They may have come into the possession of the Mulekites, who founded the city of Zarahemla, and then passed to Mosiah's grandfather when he became king of that land."[8] I agree with Tvedtnes's plausible provenance. Mosiah would have then received the stones among the ritual items featured during the merger of the Mulekites and Nephites.[9]

Although this case is plausible, it is curious that Benjamin does not mention the stones when he invests Mosiah as the next king. Part of that ceremony is the formal transmission of "the records which were engraven on the plates of brass; and

---

Jared the Urim and Thummim which he brought with him to this continent. These were separate and distinct from the Urim and Thummim had by Abraham and in Israel in the days of Aaron."

[7]Andrew H. Hedges, "Urim and Thummim," in *Book of Mormon Reference Companion*, edited by Dennis L. Largey (Salt Lake City: Deseret Book, 2003), 773, suggests: "These stones, or "interpreters," as the Book of Mormon calls them (Mosiah 8:13, 28:20; Alma 37:21; Ether 4:5), were originally given to the brother of Jared, who was commanded to seal them up with his record as a means of translating the same (Ether 3:23–24). The Nephite king $Mosiah_2$ possessed a Urim and Thummim, the origin of which is not specified in the text (Mosiah 8:13; Omni 1:20)." However, since the interpreters were sealed so that the plates could be translated, and Mosiah translated them, the parsimonious explanation is that Mosiah possessed the very interpreters sealed up for that purpose.

[8]John A. Tvedtnes, *The Most Correct Book: Insights from a Book of Mormon Scholar* (Salt Lake City: Cornerstone, 1999), 322.

[9]This appears to be Sperry's conclusion, though he also notes that it "has the weakness of not having the Nephite record drop a single word in its behalf." Sidney B. Sperry, *The Problems of the Book of Mormon* (Salt Lake City: Bookcraft, 1964), 17.

also the plates of Nephi; and also, the sword of Laban, and the ball or director, which led our fathers through the wilderness" (Mosiah 1:16). These sacred items have immense historical and religious importance: the brass plates, the plates of Nephi, the sword of Laban, and the Liahona. Why not the two stones? I hypothesize that this list consisted only of *Nephite* sacred objects. Despite the interpreters' sacredness, they were not ritually significant in the validation of the political authority of the new king.

Redaction: Why did Mormon include this particular incident in his abridgment? Of course, we have no way of comparing its significance with items that Mormon omitted. Even if we had a list of omitted items, determining significance is highly subjective. A linguist might be most interested in a description of the plates. A metallurgist might be most interested in the apparent properties of both the "gold" (a notoriously soft metal) and the silver bow in which the stones were set. But why would this incident be important to Mormon?

It is too simple to say that the incident is important because of Ether's text. Obviously, that content *is* important, but apparently not to Mormon. Mormon never abridged or edited the text and never left any indication of where he might have included that text in his work. He left it to Moroni to edit and add. At this point, Mormon includes an abbreviated conversation that says nothing about the subject matter of the plates, since Limhi and Ammon knew nothing about it. By the time he recorded this conversation, Mormon knew what the plates contained, but did not interject anything. (He later gives only the briefest of descriptions in Mosiah 28:17.) Consequently, Mormon included this exchange between Limhi and Ammon not because of the content of the plates but because it describes a seer. Mosiah's spiritual prowess is what interests Mormon, not his linguistic abilities. (See also commentary accompanying vv. 16–17.)

Mosiah 8:15

15 And the king said that a seer is greater than a prophet.

It is not unreasonable to read this verse as a verbal foil to the definition of a seer which follows. We are much more interested in Ammon's "right" definition than in Limhi's "wrong" conclusion. But why would Limhi think a seer greater than a prophet? A closer reading shows that Ammon is not correcting Limhi but agreeing with him. Ammon has described Mosiah as one who can "translate all records that are of ancient date." The significant element is the antiquity of the writing.

Why is the text's age important? Ancient Israel, ancient Mesoamerica (and likely in many other parts of the ancient world) conceived of history not merely as something that had happened but rather as part of a cycle that would recur in the future. In the words of biblical scholar H. Wheeler Robinson, "[For Israel], the unifying principle [acted] like a magnet in evoking a pattern amongst iron filings. It created a pattern of history out of all its complexities, a pattern which disclosed the previously hidden purpose of God."[10] Thus, the past revealed the form of the future. One manifestation of this patterning of life and history is the numerous ways in which the Exodus became the model for subsequent events, including Lehi's flight from Jerusalem.

Similarly, in Mesoamerica, all time ran in repeating cycles. The creation myth of the Maya and Nahua (cultural group that included the Aztecs) told of recurring cycles of destruction and new creations in which the destruction/renewal of the sun was the principal event. The serendipitous arrival of the Spanish (serendipitous for the Spanish, at least) in a year that symbolized change and renewal allowed them to be seen as the return of the divine Quetzalcoatl.[11] That same year had come and gone before, but the arrival of the Spaniards created a connection to mythological themes. Thus, a historical event became a cyclical (ritual) event, and the present repeated the past. Sadly, the most striking repetition was not Cortez's arrival as a manifestation of Quetzalcoatl's triumphant return, but the eerie way in which the destruction of the Aztec kingdom repeated the destruction of Tula—an event also linked indelibly to Quetzalcoatl in Nahua mythology.[12]

To return to our point, however, a seer was not simply one who could read about the past but who could perceive its "real truth"—how it fit as a revelation of the past and, hence, as a revelation of the future. In contrast, a prophet saw only the future, while the seer understood the larger patterns. This fact explains why Ammon did not define a seer as something else, but rather confirmed Limhi's perception of the seer's true standing. (See commentary accompanying vv. 16–18.)

Mosiah 8:16–17

> 16 And Ammon said that a seer is a revelator and a prophet also; and a gift which is greater can no man have, except he should possess the power of God, which no man can; yet a man may have great power given him from God.
> 17 But a seer can know of things which are past, and also of things which are to come, and by them shall all things be revealed, or, rather, shall secret things be made manifest, and hidden things shall come to light, and things which are not known shall be made known by them, and also things shall be made known by them which otherwise could not be known.

Ammon expands the definition of the seer. The seer has two different kinds of connection to the power of the Spirit. A seer is both a revelator and a prophet. What is the difference between these two? The prophet is one who sees the future. A revelator makes understandable aspects of the Lord's will which are hidden from

---

[10]H. Wheeler Robinson, *Inspiration and Revelation in the Old Testament* (Oxford, Eng.: Clarendon Press, 1946), 129.

[11]The tales associated with Quetzalcoatl are complicated, and the return myth is actually a questionable association. However, it underscores the Mesoamerican expectation of cycles that the Spanish used to their advantage. Brant A. Gardner, "Quetzalcoatl and the Myth of the Return," http://frontpage2k.nmia.com/~nahualli/Quetzalcoatl/Elements/Return.htm (accessed March 2007).

[12]Henry B. Nicholson, *Topiltzin Quetzalcoatl* (Boulder: University Press of Colorado, 2001), 249–54, gives a brief synopsis of the Quetzalcoatl myth. The rest of the book provides significantly more detail.

others. In this particular case, Ammon and Limhi apparently assume that the revelator applies the patterns of the past that teach about the future. The will of the Lord—past, present, and future—would become known as the revelator reveals the contents of that which is hidden—in this case in an unreadable text.

We now have three terms: prophet, seer, and revelator. The seer, according to Ammon's definition, is one who possesses the interpreters, aids not only to translation but to revealing the hidden: "He has wherewith that he can look, and translate all records that are of ancient date; and it is a gift from God. And the things are called interpreters, and no man can look in them except he be commanded, lest he should look for that he ought not and he should perish. And whosoever is commanded to look in them, the same is called seer" (Mosiah 8:13).

Although Ammon concludes with a simple functional definition of the seer as the possessor of the interpreters, his description of the interpreters is more complex. They aid in "translat[ing] all records that are of ancient date," but are so powerful that they cannot be used except by Yahweh's direct commandment, since otherwise, one might "look for that he ought not." Obviously this function goes beyond the translation of ancient languages. Why would a linguist's soul be jeopardized by translating, for example, a Hittite grocery list?[13] Clearly, the power of the interpreters is not simply in translation, but rather in revelation. One acting without the Spirit might use the interpreters to find information that he would be tempted to use unrighteously, to understand knowledge that is forbidden for good reason, and apply the lessons of the past to the exploit the future.

Mosiah 8:18

> 18 Thus God has provided a means that man, through faith, might work mighty miracles; therefore he becometh a great benefit to his fellow beings.

This explanation stresses that Yahweh reserves the use of the interpreters until he commands it so that Yahweh will be with the man who uses them. It is Yahweh's power, not man. The seer is not a translator and should not be confused as one. His function is much more than reading words; his function is revealing Yahweh. It is by revealing Yahweh and his will that the seer "becometh a great benefit to his fellow beings." (See commentary accompanying Alma 37:21–25.)

Mosiah 8:19

> 19 And now, when Ammon had made an end of speaking these words the king rejoiced exceedingly, and gave thanks to God, saying: Doubtless a great mystery is contained within these plates, and these interpreters were doubtless

---

[13]However, in at least the case of the twenty-four gold plates from which the book of Ether was translated, there was apparently information on the plates themselves that the Lord considered dangerous (Alma 37:21). The difference is that the prophet could read and understand that information but was required to keep it from the people. In this case, the danger is to the soul of the person using the interpreters, not in the information received.

> prepared for the purpose of unfolding all such mysteries to the children of men.

At this point, Limhi has no idea of the plates' contents, yet he confidently asserts that "doubtless" they contain "a great mystery" and also a precious one, since Yahweh has assured the means of revealing their content. It is a "great mystery" because Limhi expects that the past will be instructive for the present and the future.

Mosiah 8:20–21

> 20 O how marvelous are the works of the Lord, and how long doth he suffer with his people; yea, and how blind and impenetrable are the understandings of the children of men; for they will not seek wisdom, neither do they desire that she should rule over them!
> 21 Yea, they are as a wild flock which fleeth from the shepherd, and scattereth, and are driven, and are devoured by the beasts of the forest.

This conclusion seems abrupt and confusing. Limhi praises Yahweh—and well might he, at the realization that the seer, the interpreters, and the plates in an unknown tongue will shortly come together. But why does Limhi then lament the tendency of human beings to become a scattered flock, devoured by beasts?

Limhi contrasts the "marvelous . . . works of the Lord" with the "blind and impenetrable . . . understandings of the children of men." These concepts should be read together to create contrasting elements. For Limhi, the focal point is the "blind and impenetrable . . . understandings." Limhi positions himself as one of blind and impenetrable understanding, since he has the physical plates, but their meaning is impenetrable. On his own, Limhi might as well be blind, for he can understand nothing of what he assumes to be the "great mystery" they contain. In contrast are the "marvelous . . . works of the Lord" manifest in one who can read and these texts and reveal their meaning. Through this process, Yahweh reveals his wisdom.

The parallel contrast (wise and revealing Yahweh/blind and not understanding man) is further elaborated in verse 21 by expanding the description of man. Limhi's extra sentence of lament for human blindness continues to praise Yahweh through the unstated but understood contrast to Yahweh's wisdom. The structure implies that praise, even though it is not directly stated.

Verse 21 compares man without Yahweh's wisdom to a "wild flock which fleeth from the shepherd, and scattereth, and are driven, and are devoured by the beasts of the forest." The shepherd, like Yahweh, provides wisdom and order. However, the "wild flock" runs from that source of wisdom and perishes.

In the context this conversation, Limhi accepts Mosiah, sight unseen, as a seer who can reveal Yahweh's will, "a great benefit to his fellow beings" (v. 18). Mosiah, by revealing Yahweh's will, can provide the wisdom Yahweh's children require to move safely through life.

Vocabulary: Verse 20 correctly portrays wisdom as female: "They will not seek wisdom, neither do they desire that she should rule over them." Biblical wisdom refers to true divine wisdom rather than earthly understanding. Wisdom was traditionally personified as female (Prov. 1–9). Job 28:20–28 places wisdom in the beginning with God.[14] When Ammon laments to Limhi that men do not allow wisdom to rule over them, he understands wisdom as a divine quality.

Translation: Verse 21 uses the phrase: "wild flock which fleeth from the shepherd, and scattereth, and are driven." This is a fascinating mix of pastoral metaphors, as we have a shepherd, but a "wild flock which . . . scattereth." This will be the same problem we will see in the story of Ammon at the Waters of Sebus. (See commentary accompanying Alma 17:27.) The term "shepherd" suggests that we are speaking of a flock of sheep, but sheep are herding animals who do not tend to scatter when they flee. The intent of this phrase creates tension with the word "shepherd" that is used in the translation. I suggest that the intent of the phrase authentically replicates the animals with which Limhi was familiar, but that the term "shepherd" is an artifact of translation influence by the numerous references to a shepherd in the Bible. (See commentary accompanying Alma 5:59.)

---

[14]Mary Joan Winn Leith, "Wisdom," in *The Oxford Companion to the Bible*, edited by Bruce M. Metzger and Michael D. Coogan (New York: Oxford University Press, 1993), 800.

Mosiah 9

THE RECORD OF ZENIFF

An account of his people, from the time they left the land of Zarahemla, until the time that they were delivered out of the hands of the Lamanites.

Text: Mormon marks not only a change in the story, but a new source document. He indicates that he is quoting Zeniff's record in full with the headnote statement that was part of the plate text.

The wording of this summary suggests that Mormon wrote it, since it requires that the person who wrote the introduction also know the end of the story. Thus, it could not have been made by Zeniff's scribe as he began his record. The alternative is that Zeniff's record was entered into the dynastic plates of Nephi as a complete copy. With the labor required to engrave plates, this does not seem likely—another reason for seeing this headnote as Mormon's introduction.

This transition between the material in Mosiah 7–8 and Mosiah 9 is certainly Mormon's least literary shift to date in the Book of Mormon. It lacks any direct thematic relationship between the Ammon-Limhi events and Zeniff's record. In fact, the discussion of seership and Mosiah's identification as a seer are a logical introduction to the record of Ether. However, Ether's record is included only at the very end of the book, almost as an afterthought. While Mormon indicates that the record of Ether will be available, there is no indication that he personally planned to abridge it as part of his own record, intentionally leaving it to Moroni to add.

Mormon begins this insertion with direct quotations from Zeniff but ends with abridgments. Mormon certainly prized both the words of Abinadi and their effect on $Alma_1$, but those words appear in the abridged section. Mormon appears to have some sympathy for Zeniff, and the brevity of Zeniff's account certainly lent itself to copying rather than editing. However, as soon as Mormon leaves Zeniff and begins discussing his son, Noah, he changes from quoting his source to restating his source. Part of the reason is his clear antipathy to Noah, which he makes sure comes across in his editorial selections and descriptions. (See commentary accompanying Mosiah 11:1.)

Mosiah 9:1

> 1 I, Zeniff, having been taught in all the language of the Nephites, and having had a knowledge of the land of Nephi, or of the land of our fathers' first inheritance, and having been sent as a spy among the Lamanites that I might spy out their forces, that our army might come upon them and destroy them—

but when I saw that which was good among them I was desirous that they should not be destroyed.

Literature: Mosiah 9 begins with a formal declaration: "I, Zeniff, having been taught in all the language of the Nephites. . . . " This introduction echoes Nephi 1:1–2: "I, Nephi, having been born of goodly parents, therefore I was taught somewhat in all the learning of my father; and having seen many afflictions in the course of my days, nevertheless, having been highly favored of the Lord in all my days; yea, having had a great knowledge of the goodness and the mysteries of God, therefore I make a record of my proceedings in my days. Yea, I make a record in the language of my father, which consists of the learning of the Jews and the language of the Egyptians." Although the two introductions share the writer's identification of himself and his declaration of his "learning" and "language," they are still sufficiently different in that Zeniff is not, apparently, copying Nephi. Indeed, most Book of Mormon writers seem unaware of the small plates of Nephi. Therefore, we would not expect that Zeniff would have (or could have) copied 1 Nephi 1. However, Nephi may have introduced his large plates in a similar way. Perhaps Zeniff modeled his introduction on the large plates of Nephi.

This possibility becomes more probable when we realize that Zeniff has the same relation to his people (founder of the lineage and the kingdom) that Nephi did for his own people. Therefore, it was appropriate to begin a new record and make a formal declaration of identify and intention. No doubt Zeniff intended his book to continue as a record his dynasty, just as the lost book of Lehi would have included the Lehite dynasty. However, in this case, Limhi closed the three-generation dynasty by reuniting with Zarahemla and becoming a subject of Mosiah.

History: The Book of Mormon introduces Zeniff in Omni 1:27–30, although without naming him. The next mention is in Mosiah 7:9 where Limhi identifies Zeniff as his progenitor. Limhi also gives an abbreviated account of his people's history (beginning Mosiah 7:21) with a fuller account following in Mosiah, chapters 9–21, taken from the official dynastic history.

Zeniff's introduction continues by posing another mystery. The purpose of the original expedition was to spy on the Lamanites "that our army might come upon them and destroy them." Why was military action being considered? Mosiah$_1$ and his people had recently fled from the city of Nephi, so it seems likely that the Lamanites overmatched them militarily. Perhaps, now that the Zarahemlaites have swelled their population, the displaced Nephites consider that they had the military strength to "correct" their dispossession. In other words, this expedition appears to be a manifestation of both nostalgia for their former home and a grudge against those who had forced them out. Thus, this military action was mounted, apparently with Mosiah$_1$'s blessing. This expedition is the one of the rare overtly offensive actions taken by the Nephites. (See commentary accompanying Mosiah 9:17–19 for another occasion.) All other records indicate that the Nephites fought only after the Lamanites had instigated action.

Zeniff, a spy for the army, is supposed to learn about the people they want to attack, particularly the ways in which they would be most vulnerable. But what Zeniff learned changed the group's plans: "when I saw that which was good among them I was desirous that they should not be destroyed." What could have changed his mind?

We have no details about how Zeniff conducted his spying mission. It seems probable, however, that he disguised himself and went into the city of Nephi. As one who had recently lived in the land of Nephi he was able to pass as a native in both dress and language. There were at least two times that Zeniff was among the people of the city of Nephi for verse 5 mentions a second expedition. Zeniff therefore talked with some of the people and witnessed their lifestyle.

Those of the city of Nephi were linguistically Nephite but politically Lamanite. $Mosiah_1$ fled with his people from internal pressure, not external attack. Those left behind in the city of Nephi had developed the wealth and power that Jacob denounced and were almost certainly those who had conspired against Jacob. (See commentary accompanying Omni 1:12.) Their way of life would have been somewhat familiar to Zeniff, and certainly their wealth and power would have been impressive. As many soldiers have discovered, the average person who is the "enemy" is still a human being, and there is much good in all the world. Zeniff saw this first hand.

Nevertheless, Zeniff's recognition that the people were good must have had meant more than simple goodheartedness. For Zeniff to persuade a majority of the invading army that there was "much good" in these Nephites-become-Lamanites, there must have been some visible and persuasive evidence; not all who fought with Zeniff against the leader of the expedition would have entered the city and spoken with the inhabitants.

I hypothesize that the wealth and power of the inhabitants helped Zeniff's expedition see "that which was good." The foundational promise of the Nephites was that: "Inasmuch as thy seed shall keep my commandments, they shall prosper in the land of promise" (1 Ne. 4:14). Zeniff may have assumed that the reverse was also true, that evidence of prosperity was evidence of some form of keeping the commandments and of "goodness." While those of the city of Nephi had become Lamanites politically, it is doubtful that they abandoned all of their inherited religion immediately. Therefore Zeniff would see a people who still had similar beliefs and a visible prosperity to attest to their "goodness." (See "Excursus: Religion of the Nehors," following Alma 1.)

If the tentative connections between Book of Mormon cities and archaeological sites are accurate, Nephi/Kaminaljuyú was much more spectacular than Zarahemla/Santa Rosa. Internal evidence in the Book of Mormon confirms that difference in size and wealth.

Perhaps Zeniff thought that, with $Mosiah_1$'s people gone, the internal tensions had been relieved and the returning Nephites could settle peaceably in the general area, probably also accumulating some of the same wealth that characterized the city of Nephi. Indeed, the fact that the inhabitants granted lands to Zeniff's people is evidence that they felt no consuming hatred toward those who had fled with $Mosiah_1$.

Language: As with most comments involving language in the Book of Mormon, Zeniff gives us ambiguous information that we would prefer he had elaborated. He was selected as a spy because he "had a knowledge of the land of Nephi" but also because he had "been taught in all the language of the Nephites." The common origins of the Nephites and Lamanites lay nearly five hundred years in the past—plenty of time for at least one of the groups to have adopted the language of other tribes in the area or at least to be strongly influenced by other languages. Although $Mosiah_1$'s people left behind linguistic and cultural "Nephites" when they fled, those linguistic and cultural Nephites have now become political Lamanites, enemies to "the people of Nephi," who took this designation with them to Zarahemla.

Zeniff specifically notes that he was "taught" that language, probably as his natal language. The conjoining of the Nephites and the Zarahemlaites required some merging of languages. Mosiah had "Nephite" taught to the Zarahemlaites (Omni 1:18). Historically, the Zarahemlaites probably spoke Zoquean (a daughter language of Mixe-Zoque, the probable language of the Olmecs). The city of Nephi had been in an area dominated by Maya speakers. Maya and Zoque are unrelated and a meeting of two peoples with those two languages would certainly occasion the linguistic difficulties hinted at in the Book of Mormon's record of their meeting. Archaeologist John S. Henderson notes: "Interaction of Maya and Zoquean peoples continued as a historical process along a linguistic frontier that extended from the Gulf Coast through the highlands and piedmont to the Pacific Coast."[1] In the case of Zeniff, his fluency in "Nephite" qualified him as a spy.

Mosiah 9:2

> 2 Therefore, I contended with my brethren in the wilderness, for I would that our ruler should make a treaty with them; but he being an austere and a blood-thirsty man commanded that I should be slain; but I was rescued by the shedding of much blood; for father fought against father, and brother against brother, until the greater number of our army was destroyed in the wilderness; and we returned, those of us that were spared, to the land of Zarahemla, to relate that tale to their wives and their children.

We learn here that Zeniff is only a member of the party, not its leader. When he argues for making a treaty, rather than a conquest, he pits himself against the "austere and . . . blood-thirsty" leader. Naturally, this is Zeniff's perspective, but it sheds light on the nature of their conflict. $Mosiah_1$'s people probably hated those who had driven them from their homeland, thus supporting the "blood-thirsty" idea that the expedition was also one of vengeance. "Austere" is more puzzling; although

---

[1]John S. Henderson, *The World of the Ancient Maya* (Ithaca, N.Y.: Cornell University Press, 1997), 85.

it suggests that he was unswayed by the possibility of acquiring riches by less dangerous means than military conquest. It also suggests that he had no sympathy or fellow feeling for the "goodness" that Zeniff saw among the inhabitants. Zeniff's proposal of a treaty would have achieved most of the same goals as military conquest but also had the advantage of leaving social connections intact, and hence continuing the Lamanite lifestyle of the inhabitants. The choice for the rest of the expedition was thus between bloody vengeance and living peaceably in the land of their fathers.

At the end of a small civil war, Zeniff and the other like-minded survivors returned to Zarahemla to mount another venture, this time one that would return to the land of Nephi with a proposal of a treaty, not a military contest.

Mosiah 9:3

> 3 And yet, I being over-zealous to inherit the land of our fathers, collected as many as were desirous to go up to possess the land, and started again on our journey into the wilderness to go up to the land; but we were smitten with famine and sore afflictions; for we were slow to remember the Lord our God.

What does Zeniff mean by saying he was "over-zealous"?[2] A first possibility is that, writing his record with the perspective of hindsight, he contrasts early enthusiasm with his later perspective about their political dependence on the mercy of the Lamanites. Second, perhaps he merely meant that he was in such a hurry to return that his preparations were less adequate than they should have been. Support for this second possibility seems to be in his description of the journey's hardships.

Geography: Zeniff's description once again reinforces the image of the terrain between Nephi and Zarahemla as physically challenging, even treacherous. Even though Zeniff has made the trip three times (from Nephi to Zarahemla with Mosiah$_1$, then a round trip with the expedition), he and his people still "wander" through it, as will Limhi's later search party. They suffer "famine and sore afflictions" as they travel through this land.

Mosiah 9:4–5

> 4 Nevertheless, after many days' wandering in the wilderness we pitched our tents in the place where our brethren were slain, which was near to the land of our fathers.
> 5 And it came to pass that I went again with four of my men into the city, in unto the king, that I might know of the disposition of the king, and that I might know if I might go in with my people and possess the land in peace.

Because Zeniff could find the campsite of the first expedition, he was obviously not merely moving at random and had some mental map he was following. This

---

[2]Zeniff's grandson also refers to him as "over-zealous" (Mosiah 7:21). From Limhi's later position of bondage, the "over-zealousness" would have been allowing themselves to be placed in a subservient position to the Lamanites.

campsite must have been close enough to the city of Nephi to be reached by spies (first mission) and an ambassadorial party (second mission), but sufficiently far away that the inhabitants would not detect them. It must also have been a defensible location, since security would have been important to Zeniff's homesteaders, confronted as they were with the possibility that the treaty might be rejected.

Culture: Zeniff takes four men, a number that is significant in Mesoamerican documents from that area (though from later periods). However, with Zeniff as leader, the party consisted of five men. In later Mesoamerican thought, five is also an important symbolic number, since it represents the center, with the four corners of the earth surrounding it. Could five have been an equally significant number this early? Perhaps taking four men with him emphasized Zeniff as the center, the leader.

Mosiah 9:6–7

> 6 And I went in unto the king, and he covenanted with me that I might possess the land of Lehi-Nephi, and the land of Shilom.
> 7 And he also commanded that his people should depart out of the land, and I and my people went into the land that we might possess it.

Unlike Ammon's immediate arrest when he approached Limhi, Zeniff is allowed to enter the king's presence unmolested. Obviously the king felt secure (since Zeniff's small party could have easily been overpowered); but more significantly, there was no assumption of animosity. Zeniff's party was clearly not considered to be mortal enemies but kinsmen. They spoke the same language and had the same heritage, though different religious and political allegiances.

The king apparently offers Zeniff lands, again confirming that he saw no threat from these newcomers. This territory is the "land of Lehi-Nephi, and the land of Shilom," but the next verse confirms that each land also has a central city by the same name. Zeniff is thus allowed to take over an area consisting of two urban centers and their surrounding agricultural lands. It seems reasonable to suppose that the two lands are also fairly close together.

Geography: John Sorenson proposes a possible location for these two lands:

> In the Valley of Guatemala distances and topography fit markedly with the geographical statements in the Book of Mormon. The land of Nephi in the narrow sense of the term would have consisted of the upper floor of the valley occupied today by Guatemala City and its suburbs. It centered upon the sprawling ancient city that archaeologists have labeled Kaminaljuyú ("hills of the dead"). The upper valley's six square miles lie at an elevation between 4,800 and 5,500 feet. The land of Shilom, the lower level of the valley, would have lain between the curving Rio Villalobos and the north side of Lake Amatitlan. San Antonio Frutal, second largest site in the Valley, sits in this flattish zone, near 4,300 feet elevation. "Enormous mounds" found there date in part from B.C. times, although its most important remains are of Early Classic date, near the end of Book of Mormon times. It occupies a position in relation to the City of Nephi, about seven or eight miles away, which neatly fits the Book of Mormon statements involving the two. This Shilom area is about half as extensive as the Nephi portion of the valley. The hill

spoken of earlier lies about northwest (by our directions today) from San Antonio Frutal; the Book of Mormon (Mosiah 7:16) calls the direction "north."[3]

How large are these lands? How much territory would the Zeniffite party need? Although no number is suggested, this group consisted of some Nephites and some Zarahemlaites—possibly with a larger number of younger Zarahemlaites who, after several generations of settlement, might be exceeding the carrying capacity of their family's land. For the purpose of constructing a scenario, let's assign Zeniff's party a thousand people. That number might be able to leave Zarahemla without depleting it excessively, considering that Zarahemla had already lost people in its own civil strife. By settling half in each location, Zeniff would have five hundred in each town, prepared to farm its surrounding terrain. Although this population is reasonable for a "town," it would be too small for an urban center the size of the city of Nephi. Furthermore, it is very unlikely that the king would withdraw himself and all of his people from his own large city to give it up to some distant relatives.

Further indication that Lehi-Nephi and Shilom were not already powerful locations comes in the next verse, where the first tasks were to build and repair. The Zeniffites apparently received smaller lands in two separated, though probably contiguous, locations; meanwhile, the residents of Nephi stayed right where they were, keeping an eye (and thumb?) on the Zeniffites.

Mosiah 9:8

8 And we began to build buildings, and to repair the walls of the city, yea, even the walls of the city of Lehi-Nephi, and the city of Shilom.

The fact that these urban centers, though populated (since the people had to move away to make room for them), were dilapidated, suggests that the king gave Zeniff poorer lands rather than the most thriving. The Zeniffites' industry eventually allowed them to accumulate wealth and finance Noah's great building spree, but their beginnings were humble.

Mosiah 9:9

9 And we began to till the ground, yea, even with all manner of seeds, with seeds of corn, and of wheat, and of barley, and with neas, and with sheum, and with seeds of all manner of fruits; and we did begin to multiply and prosper in the land.

Botany: Daniel Ludlow notes: "Although the equivalent of the word *corn* is used in some Semitic languages to refer to various types of cereals, including wheat, Joseph Smith would probably translate it here so it would be clear to the understanding of his readers in the United States. Thus, the 'corn' here is probably maize, which is

---

[3]John L. Sorenson, *An Ancient American Setting for the Book of Mormon* (Salt Lake City: Deseret Book/Provo, Utah: Foundation for Ancient Research and Mormon Studies, 1985), 168.

frequently called corn in the Americas. It is not clear what crops are referred to by the titles of 'neas' and 'sheum.'"[4]

Sorenson explains that "sheum:"

> . . . has recently been identified as "a precise match for Akkadian s(h)e'um, 'barley' (Old Assyrian 'wheat'); the most popular ancient Mesopotamian cereal name." The word's sound pattern indicates it was probably a Jaredite term. This good North Semitic word was quite at home around the "valley of Nimrod," north of Mesopotamia, where the Jaredites paused and collected seeds before starting their long journey to America (Ether 2:1, 3). (Incidentally, the form of the word as the Book of Mormon uses it dates to the third millennium B.C., when the Jaredites left the Near East. Later, it would have been pronounced and spelled differently.) Apparently the Nephite scribe could not translate it to any equivalent grain name, nor could Joseph Smith do so when he put the text into English. The plant and its name no doubt were passed down to the Nephites/Zeniffites through survivors from the First Tradition, just as corn itself was. Since the words *barley* and *sheum* were both used in the same verse (Mosiah 9:9), we know that two different grains were involved, but what "sheum" might specifically have been in our botanical terms we cannot tell at this time. Perhaps this was amaranth?[5] [Amaranth seeds were a staple of Mesoamerican diet and used as the main ingredient in a type of bread.]

Culture: "Planting" not only relates the beginning of their important labor of self-sustenance but also states that they were continuing an agricultural lifestyle. Like most of Mesoamerica, the Zeniffites' social model comprised the central services of the town and its surrounding farming areas.

Mosiah 9:10

> 10 Now it was the cunning and the craftiness of king Laman, to bring my people into bondage, that he yielded up the land that we might possess it.

Daniel H. Ludlow suggests that "king Laman" was a throne name, much as "Nephi" became the name of all early Nephite kings (Jacob 1:11):

> Evidently the Lamanites have used the same procedure as the Nephites did in their early history of naming their kings after their earliest leader. Jacob 1:11 mentions that the kings who succeeded Nephi were known as "second Nephi, third Nephi, and so forth, according to the reigns of the kings." Thus, it should not be too surprising to discover that the king of the Lamanites in approximately 178 B.C. was still known as "King Laman" (Mosiah 10:6), although the original leader after whom the king was named had lived some four hundred years before. Also, later in the Book of Mormon we discover that the son who succeeded this king is also known as Laman (Mosiah 24:3).[6]

Ludlow is certainly correct that both father and son have the same name and that both are kings. However, it is less clear that "Laman" is not a personal name. The passage on Laman's son is: "And now the name of the king of the Lamanites was Laman, being called after the name of his father; and therefore he was called

---

[4]Daniel H. Ludlow, *A Companion to Your Study of the Book of Mormon* (Salt Lake City: Deseret Book, 1976), 181.

[5]Sorenson, *An Ancient American Setting for the Book of Mormon*, 186.

[6]Ludlow, *A Companion to Your Study of the Book of Mormon*, 181.

king Laman. And he was king over a numerous people" (Mosiah 24:3). This description does, in fact, sound like a personal name.

Since Zeniff returned to the land of Nephi not long after Mosiah$_1$'s departure from it, the political and social transformation of those remaining in the city of Nephi has occurred relatively rapidly. Despite the presence of a new ruling lineage and a new tradition, would the cultural shift required to accept a Lamanite king have occurred so quickly? It may not have been as significant a change as it might appear. Since Jacob's time, the contentions in the city of Nephi revolved around the contest between the believing and unbelieving Nephites over the degree of Lamanite acculturation. The division that split Mosiah$_1$'s people occurred on cultural lines; the believers went with Mosiah, while those who remained were presumably already pressing for greater Lamanite acculturation. The presence of a king named Laman whose father was also named Laman suggests that this was not an entirely internal fission. It is quite doubtful that the cultural hatred engrained in Nephite tradition would have seen Laman as an appropriate name. Since the king's father was also Laman, that places the father earlier than the split. It is possible, therefore, that there was some outside Lamanite influence in the events leading to Mosiah's departure, and that an outsider was sitting on the throne.

Redaction: Zeniff's description of Lamanite intention immediately follows that of his people's economic activity. The two conditions—Zeniffite prosperity and Lamanite envy—are clearly linked.

Mosiah 9:11–12

> 11 Therefore it came to pass, that after we had dwelt in the land for the space of twelve years that king Laman began to grow uneasy, lest by any means my people should wax strong in the land, and that they could not overpower them and bring them into bondage.
> 12 Now they were a lazy and an idolatrous people; therefore they were desirous to bring us into bondage, that they might glut themselves with the labors of our hands; yea, that they might feast themselves upon the flocks of our fields.

These statements, ascribing a motive for Lamanite oppression, may not be historically accurate. Zeniff is interpreting Lamanite actions, but the record does not contain any first-hand Lamanite admissions of their motives.

Zeniff bases his statement about Lamanite motives on his assumption of their economic interests. Apparently, this perception of intent became "fact" in Zeniff's mind twelve years after their settlement, but it was not clear when they first arrived to negotiate with the king. Is it an explanation after the fact, or did interactions with the Lamanites convince the Zeniffites that it was so?

Since the first attack on the Zeniffites fails, the statement about Lamanite tendencies must have been based on a different city the Lamanites successfully dominated. Arguably, only such a condition would supply Zeniff with the motives he ascribes to them. In the Mesoamerican context, exacting tribute was such an acceptable reason for a war that it required no further explanation. If the Lamanites had conquered another people, making them tributaries, Zeniff almost certainly would have known about it. This condition would explain why he calls the Lamanites "lazy." As a dominant political power, the Lamanites could live off the tribute of their subject peoples (as opposed to the Nephite ideal of working with one's own hands). Nevertheless, Zeniff's use of "lazy" is a remnant of his cultural prejudice against Lamanites. The later Aztecs of Tenochtitlan (the city of Motecuhzoma) extensively collected tribute from many city-states (the trait that Zeniff is probably critiquing), but could hardly be called lazy. Alonso de Zorita, a Spanish judge (1511–c. 1585) described some of the Nahua lords and their relationships to their people:

> The benefits these lords received were these: Their people gave them personal service in their households and brought them fuel and water, the assignment of tasks being made by the lord. Their people also worked certain fields for the lords, the size of the fields depending upon the number of people. Because of this they were exempt from service to the ruler and from working his fields, and their only other obligation to the ruler was to serve in time of war, from which none was excused. In addition, the ruler furnished them with wages, meals, and lodgings, for they served as gentlemen in waiting in his palace.
>
> These lords were responsible for the working of the fields, both for themselves and for their people, and they had overseers who saw to this. The lords also had the duty of looking after the people in their charge, of defending and protecting them. Thus these lords were appointed and intended to serve the general as well as their private good.[7]

The best explanation for the pejorative "lazy" is Zeniff's prejudice, rather than a historical fact.

What about the second adjective, "idolatrous"? This term is a religious designation: someone has abandoned the true God to worship false gods. Because of the inseparable connection between religion and culture in the ancient world, such a turning away is not only a religious but a cultural deviation. When Zeniff describes the Lamanites in the city of Nephi as rejecting belief in the God of Israel, it is a telling judgment upon the many racial/historical Nephites who were now political Lamanites. These Nephites-become-Lamanites have changed their religion as well as their political allegiance. (See "Excursus: Religion of the Nehors," following Alma 1.)

Zeniff associates the timing of the first attack with the Lamanite desire to conquer the Zeniffites before they became too powerful. This possibility does not seem particularly likely. Twelve years does not seem like an adequate time period for a people, originally seen as no military threat, to become one. Naturally more children would have been born, but young children are not soldiers. The young boys would have become warrior age, but their mature men would have become old. Rather, the only logical way for the Zeniffites to have become militarily stronger in twelve years would have been to attract smaller hamlets into dependent status or forming political alliances with allies. We have no evidence that this, in fact,

---

[7]Alonso de Zorita, *Life and Labor in Ancient Mexico: The Brief and Summary Relation of the Lords of New Spain*, translated by Benjamin Keen (Norman: University of Oklahoma Press, 1963), 47.

occurred, or even that Zeniff's attribution of this motive to the Lamanites is accurate. It is equally likely that the Lamanites, successful in battle against other people who now became tributaries, turned their attention next to the Zeniffites.

Mosiah 9:13–14

> 13 Therefore it came to pass that king Laman began to stir up his people that they should contend with my people; therefore there began to be wars and contentions in the land.
> 14 For, in the thirteenth year of my reign in the land of Nephi, away on the south of the land of Shilom, when my people were watering and feeding their flocks, and tilling their lands, a numerous host of Lamanites came upon them and began to slay them, and to take off their flocks, and the corn of their fields.

Here again (as in vv. 11–12), Zeniff assumes that Laman stirred his people up to wars and contentions. However, at least some evidence suggests that this might not have been so. Zeniff has already claimed that the Lamanites want to bring them into bondage (the state in which his grandson, Limhi, existed). Nevertheless, what Zeniff describes is a violent and murderous attack on a farming community at some distance from Nephi. Obviously, if the point is to exact tribute, it makes no sense to kill the producers—the farmers and shepherds. Rather this attack seems more characteristic of thieves and bandits. Laman certainly could have killed the Nephites and appropriated their flocks at any time in the last twelve years, so why would he have engaged in such drastic action at this point, with no history of escalating tensions and no external reason, such as a famine, driving such a short-sighted decision? While we cannot know why this band of Lamanites attacked in Shilom, it does not seem plausible to attribute responsibility to Laman.

Variant: In the manuscripts and the 1830 edition, the phrase in verse 14 was "to take *of* their flocks." This was changed in 1837 to "to take *off* their flocks." Skousen notes: "The 1837 reading 'to take **off** their flocks' does seem rather odd, which suggests that the 1837 change to *off* may have been accidental (it was not marked by Joseph Smith in the printer's manuscript)." He also notes that there are several parallel passages with "to take *of* . . . " such as 1 Nephi 16:7, "also my brethren took **of** the daughters of Ishmael to wife." Skousen suggests that the text should read "to take *of* their flocks."[8] I see the text as indicating that some of the flocks were taken rather than that all were taken.

Mosiah 9:15

> 15 Yea, and it came to pass that they fled, all that were not overtaken, even into the city of Nephi, and did call upon me for protection.

The survivors of this attack did not flee to the city of Shilom but to the city of Nephi, presumably because it was larger, more defensible, and also the seat of the

---

[8]Royal Skousen, *Analysis of Textual Variants of the Book of Mormon*, THE CRITICAL TEXT OF THE BOOK OF MORMON (Provo, Utah: Foundation for Ancient Research and Mormon Studies, 2005), Vol. 4, Part 2, 1243–44.

government. This description of flight into a town for protection underscores that this is the accepted relationship between the vulnerable outlying villages and the city with its greater concentration of people and, probably, some fortifications. (See Alonso de Zorita, commentary vv. 11–12.)

Geography: By treaty, king Laman gave the land and city of *Lehi-Nephi* to Zeniff (Mosiah 7:21). Now, however, Zeniff's people flee to the city of Nephi. Were they two different places? Sorenson thinks they were the same location. (See commentary accompanying Mosiah 7:25.) Since this verse has Nephites fleeing to the city of Nephi rather than to the city of Lehi-Nephi, it certainly appears that they are the same. Nevertheless, the evidence is not conclusive. I suggest that perhaps there was either a scribal or a transmission error at this point. Since Joseph Smith and Oliver Cowdery probably did not understand the finer points of geography and the city of Nephi and the city of Lehi-Nephi are so obviously similar, such an omission during dictation would not be unusual.

Mosiah 9:16

> 16 And it came to pass that I did arm them with bows, and with arrows, with swords, and with cimeters, and with clubs, and with slings, and with all manner of weapons which we could invent, and I and my people did go forth against the Lamanites to battle.

The catalog of Nephite weapons has already been discussed (see commentary accompanying Enos 1:21), but this verse mentions "all manner of weapons which we could invent." Did the Zeniffites literally create hitherto unknown weapons? While necessity certainly breeds inventiveness, it does not necessarily lead to completely new weapons. Note the conditions of technological inferiority England faced in the 1620s:

> Military practice had changed substantially during the 16th and early 17th centuries to the degree that some historians describe those changes as the "military revolution." Pike-trailers such as Sir Roger Williams, author of *A Briefe Discourse of Warre* (1590), warned Englishmen that they were failing to keep up with the latest technical and tactical innovations. By the time Charles I plunged into the Thirty Years' War . . . the gulf had widened between contemporary European military science and the English art of war.[9]

The resolution of the need for modernized weaponry was not adoption of the same gunpowder-based weapons as other European nations, but rather innovations on the traditional English long bow.[10] In like way, it is improbable that the Zeniffite people had the caliber of military genius required to invent entirely new weapons. It seems more likely that they manufactured weapons they knew about but did not previously possess (or, at least, had only one or two examples of). Up to this time the main Zeniffite activity seems to have been restoring buildings and working hard

---

[9]Mark Charles Fissel, "Tradition and Invention in the Early Stuart Art of War," http://www.aug.edu/mfissel/tradition.htm (accessed January 2005).

[10]Ibid.

to maintain a prosperous system of agriculture. Some support for the idea of "manufacturing" weapons with which to repel an imminent attack comes from Mosiah 10:1: "We again began to establish the kingdom and we again began to possess the land in peace. And I caused that there should be weapons of war made of every kind, that thereby I might have weapons for my people against the time the Lamanites should come up again to war against my people."

Mosiah 9:17–19

> 17 Yea, in the strength of the Lord did we go forth to battle against the Lamanites; for I and my people did cry mightily to the Lord that he would deliver us out of the hands of our enemies, for we were awakened to a remembrance of the deliverance of our fathers.
>
> 18 And God did hear our cries and did answer our prayers; and we did go forth in his might; yea, we did go forth against the Lamanites, and in one day and a night we did slay three thousand and forty-three; we did slay them even until we had driven them out of our land.
>
> 19 And I, myself, with mine own hands, did help to bury their dead. And behold, to our great sorrow and lamentation, two hundred and seventy-nine of our brethren were slain.

Redaction: How long did it take Zeniff to write or dictate this history? Did he return to it at many sittings? It sounds as if it might be a holographic record, which Mormon copied directly to his own plates. But obviously, Zeniff wrote in retrospect (as a history), not in the ongoing rush of events (as a diary). But how long after the events he records did he write them down? His record itself suggests that there were at most two sittings, and possibly only one.

A logical pause might be between verses 9–10: he has described building and planting (both cyclical processes), but the next significant event has not yet occurred. A break here does not seem likely, however, because of the structural parallel between Mosiah 9:8–12 and Mosiah 10:4–6. (See commentary accompanying Mosiah 10.) Because of this parallel, the structure of the narrative suggests that verses 8–9, rather than being closing statements, are an introduction to the story of conflict with the Lamanites. Therefore, Zeniff may have written the first part up to the end of chapter 9, then started chapter 10 at the next sitting. It is equally possible, however, that he wrote the entire record in a single sitting. I prefer this second hypothesis, not because of its logistical ease but because the narrative structure ties the two conflicts together. Furthermore, for a first-person narrative, this record omits much important history. It has the feeling of a record that Zeniff made close to the end of his life to justify his reign and actions.

History: The spiritual point of this story is that the Zeniffites defeat a superior number of Lamanites because they call upon Yahweh. Although this result of faith describes a true principle, the historical situation may have been somewhat more complex. Consider, for example, that the conflict begins when a "numerous host" (Mosiah 9:14) of Lamanites attack the Zeniffites without warning in their fields—not to force their surrender but to take their goods. This raiding party presumably left with their loot, since they were attacking farmland, which was not a fortified area that they could hold against a countering Zeniffite force. The survivors flee to Lehi-Nephi.[11] Zeniff raises an army and attacks the Lamanites (Mosiah 9:16). In other words, they are not defending their city against attack but are pursuing an aggressive policy.

Zeniff does not mention meeting an enemy army, only that they slew an enormous number of Lamanites (the casualty ratio is about 11 Lamanites for every Zeniffite) in "one day and a night" (v. 18). This description suggests a very quick battle. The 3,043 Lamanite dead might suggest a Zeniffite army of at least 3,000, but it seems very unlikely that 3,000 able-bodied men left Zarahemla or that King Laman would consider such a number to be non-threatening. At a minimum, 3,000 fighting men suggest a base population of 9,000 (one woman and one child per man).

Sorenson's reading of these verses suggests to him that the marauding army was still in the fields, caught by the Nephites as they were still taking their spoils.[12] This scenario assumes both that Shilom and Lehi-Nephi were close (his stated conclusion) but also that those who fled from the Lamanite armies were able to get to Lehi-Nephi, raise the alarm, raise the retaliatory army, and return to find the Lamanites still on the scene. While I find Sorenson's hypothesis about the distance plausible, the rest of the scenario seems less likely. If the Lamanite army were an attack force, it should have pressed its advantage. If they were marauders, they should have retreated, especially since they would have wanted to drive the captured livestock to safety without delay and without undue haste that might damage the animals. The idea that the army simply settled down in the open with its captured herd, apparently unconcerned about a counter-attack, does not seem likely.

However, a couple of alternative scenarios are possibilities. The first is that the innocent but heroic Zeniffites, after being assaulted, met and defeated a standing army of exploitive Lamanites. The second is that the Zeniffites, after being assaulted, countered by attacking hamlets occupied by Lamanites and killing them before they could raise much defense. Here is how the information fits that hypothesis:

- The Lamanite attack killed Zeniffites and therefore both justified and required the killing of Lamanites in return. Because "Lamanite" is a generic term, it does not particularly matter on which Lamanites the Zeniffites took their vengeance.
- It is more logical to see the attacking Lamanites as promptly retreating with their spoils. Once they had achieved their goal, why would they linger? Nevertheless, the Zeniffites killed three thousand Lamanites in a very short

---

[11]The text specifically calls it the city of Nephi. I suspect that this is a translation error. I see it much more likely that Lehi-Nephi was a different city from the city of Nephi. (See commentary accompanying Mosiah 7:21.)

[12]John L. Sorenson, *The Geography of Book of Mormon Events: a Source Book* (Provo, Utah: FARMS, 1990), 237–8.

period of time. This means they had to find them, and going to Lamanite settlements was the surest way of finding them, rather than engaging on an extended hunt for a group of fast-moving men in the wilderness.

- The ratio of losses indicates that the Zeniffites had the element of surprise. In hand-to-hand combat, such a vast differential in kill ratios seems unlikely unless the Zeniffites were superior in personal strength or weaponry. The record gives no indication of either characteristic (although it does not rule either out). It is quite likely that the Zeniffites were fewer in number (not just in casualties), further suggesting a surprise attack. A band of Lamanites who had attacked Nephites would certainly be prepared for retaliation or at least wary of it.
- The result of this military engagement is that the Zeniffites drive the Lamanites from the Zeniffite lands (v. 18). This description could mean forcing out a standing army, but it seems more likely to explain Lamanite families fleeing from their hamlets.

While we would prefer not to see such behavior in a people whom we identify as more sympathetic and righteous, such a scenario would be typical in the ancient world. Blood feuds are between peoples, not individuals. If Lamanites kill Zeniffites, then Zeniffites retaliate by killing Lamanites, and typically, any Lamanites, irrespective of technical guilt, would do.

Geography: Understanding both this conflict and the one in the next chapter depends heavily on forming some notion of the possible geography: the general physical relationships between Shemlon (Lamanite), Lehi-Nephi (Zeniffite), and Shilom (Zeniffite). Sorenson suggests this overview of the comparative geography of these three cities:

> From the top of Noah's "very high tower" near the temple in the city, he could "overlook" the lands of Shilom and Shemlon and "even look over all the land round about. . . . " So the distance implied from the viewing tower to, or even across, Shemlon could not be great. About twenty miles fits both this criterion and previous ones about Shilom and Shemlon. The order of elevation is: Shemlon lowest, Shilom higher, Lehi-Nephi higher still, and north of the land Shilom highest. A sound inference is that Shemlon was nearest the coast, from whence Nephi had originally come.[13]

In addition to general elevation, the cities' relative positions are important. Both Sorenson and archaeologist Richard Hauck place Lehi-Nephi north of Shilom.[14] However, each places Shemlon in a different position in relationship to Lehi-Nephi and Shilom. Sorenson locates Shemlon to the southwest, and Hauck positions it more generally east. Sorenson continues:

---

[13]Ibid., 238–39.

[14]Sorenson, *An Ancient American Setting for the Book of Mormon*, 170; F. Richard Hauck, *Deciphering the Geography of the Book of Mormon: Settlements and Routes in Ancient America* (Salt Lake City: Deseret Book, 1988), 72–3.

Shemlon was clearly the Lamanite base in the times of Zeniff, Noah, and Limhi; attacks on the Zeniffites ruled by those men always came from or through Shemlon. When the Lamanite king first welcomed Zeniff and his people, who had come up from Zarahemla, the ruler was willing to pull his own settlers out of Nephi and Shilom back to Shemlon in hopes of exploiting the Nephite returnees (Mosiah 9:6–7, 10, 12); but conflict proved inevitable. The first skirmish between the two groups came when Lamanites attacked some of Zeniff's people "watering and feeding their flocks, and tilling their lands . . . on the south of the land of Shilom" (v. 14). The Lamanite attack came "up" (Mosiah 10:6) from Shemlon. Thereafter Zeniff put a watch on the Shemlon-Shilom frontier, anticipating a renewed attack. In time the Lamanites did return, but this time they did not try to cut through Shilom on their way toward Nephi. Instead they came from Shemlon "up upon the north of the land of Shilom" (v. 8), hoping to bypass Shilom on the west and attempting to outflank the Zeniffite watch and hit Nephi without warning. Zeniff and his men knew something was brewing, having been alerted by the lookouts they had posted overlooking Shemlon. When they located the advancing enemy, they "went up" onto the hills and fought the Lamanites north of Shilom before the attackers could come around and down into Nephi proper (Mosiah 10:10).

Supposing that the city of Lehi-Nephi was Kaminaljuyú, at present-day Guatemala City, the physical details of this entire event fit perfectly. Shemlon would be the lake-side gateway to the Valley of Guatemala through which forces from the lush piedmont area would approach the city. Shemlon's attractiveness to the Lamanite elite would have included its climate, significantly warmer than at Kaminaljuyú (1,600 feet higher), yet not so oppressively hot as the adjacent lowlands, the old Lamanite base. The border between Shilom and Shemlon would obviously be the sharp bluff overlooking the lake and the curving Villalobos River. Near the river the Lamanite poachers could conveniently have got at the Nephite flocks, while the bluff would have been an ideal spot for Zeniff's watchmen. The hilly terrain on "the north of Shilom," where the Lamanite force tried to outflank the Nephite defenders, is exactly what the story calls for.[15]

Text: The 1830 edition of the Book of Mormon does not end a chapter at this point. Rather, verse 1 of chapter 10 should be read as part of the same story.

---

[15]Sorenson, *An Ancient American Setting for the Book of Mormon*, 169–71.

Mosiah 10

Mosiah 10:1

1 And it came to pass that we again began to establish the kingdom and we again began to possess the land in peace. And I caused that there should be weapons of war made of every kind, that thereby I might have weapons for my people against the time the Lamanites should come up again to war against my people.

History: The aftermath of successfully driving the Lamanites from the lands of Lehi-Nephi and Shilom results in "establish[ing] the kingdom." This phrase further emphasizes that the victory was territorial as much as it was a victory of manpower. Zeniff has firmly established his borders.

The second piece of information is that he begins to manufacture and stockpile arms. This detail corroborates the relative lack of preparation already noted (Mosiah 9:16). Zeniff rightly foresees the possibility of retaliatory attacks and is taking appropriate countermeasures.

Mosiah 10:2

2 And I set guards round about the land, that the Lamanites might not come upon us again unawares and destroy us; and thus I did guard my people and my flocks, and keep them from falling into the hands of our enemies.

Zeniff's posting of guards indicates both the military emergency and the relative size of Zeniff's people at the time. Even though children might act as sentinels, guards are necessarily of fighting age and therefore also old enough to work the fields. To designate a cadre of guards for more than a short-term emergency implies the community's ability to produce sufficient food even without the labor of these working-age males. This productivity, which probably allows Noah's extravagance, seems to be confirmed in verses 4 and 5 below. The guards are probably more like roving patrols than large garrisons at fortified outposts (see v. 7).

Mosiah 10:3

3 And it came to pass that we did inherit the land of our fathers for many years, yea, for the space of twenty and two years.

Zeniff's preparations thus deterred Lamanite retaliation for nine more years. Although it is possible to read this sentence as twenty-two years after the thirteen years mentioned in Mosiah 9:14, the Book of Mormon counts years from a major foundational event (such as establishing a new people), not lesser events in a given dynasty.

Zeniff's ability to deter further aggression highlights the complications inherent in the first attack. It could not have been a highly organized assault or it would have taken the city of Shemlon, which would have offered more spoils than just the flocks on the south of the land of Shilom. Furthermore, Zeniffite retaliation did not set off another attack by the Lamanite city of Shemlon, indicating that the attack was somehow not considered to be directed to Shemlon. While there are many unanswered and unanswerable questions concerning the first attack, it seems that the Lamanite city of Shemlon did not consider itself directly threatened by the Zeniffite retaliation. However, according to Zeniffite records, Shemlon did use the Zeniffite retaliation to justify the attack described below.

Mosiah 10:4–5

> 4 And I did cause that the men should till the ground, and raise all manner of grain and all manner of fruit of every kind.
> 5 And I did cause that the women should spin, and toil, and work, and work all manner of fine linen, yea, and cloth of every kind, that we might clothe our nakedness; and thus we did prosper in the land—thus we did have continual peace in the land for the space of twenty and two years.

Literary: These verses (4–6) are a structural parallel to Mosiah 9:9–12. As he did earlier, Zeniff sets the Lamanite actions in the context of his people's economic activities. There is no historic need to repeat that his people tilled the ground except that it serves as a metaphor for Zeniffite prosperity, which ignites Lamanite greed both earlier and here.

Mosiah 10:6

> 6 And it came to pass that king Laman died, and his son began to reign in his stead. And he began to stir his people up in rebellion against my people; therefore they began to prepare for war, and to come up to battle against my people.

While it is possible that "king Laman" is a regnal name, in this case it seems to be a personal name. (See commentary accompanying Mosiah 9:10.) The record does not mention a coronation ceremony; rather, the son named Laman simply succeeded his father. Regnal names are given after accession for the simple reason that a father cannot be certain that any given son will live to inherit the throne. If a successor-son were given a regnal name at birth but died in childhood, it could easily be interpreted as a disaster. In consequence, the regnal name is bestowed as a substitute for the personal name upon accession to the throne.

This new king $Laman_3$ apparently begins his reign by stirring up his people. Why had such agitation not occurred before his father's death? Although the Book of Mormon provides no social commentary on this event, we know three pieces of information that help explain this timing:

- Laman the father made a treaty with Zeniff.

- Zeniff led a retaliatory campaign against the Lamanites in his land, killing over three thousand. Even if such slaughter was seen as justified, the hamlets were under Shemlon's protection; therefore, Zeniff was attacking the rulership of Shemlon, though not attacking the city itself.
- Laman dies, and his son, Laman$_3$, inherits.

It is possible that Laman intended to honor his treaty, despite serious provocation in the deaths of three thousand subjects. (See commentary accompanying Mosiah 9:17–19.) While the Zeniffites no doubt felt justified in their counterattack, certainly the Lamanites felt differently, distinguishing between the "renegades" who attacked Zeniff's people and the "innocent" Lamanites who were killed. No doubt the kin of the dead Lamanites demanded retaliation in turn: life for life. The accession of new king created a potentially new situation. Laman$_3$ may have seen the treaty as a personal agreement between his father and Zeniff which was not binding upon him. If Laman$_3$ were experiencing pressure for retaliation, the death of Laman removed the brake stopping the forces that were pressing for military action.

Mosiah 10:7

7 But I had sent my spies out round about the land of Shemlon, that I might discover their preparations, that I might guard against them, that they might not come upon my people and destroy them.

This verse amplifies the information about Zeniff's guards: They are "spies. . . round about the land of Shemlon" who "guard" against the Lamanites. When the spies notice military preparations, they report their information so that the Zeniffites will not be caught by surprise.

The concept that the people would be "destroyed" by the Lamanite attack suggests a war of extermination. However, the Lamanites' actual objective, achieved during Limhi's reign, is subjugation. More likely, Zeniff sees his people's political separateness, rather than his people themselves, as being destroyed. This is, in fact what happens: political dependency and heavy tribute. It is also possible that Zeniff is using "destroy" as hyperbole to incite the Zeniffites to greater military efforts.

Geography: The elevation of Lehi-Nephi and Shilom over Shemlon provided many excellent spying vantage points in Sorenson's geographic correlation.

Mosiah 10:8

8 And it came to pass that they came up upon the north of the land of Shilom, with their numerous hosts, men armed with bows, and with arrows, and with swords, and with cimeters, and with stones, and with slings; and they had their heads shaved that they were naked; and they were girded with a leathern girdle about their loins.

Geography: In order to "[come] up upon the north of the land of Shilom," the Lamanites had to travel around Shilom and attack on the south of Lehi-Nephi. This maneuver splits the Zeniffite armies but also assumes that an attack on Lehi-Nephi would defeat Shilom's fighting effectiveness; otherwise any army from Shilom would approach the Lamanite southern flank with the army from Lehi-Nephi on the north. This military plan would create a two-front battle, complicating the Lamanites' attack.

Capturing Lehi-Nephi and the king would probably end the war. Only a plan for assuring just such a rapid capture could justify the Lamanite army's deliberately moving between two armies.

Culture: The verse tells us that the Lamanites "had their heads shaved that they were naked." Why would these warriors have shaved heads?

The pictorial convention for displaying captives was to show the victor grasping the hair of the captive. A Classic Maya vase from Nebaj, Guatemala (undated, but from the Classic period between A.D. 250 and A.D. 800), shows Lord Kan Xib Ahaw capturing warriors. Each of the three captured warriors is firmly held by his hair in the left hand of the captor.[1]

It is possible that the Lamanite shaving of the heads was a symbolic gesture indicating that they had no intention of being captured. Rather than being a raiding party bent on tribute, the Lamanites were engaged in a blood feud and bound to take vengeance. Such a scenario is certainly a possibility, given the facts known about this particular conflict. However, there is no documentation for this practice.

Mosiah 10:9

> 9 And it came to pass that I caused that the women and children of my people should be hid in the wilderness; and I also caused that all my old men that could bear arms, and also all my young men that were able to bear arms, should gather themselves together to go to battle against the Lamanites; and I did place them in their ranks, every man according to his age.

Geography: The city of Lehi-Nephi has a wilderness area in such close proximity that it will provide concealment for these women and children; as Noah's account shows, he also flees into this wilderness area, followed by his people's women and children making a last-minute escape (Mosiah 19:9). The area is sufficiently "wild" that the very geography provides protection from the army. Sorenson hypothesizes that this area is the mountainous region west of modern Guatemala City.[2]

Culture: Reinforcing the possibility that the Lamanites' shaved heads communicate their resolve to conquer or be killed is Zeniff's action in sending the women and

---

[1]Dorie Reents-Budet, *Painting the Maya Universe: Royal Ceramics of the Classic Period* (Durham, N.C.: Duke University Press, 1994), 258–9. The vase is K2352 in the Maya Vase Database, http://www.famsi.org/research/kerr/index.html (accessed January 2005).

[2]John L. Sorenson, *An Ancient American Setting for the Book of Mormon* (Salt Lake City: Deseret Book/Provo, Utah: Foundation for Ancient Research and Mormon Studies, 1985), 169–171.

children to the wilderness as a safer location than the city. He also arms the old men, trying to bolster his own numbers to match this much larger army. When Zeniff describes placing his men "in their ranks, every man according to his age," he is describing the battle ranks of massed warriors, no doubt positioned so that they could protect each others' flanks. Depth of lines would also provide immediate reinforcements as the fighters in the front fell.

Zeniff says he positioned his men according to age. Probably his most experienced and mature fighting men were in the front line, with perhaps the boys in the middle and the old men in the last row as the final defense. Such a tactic would ensure that the Lamanites would reach them only after fighting all the way through the earlier ranks, preserving the strength of the old men but still utilizing them defensively.

Mosiah 10:10

> 10 And it came to pass that we did go up to battle against the Lamanites; and I, even I, in my old age, did go up to battle against the Lamanites. And it came to pass that we did go up in the strength of the Lord to battle.

Culture: The final "rank" in the military line was Zeniff himself. Since a Mesoamerican battle was over when the king was captured, he would need to be protected as much as possible. Though old, he was physically present on the battlefield like Nephi and Benjamin before him (Jacob 1:10, W of M 1:13).

Mosiah 10:11

> 11 Now, the Lamanites knew nothing concerning the Lord, nor the strength of the Lord, therefore they depended on their own strength. Yet they were a strong people, as to the strength of men.

Literature: This verse serves as a transition from describing the Zeniffites' preparation to Zeniff's analysis of the Lamanites, particularly focusing on the concept of relying upon Yahweh's strength. He has already established that his people went to battle in Yahweh's strength. Now he describes the Lamanites as lacking such knowledge of Yahweh's power. From that point, he describes them as military opponents (strong), but concentrates on their hatred of the Zeniffites/Nephites, a second motivation that he gives for their attack upon the Zeniffites.

Mosiah 10:12–18

> 12 They were a wild, and ferocious, and a blood-thirsty people, believing in the tradition of their fathers, which is this—Believing that they were driven out of the land of Jerusalem because of the iniquities of their fathers, and that they were wronged in the wilderness by their brethren, and they were also wronged while crossing the sea;
> 13 And again, that they were wronged while in the land of their first inheritance, after they had crossed the sea, and all this because that Nephi was more faithful in keeping the commandments of the Lord—therefore he was

favored of the Lord, for the Lord heard his prayers and answered them, and he took the lead of their journey in the wilderness.
14 And his brethren were wroth with him because they understood not the dealings of the Lord; they were also wroth with him upon the waters because they hardened their hearts against the Lord.
15 And again, they were wroth with him when they had arrived in the promised land, because they said that he had taken the ruling of the people out of their hands; and they sought to kill him.
16 And again, they were wroth with him because he departed into the wilderness as the Lord had commanded him, and took the records which were engraven on the plates of brass, for they said that he robbed them.
17 And thus they have taught their children that they should hate them, and that they should murder them, and that they should rob and plunder them, and do all they could to destroy them; therefore they have an eternal hatred towards the children of Nephi.
18 For this very cause has king Laman, by his cunning, and lying craftiness, and his fair promises, deceived me, that I have brought this my people up into this land, that they may destroy them; yea, and we have suffered these many years in the land.

The long argument in verses 12–18 is constructed of smaller units. Zeniff introduces the Lamanites with a series of pejoratives ("wild . . . ferocious . . . blood-thirsty," the same trio of descriptions in the same order as in Enos 1:20), to which he appends an apparently unrelated idea: "believing in the tradition of their fathers." However, the rest of this passage explains those traditions, interpreting them as the cause of the Lamanites' moral degeneracy. In verse 18, Zeniff comes to his point, which is that the entire history of Nephite-Lamanite dealings can be explained as a result of this long-held hatred.

He begins by summarizing the history of Nephi and his brothers, Laman and Lemuel, a history with which the modern reader is familiar from the small plates, but Zeniff does not assume that his reader is as familiar, since he must summarize that history. No doubt, Lamanite traditions preserved animosity toward the Nephites. Still, Zeniff's analysis is somewhat problematic. First, he is naturally ill-disposed toward the Lamanites, given his description of the war they are currently engaged in. Still, he initially found much that was "good" among the Lamanites and resisted his first leader's policy of exterminating them (Mosiah 9:1). What has changed his mind, and how is it related to the "tradition of their fathers?"

Second, the people of Shemlon probably include people from the city of Nephi who remained behind when Mosiah led his people away. Thus, the (political) "Lamanites" would include (genetic) "Nephites." While the lineal descendents of Laman and Lemuel might hate Nephites because of this "tradition," it seems less likely that Nephites-become-Lamanites would also hate the Zeniffites, who are arguably a new tradition.

Third, why does Zeniff call the Lamanites "bloodthirsty" and "wild"? True, the Lamanites slew some Zeniffites, but far more Lamanites died in retaliation and they have not counterattacked for nine years. Arguably, the Zeniffites were also "blood-thirsty"—perhaps even blood-thirstier—if we compare their respective deaths and also if, as I have hypothesized, they attacked hamlets of unarmed civilians rather than meeting armed warriors.

Zeniff is simply repeating cultural stereotypes to which we were first introduced in Enos 1:20. Lamanites are blood-thirsty and wild simply because they are Lamanites. Zeniff blames both their traditions of hating the Nephites and their "cunning"—a sort of ancestral conspiracy theory ascribing to them the intention from the beginning to destroy the Zeniffites. He overlooks at least twelve years during which the Lamanites' more plausible purpose was to reap the economic benefits of levying tribute from the Zeniffites. Furthermore, he seems to accept without question his ability to read the Lamanite mind, even though there is no indication whatever that he has conferred with Laman₃ or received any messages/demands/threats from him. What we have are Zeniff's suppositions, filtered through his antipathy, self-justification, and mistrust—not facts.

Mosiah 10:19–21

> 19 And now I, Zeniff, after having told all these things unto my people concerning the Lamanites, I did stimulate them to go to battle with their might, putting their trust in the Lord; therefore, we did contend with them, face to face.
> 20 And it came to pass that we did drive them again out of our land; and we slew them with a great slaughter, even so many that we did not number them.
> 21 And it came to pass that we returned again to our own land, and my people again began to tend their flocks, and to till their ground.

The battle takes place "face to face" or, as modern terminology would put it, hand to hand. The Zeniffites, with Yahweh's aid, held off and drove an apparently numerically superior army away from the lands of Shilom and Lehi-Nephi. Shemlon, however, remained a strong base of Lamanite operations. The battle's resolution include a de facto truce between two close neighbors, likely including some trade and travel restrictions.

During this truce, Zeniff's people return to their normal agricultural occupations. Since the pastures and fields are more vulnerable than the cities, and since the region south of Shilom was particularly exposed, apparently the truce included an agreement with Shemlon that left the people feeling safe there, despite its exposure.

Mosiah 10:22

> 22 And now I, being old, did confer the kingdom upon one of my sons; therefore, I say no more. And may the Lord bless my people. Amen.

Zeniff does not name Noah as the son upon whom he conferred the kingdom, although this son's identity is clarified in the next verse. Zeniff assumes that his readers understand that it would have been his oldest son. This verse makes it clear, however, that he considered the transfer of power to be his final official act and consequently terminates his record.

Text: At this point, a chapter break occurs in the 1830 and modern editions. However, as Chapter 11 makes plain, the change that occasions the chapter break is more than the succession of one king by another. It is also the end of the inserted text and the beginning of a new abridgment by Mormon.

Mosiah 11

Mosiah 11:1

> 1 And now it came to pass that Zeniff conferred the kingdom upon Noah, one of his sons; therefore Noah began to reign in his stead; and he did not walk in the ways of his father.

Redaction: Zeniff's first-person account ends, and a third-person synopsis begins. Why did Mormon stop copying and begin abridging? He clearly has records from which he is taking his account but has changed his method of including information. I hypothesize that Zeniff's account was succinct, informative, and focused; an abridgment would have had few advantages over the original. But Noah's account was arguably longer. The evidence of Noah's efforts to build impressive buildings (Mosiah 11:8–12) suggests that he would have desired an impressive record to accompany his achievements. Mormon would have had no interest in recounting the political details of Noah's reign. Nevertheless, his introduction is unflattering, certainly a contrast to the tone of Noah's official record. As we continue to read Mormon's account, it will be clear that he made sure to paint Noah in the worst possible light. Mormon shifts to a third-person account because the first-person account did not fit Mormon's perception of Noah.

Mosiah 11:2

> 2 For behold, he did not keep the commandments of God, but he did walk after the desires of his own heart. And he had many wives and concubines. And he did cause his people to commit sin, and do that which was abominable in the sight of the Lord. Yea, and they did commit whoredoms and all manner of wickedness.

Because Mormon is writing this description long after the events, he is interpreting the documents before him. An official report would never cast such a pejorative light on the reigning king. Given that the tone is Mormon's, it is possible to make a few deductions about the material upon which he was basing his opinions.

Mormon was obviously offended by several qualities of Noah. He did not keep the commandments of God. He had many wives and concubines. He caused his people to commit sin and abominations, or, slightly more specifically, to commit whoredoms and "all manner of wickedness."

Later in verse 6, Mormon adds idolatry to the catalogue of Noah's sins. Except for sexual immorality, it is not clear what specific behaviors Mormon was capturing with his terms "sin," "abominations" and "all manner of wickedness." However, he also highlights Noah's materialism and preoccupation with wealth, beginning with his heavy taxations (v. 3, but especially vv. 8–14). This conjunction of religious/economic problems had also plagued the Nephites during Jacob's time (Jacob 2:12–13). Like Jacob, Mormon connects social and economic sins but definitely sees them as subcategories of religious sin, because religion encompasses all life. Both Jacob and Mormon saw an implicit association between sinful polygamy and sinful materialism.

"Whoredom" in the Book of Mormon is consistently linked either to riches (Mosiah 12:29; Alma 1:29–32; Hel. 3:14; Ether 8:16, 10:7) or to a more general category that includes contentions, strifes, and deceivings (Alma 30:18, 50:21–22; Hel. 6:22; 3 Ne. 16:10, 30:2; 4 Ne. 1:15–17; Morm. 8:31). After Helaman, the explicit connection between "whoredoms" and riches disappears, although many of the sins earlier associated with "whoredoms" continue to be mentioned.

Literature: Benjamin McGuire, a graduate student specializing in the ancient Near East and Old Testament, draws a parallel between the description of Noah as a wicked king and the Deuteronomic code for kings. He suggests that the phrase ". . . but he [Noah] did walk after the desires of his own heart. And he had many wives and concubines" is an intentional description of an evil king who violates the code found in Deuteronomy 17:17: "He must not take many wives, or his heart will be led astray. He must not accumulate large amounts of silver and gold." He sees a similar oblique reference to Deuteronomy 17:17 in the description of Riplakish as a wicked king in Ether 10:5–7.[1]

Mosiah 11:3

> 3 And he laid a tax of one fifth part of all they possessed, a fifth part of their gold and of their silver, and a fifth part of their ziff, and of their copper, and of their brass and their iron; and a fifth part of their fatlings; and also a fifth part of all their grain.

Culture: Foodstuffs appear at the end of this list of taxed items, even though a levy of food in some form is essential to provide for a hierarchy of rulers who do not farm. In the context of verse 4 that these taxes are to "support [Noah] himself, and . . . his priests, and their wives and their concubines," the mention of animals and grain show that Noah and his court ate food produced by the labor of others.

Economics: We assume that gold and silver are precious, but this entire list is specifically identified as "precious" (v. 8). Why are the other metals also precious? The presence of brass as an alloy suggests that it is their malleability that makes them precious. As noted in Jacob (see commentary accompanying Jacob 2:12–13), they are precious for what can be made with them, not simply because they exist. Like Asians, Mesoamericans apparently valued jade above gold. Historian David

[1]Benjamin McGuire, "Polygamy in the Book of Mormon, Outside Jacob 2," Post to FAIR Message Board, August 8, 2005, http://www.mormonapologetics.org/index.php?showtopic=9536&st=15. He also notes that while the original record of the Jaredites preceded Deuteronomy, the current text is heavily influenced by Moroni's redaction. He sees the similarity in vocabulary as intentional in Moroni's editing.

Drew notes: "As a precious material gold remained secondary to blue-green jade, the colour of fertility and the essence of life itself."[2]

Also as in Jacob, the metals are economically important. This land was previously inhabited by Lamanites. Had it abounded in ores that had the intrinsic value that the Spaniards assigned to gold, it seems logical that the Lamanites would have been unwilling to give up the land if gold was still readily available. Nevertheless, in a single short generation (Zeniff was already an adult when he joined the first expedition), Noah could tax specific workable metals, valuable because of the goods created from them, not because of the metals' mere existence. If these metals are sufficiently abundant that Noah can require a fifth of them, then he would not necessarily be significantly wealthier than others dealing in precious metals. Trade and the exchange of goods produces wealth; that exchange with outside communities led to wealth that, in turn, fostered social and religious divisions in the city of Nephi. Noah is back at the scene of the crime, very literally, repeating the same economic and religious errors as the Nephites of Jacob's time. (See commentary accompanying Jacob 2:12–13.)

Mosiah 11:4–5

> 4 And all this did he take to support himself, and his wives and his concubines; and also his priests, and their wives and their concubines; thus he had changed the affairs of the kingdom.
> 5 For he put down all the priests that had been consecrated by his father, and consecrated new ones in their stead, such as were lifted up in the pride of their hearts.

Culture: Mormon summarizes Noah's political tactic of replacing his father's advisors and officials with his own people. This is not an unusual procedure, not only because of personality differences, but also as a simple method of eliminating conflicts between the goals and procedures of the old and new regimes. Mormon makes it very clear that Noah introduced new ways that were so significantly different that they were sure to cause dissonance with the traditionalists. Thus, eliminating Zeniff's priests was a logical step of *realpolitik* for Noah.

Understanding the logic behind removing potential political adversaries, however, does not necessarily explain the focus on priests in particular. First, as already explained, nothing like the modern separation between church and state or privatization of religion existed in the ancient world. As Abinadi's trial shows, the priests also function as political counselors.[3] And naturally, they presided over the

---

[2]David Drew, *The Lost Chronicles of the Maya Kings* (Berkeley: University of California Press, 1999), 15. See also George E. Stuart and Gene S. Stuart, *The Mysterious Maya* (Washington, D. C.: National Geographic Society, 04/08/23 1977), 57, and Michael D. Coe, *The Maya*, 6th ed. (New York: Thames & Hudson, 1999), 29.

[3]Daniel C. Peterson, "Authority in the Book of Mosiah," *FARMS Review* 18, no. 1 (2006): 160: "Nephite priests seem to have served as a kind of council to whom the king could go for counsel and advice. Mosiah2 consulted with his priests (Mosiah 27:1), as did King Noah at his own (obviously imitative) court in the land of Nephi (Mosiah 12:17; 17:6)."

community's religious rites, which is where Mormon sees a deplorable shift from Zeniff's practices. Clearly, Noah had to deprive any men of respected standing (such as the former priests) of a position from which to voice religious misgivings about the new practices.

But where had these ideas come from, particularly the institution of polygyny (more than one wife)? Nephite culture had been decidedly monogamous from the days of Jacob (Jacob 3:5). Nevertheless, the Nephites in this region are now, for the second time, engaging in polygyny. Furthermore, in both cases the "whoredoms" included wives and concubines. Because multiple wives are more costly than one wife, the text links wealth and polygyny. Wealth provides the economic platform that allows polygyny.

Economics apart, however, this repetition of polygyny raises a question about the apparent ease with which Noah's society accepted the practice. The modern United States enjoys a level of affluence that would make polygyny economically feasible in many cases (certainly the contemporary practice of sometimes-frequent divorce and remarriage cannot be considered more cost-effective by comparison), but a very strong cultural bias forbids the practice. It remains limited as an underground, illegal practice with religious motivations that overcome the more common social prohibition. The Zeniffites should have had a similar cultural bias against polygyny. However, they lived in the same area where the Nephites of Jacob's time had also overcome their cultural prejudices and adopted polygyny. The most plausible explanation is that the other peoples of that land not only had multiple wives but that having multiple wives conferred economic benefits that Noah and his people deemed desirable. (See commentary accompanying Jacob 2:32–24 for the link between multiple wives and economic gain.)

Again the parallel to Jacob's time is instructive. Accumulating wealth in ancient societies typically depended on exchanging goods outside the community, thus providing access to items that were otherwise rare and valuable. While Noah's tax list includes foodstuffs, the rest of the taxables are workable metals. How would they increase his wealth if he exchanged them only within the community? Trading the metal back to those who had yielded it up in taxes would have been absurd; it would have no relative value to them. It seems an unavoidable conclusion that Noah's wealth came from trading with surrounding groups, presumably the Lamanites. Apparently he also traded in ideas, adopting polygyny and possibly other concepts as well.[4]

Mosiah 11:6–7

> 6 Yea, and thus they were supported in their laziness, and in their idolatry, and in their whoredoms, by the taxes which king Noah had put upon his people; thus did the people labor exceedingly to support iniquity.

---

[4]Jacob 2:35 indicates that the "Lamanites, our brethren" were monogamists while the Nephites were adopting polygyny. I argue in the commentary accompanying that verse that the particular phrase "Lamanites, our brethren" is intended to compare the Nephites to their lineal relatives and is not to be seen as a generic term in that case. The normal generic use is therefore modified with "our brethren" to distinguish them from the Lamanites who were not "our brethren."

7 Yea, and they also became idolatrous, because they were deceived by the vain and flattering words of the king and priests; for they did speak flattering things unto them.

Culture: These verses are a clear expression of Mormon's displeasure. It is his conclusion that the people labor to "support iniquity." Tellingly, it was not only Noah and his court that were "in . . . idolatry," but also the people. This issue is a critical one. Possibly Israel's most distinctive characteristic was its firm stance against idols in a world filled of religious idols. An idol, in the thought of ancient Israel, is not simply a cultural artifact or an alternative (false) religion, but an alteration in the fabric of religious thought. In a word, Noah has changed religions and caused his people to also adopt a different religion. Not only has Noah overthrown his father's political world, but also his religious world.

This factor explains the litany of transgressions Mormon records. These activities were not simply things the people decided to do, but rather a set of practices that came with the new religion/political order they had adopted.

Mosiah 11:8–9

8 And it came to pass that king Noah built many elegant and spacious buildings; and he ornamented them with fine work of wood, and of all manner of precious things, of gold, and of silver, and of iron, and of brass, and of ziff, and of copper;

9 And he also built him a spacious palace, and a throne in the midst thereof, all of which was of fine wood and was ornamented with gold and silver and with precious things.

As editor, Mormon chooses the details with which he communicates the message he wants his audience to have. In this case, his antipathy toward Noah colors how he presents this description of what could otherwise have been considered the golden age of a rising culture, marked by the erection of many richly ornamented buildings and climaxing with Noah's personal palace. However, in Mormon's eyes, the entire activity is deplorable, and Noah's palace is particularly selfish and greedy, a revelation of Noah as vain and imprudent.

Looked at more objectively, a 20 percent tax, on mostly luxury or trade items, would actually provide tax relief to many Americans. Second, most of the buildings financed by these taxes are public buildings, rather than private consumption. Third, Mormon obviously blames Noah for the people's idolatry "because they were deceived by the vain and flattering words of the king and priests" (Mosiah 11:7). Yet in this description, Mormon downplays the people's willing participation. They are not oppressed and enslaved by their selfish king; rather they have accepted the same cultural definitions as their king.[5] Those definitions defined their society; the

---

[5]Kent P. Jackson and Morgan W. Tanner, "Zeniff and Noah," in *1 Nephi to Alma 29*, edited by Kent P. Jackson, STUDIES IN SCRIPTURE (Salt Lake City: Deseret Book, 1987), Vol. 7, 232, agree that "there is no hint in the record that they saw themselves as oppressed."

public architecture would proclaim their support of that social model. It is probably not incidental that this model included general prosperity. It is probably impossible to determine if prosperity followed their adoption of a new culture and a new religion, or vice versa, but this new (idolatrous) religion certainly explains Mormon's unqualified disapproval of Noah and his reign.

Mosiah 11:10

> 10 And he also caused that his workmen should work all manner of fine work within the walls of the temple, of fine wood, and of copper, and of brass.

History: I hypothesize that this temple would follow the general pattern of Mesoamerican temples, particularly since the people would be consciously following the model of their newly adopted (idolatrous) religion. In this context, Mormon's statement that "his workmen should work all manner of fine work within the walls of the temple, of fine wood, and of copper, and of brass" merits particular scrutiny. Although modern readers might initially envision walls "of fine wood," this grammatical ambiguity can be clarified by seeing the prepositional phrase as exactly parallel to the references to copper and brass. "Fine wood," copper, and brass were ornamental, not structural materials, an interpretation corroborated by archaeological evidence that elaborate wooden carvings are part of the temple's ornamentation.[6]

Mosiah 11:11

> 11 And the seats which were set apart for the high priests, which were above all the other seats, he did ornament with pure gold; and he caused a breastwork to be built before them, that they might rest their bodies and their arms upon while they should speak lying and vain words to his people.

Culture: The typical Mesoamerican ruler's "seats" were low to the ground and would not even be described as chairs. The common native would squat or sit on the ground. A ruler would have a small raised seat or bench.[7] Elevated seats are obviously a mark of social stratification, which would be very common in the kind of society Noah was apparently building. Furthermore, Noah apparently raised not only the seat but the flooring, so that the priests occupied a space that was higher both physically and conceptually.

---

[6]Linda Schele and Peter Mathews, *The Code of Kings: The Language of Seven Sacred Maya Temples and Tombs* (New York: Scribner, 1998). The entire book is a description on the nature of the art and architecture of Classic Maya temples and other buildings. Earlier temples exhibited many of these traits. There are remains of a few elaborately carved lintels from a few temples, but unfortunately, wood is poorly preserved in the archaeological record, according to Susan Toby Evans, *Ancient Mexico and Central America: Archaeology and Culture History* (London: Thames & Hudson, 2004), 273.

[7]These ruler's benches are often depicted in pottery scenes and some have been found in the palaces of the kings. See an example in Schele and Mathews, *The Code of Kings*, 73.

Mosiah 11:12–13

> 12 And it came to pass that he built a tower near the temple; yea, a very high tower, even so high that he could stand upon the top thereof and overlook the land of Shilom, and also the land of Shemlon, which was possessed by the Lamanites; and he could even look over all the land round about.
> 13 And it came to pass that he caused many buildings to be built in the land Shilom; and he caused a great tower to be built on the hill north of the land Shilom, which had been a resort for the children of Nephi at the time they fled out of the land; and thus he did do with the riches which he obtained by the taxation of his people.

Geography: The construction of these tall towers are, again, public works with military importance. They occupy strategic locations, providing oversight of Lehi-Nephi and Shilom. They are certainly defense systems, one purpose of which is to provide a lookout.

The reference that the hill north of Shilom was "resort for the children of Nephi at the time they fled out of the land," refers to Mosiah$_1$'s departure. (See Omni 1:12ff). Sorenson suggests that the "resort" was probably a staging point, adding that "the Zeniffites likely inhabited only the local land of Nephi (and perhaps also Shilom), for the hill was convenient only to those two localities."[8]

Mosiah 11:14

> 14 And it came to pass that he placed his heart upon his riches, and he spent his time in riotous living with his wives and his concubines; and so did also his priests spend their time with harlots.

Despite Mormon's unsympathetic tone, Noah's actual record would have painted a much different picture, and his people would have regarded these activities in a much different light. Although Mormon accuses Noah of setting his heart upon riches, the people probably did the same and approved this manifestation of conspicuous consumption, from which they were also benefiting. The "wives, concubines, and harlots" is also subject to interpretation. Many ancient societies, including the Israelites, acknowledged both wives and concubines as having legal and social (not immoral) status.[9] "Harlots" definitely connotes sexual unions outside marriage or other illegal arrangements, but the Book of Mormon is unclear on terminology for sexual relations. In Jacob, taking multiple wives was equated with "whoredoms" even though they would have been legal unions. (See commentary accompanying Jacob 2:32–34.)

---

[8]John L. Sorenson, *The Geography of Book of Mormon Events: a Source Book* (Provo, Utah: FARMS, 1990), 239.

[9]Gene McAfee, "Sex" in *The Oxford Companion to the Bible*, edited by Bruce M. Metzger and Michael D. Coogan, (New York: Oxford University Press, 1993), 691. "Although concubines did not enjoy the same rights as a wife, they were socially and legally recognized in ancient Israel. A concubine's children did not share the rights of a wife's children, unless, like Hagar, sexual contact with the concubine was for the explicit purpose of producing heirs, in which case the children became the wife's children (Gen. 21:14, 25:5–6)."

In the old world, some priestesses performed such acts as part of religious service, particularly in fertility rites. Victor Ludlow describes some of these practices during Isaiah's times:

> Ancient idol worship was inseparably connected with ritual prostitution and fertility cults. Since ancient economies were founded upon agriculture, the people's dependence upon the fertility of the ground was absolute. As the pagan worship developed in ancient cultures, the belief developed that if a farmer had intercourse with a priestess at a local temple and she became pregnant, this was a sign that the fertility god would look favorably upon his crops.
>
> Also, ancient man believed that the lives and interactions of the gods were reflected in the life of man. That is, if man acted out certain activities on earth then this would facilitate their taking place in heaven. So, if people involved themselves in fertility acts in their pagan temples, then their gods would bless the land with productivity. Thus, the pagan temples usually became centers of ritual or religious prostitution.[10]

Nibley has read Alma 30:18 and 39:5 as possible references to a similar practice in the New World.[11] That practice is not known for Mesoamerican cultures, perhaps because it did not exist and perhaps because it simply was not recorded.

Certainly, this does not mean that Mormon's disapproval is incorrect. It simply suggests that the translation of the Book of Mormon may obscure culturally significant categories.

Mosiah 11:15

> 15 And it came to pass that he planted vineyards round about in the land; and he built wine-presses, and made wine in abundance; and therefore he became a wine-bibber, and also his people.

History: Alcoholic drinks in Mesoamerica have a long history,[12] but the introduction of grapes for wine is only securely known for the post-conquest period.[13] This verse probably labels as "wine" a different fermented beverage. Sorenson notes:

> Wine was apparently not made from grapes in the New World. (Certain grapes were present, but we do not know that they were used for food or drink.) However, the Book of Mormon nowhere says that "grapes" were present, only "vineyards." The Spaniards spoke of "vineyards" referring to plantings of the maguey (agave) plant from which pulque is made.

---

[10]Victor L. Ludlow, *Isaiah: Prophet, Seer and Poet* (Salt Lake City: Deseret Book, 1982), 477.

[11]Hugh Nibley, *The Prophetic Book of Mormon*, Vol. 8 of THE COLLECTED WORKS OF HUGH NIBLEY (Salt Lake City: Deseret Book/Provo, Utah: Foundation for Ancient Research and Mormon Studies, 1989), 542.

[12]Lynne V. Foster, *Handbook to Life in the Ancient Maya World* (2002; rpt. in paperback, New York: Oxford University Press, 2005), 335, documents *chicha*, a drink the Maya made from fermented maize gruel. Warwick Bray, *Everyday Life of the Aztecs* (New York: Peter Bedrick Books, 1991), 41, documents *octli* for the Aztecs, made from the fermented juice of the maguey.

[13]While the use of grapes for wine is not attested prior to the conquest, evidence of wild grapes has been discovered for the Classic period (A.D. 250–800). David L. Lentz, "Plant Resources of the Ancient Maya: The Paleoethnobotanical Evidence," in *Reconstructing Ancient Maya Diet*, edited by Christine D. White (Salt Lake City: University of Utah Press, 1999), 9.

> And various sorts of "wine" were described by the early Europeans in Mesoamerica: one from bananas in eighteenth-century Guatemala, another from pineapples in the West Indies, palm wine from the coyol palm trunk (manufactured from Veracruz to Costa Rica), and the balche of the Mayan area, made from a fermented tree bark. Clearly Noah the "wine"-bibber in the book of Mosiah could have been drinking something intoxicating besides the squeezings of the grape.[14]

Scripture: The printing of the Book of Mormon precedes Section 89 of the Doctrine and Covenants by three years. When the Book of Mormon was translated, the Lord had not given instructions to avoid alcohol, and so this verse should not be read as a deliberate violation by Noah and his court of the Word of Wisdom, even though the Lord (and Mormon) clearly disdain alcoholic excess. The Bible exhibits this same general conception of the relationship of alcohol and spirituality by prohibiting alcohol in situations of particular religious purity while it was clearly acceptable at other times.[15]

Mosiah 11:16–17

> 16 And it came to pass that the Lamanites began to come in upon his people, upon small numbers, and to slay them in their fields, and while they were tending their flocks.
> 17 And king Noah sent guards round about the land to keep them off; but he did not send a sufficient number, and the Lamanites came upon them and killed them, and drove many of their flocks out of the land; thus the Lamanites began to destroy them, and to exercise their hatred upon them.

Culture: Tensions between the Lamanites and the Noahites begin, as they had with the Zeniffites, with raiding parties, not all-out military attack. This point is significant because it allows some inferences about the political climate. First, the small-scale attacks against scattered groups in the fields show that this is not an organized assault against a political entity, but an attack against goods and secondarily against their possessors. A successful Lamanite raid yielded crops and flocks but probably not riches, since nobody would keep them in a field. These raids had no direct effect on the political balance. No king was attacked. No city was threatened. The motivation was small, not large.

Noah does not consider them to be threats against himself and his rule, but sees them for what they are—robbing bands. He reacts appropriately (sending out guards) but not effectively, because their numbers are too few to provide effective protection. Nevertheless, Mormon, possibly influenced by his personal involvement in Lamanite wars, seems to see the raids as more important than Noah did, based on his somber description of slaughter and "hatred."

---

[14]Sorenson, *An Ancient American Setting for the Book of Mormon*, 186.

[15]Michael D. Coogan, "Wine," in *The Oxford Companion to the Bible*, edited by Bruce M. Metzger and Michael D. Coogan (New York: Oxford University Press, 1993), 799: "In biblical times, the production and consumption of wine were familiar aspects of everyday life, to which the Bible refers repeatedly and, for the most part, positively."

Mosiah 11:18

> 18 And it came to pass that king Noah sent his armies against them, and they were driven back, or they drove them back for a time; therefore, they returned rejoicing in their spoil.

Apparently motivated after some time or after a "last straw" provocation to take decisive action, Noah sends "armies," which return victorious, "rejoicing in their spoil." In other words, after "guards" have proved ineffective, Noah sends not just a single "army," but "armies." Nor apparently do these armies target the raiders per se, especially if they were marginalized from the main Lamanite society. I hypothesize that Noah's armies, like Zeniff's, attacked Lamanite settlements. The fact that they return with "spoil" rather than the stolen flocks and crops suggests reprisal, rather than recovery. As such, this counterattack fits the model of Mesoamerican warfare, with its economic benefit of despoiling a conquered people. Noah avenges attacks on his farmers and herders with attacks on unspecified targets (but probably villages).

From the Lamanite perspective, such an attack is a decisively negative step in Lamanite-Noahite relationships. If the Lamanite raiders had been marauders acting outside Lamanite authority, then Noah's reprisal against what, in Lamanite terms, would be innocent civilians would justify a punitive Lamanite response. While there is no direct evidence to support such a scenario, the alternative view is that the Lamanites perpetually engaged in warfare against the Nephites because they were evil and hate-filled. That explanation seems too simplistic.

Mosiah 11:19

> 19 And now, because of this great victory they were lifted up in the pride of their hearts; they did boast in their own strength, saying that their fifty could stand against thousands of the Lamanites; and thus they did boast, and did delight in blood, and the shedding of the blood of their brethren, and this because of the wickedness of their king and priests.

Redaction: Mormon is giving his evaluation (not the Noahites') of this military aftermath. He is painting a picture of a people in apostasy, whom Abinadi will call to repentance. Thus, Mormon sees in these events the reason why Yahweh called Abinadi, who is unquestionably the main focus, with Alma, of this narrative. At this point, Mormon is explaining the wickedness of Noah and his people. Their sins include the "pride of their hearts." They have achieved a victory, but ascribe it to their own strength and forget Yahweh. Even worse, they "did delight in blood, and the shedding of the blood of their brethren."

Without Mormon's source text, this reconstruction is conjectural, of course. However, if Mormon knew that these Nephite armies were attacking numerically inferior hamlets, he may have well understood the hollowness of the "victory." Not only did it fail to target the actual marauders, but it was simply a blood payment for "crimes" against the Noahites. Thus, Mormon would have been justified in seeing their main motivation as "delight in blood" rather than self-defense.

Culture: On a social level, this passage gives us even more information. Mormon notes that the claim of the people is that: "their fifty could stand against thousands of the Lamanites." Even making allowances for the bellicose hubris, it seems apparent that the Noahites are a significantly smaller population than the Lamanites.

Furthermore, the Noahites saw their military victory as a contest against the political body of the Lamanites, not just against marauding bands. The focus of the conflict is now changing. The Lamanite raiders had picked off isolated and easy targets in the field, but the Noahites are proclaiming a "victory" against the whole Lamanite kingdom. This shift from individuals to a generalized target provides further support for the scenario of a Noahite attack against settlements under Lamanite political control. It also explains the escalation of the conflict into the major offensive that later drives Noah and his court into the wilderness.

Mosiah 11:20

> 20 And it came to pass that there was a man among them whose name was Abinadi; and he went forth among them, and began to prophesy, saying: Behold, thus saith the Lord, and thus hath he commanded me, saying, Go forth, and say unto this people, thus saith the Lord—Wo be unto this people, for I have seen their abominations, and their wickedness, and their whoredoms; and except they repent I will visit them in mine anger.

At this point, Mormon has set the scene and now begins the real story: Abinadi's two-part mission and martyrdom. The Book of Mormon supplies virtually no information about Abinadi's pre-mission life, but John Tvedtnes proposes an interesting hypothesis:

> When Noah replaced his father Zeniff as king of the Nephites living in the land of Nephi, "he put down all the priests that had been consecrated by his father, and consecrated new ones in their stead, such as were lifted up in the pride of their hearts" (Mosiah 11:5). . . .
>
> We know that Abinadi "spake with power and authority from God" (Mosiah 13:6). Amid the political and religious corruption in the land of Nephi, how did he receive this divine authority? It is possible that he was one of the deposed priests who had served under the righteous king Zeniff, but, alas, the record is silent on this matter.[16]

Rodney Turner, professor of religion at Brigham Young University, suggests that Abinadi's mission has parallels to that of John the Baptist in the New Testament: "Abinadi is the John the Baptist of the Book of Mormon. Like John, he was a lone prophet who briefly ministered to a people committed to the law of Moses who knew little of the Messiah to come and nothing of his actual divinity. Like John, Abinadi preached repentance, warned of the impending judgments of God, and testified of the Messiah to come. Both prophets were opposed by the religious leaders of their day; both were victims of priestcraft—the ultimate

---

[16]Tvedtnes, *The Most Correct Book*, 323–4.

hypocrisy. Both denounced the immoral conduct of their respective kings and died violent deaths at their hands."[17]

Culture: Abinadi is clearly a member of the Noahite society, "a man among them." He may have come from Zarahemla with Zeniff. We probably all have a clear image of him as elderly, thanks to the popular Arnold Friberg painting, but the text itself provides no indication of his age. He certainly is not one of those who has abandoned Yahweh and adopted the new idolatry. He preaches against "abominations, wickedness, and whoredoms," all of which resulted from the conjectured adoption of the indigenous culture/religion. Abinadi comes to call them back to the worship of the true God.

Mosiah 11:21–23

> 21 And except they repent and turn to the Lord their God, behold, I will deliver them into the hands of their enemies; yea, and they shall be brought into bondage; and they shall be afflicted by the hand of their enemies.
> 22 And it shall come to pass that they shall know that I am the Lord their God, and am a jealous God, visiting the iniquities of my people.
> 23 And it shall come to pass that except this people repent and turn unto the Lord their God, they shall be brought into bondage; and none shall deliver them, except it be the Lord the Almighty God.

Literature: It is tempting to see these verses as a type of chiasm, but the verses have a subtle change of reference suggesting that the third verse builds upon the first rather than simply reflecting it. In verse 21 the message is: Repent and turn to Yahweh, or the people will be brought into bondage by their enemies.

This is the first part of the prophecy. It begins with a people who are not in bondage and offers them freedom from the threat of bondage if they will repent.

Verse 22 appears to indicate Yahweh's foreknowledge that they would not repent and, hence, will suffer bondage and afflictions. In the model familiar from the Old Testament, Yahweh plays an active role in afflicting and chastening his unrepentant people. This claim should be seen as a rhetorical device, however, because the situation is obviously one, rather, of Yahweh's nonintervention while the natural consequence of the people's sinful behavior plays itself out.

In verse 23 Abinadi again mentions repentance; but rather than replicating the message of verse 21, this verse expresses different timing: You will be brought into bondage; only Yahweh will relieve you from that bondage.

While the language is parallel to that in verse 21, the theme is progressive through time, with the final pronouncement indicating Yahweh's foreknowledge of their bondage and affliction. Despite the people's willful rebellion and the chastisement of this pessimistic prophecy, Yahweh still holds hope before the people of Noah. When they repent, Yahweh will deliver them. We have already seen the fulfillment of this prophecy in the account of the public penance,

---

[17]Rodney Turner, "Two Prophets: Abinadi and Alma," in *1 Nephi to Alma 29*, edited by Kent P. Jackson, STUDIES IN SCRIPTURE (Salt Lake City: Deseret Book, 1987), Vol. 7, 240.

repentance, and preparation for salvation that Limhi's people engaged in after Ammon's arrival (Mosiah 7:18–33).

Mosiah 11:24–25

> 24 Yea, and it shall come to pass that when they shall cry unto me I will be slow to hear their cries; yea, and I will suffer them that they be smitten by their enemies.
> 25 And except they repent in sackcloth and ashes, and cry mightily to the Lord their God, I will not hear their prayers, neither will I deliver them out of their afflictions; and thus saith the Lord, and thus hath he commanded me.

Why would a kind and loving God be slow to hear the cries of his children? Why does he not respond immediately? This prophecy captures the fact that the Lord works on multiple levels. This particular promise of being "slow to hear their cries" comes only after the second failure of the Noahites to repent. In the first place, they had not repented with sufficient sincerity to avert their bondage; their second failure came because they lamented the bondage itself, not their sin. Thus, they had not yet truly turned to Yahweh.

The social transformation of the faithful people of Zeniff into the idolatrous people of Noah is a great change, and the seduction of the wealth and prestige, bolstered by real or imagined "victories," would have created powerful reasons not to repent. This "repentance" was not simply a regret for their individual sins but the renunciation of a highly profitable culture/religion as a people, and their individual and collective rededication to Yahweh. Like Israel under Moses, it took time to cast the seductive images of Egyptian leeks and seething pots out of the hearts of this smaller Israel laboring under a different kind of bondage.

Mosiah 11:26

> 26 Now it came to pass that when Abinadi had spoken these words unto them they were wroth with him, and sought to take away his life; but the Lord delivered him out of their hands.

As readers, we may well regret that Mormon pressed on with his story instead of giving us the details of Abinadi's deliverance. It takes little imagination to understand why those who had embraced the new culture/religion would want to remove Abinadi. After all, he was denouncing their very lifestyle and all that they believed that they had achieved. The people themselves—not court officials—rejected Abinadi. Verse 26 suggests that the people to whom Abinadi was preaching sought his life, but Noah had not apparently heard of Abinadi at this point, as verse 27 clarifies. Although it is convenient to blame Noah for the people's apostasy, they brought their own bondage upon themselves.

Mosiah 11:27–28

> 27 Now when king Noah had heard of the words which Abinadi had spoken unto the people, he was also wroth; and he said: Who is Abinadi, that I and

> my people should be judged of him, or who is the Lord, that shall bring upon my people such great affliction?
> 28 I command you to bring Abinadi hither, that I may slay him, for he has said these things that he might stir up my people to anger one with another, and to raise contentions among my people; therefore I will slay him.

Noah is echoing, not initiating, the people's reaction to Abinadi; but he specifically commands Abinadi's capture so that he can be executed on a charge of sedition: Abinadi "raise[s] contentions among my people." Despite the people's rejection of Abinadi and his message, obviously some believed or there would be no contention. In spite of Noah's decree, however, Abinadi lives safely in hiding for two years before he commences the second half of his mission (Mosiah 12:1).

Mosiah 11:29

> 29 Now the eyes of the people were blinded; therefore they hardened their hearts against the words of Abinadi, and they sought from that time forward to take him. And king Noah hardened his heart against the word of the Lord, and he did not repent of his evil doings.

Text: There is no chapter break at this point in the 1830 edition. This verse provides an essential preface to the next chapter of the editions from 1879 to 1981 of the Book of Mormon and is discussed with Mosiah 12:1.

Mosiah 12

Mosiah 11:29–Mosiah 12:1

> 29 Now the eyes of the people were blinded; therefore they hardened their hearts against the words of Abinadi, and they sought from that time forward to take him. And king Noah hardened his heart against the word of the Lord, and he did not repent of his evil doings.
>
> 1 And it came to pass that after the space of two years that Abinadi came among them in disguise, that they knew him not, and began to prophesy among them, saying: Thus has the Lord commanded me, saying—Abinadi, go and prophesy unto this my people, for they have hardened their hearts against my words; they have repented not of their evil doings; therefore, I will visit them in my anger, yea, in my fierce anger will I visit them in their iniquities and abominations.

Mormon summarizes the social climate for Abinadi's second mission: the people, not just the king, opposed Abinadi and sought his life. They do not repent. Consequently, the judgments of God will surely come upon them.

Abinadi returns in disguise, so why then does he openly announce his name? As Mosiah 11:29 explains, Abinadi would have been attacked on sight. The disguise was necessary to allow him to penetrate the community and to make his announcement in the most public possible manner. Whether Abinadi understood that martyrdom awaited him, Yahweh's purposes required that Abinadi testify before Noah's court. As a result, he had to publicly preach and identify himself, triggering a formal arrest rather than merely mob murder. His trial before Noah was the true purpose of his mission. The disguise was necessary to achieve that direct confrontation.

Text: Mormon did not create a chapter break at this point. I have repeated Mosiah 11:29 in order to provide some of the context that was lost in the chapter divisions, beginning in 1879. Mormon is taking this part of his account from some source that is more sympathetic to Abinadi than King Noah's official court records would have been. (See commentary accompanying Mosiah 17:3–4.)

Mosiah 12:2

> 2 Yea, wo be unto this generation! And the Lord said unto me: Stretch forth thy hand and prophesy, saying: Thus saith the Lord, it shall come to pass that this generation, because of their iniquities, shall be brought into bondage, and shall be smitten on the cheek; yea, and shall be driven by men, and shall be

> slain; and the vultures of the air, and the dogs, yea, and the wild beasts, shall devour their flesh.

During Abinadi's first mission Yahweh had him call the people to repentance. This mission is different. Abinadi does not deliver a prophetic *if* but rather a prophetic *will*. Abinadi now foretells their bondage and suffering. The people have made their decision, and Yahweh has made his. Abinadi simply describes the imminent future of the unrepentant population. These fearsome calamities will all too soon become the reality of their lives.

Text: Mormon appears to be quoting Abinadi's speech. However, internal evidence shows that there was no single record of this speech (vv. 10–12), which is logical, since he delivered this discourse to an audience that was not expecting him. It would have been highly improbable for a trained scribe to be on the spot with writing materials at that exact moment. Hence, Mormon is using Noah's official record, which must be based on the memories of those in the crowd. The inevitable discrepancies between witnesses explain the slightly different versions of what he said.

Mosiah 12:3

> 3 And it shall come to pass that the life of king Noah shall be valued even as a garment in a hot furnace; for he shall know that I am the Lord.

Abinadi bleakly and literally foretells the fate of the king.

Literature: Perhaps both the form and the metaphor of this curse derive from Old World sources. Although specific Nephite remembrance of Old World customs were certainly limited, the retention of certain literary structures, passed intact through the generations, is not beyond possibility, just as ritual practices from the law of Moses could also be retained. In this context, John Tvedtnes summarized Mark Morrise's research and commented:

> In Mosiah 12:3, Abinadi prophesied "that the life of king Noah shall be valued even as a garment in a hot furnace." Noah's priests reported the words a little differently, "thy life shall be as a garment in a furnace of fire" (Mosiah 12:10). The prophecy was fulfilled when King Noah was burned to death (see Mosiah 19:20).
>
> Mark J. Morrise has shown that Abinadi's words fit the pattern of a simile curse, in which the subject of the curse is likened to a specific event; Morrise provides many examples, such as the following from an Aramaic treaty of approximately 750 B.C.:
>
> ["] Just as this . . . is burned by fire, so shall Arpad be burned. ["]
>
> Hugh Nibley suggested that Abinadi borrowed from the simile curse in Isaiah 50:9, 11 (cited in 2 Ne. 7:9, 11): "Who is he that shall condemn me? lo, they all shall wax old as a garment, and the moth shall eat them up. . . . Behold, all ye that kindle a fire, that compass yourselves about with sparks: walk in the light of your fire, and in the sparks that ye have kindled."
>
> But the Isaiah parallel is only a partial one, for verse 11 (which mentions fire) has nothing to do with the garment which is consumed by the moth, not the fire. If there are parallels to be found, one might expect them to include both the garment and the fire and possibly the furnace. Yet no such complete parallels are forthcoming from the Old

Testament or other ancient Near Eastern literature. Nevertheless, there are some partial parallels.

The Law of Moses provides that a garment visibly tainted by the plague is to be burned (see Leviticus 13:52, 57; compare Jude 1:23). While the Lord knew about germs, the ancient Israelites did not. Therefore, the burning of garments to prevent the spread of disease would not have been reasonable before the nineteenth century, when people learned that microorganisms caused diseases. But the burning of a man's possessions after his death is very common in "primitive" cultures throughout the world. Typically, all his personal possessions would be brought into his house (usually a rather insubstantial structure in such societies), which would then be set on fire. In this way, the deceased would not be able to find his possessions and would be free to move on to the world of spirits. In such cases, we have the garment and the fire, but not the furnace.

A ceremonial burning of worn-out priestly clothing took place in the Jerusalem temple of Christ's time during the Feast of Tabernacles. Located above the court of the women were huge cups in which olive oil was burned; these garments served as wicks. Just as priests who developed bodily infirmities were disqualified from performing priestly functions under the Law of Moses (see Lev. 21:17–23), so, too, their worn clothing became unsuited for temple service.[1]

Mosiah 12:4–5

4 And it shall come to pass that I will smite this my people with sore afflictions, yea, with famine and with pestilence; and I will cause that they shall howl all the day long.

5 Yea, and I will cause that they shall have burdens lashed upon their backs; and they shall be driven before like a dumb ass.

These calamities do not occur simultaneously. Some come during their military subjugation, others in the aftermath. But all come to pass. Ammon arrives during the stage when they are burdened and driven, a scene we have already read, but which lies in the future from Abinadi's pronouncement.

Translation: Abinadi uses the phrase "they shall be driven before like a dumb ass"—or in other words, be treated as beasts of burden, which is the state in which Ammon finds the Limhites. However, there were no asses in the Western Hemisphere prior to European contact and no known beasts of burden in Mesoamerica. Thus both the specific animal and the concept of a draft animal would be foreign to Abinadi. Obviously, this case is another of Joseph Smith's translating the meaning, rather than the specific words. The modern reader clearly understands this image but would probably be puzzled by a more culture-specific phrase, such as "tributaries with a tumpline." (A tumpline around the forehead to help support and balance a heavy burden on the back is the standard mode of transport in Mesoamerica.) Hence, this translation of the concept is consistent with the less-than-literal translation mode that I argue for in this commentary.

---

[1]John A. Tvedtnes, "As a Garment in a Hot Furnace," in *Pressing Forward with the Book of Mormon*, edited by John W. Welch and Melvin J. Thorne (Provo, Utah: FARMS, 1999), 127–28.

Mosiah 12:6–7

6 And it shall come to pass that I will send forth hail among them, and it shall smite them; and they shall also be smitten with the east wind; and insects shall pester their land also, and devour their grain.
7 And they shall be smitten with a great pestilence—and all this will I do because of their iniquities and abominations.

Sorenson comments that this prophecy, the fulfillment of which is not recorded in the Book of Mormon,

> turns out to be a valid one on the Guatemalan scene where it seems to have been uttered. The conditions foretold are phrased in such a way as to indicate they were within the realm of nature's recognized potential, yet they were so rare that the listeners normally did not contemplate such a combination of calamities as a serious possibility. Highland Guatemala does occasionally suffer just those prophesied conditions under unusual circumstances. Abinadi's point was that God would cause these rare phenomena to come about jointly as unusual punishment for the Zeniffites' gross wickedness.
>
> Geographer F. W. McBryde explains that certain meteorological situations produce an extremely drying north or northeast wind. (Recall that the "east" among pre-Columbian peoples in highland Guatemala coincided with what on our present maps is north or northeast.) These freak "norte" winds hold back the moist air from the Pacific side that normally flows into the highland valleys daily. As a result, the normal pattern of life-giving showers is upset. Fire danger heightens under these unusual conditions, with drying gusts reaching as high as 35 miles an hour. Great hailstorms occasionally (March through May) accompany these winds, as the strong surge of dry air converges along the coast with moist Pacific air, forming huge hail-generating thunderheads that drift inland above the north ("east") wind. Thus, a period of "east wind" could cause disastrous weather problems in Guatemala/Nephi, in just the terms the prophet said.
>
> He also warned that insects would come to attack the crops. Migratory locusts periodically caused great destruction to corn fields in the Yucatan Peninsula and highland Guatemala. The dry interior Motagua River valley, only 15 miles "east" from our Nephi, had a climate that particularly favored the pests. The dry "norte" winds could drive the swarms those few miles onto the Zeniffites' fields. The *Annals of the Cakchiquels*, one of the traditional histories from the highlands, mentions two locust infestations shortly before the Spanish conquest, and there must have been many more. Food shortages that result from destructive weather and locust infestations are known historically to have brought malnutrition and pestilence in their wake. As Abinadi foretold, the pattern of wind, hail, insects, and famine, which on the surface seems rather arbitrary, turns out to be logically, integrally linked when we have our geography correct. They could happen, and would be devastating, if the Lord chose to trigger them.[2]

Mosiah 12:8

8 And it shall come to pass that except they repent I will utterly destroy them from off the face of the earth; yet they shall leave a record behind them, and I will preserve them for other nations which shall possess the land; yea, even this will I do that I may discover the abominations of this people to other nations. And many things did Abinadi prophesy against this people.

---

[2]John L. Sorenson, *An Ancient American Setting for the Book of Mormon* (Salt Lake City: Deseret Book/Provo, Utah: Foundation for Ancient Research and Mormon Studies, 1985), 183.

While general destruction is a typical prophecy of doom, this particular prophecy includes the unusual idea that a record will be made of their annihilation. In other words, Abinadi warns the people that they are not only are headed for destruction but will be used as an object lesson for future peoples. No wonder they were outraged (v. 9).

Mosiah 12:9

> 9 And it came to pass that they were angry with him; and they took him and carried him bound before the king, and said unto the king: Behold, we have brought a man before thee who has prophesied evil concerning thy people, and saith that God will destroy them.

Although the people are angry, they do not kill Abinadi. They take him before the king, which is the desired outcome of his mission.

Mosiah 12:10–12

> 10 And he also prophesieth evil concerning thy life, and saith that thy life shall be as a garment in a furnace of fire.
> 11 And again, he saith that thou shalt be as a stalk, even as a dry stalk of the field, which is run over by the beasts and trodden under foot.
> 12 And again, he saith thou shalt be as the blossoms of a thistle, which, when it is fully ripe, if the wind bloweth, it is driven forth upon the face of the land. And he pretendeth the Lord hath spoken it. And he saith all this shall come upon thee except thou repent, and this because of thine iniquities.

Text: Although verse 3 reports that Abinadi compared Noah's life to a garment in a hot furnace, these reports include two additional images of fragility and impermanence. Whether the original text split up the details as they appear in these two reports or whether Mormon simply emphasized the garment in the furnace because he knew that death by fire would, in fact, be Noah's fate, we cannot tell. I tend to see Mormon as underscoring the image of the garment to stress how exactly Abinadi's prophecy was fulfilled.

Mosiah 12:13–15

> 13 And now, O king, what great evil hast thou done, or what great sins have thy people committed, that we should be condemned of God or judged of this man?
> 14 And now, O king, behold, we are guiltless, and thou, O king, hast not sinned; therefore, this man has lied concerning you, and he has prophesied in vain.
> 15 And behold, we are strong, we shall not come into bondage, or be taken captive by our enemies; yea, and thou hast prospered in the land, and thou shalt also prosper.

Text: Possibly Mormon is simply quoting a speech of accusation, exactly as it appeared in Noah's court records, or possibly a formal bill of charges was drawn up, which Mormon recasts as a speech. It is not unusual in ancient literature for an author to create the words that would have been said to give a dramatic context. Richard Neitzel Holzapfel, professor of Church history and doctrine at Brigham Young University, describes this process:

> One may be puzzled by Josephus's access to speeches and private conversations, such as discussions between Herod and Octavian and remarks made by Herod and his wives in their bedroom. Certainly Josephus followed the practice introduced by the ancient Greek historian Thucydides. Thucydides stated that since it was impossible to always give a verbatim report of speeches, he put into the speaker's mouth the thoughts "given in the language in which, as it seemed to me, the several speakers would express, on the subjects under consideration, the sentiments most befitting the occasion, though at the same time I have adhered as closely as possible to the general sense of what was actually said.[3]

Since the speech is attributed to the people, who certainly would not have recited this speech in unison, it seems likely that Mormon has used the source material to reconstruct a dramatic setting and the related speech.

The accusations focus on Abinadi's condemnation of the king and the destruction of his political order. From their perspective, Abinadi has committed sedition.

Mosiah 12:16

> 16 Behold, here is the man, we deliver him into thy hands; thou mayest do with him as seemeth thee good.

This scene shows an orderly society responding to disorder in an orderly way. While Mormon's portrait of Noah's people is highly unsympathetic, his censoriousness stems from his religious perspective. From their own perspective, they are not a disorderly and impulsive mob; they recognize proper authority and make formal complaints with which the law can deal. Despite Abinadi's threats against the king and the society, he will not be executed without a trial.

Mosiah 12:17–19

> 17 And it came to pass that king Noah caused that Abinadi should be cast into prison; and he commanded that the priests should gather themselves together that he might hold a council with them what he should do with him.
> 18 And it came to pass that they said unto the king: Bring him hither that we may question him; and the king commanded that he should be brought before them.
> 19 And they began to question him, that they might cross him, that thereby they might have wherewith to accuse him; but he answered them boldly, and withstood all their questions, yea, to their astonishment; for he did withstand them in all their questions, and did confound them in all their words.

This part of the record continues to provide evidence of order, if not formal law. Rather than a summary execution, Abinadi is granted a hearing. But why? I

---

[3]Richard Neitzel Holzapfel, "King Herod," in *Masada and the World of the New Testament*, edited by John F. Hall and John W. Welch (Provo, Utah: BYU Studies, 1997), 4.

hypothesize that, even though the people themselves turned him over to the king, showing a certain lack of popular support, Abinadi likely had some sympathizers among the people, even if they were a minority. The conflict between religious systems (meaning politico-religious systems) means that Abinadi's claims to speak for Yahweh in denouncing the political rulers are appropriately heard by the court priests.

Abinadi is posing a religious challenge. The priests must "cross him" or show the incorrectness of Abinadi's ideas, thus discrediting him with his sympathizers. This victory will consolidate the rule of the new order over all of the people. Discrediting him will be a public relations victory that could not be achieved by simply killing him in a private dungeon.

This tactic backfires, however, as Abinadi "did withstand them in all their questions, and did confound them in all their words." Granted, this praise of Abinadi's skill may reflect primarily Mormon's sympathy, since the priests consider him to have condemned himself and declare themselves the victors of the debate.

Mosiah 12:20–24

> 20 And it came to pass that one of them said unto him: What meaneth the words which are written, and which have been taught by our fathers, saying:
> 21 How beautiful upon the mountains are the feet of him that bringeth good tidings; that publisheth peace; that bringeth good tidings of good; that publisheth salvation; that saith unto Zion, Thy God reigneth;
> 22 Thy watchmen shall lift up the voice; with the voice together shall they sing; for they shall see eye to eye when the Lord shall bring again Zion;
> 23 Break forth into joy; sing together ye waste places of Jerusalem; for the Lord hath comforted his people, he hath redeemed Jerusalem;
> 24 The Lord hath made bare his holy arm in the eyes of all the nations, and all the ends of the earth shall see the salvation of our God?

Text: Verse 19 states that Abinadi withstands the priests' questions, while verse 20 begins with "and it came to pass." It seems likely that we do not have a full record of the debate, simply Mormon's choice of one sample. It is, perhaps, the concluding response of the questioning.

The priests' quotation of Isaiah 52:7–10 is identical to the King James Version of those verses. The quotation reveals that the Zeniffite expedition brought a copy of all or parts of the brass plates.[4] Even though the record does not say whether the priests read from a written record or quoted this passage from memory, a copy still had to be available, since (even assuming that part of priestly duties was memorizing the scriptures) Noah had removed the former priests and his new priests had to have a way of learning the texts.

Why did the priests ask Abinadi this particular question? Because they were trying to "cross" Abinadi, we can eliminate the possibility that they sincerely

---

[4]The brass plates themselves stayed in Zarahemla, since Benjamin passed them on to Mosiah (Mosiah 1:16).

wanted to understand the answer. The text must contain a conflict that the priests planned to use against the prophet. But what could this conflict have been?

Context 1: Although any reconstruction must be conjectural, I hypothesize that the contrast is between Noah's people as a victorious Jerusalem versus Abinadi's depiction of inevitable calamities. The watchmen are shouting for joy, while Lord "hath comforted his people, he hath redeemed Jerusalem." Noah's kingdom has won a decisive victory over the Lamanites and is enjoying prosperity and peace. Have the priests used this text as evidence that Yahweh is protecting the people? If so, then Abinadi is denying and rejecting scripture. John W. Welch argues for a similar interpretation: "It appears that the priests intended . . . to catch him in conflict with that scripture and thereby convict him of false prophecy—a capital offence under the Law of Moses (Deut. 18:20). In essence, they were apparently asking Abinadi why he bore tidings of doom and destruction when Isaiah had declared that the beautiful and true prophet brings good tidings and publishes peace."[5]

Context 2: This context, also hypothetical, assumes that both the priests and Abinadi knew the context of the verses in addition to the verses themselves. Indeed, Abinadi's response strongly suggests that he understood the larger context, because he quotes Isaiah 53, which continues the message of chapter 52. Abinadi may be taking advantage of the fact that verse 21 stresses the role of the servant in publishing tidings of peace. Does Abinadi see his role in that context? If so, then this contest may be replicating aspects of the conflict between Sherem and Jacob (Jacob 7). Abinadi's response clearly proclaims the Messiah. If Noah's priests understand the Mosaic law in the manner that Sherem did, then they would preach the law of Moses (as they do in verse 28) but deny the role of the Messiah. As Nephites, however, they would surely know of its Messianic emphasis, expect Abinadi to interpret this text messianically, and condemn Abinadi for his "false" interpretation. (See "Excursus: Religion of the Nehors," following Alma 1.)

It is interesting that the Zeniffites' return to the land of Nephi not only seems to prompt a revival of polygamy but perhaps also a revival of Sherem's religious philosophy. Perhaps the local Lamanites had adopted a particular form of religious synthesis with these characteristics.

Mosiah 12:25

> 25 And now Abinadi said unto them: Are you priests, and pretend to teach this people, and to understand the spirit of prophesying, and yet desire to know of me what these things mean?

Rhetoric: Rather than taking the priests' bait, Abinadi takes the question as a request for information they should have known. By coloring their question as a request for information they did not possess, Abinadi can respond by teaching them the true gospel.

---

[5]John W. Welch, "Isaiah 53, Mosiah 14, and the Book of Mormon," in *Isaiah in the Book of Mormon*, edited by Donald W. Parry and John W. Welch (Provo, Utah: FARMS, 1998), 294.

Mosiah 12:26

> 26 I say unto you, wo be unto you for perverting the ways of the Lord! For if ye understand these things ye have not taught them; therefore, ye have perverted the ways of the Lord.

This verse pushes Abinadi's accusation a step further: They are perverting the true religion. By their own admission, they do not understand the scripture and therefore have taught falsehood. These priests' teachings were close enough to the inherited gospel that the people would accept the changes, but sufficiently diminished by interpretation and acceptance of outside influences that they no longer reflect truth.

Mosiah 12:27–28

> 27 Ye have not applied your hearts to understanding; therefore, ye have not been wise. Therefore, what teach ye this people?
> 28 And they said: We teach the law of Moses.

The priests, by asking a question of scriptural interpretation, have allowed Abinadi to shift the grounds of the attack from his sedition to their competency. When Abinadi asks what they teach, they answer that they teach the law of Moses. Why do they say this? I propose that Noah's religion has apostatized from Zeniff's because he has adopted foreign aspects, resulting in "whoredoms" and "idolatry." Yet it seems unlikely that the altered religion is a completely new one. Even under the duress of outright conquest, conquered peoples still attempt to retain some of their previous culture and religion. Doubtless the apostate elements included a foundation of the Mosaic law, with interpretations of that law to justify it. It seems logical that Noah's courts justified their polygamy by appealing to Solomon's and David's practices, since this is also what occurred during Jacob's time. Thus, the priests' quick answer that they teach the law of Moses positions themselves as defenders of that law of Moses, while, in contrast, Abinadi would be guilty of opposing it. (See "Excursus: Religion of the Nehors," following Alma 1.)

Variant: The 1830 text for verse 27 reads "... therefore what *teachest thou* this people." This has been changed to "therefore what *teach ye* this people?"[6] The shift from "thou" (singular) to "ye" (plural) recognizes that Abinadi is addressing a group, but the meaning does not change. In fact, modern usage reflects the underlying text better than the 1830 edition. Joseph Smith could easily make the error since Jacobean English was not native to him, despite his undoubted familiarity with the King James Bible.[7] Like

---

[6] *Book of Mormon Critical Text: A Tool for Scholarly Reference*, 3 vols. (Provo, Utah: FARMS, 1987), 2:428; italics mine.

[7] Curt van den Heuvel, "The Book of Mormon and the King James Version," downloaded from http://www.infidels.org/library/modern/curt_heuvel/bom_kjv.html (accessed January 2005). "One can find numerous examples of inconsistent application of the Jacobean personal noun case in the Book of Mormon." (See the section entitled "Affected Style.")

Van den Heuvel is decidedly anti-Book of Mormon, but his observation is correct. Unfortunately, he supposes that the translation method ought to have produced a perfect English rendition. Rather than examine the text to discover the nature of translation, he uses his assumption of what it should have been to criticize it when it doesn't match his original assumption. Nevertheless, when the article

similar errors in the Book of Mormon text, the best explanation is that, while the translation remains faithful to the text's meaning, the method of translation allowed the expression of those ideas in Joseph's language.

Mosiah 12:29

> 29 And again he said unto them: If ye teach the law of Moses why do ye not keep it? Why do ye set your hearts upon riches? Why do ye commit whoredoms and spend your strength with harlots, yea, and cause this people to commit sin, that the Lord has cause to send me to prophesy against this people, yea, even a great evil against this people?

Abinadi declares that the priests of Noah are not correctly interpreting the law of Moses. Rather than being intimidated by the priests' claim, Abinadi affirms himself as the law's champion, thereby placing the priests in exactly the position they had attempted to place him. He then lists three ways in which they violate the law of Moses: They set their hearts upon riches, commit whoredoms, and cause the people to sin.

Greed is certainly reprehensible, but how does it violate the law of Moses? The law does not prevent people from being well-to-do or suggest that poverty is preferable to affluence. The explanation lies in the Book of Mormon's two earlier examples of prophetic warnings against riches. Jacob had not objected to riches *per se*, but to their unequal distribution (Jacob 2:17–19). Similarly Benjamin had stressed the responsibility of those who have toward those who have not (Mosiah 4:16–25). Thus, Abinadi follows what appears to be a consistent Nephite reading of the law of Moses: that it desires the common good of the people and counsels against the social and economic separation that riches can bring.[8] The priests violate this principle, not by their possession of riches but by their desire. In addition to desiring riches, they also desire superiority to the people. Their seats are even elevated above those of ordinary worshippers (Mosiah 11:11). This inequality violates the law as the great Nephite prophets have interpreted it.

Abinadi's second accusation concerns whoredoms and harlots. As did Jacob, Abinadi would not be arguing against the principle of polygyny, but rather against the specifics of the Noahite practice. As previously noted, the people of Noah have returned to the same geographic area that saw these same social pressures develop in early Nephite society (as reported in Jacob). As in Jacob's time, at least some of these wives may have been indigenous women and, accompanying the marriages, may have

---

is sticking to the facts rather than interpretation of those facts, it provides useful examples of the relationship of the English text to what the underlying text must have been.

[8]The Nephite ideal of social egalitarianism appears to be more solidly based on Isaiah than the law of Moses. (See commentary accompanying 2 Nephi 15:8.) However, I suggest that Abinadi conflated correct principles with the gospel law he was living. For Abinadi, Isaiah was a prophet who defended and explained the law of Moses, hence the principles taught were part of that law, much as the Church of Jesus Christ of Latter-day Saints believes that pronouncements by modern prophets are still part of the restored gospel even if they were not part of the understanding that Joseph Smith revealed at the beginning of this dispensation.

been the adoption of foreign religious practices. (See commentary accompanying Mosiah 11:14; Jacob 2:12–13, 32–34.) They are not simply committing sexual sin, serious though that is, but open acts of rebellion against Yahweh.

Abinadi's third accusation is that the priests are teaching these things to the people. Clearly the priests have grafted new practices and ideas onto the inherited religion. They are directly responsible for "perverting" the people's beliefs to the point that they not only fail to recognize Yahweh's prophet but willingly capture him and deliver him up to a trial that will inevitably end in his death. In this accusation, Abinadi foreshadows the Messiah's teaching on the Sermon on the Mount: "Whosoever therefore shall break one of these least commandments, and shall teach men so, he shall be called the least in the kingdom of heaven" (Matt. 5:19).

Mosiah 12:30–31

> 30 Know ye not that I speak the truth? Yea, ye know that I speak the truth; and you ought to tremble before God.
> 31 And it shall come to pass that ye shall be smitten for your iniquities, for ye have said that ye teach the law of Moses. And what know ye concerning the law of Moses? Doth salvation come by the law of Moses? What say ye?

Abinadi applies his prophetic message of coming calamities directly to the priests, declaring that Yahweh condemns them. Abinadi may not understand that these priests will escape some of the bondage and oppression from the Lamanites that the people will suffer; but their ultimate punishment will be at Yahweh's hand.

Rhetoric: Abinadi uses the priests' tactic of laying a verbal trap by asking if salvation comes through the law of Moses. This question goes to the crux of their apostasy. He knows that salvation comes only through the Messiah and also knows that this was the original religious understanding of these priests. However, like Sherem, they have altered the teachings, eliminating the Messiah as savior and privileging the law of Moses (Jacob 7:2).

Mosiah 12:32–33

> 32 And they answered and said that salvation did come by the law of Moses.
> 33 But now Abinadi said unto them: I know if ye keep the commandments of God ye shall be saved; yea, if ye keep the commandments which the Lord delivered unto Moses in the mount of Sinai, saying:

The priests can give no other response. They have been teaching the law of Moses, excluding the Messianic revelations of the Nephite prophets. To be consistent, they *must* conclude that the law is sufficient to bring salvation.

Mosiah 12:34–36

> 34 I am the Lord thy God, who hath brought thee out of the land of Egypt, out of the house of bondage.
> 35 Thou shalt have no other God before me.

36 Thou shalt not make unto thee any graven image, or any likeness of any thing in heaven above, or things which are in the earth beneath.

Rhetoric: Abinadi explains their error to them by beginning with the Mosaic law, the point on which they agree.

Reference: Abinadi quotes Exodus 20:2–4 with only minor changes (additions in bold, deletions in strikethrough):

> I am the Lord thy God, which have brought thee out of the land of Egypt, out of the house of bondage.
>
> Thou shalt have no other **God** ~~gods~~ before me.
>
> Thou shalt not make unto thee any graven image, or any likeness of any thing ~~that is~~ in heaven above, ~~or that is~~ **or things which are** in the earth beneath, ~~or that is in the water under the earth~~.

In the 1611 edition of the King James Bible, the word "is" (in the phrase "that is") was not italicized, but it is other editions.[9] It is still most likely that the deletion of "that is" was occasioned by the italicized word "is" and that the word "that" had to be removed along with it. There is no damage done to the sense of the verse with that change. There is no particular reason for the deletion of the last phrase. A more interesting change is that the KJV designates "gods" while Abinadi specifies "God." This change may be another simplification measure, but it may also be Abinadi's deliberate adaptation to his trial before the priests. Because they were building new religious elements on the fundamental law of Moses, they probably had not attempted to alter with its most basic belief in one God, even if the people included converts from polytheistic cultures. In fact, such converts are typically even more protective of their new religious principles than lifetime believers. Thus, it seems unlikely that the priests of Noah had attempted to introduce new gods. Rather they had probably reinterpreted the law to effectively deny the salvific role of that one God. (See "Excursus: Religion of the Nehors," following Alma 1.)

Because Abinadi's defense of the Messiah accuses them of departing from that belief, he may have deliberately shifted to the singular form ("God") rather than quoting the original ("gods") because it would be easy for the priests to deny that they worshipped multiple gods. However, Abinadi's point is not polytheism but a perversion of the worship of the One God.

Mosiah 12:37

37 Now Abinadi said unto them, Have ye done all this? I say unto you, Nay, ye have not. And have ye taught this people that they should do all these things? I say unto you, Nay, ye have not.

Abinadi forces home his point. They *should* believe in the one God who brought his children from bondage in Egypt and gave the law to Moses; but they do not. In essence, he is accusing them of blasphemy.

---

[9]*Book of Mormon Critical Text: A Tool for Scholarly Reference*, 3 vols. (Provo, Utah: FARMS, 1987), 2:431.

Text: The chapter break in the 1879 edition at this point is unfortunate. The 1830 edition continues without interruption, thus not allowing a conceptual gap between Abinadi's remarkable accusation and its effect on the priests. This chapter should always be read with the next one to retain the power of the argument and drama of the situation.

Mosiah 13

Mosiah 12:37–13:1

> 37 Now Abinadi said unto them, Have ye done all this? I say unto you, Nay, ye have not. And have ye taught this people that they should do all these things? I say unto you, Nay, ye have not.
> 1 And now when the king had heard these words, he said unto his priests: Away with this fellow, and slay him; for what have we to do with him, for he is mad.

Abinadi has effectively accused Noah and his priests of blasphemy—of not understanding or teaching the very law that they claim to be upholding. Although the priests' reaction is not directly described, Noah, who has been silent up to this point, is greatly offended, instantly declares Abinadi's guilt, and commands that he be removed and executed.

Vocabulary: Assistant professor of English at Brigham Young University Don Norton notes that the contemporary definition of "fellow" in Joseph Smith's day (according to Webster's definition) was "a man without good breeding or worth; an ignoble man."[1] In the context of Noah's certain disdain for Abinadi, this more archaic reading would provide deeper color to the recorded statement.

Mosiah 13:2–3

> 2 And they stood forth and attempted to lay their hands on him; but he withstood them, and said unto them:
> 3 Touch me not, for God shall smite you if ye lay your hands upon me, for I have not delivered the message which the Lord sent me to deliver; neither have I told you that which ye requested that I should tell; therefore, God will not suffer that I shall be destroyed at this time.

Apparently the court functionaries made a move to seize Abinadi, since he commands them not to touch him until he has completely delivered his message. Revealingly, he affirms that he will not be "destroyed at this time." He clearly understands that his is a fatal mission. Even in his prophetic foreknowledge of death, Abinadi accepts Yahweh's mission.

Mosiah 13:4

> 4 But I must fulfil the commandments wherewith God has commanded me; and because I have told you the truth ye are angry with me. And again, because I have spoken the word of God ye have judged me that I am mad.

---

[1]Don Norton, "A Reader's Library," *Journal of Book of Mormon Studies* 13, nos. 1–2 (2004): 162.

Abinadi responds directly to Noah's outburst, declaring that his words are Yahweh's. Thus, in accusing Abinadi of madness, Noah is accusing Yahweh of being mad, a blasphemous assertion on its face.

Mosiah 13:5

> 5 Now it came to pass after Abinadi had spoken these words that the people of king Noah durst not lay their hands on him, for the Spirit of the Lord was upon him; and his face shone with exceeding luster, even as Moses' did while in the mount of Sinai, while speaking with the Lord.

This passage records the fear that came upon Noah's court as they witness a visible transformation in Abinadi—a shining "luster"—through the power of the Spirit. Abinadi's warning not to touch him echoes Nephi's experience in building the ship when he warns off his angry brothers. The brothers received that message just as clearly as Noah's court (1 Ne. 17:47–49). Moses's face, after he descended from Mount Sinai, shone so brightly that he veiled himself (Ex. 34:30). Heavenly beings are frequently described in terms of "light" (see, for instance, JS—History 1:16, 30). Manifestations from the spiritual realm may be accompanied by what we perceive as light, and the powerful presence of the Spirit with Abinadi transformed and lighted his face. Possibly the light extended to his entire person but was most evident in his face as that would be where the priests would naturally concentrate their vision.

Text: Daniel H. Ludlow comments on the comparison between Abinadi's "luster" and Moses's visage:

> This statement is of particular interest because of the controversy among biblical scholars and translators concerning the facial appearance of Moses after he had talked with the Lord on the mount of Sinai. The King James Version renders Exodus 34:30 as follows: "And when Aaron and all the children of Israel saw Moses, behold, the skin of his face shone; and they were afraid to come nigh him." However, the Catholic translators of the Douay Version followed the pattern of the Septuagint Bible by translating the same verse as follows: "And he knew not that his face was horned from the conversation with the Lord. And Aaron and the children of Israel seeing the face of Moses horned, were afraid to come near." Because of this faulty interpretation, the great sculptor Michelangelo put horns on his famous statue of Moses![2]

John Gray, professor of Hebrew and Semitic languages at the University of Aberdeen, Scotland, provides background on the events in Exodus 34:29:

> The word translated as veil, used only here, probably means a cult mask—such as is well attested in antiquity and among the Arabs in connection with prophecy—which Moses used to use when speaking an oracle from Yahweh. Since the tradition was embarrassing to later orthodoxy (cf. Ezek. 13:18) the P author [Priestly author in the documentary hypothesis] explains the mask as worn on only one occasion to cover the awesome afterglow on Moses' face resulting from the divine encounter (cf. Paul's explanation, 2 Cor. 3:13). In vs. 35a, however, omission in the LXX [Septuagint] of the

---

[2]Daniel H. Ludlow, *A Companion to Your Study of the Book of Mormon* (Salt Lake City, Utah: Deseret Book, 1976), 182.

> skin of Moses' face suggests that these words were repeated by an editor from vss. 29–30 and that the meaning is rather that the face of Moses . . . shone when he was wearing the mask. No doubt it was made of burnished metal—cf. an Arab cult mask of gold—or decorated with metal pieces, perhaps from the ornaments contributed by the people ([Ex.] 33:1–6). "Shone" translates a rare word which contains the consonants of horn and was so rendered in the Vulg[ate]—whence Michelangelo's famous statue of Moses with horns. Possibly vs. 35a originally described the mask as having horns.[3]

If John Gray is correct, the transformation of understanding from "cult mask" to simply "shining" had occurred by the time of Ezekiel, who preaches in the early years of the Babylonian exile. This suggests that the change had occurred by Lehi's time and that shining was religiously and culturally understood as a reflection of the Spirit among the Nephites.

Mosiah 13:6–8

> 6 And he spake with power and authority from God; and he continued his words, saying:
> 7 Ye see that ye have not power to slay me, therefore I finish my message. Yea, and I perceive that it cuts you to your hearts because I tell you the truth concerning your iniquities.
> 8 Yea, and my words fill you with wonder and amazement, and with anger.

Abinadi has not yet delivered the part of his message that is so essential that he cannot be touched, but already the reaction of his listeners is so intense that he accurately describes them as cut "to your hearts because I tell you the truth." The effect of hearing the truth on those who have justified their actions is to awaken the sharp pain of recognizing their sin. Anger at the messenger is a very typical reaction to such pain, an attempt to displace the pain and project it outward. However, to feel pain they had to be able to feel at least some of the Spirit; otherwise, Abinadi's message would have been irrelevant, not a personal conflict. This pain of recognition is the first step in repentance, but certainly does not guarantee repentance. Of all of the priests pierced by this painful awakening, only Alma is known to have accepted it and moved on toward full repentance.

Mosiah 13:9–10

> 9 But I finish my message; and then it matters not whither I go, if it so be that I am saved.
> 10 But this much I tell you, what you do with me, after this, shall be as a type and a shadow of things which are to come.

Abinadi has already told the priests that he cannot be captured until he finishes his message. Now he announces that he *will* finish it. Abinadi allows for the possibility

---

[3]John Gray, "The Book of Exodus," in *The Interpreter's One-Volume Commentary on the Bible*, edited by Charles M. Laymon (Nashville, Tenn.: Abingdon Press, 1971), 67. Bold in original. Everett Fox, *The Five Books of Moses*, Vol. 1 of THE SCHOCKEN BIBLE (New York: Schocken Books, 1995), 459, notes: "There have now been found other ancient Near Eastern texts that support [the reading of 'horned'], although the present context and comparative religion seem also to throw weight to 'radiating.'"

that he may not survive this encounter with Noah. In a voice of prophetic warning, he assures them that they will reap in their personal lives whatever fate they inflict on him. He is holding out options to them. Yahweh left room for the exercise of agency and repentance, even to the last moment. If all had repented like Alma, then Abinadi would have been freed and the toppling of Noah's regime (including his own death) might have been avoided. If Noah or any of the priests saw this option, however, they did not take it.

Mosiah 13:11

> 11 And now I read unto you the remainder of the commandments of God, for I perceive that they are not written in your hearts; I perceive that ye have studied and taught iniquity the most part of your lives.

After this declaration that he will read "the remainder of the commandments of God," Abinadi recites a version of the Decalogue. Those are certainly "the commandments of God" that the priests likely declared they taught as the law. The essential message, however, will come in verses 28–31.

Why does Abinadi declare that he will "read" the text that has he been quoting up to this moment? The record gives no indication that he was already reading, nor that he had earlier read the earlier Isaiah passage. Perhaps Mormon had omitted this detail. Abinadi could have asked for the scriptures and then read from them. He could even have walked over to the priests' section of the court, cowing them with his glowing visage and obvious authority and appropriating a book of scripture from which he continues his discourse. Another possible explanation is a broader interpretation of "read," and Abinadi is "reading" them the law just as one might be "read" his rights.

Of course Abinadi was literate, or he would have had much more difficulty in memorizing the lengthy passages he does quote. His literacy also strengthens Tvedtnes's suggestion (see commentary accompanying Mosiah 11:20) that Abinadi might have been a deposed priest of Zeniff—both literate and with access to the scriptures.

Mosiah 13:12

> 12 And now, ye remember that I said unto you: Thou shall not make unto thee any graven image, or any likeness of things which are in heaven above, or which are in the earth beneath, or which are in the water under the earth.

Rhetoric: Abinadi is refocusing the discussion at the point where he was earlier interrupted (Mosiah 12:34–36). After quoting this particular commandment, he began his commentary about how the priests were failing to teach this commandment. Now he repeats not only this prohibition against graven images but the rest of the Ten Commandments listed in Exodus. Obviously, he is reminding his listeners about the most basic elements of the Mosaic law, making it clear that he, too, is a master of the law. Yet he is not seeking to show points of unity with his accusers but rather showing that they have ignored the point of the law, which is the Messiah's atonement. The fact that he must preach the Messiah to them constitutes evidence that they have rejected the Messianic part of the Nephite religion, retaining only its Mosaic component.

Abinadi had earlier stopped his recitation after this commandment to have no other God(s) before the Lord because that single command is the crux of his message. The Noahites are believing in the wrong god, even though they claim to accept the law of Moses. Abinadi continues with the rest of what we call the Ten Commandments to demonstrate that the priests' understanding is mistaken. Of course, the law of Moses consists of more than these few quotations, but they form the moral basis of the law, and, hence, are a proper departure point for the argument Abinadi is building.

Translation: Although Abinadi may be either reading or quoting, comparing his two versions of this passage suggests that Joseph Smith may have rendered them differently in translation. In Mosiah 12:36, "that is" is replaced by "which are," making it agree with the plural "things" which is singular in both Exodus and Mosiah 12:36. The sense of the verse has not changed, and the slight singular/plural alteration suggests oral translation/dictation rather than a change in the underlying text. Assuming that this hypothesis is true, did Joseph introduce it as he dictated or did Oliver mishear it as he wrote? It is impossible to tell, of course, but Oliver did hear other phrases incorrectly, then corrected them, so this slight change may reflect a scribal variation.[4]

Mosiah 13:13

> 13 And again: Thou shalt not bow down thyself unto them, nor serve them; for I the Lord thy God am a jealous God, visiting the iniquities of the fathers upon the children, unto the third and fourth generations of them that hate me;

Translation: The introductory phrase "and again" is not in Exodus 20:5. It is most likely Abinadi's oral addition, even if he were reading. The second change is again a shift from the singular "iniquity (Exodus) to the plural "iniquities" (Abinadi). Like the earlier change in number, this alteration probably results from the translation process, not a difference in the versions of the document, although Tvedtnes does note that the Hebrew word for "iniquity," though grammatically singular, may be used in a collective sense.[5]

Mosiah 13:14–24

> 14 And showing mercy unto thousands of them that love me and keep my commandments.

---

[4]Royal Skousen, "How Joseph Smith Translated the Book of Mormon: Evidence from the Original Manuscript," in *Journal of Book of Mormon Studies* 7, no. 1 (1998): 25.

[5]John A. Tvedtnes, "Isaiah Textual Variants in the Book of Mormon," FARMS Reprint Series (Provo, Utah: FARMS, 1981), 92: "[The Masoretic Text] has *cwn* which, while singular in form, may be used in a collective sense. Note that [the Septuagint] has the plural (*tais amartias*), agreeing with [the Book of Mormon]," text in brackets expands abbreviations in the original.

> 15 Thou shalt not take the name of the Lord thy God in vain; for the Lord will not hold him guiltless that taketh his name in vain.
> 16 Remember the sabbath day, to keep it holy.
> 17 Six days shalt thou labor, and do all thy work;
> 18 But the seventh day, the sabbath of the Lord thy God, thou shalt not do any work, thou, nor thy son, nor thy daughter, thy man-servant, nor thy maid-servant, nor thy cattle, nor thy stranger that is within thy gates;
> 19 For in six days the Lord made heaven and earth, and the sea, and all that in them is; wherefore the Lord blessed the sabbath day, and hallowed it.
> 20 Honor thy father and thy mother, that thy days may be long upon the land which the Lord thy God giveth thee.
> 21 Thou shalt not kill.
> 22 Thou shalt not commit adultery. Thou shalt not steal.
> 23 Thou shalt not bear false witness against thy neighbor.
> 24 Thou shalt not covet thy neighbor's house, thou shalt not covet thy neighbor's wife, nor his man-servant, nor his maid-servant, nor his ox, nor his ass, nor anything that is thy neighbor's.

Abinadi quotes these verses to complete the foundation for his challenge to the priests' declaration that they teach the law of Moses (Mosiah 12:28). Abinadi begins by reciting the compact form of the law of Moses.

Text: In the 1830 edition, a chapter break occurs here. While this separation seems awkward to the modern reader because it interrupts a continuous speech, it nevertheless seems to be consistent with one of Mormon's most regular editorial practices. Up to this point, he is quoting his source. At the quotation's end and before Mormon interjects his own explanation, the chapter ends.

Translation: These verses are included with no changes except spelling from the King James Version (for example, "shewing/showing," "neighbour/neighbor").

Mosiah 13:25

> 25 And it came to pass that after Abinadi had made an end of these sayings that he said unto them: Have ye taught this people that they should observe to do all these things for to keep these commandments?

Text: Mormon interjects a comment between two quotations from his source. Abinadi finished reading the Ten Commandments and will now press home his essential message, the one that he came to this trial to deliver. There is no event in the record of the trial that suggests a reason for Mormon's chapter break. The only thing that marks this new chapter is the essential message. Perhaps Mormon created the chapter to conceptually set the message apart from the preliminary verbal sparring that led up to it.

After reading the Ten Commandments to the priests, Abinadi recapitulates the form of his opening argument. His quotation of the Ten Commandments parallels the question/response from Mosiah 12:31–32: "And what know ye concerning the law of Moses? Doth salvation come by the law of Moses? What say ye? And they answered and said that salvation did come by the law of Moses." In the current verse 25 he asks "Have ye taught this people that they should observe to do all these things for to keep the commandments?" In 12:37 he had queried: "And have ye taught this people that they should do all these things?

Abinadi's argument in chapter 12 was leading up to his message. Chapter 13 begins with King Noah's reaction and Abinadi's command that they not touch him. Thus, Abinadi was about to deliver his essential message when the king attempted to seize him. After that flurry of activity, Abinadi returned to his message, setting it up exactly as before the interruption.

Mosiah 13:26

> 26 I say unto you, Nay; for if ye had, the Lord would not have caused me to come forth and to prophesy evil concerning this people.

Abinadi is simply pointing out an inexorably logical position. If the priests had been teaching the gospel correctly, Yahweh would not have called Abinadi to stand before them. (See the parallel statement in Mosiah 12:37.) His words are poignant. He has come to "prophesy evil"—the calamitous events that he has foretold. Those events indeed would be seen as "evil" by the Limhites who had endured them by the time Ammon arrived (see Mosiah 7:24–28, especially v. 25).

Mosiah 13:27

> 27 And now ye have said that salvation cometh by the law of Moses. I say unto you that it is expedient that ye should keep the law of Moses as yet; but I say unto you, that the time shall come when it shall no more be expedient to keep the law of Moses.

Abinadi reaches the crux of his discourse. He has declared that the priests' teachings are not correct, has recited a succinct catalog of the Mosaic law's prescriptions, and has recognized that the priests claim that these are precisely the things they say they have taught. How will Abinadi testify that the priests have not taught what they claim to have taught?

He first asserts that salvation comes through the law of Moses. This is an essential point; if the law were sufficient for salvation, then the priests' teachings would be correct. His first instruction confirms the value of the law: "It is expedient that ye should keep the law of Moses as yet." "Expedient" indicates a response to temporary conditions, which "as yet" underscores. Future conditions will be different. We can hear in Abinadi's argument an echo of Christ's own explanation of his approach to the law: "Think not that I am come to destroy the law, or the prophets: I am not come to destroy, but to fulfil" (Matt. 5:17).

Abinadi is blunter, however, in spelling out the fact that, at some future point, they will not need to obey the law of Moses. This is a different concept from Christ's message, which emphasizes the continuation *and* transformation of the law—that he will not destroy but fulfill it (Matt. 5:17, 3 Ne. 12:17). In contrast, Abinadi suggests that the law is good now but will not be in the future.

On their face, the two statements seem contradictory, but both express the revealed reality. Jesus calls it "fulfilling," but that operation required abandoning some features of the law in accepting the gospel. Abinadi also explains the future nonoperational status of the law of performances but acknowledges its transformation. He did not bother to couch his message in more subtle terms, as Christ did, apparently feeling no compunction about further antagonizing his captors.

Mosiah 13:28

> 28 And moreover, I say unto you, that salvation doth not come by the law alone; and were it not for the atonement, which God himself shall make for the sins and iniquities of his people, that they must unavoidably perish, notwithstanding the law of Moses.

This is the point of contention between Abinadi's religion and the priests'. The priests teach the Sherem religion, later described as "the religion of the Nehors." (See "Excursus: Religion of the Nehors," following Alma 1.) This brass-plates' religion lacks the Messianic prophecies of the Nephite prophets.

Abinadi assumes that the priests know about these Messianic teachings and have heard of the atonement. If Abinadi were one of Zeniff's priests, as Tvedtnes suggests (see commentary accompanying Mosiah 11:20), then this assumption would be based on his personal knowledge. Abinadi proceeds, not by revealing things that they have never known, but by explaining teachings they have chosen to disregard. They are not sinning in ignorance, but by choice, and perhaps by avarice.

Abinadi makes two important points. First, the atonement provides salvation. The reason for living the law of Moses comes because of the atonement, not apart from it. The second, and perhaps most interesting, is his statement that "God himself" will effect the atonement. It is clear from the following verses (especially v. 34) that Abinadi sees Yahweh and the Messiah as the same being. (See commentary accompanying 1 Nephi 11:15–18 for the Nephite concept of God.) This is the reason for Abinadi's alteration of "gods" (Ex. 20:3) to "God" when he quotes the same passage (Mosiah 12:35).

When Abinadi speaks of the Messiah as "God himself" atoning for humankind, he is probably demonstrating that the priests are teaching a false god because they are denying Yahweh's Messianic role. In other words, he is purposefully exposing the priests of Noah as ranking a false god before the true God, the God-who-will-be-Messiah. Rodney Turner notes:

> The central message of Abinadi to King Noah was essentially the same message an angel of the Lord was to deliver to King Benjamin over twenty years later: "God himself"—"the Lord Omnipotent"—was to come to earth as the Redeemer of mankind (see Mosiah 3:5; 15:1). . . .

> Although the Redeemer was known to the Nephite prophets by different titles (God of Jacob, Holy One of Israel, Great Creator, Lamb of God, Messiah, Christ, and so on), in every instance, they were referring to one and the same person.[6]

Mosiah 13:29–30

> 29 And now I say unto you that it was expedient that there should be a law given to the children of Israel, yea, even a very strict law; for they were a stiffnecked people, quick to do iniquity, and slow to remember the Lord their God;
> 30 Therefore there was a law given them, yea, a law of performances and of ordinances, a law which they were to observe strictly from day to day, to keep them in remembrance of God and their duty towards him.

Abinadi's comment echoes Paul's similar explanation of the relationship between the law of Moses and the law of the gospel: "Wherefore the law was our schoolmaster to bring us unto Christ, that we might be justified by faith" (Gal. 3:24). Although the two statements mean essentially the same thing, their perspectives are different. Paul's statement is more positive: The law was necessary, but it was simply a teacher; the gospel would bring a more important way. Abinadi's statement is less positive, showing the law as necessary for a "stiffnecked" people. As a "law of performances and ordinances," it allowed these "children" to learn slowly, with rigid instructions about daily practices keeping them from error. This rigidity of practice will be replaced by the freedom of the gospel.

It is easy to understand why the two prophets explained the law in different terms. Paul was trying to win converts and nurture newly converted members; therefore, he focuses on a smoother transition from one law to the other. Abinadi, in contrast, is condemning false teachers who are placing the law above the gospel. He is harsh in order to be clear. He wants to show the priests how and why they are mistaken in eliminating Christ from their teachings. Therefore, he must show that the law of Moses is not as powerful or salvific as they preach.

Mosiah 13:31

> 31 But behold, I say unto you, that all these things were types of things to come.

The Mosaic ordinances were schoolteachers because they were symbolic precursors to—or "types" of—the Savior's mission. Abinadi allows himself no more than this succinct explanation, presumably because the theological arguments that explained the symbolic relationship of Mosaic practices to the revealed Messianic mission were part of what the priests had knowingly eliminated in the Noahite religion. Were this information completely new, no doubt Abinadi would have developed and illustrated his meaning. Because he does not, we deduce that his audience had heard the debate before and understood this argument from a quick reference alone.

---

[6]Rodney Turner, "Two Prophets: Abinadi and Alma," in *1 Nephi to Alma 29*, edited by Kent P. Jackson, STUDIES IN SCRIPTURE (Salt Lake City: Deseret Book, 1987), Vol. 7, 244–45.

Apocryphal Literature: The first-century letter of Barnabas is a post-Christian examination that interprets the Mosaic symbols in a Christian context, as Abinadi suggests can be done.[7] Nevertheless, Bart D. Ehrman, chair of the Department of Religious Studies at the University of North Carolina at Chapel Hill, notes that the letter of Barnabas had a distinctly anti-Jewish tone of which neither Abinadi nor Mormon would have approved.[8]

Mosiah 13:32

> 32 And now, did they understand the law? I say unto you, Nay, they did not all understand the law; and this because of the hardness of their hearts; for they understood not that there could not any man be saved except it were through the redemption of God.

The Jews did not understand the law because they missed an essential element, a true understanding of the Messiah's atoning mission. Their hardheartedness on this point would not have been included in the brass plates. While texts from the brass plate texts certainly contained calls to repentance, the people's sin is never clearly identified as a rejection of the Atoning Messiah, even though for much of its history, Israel expected a conquering Messiah rather than an atoning one. Why, then, does Abinadi declare that the Jews were hardhearted about this part of the gospel? One logical source would be direct revelation. The second would be Nephi's revelation. On the small plates, both Nephi and Lehi affirm that the Jews reject the Atoning Messiah (1 Ne. 10:11, 15:17).

Did Abinadi have access to the small plates? It seems unlikely. The plates almost certainly were given to Mosiah after the departure of Zeniff (Noah's father) to the land of Lehi-Nephi. However, if Nephi condensed Lehi's prophecies on his own small plates, then the book of Lehi on the large plates would have contained a fuller version. As I have already hypothesized, Zeniff and his party brought a copy of this work and the brass plates with them from Zarahemla.

Interesting, too, is the fact that Abinadi refers to the hard-heartedness as occurring in the past, even though the evidence for it lies in the future. This rhetorical device is known as the prophetic past, or prophetic perfect. According to Donald W. Parry, an associate professor of Hebrew language and literature at

---

[7]This work should not be confused with a later Gospel of Barnabas that exists only in an Italian copy from the late 1500s and is generally not accepted as authentic. A convenient source for the first-century "Barnabas" is in *The Lost Books of the Bible and the Forgotten Books of Eden* (New York: World Publishing, 1973), 145–65.

[8]Bart D. Ehrman, *Lost Christianities: The Battles for Scripture and the Faiths We Never Knew* (New York: Oxford University Press, 2005), 146:

> As became typical among his proto-orthodox successors, the author of the letter does not spurn the Jewish Scriptures per se. He instead embraces them, insisting that when the prophets of Scripture attack the people of Israel for their opposition to God, their words are to be taken as literal truth. Because Jews rebelled against God from the very beginning, this author claims, they were misled into thinking that scriptural laws concerning how to live and worship were to be taken literally. But these biblical laws concerning sacrificial rites, ritual practices, and sacred institutions, he avers, were meant to be taken figuratively, pointing forward to the salvation to be brought to the world by Christ.

Brigham Young University, "The 'prophetic perfect' is the use of the past tense or the past participle verb forms (present and past perfect tenses) when referring to future events in prophecy. On occasion, Old Testament prophets prophesied using these forms 'to express facts which are undoubtedly imminent, and therefore, in the imagination of the speaker, already accomplished.'"[9]

Rhetoric: Abinadi is pounding home the essential point of his discourse—that the Messiah's mission is essential even for the law of Moses. He stresses that the priests' religion cannot save because it denies the Messiah, as have the Jews.

Mosiah 13:33

> 33 For behold, did not Moses prophesy unto them concerning the coming of the Messiah, and that God should redeem his people? Yea, and even all the prophets who have prophesied ever since the world began—have they not spoken more or less concerning these things?

It is not clear to which prophecy of Moses Abinadi is referring. The book of Moses "translated" by Joseph Smith is certainly clear on this point, but it does not correspond to our received text of Genesis.[10] Perhaps the brass plates included more specific prophecies from Moses that we do not now have. However, they must have been couched in ways that the priests could accept the brass plate religion and yet deny the Atoning Messiah.

Mosiah 13:34–35

> 34 Have they not said that God himself should come down among the children of men, and take upon him the form of man, and go forth in mighty power upon the face of the earth?
> 35 Yea, and have they not said also that he should bring to pass the resurrection of the dead, and that he, himself, should be oppressed and afflicted?

Abinadi again assumes that the priests understand his argument. He asserts that many prophets have given specific testimonies about the Messiah's mission; the next section of his discourse provides an example. The insertion of a chapter break in the 1879 edition perhaps muffles the connection between the Isaiah quotation and Abinadi's exegesis that it is evidence of much prophetic knowledge about the Messiah's earthly mission. Contemporary readers of this passage have knowledge of Christ's mission that Abinadi does not have, so his understanding of Isaiah must

---

[9]Donald W. Parry, "Hebraisms and Other Ancient Peculiarities in the Book of Mormon," in *Echoes and Evidences of the Book of Mormon*, edited by Donald W. Parry, Daniel C. Peterson, and John W. Welch (Provo, Utah: Foundation for Ancient Research and Mormon Studies, 2002), 164. The internal reference cites Friedrich Heinrich Wilhelm Gesenius, *Gesenius' Hebrew Grammar* (Oxford: Carendon, 1970), 312–13.

[10]Joseph Smith's work on Moses began about June 1830 and continued until March 1835. *Joseph Smith's New Translation of the Bible: Original Manuscripts*, edited by Scott H. Faulring, Kent P. Jackson, and Robert J. Matthews (Provo, Utah: BYU Religious Studies Center, 2004), 57–58.

come from his own prophetic experience or from his understanding of the prophetic experience and writings of other Nephite prophets like Lehi and Nephi.

Text: Because the 1830 edition of the Book of Mormon makes no chapter break at this point, the Isaiah passage should be read as a continuation of the witness that many earlier prophets made of Messianic prophecies.

Mosiah 14

Mosiah 14:1

> 1 Yea, even doth not Isaiah say: Who hath believed our report, and to whom is the arm of the Lord revealed?

Text: The chapter break inserted at this point in 1879 separates this quotation of Isaiah 53:1–12 from Abinadi's speech; but the 1879 versification and chapter designations are clearly designed to replicate biblical chapters and verses. Like Nephi and Jacob, Abinadi uses Isaiah as a springboard for his current purpose rather than as an explanatory commentary. At this point, this commentary concentrates on the Isaiah passages themselves and their position in Abinadi's discourse.

Abinadi introduces the quotation with a short statement: "Yea, even doth not Isaiah say . . . " which ties Abinadi's previous statements to the following Isaiah quotation. Because that context is important, I repeat those verses here: "Have they not said that God himself should come down among the children of men, and take upon him the form of man, and go forth in mighty power upon the face of the earth? Yea, and have they not said also that he should bring to pass the resurrection of the dead, and that he, himself, should be oppressed and afflicted?" (Mosiah 13:34–35).

Abinadi quotes Isaiah as an example of a prophet who has foretold the Messiah's mortal mission. Once again, our modern perspective can easily obscure the potential theological differences that Abinadi would face. While Noah's priests might agree that a Triumphant Messiah would come at the end of time, they deny his mortal (atoning) mission. In other words, from Abinadi's perspective, there are two future "comings" of the Messiah: the first (mortal) and the second (triumphant). While from our perspective, we know that the first has already occurred and await the second, it is not surprising that Abinadi's listeners could have easily confused these two future "comings" involving the same figure or had trouble reconciling the Triumphant Messiah of the second coming with the scorned and rejected Messiah of the first.

Abinadi begins his argument with Isaiah 53:1. As Welch notes:

> Although some scholars have wondered whether the song of the suffering servant should begin at Isaiah 53:1 or 52:13, the fact that Abinadi began quoting at Isaiah 53:1 implies that he and the ancient Nephites understood that a poetical unit began at Isaiah 53:1, as it does today in the traditional chapter divisions in the Bible, not at Isaiah 52:13, as has been suggested by such scholars as Dion and Clines. Indeed, other biblicists,

including Orlinsky and Whybray, have argued in favor of commencing the unit at 53:1, the traditional starting point.[1]

In addition to these technical arguments for seeing Isaiah 53:1 as the beginning point, there is another reason why Abinadi might begin his quotation here. Welch implies that Abinadi would prefer to start at the "beginning" of a poetical unit. Certainly Nephi and Jacob follow this pattern in their Isaiah quotations (see "Excursus: Isaiah on the Small Plates," following 1 Nephi 19), but Abinadi seems less constrained. Here, I suggest that a more important fact is that Isaiah 53:1 asks Abinadi's very question: "Who hath believed our report . . . ?" If 52:13 were seen as the beginning point, then this question refers to the beginning of the "report" which discusses the "servant." But if 53:1 is the beginning point, then the question must refer to the answer which follows, not to a previous text.

In either case, it is the question that is most important. Abinadi is using it as a text that comments on his previous statement about the numerous prophets who have predicted this suffering Messiah. Now he asks, in Isaiah's words, "Who hath believed our report?" While Isaiah's reference was general, Abinadi's is a loaded gun pointed at Noah's priests. Abinadi has declared that there will be a suffering Messiah, a first-coming Messiah, and claims the support of other prophets who have made the same prediction. Abinadi is stressing that it is the unbelieving priests, not he, who are in conflict with the scriptures.

Victor Ludlow, professor of ancient scripture at Brigham Young University, sees Isaiah 53:1 in precisely the way Abinadi uses it—as a declaration that other prophets have testified of the Savior:

> Isaiah asks a second question at the beginning of verse 1: "In whom has the arm of the Lord been revealed?" He implies that the servant will be revealed by the "arm" or power of the Lord. (See Isa. 52:10, John 12:37–38, 1 Ne. 22:10–11, D&C 45:47.) Isaiah spends the rest of the chapter answering this second question.
>
> The servant to be revealed by the Lord's power is not named, but both the prophet Abinadi and the evangelist Philip identify him as Jesus Christ (Mosiah 15, Acts 8:26–35). In addition, Matthew, Peter, and Paul apply various verses of Isaiah 53 to Christ (Matt. 8:17, 1 Pet. 2:24–25, Rom. 4:25).[2]

Mosiah 14:2

> 2 For he shall grow up before him as a tender plant, and as a root out of dry ground; he hath no form nor comeliness; and when we shall see him there is no beauty that we should desire him.

This verse makes three symbolic/descriptive comparisons to the coming Messiah: (1) a "tender plant," (2) a "root" from "dry ground," and (3) a lack of "beauty that we should desire him." These passages are typically labeled the "suffering servant" songs; and in traditional Jewish interpretation, Israel is the suffering servant.

---

[1]John W. Welch, "Isaiah 53, Mosiah 14, and the Book of Mormon," in *Isaiah in the Book of Mormon*, edited by Donald W. Parry and John W. Welch (Provo, Utah: FARMS, 1998), 295.

[2]Victor L. Ludlow, *Isaiah: Prophet, Seer and Poet* (Salt Lake City: Deseret Book, 1982), 448.

Ludlow suggests that the image of the Messiah as a tender plant is the infant Jesus, growing up as all children must.[3] This image may perhaps echo the metaphor of the Messiah as a "branch" (Isa. 11:1; Jer. 23:5, 15). Both are botanical references, suggesting at least an association that should be considered.

The second image focuses on the plant's root, rather then the tender stem and foliage. Again, it may echo such established Messianic imagery as Isaiah 11:10: "And in that day there shall be a root of Jesse, which shall stand for an ensign of the people; to it shall the Gentiles seek: and his rest shall be glorious." Here the "root" clearly personifies the Triumphant Messiah while in Isaiah 53:2, the "root" is the suffering Messiah. Nevertheless, the similarity is so close that Isaiah probably not only used them purposefully but understood that the suffering Messiah and the Triumphant Messiah were indeed the same person.

The dry ground contrasts with fertile soil, communicating that the Messiah's environment will be grudging and harsh, inhospitable to his message and unwilling to accept him.

The third image describes a being who lacks physical beauty (as the KJV translates it). Joseph Fielding Smith interprets this passage: "There was nothing about him to cause people to single him out. In appearance he was like men; and so it is expressed here by the prophet that he had no form or comeliness, that is, he was not so distinctive, so different from others that people would recognize him as the Son of God. He appeared as a mortal man."[4] This interpretation is less pejorative and more neutral in its interpretation. However, while it is certainly true that Jesus did not attract others because of his striking physical beauty, Isaiah may be suggesting that this lack of comeliness paralleled the other "negatives" of the suffering servant. Certainly the earthly Jesus labored with his hands. Mark describes him as a *tekton* in Greek (Mark 6:3), which has been traditionally translated as a carpenter. John Dominic Crossan's study of the first-century social context of the carpenter suggests that it may have been a rather undesirable profession, connoting a landless man. He also reads other statements by writers of the Gospels as hints that they may have been somewhat embarrassed by their leader's less-than-admirable profession.[5] (See commentary accompanying 3 Nephi 14:24–27.) James D. Tabor, chair of the Department of Religious Studies at the University of North Carolina at Charlotte, agrees with this vision of Jesus's occupation: "To be *tekton* meant first and foremost that one had no land and took work as one could find it with no guarantees of security. These itinerant peasants were left to eke out a subsistence existence on two or three sesterces a day—barely enough to sustain a slave."[6] The more negative aspects of Isaiah's descriptions might also apply to the mortal Messiah.

---

[3]Ibid.

[4]Joseph Fielding Smith, *Doctrines of Salvation*, edited by Bruce R. McConkie, 3 vols. (Salt Lake City: Bookcraft, 1977), 1:23.

[5]John Dominic Crossan, *The Birth of Christianity: Discovering What Happened in the Years Immediately after the Execution of Jesus* (San Francisco: HarperSanFrancisco, 1998), 349.

[6]James D. Tabor, *The Jesus Dynasty: The Hidden History of Jesus, His Royal Family, and the Birth of Christianity* (New York: Simon & Schuster, 2006), 90.

A further indication that Isaiah meant to provide a contrast between the divine nature and the physical appearance of the Atoning Messiah lies in the Hebrew word (*hadar*) that was translated as "comeliness" in the KJV. Kevin Barney, an attorney and student of the scriptures, notes: "Hadar means 'ornament, splendour, honor.' It is used, for example, to refer to grey hair for old men (Prov. 20:29), in Exodus 16:14 figuratively of the ornaments of Jerusalem as the bride of Yahweh, and in Leviticus 23:40 of the fruit of goodly (i.e., ornamental, beautiful) trees. Here it seems to mean that he had no splendour or majesty."[7] Isaiah is contrasting the Messiah's real splendor with his lack of apparent earthly glory. This poetic contradiction is a stylistic feature of many of Isaiah's writings.

Mosiah 14:3

> 3 He is despised and rejected of men; a man of sorrows, and acquainted with grief; and we hid as it were our faces from him; he was despised, and we esteemed him not.

This verse follows naturally from verse 2. Ancient Mediterranean cultures placed heavy emphasis on honor and shame. This verse describes one who has been shamed. Bruce J. Malina, professor of biblical studies at Creighton University, explains: "People get shamed (not have shame) when they aspire to a certain status and this status is denied them by public opinion. At the point a person realizes he is being denied the status, he is or gets shamed, he is humiliated, stripped of honor for aspiring to an honor not socially his."[8] It is not the suffering servant who turns his head, but the rest of society. He is despised and not esteemed. These are the reactions of people who have shamed him. Under Malina's model, to what social position does this suffering servant aspire? Assuming the Messianic context, the servant "aspires" to be known as the true Messiah, yet society rejects him and shames him for the attempt.

Victor Ludlow suggests:

> [Jesus] experienced constant sorrow and rejection throughout his life (Matt. 23:37). Members of his own family and the people in his hometown rejected him at first (John 7:5, Luke 4:16–30). His own chosen people, the Jews, rejected his messianic calling (John 1:11, 5:18). As his mortal ministry neared completion, one of his apostles betrayed him and another temporarily denied any knowledge of him (Luke 22:48, 54–62). This constant persecution and rejection must have caused Christ great sorrow, for the very people he came to save first turned away from him (see Mark 9:12, 1 Ne. 19:7–10).[9]

Mosiah 14:4

> 4 Surely he has borne our griefs, and carried our sorrows; yet we did esteem him stricken, smitten of God, and afflicted.

---

[7]Kevin Barney, "Translation Question on Isaiah 53:3," Scripture-L list, October 30, 1998, archived copy in my possession.

[8]Bruce J. Malina, *The New Testament World: Insights from Cultural Anthropology* (Atlanta, Ga.: John Knox Press, 1981), 46.

[9]V. Ludlow, *Isaiah: Prophet, Seer and Poet*, 449.

By bearing our griefs and carrying our sorrows, the Messiah's atoning mission comes into focus as the mark of his first coming. He comes not to rule the world, but to redeem the individual. Isaiah highlights the poignant incongruity that Israel rejects the very one who had come to lift their burdens. As Barney notes, the Hebrew word for "sorrows" could be rendered more literally as "pains," while "sickness" is a more literal translation of the word rendered in King James English as "grief."[10]

Barney also suggests that the reversal of the two elements "sorrows/pains" and "grief/sickness" creates a tighter poetic coupling between verses 3 and 4, with a chiastic reversal of the elements from one verse to the next. This structuring suggests that a poetic point is being made, probably on the meanings of "pains/sickness." The Atoning Messiah is a man of pain and sickness because he is mortal; his understanding of our pain and sickness allows him to carry those burdens for us. We may be seeing here the tendency among the King James translators to emphasize Christ's perfection, distancing him from physical ailment, sickness, or perhaps even the sweat and fatigue of manual labor. This tendency in traditional Christianity to mask Jesus's humanity but exalt his divinity does not correspond with Isaiah's Messiah, who was both human and divine, a God subject to physical ailments. That contradictory image of humanity and divinity lies at the heart of Isaiah's declaration.

Mosiah 14:5

> 5 But he was wounded for our transgressions, he was bruised for our iniquities; the chastisement of our peace was upon him; and with his stripes we are healed.

These verses are poetic but also literal in their description of physical harm. Certainly Christ was "wounded," "bruised," and "striped" as his life ended. Although the KJV "stripes" seems to suggest Jesus's flogging, other translations usually render the Hebrew *chaburah* as "wounds," a more generic, though still appropriate term. Perhaps the KJV translators were reading into their selection of terms their New Testament knowledge. Isaiah specialist Avraham Gileadi interprets this passage as "he was pierced for our transgressions," which also seems to inform the translation with New Testament knowledge.[11]

For a time during the early 1990s, there was much excitement about a reconstructed passage in the Dead Sea Scrolls that apparently discussed a Messianic figure who would be (or was) put to death.[12] Further scholarship, however, now indicates that this reading was probably erroneous:

> "Rediscovered" among the unpublished fragments of the scrolls when they first became available late in 1991, 4Q285 frag. 5 of The War of the Messiah created a flurry of

---

[10]Barney, "Translation Question on Isaiah 53:3."

[11]Avraham Gileadi, *The Book of Isaiah: A New Translation with Interpretive Keys from the Book of Mormon* (Salt Lake City: Deseret Book, 1988), 201.

[12]Robert Eisenman and Michael Wise, *The Dead Sea Scrolls Uncovered* (New York: Barnes and Noble, 1994), 24–29.

excitement and generated front-page headlines all over the world. Line 4 of the fragment is ambiguous in the original Hebrew, which is written without vowels. According to the vowels mentally supplied by the Hebrew reader, 1.4 could say either "they (the enemy) will put the Leader of the community to death" or "the Leader of the community will have him (the enemy leader) put to death." The Leader of the community is a messianic figure known from other Dead Sea Scrolls. Thus, following the first option, fragment 5 appeared to be describing the execution of a messiah, and the obvious parallels to Jesus of Nazareth were drawn.

The excitement has since died down. After a whirlwind of research activity and a number of critical assessments, scholarly consensus has rejected the first option and settled on the second. Even the primary exponent of the "dying messiah" interpretation, Robert Eisenman, has publicly recanted, saying that in fact he never really believed it in the first place.[13]

Although the "pierced" Messiah is not present in the Dead Sea Scrolls, they nevertheless appear to preserve the same belief in an Atoning Messiah as do the Nephites. John A. Tvedtnes notes:

> A messianic scroll from Cave 11, called 11QMelch or 11Q13 by scholars, casts Melchizedek in a divine saving role similar to that given to Jesus in the New Testament. Jesus is compared to Melchizedek in Hebrews 5:6, 10; 6:20; 7:1, 10–11, 15, 17, 21. Melchizedek, whose name can mean "legitimate king," is the archetypical king in the Old Testament and is therefore a fitting symbol of the Messiah. . . .
>
> Other portions of the Dead Sea Scrolls are even stronger in their support of the view that a knowledge of a savior-messiah was had in ancient Israel. An Aramaic scroll, 4Q246, is of particular interest because it contains concepts found in the angel Gabriel's announcement of Christ's birth in Luke 1 and even parallels some of the language of that chapter.[14]

Mosiah 14:6

> 6 All we, like sheep, have gone astray; we have turned every one to his own way; and the Lord hath laid on him the iniquities of us all.

Isaiah contrasts the general apostasy and sinfulness of the people with the purity of the Atoning Messiah who removes our sins. The phrase "the Lord hath laid on him the iniquities of us all" is very clearly a reference to the atonement. The reference to Israel as sheep turning away establishes a contrast with the "lamb" of verse 7. Implicitly, Jesus is the shepherd and his sheep have turned away from him. This concept reprises the shaming of the suffering servant by the community.

Variation: The Book of Mormon text has "iniquities," while the KJV text has "iniquity." While this plural/singular variation may simply be a dictation error (see discussion accompanying Mosiah 13:13), Tvedtnes notes that the Hebrew term may be used as a collective. In other words, while grammatically singular, it may be legitimately translated as a plural in languages where the translated word is not a collective.[15]

---

[13]Michael Wise, Martin Abegg, Jr. and Edward Cook, *The Dead Sea Scrolls: A New Translation* (San Francisco: HarperSanFrancisco, 1996), 291–92.

[14]John A. Tvedtnes, *The Most Correct Book: Insights from a Book of Mormon Scholar* (Salt Lake City: Cornerstone, 1999), 330, 331.

[15]John A. Tvedtnes, "Isaiah Textual Variants in the Book of Mormon," FARMS Reprint Series (Provo, Utah: FARMS, 1981), 92.

Mosiah 14:7

7 He was oppressed, and he was afflicted, yet he opened not his mouth; he is brought as a lamb to the slaughter, and as a sheep before her shearers is dumb so he opened not his mouth.

These specific events literally occurred in Jesus's trial.[16] "Lamb" is not simply a literary echo of verse 6 but another layering of symbolic meaning. Mosaic law establishes the lamb as a sacrifice for Israel:

> And the Lord spake unto Moses and Aaron in the land of Egypt, saying,
> This month shall be unto you the beginning of months: it shall be the first month of the year to you.
> Speak ye unto all the congregation of Israel, saying, In the tenth day of this month they shall take to them every man a lamb, according to the house of their fathers, a lamb for an house:
> And if the household be too little for the lamb, let him and his neighbour next unto his house take it according to the number of the souls; every man according to his eating shall make your count for the lamb.
> Your lamb shall be without blemish, a male of the first year: ye shall take it out from the sheep, or from the goats:
> And ye shall keep it up until the fourteenth day of the same month: and the whole assembly of the congregation of Israel shall kill it in the evening.
> And they shall take of the blood, and strike it on the two side posts and on the upper door post of the houses, wherein they shall eat it. (Ex. 12:1–7)

While the correspondence is not exact since Isaiah includes a lamb before the shearers (an image of humiliation?—see commentary accompanying 2 Nephi 17:30), the death of a lamb united with concept of bearing the "iniquities of all" is a powerful image of redemption.

Mosiah 14:8

8 He was taken from prison and from judgment; and who shall declare his generation? For he was cut off out of the land of the living; for the transgressions of my people was he stricken.

Translation: The New International Version (NIV) renders this passage: "By oppression and judgment, he was taken away. And who can speak of his descendants? For he was cut off from the land of the living; for the transgression of my people he was stricken."

Gileadi's translation reads: "By arrest and trial he was taken away. Who can apprise his generation that he was cut off from the land of the living for the crime of my people, to whom the blow was due?"[17]

The New English Bible (NEB) reads: "He was arrested and sentenced and taken away, and who gave a thought to his fate—how he was cut off from the world of the living, stricken to death for my people's transgression?"

---

[16]Matt. 26:62–63, 27:12–14; John 19:9–11; Luke 23:8–10; see also V. Ludlow, *Isaiah: Prophet, Seer, and Poet*, 454.

[17]Gileadi, *The Book of Isaiah*, 202.

All renditions of the verse agree on judgment. Most agree that he was taken away by judgment, but the KJV has him taken from prison. It would appear that it is a better translation to have the judgment applied against him, rather than the judgment removing him from prison. Blenkinsopp notes: "The phrase describing how he was taken away . . . is difficult; in the only other occurrence of *me'oser*, the preposition signifies instrumentality (Ps. 107:39 "brought low by oppression")."[18] Blenkinsopp therefore renders the phrase: "By oppressive acts of judgment he was led away. . . . "[19]

The next focal point of translation differences is the concept of "generations." The NEB reads "generations" as focusing on the future and therefore on the fate of the servant. Blenkinsopp uses the same translation.[20] The KJV assumes that "generations" refers to forebears, while the NIV assumes descendants. Gileadi interprets "generations" to mean his contemporaries. That is a wide range of possibilities.

Based on the question in which this critical term appears, and the correlation to Isaiah 53:1 that began with a question, we may assume that Isaiah intends that we see parallels in his prose. Since the first rhetorical question dealt with the past (past prophets who made declarations but who were not believed) this reference may be the reversal, referring to descendants (or the genericized "fate"), LDS scholar Sidney Sperry opts for the interpretation of "generations" as descendants.[21]

The final point of the verse is dramatically clear. This suffering servant will be put to death for the sins of the people. Even the KJV's somewhat oblique "cut off out of the land of the living" is still recognizable as a metaphor for death.

Mosiah 14:9

> 9 And he made his grave with the wicked, and with the rich in his death; because he had done no evil, neither was any deceit in his mouth.

Gileadi uses his Christian perspective to render this more clearly: "He was appointed among the wicked in death, among the rich was his burial; yet he had done no violence, and deceit was not in his mouth."

Isaiah is creating a poetic contrast between the righteousness of the suffering servant and the circumstances of his death. The first incongruity is that the righteous man would be "among the wicked in death." It is probable that, given Isaiah's opinion of the rich, that we should read "rich" as synonymous with "wicked." Christ fulfilled this contradiction when he was crucified among thieves and buried in the tomb of Joseph of Arimethea.

Comparison: The KJV has "violence" where the Book of Mormon has "evil": "Because he had done no ~~violence~~ **evil**." Tvedtnes notes that the Masoretic text reads

---

[18]Joseph Blenkinsopp, *Isaiah 40–55*, THE ANCHOR BIBLE (New York: Doubleday, 2002), 348.
[19]Ibid., 345.
[20]Ibid.
[21]Sidney B. Sperry, *Book of Mormon Compendium* (Salt Lake City: Bookcraft, 1968), 304.

mrmh which means both "evil" and "violence."[22] The KJV translation stresses the lack of reason for capital punishment, while the Book of Mormon emphasizes the suffering servant's purity (lack of evil).

Mosiah 14:10

> 10 Yet it pleased the Lord to bruise him; he hath put him to grief; when thou shalt make his soul an offering for sin he shall see his seed, he shall prolong his days, and the pleasure of the Lord shall prosper in his hand.

This verse creates a conceptual break in that it shifts from the past tense to the future. The past tense describes the suffering; the future describes the glory.[23] This verse views the suffering servant from the Lord's perspective. It indicates that the Lord allowed the suffering because it achieved a larger purpose. What is most fascinating here is the juxtaposition of the death imagery of verses 8 and 9 and the clearly life-affirming statement that the Lord "shall prolong his days . . . " even that "he shall see his seed. . . . " As with other contradictory statements in this passage, it was intended to be seen as a paradox. For instance, it would be hard to imagine how a grave among the wicked could also be a grave among the rich—unless one understands how Christ fulfilled that prophecy. Similarly, it is intended to be contradictory that there should be a death and a prolonging of days. The poetic attempt of this verse is to declare the resurrection. The resurrection is the part of the atonement that extends Jesus's days after death.

Who then are his "seed?" Sperry sees the "seed" as the future believers, partly based on Ether 3:14: "In me shall all mankind have life, and that eternally, even they who shall believe on my name; and they shall become my sons and my daughters."[24] In this reading, the verse predicts a resurrected Christ who witnesses "generations" of the faithful who follow him and have become his sons and daughters through faith on his name.

Mosiah 14:11

> 11 He shall see the travail of his soul, and shall be satisfied; by his knowledge shall my righteous servant justify many; for he shall bear their iniquities.

The two individuals referenced in this verse are the Most High God and Jesus, and God the Most High is the one who "shall see the travail" of Jesus's soul. The important phrase is "and shall be satisfied." The point of this verse is that the Most High God will accept Jesus's atoning sacrifice and that it will become possible for the sins of the world to be borne away.

Mosiah 14:12

> 12 Therefore will I divide him a portion with the great, and he shall divide the spoil with the strong; because he hath poured out his soul unto death; and he

---

[22]Tvedtnes, "Isaiah Textual Variants in the Book of Mormon," 93.
[23]V. Ludlow, *Isaiah: Prophet, Seer and Poet*, 455.
[24]Sperry, *Book of Mormon Compendium*, 304.

> was numbered with the transgressors; and he bore the sins of many, and made intercession for the transgressors.

Isaiah returns to literary contrasts to finish this section. Though the suffering servant dies among the wicked, he receives a reward with the great. Though he was numbered with the transgressors (here referring to his death, not to his personal qualities), he will be the salvation for those transgressors (indicating his great position above them). This is the ultimate resurrected and exalted Savior, who has taken his seat by God's side.

Comparison: Here is another number difference between the KJV ("the sin of many") and the Book of Mormon ("the sins of many"). This is another area where the underlying text is a collective and where either translation is correct.[25]

Text: There is no chapter break at this point in the 1830 edition. While we have seen breaks between cited text and a return to narrative, this occasion does not really fit that model for Mormon's chapter breaks. While Abinadi changes referents here, Mormon does not. Mormon is still working with copied text. The break will come when Mormon shifts to narrative from copying text (our chapter 16).

---

[25]Tvedtnes, "Isaiah Textual Variants in the Book of Mormon," 93.

Mosiah 15

Mosiah 15:1

1 And now Abinadi said unto them: I would that ye should understand that God himself shall come down among the children of men, and shall redeem his people.

Notice how the citation from Isaiah is bracketed in Abinadi's argument:

> Have they not said that God himself should come down among the children of men, and take upon him the form of man, and go forth in mighty power upon the face of the earth? Yea, and have they not said also that he should bring to pass the resurrection of the dead, and that he, himself, should be oppressed and afflicted? (Mosiah 13:34–35)

The quotation of Isaiah 53:1–12, constitutes Mosiah 14 .

> And now Abinadi said unto them: I would that ye should understand that God himself shall come down among the children of men, and shall redeem his people. (Mosiah 15:1)

Both leading into and coming out of the Isaiah proof text, Abinadi's message is that "God [Yahweh] himself" will come down and effect the atonement. While most LDS commentaries remain relatively silent on the phrase "God himself," that is nevertheless the driving point behind Abinadi's entire argument.[1] This phrasing is part of his counter-attack on the priests of Noah, particularly his discussion of the commandment to have no other gods. (See commentary accompanying Mosiah 12:35–37.)

Abinadi is facing priests who deny the Atoning Messiah while claiming to believe in the law of Moses. Abinadi is using that law against them, turning their assumptions back on them. While they assume that they have no other gods, Abinadi is showing them that they have essentially created a new god because they deny the revealed traits of the God of Moses.

For latter-day readers, this verse and the next few present some theological confusion because of Abinadi's apparent conflation of Jesus and God. The Nephite understanding was that the Jehovah would come to earth as the Messiah. Modern

---

[1]Reynolds and Sjodahl simply reiterate the statement without explanation. Most commentators save their discussion for the Father/Son text in verse 2. George Reynolds and Janne M. Sjodahl, *Commentary on the Book of Mormon*, edited and arranged by Philip C. Reynolds, 7 vols. (Salt Lake City: Deseret Book, 1955–61), 2:164. Rodney Turner does address the concept directly, however. See Rodney Turner, "Two Prophets: Abinadi and Alma," in *1 Nephi to Alma 29*, edited by Kent P. Jackson, STUDIES IN SCRIPTURE (Salt Lake City: Deseret Book, 1987), Vol. 7, 244–45.

readers read "Jehovah" as the premortal designation for Christ, and, hence, agree with the Nephites. (See "Excursus: The Nephite Understanding of God," following 1 Nephi 11 for more information on Yahweh as Father.)

Rhetoric: It is tempting to characterize Abinadi's use of Isaiah 53 as a commentary. It is not. Abinadi paraphrases and expands Isaiah. He uses the Isaiah text as his base, returning to it more frequently than Nephi and Jacob did when they used Isaiah. Abinadi uses Isaiah to further his own arguments; he does not explain Isaiah so that it may be understood.

Mosiah 15:2–4

> 2 And because he dwelleth in flesh he shall be called the Son of God, and having subjected the flesh to the will of the Father, being the Father and the Son—
> 3 The Father, because he was conceived by the power of God; and the Son, because of the flesh; thus becoming the Father and Son—
> 4 And they are one God, yea, the very Eternal Father of heaven and of earth.

Ancient Context: This passage is the logical continuation of Abinadi's assertion that God [Yahweh] himself would come among humankind. This particular explanation is necessitated by the title "Son of God." The "Son of God" title might lead some to believe that Jehovah and the Messiah were two different people, a misapprehension that would undermine Abinadi's contention that Yahweh himself was going to come among men. In other words, it is confusing to modern readers for the very reason Abinadi brought it up in the first place.

In Nephite theology, the Father/Son distinction that modern LDS readers make existed between the Most High God and Jehovah. The Father/Son relationship reference here is one between a heavenly Jehovah and an earthly being (the Messiah). The application of "father" to Jehovah and "son" to those who dwell on earth is unusual for modern readers, but it is both consistent and conceptually clear in Nephite theology. (See "Excursus: The Nephite Understanding of God," following 1 Nephi 11.)

Modern Context: Daniel Ludlow provides the following explanation of how this verse may be understood in the light of our modern understanding of the nature of the godhead:

> Jesus Christ is referred to several times in the Book of Mormon as both the Father and the Son. (Mosiah 15:1–4, Ether 3:14.) The question might well be asked: In what way (or in what sense) is Jesus Christ both the "Father" and the "Son"? The words Father and Son are titles rather than names; thus they may be used to refer to more than one person. The term Father may rightfully be used to refer to Jesus Christ in the following areas:
>
> 1. Jesus Christ is the Father of those who accept the gospel because it is through his atonement that the gospel is made active on this earth (Mosiah 5:7, 15:10–13; see also D&C 25:1, 39:1–4; and Ether 3).

2. Jesus Christ is the Father of this earth in the sense that he created this earth under the direction of his Father (Mosiah 15:4, 16:15; see also Alma 11:38–39, 3 Ne. 9:15, Ether 4:7, D&C 45:1).
3. Jesus Christ is the Father because of divine investiture of power—that is, Jesus Christ has been given the power to act for and represent his Father on this earth (read particularly D&C 93:2–4, 17).
4. Other dictionary definitions of Father that might be used to refer to Jesus Christ are as follows: "one to whom respect is due"; "one who cares as a father might"; "an originator, source, or prototype"; "one who claims or accepts responsibility."

The term Son also has varied meanings. Jesus Christ is rightfully referred to as the Son in the following senses: (1) Jesus Christ is the firstborn of God in the spirit (Col. 1:15–19, D&C 93:21); (2) Jesus Christ is the Only Begotten Son of God in the flesh (Jacob 4:5, 11; Alma 12:33–34; 13:5; John 1:18, 3:16); (3) Jesus Christ submitted his will to the will of his Father (Mosiah 15:2–7).[2]

Mosiah 15:5

> 5 And thus the flesh becoming subject to the Spirit, or the Son to the Father, being one God, suffereth temptation, and yieldeth not to the temptation, but suffereth himself to be mocked, and scourged, and cast out, and disowned by his people.

At this point Abinadi begins to restate Isaiah. The clarity of Abinadi's recasting of Isaiah suggests that he has a prophetic understanding of how the Messiah completed Isaiah's visual picture. (Nephi certainly understood these details, for he discusses them in 1 Nephi 11.) Abinadi reprises the suffering servant images from Isaiah and directly relates them to the Son of God[3]—the "God himself" who would come down. The scourging and casting out also reprise Isaiah (Isa. 53: 4–5).

Abinadi's addition to Isaiah is that the Messiah will not yield to temptation. The idea of an innocent Messiah may lie behind the Book of Mormon rephrasing for Isaiah 53:9 which stresses that the servant has done no evil, in contrast to the KJV's no "violence." (See commentary accompanying Mosiah 14:9.)

Mosiah 15:6–7

> 6 And after all this, after working many mighty miracles among the children of men, he shall be led, yea, even as Isaiah said, as a sheep before the shearer is dumb, so he opened not his mouth.
> 7 Yea, even so he shall be led, crucified, and slain, the flesh becoming subject even unto death, the will of the Son being swallowed up in the will of the Father.

---

[2]Daniel H. Ludlow, *A Companion to Your Study of the Book of Mormon* (Salt Lake City: Deseret Book, 1976), 183–84.

[3]Royal Skousen, ed., *The Printer's Manuscript of the Book of Mormon*, THE CRITICAL TEXT OF THE BOOK OF MORMON (Provo, Utah: Foundation for Ancient Research and Mormon Studies, 2001), Vol. 2, Part 1, 332, confirms the presence of the capitalization "Son of God." The original manuscript is not extant at this point. I suggest that a better transcription would be "son of God," to correspond better to the Nephite understanding of the realms in which Yahweh operated.

This paraphrase introduces the conclusions that Abinadi wants to draw from Isaiah. Abinadi recasts Isaiah to position his own interpretation in harmony with the revered brass plate prophet. The priests of Noah claim to believe in the brass plates; hence, they must believe Isaiah. If they believe Isaiah, they must also believe Abinadi.

At this point, Abinadi summarizes the trial and crucifixion of the Savior. Isaiah also includes the element of death (Isa. 53: 8–9/Mosiah 14:8–9) but detail of crucifixion is unique to the Nephite prophets.[4]

A phrase deserving of some notice is "the will of the Son being swallowed up in the will of the Father." We might easily read this phrase with our modern understanding that the Father and the Son are separate individuals and therefore assume that this phrase simply depicts proper filial behavior. However, in Abinadi's usage, both personages are the same, and it is the context that is different. Abinadi uses the phrase symbolically to indicate that the flesh submits to the spirit's will.

Mosiah 15:8–9

> 8 And thus God breaketh the bands of death, having gained the victory over death; giving the Son power to make intercession for the children of men—
> 9 Having ascended into heaven, having the bowels of mercy; being filled with compassion towards the children of men; standing betwixt them and justice; having broken the bands of death, taken upon himself their iniquity and their transgressions, having redeemed them, and satisfied the demands of justice.

Isaiah 53:10 (Mosiah 14:10) hinted at the resurrection. Abinadi explicates it clearly. He is now dealing with the resurrected Messiah who returns to the realm where he is known as the Father. This passage is the prelude to Abinadi's answer to the priests' question about Isaiah 52:7–10.

Isaiah briefly mentions the Messiah as an intercessor for transgressors (Isa. 53:12). Abinadi clarifies that text by explicitly describing the Messiah as the judge "standing betwixt [the children of men] and justice."

Text: While Abinadi's explanation of Isaiah makes sense in Abinadi's discourse, it does not follow the order of verses in Isaiah. This explanation expands Isaiah 53:12, while the following verse expands on Isaiah 53:10. That Abinadi would elucidate Isaiah but not carefully follow Isaiah's sequence merely highlights the use that Abinadi is making of Isaiah. The intent is not so much a commentary as a restatement. Abinadi artfully uses the phrases in Isaiah as a touchstone for the message he is delivering. In short, this passage is not a commentary on Isaiah but a commentary on the priests of Noah, using Isaiah as a base text.

---

[4]The crucifixion is stated explicitly in 1 Nephi 19:13, 2 Nephi 6:9, 10:3, 25:13, sources that predate Abinadi and to which he must have had some access. Since it is unlikely that Abinadi had access to the small plates, we may suppose that this information also appeared on the large plates which would have served as Abinadi's source.

Mosiah 15:10

> 10 And now I say unto you, who shall declare his generation? Behold, I say unto you, that when his soul has been made an offering for sin he shall see his seed. And now what say ye? And who shall be his seed?

We saw in the discussion of Mosiah 14:10/Isaiah 53:10 that Isaiah's use of "generation" can be seen in several ways. It may look back to ancestors, it may be a declaration about his contemporaries, or it may point to his descendants. Despite this range of possibilities, however, Abinadi clearly reads this instance of "generation" as descendants. He has powerful reasons for wanting to do so. By declaring that this "generation" parallels the Messiah's seeing his seed, he can focus his discourse on that seed.

Abinadi may obliquely relate sowing the seed to publishing peace. He ends this part of the discourse with a return to the original question he was asked. By the time he returns, "seed" and "publishing peace" have the same meaning. Perhaps in Abinadi's language, some underlying word play relates sowing to publishing. Publishing might be seen as similar to planting seeds by broadcasting them on the ground, though this is not the method for planting the Mesoamerican staples of corn and beans.

Mosiah 15:11

> 11 Behold I say unto you, that whosoever has heard the words of the prophets, yea, all the holy prophets who have prophesied concerning the coming of the Lord—I say unto you, that all those who have hearkened unto their words, and believed that the Lord would redeem his people, and have looked forward to that day for a remission of their sins, I say unto you, that these are his seed, or they are the heirs of the kingdom of God.

The agricultural imagery of the process of growth is fused with the biological process of fathering a child. The seed is planted, and the planter becomes father to the new growth. It is the prophets who create the conditions whereby a human being may become the "seed" or children of the Father. Abinadi has declared that the prophets have declared the Atoning Messiah (Mosiah 13:33–35). Their teachings prepared the people for the Messiah's mortal mission. When the people are thus prepared, they become the fallow ground for growing this seed. Abinadi's conclusion that they are "heirs of the kingdom of God" depends on the father-child relationship that he declares is created through this process. The "seed" are heirs because they are children of their father, and inheritance is the children's right.

Mosiah 15:12–13

> 12 For these are they whose sins he has borne; these are they for whom he has died, to redeem them from their transgressions. And now, are they not his seed?

> 13 Yea, and are not the prophets, every one that has opened his mouth to prophesy, that has not fallen into transgression, I mean all the holy prophets ever since the world began? I say unto you that they are his seed.

Rhetoric: The prophets certainly accept the Atoning Messiah's mission. It is they who know it best. This point is critical in Abinadi's argument. He must answer the question about those who publish peace, and for him the obvious answer is the prophets. However, since Abinadi's real purpose is to hammer home the priests' apostasy in denying the Messiah, he must clearly define the prophets as believers. Then, when he returns to the original question asked of him, his rhetorical gun is fully loaded with powerful ammunition. He can now focus all of the priests' agenda against them and their greatest heresy.

Mosiah 15:14–17

> 14 And these are they who have published peace, who have brought good tidings of good, who have published salvation; and said unto Zion: Thy God reigneth!
> 15 And O how beautiful upon the mountains were their feet!
> 16 And again, how beautiful upon the mountains are the feet of those that are still publishing peace!
> 17 And again, how beautiful upon the mountains are the feet of those who shall hereafter publish peace, yea, from this time henceforth and forever!

Rhetoric: Abinadi finally comes to the point of answering the question earlier asked of him by expanding on Isaiah 52:7/Mosiah 12:21. He recites and expounds the theme of that verse so that it is clear that he is answering the question, but that he is doing so in the light of the rest of his discourse. The original verse reads: "How beautiful upon the mountains are the feet of him that bringeth good tidings; that publisheth peace; that bringeth good tidings of good; that publisheth salvation; that saith unto Zion, Thy God reigneth" (Mosiah 12:21/Isaiah 52:7).

Abinadi's connection between his discourse and this verse rests on three assumptions: the idea that "feet" represent an action;[5] that Isaiah's trilogy of publishing peace, good tidings, and salvation are all terms for the same thing; and that this peace/good tidings/salvation is the atonement through the Messiah who is to come.

It is particularly important that Abinadi quotes the end of Isaiah 52:7 (Mosiah 12:21): "Thy God reigneth." Since Abinadi's point has been that God himself

---

[5]Bruce J. Malina, *The New Testament World: Insights from Cultural Anthropology* (Atlanta, Ga.: John Knox Press, 1981), 61, discusses the Mediterranean culture area's tendency to use parts of the body to represent either "inmost reactions (eyes-heart) . . . language (mouth-ears) and/or outwardly realized . . . activity (hands-feet)." In this case, the use of "feet" would represent a coming action. Claus Westermann applies this concept to this particular verse: "North comments laconically, 'but feet are hardly beautiful.' But this fails to see that 'the beautiful' means something different in Hebrew thought than it does for us. The beautiful is something that comes about; and in 52:7 is a particularly clear example of this idea of it. The messenger's feet are not objectively beautiful. Their beauty consists in their intimation of the beauty of the coming of the tidings; and this is beautiful because it awakens jubilation." Claus Westermann, *Isaiah 40–66* (Philadelphia: Westminster Press, 1969), 251.

should come down to atone, he interprets Isaiah's declaration as directly referring to the Messiah. For Abinadi, Isaiah's statement is a direct declaration of the Messiah as God and of the triumph of this God who is the Messiah.

Not only can the priests not properly keep the law of Moses without teaching about the coming Messiah, but they do not even understand that the verses they are using to trap Abinadi declare the very Messiah they deny.[6]

Mosiah 15:18

> 18 And behold, I say unto you, this is not all. For O how beautiful upon the mountains are the feet of him that bringeth good tidings, that is the founder of peace, yea, even the Lord, who has redeemed his people; yea, him who has granted salvation unto his people;

Now Abinadi expands the definition of those who publish peace. It is not simply the prophets who declare the coming of the Atoning Messiah but the Messiah himself who is the ultimate publisher of peace. Where the prophets merely speak of coming good news, the Messiah actually provides (publishes) salvation. In his life it is an accomplished action—not a promised action.

Mosiah 15:19

> 19 For were it not for the redemption which he hath made for his people, which was prepared from the foundation of the world, I say unto you, were it not for this, all mankind must have perished.

How does Messiah publish peace? He redeems his people. This is such an essential act that without it humankind "must have perished." The priests cannot claim salvation through the law of Moses because, even with the law, there is no salvation without the atonement. Abinadi is reiterating the point he began in Mosiah 12:31 when he asked the priests if they believed that salvation came through the law of Moses. (They answered affirmatively [v. 32]). Abinadi has stressed that point to the priests' condemnation. They have said they believe that salvation can come through the law. Abinadi boldly declares that even with the law there is no salvation except through the Messiah's atonement.

Mosiah 15:20

> 20 But behold, the bands of death shall be broken, and the Son reigneth, and hath power over the dead; therefore, he bringeth to pass the resurrection of the dead.

Abinadi's next allusion to and expansion of Isaiah comes from the idea of the Messiah seeing his seed after death. Abinadi has first used that phrase (Mosiah 14:10/

---

[6]Modern readers may understand "Thy God reigneth" as God the Father. However, that would weaken Abinadi's logic. All of his rhetorical direction has led to this point where he can add his prophetic declaration to Isaiah's and declare the Atoning Messiah as God himself. (See Mosiah 15:1 and accompanying commentary. See also "Excursus: The Nephite Understanding of God," following 1 Nephi 11.)

Isa. 53:10) to describe who the seed are (v. 13). Now he uses a contextual implication of that phrase to emphasize the resurrection of the Atoning Messiah.

Mosiah 15:21

> 21 And there cometh a resurrection, even a first resurrection; yea, even a resurrection of those that have been, and who are, and who shall be, even until the resurrection of Christ—for so shall he be called.

Rhetoric: Abinadi is about to get very personal. While we might read these verses simply as describing the resurrection, in the context of Abinadi's discourse, this passage is a direct accusation against the priests. Abinadi's entire discourse has turned the priests' accusations back on them. From this point to the end of our chapter 16 is Abinadi's final prophetic condemnation of the priests.

Scripture: Abinadi first uses the Messiah's resurrection as the beginning point for the resurrection of all of humanity. Isaiah's text allows only for the resurrection of the Messiah, so Abinadi is relying here on other teachings, such as those of Lehi (2 Ne. 2:8) and Jacob (2 Ne. 9:6). Since Abinadi does not argue the point, he must assume that the priests of Noah understand that the resurrection is for all, and not just of the Messiah.

While resurrection is for all, it nevertheless has a component in it that divides the righteous from the unrighteous. Both the righteous and the unrighteous are resurrected, but the nature of the resurrection differentiates between the righteous and the unrighteous. The first resurrection is for the righteous and the second for the unrighteous. True, Abinadi does not make it clear that the resurrection requires Yahweh's final judgment, but that point is implied.

Mosiah 15:22–23

> 22 And now, the resurrection of all the prophets, and all those that have believed in their words, or all those that have kept the commandments of God, shall come forth in the first resurrection; therefore, they are the first resurrection.
> 23 They are raised to dwell with God who has redeemed them; thus they have eternal life through Christ, who has broken the bands of death.

Rhetoric: Since there are two resurrections, first of the righteous and second of the unrighteous, Abinadi can use those labels to define the types of people who will be resurrected. Pointedly, he says that the prophets, who have all testified of the Atoning Messiah (Mosiah 13:33), will take part in this first resurrection. Abinadi is emphasizing that those prophets—those who have published peace; those who have testified of the Atoning Messiah—are the righteous.

Mosiah 15:24–25

> 24 And these are those who have part in the first resurrection; and these are they that have died before Christ came, in their ignorance, not having salvation declared unto them. And thus the Lord bringeth about the

> restoration of these; and they have a part in the first resurrection, or have eternal life, being redeemed by the Lord.
> 25 And little children also have eternal life.

The prophets are the first to arise in the resurrection. Even if this is not technically accurate, it is symbolically apt. The prophets are quintessentially righteous. Abinadi emphasizes that there two classes of people will also be saved with the righteous, even though they did not believe.

The first are those who "have died before Christ came" and who were therefore ignorant of his coming mission. This is important, not only because it provides the theological assurance that Yahweh is just and will not condemn his children for what they did not know, but also because Abinadi and the priests are among those who are living before "Christ came." Abinadi is speaking of people now alive (including his audience) who might be saved. First are the prophets (and by implication those who believe as they do) and second are those who do not believe because they have not heard. All these are saved. Next Abinadi adds "little children." Once again there is theological comfort for us in knowing this, but Abinadi's purpose in mentioning this is not to comfort future generations, but rather to condemn a current one.

Mosiah 15:26

> 26 But behold, and fear, and tremble before God, for ye ought to tremble; for the Lord redeemeth none such that rebel against him and die in their sins; yea, even all those that have perished in their sins ever since the world began, that have wilfully rebelled against God, that have known the commandments of God, and would not keep them; these are they that have no part in the first resurrection.

Abinadi pulls the trigger. While the ignorant and even "incapable" children will be saved with the righteous, the priests of Noah will not because they are in a group that is not among the righteous of the first resurrection. They are not believers, but they are also not ignorant. They "rebel against him and die in their sins." Abinadi knows that the priests understand the Atoning Messiah's mission, evidenced at several points in the text where Abinadi assumes their understanding. He is not preaching new information to them but reminding them of a doctrine against which they have "willfully rebelled."

Abinadi began his discourse by noting: "Have ye done all this? I say unto you, Nay, ye have not. And have ye taught this people that they should do all these things? I say unto you, Nay, ye have not" (Mosiah 12:37). Now he declares that the unrighteous are they "that have known the commandments of God, and would not keep them." Abinadi accuses the priests of Noah of the very sin of which he stands accused.

Mosiah 15:27

> 27 Therefore ought ye not to tremble? For salvation cometh to none such; for the Lord hath redeemed none such; yea, neither can the Lord redeem such; for he cannot deny himself; for he cannot deny justice when it has its claim.

In Mosiah 12:32 the priests declare that salvation comes through the law of Moses and that they preach that law. The priests would therefore assume that they were saved. Abinadi makes it clear that their belief not only will not save them but also that their particular form of living that law (denying the Messiah) will condemn them.

Mosiah 15:28–31

> 28 And now I say unto you that the time shall come that the salvation of the Lord shall be declared to every nation, kindred, tongue, and people.
> 29 Yea, Lord, thy watchmen shall lift up their voice; with the voice together shall they sing; for they shall see eye to eye, when the Lord shall bring again Zion.
> 30 Break forth into joy, sing together, ye waste places of Jerusalem; for the Lord hath comforted his people, he hath redeemed Jerusalem.
> 31 The Lord hath made bare his holy arm in the eyes of all the nations; and all the ends of the earth shall see the salvation of our God.

Rhetoric: To this point, Abinadi still had not answered the implicit questions posed to him by the final three verses of Isaiah 52. He now focuses on that passage. With the salvation of humankind as the backdrop, Abinadi interprets the joy of Zion as the salvation that has come through the Messiah. He sets up this interpretation in verse 28, and then simply repeats the verses. In his context, they now become self-evident. Abinadi does not deal with most of these verses directly, but rather extracts the phrase "see eye to eye" from verse 29 to form the basis of his concluding declaration (our chap. 16).

Text: The 1830 edition does not break a chapter here. This break awkwardly divides Abinadi's discourse from his conclusion. Chapter 16 should be read with Chapter 15.

Mosiah 16

Mosiah 16:1

> 1 And now, it came to pass that after Abinadi had spoken these words he stretched forth his hand and said: The time shall come when all shall see the salvation of the Lord; when every nation, kindred, tongue, and people shall see eye to eye and shall confess before God that his judgments are just.

The textual base for this part of Abinadi's discourse is: "Yea, Lord, thy watchmen shall lift up their voice; with the voice together shall they sing; for they shall see eye to eye, when the Lord shall bring again Zion" (Mosiah 15:29). From this verse he extracts the phrase "see eye to eye" and describes what they will be seeing. Of course, what they see is the resurrected Messiah who is the embodiment of salvation. The Messiah who brings Zion is the Messiah who will have brought salvation. This Messiah may sit in judgment precisely because such judgment flows from the salvation he has wrought.

Mosiah 16:2

> 2 And then shall the wicked be cast out, and they shall have cause to howl, and weep, and wail, and gnash their teeth; and this because they would not hearken unto the voice of the Lord; therefore the Lord redeemeth them not.

The emphasis on this part of the verse is the result of judgment. In this case, it is the fate of the wicked to "weep, and wail, and gnash their teeth." Why do the wicked suffer this punishment? It is because "they would not hearken unto the voice of the Lord; therefore the Lord redeemeth them not." In the context of Abinadi's argument, this conclusion is inevitable. Those who are not redeemed are those who choose not to listen to the gospel of the Messiah. Specifically, those who are not redeemed (who shall weep, and wail, and gnash their teeth) are Noah's priests who have denied the Messiah.

Mosiah 16:3

> 3 For they are carnal and devilish, and the devil has power over them; yea, even that old serpent that did beguile our first parents, which was the cause of their fall; which was the cause of all mankind becoming carnal, sensual, devilish, knowing evil from good, subjecting themselves to the devil.

Those who knowingly reject the Atoning Messiah (the priests of Noah) are "carnal [and] devilish." While we do not know if Abinadi has specifically accused the priests of succumbing to the temptations of the flesh, certainly Mormon characterized them that way (Mosiah 11, esp. v. 14). If Abinadi had not made a prior accusation, he is probably articulating a perception common among the people who did not embrace Noah's reforms.

As Abinadi builds to his climax, he reinforces the Messiah's mission from yet another angle. Since the issue at hand is the requirement that even the Mosaic law recognizes this Atoning Messiah, Abinadi begins with another point of agreement between himself and the priests: the fall of Adam and Eve. As part of the text on the brass plates, this doctrine must be one that the priests believe and teach.

Abinadi points out, not the fall from Yahweh's grace, but the fall from innocence before Yahweh. He emphasizes the state of sin into which Adam and all humanity fell. First, Abinadi notes that, after the fall, Adam (and humanity) knew good from evil. Such knowledge is an essential component of his argument, because Abinadi has already stressed the salvation of innocents (Mosiah 15:24–25). Adam and humankind have fallen into a state of knowledge. Being under the sway of sin, they are also under the influence of Satan.

Mosiah 16:4

> 4 Thus all mankind were lost; and behold, they would have been endlessly lost were it not that God redeemed his people from their lost and fallen state.

The fall created a gulf between Yahweh and his people. Nephi described the reason for this gulf: "But behold, I say unto you, the kingdom of God is not filthy, and there cannot any unclean thing enter into the kingdom of God" (1 Ne. 15:34). The fall of humankind creates a condition which requires resolution. If nothing is done, humanity will be irretrievably lost. Once they have sinned, they are forever cut off from Yahweh. Yahweh would send his children to this earth, but they would unavoidably be lost and subject to the devil.

Of course, such an outcome is inconceivable, so a plan to redeem humankind must be part of Yahweh's understanding from the beginning. Indeed, the Messiah as the lamb slain from the foundation of the world (Rev. 13:8) is the sacrifice who removes the sin from all the world and allows reconciliation. It is in symbolically enacting this event that the performances of the law of Moses become a type of this Messiah who is to come. In fact, Abinadi argues that the law is a type for the Messiah (Mosiah 13:10).

Mosiah 16:5

> 5 But remember that he that persists in his own carnal nature, and goes on in the ways of sin and rebellion against God, remaineth in his fallen state and the devil hath all power over him. Therefore, he is as though there was no redemption made, being an enemy to God; and also is the devil an enemy to God.

Yahweh-Messiah's atonement is effective only for a certain portion of humanity. Specifically excluded is "he that persists in his own carnal nature, and goes on in the ways of sin and rebellion against God"—in other words, the priests of Noah.

Mosiah 16:6

> 6 And now if Christ had not come into the world, speaking of things to come as though they had already come, there could have been no redemption.

Text: Abinadi speaks as if the Messiah had already come, when his birth lies in Abinadi's future. As Daniel Ludlow explains: "Often when ancient prophets would speak of future events or prophecies, they would use a verb form sometimes called the 'prophetic past tense.' That is, they would talk about the future as though the event had already happened."[1] Here Abinadi explains that he is "speaking of things to come as though they had already come." He does this not only because his intimate knowledge of the prophecies makes the event seem real and already accomplished, but also because his argument requires that the atonement be accomplished. The divine promise of the future atonement is sufficient to supply the benefits in Abinadi's present. Neither Abinadi nor anyone else must wait for the atonement to be able to repent.

Mosiah 16:7–8

> 7 And if Christ had not risen from the dead, or have broken the bands of death that the grave should have no victory, and that death should have no sting, there could have been no resurrection.
> 8 But there is a resurrection, therefore the grave hath no victory, and the sting of death is swallowed up in Christ.

These two verses should be read together. They form an opposed pair, with the first declaring the situation had there been no atonement, and the second declaring those consequences void because there is an atonement. The return to the theme of the resurrection is a return to a thematic element in Isaiah.

Mosiah 16:9

> 9 He is the light and the life of the world; yea, a light that is endless, that can never be darkened; yea, and also a life which is endless, that there can be no more death.

---

[1]Daniel Ludlow, *A Companion to Your Study of the Old Testament*, 301. See also Donald W. Parry, "Hebraisms and Other Ancient Peculiarities in the Book of Mormon," in *Echoes and Evidences of the Book of Mormon*, edited by Donald W. Parry, Daniel C. Peterson, and John W. Welch (Provo, Utah: Foundation for Ancient Research and Mormon Studies, 2002), 164, discussed above accompanying Mosiah 13:32.

[No author identified], "Hebrew Tenses," http://www.iclnet.org/pub/resources/text/m.sion/hebrtens.htm (accessed March 2007), notes:

> There is no such thing as "tense" in biblical Hebrew. (Modern Hebrew, on the other hand, does have tenses.) Biblical Hebrew is not a "tense" language. Modern grammarians recognize that it is an "aspectual" language. This means that the same form of a verb can be translated as either past, present, or future depending on the context and various grammatical cues. The most well known grammatical cue is the "vav-consecutive" that makes an imperfective verb to refer to the past.
>
> Therefore it is wrong to say that Isaiah 53 or other prophecies are in the "past tense." Biblical Hebrew has no tenses. There are many examples of what is wrongly called the "past tense" form (properly called "the perfective" or "perfect") being used for future time.
>
> This fact was recognized by the medieval commentators as well as by modern grammarians.

The article supplies several examples.

The resurrection from death is absolute. In Yahweh-Messiah is "a life which is endless, that there can be no more death." The mission of the Atoning Messiah is required, but only once.

Mosiah 16:10

> 10 Even this mortal shall put on immortality, and this corruption shall put on incorruption, and shall be brought to stand before the bar of God, to be judged of him according to their works whether they be good or whether they be evil-

Abinadi must next make clear the distinction between resurrection and salvation. Resurrection is a gift given to all. Yahweh-Messiah has broken the bands of death for all. The condemnation of the priests does not come from their denial of the resurrection, but from their lack of understanding the quality of that resurrection: the resurrection of the righteous or the wicked.

Reference: This text is clearly dependent upon 1 Corinthians 15:53–54: "For this corruptible must put on incorruption, and this mortal must put on immortality. So when this corruptible shall have put on incorruption, and this mortal shall have put on immortality, then shall be brought to pass the saying that is written, Death is swallowed up in victory."[2]

How can Abinadi quote Paul? The answer is that he clearly cannot, because Paul's text comes more than a century later and literally half a world away. The text owes its parallels to the similarity of concepts; when Joseph Smith recognized those similarities, he couched his translation of Abinadi in Paul's language. This same phenomenon has occurred in other places, where Joseph's familiarity with the New Testament produces text that alludes to or quotes from the New Testament.

Mosiah 16:11–12

> 11 If they be good, to the resurrection of endless life and happiness; and if they be evil, to the resurrection of endless damnation, being delivered up to the devil, who hath subjected them, which is damnation—
> 12 Having gone according to their own carnal wills and desires; having never called upon the Lord while the arms of mercy were extended towards them; for the arms of mercy were extended towards them, and they would not; they being warned of their iniquities and yet they would not depart from them; and they were commanded to repent and yet they would not repent.

There are two resurrections, one to "endless life and happiness: and the other to "endless damnation."[3] Those subjected to endless damnation have been carnal and

---

[2]The corruptible/incorruptible vocabulary occurs several times in the Book of Mormon: 2 Ne. 2:11, 9:7; Mosiah 16:10; Alma 5:15, 40:2, and 41:4.

[3]The Lord has clarified the meaning of "endless damnation" in modern times. Doctrine and Covenants 19:10–12 states:

> For, behold, the mystery of godliness, how great is it! For, behold, I am endless, and the punishment which is given from my hand is endless punishment, for Endless is my name. Wherefore—

have "never called upon the Lord." Abinadi makes it clear that these people have had the opportunity to accept the redeeming Messiah, but have chosen not to.

Mosiah 16:13

> 13 And now, ought ye not to tremble and repent of your sins, and remember that only in and through Christ ye can be saved?

Abinadi repeats his question: "Ought ye not to tremble and repent of your sins?" Like previous parts of the discourse, he aims this discussion of the fate of the wicked directly at the priests. Their particular sin is emphasized in Abinadi's description of how to avoid this fate: "Remember that only in and through Christ ye can be saved." While the entire discourse damns the priests, it does so while holding out the option of repentance. Indeed, the major event that comes from this discourse is a repentant priest, Alma.

Mosiah 16:14–15

> 14 Therefore, if ye teach the law of Moses, also teach that it is a shadow of those things which are to come—
> 15 Teach them that redemption cometh through Christ the Lord, who is the very Eternal Father. Amen.

Abinadi ends his discourse by returning to the beginning. If the priests of Noah are to truly teach of the Mosaic law, they must also teach about the Atoning Messiah, "Christ the Lord, who is the very Eternal Father." The emphasis on the Eternal Father reprises another of Abinadi's arguments; that the Messiah is "God himself [who] shall come down among the children of men, and shall redeem his people" (Mosiah 15:1).

Text: This concludes Abinadi's discourse. Mormon created a break at this place because he has completed his quotation from Abinadi and now returns to narrative.

Endless punishment is God's punishment.

Mosiah 17

Mosiah 17:1

> 1 And now it came to pass that when Abinadi had finished these sayings, that the king commanded that the priests should take him and cause that he should be put to death.

Having finished his message, the powerful protection of the Spirit has withdrawn. Abinadi may now be apprehended, and Noah condemns him to death.

Text: The chapter break occurs at this point because Mormon shifts from citation to description. Abinadi's speech was important, so Mormon included it in its entirety, but the narrative is significant only in describing the aftermath of Abinadi's speech.

Mosiah 17:2

> 2 But there was one among them whose name was Alma, he also being a descendant of Nephi. And he was a young man, and he believed the words which Abinadi had spoken, for he knew concerning the iniquity which Abinadi had testified against them; therefore he began to plead with the king that he would not be angry with Abinadi, but suffer that he might depart in peace.

Mormon introduces us to Alma, one of the most influential figures in Nephite history. This verse tells us only that he is a descendant of Nephi, and was "one among them," meaning that he was not only counted among Noah's priests but that he was of a mind with them. The most perplexing comment is that "he was a young man." According to the chronology worked out and discussed accompanying Mosiah 7:1, Alma would have been born in 159 B.C. and died at age eighty-two in 77 B.C. According to this same chronology, Mosiah_1 left the city of Nephi in 148 B.C. and Zeniff left Zarahemla in approximately 143 B.C. Alma would have been eleven when Mosiah_1 left the city of Nephi and would have returned with Zeniff when he was sixteen. Thus, he would have been thirty-six when Zeniff died and Noah took power. Abinadi's mission could not reasonably have occurred much before five years later, and ten years seems more likely, considering the cultural changes that occurred, thus making Alma forty or forty-five. How could Mormon have called Alma "young"? Perhaps Mormon never bothered to work out the dates and his sources were incomplete. We may simply be seeing a mistaken assumption on Mormon's part that only a comparatively young man could have achieved Alma's great feats.

Mormon also seems to have access to information that could not have been in the texts concerning this immediate story, for example, that Alma was a descendant of Nephi. Did Mormon mean that Alma was of Nephi's direct lineage, or does he simply mean that Alma was a Nephite? The first meaning requires a very specific genealogy, which Mormon never acknowledges but which probably was recorded in some document, most likely dating from the Zarahemla period. However, it is also possible that by "Nephite" Mormon meant that Alma was a lineal Nephite rather than a descendant of one of the people from Zarahemla or the "others" who would have entered into the Nephite culture before this time.

That Alma was "one among them"—one of the priests confronting Abinadi—is clear because he was present for Abinadi's sermon. He therefore could not have been Zeniff's priest, since Noah "put down all the priests that had been consecrated by his father, and consecrated new ones in their stead" (Mosiah 11:5). Rather, Alma must have been a follower of Noah's reforms (or apostasy). Alma required conversion, and Abinadi's discourse and the witness of the Spirit converted him. The message reached Alma even though it did not reach any other priest (as far as we know from the text). Perhaps Alma's patience with his own son later in life had roots in his own conversion experience. He would clearly understand how one might be deceived—that adopting attractive cultural changes could lead to religious change. He would also clearly understand how one could be turned completely by an experience with Yahweh's power. He would understand his son better than his son would know.

Abinadi comes to the city of Lehi-Nephi to preach, apparently with miniscule results, although we do not know what influence he may have had on those who eventually follow Alma out to the wilderness. Abinadi comes before the court of Noah, and preaches so powerfully that they are unable to lay a hand on him. Why is this message so important that it must be delivered? The message had no impact on Noah. The message had no impact on any known priest except Alma. Alma may have been in a state of apostasy at the time, but he would prove to be one of the most important figures in Nephite history. It appears that Abinadi was sent on a mission that spelled certain personal doom because Yahweh needed to touch one man: Alma. Is there any more powerful case for Yahweh's concern with an individual?

As with Christ's painful crucifixion, the glory of God's purposes can meet with terrible human reactions. God sends the messenger to deliver the message. It is base humanity that kills the prophets.

Mosiah 17:3–4

> 3 But the king was more wroth, and caused that Alma should be cast out from among them, and sent his servants after him that they might slay him.
> 4 But he fled from before them and hid himself that they found him not. And he being concealed for many days did write all the words which Abinadi had spoken.

By pleading for Abinadi, Alma also became an enemy to Noah, whose first command was banishment and whose second was assassination. It is not clear why

Noah changed his mind, since he could have ordered Alma executed on the spot. Perhaps Noah wished to distance himself from the murder.

Redaction: Alma finds a way to avoid those who searched for him. While in hiding, he records Abinadi's words, and this record was probably Mormon's main source for Abinadi's defense before the priests. The positive statements about Abinadi's effect on the court and the description of Yahweh's power seem logical in Alma's record but odd in Noah's official record.

Nevertheless, Mormon is using more than one account here, since he recorded events that occurred immediately after Alma's banishment. There is no reasonable way that Noah's court records would have ended up in Alma's hands. The information describing what happened after Alma's banishment was probably oral and came from someone in the court, but not a member of the priests. Perhaps one of the guards also believed and eventually joined with Alma and then provided the more complete account. Perhaps Limhi's records filled in the gap for Mormon.

Text: Robert J. Matthews notes:

> Although Alma wrote "all" of Abinadi's words, Mormon did not include all of them in the abridged account in Mosiah 11–17. Mosiah 12:18–19 states that Abinadi answered all the questions of the priests, yet the record deals only with the questions about Isaiah 52:7–10. Furthermore, the prophet Mormon later spoke of the "sorceries, and witchcrafts, and magics" in the land, "fulfilling . . . all the words of Abinadi" (Morm. 1:19). The Book of Mormon record contains no such prophecy of Abinadi.[1]

Mosiah 17:5

> 5 And it came to pass that the king caused that his guards should surround Abinadi and take him; and they bound him and cast him into prison.

Because Abinadi was first imprisoned rather than being executed on the spot suggests a parallel with Alma's banishment, followed by the order for his execution. Perhaps there was a legal or religious prohibition against killing in the court itself.

Mosiah 17:6–8

> 6 And after three days, having counseled with his priests, he caused that he should again be brought before him.
> 7 And he said unto him: Abinadi, we have found an accusation against thee, and thou art worthy of death.
> 8 For thou hast said that God himself should come down among the children of men; and now, for this cause thou shalt be put to death unless thou wilt recall all the words which thou hast spoken evil concerning me and my people.

Abinadi himself had predicted this inevitable outcome (Mosiah 13:3, 7–10). The official charge was probably blasphemy. It is couched in the terms that Abinadi insisted on: that Yahweh himself should come down among men. Noah and the

---

[1]Robert J. Matthews, "Abinadi," in *Book of Mormon Reference Companion*, edited by Dennis L. Largey (Salt Lake City: Deseret Book, 2003), 23.

priests must deny this assertion or admit that they had been teaching false doctrine. Ironically, Abinadi was sentenced to death on the very charge that he had leveled against Noah and his priests.

Why did Noah give Abinadi the chance to recant? Perhaps he was uneasy about the possibility that Abinadi, as a martyr, would become a rallying point for religious opposition to Noah. If Abinadi recanted, then the threat would be eliminated.

Mosiah 17:9–10

> 9 Now Abinadi said unto him: I say unto you, I will not recall the words which I have spoken unto you concerning this people, for they are true; and that ye may know of their surety I have suffered myself that I have fallen into your hands.
> 10 Yea, and I will suffer even until death, and I will not recall my words, and they shall stand as a testimony against you. And if ye slay me ye will shed innocent blood, and this shall also stand as a testimony against you at the last day.

Abinadi refuses this option and declares that his death will testify against Noah (and his priests). In verse 9 Abinadi clearly declares that, while Noah's men may have physically brought him to the court, he came intentionally and voluntarily. The result is to stress that he understood his mission to be his sermon before the priests which converted Alma and condemned the rest.

Mosiah 17:11–12

> 11 And now king Noah was about to release him, for he feared his word; for he feared that the judgments of God would come upon him.
> 12 But the priests lifted up their voices against him, and began to accuse him, saying: He has reviled the king. Therefore the king was stirred up in anger against him, and he delivered him up that he might be slain.

Noah is shaken by Abinadi's words and the power of the Spirit. The condemnation frightens him to the point that he is on the verge of withdrawing his own decree. But the priests do not allow it. As the focus of Abinadi's accusations was that they had taught false doctrine, they had the greatest hatred for Abinadi. They push Noah by reminding him that Abinadi has spoken against the king. The belief in the king's divinity, common throughout most of the ancient world,[2] made Abinadi's words tantamount to blasphemy. By appealing to Noah's pride (and perhaps subtly reminding him that his own status was challenged), they assured Abinadi's execution.

Mosiah 17:13

13 And it came to pass that they took him and bound him, and scourged his skin with faggots, yea, even unto death.

---

[2]Mircea Eliade, *Patterns in Comparative Religion*, translated by Rosemary Sheed (New York: Meridian, 1963), 63, 65.

Translation: This verse is somewhat confusing because it suggests that faggots were used to strike Abinadi (the meaning of scourge). A faggot is a bundle of sticks, usually fuel for a fire. Verse 14 clarifies that Abinadi died by fire. However, "scourge" on the face of it represents a blow to the skin, not the effect of a flame on the skin.

There are two possible explanations for this passage. Some evidence in Mesoamerican documents shows that beating with firebrands was a traditional punishment for certain crimes. The Codex Mendoza is a richly illustrated ethnographic record of Aztec daily life that was produced in Mexico City around 1541. One of the scenes painted in that codex depicts a youth being beaten with sticks with an attached label reading *tlequahuitl*, or "firewood." The translators render the term "burning firebrand:" "Masters of youths [*telpuchtlato*]: the two *telpuchtlato*, who are masters who govern youths, punished a youth who had been living with a woman by beating him with burning firebrands."[3]

A second possibility is that "scourged" is a scribal error. Royal Skousen makes the general observation: "Very often in my work on the critical text of the Book of Mormon, I have discovered cases where the text reads inappropriately. Book of Mormon researchers have typically attempted to find some circumstance or interpretation to explain a difficult reading, but in many cases I have found that difficult readings are actually the result of simple scribal errors."[4] Thus, he discourages efforts at complicated or far-fetched interpretations of terms that may fall in this category.

Commenting on "scourged" in Mosiah 17:3, Skousen notes the incongruity of verse 13's implied beating with the clear evidence for death by burning in all other texts. He next notes that Oliver Cowdery frequently misspelled "scourge" as "scorge" in several locations. He therefore argues for scribal error: "One possibility is that when Oliver Cowdery came to copy this passage into the printer's manuscript, he mistakenly read scorched as scourged. This misreading would have been facilitated by Oliver's frequent misspelling of scourge(d) as scorge(d)."[5]

Skousen also notes that the same type of scribal error might have entered the printed text in another way: "Another possibility is that this transmission error occurred during the dictation of the text. In this instance the scribe for the original manuscript might have misheard Joseph Smith's dictated scorched as scourged. Note, in particular, the similarity in sound between the final ch and j sounds in scorch and scourge."[6]

Skousen's third possibility for scribal error comes from the New Testament influence that we have already seen in multiple locations in the translation of the Book of Mormon:

---

[3]Frances F. Berdan and Patricia Rieff Anawalt, eds. and trans., *The Essential Codex Mendoza*, Vols. 2 and 4 of the full edition, bound together (Berkeley: University of California Press, 1997), 4:131. See also Brant Gardner, "Scourging with Faggots," *Insights* 21, no. 7 (2001): 2–3.

[4]Royal Skousen, "'Scourged' vs. 'Scorched' in Mosiah 17:13," *Insights* 22, no. 3 (2002): 2–3.

[5]Ibid., 3.

[6]Ibid.

> We should also note one additional factor that may have led scorched to be replaced by scourged—namely the parallel sentence construction between John 19:1 and the current text for Mosiah 17:13:
>
> Pilate . . . took Jesus . . . and scourged him. . . .
> They took him and bound him and scourged his skin. . . .
>
> In other words, the familiarity of the language of the Gospels describing Christ's scourging may have led Oliver Cowdery to substitute the familiar scourged for the unfamiliar scorched in Mosiah 17:13."[7]

Neither of these explanations—a Mesoamerican practice or scribal error—is completely satisfying. The parallel Mesoamerican practice dates about a thousand years after Abinadi's case and comes from a different culture. Added to that problem is the potential difficulty in reconciling beating with firebrands to the full immolation implied in the other verses.[8]

Skousen's explanation has the advantage of following explanations that are obvious for other passages, that is, that there was an error between plate text and text on the printer's manuscript. (The original manuscript is not extant for this passage.) Skousen's explanation is certainly simpler and fits the contextual information, but we still have the problem of a term that is out of place in the text and which Joseph Smith never corrected. An option Skousen does not entertain is that the translation error could have happened because Joseph Smith, not Cowdery, was influenced by the New Testament text. In that case, Joseph would have misread the word but Oliver wrote it down correctly. Even that possibility is difficult because it assumes that Joseph understood the plate text correctly, but did not completely understand the connotations of the word "scourged."

Mosiah 17:13 will continue to be enigmatic although possibilities do exist that may explain the presence of this anomalous term.

Mosiah 17:14–15

> 14 And now when the flames began to scorch him, he cried unto them, saying:
> 15 Behold, even as ye have done unto me, so shall it come to pass that thy seed shall cause that many shall suffer the pains that I do suffer, even the pains of death by fire; and this because they believe in the salvation of the Lord their God.

---

[7]Ibid.

[8]Royal Skousen, *Analysis of Textual Variants of the Book of Mormon*, THE CRITICAL TEXT OF THE BOOK OF MORMON (Provo, Utah: Foundation for Ancient Research and Mormon Studies, 2005) , Vol. 4, Part 3, 1393, states: "Although the textual and linguistic evidence is very clear that in Mosiah 17:13 *scourged* is a mishearing for *scorched* . . . , yet some have defended the current reading *scourged* by hunting for examples of people being beaten with burning sticks or of people being beaten prior to being burned at the stake. For one example see Brant Gardner's 'Sourging with Faggots'. . . . In my own textual analyses of the Book of Mormon, I avoid using cultural evidence simply because it can always be found." Unfortunately, editorial changes made that published note sound more like Skousen's description of hunting for evidence rather than the caution I actually suggest.

The same basic paragraph is also included in Royal Skousen, "Conjectural Emendation in the Book of Mormon," *FARMS Review* 18, no. 1 (2006): 200.

This curse might appear to be the same as that in verse 18 below, which is fulfilled in Mosiah 19:20–21 when Noah's subjects burn him alive. This event clearly parallels Abinadi's death. However, Abinadi's curse does not actually seem to refer to this particular prophecy and therefore is not its fulfillment.

In Abinadi's prophecy, it is the faithful who will suffer death by fire, not the unfaithful (as was Noah). The language is possibly ambiguous, but the prophecy seems to state that the seed of these wicked people (whether actual seed, spiritual seed, or both, is not clear) will cause the faithful to suffer the pangs of death by fire. This event is probably that witnessed by Alma and Amulek and is recorded in Alma 14:8.

Mosiah 17:16–17

> 16 And it will come to pass that ye shall be afflicted with all manner of diseases because of your iniquities.
> 17 Yea, and ye shall be smitten on every hand, and shall be driven and scattered to and fro, even as a wild flock is driven by wild and ferocious beasts.

Abinadi is pronouncing this curse upon those who are present. Mormon does not list who they are, but it appears to be more than the priests and King Noah. While the priests do suffer during their flight through the wilderness, they eventually join with the Lamanites. Thus, their ultimate fate does not seem to fulfill this prophecy. Rather, in this public setting, Abinadi is speaking to those who will become the people of Limhi. They certainly suffered from bondage to the Lamanites, and fleeing from their homes to Zarahemla would fulfill the prophecy of the scattering.

In the ancient world (and until relatively recently), executions were typically public. In Mesoamerica, human sacrifice was publicly performed. The social reasons for public execution include the emphasis on the social sanction against the person and public disapproval of his crime. The punishment stands as a clear and present warning to all who might have sympathized with the one being executed. In this case, Abinadi was seen as a threat and therefore was publicly executed to demonstrate the fate of those who oppose the king.

Mosiah 17:18–19

> 18 And in that day ye shall be hunted, and ye shall be taken by the hand of your enemies, and then ye shall suffer, as I suffer, the pains of death by fire.
> 19 Thus God executeth vengeance upon those that destroy his people. O God, receive my soul.

In contrast to the public condemnation, this prophecy is probably directly targeted at Noah, for he had already prophesied that this would be Noah's end. Noah's death by fire was first proclaimed in Mosiah 12:3: "And it shall come to pass that the life of king Noah shall be valued even as a garment in a hot furnace; for he shall know that I am the Lord." Abinadi's statement, "Thus God executeth vengeance upon those that destroy his people. O God, receive my soul" (Mosiah 17:19), reiterates that prophesy (which is fulfilled in Mosiah 19:20–21).

Yahweh's vengeance is certain, but certainly not always immediate nor apparent. The ultimate "vengeance" of Yahweh is the denial of the blessings of the celestial kingdom, a process brought upon those whose actions merit that judgment. It is not an emotional and uncharacteristic outburst from an otherwise loving God. Abinadi exercises the same poetic license as other prophets who speak against humankind's worldly ways.

In this case, the actions of the people will bring these calamities upon themselves and Abinadi uses them as a sign of Yahweh's righteousness. However, we know that evil frequently goes unpunished in this world, awaiting that final judgment. Dire consequences do not immediately follow evil and frequently do not follow at all in this lifetime. Were they to do so, it would become rather obvious and uncomfortable to be a sinner. If unpleasant consequences always came as noticeably as the calamities Abinadi prophesied on Noah's people, human agency would be short-circuited and become of lessened value.

Mosiah 17:20

> 20 And now, when Abinadi had said these words, he fell, having suffered death by fire; yea, having been put to death because he would not deny the commandments of God, having sealed the truth of his words by his death.

Text: There is no chapter break at this point in the 1830 edition of the Book of Mormon. While Abinadi's death does seem to end a story, Mormon is actually telling Alma's story. Abinadi's narrative is only its essential prologue. Alma's story is just beginning.

Mosiah 18

Mosiah 18:1

> 1 And now, it came to pass that Alma, who had fled from the servants of king Noah, repented of his sins and iniquities, and went about privately among the people, and began to teach the words of Abinadi—

Mormon does not describe Alma's repentance, but it certainly required a complete change of mind and ways. Alma was converted in the true sense of being changed from one state to another.[1] Once a presumably firm supporter of the king and his apostate religion, he now teaches the gospel as Abinadi had explained it, especially its primary belief in the Atoning Messiah. There is no indication that Alma needed to learn any other doctrine to understand and teach the gospel.

Alma must have known that his life was in danger. Regardless, he "went about privately among the people." Perhaps people were willing to listen to Alma where they had not listened to Abinadi because Alma had been one of the court priests. Perhaps they listened because they understood that Alma was giving up earthly prestige, position, rank, and wealth—and risking his life—to follow the heavenly message. He was a walking testimony to the power of Abinadi's message.

Mosiah 18:2

> 2 Yea, concerning that which was to come, and also concerning the resurrection of the dead, and the redemption of the people, which was to be brought to pass through the power, and sufferings, and death of Christ, and his resurrection and ascension into heaven.

Mormon's first declaration is that Alma taught "that which was to come." What was that? It was the coming of the Atoning Messiah.[2] That concept was the essence of Abinadi's message. Understanding that message had converted Alma. Alma is preaching the Atoning Messiah.

Mosiah 18:3

> 3 And as many as would hear his word he did teach. And he taught them privately, that it might not come to the knowledge of the king. And many did believe his words.

---

[1]Alma the Younger similarly experienced a life-changing conversion. See Mosiah 27:24–31.

[2]This phrase occurs with the same meaning in Enos 1:19; Mosiah 3:1, 18; 4:11; Alma 5:48; 7:6; 30:13; 58:40; Hel. 8:22–23.

Mormon does not explain how Alma found those who "would hear his word." He probably exercised considerable caution, so as not to draw attention to himself and to teach only those he could trust not to betray him. The adverb "privately" also implies "secretly." This was a careful and clandestine preaching of the gospel. Abinadi had already died for this gospel, and Alma was under a death sentence. Probably those who listened understood that they might also share Abinadi's fate if they were caught. It is a strong testimony to their faith that they were not only willing to believe, but willing to believe under such harsh circumstances.

Mosiah 18:4

> 4 And it came to pass that as many as did believe him did go forth to a place which was called Mormon, having received its name from the king, being in the borders of the land having been infested, by times or at seasons, by wild beasts.

Geography: The people go to a place called Mormon. This name refers to an entire region: "And now it came to pass that all this was done in Mormon, yea, by the waters of Mormon, in the forest that was near the waters of Mormon; yea, the place of Mormon, the waters of Mormon, the forest of Mormon" (Mosiah 18:30).

This gathering place was not a town. They were leaving their homes and going into the wilderness. They gave up material comfort for the gospel and accepted official condemnation from their ruler, as witnessed by the fact that they went to the "place which was called Mormon" to avoid detection.

The fact that Mormon had "received its name from the king" could mean either that the king declared its name to be Mormon or that the king's name was Mormon. Mormon can be a man's name, although our Mormon-the-abridger was named after the land, not a person (3 Ne. 5:12). But if the king were named Mormon, which king was it? No king in the record is named Mormon, and Nephite kings before $Mosiah_1$ were called Nephi (Jacob 1:11), although Mormon might possibly have been a "Nephi's" birth name. It seems more likely, however, that Mormon was the name of a Lamanite king and that Alma deliberately led his people out of Noah's realm. Mormon may have been a region unassociated with the ancestral Nephites—in other words, a territory into which Noah was not likely to follow for long, both because of a lesser knowledge of the area and the possibility of angering neighboring Lamanite populations.

It is also important that Mormon was "infested, by times or at seasons, by wild beasts." The word "infested" suggests that it was not a hunting ground and that these wild beasts did not provide food. In fact, the connotation is of a nuisance, or even dangerous predators who would prey upon human beings. Mesoamerica is home to a number of larger cats, the most powerful of which is the jaguar. The jaguar was sacred in most Mesoamerican cultures. While it would probably not have been common for the jaguar to hunt human beings, it also must have happened at least occasionally. The forests of Mormon might easily have also harbored the smaller ocelot. For these reasons, it may have been an unfavorable location for a settled population, characteristics that would make it ideal for Alma's purposes.

Mosiah 18:5

> 5 Now, there was in Mormon a fountain of pure water, and Alma resorted thither, there being near the water a thicket of small trees, where he did hide himself in the daytime from the searches of the king.

Geography: John Sorenson pieces together the clues from the description to provide a possible Mesoamerican location for Mormon:

> The waters of Mormon "in the borders of the land" of Nephi (Mosiah 18:4, 31) was [the] rendezvous [for Alma's people]. This spot had to be far enough from the City of Nephi that reports of what they were up to would not readily get back to Noah's court. Events demonstrated that Mormon was located on the Zarahemla side of Nephi. We know this because when the time came that Alma's group had to flee, they got on their way to Zarahemla from Mormon with a significant head start over Noah's army, which pursued them. Alma at Mormon got word about the approaching force after they were en route, yet the people still had time to pack up and make an unhindered escape in the direction of Zarahemla (Mosiah 18:34). Approximately two days of routine travel, or one and a half under pressure, seems satisfactory for the distance from Nephi to Mormon.
>
> The relationship of Nephi and Mormon becomes clearer when we look at the geography of highland Guatemala. With the City of Nephi at Kaminaljuyú (Guatemala City), the only body of water in the direction of Zarahemla that could serve as the waters of Mormon was Lake Atitlan. It is about nine by four miles in dimension. Only a sizable lake would do as the Book of Mormon "waters," for two reasons: (1) the same body of water, it appears, later rose enough to submerge the city of Jerusalem (3 Ne. 9:7), a Lamanite center built after Alma's departure, and (2) it was "away joining the borders of Mormon" (Alma 21:1), implying that the two spots were some little distance apart. The distances and directions relating Nephi, Mormon and Jerusalem are appropriate if the latter two were on Lake Atitlan. Nephi at Kaminaljuyú would be approximately 40 air miles from Lake Atitlan.[3]

Culture: Sorenson stresses the description of "pure water" for the waters of Mormon. The next community Alma founds is also noted for its "pure water" (Mosiah 23:4). Sorenson suggests a possible connection to the Mesoamerican reverence for waters of the underworld, which were considered sacred.[4] The concept of waters underneath the surface of the earth is, of course, widespread, appearing in the mythology of Babylon and other Levantine civilizations.[5] This Levantine concept of waters under the earth was also part of Israelite cosmology: "The biblical reflexes of the Ugaritic traditions of El's dwelling are not hard to discern," comments Richard Clifford. ". . . El's residence as the source of all

---

[3]John L. Sorenson, *An Ancient American Setting for the Book of Mormon* (Salt Lake City: Deseret Book/Provo, Utah: Foundation for Ancient Research and Mormon Studies, 1985), 176.

[4]Ibid., 176–79.

[5]See Geo Widengren, *The King and the Tree of Life in Ancient Near Eastern Religion* (Uppsala, Sweden: A.-B. Lundequistska Bokhandeln, 1951), 35; and Richard J. Clifford, "The Temple and the Holy Mountain," in *The Temple in Antiquity*, edited by Truman G. Madsen (Provo, Utah: BYU Religious Studies Center, 1984), 111.

fertilizing waters is echoed in Genesis 2:10–14, which discusses the four rivers that rise in Eden, and in Ezekiel 47:1–12, describing the river that flows from the temple on the mountain."[6]

John Lundquist, the Susan and Douglas Dillon Chief Librarian of the Asian and Middle Eastern Division at the New York Public Library, expands on the connection between the temple and the waters:

> The temple is often associated with the waters of life which flow from a spring within the building itself—or rather the temple is viewed as incorporating within itself such a spring or as having been built upon the spring. The reason such springs exist in temples is that they were perceived as the primeval waters of creation, Nun in Egypt, abzu in Mesopotamia, tehom in Israel. The temple is thus founded upon and stands in contact with the waters of creation. These waters carry the dual symbolism of the chaotic waters that were organized during the creation and of the life-giving, saving nature of the waters of life.[7]

These ancient Near Eastern ideas would have blended well with general Mesoamerican water/mountain/temple symbolism. The mythic connection with the "pure" waters of the underworld persists to the Maya present. Note the nature of the water in this description of a modern Maya rite, recorded by anthropologists in 1989: "All participants brought the dough made with corn ground by their womenfolk for the sacred breads that are layered, like heaven and the underworld, on the altar, as well as the cooked meats, and the 'wine' made from honey and 'virgin water' from a deep natural well."[8]

The characteristic that made this modern water "virgin" was that it came from a deep natural well, not flowing on the surface. Something similar may have characterized Alma's "pure waters." In any case, the locations were understood as sacred. Whether drawing upon the more immediate Mesoamerican understanding or an archetypal remembrance of the Old World meanings through the brass plates makes little difference. Alma would easily have understood the sacred relationships of mountains and waters. Founding a religious community in such a sacred place would be both appropriate and powerful.

Mosiah 18:6–7

> 6 And it came to pass that as many as believed him went thither to hear his words.
> 7 And it came to pass after many days there were a goodly number gathered together at the place of Mormon, to hear the words of Alma. Yea, all were gathered together that believed on his word, to hear him. And he did teach them, and did preach unto them repentance, and redemption, and faith on the Lord.

---

6 Clifford, "The Temple and the Holy Mountain," 111.

7 John M. Lundquist, "The Common Temple Ideology of the Ancient Near East," in *The Temple in Antiquity*, edited by Truman G. Madsen (Provo, Utah: BYU Religious Studies Center, 1984), 66.

8 David Freidel, Linda Schele, and Joy Parker, *Maya Cosmos: Three Thousand Years on the Shaman's Path* (New York: William Morrow and Company, 1993), 31.

Alma spent an unspecified period preaching to the Noahites secretly in their homes. Such an arrangement, though essential, would have been frustrating for believers, since they would inevitably desire to participate in a community who shared common understandings. Yet larger gatherings in Noah's politically charged atmosphere would have been dangerous, perhaps suicidal. To openly live their new belief, the converts had to leave their established community and begin a new one. Those who go to the land of Mormon are already converted, not merely interested investigators. Likely the community's location was also kept secret and known only to the faithful, for fear of betrayal.

Just as Joseph Smith's earliest converts found that gathering to a new community gave them the opportunity to openly share their religion with others of the same beliefs, so did this community of Alma's believers. They had left their homes, and possibly their families, and gone to a relative wilderness—not to seek riches, but to seek Yahweh's kingdom. The place might be beautiful, but it was also dangerous because of Noah's religious oppression and the wild beasts (v. 4). Gathering would have taken several days, some spent in preparation and others in travel; some were taken up in preparations for that travel. By the time they left the land of Mormon, 450 believers had joined Alma (v. 35). This count presumably included only adults, as the record does not mention children and converted parents would certainly bring their offspring. A count of 450 adults probably means somewhat more than half of that number as households, which would create a hamlet. Of course if the count follows the general Old World custom of counting adult males only (a distinct possibility since the Book of Mormon is so studiously quiet about women), then the village would have been a more substantial one. In either case, their departure could not fail to be noticed and would certainly have generated the official concern that the history records.

Our quick introduction to the essential difference in what Alma taught from that which they might have learned in Lehi-Nephi is found in the final sentence of verse 7. They learn "repentance, and redemption, and faith on the Lord." These phrases are sufficiently common for modern Christians that it is easy to gloss over their significance for Alma's community. What Alma preaches is the Atoning Messiah—precisely the message that Abinadi delivered but which was rejected. Abinadi's conversion of Alma succeeded in doing what Abinadi had been unable to do—to convert some of the Noahites to a true understanding of the connection between the law of Moses and the future mission of the Atoning Messiah.

It is equally probable that modern Latter-day Saints also miss the fact that Alma's group provides the first clear evidence in the Book of Mormon of what we would call a church.[9] Alma organizes a community of believers that eventually sets

---

[9]See Daniel C. Peterson, "Priesthood in Mosiah," in *The Book of Mormon: Mosiah, Salvation Only Through Christ*, edited by Monte S. Nyman and Charles D. Tate, Jr. (Provo, Utah: BYU Religious Studies Center, 1991), 187–210, for an important discussion of priesthood and church in this period of the Book of Mormon.

the pattern for all Nephite religious practices. Alma will become the most important religious innovator in Nephite history.

Mosiah 18:8–10

8 And it came to pass that he said unto them: Behold, here are the waters of Mormon (for thus were they called) and now, as ye are desirous to come into the fold of God, and to be called his people, and are willing to bear one another's burdens, that they may be light;
9 Yea, and are willing to mourn with those that mourn; yea, and comfort those that stand in need of comfort, and to stand as witnesses of God at all times and in all things, and in all places that ye may be in, even until death, that ye may be redeemed of God, and be numbered with those of the first resurrection, that ye may have eternal life—
10 Now I say unto you, if this be the desire of your hearts, what have you against being baptized in the name of the Lord, as a witness before him that ye have entered into a covenant with him, that ye will serve him and keep his commandments, that he may pour out his Spirit more abundantly upon you?

History: These verses introduce us to Alma baptizing in the waters of Mormon, a scene corresponding so closely with our modern understanding of baptism that we may easily miss how revolutionary it was. The level of detail with which Mormon records it, however, shows that he fully appreciated what Alma was doing.

Alma introduces baptism to his believers. The concept of a whole-body washing for personal purity, or *miqveh*, had long been part of Israelite religion.[10] It was probably this ancient Jewish rite that John the Baptist expanded into baptism.[11] Adopted by the Christian community, it underwent a theological evolution when it became associated with Jesus's death and resurrection, a symbolism it could not have had during John the Baptist's ministry (Col. 2:12; Rom. 6:3).

In the New World, Nephi taught baptism (2 Ne. 31:4–5). To review the commentary accompanying that passage, the Jewish ritual washing by immersion symbolized purity. Christian baptism retains this image as a symbol that the baptized one is cleansed from sin. It adds to purification, however, the formal covenant of entry into a community of believers, an element stressed by the writers of the Dead Sea Scrolls.[12] This second function distinguished Nephi's baptism from the later baptisms by the Qumran community. While Qumran baptized for entrance into a community, Nephi's community already existed. Baptism was added on to the whole community's belief structure.

---

[10]Joan E. Taylor, *The Immerser: John the Baptist within Second Temple Judaism* (Grand Rapids, Mich.: William B. Eerdmans Publishing, 1997), 64–69, argues that while the *miqveh* functioned for both ritual cleansing and for proselyte baptisms, the function of the washing was always cleansing rather than a rite of initiation. That is, the ritual immersion cleansed the person but did not indicate that he or she had crossed a social boundary.

[11]Ibid., 63.

[12]Geza Vermes, *The Dead Sea Scrolls in English* (New York: Penguin Books, 1975), 45.

Alma's baptism, however, differs from Nephi's and follows that of the Qumranians by becoming the symbol of community-creation. He and his followers had been part of a community religion (Noah's) and are now accepting a new interpretation of that religion by accepting Abinadi's teachings on the Atoning Messiah as an integral part of their Mosaic observances and beliefs. Baptism not only represents a covenant of cleansing but one of entrance into this specialized community of belief. Alma is a major religious reformer, not in the sense of teaching unknown doctrines, but in teaching a new socioreligious structure previously unknown in the Book of Mormon.

Daniel C. Peterson notes:

> Although Nephi makes it clear that baptism is the first step on the path toward eternal life (2 Ne. 31:9, 18), it is not self-evident that baptism has always signified entrance into a church, or that entrance to a church has always been a part of that path.
>
> I propose that before the ordinance of baptism signified membership in the Church the early Nephites found their primary social and religious identification in the very fact that they were Nephites. In the earliest days of the Nephites in the New World, following Nephi required a deliberate commitment which demanded sacrifice from those who made it. Baptism was preached, and, indeed, stressed to these early Nephites as something pleasing to God and as a necessity for salvation in his kingdom—but it would be easy for unbaptized Nephites to think of themselves as members of God's people strictly because of their heritage.[13]

Alma takes this group, self-selected from the dominant culture, and reintegrates a religious community from it. Later, as chief priest, he will organize other sub-communities bound by shared religious beliefs that are covenantally witnessed by baptism. This rite will symbolize both individual cleansing and entrance into the community of believers. These churches will exist for the first time in the Book of Mormon because of his action. In the larger "Nephite" population represented by the communities attached to Zarahemla, baptism as an entrance into a church allows for the coexistence of differing religious ideas in the political entity of Zarahemla. It will also account for specific missions to bring dissidents back to the fold.

One further symbolism attached to Christian baptism is Paul's distinctive preaching that associates the believer's baptism with Christ's death and resurrection:

> Know ye not, that so many of us as were baptized into Jesus Christ were baptized into his death?
>
> Therefore we are buried with him by baptism into death: that like as Christ was raised up from the dead by the glory of the Father, even so we also should walk in newness of life.
>
> For if we have been planted together in the likeness of his death, we shall be also in the likeness of his resurrection:
>
> Knowing this, that our old man is crucified with him, that the body of sin might be destroyed, that henceforth we should not serve sin.

---

[13]Peterson, "Priesthood in Mosiah," 202.

> For he that is dead is freed from sin.
> Now if we be dead with Christ, we believe that we shall also live with him:
> Knowing that Christ being raised from the dead dieth no more; death hath no more dominion over him.
> For in that he died, he died unto sin once: but in that he liveth, he liveth unto God.
> Likewise reckon ye also yourselves to be dead indeed unto sin, but alive unto God through Jesus Christ our Lord. (Rom. 6:3–11)

Note how thoroughly Paul develops the imagery of Christ's death and resurrection. From at least Paul's time, therefore, one of the symbols attached to baptism has been burial and resurrection. When one enters the water, it is not only the water of cleansing but also the grave of the former self, from which a resurrected/renewed soul arises. Significantly, this symbol absolutely requires that the death and resurrection of Christ be already accomplished. In the Book of Mormon, this symbolic connection is absent. Obviously, because Abinadi/Alma's teachings occurred so long before Christ's earthly mission, the emphasis on the Atoning Messiah rather than Paul's dying Savior formed a more coherent message.

Mosiah 18:11

> 11 And now when the people had heard these words, they clapped their hands for joy, and exclaimed: This is the desire of our hearts.

Redaction: Mormon interrupts his description to quote Alma directly. The only firm indication that Alma made a record is Mosiah 17:4; that record specifies that he wrote about Abinadi. However, it seems safe to assume that Alma also made a record of his people in the land of Mormon.

Mormon quoted Alma's record for Abinadi's words but abridges the record of events in the land of Mormon. It is possible to offer some tentative speculations on Alma's record based on Mormon's abridgment. Obviously, Mormon is quite willing to record an original document (e.g., Zeniff's record, beginning in Mosiah 9), or a lengthy discourse (e.g., Abinadi's address to the court); but in this section, Mormon quotes significant passages such as the baptismal covenant but more typically provides description and summary, which continues through the end of this chapter and summarizes Alma's post-baptismal sermon.

Why doesn't Mormon quote the full sermon? The topics appear to be important, and in similar instances, Mormon has copied the original text. Therefore, I hypothesize that Alma created a narrative description, including a summary of his own sermon, which Mormon easily condensed. When Alma quoted Abinadi, so did Mormon. When Alma summarized, so does Mormon.

History: The people's enthusiastic response to the offer of baptism, while apparently straightforward, does not account for all of the information. For example, an interesting detail is that they unitedly clap their hands for joy. Why? Because the record does not clarify, I offer only a speculative suggestion. Angel Miguel Rodríguez of the Biblical Research Institute summarizes hand-clapping in the Bible:

1. It is an expression of joy at the ascension of the king: This is a social function of the gesture. When Joash was introduced as the legitimate heir to the throne, those who were present clapped their hands and shouted, "Long live the king!" (2 Kgs. 11:12, NIV). A religious usage is found in Psalm 47:1, where the psalmist invites all peoples to clap their hands because the Lord is being proclaimed as king over the earth. In Psalm 98:8 the people are exhorted to praise the Lord and the hills to clap their hands because the Lord is coming as king and judge of the earth.

2. It is an expression of joy on account of God's saving actions: The return of the people of God from their captivity in Babylon is described by Isaiah as an act of redemption. What the Lord will do for His exiled people is so wonderful and glorious that even nature will rejoice. In this context the prophet personifies the trees of the field and describes them as clapping their hands as a gesture of joy (Isa. 55:12).

3. It is an expression of disgust and anger: Balak was angry because Balaam blessed the people of Israel instead of cursing them, and he showed his displeasure by clapping his hands (Num. 24:10). Ezekiel clapped his hands in disgust after seeing the evil practiced in Judah (Ezek. 6:11). The Lord clapped His hands in anger and disgust as a reaction to dishonest gain and to the blood spilled by His people in Jerusalem (Ezek. 22:13; 21:14, 17). This symbolic action on God's part is followed by His judgment against unrepentant sinners.

4. It is an expression of malicious glee: This meaning is found exclusively in the context of defeated enemies. In the prophecy against Nineveh God announces that all those who will hear about His judgments will clap their hands over the city and its misfortune (Nahum 3:19). The Ammonites clapped their hands and rejoiced with malice when Israel was being destroyed by the Babylonians (Ezek. 25:6). It is this same contempt and hostility that those passing by the ruins of Jerusalem expressed by clapping their hands (Lam. 2:15). This gesture was indeed a sign of hostility and derision.[14]

Of these four examples, three are communal. Only one, the expression of derision, is individual. The communal versions are positive and have some relationship to deity (joy at the ascension of the king as representative of the divine, joy in God's saving actions, or joy in God's victory over an enemy). I suggest that this communal action best explains Mosiah 18:11, and that it draws its meaning from the sound of a large number of people clapping. An early association of Yahweh is with storms.[15] Clapping by a large congregation may invoke the sound of thunder and therefore the symbolic presence of the God. I suggest, therefore that this practice was subliminally transferred across the ocean and made its appearance when the divine was being communally recognized.

As we saw in the discussion of Benjamin's speech (see commentary accompanying Mosiah 4:1), collective action can either be ritual or spontaneous. Which might this one be? While the first possibility cannot be disproven, it seems unlikely that both Alma and Mormon would record such a detail. It is more likely that this is a spontaneous action, remarkable in its spontaneity, and therefore noteworthy to both Alma and Mormon. Such a spontaneous expression of joy can

---

[14]Angel Miguel Rodríguez, "The Place for Applause," http://biblicalresearch.gc.adventist.org/Biblequestions/applause.htm (accessed February 2005).

[15]Frank Moore Cross, *Canaanite Myth and Hebrew Epic* (Cambridge, Mass.: Harvard University Press, 1973), 156–77.

be a natural human reaction, thus reinforcing the possibility that it was an unplanned public event.

But why was this event spontaneous? Spontaneous clapping is typically not only connected to joy, but to surprise. Little children at Christmas might clap for joy when they see something that really excites them. When they see that same thing later, they may continue to be excited and joyful, but they seldom repeat the hand-clapping. What would be unexpected in Alma's invitation to baptism? I argue that they do not expect baptism as part of their commitment to follow Alma. Nephi's introduction of a more Christian baptism would have supplanted the ritual washing of the *miqveh*. (See commentary accompanying vv. 8–10.) However, it seems likely that Noah's religion did not include the rite of redemptive baptism. Therefore, Alma's converts greeted this opportunity to expunge their sins as a joyful and welcome surprise. Despite the distance that still separated them from the Atoning Messiah, Alma was offering them immediate access to the atonement that they had recently come to understand. They had given up their homes, comforts, and safety because of their understanding of this atonement. Now they had the opportunity to participate in it directly and personally. No wonder the offer of baptism was not only surprising, but also an occasion of tremendous joy.

Mosiah 18:12–14

> 12 And now it came to pass that Alma took Helam, he being one of the first, and went and stood forth in the water, and cried, saying: O Lord, pour out thy Spirit upon thy servant, that he may do this work with holiness of heart.
> 13 And when he had said these words, the Spirit of the Lord was upon him, and he said: Helam, I baptize thee, having authority from the Almighty God, as a testimony that ye have entered into a covenant to serve him until you are dead as to the mortal body; and may the Spirit of the Lord be poured out upon you; and may he grant unto you eternal life, through the redemption of Christ, whom he has prepared from the foundation of the world.
> 14 And after Alma had said these words, both Alma and Helam were buried in the water; and they arose and came forth out of the water rejoicing, being filled with the Spirit.

Culture: The waters of Mormon are described as a "fountain of pure water" (v. 5). In Jacobean English, the "fountain" might have been a stream or a spring, although that does not seem to fit the plausible location in the New World. John L. Sorenson has argued that the waters of Mormon may have been Lake Atitlán, pointing out that Jerusalem, which was in the borders of the land of Mormon, was submerged in the cataclysm accompanying Christ's appearance in the New World.[16] Perhaps the word "fountain" is due to Joseph Smith's biblical vocabulary rather than an accurate representation of the type of water represented in the text.

There is an interesting difference between Old World and New World conceptions about water that may be relevant. The *Didaché* (a "church manual"

[16]Sorenson, *An Ancient American Setting for the Book of Mormon*, 179, 224.

dating to soon after A.D. 100) indicates that one should be baptized in running water: "Now about baptism: this is how to baptize. Give public instruction on all these points, then 'baptize' in running water, 'in the name of the Father and of the Son and of the Holy Spirit.' If you do not have running water, baptize in some other. If you cannot in cold, then in warm."[17]

In the Old World, the most desirable baptismal water was natural (cold, not warm) and "living" (with a current, not stagnant). In the New World, the conceptual meanings favored the still water rather than the running water. The following description is for modern Quiché Maya, but the anthropologists have discovered that there is much in the retained worldview of the modern Mesoamericans that traces directly to the ancient beliefs:

> A common divination method directly linked to this function and to water was scrying. This technique involved interpreting the light seen on reflective surfaces such as natural bodies of pooled water (particularly those found within caves), the liquid in a bowl and a circular mirror which was often placed in the bottom of a bowl. In addition, the lots used in divination casting were sometimes placed in a bowl of liquid. As the reflective surfaces of these circular divination tools represented the pooled water of the sea, the implication is that divination knowledge was linked to the waters of the sea and, by extension, to the creator grandparents who lived there. . . .
>
> The belief that water plays a fundamental role in divination is found in the world view, initiation rituals and divination methods of the modern Quiché. Like many traditional Maya communities, the Quiché of Momostenango have sacred mountains that define their community. They also have four sacred lakes, one for each direction. Their directional nature and locations at the edges or beyond the limits of the Momostenango community strongly suggest that each lake represents one quadrant of the mythological sea. . . . Dreaming of a lake is one indication that the ritual specialist is ready to receive divination knowledge. The lake is described as a mirror.[18]

Given this cultural background, Alma may have preferred to baptize in a lake rather than a stream. The Old World symbolism attached to a river had a symbolic counterpart in New World lakes. Since Alma's converts had been influenced by Noah's apostate religion, it would not be surprising if they had absorbed at least the general conception of the lake as a sacred location with greater connections to the divine than a stream or a river.

History: Helam (v. 12) is introduced as "being one of the first. . . . " Because he clearly is the first to be baptized, this reference to being one of the first cannot refer to Helam's order of baptism. Since a land was named for him (Mosiah 23:19), we may assume that Helam was a man of some importance in Lehi-Nephi, thus warranting the honor of being baptized first. (See commentary accompanying Mosiah 23:19.)

Scripture: What was the source of Alma's authority? Had he been previously baptized? Joseph Fielding Smith suggests:

---

[17]Cyril C. Richardson, ed., "Didaché," in *Early Christian Fathers* (New York: Macmillan Publishing, 1970), 174.

[18]Karen Bassie, Unpublished, untitled manuscript, 1999, photocopy in my possession. Used by permission. Internal references removed.

> We may conclude that Alma held the priesthood before he, with others, became disturbed with King Noah. Whether this is so or not makes no difference because in the Book of Mosiah it is stated definitely that he had authority. . . .
>
> If he had authority to baptize that is evidence that he had been baptized. Therefore, when Alma baptized himself with Helam that was not a case of Alma baptizing himself, but merely as a token to the Lord of his humility and full repentance. In Alma 5:3 we learn that Alma was consecrated the high priest over the Church under his father. Now Alma did not organize the Church with the idea that they had no church before that time. They had a church from the days of Lehi and Alma only set things in order.
>
> Remember that the Book of Mormon is an abridgment of former records, and like the Bible, does not furnish many details. If I remember correctly, there is no reference to the baptism of Alma the elder or Helaman nor of Nephi and his brother Jacob, but we know they were baptized as were all the faithful members in the Church.[19]

Daniel Ludlow, commenting on the same verse, suggests: "The Book of Mormon does not specifically state whether or not Alma had been baptized before or how he got his authority to baptize. The record merely says that Alma immersed himself in the water when he baptized Helam (Mosiah 18:14–15) and that 'Alma, having authority from God, ordained priests' (Mosiah 18:18.) Alma may have been ordained by Abinadi, but the record is not clear on this point."[20]

The first point on which both authors are clear and the basis upon which this discussion must rest is that there is no definitive answer. Information gleaned from the text is not clear, so all answers are speculative. Joseph Fielding Smith's interpretive model is clearly that of the modern church, which he is reading back into the record, hence his assertion: "We may conclude that Alma held the priesthood before he, with others, became disturbed with King Noah . . . " and "we know they were baptized as were all the faithful members in the Church." Ludlow agrees with Smith on the possibility of an ordination and suggests that Abinadi may have performed it, though leaving unanswered the question of when it might have been possible.

However, neither possibility appears probable. Alma was a priest of Noah and therefore could not have been Zeniff's priest, since Noah had "put down all the priests that had been consecrated by his father, and consecrated new ones" (Mosiah 11:5). Could Alma have received the priesthood from Abinadi, as Ludlow suggests? There is no known time that Abinadi and Alma were together save in the court. There was certainly no possibility of any ordination after the end of the trial, since Alma fled and Abinadi was put to death, apparently immediately. Indeed, it seems that Abinadi's mission was to convert Alma; otherwise, his martyrdom was meaningless. Rather, the record seems to indicate that Alma was indeed in a state of apostasy and that Abinadi's preaching converted him.

---

[19]Joseph Fielding Smith, *Answers to Gospel Questions*, 5 vols. (Salt Lake City: Deseret Book, 1957–66), 3:203.

[20]Daniel H. Ludlow, *A Companion to Your Study of the Book of Mormon* (Salt Lake City: Deseret Book, 1976), 188.

Where did Alma get his authority? Alma specifically declares that he has "authority from the Almighty God" (v. 13). The question would be when and how it was received. Daniel C. Peterson of Brigham Young University suggests that as with other priests, Alma received his ordination at the hands of the king. At that time it was Noah. Peterson continues:

> The fact that Noah was not righteous and that Alma himself seems to have violated the laws of God during his early ministry has nothing to do with Alma's priesthood authority. Unless and until superior priesthood authority withdraws permission to exercise priestly functions, a legitimately ordained holder of the priesthood may continue to perform valid priesthood ordinances—however unrighteous he may personally be, however dead to spiritual promptings, and however unlikely it may be that he will ever actually exercise his priesthood.[21]

The right to ordain priests was transmitted from Zeniff to Noah and Noah to Limhi. Alma received his priesthood from the king, just as all other priests had done. Clearly, his heart underwent a spiritual transformation and the earthly ordination was clearly confirmed by a spiritual witness, hence he could declare that he operated under "authority from the Almighty God" (v. 13).

What of Alma's prior baptism? Joseph Fielding Smith argues that he must have been baptized because he was a faithful member of the church. This assertion is problematic, both because of baptism's role in the Book of Mormon and Alma's apostate standing during Abinadi's trial. The very logic of his assertion depends on accepting the Book of Mormon as an earlier version of the modern Church, an assertion not supported by various aspects of the text, the issue of baptism being one of them. (See commentary accompanying 2 Nephi 31:5.)

The baptism of Alma and Helam in these verses parallels the later experience of Joseph Smith and Oliver Cowdery:

> We still continued the work of translation, when, in the ensuing month (May, 1829), we on a certain day went into the woods to pray and inquire of the Lord respecting baptism for the remission of sins, that we found mentioned in the translation of the plates. While we were thus employed, praying and calling upon the Lord, a messenger from heaven descended in a cloud of light, and having laid his hands upon us, he ordained us, saying:
>
> Upon you my fellow servants, in the name of Messiah, I confer the Priesthood of Aaron, which holds the keys of the ministering of angels, and of the gospel of repentance, and of baptism by immersion for the remission of sins; and this shall never be taken again from the earth until the sons of Levi do offer again an offering unto the Lord in righteousness.
>
> He said this Aaronic Priesthood had not the power of laying on hands for the gift of the Holy Ghost, but that this should be conferred on us hereafter; and he commanded us to go and be baptized, and gave us directions that I should baptize Oliver Cowdery, and that afterwards he should baptize me.
>
> Accordingly we went and were baptized. I baptized him first, and afterwards he baptized me—after which I laid my hands upon his head and ordained him to the Aaronic Priesthood, and afterwards he laid his hands on me and ordained me to the same Priesthood—for so we were commanded. (JS—H 1:68–71)

---

[21]Peterson, "Authority in the Book of Mosiah," 164–65.

Joseph Smith's account provides more details than Alma's, but the baptism of the first two is clearly similar, even though Alma and Helam submerged themselves simultaneously while Joseph and Oliver baptized each other in turn. Still, the previously unbaptized performs a baptism. Joan E. Taylor (lecturer in religious studies at the University of Waikato, Hamilton, New Zealand), comments in her work on John the Baptist: "It is possible that John went underwater at the same time as the person he was causing to be immersed. In Acts 8:36–39 the Christian *diakonos* ('servant' or 'assistant') Philip baptizes the Ethiopian eunuch by going down into the river with him, immersing himself at the same time."[22] Joseph Smith explicitly claims that he and Oliver received verbal authority to perform the baptism while the Book of Mormon is silent, but the Lord could easily have provided the necessary authority in the same way. The similarities in form suggest a similarity of occasion as well: the introduction of priesthood-authorized baptism to a new generation.

Baptism and the Spirit: One of the distinguishing differences between the baptism of John and the baptism of Jesus was the accompanying "baptism" by the Spirit. Joan Taylor explains:

> It may be that in the early Gentile Church John's baptism was counted with Christian baptism as being in some way initiatory. A Gentile understanding of the gospel stories could easily have led to this assumption. In Acts, John's baptism seems to have been considered adequate for participation in the community of Jesus' first disciples, though after Pentecost and the reception of the Holy Spirit, distinctive Christian baptism had a different, two-pronged character: it involved water and the Holy Spirit, as opposed to water alone (though Philip was permitted to continue a water-only baptism by full immersion, as long as apostles such as Peter and John made sure to follow in his tracks). The idea that being immersed with the "immersion of John" gave one a certain status in the community of Jesus' disciples is reflected in the story that the man chosen to replace Judas had to be someone who had been with Jesus and the others "beginning with [or: from] the immersion of John" (Acts 1:22; cf. John 1:35–51). Yet there is the idea that those who were baptized by John—or were immersed in accordance with the kind of baptism John performed—had only an inferior sort of immersion and had to be baptized again with the Holy Spirit. The Pentecost experience apparently completed the process, so that those immersed were immersed not only in water but also by the Holy Spirit (Acts 2:1–4).[23]

Alma says: "O Lord, pour out thy Spirit upon thy servant, that he may do this work with holiness of heart" (v. 12), which may be interpreted as a direct invocation of this later concept of baptism. Alma does not have a separate ordinance of baptism followed by a laying on of hands, but he does invoke the Spirit in a way that uses a form of water imagery to describe the effect of the Spirit: "pour out thy Spirit. . . . "

However, there are insufficient details to determine whether Alma's baptism precisely foreshadowed the Christian double-pronged "immersion" in water and spirit. Even if Alma was not conferring the Spirit, he was certainly invoking it. This

---

[22]Taylor, *The Immerser*, 52.
[23]Ibid., 71–72.

difference may be small, but it is important in understanding the development of baptism in the Book of Mormon.

Variant: The printer's manuscript for verse 12 contains the name Helaman rather than Helam, but also the handwritten correction to Helam, which appears in the first printed edition. This correction of Helaman to Helam occurs twelve times in the corrections to the printer's manuscript: Mosiah 18:12, 13, 14; Mosiah 23:19, 20, 25, 26, 29, 35, 37, 38, 39.[24] Up to this point, each textual reference to Helaman was changed to Helam. This pattern in the printer's manuscript changes with the next two references to our current Helam: Mosiah 27:16, Alma 24:1.[25] The pattern here indicates that the first twelve occurrences of Helaman were an error, which was caught by the time the printer's copy was written up to Mosiah 27:16. All of the "errors" were corrected simultaneously to read "Helam."

This portion of the printer's manuscript cannot be checked against the original, which has not survived; so it is possible that Oliver simply misread the name while he was copying and substituted the name of Helaman, with which he would have been familiar from his work on the original manuscript.

The only argument against this scenario is large number of times the error is repeated. We expect scribal errors to be localized and more limited. While the changes are confined to two locations, those locations are separated by a fair amount of text. If, and only if, the transcription of "Helaman" accurately reflected the original manuscript, this fact would call into question some of the evidence from the original that is used to show that there was close control over the spelling.[26] We cannot know, however, what was on the original, and what the source of this mistranscription was. In the absence of any other hypothesis, the best answer is that Oliver Cowdery erred while copying the printer's manuscript from the original. Skousen argues:

> The original manuscript is not extant for any portion of the book of Mosiah. One could argue that for Mosiah 23 the original manuscript actually read *Helaman* in all 11 cases [that were changed to *Helam*] and that this is why Oliver Cowdery originally copied it consistently as *Helaman* into [the printer's manuscript] and did not immediately correct it to *Helam*. This interpretation would imply that Oliver later decided that *Helaman*, both in [the original manuscript] and [the printer's manuscript] for Mosiah 23, was a mistake for *Helam* and that he therefore systematically emended the text. But such an innovative decision on Oliver's part seems unlikely. A more plausible explanation, in my view, is that when Oliver got to copying Mosiah 23, he read *Helam* in [the original manuscript] but decided it was an error for *Helaman*, not realizing that the land and city of Helam had been named after the Helam that Alma had baptized in Mosiah 18.[27]

---

[24]*Book of Mormon Critical Text: A Tool for Scholarly Reference*, 3 vols. (Provo, Utah: FARMS, 1987), 2:453–54; 2:475–79.

[25]Ibid., 2:497, 2:670.

[26]Royal Skousen, "How Joseph Smith Translated the Book of Mormon; Evidence from the Original Manuscript," in *Journal of Book of Mormon Studies* 7, no. 1 (1998): 27.

[27]Royal Skousen, *Analysis of Textual Variants of the Book of Mormon*, THE CRITICAL TEXT OF THE BOOK OF MORMON (Provo, Utah: Foundation for Ancient Research and Mormon Studies, 2005), Vol. 4, Part 3, 1371.

Mosiah 18:15

> 15 And again, Alma took another, and went forth a second time into the water, and baptized him according to the first, only he did not bury himself again in the water.

On this second baptism, Alma did not immerse himself as he had with Helam. This baptism had two functions, to remit sin and to enter the new church. Both functions were required only once, so Alma did not need to repeat it for himself.

Mosiah 18:16

> 16 And after this manner he did baptize every one that went forth to the place of Mormon; and they were in number about two hundred and four souls; yea, and they were baptized in the waters of Mormon, and were filled with the grace of God.

Alma similarly baptized "every one that went forth to the place of Mormon"—the 204 believers who had followed him out of Lehi-Nephi. Mormon gives few details about the history of this community, but when they depart for the land of Zarahemla, he records that they number "four hundred and fifty souls" (v. 35). While we do not know precisely how long they stayed in the land of Mormon, it would be unrealistic for the population to more than double through births only. There must have been some way to communicate to friends and loved ones in Lehi-Nephi and ongoing conversions as a result. Since the land of Mormon was uninhabited (the very reason that Alma and his people went there), these converts must have come from Lehi-Nephi.

Mosiah 18:17

> 17 And they were called the church of God, or the church of Christ, from that time forward. And it came to pass that whosoever was baptized by the power and authority of God was added to his church.

Culture: This verse parallels the historical event recorded in Acts 11:25: "And the disciples were called Christians first in Antioch." In the Old World, the earliest term for Christ's followers was "The Way."[28] When Paul is speaking to Felix, he states: "However, I admit that I worship the God of our fathers, as a follower of the Way, which they call a sect . . . " (Acts 24:14, New International Version).

The shift from "the Way" to "Christians" signaled not only an internal/external designation, but a recognition that a more formal structure had evolved. Richard A. Horsley, professor of religion at the University of Massachusetts, and Neil Asher Silberman, historian of the ancient Near East, note: "Just as the acolytes of the imperial cult were known as Augustiani, and just as the adherents of the various mystery religions were known by the name of the patron deities who were invoked in their secret, communal meals and ceremonies, the faithful followers of

---

[28]Raymond E. Brown, *An Introduction to the New Testament* (New York: Doubleday, 1997), 81.

Jesus in the city—both Jews and Greeks—came to be known as *Christianoi*, or 'Christians,' to the people of Antioch."[29]

Just as this Old World shift in terminology formalized the outward perception that the Christian community had become a "church," so this name for Alma's people denotes the creation of a new entity: the "church of God," or "the church of Christ." In the Nephite theology, a more exact translation might be the "church of Yahweh" and "church of the Messiah," since they understood God and Messiah to be the same being. (See "Excursus: The Nephite Understanding of God," following 1 Nephi 11.)

"Church" is the English translation for the Greek *ekklesia*, but of course, Mormon would not have written *ekklesia* on the plates. How could there be a church in the Book of Mormon before there was a church in the New Testament? The Greek word means a group of citizens called out to assemble for political purposes, outside of the religious use of the term.[30] It is used in the Septuagint interchangeably with "synagogue" to translate the Hebrew word for "assembly."[31]

Although the Hebrew *qahal* "assembly," could be the basis for the translation to the English "church" in the Book of Mormon, any argument based on specific words in the Book of Mormon ignores the problems of translation. We do not know what word Mormon wrote. We know only that Joseph Smith translated it as "church."

Although "church" in Alma's account bears the meaning of a specific organization, religion was inextricably intertwined in all aspects of life in the ancient world. The concept of "belonging" to a religion was foreign to most of the ancient world. Religion provided their definition of reality. It was their science, their definition of the way the world worked.[32] In smaller communities, everyone would have the same worldview or the same religion. Of this early form of religion, Daniel C. Peterson suggests "the possibility that early Nephite priesthood was mediated and given structure through family and clan organization, rather than through a church structure."[33]

What we see happening with Alma is the formalization of a particular type of belief that might be separate from the worldview of others in the community. This differing participation in worldview necessitated a new structure in which to mediate the subcommunity's commonalities that were yet opposed to the surrounding beliefs of their own people. While all of Alma's people had relocated to form a new community, they were aware of those left behind and the differences

---

[29]Richard A. Horsley and Neil Asher Silberman, *The Message and the Kingdom: How Jesus and Paul Ignited a Revolution and Transformed the Ancient World* (New York: Grosset/Putnam, 1997), 128.

[30]Daniel N. Schowalter, "Church," in *The Oxford Companion to the Bible*, edited by Bruce M. Metzger and Michael D. Coogan (New York: Oxford University Press, 1993), 121.

[31]Ibid.

[32]Peterson, "Authority in the Book of Mosiah," 173, uses a similar social definition of early Nephite religion: "I propose that the early Nephites found their primary social and religious identification in the very fact that they were Nephites."

[33]Ibid.

between their current beliefs and those of their former community. When this community is integrated into Zarahemlan society, it brings with it the ability to define a subset of a community by religion. That separability became important in the socially and religiously diverse Zarahemla. The church became a mediating function among the pressures for those diverse religious and social impulses.

This important distinction was probably not available in most Mesoamerican communities. King Benjamin's speech instituting social reform in Zarahemla followed a period of social unrest and the defection of the dissenters to the Lamanites. In Benjamin's case, there was no mechanism for establishing internal divisions that could remain separate, yet part of the community. Yet it is this concept of a separate entity that can exist within a larger community that is Alma's religious innovation, one he will introduce into Zarahemla. In that setting, it allows for the continuation of a body of believers in a larger setting that does not always uniformly adhere to those beliefs, even though there may be a political tie to Zarahemla.

Mosiah 18:18

> 18 And it came to pass that Alma, having authority from God, ordained priests; even one priest to every fifty of their number did he ordain to preach unto them, and to teach them concerning the things pertaining to the kingdom of God.

Culture: Alma not only created a church but a community. He organized both a system of belief and a system of communal care. By assigning a priest to every fifty people, Alma was organizing his people so that they could be cared for and governed. The number fifty provides a reasonable division of his people (four priests and eight "fifties") while allowing for future growth. Why fifty? Perhaps from the brass plates: "Moreover thou shalt provide out of all the people able men, such as fear God, men of truth, hating covetousness; and place such over them, to be rulers of thousands, and rulers of hundreds, rulers of fifties, and rulers of tens" (Ex. 18:21). Alma's people were few enough that there was no reason for the larger divisions, and perhaps not even the "rulers of tens." The rulers of fifty did have divine sanction and may have been his source.

Mosiah 18:19–20

> 19 And he commanded them that they should teach nothing save it were the things which he had taught, and which had been spoken by the mouth of the holy prophets.
> 20 Yea, even he commanded them that they should preach nothing save it were repentance and faith on the Lord, who had redeemed his people.

Mormon gives a brief description of Alma's religious teachings. While it is tempting to see the admonition to "preach nothing save it were repentance and faith on the Lord" as a general command to preach only the basic doctrines, in the historical context of Alma's community these verses have a deeper color.

Alma had been a priest of Noah and had previously taught a religion that denied the Atoning Messiah. He now teaches repentance and faith on the "Lord"—the Atoning Messiah. Alma is making sure that his people are hearing the correct message of Yahweh—as the prophets received it, as Abinadi declared it, and as Alma came to know it. When Alma commands that they preach "nothing save it were repentance and faith on the Lord," he is telling them the most important thing to preach. It is a positive commandment, not a list of things that should not be taught. These people were acquainted with the law of Moses but had previously believed it in a version that denied the Messiah. Alma wants to make sure that his congregation understands the critical mission of this coming Messiah. Therefore, his people are to preach nothing else.

Mosiah 18:21–22

> 21 And he commanded them that there should be no contention one with another, but that they should look forward with one eye, having one faith and one baptism, having their hearts knit together in unity and in love one towards another.
>
> 22 And thus he commanded them to preach. And thus they became the children of God.

Redaction: When Mormon states that Alma commanded that "there should be no contention one with another, but that they should look forward with one eye, having one faith and one baptism, having their hearts knit together in unity and in love one towards another," it is either Mormon's synopsis of the intent of Alma's teaching, or a direct quotation. With Mormon's clear (and well-deserved) admiration for Alma, one would suspect that Mormon would take the opportunity to insert some of Alma's words here. However, it is most likely a description rather than a quotation. It says what Alma said but does not replicate the precise wording.

Of course, the "one faith, one baptism" phrase echoes Ephesians 4:5: "One Lord, one faith, one baptism." Probably, this phrasing again displays Joseph's Smith familiarity with Paul's writings, but the concept of communal unity resulting from baptismal covenants is completely harmonious with Alma's context. Even though the specific wording owes a debt to Paul, the meaning is Alma's, describing his hope for this new community.

Scripture: Mormon indicates that his people became "children of God" through the unity of their faith and baptism. Embedded in Mormon's argument as it is, this phrase suggests that it is Mormon's, rather than Joseph Smith's. Mormon is summarizing the people's conversion process, indicating that Alma's people have undergone the great change described by Benjamin: "And now, because of the covenant which ye have made ye shall be called the children of Christ, his sons, and his daughters; for behold, this day he hath spiritually begotten you; for ye say that your hearts are changed through faith on his name; therefore, ye are born of him and have become his sons and his daughters" (Mosiah 5:7). Because the Nephites understood that Yahweh and the

Messiah were the same, I see "children of God" and "children of Christ" as equivalent phrases.

Mosiah 18:23

> 23 And he commanded them that they should observe the sabbath day, and keep it holy, and also every day they should give thanks to the Lord their God.

It is not clear why Mormon took the time to record this particular commandment of Alma to his people. We would expect that they observed the Sabbath routinely, as part of their observance of the Mosaic law. Perhaps this practice had become corrupted along with other concepts? Even if this were the case, Sabbath observance did not divide the week into secular and religious days, for on other days they were also to give thanks to Yahweh. Alma's people were to renew their covenant to be Yahweh's people. They honored the Sabbath, but every day honored Yahweh.

Mosiah 18:24

> 24 And he also commanded them that the priests whom he had ordained should labor with their own hands for their support.

While this command echoes King Benjamin's declaration that he had supported himself with his own labor (Mosiah 2:14), it probably draws its immediate strength from contrast with Noah's priests, who had obviously accumulated their wealth at the expense of the people (Mosiah 11:4–6). Alma here forbids the possibility of a socially segregated priestly class.

Mosiah 18:25

> 25 And there was one day in every week that was set apart that they should gather themselves together to teach the people, and to worship the Lord their God, and also, as often as it was in their power, to assemble themselves together.

Mormon has already noted Sabbath observance as a feature of Alma's church (v. 23). Was this "one day in every week that was set apart" the Sabbath or an additional day of worship? Obviously the day of rest from one's labor would be the most convenient time for farmers to leave their fields and assemble. Given the relatively small group and the need for the new community to be self-sustaining, it seems likely that the community gathered on the labor-free Sabbath, which was probably the Israelite Sabbath. (See commentary accompanying Moroni 6:5.)

In addition to the decreed day of assembly/teaching, they were also "as often as it was in their power, to assemble themselves together." Alma created social structures that emphasized both the community and the community's religious foundation. In contrast to the social segregation of Noah's reign, Alma fostered a sharing group, one without social hierarchies. The only social division is between teacher and student. He expressly forbids a distinction between economic-producer and consumer (v. 26).

Mosiah 18:26

> 26 And the priests were not to depend upon the people for their support; but for their labor they were to receive the grace of God, that they might wax strong in the Spirit, having the knowledge of God, that they might teach with power and authority from God.

Redaction: This verse repeats the information in verse 24, but the repetition cannot be explained by structural or poetic parallelism. I hypothesize that this information was originally in two places that were much farther apart in Mormon's source, but which his abridging brought close. The next verse begins "and again," suggesting that Alma was reading a set of regulations for the community that Mormon is simply summarizing.

Mosiah 18:27–28

> 27 And again Alma commanded that the people of the church should impart of their substance, every one according to that which he had; if he have more abundantly he should impart more abundantly; and of him that had but little, but little should be required; and to him that had not should be given.
> 28 And thus they should impart of their substance of their own free will and good desires towards God, and to those priests that stood in need, yea, and to every needy, naked soul.

Culture: Alma did not hear King Benjamin's sermon, but their social programs are remarkably similar. King Benjamin told his people in Zarahemla:

> And also, ye yourselves will succor those that stand in need of your succor; ye will administer of your substance unto him that standeth in need; and ye will not suffer that the beggar putteth up his petition to you in vain, and turn him out to perish.
>
> Perhaps thou shalt say: The man has brought upon himself his misery; therefore I will stay my hand, and will not give unto him of my food, nor impart unto him of my substance that he may not suffer, for his punishments are just—
>
> But I say unto you, O man, whosoever doeth this the same hath great cause to repent; and except he repenteth of that which he hath done he perisheth forever, and hath no interest in the kingdom of God. (Mosiah 4:16–18)

In both communities, communal sharing was the economic ideal. However, Benjamin was leveling a society that had become economically stratified, while Alma's converts removed themselves from the social strata of Lehi-Nephi. Except for whatever food or other material resources they had brought with them, all members of this new community were starting over on the same footing. Thus, they were sharing from economic necessity. Almost immediately, even those who had managed to bring some goods with them would also be required to farm. Their principles were egalitarian, but the land is notoriously chancy and inegalitarian. Alma's people had no one else to rely on; they had to share or risk starvation. True,

Benjamin advocated imparting to the needy, but this practice was not the same as the complete communal ownership of goods that Alma's community was practicing.

This fact suggests that the communitarianism of the early Christians in Jerusalem may have emerged from a similar necessity. Even though the Jerusalem Christians were surrounded by a larger Judean population, the economic and physical needs of the dispossessed were similarly provided through a gospel-based change from selfishness to selflessness.[34] Although the Gentile Christians did not apparently pool resources in the same way, they did stress the bonds of brotherhood and sent financial aid to the Christian poor in Jerusalem.[35] Such communitarianism brings social as well as economic benefits, foremost among them God-like love and neighborly compassion.

Mosiah 18:29

> 29 And this he said unto them, having been commanded of God; and they did walk uprightly before God, imparting to one another both temporally and spiritually according to their needs and their wants.

Scripture: Mormon has been speaking of communal sharing in what might be considered a rather temporal context, yet here he explicitly extends their sharing from the physical to the spiritual. In addition to sharing food, they shared the gospel; in addition to sharing meals, they shared spiritual understanding. In any community, some will have more economic goods and some more spiritual understanding. All shared, each as he or she was able, to build up both body and soul.

Mosiah 18:30

> 30 And now it came to pass that all this was done in Mormon, yea, by the waters of Mormon, in the forest that was near the waters of Mormon; yea, the place of Mormon, the waters of Mormon, the forest of Mormon, how beautiful are they to the eyes of them who there came to the knowledge of their Redeemer; yea, and how blessed are they, for they shall sing to his praise forever.

Mormon is not satisfied with simply recording the place in which Alma's disciples became a community. Instead, he uses poetic repetition, unusual for him, to describe the general area. Thus, it is "Mormon, yea, by the waters of Mormon, in the forest that was near the waters of Mormon." This literary device expands the initial statement by modifiers, a technique seen in later Mexica poetry.[36]

---

[34]Horsley and Silberman, *The Message and the Kingdom,* 102–3. A trend of communalism has also been documented in the community of the Dead Sea Scrolls. Lawrence H. Schiffman, *Reclaiming the Dead Sea Scrolls* (New York: Doubleday, 1995), 106–10.

[35]For an analysis of *koinonia* ("community or fellowship"), see Brown, *An Introduction to the New Testament*, 286–88.

[36]Angel María Garibay K., *Historia de la Literatura Nahuatl*, 2 vols. (Mexico: Editorial Porrúa, S. A., 1971), 1:65–66.

At this point, Mormon has located the people in a place. However, his interest is not geography, but spirituality. To make a transition from the more mundane concept of physical location, he repeats the triple description, but this repetition becomes a spiritual location. The words are the same, but they are metaphorically expanded by the phrase "how beautiful are they to the eyes of them who there came to the knowledge of their Redeemer."

We cannot know how much of the joy of the people came from Mormon's sources or how much he simply surmised from his own experience in coming to know the Redeemer. Regardless of the source, he was likely quite accurate in describing the excitement of this new community.

Mosiah 18:31

> 31 And these things were done in the borders of the land, that they might not come to the knowledge of the king.

The death sentence on Alma likely extended to any of his followers. Since Alma was actively preaching against Noah's social, religious, and economic rule, he would be even more hated and hunted than when he first fled from the court.

The "borders of the land" had to include Mormon, since the record specifies that they were in Mormon. However, Mormon, although on the fringes of the land, is not out of touch with Lehi-Nephi. Alma's people have not completely lost connection with the city.

Redaction: This verse is a transition from the story of Alma's people to the next story, Noah's death. Their remote location provides context for the armies of Noah who are searching for them.

Mosiah 18:32

> 32 But behold, it came to pass that the king, having discovered a movement among the people, sent his servants to watch them. Therefore on the day that they were assembling themselves together to hear the word of the Lord they were discovered unto the king.

What was the "movement among the people" that Noah saw? From the context, it was not merely a change of opinions and religious beliefs, but rather a physical movement—probably the hundreds of people who were quietly disappearing from the city. Some disappeared permanently, while others came and went. Noah ordered spies to trace those movements, and they followed them to the land of Mormon or perhaps posed as believers to infiltrate the group while in the city.

Much later, Mosiah 23:1 specifies: "Now Alma, having been warned of the Lord that the armies of king Noah would come upon them, and having made it known to his people, therefore they gathered together their flocks, and took of their grain, and departed into the wilderness before the armies of king Noah." Since the believers still had access to their herds and storage, Alma's preaching did not create an immediate and irrevocable separation from Lehi-Nephi. It was obviously the believers who came and went between Lehi-Nephi whose "movement" Noah observed and whom the spies followed.

It is also obvious that they were conducting missionary work in Lehi-Nephi, or their numbers could not have grown from two hundred to four hundred and fifty in a relatively short time. Whether overtly or covertly, those who had accepted the Messiah returned to Lehi-Nephi and found others who were willing to accept the Messiah. These new converts accompanied their missionaries to Mormon where they were baptized into Yahweh's church.

Mosiah 18:33

> 33 And now the king said that Alma was stirring up the people to rebellion against him; therefore he sent his army to destroy them.

Nothing in Alma's recorded preaching directly supports Noah's assertion that Alma was preaching rebellion. Nevertheless, it was true that what Alma preached was antithetical to Noah's religious and political order. Even if Alma had not mentioned resistance to Noah and his priests, the teachings themselves would have caused a schism. Some type of rebellion was inevitable. Although the movement of Lehi-Nephi residents to Mormon and their baptism is not, from our perspective, a rebellion, it could only have been a matter of time.

Mosiah 18:34

> 34 And it came to pass that Alma and the people of the Lord were apprised of the coming of the king's army; therefore they took their tents and their families and departed into the wilderness.

This verse parallels Mosiah 23:1: "Now Alma, having been warned of the Lord that the armies of king Noah would come upon them, and having made it known to his people, therefore they gathered together their flocks, and took of their grain, and departed into the wilderness before the armies of king Noah." Each verse tells the same story. Mosiah 23:1 must repeat this information because it is physically removed from the story. Limhi's interpolated story must be completed before Mormon returns to Alma's account.

Mosiah 18:35

> 35 And they were in number about four hundred and fifty souls.

Although it is not clear how long Alma's group has been in existence, it has doubled in size. While many of the members of the church would have lived with Alma, many still lived in Lehi-Nephi, as discussed above.

Text: There is no break at this point in the 1830 edition. While modern readers see a clear break between the stories of Alma and the next one of Limhi, Mormon did not separate them. Perhaps he placed them in the same chapter because they were happening almost simultaneously. The army that is sent to destroy Alma's people causes Alma's people to leave but also figures in the story of Limhi.

Mosiah 19

Mosiah 19:1

1 And it came to pass that the army of the king returned, having searched in vain for the people of the Lord.

Text: This chapter division was added in 1879. This verse is directly related to Mosiah 18:32 which described the army's search for Alma's people. At the end of chapter 18, Alma, warned of the army's approach, leads his people away. This transition shifts from Alma's people to Limhi's, leaving Alma's temporarily suspended, in the limbo of departure. Mormon resumes their account in Mosiah 23.

Mosiah 19:2–3

2 And now behold, the forces of the king were small, having been reduced, and there began to be a division among the remainder of the people.
3 And the lesser part began to breathe out threatenings against the king, and there began to be a great contention among them.

Mormon has most certainly omitted an important historical episode somewhere between the story of Abinadi and this point. At the beginning of Abinadi's story, Noah is a powerful ruler, controlling the labor force and sponsoring large building projects. He appears to have fairly uniform popular support. Yet this passage describes a king losing his authority.

How has the unity of Noah's people disintegrated into internal factionalism and a reduction of the army? Have unspecified battle losses caused the military reduction? It seems unlikely, since verse 6 specifies a Lamanite attack with no indication of any previous attack. Rather, the army seems to have dwindled through defections. In that case, it would be directly related to the internal dissension. Those who agreed with the dissenters are leaving Noah's service.

We have even less information for recreating the internal disorder. It is tempting to speculate that Alma's teachings have created religious (and therefore political) dissatisfaction with Noah. However, Alma's adherents seem to be a separate faction, one that operates secretly and physically leaves the city. Thus, those who remain in open contention are probably not Alma's followers, but they are also clearly no longer Noah's.

It is possible that this faction (or factions) had been in existence before Abinadi's mission, glossed over in Mormon's abridgment because it served his editorial interests to show the entire population as apostate. Against this simpler backdrop, Mormon could then create a more dramatic story of Abinadi's rejection, arrest, and trial.

Because Mormon is making narrative selections based on historic documents, no doubt including Noah's official records, we have some leeway in reconstructing the most probable social situation because the official record would have made the situation appear more uniform. Clearly Noah had a dominant political position and probably the support of the majority for his religious innovations. However, it is unlikely that all of Zeniff's followers would have completely abandoned their previously held religion. They would have constituted a smoldering faction that could easily erupt after Abinadi's cruel death. Also probably, the high taxation that financed the building projects created economic pressure that would have chafed those who disagreed with the political and social statement behind those buildings projects.

Almost certainly, these still-loyal followers of Zeniff would have been receptive to Abinadi's preaching, more likely to recognize him as a prophet. Although this scenario is certainly speculative, it would explain how Mormon's few reported details could lead to the relatively quick erosion of Noah's authority. Perhaps such a sequence appeared so natural to Mormon that he saw no reason to explain it. Or perhaps this episode is simply another example of how Mormon's interest in spiritual things led him to omit many things that a historian would love to know.

Mosiah 19:4

> 4 And now there was a man among them whose name was Gideon, and he being a strong man and an enemy to the king, therefore he drew his sword, and swore in his wrath that he would slay the king.

Gideon appears abruptly in the narrative, without any background. From his actions, we can easily surmise his military experience. Verse 22 mentions the "men of Gideon," clearly positioning him as a leader. Mosiah 20:21 shows that Gideon knows Abinadi's prophecy about Noah and his people. These bits of information let us deduce that Gideon was a man of physical action, skilled in handling weapons, not a man given to political intrigue. He must have been assigned to the palace and either heard Abinadi's statements directly or through the palace gossip network. His dissatisfaction with Noah, combined with the knowledge of Abinadi's prophecy suggests that he had left Noah's military service and would have been sympathetic to the dissenters. It also seems likely that his military unit defected with him, helping to account for the reduction of Noah's army.

Mosiah 19:5

> 5 And it came to pass that he fought with the king; and when the king saw that he was about to overpower him, he fled and ran and got upon the tower which was near the temple.

Modern Saints, primed by Arnold Friberg's memorable painting, probably picture Noah as overweight and out of shape. This verse suggests both competence in handling weapons and a fair amount of physical conditioning to be able to ascend a tower-pyramid rapidly enough to stay ahead of a certainly well-conditioned military man. Gideon was obviously competent. For Noah to survive his attack unwounded, even though he was about to be overpowered, suggests a fair level of physical ability.

There is no suggestion that Gideon had to fight past Noah's guards to reach the king, further suggesting that Gideon had rank and respect from the palace guard. If he had been fighting his way to Noah from outside the palace, Noah would have been alerted and either fled sooner or marshaled a larger guard. In fact, Gideon was apparently leading a palace coup, supported by his own men. If he could reach Noah virtually unhindered, it seems clear that Noah's rule was over and that Gideon had already effectively seized the government.

Mosiah 19:6

> 6 And Gideon pursued after him and was about to get upon the tower to slay the king, and the king cast his eyes round about towards the land of Shemlon, and behold, the army of the Lamanites were within the borders of the land.

These watchtowers had been built specifically to provide warnings of Lamanite incursions (Mosiah 11:12), and that's exactly what happened. Noah saw the Lamanites in the distance. But why would Noah run up a tower, rather than toward open ground where he would have a better chance of escape? It seems that he "treed" himself. It seems likely that Gideon had effectively seized control of the palace exits. Therefore, Noah's only hope would have been to find higher ground where he could defend himself. Given the narrow and steep steps of Mesoamerican temples and assuming a similar architecture, it is easy to see how such a "tower" might offer defense possibilities, with Noah on the flat top and Gideon attempting an uphill fight on narrow stairs. From Mormon's brief hints, it seems that Noah took the only action with any chance of saving his life.

Mosiah 19:7–8

> 7 And now the king cried out in the anguish of his soul, saying: Gideon, spare me, for the Lamanites are upon us, and they will destroy us; yea, they will destroy my people.
> 8 And now the king was not so much concerned about his people as he was about his own life; nevertheless, Gideon did spare his life.

Gideon chooses not to kill Noah, even though that was clearly his intention. Why is the presence of the Lamanites enough to change his mind? Was there some reason he could not first kill Noah, then meet the Lamanite threat? If the scenario I have hypothesized is correct, dispatching Noah would not have been either quick or easy. In fact, he may well have been able to kill Gideon, which would have left the defense of the city in great danger without Gideon to lead his men. Given the choice between a protracted delay while he killed the king, or the immediate ability to rally forces to meet a much larger challenge, Gideon chose the more pressing immediate threat of the Lamanites. This decision further suggests that Gideon was fairly firmly in control of the government, so that he could rally the military forces without worrying about Noah attempting to wrest back control.

Mosiah 19:9

> 9 And the king commanded the people that they should flee before the Lamanites, and he himself did go before them, and they did flee into the wilderness, with their women and their children.

Almost certainly, Gideon was not one of those who fled with Noah before the Lamanite advance. Indeed, his character seems to preclude such a cowardly flight. Rather, it seems most likely that Gideon and those loyal to him would have stayed behind, defending the city, while Noah and those loyal to him (or those who panicked) fled into the wilderness in the opposite direction from the Lamanite advance. The fleeing population of an entire city would have presented a remarkably easy target for the Lamanites. There would have been no time to prepare to flee, so probably it was only Noah and those closest to him, either in his court or families in the immediate vicinity of the palace (or those who saw them running and raced to join them) who fled. Mesoamerican housing patterns show homes clustered in kin-based compounds. Thus, Noah could have alerted his kinsmen. As it was, even this group was destined to be caught.

Mosiah 19:10

> 10 And it came to pass that the Lamanites did pursue them, and did overtake them, and began to slay them.

The text does not make it clear how the Lamanites discovered those who fled. Perhaps they arrived with sufficient rapidity and the flight took enough time that the Lamanites had arrived close enough to see clearly those who were fleeing from the other side of the city. Because Mesoamerican wealth was displayed as part of their clothing, the fleeing group might easily be seen as the elite class and therefore the more desirable target, if not the easier. Assuming that Gideon was ready to defend the city, the Lamanites might easily have elected to capture elite prisoners who seemed unarmed rather than fight a military force entrenched in defensive positions.

Mosiah 19:11

> 11 Now it came to pass that the king commanded them that all the men should leave their wives and their children, and flee before the Lamanites.

Mormon had asserted that Noah was cowardly: "And now the king was not so much concerned about his people as he was about his own life . . . " (v. 8), and this incident, which he would have known about before writing the abridgment, provides proof of Noah's character flaw.

Yet possibly there was something else behind this apparently cowardly command. Schele and Mathews discuss the settlement of Chichén Itzá (a city settled long after the close of the book of Mormon): "We also suspect that most of the refugees/migrants were nobles, because the accounts say that the migrants went without their wives so that they married local women during their migrations."[1]

Although this account of the Itzá residents' travels is much later, it provides a potential parallel context for Noah's command. If Noah realized that they had lost both city and position (how likely was it that Gideon would let him live, let alone restore him to the throne?), he may have quickly grasped the slim possibility of fleeing to a different location and re-creating his dynasty there. Intermarriage with the local women would give them some connection to the area; and in fact, Noah's priests seem to have done something like this later in the story (Mosiah 20:1–5).

Mosiah 19:12

> 12 Now there were many that would not leave them, but had rather stay and perish with them. And the rest left their wives and their children and fled.

This verse documents yet another division among Noah's loyalists: those who would obey him and abandon their families, and those who rejected his leadership and remained with their families.

Mosiah 19:13–14

> 13 And it came to pass that those who tarried with their wives and their children caused that their fair daughters should stand forth and plead with the Lamanites that they would not slay them.
> 14 And it came to pass that the Lamanites had compassion on them, for they were charmed with the beauty of their women.

Possibly women and children were totally expendable in this male-centered world. But a possible defense of those who abandoned their families is that Noah and his male followers hoped for exactly this solution. Perhaps there was some tradition of nonviolence against women that they hoped would come into play. It may be too far removed in time to have become precedent, but Nibley suggested that the pleading of Ishmael's daughters for Nephi's life was a recognized Near Eastern practice.[2] It was a mechanism that apparently allowed men to find an acceptable way out of the conflict by acquiescing to the women's desires. Perhaps some of this custom was retained. (See commentary accompanying 1 Nephi 7:17–19.) Even those men who remained with their families seized upon the expedient of having their women act as intermediaries, rather than proceeding straight to battle.

Mormon explains that the Lamanites were "charmed" by the beauty of the Nephite women. It is hard to understand how a marauding army would be so touched by beauty in whatever degree to the point of abandoning hostilities. Rather, it seems more probable that the women provided a cultural excuse under

---

[1]Linda Schele and Peter Mathews, *The Code of Kings: The Language of Seven Sacred Maya Temples and Tombs* (New York: Scribner, 1998), 202.

[2]Hugh Nibley, *Teachings of the Book of Mormon—Semester 1: Transcripts of Lectures Presented to an Honors Book of Mormon Class at Brigham Young University, 1988–1990* (Provo, Utah: Foundation for Ancient Research and Mormon Studies, 1993), 169.

which a surrender might be negotiated. Given the desired outcome of Lamanite warfare, it is unlikely that they would have killed the men. What they wanted was capture, not only for the possession of captives, but the possession of the city over which they ruled. From this point on, Lehi-Nephi passed under Lamanite rule. Even though there had been a Gideon-led rebellion, it does not appear that the rebels were in sufficient control to claim to have deposed their government. The capture of the fleeing king accomplished the task of capturing the city.

Mosiah 19:15

> 15 Therefore the Lamanites did spare their lives, and took them captives and carried them back to the land of Nephi, and granted unto them that they might possess the land, under the conditions that they would deliver up king Noah into the hands of the Lamanites, and deliver up their property, even one half of all they possessed, one half of their gold, and their silver, and all their precious things, and thus they should pay tribute to the king of the Lamanites from year to year.

History: Rather than the typical European model of conquest, plunder, and dispossession, this story reflects the Mesoamerican mode of ending a conflict. It is important to note that the captives were carried back to the land of Nephi, not the city of Lehi-Nephi. Noah and Limhi remained in Lehi-Nephi, but the Lamanites appear to have taken some ranking members of society back to their own lands. In the Mesoamerican context this is exactly as expected. The future of those captives would not be pleasant. (See commentary accompanying Alma 24:9–11.)

In the city of Lehi-Nephi, however, the situation is much better. The city is allowed to continue, with the sole penalty of a heavy annual tribute to the Lamanites.

Mosiah 19:16

> 16 And now there was one of the sons of the king among those that were taken captive, whose name was Limhi.

Mormon reintroduces Limhi, whom we first met at the beginning of historical flashback (Mosiah 7). Limhi's presence in the fleeing party strengthens the idea that those who fled were Noah's family and retainers. Limhi certainly would have gone with his clan, even though his moral character is certainly an improvement over his father's, a fact Mormon also notes (v. 17).

The presence of both the king and the future king in the same group provides yet another reason, both for the Lamanite decision to pursue this group and the relatively peaceful conclusion of the conflict. Noah was not captured but Limhi was. Noah's absence created a power vacuum that Limhi filled. This was a change that may have been in the Lamanites' favor, as Limhi had never been an independent king. From the beginning of his reign, he would have made accommodations to the new overlords.

Mosiah 19:17

> 17 And now Limhi was desirous that his father should not be destroyed; nevertheless, Limhi was not ignorant of the iniquities of his father, he himself being a just man.

This verse is difficult to place in context. If it serves as a conclusion to the previous verses, then Mormon is commenting on Limhi's mixed feelings about replacing his father as ruler. If, however, Mormon meant it as the prelude to Gideon's actions, then it suggests that Limhi asked Gideon and his men to find his father and bring him back to the city; but in light of Gideon's determined attempt to kill Noah, this possibility seems unlikely. Even if Limhi did not know that Gideon had attacked Noah, it seems likely, given Gideon's character, that he would have filled Limhi in on the details of the coup. Even if Limhi, an honorable man himself, had trusted Gideon to carry out this assignment honorably, it hardly seems like that Noah would have surrendered to Gideon, whose intentions he had so recently experienced.

It seems easier to view this expedition as having been sent from the city after the return of Limhi's people. Gideon would have been in the city and therefore would have initiated the search party as a continuation of his attempt to overthrow Noah. It is therefore quite probable that, when the party began hunting those who fled, their goal was killing Noah. At this point, Limhi had not been formally recognized as king by Gideon or his men. A restabilization of the government must have come afterward, when events had settled and the city's safety was assured.

Mosiah 19:18

> 18 And it came to pass that Gideon sent men into the wilderness secretly, to search for the king and those that were with him. And it came to pass that they met the people in the wilderness, all save the king and his priests.

Note that Gideon sends the men "secretly." Perhaps it means that they were going cautiously, or perhaps he was acting without Limhi's approval or authorization. The search party meets men returning toward the city—evidently a substantial number since only the king and the priests remained behind.

Mosiah 19:19–21

> 19 Now they had sworn in their hearts that they would return to the land of Nephi, and if their wives and their children were slain, and also those that had tarried with them, that they would seek revenge, and also perish with them.
> 20 And the king commanded them that they should not return; and they were angry with the king, and caused that he should suffer, even unto death by fire.
> 21 And they were about to take the priests also and put them to death, and they fled before them.

The contentions eating at all of Lehi-Nephi now penetrate the last of Noah's loyalists. Among this self-selected group of men, only the king and the priests appear to stand together. The rest desert him. The official reason was their desire to avenge the deaths of their wives and children; but obviously, they are rejecting Noah's authority. It is the final act of political rebellion. The king was definitively shown as less than infallible and certainly less than divine, which he might have claimed in Mesoamerican tradition.[3]

These newly minted rebels decide to remove the government that had led them into embarrassment by killing the king. They would have also killed the priests if the priests had not escaped in some way Mormon failed to record.

Mosiah 19:22

> 22 And it came to pass that they were about to return to the land of Nephi, and they met the men of Gideon. And the men of Gideon told them of all that had happened to their wives and their children; and that the Lamanites had granted unto them that they might possess the land by paying a tribute to the Lamanites of one half of all they possessed.

The initial meeting of these two groups was probably not as calm and easy as Mormon makes it sound. If Gideon's men were bent on killing the king, they would be ready for a fight. The returning men would be tired but apprehensive, perhaps not sure immediately whether they were seeing Nephites or Lamanites. As the distance narrowed, however, at least some in each party would recognize men in the other party, although it is less clear that they would have assumed friendship.

Clearly the returning men would be anxious about their abandoned families. After the unmentioned means of reconciling the potentially violent anxieties, Gideon's party removes another anxiety by informing the men of the fate of their families and city.

Mosiah 19:23–24

> 23 And the people told the men of Gideon that they had slain the king, and his priests had fled from them farther into the wilderness.
> 24 And it came to pass that after they had ended the ceremony, that they returned to the land of Nephi, rejoicing, because their wives and their children were not slain; and they told Gideon what they had done to the king.

Verse 24 contains the unique phrase "after they had ended the ceremony. . . ." What ceremony would this have been? A ceremony of greeting? A ceremony of surrender to Gideon's men? Perhaps it described some kind of truce under which information could be safely exchanged and the two groups could realize that they had no hostile intent toward each other. A fourth possibility is that Mormon has conflated the meeting with the exchange of oaths (v. 25) and called both the "ceremony." Gideon may have sent his men "secretly" while the rest of the city was occupied in the "ceremony" of formal submission to the Lamanites.

---

[3]We do not have a term better than *divine* to describe the way Mesoamericans would have seen their king. Noah would not have been a divine king in the Western European sense, but more in the sense that Roman emperors claimed divinity. When Ammon is before King Lamoni, Lamoni fears that Ammon is one of these divinities on earth. See commentary accompanying Alma 18:2.

John Tvedtnes has suggested the possibility of a purification ceremony that would have returned the men to ritual cleanliness after murdering the king.[4] This suggestion makes sense in terms of Jewish halakic (purity) laws but not necessarily for the biblically prescribed result of a killing. As Tvedtnes points out, the murderer would not be allowed to live under the law of Moses. While killing by accident allowed the slayer to seek a city of refuge, Noah's death did not qualify as accidental. Nevertheless, some aspect of Nephite culture (or at least this branch of it) may have provided for the ritual cleansing of those who had committed a similar act.

Skousen sees the problematic reading as a possible error in recording the dictation. He speculates (with evidence) that the word *ceremony* should have been *sermon*. He notes:

> The critical text will therefore accept the proposed emendation *sermon* for Mosiah 19:24, not with the modern meaning but instead with the earlier meaning of "talk, discourse." The reading *ceremony* is most likely the result of an early error in the transmission of the text, beginning with the misspelling of *sermon* as *cermon* in [the original manuscript] and followed by the misinterpretation of *cermon* as *ceremony* when Oliver Cowdery could not recognize *cermon* as *sermon*, since for him a sermon would have been either a minister's prepared discourse on a religious subject or, more generally speaking, an exhortation or even an harangue.[5]

Mosiah 19:25–26

> 25 And it came to pass that the king of the Lamanites made an oath unto them, that his people should not slay them.
> 26 And also Limhi, being the son of the king, having the kingdom conferred upon him by the people, made oath unto the king of the Lamanites that his people should pay tribute unto him, even one half of all they possessed.

There is no conceptual break between verses 24 and 25, but the place, occasion, and meaning all change between these verses. These verses have two actors—the Lamanite king and Limhi, who just became king, not only because he was Noah's son but also because the kingdom was "conferred upon him by the people." (See "Excursus: The Voice of the People," following Mosiah 29.) The two rulers have a formal exchange, the one imposing and the other accepting the terms of subjugation (paying tribute). This imposition of tribute is, ironically, the very thing that Zeniff had, two generations earlier, feared as the Lamanites' ultimate goal (Mosiah 9:12).

Mosiah 19:27–29

> 27 And it came to pass that Limhi began to establish the kingdom and to establish peace among his people.

---

[4]John A. Tvedtnes, *The Most Correct Book: Insights from a Book of Mormon Scholar* (Salt Lake City: Cornerstone, 1999), 176–77.

[5]Royal Skousen, *Analysis of Textual Variants of the Book of Mormon*, THE CRITICAL TEXT OF THE BOOK OF MORMON (Provo, Utah: Foundation for Ancient Research and Mormon Studies, 2005), Vol. 4, Part 2, 1394.

28 And the king of the Lamanites set guards round about the land, that he
might keep the people of Limhi in the land, that they might not depart into
the wilderness; and he did support his guards out of the tribute which he did
receive from the Nephites.
29 And now king Limhi did have continual peace in his kingdom for the space
of two years, that the Lamanites did not molest them nor seek to destroy them.

These verses describe the tribute arrangement, enforced by Lamanites "guards" left behind. However, the Lamanites have no interest in establishing their own rule. Limhi is allowed to govern his people with no implication of other political consequences or pressures.

Text: There is no chapter break at this point in the 1830 edition of the Book of Mormon.

Mosiah 20

Mosiah 20:1–2

1 Now there was a place in Shemlon where the daughters of the Lamanites did gather themselves together to sing, and to dance, and to make themselves merry.
2 And it came to pass that there was one day a small number of them gathered together to sing and to dance.

Text: Although Mormon did not break chapters between our current chapters 19 and 20, there is clearly a change of subject. Perhaps he is following the organization of his source material. At this point, Limhi's story pauses (Mosiah 19:29) while the story of Noah's priests picks up.

This transition is marked by "Now," the signal of a new subject happening at approximately the same time as the other events. While Limhi was being installed, the priests cease their flight and begin building new lives. Their most important activity was at Shemlon, where Mormon sets the scene with the singing and dancing Lamanite young women.

Geography: While we do not know which direction the priests fled, it was almost certainly not toward Shemlon, as the Lamanite armies were coming from that direction (Mosiah 19:6). Presumably, then, the original path of flight for Noah, the priests, and those with them, would have been in the exact opposite direction. Obviously, then, the priests fleeing from the Nephites who killed Noah would not have found themselves immediately in the vicinity of Shemlon. This incident, therefore, took place at some later date—after they had time to assess their situation and double back.

Culture: From Mormon's brief description, it seems obvious that

- Shemlon was a common locale for women to gather for the express purpose of singing and dancing.
- On this particular day ("one day"), only "a small number" had gathered, implying that at other times there would be many.
- There were no men present.

These hints suggest that the women were engaged in a religious ritual that was held at regular intervals, that the ritual itself forbade the presence of men, and that it was held at sufficiently frequent intervals that not all women felt required to attend every time as a religious duty. Probably the location had a religious shrine and, most likely, it was to a goddess. The women were almost certainly of marriageable age, since the priests would not have seen children or aged women as potential wives. I therefore speculate that the gathering was a puberty rite that welcomed girls across the threshold into womanhood with ritualized singing and dancing.

Judges 21 describes what seems to be a similar event:

> Then the elders of the congregation said, How shall we do for wives for them that remain, seeing the women are destroyed out of Benjamin?
>
> And they said, There must be an inheritance for them that be escaped of Benjamin, that a tribe be not destroyed out of Israel.
>
> Howbeit we may not give them wives of our daughters: for the children of Israel have sworn, saying, Cursed be he that giveth a wife to Benjamin.
>
> Then they said, Behold, there is a feast of the Lord in Shiloh yearly in a place which is on the north side of Bethel, on the east side of the highway that goeth up from Bethel to Shechem, and on the south of Lebonah.
>
> Therefore they commanded the children of Benjamin, saying, Go and lie in wait in the vineyards;
>
> And see, and, behold, if the daughters of Shiloh come out to dance in dances, then come ye out of the vineyards, and catch you every man his wife of the daughters of Shiloh, and go to the land of Benjamin.
>
> And it shall be, when their fathers or their brethren come unto us to complain, that we will say unto them, Be favourable unto them for our sakes: because we reserved not to each man his wife in the war: for ye did not give unto them at this time, that ye should be guilty.
>
> And the children of Benjamin did so, and took them wives, according to their number, of them that danced, whom they caught: and they went and returned unto their inheritance, and repaired the cities, and dwelt in them. (Judg. 21:16–23)

The similarity of these two episodes is so strong that the priests of Noah might conceivably have got the idea from this passage on the brass plates. Alan Goff notes:

> Some Book of Mormon critics have seen the parallels between the two stories and concluded that Joseph Smith merely copied the story from Judges. They conclude that any similarities in stories indicate plagiarism. Biblical scholars take a more sophisticated approach than do these critics to texts that may appear to borrow from other texts. Scholars often see similarities between stories as evidence of the writer's sophistication and of the richness of the text. . . . I believe that, in a similar way, the story of the abduction in Mosiah means more when we see it in light of the story in Judges. I feel that the author of the story in Mosiah borrowed consciously from the story in Judges, which he knew from the plates of brass, to help make his point.[1]

Goff's conclusion is strengthened when we remember that Mormon could not have had a first-hand account of the abduction, and therefore was required by circumstances to create the text himself. In such a case, structuring the story to fit text from the brass plates would be perfectly understandable.

Tvedtnes suggests that the "feast of the Lord" in Judges 21:19 suggests that the Book of Mormon event may have been a feast as well, probably the Feast of

---

[1]Alan Goff, "The Stealing of the Daughters of the Lamanites," in *Rediscovering the Book of Mormon*, edited by John L. Sorenson and Melvin J. Thorne (Provo, Utah: FARMS, 1991), 69–70.

Tabernacles.[2] John W. Welch, Robert F. Smith, and Gordon C. Thomasson suggest that this festival might have occurred on the fifteenth of Av, an ancient "matrimonial holiday for youth" during which maidens would dance.[3] Both of these suggestions have merit in that the Book of Mormon certainly implies a festival occasion. However, it seems unlikely that an Old World festival continued to be practiced more than 450 years later among the Lamanites, who apparently engaged in fairly wholesale rejection of their ancestral religion. Even among the Nephites, the endurance of such a custom seems unlikely. Furthermore, the matrimonial festival on the fifteenth of Av virtually requires the presence of young men to watch and thereby be attracted to the maidens—a detail that contradicts an essential element of the Book of Mormon story in which not even guards were present, even respectfully out of sight of the actual dancing.

Mosiah 20:3

> 3 And now the priests of king Noah, being ashamed to return to the city of Nephi, yea, and also fearing that the people would slay them, therefore they durst not return to their wives and their children.

The priests' fears are not without merit. They had no doubt witnessed or at least been aware of Noah's execution by those who had followed him and abandoned their wives. Given that wrath from those who had been most favorable politically and religiously to the priests, it is no wonder they concluded that the city would be even less inclined to welcome them back.

Clearly, however, they also feared the Lamanites. They did not seek asylum at Shemlon among the Lamanites. They saw themselves as without a nation, required to make their way on their own. This would have been a difficult situation for men accustomed to luxury. They would now be entirely on their own for everything. Understanding their isolation, they would want women to complete their community.

It is also important that they did not attempt to lure away the wives they had abandoned or, at least, capture women from their own culture. It seems probable that they understood their act as a criminal one and perpetrated it upon an enemy rather than upon their own people, possibly rationalizing their act as a raid in which the women became a kind of spoils of war.

Mosiah 20:4–5

> 4 And having tarried in the wilderness, and having discovered the daughters of the Lamanites, they laid and watched them;
> 5 And when there were but few of them gathered together to dance, they came forth out of their secret places and took them and carried them into the

[2]John A. Tvedtnes, *The Most Correct Book: Insights from a Book of Mormon Scholar* (Salt Lake City: Cornerstone, 1999), 183–86.

[3]John W. Welch, Robert F. Smith, and Gordon C. Thomasson, "Dancing Maidens and the Fifteenth of Av," in *Reexploring the Book of Mormon*, edited by John W. Welch (Provo, Utah: FARMS, 1992), 139–41.

> wilderness; yea, twenty and four of the daughters of the Lamanites they carried into the wilderness.

These two verses reveal that the priests were previously unaware of the ritual or that it took place in this particular location, since they "discovered" the women there. After this initial discovery they apparently they continued their observations on more than one occasion, waiting until "but few of them gathered together to dance."

Because the priests were in Lamanite territory, they had already made the decision to raid the Lamanites for women. Fearing both Limhites and Lamanites, there would be no other reason to be near Shemlon. They may have been seeking women engaged in some isolating activity, such as bathing, doing laundry at the river, etc. The ritual dance spot fit perfectly into their plans.

Text: It is not clear how Mormon learned this information. The Lamanite king's accusation to Limhi, and Gideon's quick deduction about what had really happened, would have supplied the general facts of the abduction. Limhi may have speculated on or reconstructed these events, later confirmed by information Alma's people transmitted when they joined the Nephites and Limhites at Zarahemla. Certainly there would be no contemporary record created by the priests themselves in Limhi's (or Alma's) possession that would have served as Mormon's source. Mormon may have been supplying a firmer historical description than would have been available contemporaneously.

Culture: While the abduction of twenty-four women suggests an approximate number of priests, an exact numeric match seems improbable. However, it is unlikely that the priests outnumbered the women, since otherwise they would have simply waited for a ritual occasion when more women came to the dancing place. But since these priests had likely practiced polygamy (or concubinage), a scenario in which women outnumbered men, giving some of them more than one wife, seems likely.

Mosiah 20:6–7

> 6 And it came to pass that when the Lamanites found that their daughters had been missing, they were angry with the people of Limhi, for they thought it was the people of Limhi.
>
> 7 Therefore they sent their armies forth; yea, even the king himself went before his people; and they went up to the land of Nephi to destroy the people of Limhi.

The phrase "when the Lamanites found that their daughters had been missing . . . " is both interesting and significant. The Lamanites expected their daughters to be off on their own for some time, thus reinforcing the hypothesis that the young women were participating in a known ritual at a known time. Their parents were concerned only after the expected time had elapsed.

Second, it is also clear that there was no direct supervision over the dancers, which doubtless facilitated the abductions.

The next similarly small but important point is that the Lamanites immediately suspected Limhi's people. Why? The most common assumption is that the traditional hatred between Lamanites and Nephites meant that the Lamanites immediately blamed the Nephites for anything untoward. That assumption is unsatisfying. Historical and archaeological studies confirm that conflict was a way of life in Mesoamerica and not all conflicts could possibly have been between Lamanite and Nephite. There were other inter-city hatreds that are not part of our Book of Mormon.

If we assume that there were other populations in the vicinity (all subsumed under the rubric of "Lamanites" in the Book of Mormon) we may legitimately ask why the Limhites were so immediately suspect. Certainly the answer lies in the conflict just resolved between the two peoples. The Lamanites had attacked Lehi-Nephi; and even though a tribute treaty had been imposed and accepted, it would not be completely out of the question that some resentful Nephites might retaliate by taking the Lamanite women, although what they hoped to gain by this action is not clear. Thus the accusation is logical against the Limhites, but not because they were absolutely the only choice. They were only the most logical choice, possessing both motive and opportunity.

The third important item in these two verses is the direct participation of the Lamanite king. He personally led the army bent on destroying Lehi-Nephi. In contrast, no king is mentioned in the army of conquest that had so recently conquered the Limhites and imposed the tribute treaty. Why would the king be so personally involved at this point?

There are likely compounding reasons for the king's participation. One would be the necessity to forcefully suppress an attempted rebellion, lest other tributaries take heart from a successful uprising. Second, because the dancers were probably involved in a religious rite, their abduction partook of blasphemy, thus requiring retribution to cancel out the insult to their gods.

Significant, but probably less important than the military and religious motivations, would have been anger over the loss of the daughters. While modern societies would assume that anguish for a child would be a paramount emotion, this may not have been the case in the ancient world. Not only was life cheaper in many ways in the ancient world, but there is no indication that the king was personally related to any of the dancers. The absence of kinship would have reduced his level of personal concern. Additionally, given the secondary social status accorded women in ancient societies, the fact that this loss was of "only women" should have diminished the response, not heightened it. Therefore, chivalry may be discounted as a reason for the king's personal involvement. Although assigning motivations can be only speculative, it seems most likely that the Lamanites marching against Limhi were retaliating for political and religious reasons, not simple parental love.

Mosiah 20:8–9

8 And now Limhi had discovered them from the tower, even all their preparations for war did he discover; therefore he gathered his people together, and laid wait for them in the fields and in the forests.

9 And it came to pass that when the Lamanites had come up, that the people of Limhi began to fall upon them from their waiting places, and began to slay them.

As the incident with Gideon and Noah shows, this tower gave a view of Lamanite lands. Therefore, Limhi was warned about the approach of this army which was no doubt large and which evidently made no attempt at a stealthy approach. In Mesoamerican warfare, a significant tactic was intimidating the enemy by a show of numbers and impressive regalia, and there is no reason to see these pre-encounter maneuvers as different.

Unlike Noah, who was on the tower by coincidence, Limhi was there because the recent hostilities between the two city-states and his resultant wariness about another attack. When he saw this one developing, he promptly launched an ambush to regain the tactical advantage. This maneuver suggests that he had significantly fewer fighting men than the Lamanite king. Verse 11 confirms that Limhi's army was "not half so numerous as the Lamanites." He was thus skillfully evening the odds.

Mosiah 20:10–11

10 And it came to pass that the battle became exceedingly sore, for they fought like lions for their prey.

11 And it came to pass that the people of Limhi began to drive the Lamanites before them; yet they were not half so numerous as the Lamanites. But they fought for their lives, and for their wives, and for their children; therefore they exerted themselves and like dragons did they fight.

Literature: The zoological reference to lions, while communicating accurately to an American audience, is not culturally accurate for Mesoamerica where the biggest feline was a jaguar. Joseph Smith likely substituted a well-known big cat for the less well known predator that was also a big cat. In other words, the underlying text was probably "jaguar," but the translation is "lion." It is easier to see explain this word as Joseph's mislabeling than Mormon's failure to correctly identify a jaguar.

The more common English idiom of fighting lions in verse 10 gives way to a much more awkward description in verse 11 of fight "like dragons." (The reference to fighting like dragons will also appear as a description of the Lamanites in Alma 43:44.) In English literature, the dragon appears as the maiden-devouring, fire-breathing foe of St. George and other fairytales. (In contrast, the Chinese dragon represents wisdom and longevity, rather than ferocity.) Furthermore, while the image of English dragons is always negative (a vicious enemy to the innocent), Mormon clearly uses the term to praise Limhi's soldiers. Why? The best explanation relies upon a Mesoamerican context. Mesoamerican culture contains a fictive animal that combines elements of both serpent and bird (wings and feathers). During Mormon's time, this feathered serpent could have been seen as a symbol *par excellence* of valiant warriors. The Temple of the Feathered Serpent at Teotihuacan clearly presents the symbol in this military context.[4]

Thus, recasting verses to reflect their Mesoamerican context might yield this retranslation:

> And it came to pass:
> The battle became violent and noisy
> They fought [for their families]
> Like God's jaguars for their prey.
> And it came to pass:
> The Limhites began to drive away the Lamanites
> Though they were not half so many.
> They fought for lives, wives, and children.
> They fought mightily.
> They fought like God's feared war serpent.

Of course this "translation" takes great liberties with the English text. I do not argue that it represents the actual underlying text but rather that it may simulate that text. In both Maya and Nahua poetry, the imagery comes in shorter and more powerful phrasings, so I have restructured the English ideas to provide a more Mesoamerican poetic flavor.

Mormon is clearly creating a poetic parallel between the lions and the dragons. When we add the religious/military significance of those images in Mesoamerica, the description of the Limhites' fighting fury takes on new meanings. In addition to the strength of arms alone is the implication of a divine presence ("God's"). In poetic terms, Mormon not only describes their efforts but also emphasizes the role God played in the victory.

John Sorenson has also identified the dragon as a Mesoamerican motif but missed the parallel to the lion and suggested that the dragon is the caiman or the earth monster.[5] While the caiman is certainly a respectable candidate for the dragon, being one of the few large predators of the area, its association with earth ignores the significant military associations of the war serpent of Mormon's time. Clearly there is not enough evidence to draw firm conclusions, but the war serpent appears to fit the context better.[6]

---

[4]Saburo Sugiyama, "Rulership, Warfare, and Human Sacrifice at the Ciudadela: An Iconographic Study of Feathered Serpent Representations," in *Art, Ideology, and the City of Teotihuacán*, edited by Janet Catherine Berlo (Washington, D.C.: Dumbarton Oaks Research Library and Collection, 1992), 209–10. This temple was constructed around A.D. 200. The imagery of the war serpent continued to be important in Mormon's times.

[5]John L. Sorenson, *An Ancient American Setting for the Book of Mormon* (Salt Lake City: Deseret Book/Provo, Utah: Foundation for Ancient Research and Mormon Studies, 1985), 187. The caiman is a species of crocodile indigenous to Central America.

[6]David Freidel, Linda Schele, and Joy Parker, *Maya Cosmos: Three Thousand Years on the Shaman's Path* (New York: William Morrow and Company, 1993), 309, note that the war serpent was imported into Maya culture from Teotihuacán. This makes it a late symbol and not present when these events

Translation: What are the implications of this passage for Joseph Smith's translation process? While acknowledging the speculative nature of my poetic recasting, recasting the verses increases their meaning by incorporating the appropriate Mesoamerican context (lions = jaguars/ dragons = war serpents). Thus, this passage is another example to reinforce the idea that our current English text relates to the underlying original language on the basis of meaning, rather than literal translation.

Mosiah 20:12

> 12 And it came to pass that they found the king of the Lamanites among the number of their dead; yet he was not dead, having been wounded and left upon the ground, so speedy was the flight of his people.

Culture: There are two important parts of the battle's description: first, the Lamanites flee, leaving their wounded king behind; and second, he is wounded, not dead. While both of these facts are not necessarily foreign to modern warfare, they are more understandable in the context of Mesoamerican warfare.

First, even though the Limhites were not half so numerous as the Lamanites, their ambush is effective. Warfare of the time was essentially hand-to-hand, not long distance. Thrown arrows (employing the atlatl) might wound from a distance, but not necessarily kill the foe, if he were wearing the defensive padded shirt that was used for armor. (See commentary accompanying Alma 43:18–20.) Once the initial surprise of the attack from ambush has had its effects, the two armies would engage in hand-to-hand combat. The net effect of two Lamanites for every Limhite suggests that the ambush had not completely evened the odds or incapacitated half of the Lamanite army.

The ambush succeeded because the Limhites break through to the king and wounded him severely enough to incapacitate him. This stroke appears to have ended the battle, and the surviving Lamanites "speedily" retreated.

Next, we note that the king was only wounded. While there were certainly casualties in Mesoamerican warfare, both intent and characteristics of the weapons were more likely to inflict injury than death. Given Mesoamerican culture, it is predictable that the Limhites would attempt to capture the king rather than kill him.

Mosiah 20:13

> 13 And they took him and bound up his wounds, and brought him before Limhi, and said: Behold, here is the king of the Lamanites; he having received a wound has fallen among their dead, and they have left him; and behold, we have brought him before you; and now let us slay him.

After promptly treating the king's wounds, Limhi's soldiers deliver him for a face-to-face meeting. This king-to-king exchange represents, not a military conflict, but

---

took place. It was, however, a symbol with which Mormon would have been painfully familiar. (See Helaman, Part 1: Context, Chapter 3, "The Gadianton Robbers in Mormon's Theological History: Their Structural Role and Plausible Identification.")

a political one. Even though the Lamanite king, by being defeated, has admittedly lost his divine mandate, Limhi honors the protocol of such an exchange.

Yet if capturing the king is a Mesoamerican tradition, then why does Limhi's army immediately ask permission to kill him? Although an answer is necessarily speculative, perhaps such a threat is a formal aspect of the presentation. The Lamanite king is ritually presented as a forfeited life, so that the conquering king is clearly recognized as having power of life and death over him.

A second, and simpler, possibility is that the army, still aroused to blood lust, simply wanted to kill the man responsible for the deaths of their comrades in arms. In that case, however, taking the care to staunch his wounds would seem both unnecessary and unlikely.

Redaction: Mormon shifts his narration here from description to quotation (although his description of the battle may have also been quoted from a text). He must have been reading an official text of this exchange.

Mosiah 20:14

> 14 But Limhi said unto them: Ye shall not slay him, but bring him hither that I may see him. And they brought him. And Limhi said unto him: What cause have ye to come up to war against my people? Behold, my people have not broken the oath that I made unto you; therefore, why should ye break the oath which ye made unto my people?

Literature: There is a direct parallel between the end of verse 13 ("we have brought him before you; and now let us slay him") and the beginning of 14 ("Ye shall not slay him, but bring him hither"). These two phrases are an intentionally contrasting parallel. Even though Mormon is quoting the conversation from his source, someone had to record it. It is quite likely that we are seeing only bits and pieces of some of the original text's structure. As part of the official royal record, it is not surprising that conversations would be "enhanced" by literary devices.

Mosiah 20:15–16

> 15 And now the king said: I have broken the oath because thy people did carry away the daughters of my people; therefore, in my anger I did cause my people to come up to war against thy people.
> 16 And now Limhi had heard nothing concerning this matter; therefore he said: I will search among my people and whosoever has done this thing shall perish. Therefore he caused a search to be made among his people.

The Lamanite invasion violated a solemn treaty. The question between the kings therefore focuses on that violation. The treaty oath should only have been breached for cause. Upon finding out that there was indeed a breach of the treaty, Limhi declares that he will search out the perpetrators among his people.

In short, rather than declaring himself the winner and rejoicing over his conquered opponent, Limhi focuses, not on the battle, but on a broken oath. When Limhi learns that his own people might have been the oath-breakers, the entire situation changes. Rather than triumphant victors, the Limhites are now tainted with shame. Limhi's honor requires the resolution of this situation. The issue is no longer warfare but integrity.

Mosiah 20:17–18

> 17 Now when Gideon had heard these things, he being the king's captain, he went forth and said unto the king: I pray thee forbear, and do not search this people, and lay not this thing to their charge.
> 18 For do ye not remember the priests of thy father, whom this people sought to destroy? And are they not in the wilderness? And are not they the ones who have stolen the daughters of the Lamanites?

Gideon probably heard the account, not only because he was the king's captain, but probably because Limhi assigned him to conduct the search. This indication of Gideon's title and authority reinforces the suggestion that he had held a similar position of power under Noah. Gideon does not know that the priests have stolen the Lamanite women; but as the captain of city guard, he almost certainly would know if any group of men had left the city and especially when they returned with strange and no doubt resistant Lamanite women. The entire city was vigilant (recall Limhi's discovery of the Lamanite preparations), so it would make sense that, while Gideon could not prove that it was the priests, he would have known that it was not the Limhites.

Mosiah 20:19–21

> 19 And now, behold, and tell the king of these things, that he may tell his people that they may be pacified toward us; for behold they are already preparing to come against us; and behold also there are but few of us.
> 20 And behold, they come with their numerous hosts; and except the king doth pacify them toward us we must perish.
> 21 For are not the words of Abinadi fulfilled, which he prophesied against us—and all this because we would not hearken unto the words of the Lord, and turn from our iniquities?

The Lamanite king had been lost and was presumed dead. That situation would require that a new king be selected. The battle was lost when the king was lost, but that does not mean that the entire war was doomed. With a new king and no other ill effect from their defeat in battle, they might be expected to return to their original purpose. The oath had been breached, and the women were still missing. Thus, it is not surprising that the Lamanites were preparing for another assault on Lehi-Nephi.

In this situation, Gideon sees the fulfillment of prophecy. They will all be killed unless, as Gideon proposes, the reason for the war can be eliminated. The conflict is justified only because of the breach of an oath. If Limhi's people did not break their oath, then there is no reason for war. The Lamanite king's pleading for the Limhites will satisfy the claims of honor by declaring the Limhites innocent of oath-breaking.

Mosiah 20:22

> 22 And now let us pacify the king, and we fulfil the oath which we have made unto him; for it is better that we should be in bondage than that we should lose our lives; therefore, let us put a stop to the shedding of so much blood.

Gideon spells out the plan for ending the war. The Limhites will "fulfil the oath which we have made unto him." Modern readers may be bemused at the spectacle of the victors concerned primarily with honoring an oath made to the man they have captured and who is completely at their mercy. Furthermore, the honorable fulfillment of the oath will place the Limhites again in "bondage." Of course, Gideon clearly sees that the military options are restoration of the original bondage or annihilation by the larger army. Nevertheless, the issue is the oath, with all of its consequences.

Mosiah 20:23–24

> 23 And now Limhi told the king all the things concerning his father, and the priests that had fled into the wilderness, and attributed the carrying away of their daughters to them.
> 24 And it came to pass that the king was pacified toward his people; and he said unto them: Let us go forth to meet my people, without arms; and I swear unto you with an oath that my people shall not slay thy people.

The confrontation between the two kings appears to place the Lamanite king in the superior position. Limhi is appeasing the Lamanite king. While there are mitigating circumstances (such as the large Lamanite army), it is still unusual for a captive to be in a superior bargaining position in modern times and probably most ancient times as well. It occurs here because Limhi recognizes the legitimate Lamanite assumption that the oath had been broken. The injury caused by breaking the first oath will be healed by the second oath that the Lamanite king now makes to Limhi.

Mosiah 20:25–21:1

> 25 And it came to pass that they followed the king, and went forth without arms to meet the Lamanites. And it came to pass that they did meet the Lamanites; and the king of the Lamanites did bow himself down before them, and did plead in behalf of the people of Limhi.
> 26 And when the Lamanites saw the people of Limhi, that they were without arms, they had compassion on them and were pacified toward them, and returned with their king in peace to their own land.
> 1 And it came to pass that Limhi and his people returned to the city of Nephi, and began to dwell in the land again in peace.

This brief description certainly does not paint the full picture of what happened. Mormon's interest terminates when he demonstrates that both parties behaved honorably. However, the statement that the Lamanites forgave because they were motivated by compassion is too simple. The actual reconciliation had to have occurred with the reinstatement of the original oath-treaty. I include Mosiah 21:1

because it is more logically a conclusion to this section than a beginning to the next story.

Text: There is no chapter break here in the 1830 edition. The current break between chapters 20 and 21 is arbitrary. From a literary standpoint, however, verse 1 of chapter 21 belongs with the current unit, since it concludes the story with the restoration of peace. The next literary unit begins another story of conflict.

Mosiah 21

Mosiah 21:1

> 1 And it came to pass that Limhi and his people returned to the city of Nephi, and began to dwell in the land again in peace.

Text: As noted at the end of chapter 20, this verse is misplaced. Since there is no break in the 1830 edition, Mormon did not create this division in the sentences and would have read this verse as part of the previous unit. Verse 2 below is the proper starting point of the new unit.

Mosiah 21:2

> 2 And it came to pass that after many days the Lamanites began again to be stirred up in anger against the Nephites, and they began to come into the borders of the land round about.

It is not clear how much time passed between the resolution of the previous war and these new hostilities. "After many days" could mean anywhere from a few days to perhaps a few months. It was probably not as much as a year, since that time-unit would have been easier to note than "many days," particularly since the large plates were apparently kept by years. (See commentary accompanying Mosiah 6:7.)

Thus, it seems likely that the increase in hostilities is relatively close in time and, therefore, likely to be based on the same reasons. Since the previous conflict regarded the oath, what is creating this conflict? Mormon does not say. I speculate, however, that while the Lamanites recognized that the Limhites were probably not guilty of oath-breaking by abducting the Lamanite young women, the issue was still unresolved because it had not been determined that Noah's priests were the real culprits. In this situation, the treaty had been officially reinstated, but individual Lamanites no doubt still harbored suspicious about the Limhites' innocence. After all, the priests of Noah had come from this city. If they believed that the Limhites were indeed guilty (if only by association), the resumption of hostilities is understandable.

Mosiah 21:3

> 3 Now they durst not slay them, because of the oath which their king had made unto Limhi; but they would smite them on their cheeks, and exercise authority over them; and began to put heavy burdens upon their backs, and drive them as they would a dumb ass—

Whether there was explicit information in the plates on this point, we have no way of knowing, but Mormon understands that this increase in hostility is not government-sanctioned punishment. Rather, individuals are pushing the limits of their treaty, restrained from actually killing them only by the treaty-oath. They manifest their desire to harm, not in military situations, but as individual harassments of slapping and overburdening. Either Mormon is interpreting the situation based on his reading, or his source spelled out the implications, which Mormon reports.

Given those two options, it seems more likely to me that Mormon is the interpreter. The actions of the Limhites suggest that they did not fully understand what motivated the attacks on them but to which they respond militarily.

Mosiah 21:4–5

> 4 Yea, all this was done that the word of the Lord might be fulfilled.
> 5 And now the afflictions of the Nephites were great, and there was no way that they could deliver themselves out of their hands, for the Lamanites had surrounded them on every side.

Redaction: Verse 4 is clearly Mormon's comment. The Limhites may not have explicitly connected their current burdens with their past actions and Abinadi's prophecy, but Mormon knew the whole story and certainly saw its cause as their departure from Yahweh, Yahweh's punishment for their apostasy, and the people's repentance and reconciliation to Yahweh—in short, as a moral tale.

Verse 15 sets up the conflict of the current story with Mormon's synopsis: The oppressed Limhites require deliverance. They cannot rescue themselves because the Lamanites have them surrounded. However, while *Mormon* knows this, the Limhites see things differently because they respond by attacking the Lamanites, not once but three times. Surely, if they expected total failure, this is not the course they would have chosen. But Mormon knows that their attempts failed.

Mosiah 21:6–7

> 6 And it came to pass that the people began to murmur with the king because of their afflictions; and they began to be desirous to go against them to battle. And they did afflict the king sorely with their complaints; therefore he granted unto them that they should do according to their desires.
> 7 And they gathered themselves together again, and put on their armor, and went forth against the Lamanites to drive them out of their land.

The people were naturally unhappy with how they were treated. On top of the burdensome tribute, they had to endure taunts and physical harassment. It is not at all surprising that they sought deliverance, nor that they sought it through a military means. After all, they had achieved notable military success, previously beating back Lamanite advances and, mostly recently, having successfully ambushed an army and put it to flight. Given their concentrated pleading, it is also not surprising that Limhi gave permission for the military effort.

Mosiah 21:8

> 8 And it came to pass that the Lamanites did beat them, and drove them back, and slew many of them.

It is not surprising that the Lamanites repelled their attack with considerable loss of life, forcing them to retreat to their city. Mosiah 19:2 explained that the army was greatly reduced during Noah's destruction. Alma's disciples almost certainly included a number of able-bodied men. And finally, despite the successful ambush, no doubt the Limhites, already outnumbered two to one (Mosiah 20:11), had suffered casualties. With the Lamanites surrounding the Limhites geographically, with clear numerical superiority, and with an expectation of violence (and perhaps even the hope of provoking it) the battle to which the Limhites sallied forth was doomed from the start.

As an insight into Mesoamerican culture, however, the battle ends when the defeated Limhites retreat to their city. There is no further attack. The tribute function was still important, and the Lamanites' military goal was no doubt to suppress rebels and compel them to accept their tributary status. While Western history might predict retaliatory destruction, it did not happen.

Geography: The Lamanites are able to surround the Limhites, and apparently all Limhite action came from a single location, presumably the city of Lehi-Nephi. Zeniff was also granted the land of Shilom (Mosiah 9:6) and Noah had a building project in Shilom (Mosiah 10:13), but Limhi's record does not mention Shilom. Somewhere, Shilom passed back into Lamanite hands—perhaps at the time of Noah. Perhaps it was the site of a separate battle, perhaps the one that resulted in the reduction of the Nephite army (Mosiah 19:2). In any case, Shilom is lost, and Lehi-Nephi is completely surrounded. It is to that one remaining city that Ammon will come.

Mosiah 21:9–10

> 9 And now there was a great mourning and lamentation among the people of Limhi, the widow mourning for her husband, the son and the daughter mourning for their father, and the brothers for their brethren.
> 10 Now there were a great many widows in the land, and they did cry mightily from day to day, for a great fear of the Lamanites had come upon them.

In addition to the obvious sorrow of losing husbands, brothers, and sons, the Limhites experienced "great fear of the Lamanites." No doubt they already feared Lamanite might, but the great defeat had given them new cause for terror. Always before they had been victorious, even with smaller numbers. Now they were clearly vulnerable.

Mosiah 21:11–14

> 11 And it came to pass that their continual cries did stir up the remainder of the people of Limhi to anger against the Lamanites; and they went again to battle, but they were driven back again, suffering much loss.

12 Yea, they went again even the third time, and suffered in the like manner;
and those that were not slain returned again to the city of Nephi.
13 And they did humble themselves even to the dust, subjecting themselves to
the yoke of bondage, submitting themselves to be smitten, and to be driven to
and fro, and burdened, according to the desires of their enemies.
14 And they did humble themselves even in the depths of humility; and they
did cry mightily to God; yea, even all the day long did they cry unto their God
that he would deliver them out of their afflictions.

This passage describes the transformation of Limhite pride into humility. While verse 10 suggests that they were becoming humble, the second and third military failures (vv. 11–12) stripped away the last vestiges of pride in their military prowess and forced them to accept the reality of their altered circumstances.

The Limhite humility took two forms. First, they resigned themselves to Lamanite domination, allowing themselves to be "smitten, and to be driven to and fro, and burdened." While their abandonment of any kind of resistance is a logical consequence of the terrible military losses they have suffered, the most important form of humility (v. 14) is when they humble themselves before the Lord, realizing that only he can save them. They no longer have pride in their strength or skill. They no longer believe they can extricate themselves. In their utmost extremity, they finally call upon Yahweh.

Mosiah 21:15

15 And now the Lord was slow to hear their cry because of their iniquities; nevertheless the Lord did hear their cries, and began to soften the hearts of the Lamanites that they began to ease their burdens; yet the Lord did not see fit to deliver them out of bondage.

Human beings do not understand the Lord's timetable. He hears and answers prayers but clearly does so according to his own wisdom. He did not immediately deliver the Limhites but, by "soften[ing]" the Lamanites' hearts, the Limhites' burdens became easier. Obviously this is Mormon's assessment and also his style: to credit Yahweh for easing the sufferings and burdens of an oppressed people.

But such a development is also relatively normal. As time passed and the armed conflict receded into the past, immediate tensions obviously lessened. The longer the Limhites lived with their burdens, the more "normal" they became and the more easily they could live with lowered expectations of either comfort or superiority.

Mosiah 21:16–17

16 And it came to pass that they began to prosper by degrees in the land, and
began to raise grain more abundantly, and flocks, and herds, that they did not
suffer with hunger.
7 Now there was a great number of women, more than there was of men;
therefore king Limhi commanded that every man should impart to the support

> of the widows and their children, that they might not perish with hunger; and this they did because of the greatness of their number that had been slain.

Verses 16 and 17 are probably causally connected. The ability to increase productivity with fewer able-bodied men would necessitate adjusted social roles. The women likely took on more responsibilities for farming and herding, naturally increasing the productivity of both. Obviously households without an able-bodied male were disadvantaged, even with the expanded labor of women and children, simply because there would have been fewer hands for the work. A widow might be able to grow corn, but she could not cultivate as much land as she and her husband could have done together.

Given these economic constraints, Limhi introduces a policy of communal sharing, somewhat similar to that described by Alma and his people. It is not necessarily a religious response (although religion provides a powerful motivation for such sharing). The reduced population means that individuals would have a greater number of contacts, better information about each person's well-being, and obviously a greater need to share rather than create divisions based on the creation or distribution of life's basic necessities.

Mosiah 21:18

> 18 Now the people of Limhi kept together in a body as much as it was possible, and secured their grain and their flocks;

Obviously keeping together was a means of mutual protection. Because of the treaty, they probably did not need protection against official Lamanite attack but rather from hostile bands or resentful individuals. Lamanites who burdened and beat the Limhites would certainly continue to do so but would be somewhat restrained by the presence of a larger group.

Mosiah 21:19

> 19 And the king himself did not trust his person without the walls of the city, unless he took his guards with him, fearing that he might by some means fall into the hands of the Lamanites.

This verse explains the circumstances that Ammon encountered (Mosiah 7:7–8).

Mosiah 21:20–21

> 20 And he caused that his people should watch the land round about, that by some means they might take those priests that fled into the wilderness, who had stolen the daughters of the Lamanites, and that had caused such a great destruction to come upon them.
> 21 For they were desirous to take them that they might punish them; for they had come into the land of Nephi by night, and carried off their grain and many of their precious things; therefore they laid wait for them.

Limhi seems less concerned about the Lamanites as a threat than the priests of Noah, who are the direct cause of their current level of distress. Finding them and their Lamanite wives would conclusively demonstrate the innocence of the Limhites, thus lessening the anger of their Lamanite guards, even though such a determination would not change the conditions of the original treaty.

As for Limhi's second cause of concern—raids by the priests—it is not clear how he knows the raiders are the priests and not the Lamanites. If anyone had spotted and identified them, this record does not say so. Logically, the Lamanites have no need to steal, while the priests would be in greater need and would not have had enough time to plant and grow food. Thus, their thievery is understandable.

Mosiah 21:22

> 22 And it came to pass that there was no more disturbance between the Lamanites and the people of Limhi, even until the time that Ammon and his brethren came into the land.

Redaction: Mormon concludes his lengthy flashback. He resolves the literary problem of picking up the story where he left Ammon at the end of chapter 8 by simply repeating the Ammon/Limhi meeting. Thus, the story is told twice, once from Ammon's perspective, and once from Limhi's.

Mosiah 21:23–24

> 23 And the king having been without the gates of the city with his guard, discovered Ammon and his brethren; and supposing them to be priests of Noah therefore he caused that they should be taken, and bound, and cast into prison. And had they been the priests of Noah he would have caused that they should be put to death.
> 24 But when he found that they were not, but that they were his brethren, and had come from the land of Zarahemla, he was filled with exceedingly great joy.

This second telling adds the detail that Limhi and his guards mistook Ammon and his companions for Noah's priests. In Mosiah 7, the impression was that Limhi thought they were Lamanites. After understanding Limhi's story, however, we understand that this could not be true. The Limhites were tributaries to the Lamanites, and capturing Lamanites would have been an act of war. However, he is on the alert for Noah's priests and quickly has Ammon, Amaleki, Helem, and Hem captured and imprisoned (Mosiah 7:6–7).

This detail also suggests that Limhi's guard had not been part of Noah's court or they would have recognized Noah's priests. During Ammon' s two days in prison (Mosiah 7:8), it must have been clear that they were neither Noah's priests nor Lamanites. Limhi thus summons Ammon to identify himself (Mosiah 7:9–13).

Mosiah 21:25–27

> 25 Now king Limhi had sent, previous to the coming of Ammon, a small number of men to search for the land of Zarahemla; but they could not find it, and they were lost in the wilderness.

> 26 Nevertheless, they did find a land which had been peopled; yea, a land which was covered with dry bones; yea, a land which had been peopled and which had been destroyed; and they, having supposed it to be the land of Zarahemla, returned to the land of Nephi, having arrived in the borders of the land not many days before the coming of Ammon.
> 27 And they brought a record with them, even a record of the people whose bones they had found; and it was engraven on plates of ore.

Redaction: Why does Mormon repeat the story already told in Mosiah 8:6–11? Nothing about it returns us to Ammon's essential story—which is his meeting with and eventual liberation of the Limhites. In the previous story, it fit well into the context but seems out of place here.

I see the most plausible answer as lying in a source shift. Mosiah 8 tells the story from Ammon's point of view. That story made sense because Ammon knew of King Mosiah's abilities with the Urim and Thummim. However, in Mosiah 21 Mormon is writing the story from Limhi's account, which also records the incident of the men who searched for Zarahemla. Limhi includes this detail because of the great contrast between their sorrowful conclusion that Zarahemla had been destroyed (v. 26) and their joy at learning from Ammon that Zarahemla survived.

A modern reader does not need this repetition; but in the context of Mormon's two sources, both tellings are appropriate. We are left now only with the question of why Mormon decided to include it. I deduce that, although he felt free to provide synopses, he also remains relatively faithful to his source documents and, hence, included the event both times.

Mosiah 21:28

> 28 And now Limhi was again filled with joy on learning from the mouth of Ammon that king Mosiah had a gift from God, whereby he could interpret such engravings; yea, and Ammon also did rejoice.

In Mosiah 8:19–21, Limhi had joyfully exclaimed:

> And now, when Ammon had made an end of speaking these words the king rejoiced exceedingly, and gave thanks to God, saying: Doubtless a great mystery is contained within these plates, and these interpreters were doubtless prepared for the purpose of unfolding all such mysteries to the children of men.
>
> O how marvelous are the works of the Lord, and how long doth he suffer with his people; yea, and how blind and impenetrable are the understandings of the children of men; for they will not seek wisdom, neither do they desire that she should rule over them!
>
> Yea, they are as a wild flock which fleeth from the shepherd, and scattereth, and are driven, and are devoured by the beasts of the forest.

Limhi obviously expected information on the plates that might show his people their own future.

Variant: The printer's manuscript and the 1830 edition of the Book of Mormon read "that king Benjamin had a gift from God. . . . " "Benjamin" became "Mosiah," beginning in the 1837 edition.[1] Ammon left Zarahemla after the coronation of Mosiah (Mosiah 7:2–3) but perhaps before Benjamin's death three years after the coronation (Mosiah 6:5). Skousen notes that Benjamin lives three years after Mosiah's coronation and Ammon's party departs after three years of peace at the beginning of Mosiah's reign. The timeline is close enough that "some overlap is possible. Perhaps Ammon and his men left not knowing that Benjamin had died, or perhaps he was still alive when they left."[2]

Part of the coronation was Benjamin's transmittal to Mosiah of religious and royal objects: "And moreover, he also gave him charge concerning the records which were engraven on the plates of brass; and also the plates of Nephi; and also, the sword of Laban, and the ball or director, which led our fathers through the wilderness, which was prepared by the hand of the Lord that thereby they might be led, every one according to the heed and diligence which they gave unto him" (Mosiah 1:16). The interpreters do not appear on this list. Perhaps they were not part of the transfer of kingship. Benjamin may have retained the interpreters and his prophetic functions, passing only the governing function to his son. Therefore, the printer's manuscript's mention of "Benjamin" would have been correct in identifying the interpreters as being in his possession, not Mosiah's (at least when Ammon left Zarahemla). All of this is plausible, but perhaps not the best explanation for this particular variant.

Looking past the modern manuscript text and its variants, we must also deal with the sources Mormon used to compile his plate text. In this case, there are two possible records, that of Limhi and that of Ammon. Most of chapter 21 must come from the records of Limhi's people, even though it is quite probable that Mormon supplemented his sources with some record from Ammon, which is imputed from what must have been available but is never explicitly mentioned. I suggest that the original conversation from Ammon was that "the king" had the "gift from God, whereby he could interpret such engravings" (Mosiah 21:28) and did not mention the name of the king. The people of Limhi would remember only Benjamin, their first leader, Zeniff, having departed during Benjamin's reign (Omni 1:24–29). The recorders for Limhi's records entered their own idea of who the unnamed king was and wrote Benjamin into the record. Mormon used that record and therefore that name.

This same issue also occurs in Ether 4:1, where Moroni writes *Benjamin* and the text has been emended to read *Mosiah*. Of that textual issue, Skousen notes:

> The passage in Ether 4:1 causes more difficulties than the one on Mosiah 21:28. The Ether passage implies that king Benjamin had some control over the Jaredite record, which means, of course, that he must have still been alive when king Limhi handed over these newly found records to king Mosiah (Mosiah 22:13–14).[3]

---

[1]*Book of Mormon Critical Text: A Tool for Scholarly Reference*, 3 vols. (Provo, Utah: FARMS, 1987), 2:469.

[2]Royal Skousen, *Analysis of Textual Variants of the Book of Mormon*, THE CRITICAL TEXT OF THE BOOK OF MORMON (Provo, Utah: Foundation for Ancient Research and Mormon Studies, 2005), Vol. 4, Part 3, 1418.

[3]Ibid., 3:1419.

Rather than a significant textual issue, however, I see Moroni's reference as a reflection of the presence of *Benjamin* in Mosiah 21:28. Rather than an independent witness, Moroni is a dependent witness. Moroni simply uses the information as it appeared in his father's text on the plates Moroni had with him.[4]

Mosiah 21:29

> 29 Yet Ammon and his brethren were filled with sorrow because so many of their brethren had been slain;

Redaction: Ammon's version does not mention sorrow at the slain Limhites. Certainly he and his party sorrowed, but the slain would have been strangers to them. While their grief was general—and Limhi recorded it as an appropriate response—it was apparently less important to Ammon. In short, this passage is not a mere copy of Mosiah 8. Rather, it shows the subtle variations of a different writer with a different perspective on the same event.

Mosiah 21:30

> 30 And also that king Noah and his priests had caused the people to commit so many sins and iniquities against God; and they also did mourn for the death of Abinadi; and also for the departure of Alma and the people that went with him, who had formed a church of God through the strength and power of God, and faith on the words which had been spoken by Abinadi.

In the previous version from Ammon's records, he notes Limhi's description of Noah's improper reign and Abinadi's death (Mosiah 7:25–28) but does not mention Alma specifically. Nevertheless, Alma's activities were clearly important to Limhi as part of Abinadi's mission, so he certainly would have discussed it. The value that Limhi placed on Alma is evidenced in the last part of the verse. While the words are Mormon's, it is not difficult to read them as accurately echoing the original source of this prophet "who had formed a church of God through the strength and power of God." Limhi's people in their humbled state would certainly have recognized the power of Abinadi's prophecies about Noah and their own future. They would also have accepted his teachings about the Atoning Messiah. They must have seen in Alma's church and in his instituting baptism a further fulfillment of Abinadi's prophecy (v. 33).

Mosiah 21:31

> 31 Yea, they did mourn for their departure, for they knew not whither they had fled. Now they would have gladly joined with them, for they themselves had entered into a covenant with God to serve him and keep his commandments.

---

[4]Skousen's final comment is: "The occurrence of *Benjamin* instead of *Mosiah* cannot be readily explained as an error in the early transmission of the text; moreover, the text can be interpreted so that Benjamin was still alive when the plates of Ether were delivered by king Limhi to king Mosiah, who then gave the Jaredite record to his father, king Benjamin, for his examination and safekeeping." Ibid., 3:1420–21. As I note above, I disagree with this conclusion.

Limhi and his people would have joined Alma, not simply to be out from under the oppression of the Lamanites as Alma's people were, but because Limhi and his people recognized that Alma's people have made a covenant with Yahweh, and are under Yahweh's protection. They now want that covenant for themselves.

Mosiah 21:32–33

> 32 And now since the coming of Ammon, king Limhi had also entered into a covenant with God, and also many of his people, to serve him and keep his commandments.
> 33 And it came to pass that king Limhi and many of his people were desirous to be baptized; but there was none in the land that had authority from God. And Ammon declined doing this thing, considering himself an unworthy servant.

Limhi sees Ammon as a means of entering into the same covenant that Alma had made with Yahweh and into which he had introduced his people. Indeed, the Limhites had already made the covenant in their hearts (v. 32) but were awaiting the ordinance of baptism which would seal the covenant. Having seen (or at least heard reports of) Alma and his church, they wanted that same benefit for themselves and hoped that Ammon could give them the benefits of Alma's baptism. Ammon declines, not because he lacks authority, but because he sees himself as "an unworthy servant." Daniel C. Peterson suggests that Ammon felt "unworthy" because he was a warrior.[5] I believe that there were even more forces at play.

The Limhites have already delayed baptism because "there was none in the land that had authority from God." They assumed that Ammon, coming from Zarahemla, would possess such authority. Ammon neither confirms nor denies that point. Ammon appears to hesitate for reasons more complex than just the worthiness to perform a baptism. (See commentary following vv. 34–35.)

Mosiah 21:34–35

> 34 Therefore they did not at that time form themselves into a church, waiting upon the Spirit of the Lord. Now they were desirous to become even as Alma and his brethren, who had fled into the wilderness.
> 35 They were desirous to be baptized as a witness and a testimony that they were willing to serve God with all their hearts; nevertheless they did prolong the time; and an account of their baptism shall be given hereafter.

Alma's baptism became the sign of entering into a church, which was being organized on the spot. Since the Limhites' understanding of religion at that point consisted of the obviously apostate version of Noah and the obviously Yahweh-approved church of Alma, naturally the Limhites wanted to follow Alma's example in becoming a church. There is no clear indication that a church existed in

---

[5]Daniel C. Peterson, "Priesthood in Mosiah," in *The Book of Mormon: Mosiah, Salvation Only through Christ*, edited by Monte S. Nyman and Charles D. Tate Jr. (Provo, Utah: BYU Religious Studies Center, 1991), 201.

Zarahemla at this time. The first mention occurs in Mosiah 25:18–19 after Alma's arrival and ministry in Zarahemla. It seems likely to me that Ammon is balking, not over the smaller issue of authority to baptize, but rather at the greater authority of forming a church. Being asked to perform a baptism in the context of creating a church would have been unfamiliar territory and a place where Ammon declined to go without more specific instruction from King Mosiah.[6] Otherwise, if Ammon had the priesthood and the authority to baptize, it is hard to imagine why he would deny the ordinance to a people who were so clearly prepared for and desirous of it.

Mosiah 21:36

> 36 And now all the study of Ammon and his people, and king Limhi and his people, was to deliver themselves out of the hands of the Lamanites and from bondage.

Text: This verse provides a transition to a new literary unit. Mormon is closing the flashback portion of the text and now begins new material. That new material appears in a separate chapter in both the 1830 and modern editions, a literary signal of the return to the main story line.

[6]Ibid. 200. Peterson specifically notes that the church was Alma's innovation.

Mosiah 22

Mosiah 22:1

1 And now it came to pass that Ammon and king Limhi began to consult with the people how they should deliver themselves out of bondage; and even they did cause that all the people should gather themselves together; and this they did that they might have the voice of the people concerning the matter.

Culture/History: It is significant that Ammon and Limhi consulted the "voice of the people." (See "Excursus: The Voice of the People," following Mosiah 29.) Obviously, this decision lay beyond the king's normal authority, otherwise the consultation would not have been necessary. When Noah was king, given the size of the city (and Noah's probable proclivities), the king would simply decide and declare that decision. In this case, the entire population will be affected by the decision. In fact, it is quite likely that the options had already been thoroughly discussed, and the meeting was really held to let the people participate in confirming a decision that would uproot them from their homes.

A second important piece of information is that, while they were under Lamanite guard, the Lamanites were not in the city or close enough that the gathering attracted their attention. It seems clear that the Limhites conducted their discussion without special precautions against its coming to the Lamanites' attention.

Mosiah 22:2

2 And it came to pass that they could find no way to deliver themselves out of bondage, except it were to take their women and children, and their flocks, and their herds, and their tents, and depart into the wilderness; for the Lamanites being so numerous, it was impossible for the people of Limhi to contend with them, thinking to deliver themselves out of bondage by the sword.

A military solution has not only failed three times but resulted in punishing losses of their adult men each time. Negotiation is not an option either; they have nothing to negotiate with. Thus, flight is the only way out of their bondage.

Mosiah 22:3–5

3 Now it came to pass that Gideon went forth and stood before the king, and said unto him: Now O king, thou hast hitherto hearkened unto my words many times when we have been contending with our brethren, the Lamanites.
4 And now O king, if thou hast not found me to be an unprofitable servant, or if thou hast hitherto listened to my words in any degree, and they have been of

> service to thee, even so I desire that thou wouldst listen to my words at this time, and I will be thy servant and deliver this people out of bondage.
> 5 And the king granted unto him that he might speak. And Gideon said unto him:

Redaction: While it is possible that Mormon created dialogue, it seems that he prefers to copy it from his sources. Of course, the author of the source document may have exercised creativity (or literary formulae) in recording the dialogue.

In this particular case, it seems to be authentic to the period. Rather than tersely introducing the topic, Gideon gives an elaborate introduction why he should be allowed to speak. He reminds the king that his valuable past services and useful advice. Of course, Limhi already knows this, so Gideon's introduction is entirely useless as information. However, it is entirely appropriate as revealing the protocol required for a formal occasion. Mormon's style tends to be more direct. If Mormon had invented this speech, he would have more likely moved quickly to the point.

Mosiah 22:6

> 6 Behold the back pass, through the back wall, on the back side of the city. The Lamanites, or the guards of the Lamanites, by night are drunken; therefore let us send a proclamation among all this people that they gather together their flocks and herds, that they may drive them into the wilderness by night.

Gideon's knowledge of Lamanite drunkenness tells us that Gideon has some system of espionage. The fact that the Lamanites seem to have frequently, or even habitually, gotten drunk is interesting and may have been interpreted, even among the Lamanites, as a moral failing. Jacques Soustelle, who analyzed the Mexica (Aztec) laws from the time of the Conquest concerning drunkenness, observed:

> When one studies the literature upon the subject, one has the feeling that the Indians were very clearly aware of their strong natural inclination to alcoholism, and that they were quite determined to work against this evil, and to control themselves, by practising an extraordinarily severe policy of repression. "Nobody drank wine (octli) excepting only those who were already aged, and they drank a little in secret, without becoming drunk. If a drunk man showed himself in public, or if he were caught drinking, or if he were found speechless in the street, or if he wandered about singing or in the company of other drunkards, he was punished, if he were a plebeian, by being beaten to death, or else he was strangled before the young men (of the district) by way of an example and to make them shun drunkenness. If the drunkard were noble, he was strangled in private."
>
> There were ferocious laws against public drunkenness. The statutes of Nezaualcoyotl punished the priest taken in drunkenness with death; and death was the punishment for the drunken dignitary, official or ambassador if he were found in the palace: the dignitary who had got drunk without scandal was still punished, but only by the loss of his office and his titles. The drunken plebeian got off the first time with no more than having his head shaved in public, while the crowd jeered at him; but the backslider was punished with death, as the nobles were for their first offence.
>
> Here we have an exceedingly violent case of socially defensive reaction against an equally violent tendency, whose existence has been historically proved, for when the

> conquest had destroyed the moral and judicial underpinning of Mexican civilisation, alcoholism spread among the Indians to an extraordinary degree.[1]

While this example comes over a thousand years later than the Book of Mormon and from an entirely different culture, there is no reason to suppose that the potential problem with alcohol was much less in earlier times and different cultures. The severe laws against public drunkenness demonstrate a known disposition to drink (similar to virtually all societies which have discovered alcohol). The laws don't tell us that the drinking stopped, but that it was considered a widespread problem.

As Gideon describes the situation, the Lamanites responsible for guarding "the back gate" get drunk nightly. Gideon does not mention that any other group of guards had this problem—although, since he was interested only in the back gate as an escape route, there would have been no reason for him to comment on Lamanite guards in general. I hypothesize that the comparative isolation of this group allowed them to escape the rigorous injunction against drunkenness (admittedly also hypothetical). Because Gideon also speaks of a secret pass (v. 7), the region may have been generally considered impassible, except perhaps at the one location guarded by the Lamanites. Therefore, these negligent guards apparently anticipated no efforts that their captives would escape, and especially not at night.[2] This Lamanite complacency would be increased by the lack of probable trouble as well as the lack of recent troubles. When combined with their relative isolation, it would appear that they literally let their guard down.

Mosiah 22:7

> 7 And I will go according to thy command and pay the last tribute of wine to the Lamanites, and they will be drunken; and we will pass through the secret pass on the left of their camp when they are drunken and asleep.

Because wine is a consistent tribute to the Lamanites, it is clear that, if there were any stringent prohibitions such as were seen among the later Aztecs, it was against public drunkenness and not against drinking. In fact, the Aztecs drank. Modern laws similarly distinguish between drinking and drinking to excess. In the case of the Lamanite guards, it appears that they not only drank, but were known to drink to excess. Gideon's two-part plan begins with assuring that the habitually drunken guards will truly be incapacitated, and the second part is to use the "secret pass." How "secret" was it? Gideon knew about it, but obviously the Lamanites didn't, since their encampment would have been squarely athwart the most obvious route out of the land.

Mosiah 22:8

> 8 Thus we will depart with our women and our children, our flocks, and our herds into the wilderness; and we will travel around the land of Shilom.

---

[1]Jacques Soustelle, *The Daily Life of the Aztecs* (Stanford, Calif.: Stanford University Press, 1961), 156–57.

[2]The difficulties of traveling at night meant that military marches rarely took place at night. Ross Hassig, *Aztec Warfare* (Norman: University of Oklahoma Press, 1988), 95.

Geography: Sorenson admits that Gideon's information is too scanty to reconstruct the route out of Lehi-Nephi. However, he suggests a plausible route that bends toward Shilom on the south, then reaches a more passable valley system leading northward to Zarahemla.[3] The relative locations of Shemlon, Shilom, and Lehi-Nephi suggest that Shilom lay between Shemlon and Lehi-Nephi. All of Limhi's people are currently living in Lehi-Nephi. Either Shilom is uninhabited or, more probably, is inhabited by Lamanites who seem to be expanding and who would have found desirable Noah's elaborate architectural experiments (Mosiah 11:13).

Keeping this arrangement in mind, then, the most likely "back gate" would be the one farthest from Shemlon and Shilom, thus allowing the people to put the city between them and the largest force of the Lamanites. They would not go nearer Shemlon than they had to. In Sorenson's geography, their path would go down-valley to the south-southwest before connecting with the northwesterly valley. This route would eliminate the need to take their herds across mountains—possibly a safer, but certainly a more difficult route. Thus, this turn toward Shilom makes geographic sense, though less from the perspective of safety.

Mosiah 22:9–10

> 9 And it came to pass that the king hearkened unto the words of Gideon.
> 10 And king Limhi caused that his people should gather their flocks together; and he sent the tribute of wine to the Lamanites; and he also sent more wine, as a present unto them; and they did drink freely of the wine which king Limhi did send unto them.

Limhi gives the Lamanites the regular portion of tribute wine. As previously noted (see commentary accompanying Mosiah 22:6), this drink was probably *pulque* (or *octli,* in the Nahuatl language) the standard Mesoamerican intoxicant, made by fermenting the sap of the maguey plant, rather than wine made from grapes. Limhi also gives them an extra portion, a certain encouragement to overindulgence.

Text: Both the printer's manuscript and the 1830 edition of the Book of Mormon begin this sentence with "And it came to pass that king Limhi. . . . " The phrase was deleted in all editions from 1837 through the present.[4]

Mosiah 22:11

> 11 And it came to pass that the people of king Limhi did depart by night into the wilderness with their flocks and their herds, and they went round about the land of Shilom in the wilderness, and bent their course toward the land of Zarahemla, being led by Ammon and his brethren.

Geography: Limhi's people exit from the "back" of the city through a secret pass between mountains, apparently leading toward Shilom. Since the topography

---

[3]John L. Sorenson, *An Ancient American Setting for the Book of Mormon* (Salt Lake City: Deseret Book/Provo, Utah: Foundation for Ancient Research and Mormon Studies, 1985), 175.

[4]*Book of Mormon Critical Text: A Tool for Scholarly Reference*, 3 vols. (Provo, Utah: FARMS, 1987), 2:472.

suggests that Shilom is at a lower elevation than Lehi-Nephi, the group would be traveling down a valley, perhaps a drainage, toward Shilom. Thus, they go "round about the land of Shilom." They do not get all of the way to Shilom, because they remain "in the wilderness," meaning unpopulated land. However, it is certainly not desolate. It would have had trees, pasturage for their flocks, and other types of cover. Although they were following no road, the bottom of the valley, ravine, or drainage provided a reasonable pathway.

At some point before reaching Shilom and at a safe distance from that city, they were able to "bend their course toward the land of Zarahemla," suggesting skirting some foothills. Sorenson's map depicts precisely this arrangement of mountains and valleys.[5]

Mosiah 22:12

12 And they had taken all their gold, and silver, and their precious things, which they could carry, and also their provisions with them, into the wilderness; and they pursued their journey.

Culture: "Gold and silver, and . . . precious things" are probably raw trade materials—luxury goods. Even though they were not *money*, they had trade value. Doubtless the Limhites expected to need to have the ability to acquire goods in Zarahemla and they took with them the means of exchange. (See commentary accompanying Jacob 2:12–13 for more information on the early Nephite economy.)

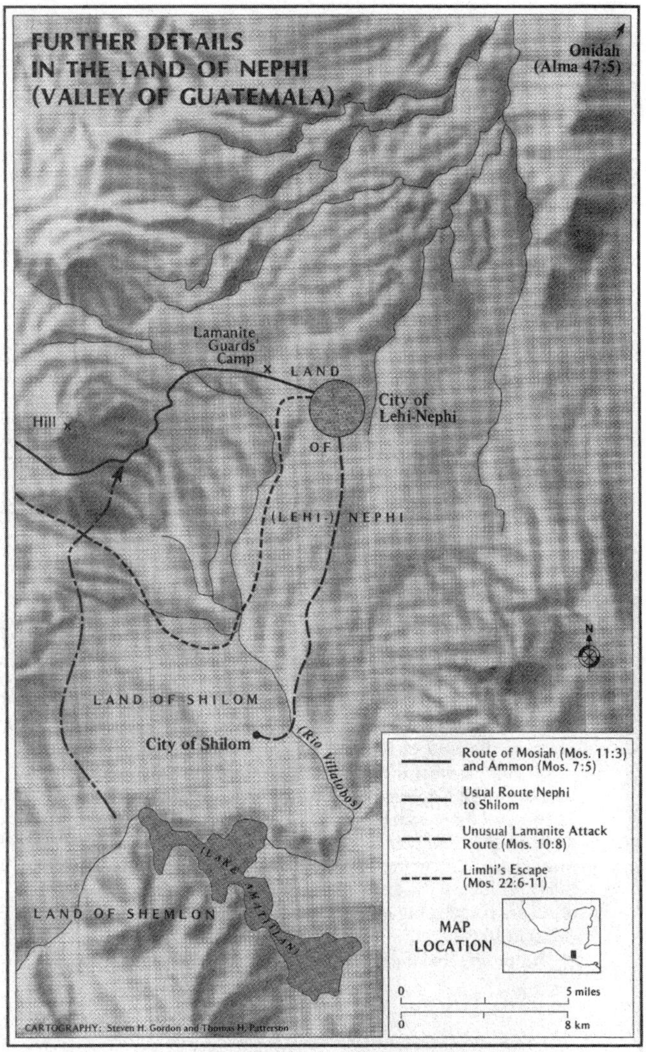

[5]Sorenson, *An Ancient American Setting for the Book of Mormon*, 170.

Mosiah 22:13

13 And after being many days in the wilderness they arrived in the land of Zarahemla, and joined Mosiah's people, and became his subjects.

Few details are reported about the trip itself, but it was no doubt arduous. Probably they followed a path similar to the one Ammon took to find them. They probably followed the correct river rather than the plausible error of the Limhite search party that had attempted to find Zarahemla. (See commentary accompanying Mosiah 8:8.)

Upon their arrival in Zarahemla, Limhi recognizes Mosiah's right to rule, probably because (1) the Limhites were coming as strangers to a city with a greater population, (2) the historical fact that Limhi's ancestors had been subject to $Mosiah_1$, and (3) the recognition that Zarahemla was rescuing the Limhites.

Variant: The reading "joined *Mosiah's* people," was first introduced in the 1920 edition. Up to that date, the text had read "joined *his* people."[6] The clear intent is to reference the king of the land. The original "his" follows "arrived in the land of Zarahemla." Because the land and city of Zarahemla were apparently named for the man Zarahemla who was the leader/ruler of the land prior to the Nephite arrival, the intent of the phrase is certainly to reference the king of the land. Of course, at this time the king was Mosiah, not Zarahemla. The change to *Mosiah's* people makes the intent clear, but creates a situation where an anomalous construction was added to the text. All other designations of a people are "the people of . . . ,"[7] not "someone's people."

Mosiah 22:14

14 And it came to pass that Mosiah received them with joy; and he also received their records, and also the records which had been found by the people of Limhi.

Text: The twenty-four gold plates now translated as our book of Ether are mentioned, but they are not the only plates given to Mosiah. The record of Zeniff (Mosiah 25:5), which probably also included Noah's and Limhi's histories, was also given to Mosiah, who read these accounts to his people.

The fact that the record is named for Zeniff, even though it encompassed the reign of three kings, is analogous to the books on the plates of Nephi as dynastic records. (See Mosiah, Part 1: Context, Chapter 2, "Mormon's Structural Editing: Chapters and Books.") The official lineage record would be named for the founding ancestor and the name of the "ancestor book" would not be changed until a change in dynasty occurred. This is what we see occurring in the book of Mosiah, which begins a new dynasty and also contains the accounts of three kings ($Mosiah_1$, Benjamin, and $Mosiah_2$).

---

[6]Royal Skousen, *Analysis of Textual Variants of the Book of Mormon*, THE CRITICAL TEXT OF THE BOOK OF MORMON (Provo, Utah: Foundation for Ancient Research and Mormon Studies, 2005), Vol. 4, Part 3, 1428.

[7]Ibid., 3:1429.

Culture: While Mosiah received the Limhites "with joy," their social and economic integration no doubt presented a difficult task. Since they were an entire community, complete with their own clans, history, and experiences, they would probably wish to remain together. Mosiah thus probably had to find a way to include a new city inside his jurisdiction. The Limhites would therefore be sent to add to a small population, or to begin a new village in the land of Zarahemla, but would not remain in the city of Zarahemla. The presence of a city and land of Gideon may indicate their ultimate location (Alma 6:7).

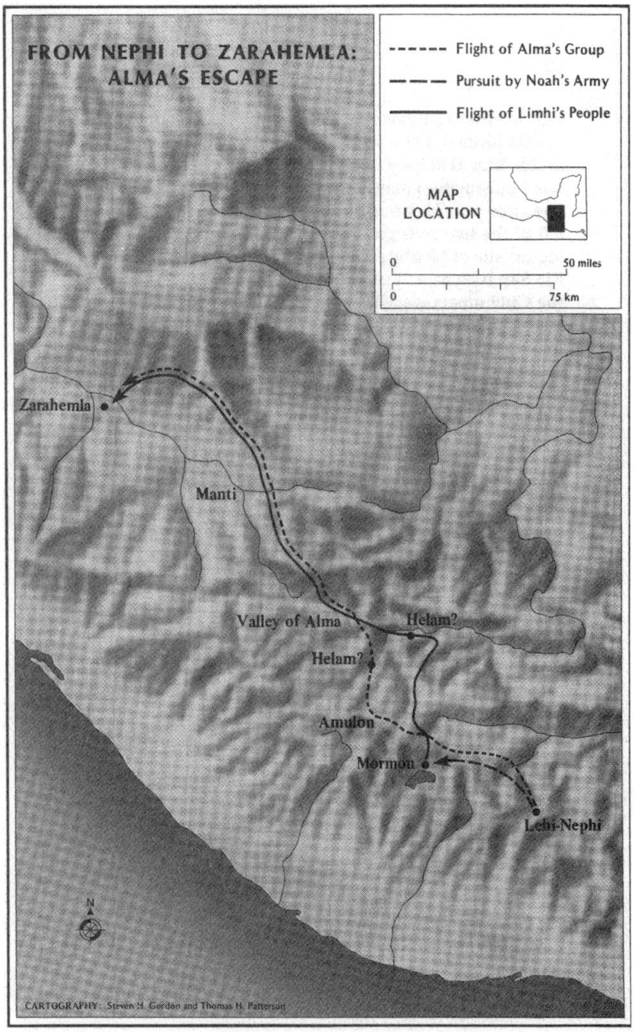

Translation: It is possible that "received them with joy" is the formal phrase used for the integration of one people into another, because virtually the identical phrase recurs when Alma's people come to Zarahemla: "And after they had been in the wilderness twelve days they arrived in the land of Zarahemla; and king Mosiah did also receive them with joy" (Mosiah 24:25). If this is not a formal acceptance phrase, then it is possible that Mormon is making a literary parallel to indicate that both the Limhites and Almaites were accepted equally.

Mosiah 22:15–16

15 And now it came to pass when the Lamanites had found that the people of Limhi had departed out of the land by night, that they sent an army into the wilderness to pursue them;
16 And after they had pursued them two days, they could no longer follow their tracks; therefore they were lost in the wilderness.

There is no indication that Limhi (or Mormon) knew this information. Perhaps some scouts brought up the rear of the Limhite retreat and observed both the pursuit and when it ended. Why did the tracks of so large a people become untraceable after two days? They passed through a mountainous forest, and the broken vegetation, animal dung, and footprints of so many people would have surely left their mark. It would seem nearly impossible for a following army to "lose" the trail. However, this is a record that is recorded by Limhi. He and his people did not know *why* they were no longer followed. They knew only that they were not. Whether the speculation on how the army failed to follow them was Limhi's speculation or a later insertion by Mormon cannot be known.

Text: This is also the end of a chapter in the 1830 edition of the Book of Mormon.

Mosiah 23

An account of Alma and the people of the Lord, who were driven into the wilderness by the people of King Noah.

Text: This inserted notation about the following chapter probably comes from the text on the plates and is a direct structural parallel to the preface before our Mosiah 9 that introduces the record of Zeniff.

Mormon's inclusion of these introductory phrases signals that he is beginning a major divergence in his story line. In Zeniff's case, it also certainly denoted a change in the source material for his text, which is taken from the plates of Zeniff. This chapter also indicates a clear change in source material. Mormon has been telling the story of Zeniff through Limhi, most of which would have come from the official Zeniffite dynasty records with additions from the records of the sons of Mosiah (probably Ammon's). Now Mormon tells the story of Alma. Mormon does not specifically mention his source; but since Alma's people have departed from the land where the Zeniffite records were kept, their story could not have been on the Zeniffite records.

In the 1830 edition of the Book of Mormon, this introduction presents chapter 11. That single chapter is now represented by Mosiah 23–27, inclusive. The text in the 1981 edition indicating that this introduction covers only our chapters 23 and 24 is a misreading of Mormon's intent.

If we assume that chapter breaks are Mormon's own textual divisions (see Mosiah, Part 1: Context, Chapter 2, "Mormon's Structural Editing: Chapters and Books") then Mormon is considering our current chapters 23–27 as an entire unit. This unit is not simply the story of Alma before he arrived in Zarahemla. It is the story of Alma's importance to Zarahemla. Alma is a pivotal character in the Book of Mormon, even though no "book" is named for him as one is for his son, $Alma_2$.

The two summaries give us only a little more information about the way Mormon was organizing his records. Both Zeniff's record and Alma's are separate document traditions from the large plates of Nephi, yet Mormon includes both records under the "book" heading from the large plates of Nephi (which is the book of Mosiah from the large plates, named for $Mosiah_1$). Mormon's conceptual pattern follows the overall structural lead of the large plates of Nephi and fills in important pieces with supplemental records such as those of Zeniff and Alma. Of course, it is quite probable that these external sources were physically included in the large plates, allowing Mormon access to the separate traditions even though he was consulting only the official large plates.

Mosiah 23:1

1 Now Alma, having been warned of the Lord that the armies of king Noah would come upon them, and having made it known to his people, therefore they gathered together their flocks, and took of their grain, and departed into the wilderness before the armies of king Noah.

Mormon now returns to the story of Alma after a long detour since chapter 18. He had concluded that part of Alma's story with: "And it came to pass that Alma and the people of the Lord were apprised of the coming of the king's army; therefore they took their tents and their families and departed into the wilderness. And they were in number about four hundred and fifty souls" (Mosiah 18:34–35). He picks up that story by repeating the basic information.

Mosiah 23:2

2 And the Lord did strengthen them, that the people of king Noah could not overtake them to destroy them.

Alma's account states that Yahweh warned Alma of the army's approach (Mosiah 18:34, 23:1). With such divine protection, it is not surprising that Yahweh would also assist in their travel. Alma's people, traveling with families and flocks, managed to outdistance a military expedition, or at least move away with sufficient speed that the army could not find them. This protection resembles that enjoyed by the fleeing Limhites. Alma's group had repented as part of their community formation. By the time the Limhites left Lehi-Nephi, they, too, had been humbled, had repented, and had covenanted with Yahweh. Yahweh protected both.

Mosiah 23:3–4

3 And they fled eight days' journey into the wilderness.

4 And they came to a land, yea, even a very beautiful and pleasant land, a land of pure water.

How far did they actually travel? Sorenson suggests an average speed of no more than eleven miles per day, based on comparative estimates for similar situations.[1] Eight days' travel, then, would position them approximately eighty-eight miles from Mormon, which was another three days (fifteen to forty) miles from Lehi-Nephi.[2] Since they were fleeing from Noah's army, they certainly would not gone toward Lehi-Nephi (and therefore Shilom), and they apparently were going in the general direction of Zarahemla, since they could continue to Zarahemla from this new location without doubling back.

They reach a location of "pure water," the phrase used to describe the waters of Mormon. (See commentary accompanying Mosiah 18:5.) As mentioned in the

---

[1]John L. Sorenson, *Mormon's Map* (Provo, Utah: FARMS, 2000), 56.
[2]Ibid., 56.

commentary on that verse, the phrase may allude to a Mesoamerican conception that waters from earthly sources are pure.[3]

Variant: The printer's manuscript and 1830 edition of the Book of Mormon both begin this passage with: "And it came to pass that they fled. . . . " This was deleted from all editions from the 1837 through the present.[4]

Mosiah 23:5

> 5 And they pitched their tents, and began to till the ground, and began to build buildings; yea, they were industrious, and did labor exceedingly.

This verse bears superficial similarities to 2 Nephi 5:7, 11, in which Nephi describes the foundation of his city. Alma's record is similarly sparse. His people pitch their tents (as they did in 2 Ne. 5:7) and begin to till the ground (as in 2 Ne. 5:11).

These people assume that they will stay in this location. Even though we know that they will eventually reach Zarahemla, they are now attempting to create their own city. When they have met their most immediate needs (shelter and food), they take up the task of constructing buildings, or laying out a permanent village. The first building Nephi's people worked on was their temple (2 Ne. 5:16). We might speculate that Alma's people similarly began construction of a religious building, given the religious orientation of this new colony.

Text: Both the printer's manuscript and the 1830 edition of the Book of Mormon begin this text with "And it come to pass that they pitched. . . . " This phrase disappeared from all editions, beginning in 1837. Another more interesting deletion also occurs in this text. The phrase: "began to build buildings &c." was removed in the 1920 edition.[5] The removal of the "&c" does not change the essential meaning of the text, but it is curious that it was there at all, communicating as it does an additional, but nonspecific, construction. Any guess about what this common English abbreviation of the Latin "et cetera" may have represented on the plates is absolutely conjectural, but it is unusual for Mormon to generalize in this way. Perhaps the word being translated had a meaning of "build buildings and other evidences of civilization." Such a hypothetical word might exist, and might be reasonably translated as "build buildings &c."

The other possibility for "&c" is that Joseph or Oliver tired of writing something out, and simply abbreviated. The use of "&c" is typically for things that should be understood and therefore do not need saying. But this second hypothesis seems less likely. If they had not wearied of writing out so much of Isaiah, whose text is identical to the KJV, why would they have then reached for an abbreviation about building a city? Barring a third hypothesis I have not thought of, the first possibility seems likelier. Conceivably Mormon might have thought that the essentials of city establishment could warrant the "&c" even if we might wish for more elaboration.

---

[3]John L. Sorenson, *An Ancient American Setting for the Book of Mormon* (Salt Lake City: Deseret Book/Provo, Utah: Foundation for Ancient Research and Mormon Studies, 1985), 176–79.

[4]*Book of Mormon Critical Text: A Tool for Scholarly Reference*, 3 vols. (Provo, Utah: FARMS, 1987), 2:473.

[5]Ibid.

Mosiah 23:6–8

> 6 And the people were desirous that Alma should be their king, for he was beloved by his people.
> 7 But he said unto them: Behold, it is not expedient that we should have a king; for thus saith the Lord: Ye shall not esteem one flesh above another, or one man shall not think himself above another; therefore I say unto you it is not expedient that ye should have a king.
> 8 Nevertheless, if it were possible that ye could always have just men to be your kings it would be well for you to have a king.

Alma also echoes Nephi on governance. Alma's people, like Nephi's, wanted him to be king: "And it came to pass that they would that I should be their king. But I, Nephi, was desirous that they should have no king; nevertheless, I did for them according to that which was in my power" (2 Ne. 5:18).

Alma and Nephi share some of the same circumstances in beginning their colonies. The biggest difference is that Nephi agreed to become king but Alma refuses. Nephi never indicated any dislike for the position of king per se, but Alma is adamantly opposed to the institution itself.

Nephi had had first-hand experience with an unjust and tyrannous ruler—Laban or perhaps Josiah. (See 1 Nephi, Part 1: Context, Chapter 1, "The Historical Setting of 1 Nephi.") He apparently had other models of righteous rulers from which to draw (or at least an Israelite tradition that accepted some kings as righteous). By contrast, Alma's experience with king Noah had fostered in him a dislike of kingship per se, not simply the person who might occupy that position. This distinction is an important one, because Alma will influence Zarahemla to replace its system of hereditary rulers with the reign of the judges. (See commentary accompanying Mosiah 29:12–13.)

Part of his argument against kings comes from his interpretation of a divine commandment: "for thus saith the Lord: Ye shall not esteem one flesh above another, or one man shall not think himself above another." Since this particular commandment appears only in this passage, it is impossible to tell whether Alma is quoting a source lost to us or announcing a new revelation. Certainly the argument is an extrapolation. Apparently, the "commandment" was "ye shall not esteem one flesh above another, or one man shall not think himself above another." But the conclusion ("therefore I say unto you it is not expedient that ye should have a king") appears to be Alma's interpretation of the commandment.

It is interesting that Alma dismisses kingship because it can lead to presumed personal superiority and social hierarchies. He is certainly thinking of King Noah here. Nephi could not be accused of this fault nor could Benjamin (though Alma did not and could not have known Benjamin), and Alma quickly points out that a good man could be a good king. Possibly Alma was including the Lamanite kings along with Noah.

But Alma was concerned with more than the occupier of the throne. Kingship led to social stratification along economic lines as it had in the land of Nephi. When a bad man ruled, the institution itself could be disastrous, since it did not check the temptation to indulge in stratification.

Text: The printer's manuscript and the 1830 edition of the Book of Mormon begin this text with "And it came to pass that. . . . " This phrase was removed from all editions from the 1837 through the present.[6]

Mosiah 23:9–11

> 9 But remember the iniquity of king Noah and his priests; and I myself was caught in a snare, and did many things which were abominable in the sight of the Lord, which caused me sore repentance;
> 10 Nevertheless, after much tribulation, the Lord did hear my cries, and did answer my prayers, and has made me an instrument in his hands in bringing so many of you to a knowledge of his truth.
> 11 Nevertheless, in this I do not glory, for I am unworthy to glory of myself.

Alma reinforces his argument with a brief description of his conversion. He asserts that his behavior required repentance. Simply hearing Abinadi did not transform him from nonbeliever to believer without undergoing "sore repentance" (v. 9). It fills in his autobiography immediately after he escaped from the palace during Abinadi's trial. We now know that he underwent a trial of his own, recognized that his behavior violated God's will, understood the gravity of his actions, and desired change. This is the process of repentance. (See "Excursus: The Principle of Repentance," following 3 Nephi 18.) We do not know what exactly that "sore" repentance required of him, although it included "much tribulation," but the effect on his soul was tremendous. Once repentant and converted, Alma experienced the exquisite pleasure of being accepted by Yahweh and becoming his instrument for teaching these who also hearkened to the message of Abinadi (through Alma).

In addition to the interest of the information itself, it is interesting that this description of repentance comes as part of his argument against kingship. The repentance was from Yahweh, but the need for repentance came from the excesses of kingship. While Alma's first argument against kingship was the risk of social stratification, he now attacks the personal effect of a king who has departed from Yahweh's ways.

Ancient kingship was both religious and political. As religious leader, Noah was responsible to lead his people to Yahweh. Instead he led them away. Alma is not just adding a personal reflection, but making another argument about the dangers—this time spiritual ones—of kingship.

Mosiah 23:12

> 12 And now I say unto you, ye have been oppressed by king Noah, and have been in bondage to him and his priests, and have been brought into iniquity by them; therefore ye were bound with the bands of iniquity.

Rhetoric: Alma uses his experience as a bridge to his listeners' experience. Alma was in bondage; they were in bondage. Alma was influenced by King Noah; they

---

[6] Ibid., 2:474.

were "oppressed by king Noah." The connection here is entirely spiritual. For at least some of the time, the people willingly followed Noah. Mosiah 11:7 at least implies that they began to accept Noah's methods. They rejoiced in defeating the Lamanites, which they would have interpreted as divine approval of Noah's ways (Mosiah 11:17–19).

But the bondage that concerns Alma is not Noah's burdensome taxes (Mosiah 11:3) but the burden of iniquity that he caused them to bear. Because he was king, they were "brought into iniquity." Alma is talking about spiritual evil, not political nor economic. In the end, Alma's major argument against kingship is the danger of a king who turns away from Yahweh and leads his people astray.

Mosiah 23:13

> 13 And now as ye have been delivered by the power of God out of these bonds; yea, even out of the hands of king Noah and his people, and also from the bonds of iniquity, even so I desire that ye should stand fast in this liberty wherewith ye have been made free, and that ye trust no man to be a king over you.

Rhetoric: Alma concludes by pointing out that Yahweh has delivered them from their "bonds of iniquity" (v. 12). The king led them away from Yahweh and Yahweh led them away from a king. As a final logical argument, Alma is saying to his people that, since Yahweh led them away from a king who caused them to stray from God, they should honor Yahweh by staying away from kings. Alma tells his people, "I desire that ye should stand fast in this liberty wherewith ye have been made free." He is not contrasting two political systems: monarchy and democracy. He is rather contrasting the freedom of Yahweh to the tyranny of a king who did not follow Yahweh.

If Alma's concerns are so clearly religious, why does he focus those concerns on the king rather than the people's individual righteousness? Part of the answer lies in the intimate connection between the king's roles as both political ruler and anointed religious ruler. Ancient kings were considered to rule under a divine mandate. It was because of this religious power that Noah had the ability to bring the people into the "bondage of iniquity."

Kings over Lamanite cities may have also fit Alma's argument. The elaboration of the Maya concept of kingship occurs in the Late Preclassic (500 B.C. to A.D. 250). Schele and Freidel discuss the archaeological evidence for the rise of kingship in a site named Cerros in present-day Belize (near Chetumal Bay) dating to around 50 B.C.[7] Although kings had been known in Mesoamerica for a thousand years, Cerros saw a distinctive elaboration of the ruler's social role, caused by social stratification.[8] Schele and Freidel note:

---

[7]Linda Schele and David Freidel, *A Forest of Kings: The Untold Story of the Ancient Maya* (New York: William Morrow and Company, 1990), 103.

[8]Ibid., 97.

> We know that the problem the Maya were trying to resolve was one of social inequality because that is precisely the state of affairs that the institution of ahau ["lord"] defines as legitimate, necessary, and intrinsic to the order of the cosmos. The development of a high civilization always creates problems of social inequality, but such differences between people need not be manifested negatively. For the Maya, kingship became the primary symbol of and rationale for the noble class, the *ahauob* ["lords," plural of *ahau*]. Kingship addressed the problem of inequality, not by destroying or denying it, but by embedding the contradictory nature of privilege into the very fabric of life itself.[9]

Noah's reign was characterized by increasing class distinctions. Neither Noah nor his priests worked with their own hands (the traditional Nephite egalitarian ideal). The proliferation of expensive buildings created visual monuments to the ruler's power and parallel the manifestations for social stratification that Schele and Freidel see in Cerros. It seems reasonable that Noah's excesses mimicked the social style of other kings he might have seen or heard about. Hence, Alma's mistrust was not of Noah alone but of the entire social, political, and religious ideology that had become identified with Noah as monarch. He feared that, if his people insisted on reestablishing the institution of kingship, they would also accept social stratification (Alma's first reason) and ultimately the erosion of their religion (Alma's second reason).

Mosiah 23:14

> 14 And also trust no one to be your teacher nor your minister, except he be a man of God, walking in his ways and keeping his commandments.

Alma makes it clear that his ultimate concern is religious rather than political. In addition to eschewing kingship, the people should not tolerate unrighteous or unorthodox teachers or ministers. Obviously he sees, as the ultimate danger, losing the relationship with Yahweh that they had so recently gained and which they had confirmed by their baptism.

Mosiah 23:15

> 15 Thus did Alma teach his people, that every man should love his neighbor as himself, that there should be no contention among them.

This teaching of neighborly love and peace is Alma's summary to the previous text. He does not elaborate on the dangers of godless teachers but pleads for social unity rather than social stratification. He probably saw loving one's neighbor as the antithesis to social stratification, which resulted in seeing oneself as better or worse than one's neighbor (v. 7: "Ye shall not esteem one flesh above another, or one man shall not think himself above another").

Mosiah 23:16

> 16 And now, Alma was their high priest, he being the founder of their church.

---

[9]Ibid., 98.

When Mormon interjects "And now . . . " it typically signals that he is changing subjects. (See commentary accompanying 1 Nephi 1:19–20.) Thus, the literary unit on the political organization of Alma's people has ended, and Mormon will discuss their religious organization. Mormon has recorded Alma's discourse against kingship, but he does not describe the kind of government that they did institute.

It is possible, however, to offer some speculations. Alma's influence over the people was tremendous. He was their gospel teacher and the symbol of their unity, manifest not only in their religious community but also in the physical creation of their city. It is hard to see him as any but the de facto ruler, whatever his title—here, high priest, which undoubtedly indicates both a religious and political position. Noah's priests also held religious/political posts, although they were clearly subservient to Noah. Alma is simply choosing a religious title rather than a political one.

What significance does Alma attach to this different title since, for all practical purposes, he still represents one-man rule? The difference is the central role of the gospel. Alma's greatest argument against monarchy was the king's tendency to lead people away from Yahweh. As a high priest, Alma is aligned with Yahweh and affirms that gospel principles will inform public life. It is not the locus of power, but the righteousness of power that makes the difference.

Mosiah 23:17

> 17 And it came to pass that none received authority to preach or to teach except it were by him from God. Therefore he consecrated all their priests and all their teachers; and none were consecrated except they were just men.

As modern readers, we see here the affirmation of priesthood power by the authority of God. While this is a true principle, it does not explain all that was happening in Alma's community. In addition to priesthood authority from Yahweh, Alma organized his community to support righteousness rather than to foster the potential unrighteousness of a kingship. Alma is a just man and appoints other just men as teachers and priests.

Politically, these appointments imply that the designation of public offices flows from Alma's personal authority, not from a democratic election. While Alma will be instrumental in the change from kinship to judges in Zarahemla, it is a mistake to assume that his political views were similar to the modern concept of a democracy. Probably Alma's government included the "voice of the people" that operated in Nephite society; however, it is quite different from a modern voting democracy. (See "Excursus: The Voice of the People," following Mosiah 29.)

Mosiah 23:18

> 18 Therefore they did watch over their people, and did nourish them with things pertaining to righteousness.

It is too easy to see Alma's priests and teachers in the same light as our modern priesthood offices. We probably read into "they did watch over their people" some view of modern home and visiting teaching programs. For Alma's people, however, this "watching over" would have been much more literal. These priests and teachers *were* the government and, as the ruling organization, literally watched over the people. There is no indication of any other type of political organization; therefore, all aspects of community life are being directed by a group of men who have primary religious responsibilities and only secondarily political ones. This situation parallels the secular functions of the Aaronic Priesthood in the Salt Lake Valley when the Saints were both the political and religious authorities.[10]

Mosiah 23:19

> 19 And it came to pass that they began to prosper exceedingly in the land; and they called the land Helam.

Helam was the first man whom Alma baptized at Mormon (Mosiah 18:12–13). That the land should be named Helam suggests his importance among Alma's people, probably a status that he had in Lehi-Nephi. Even though Alma's society reduced economic differentiations, it could not have eliminated manifestations of social respect. This conjecture suggests that much of Helam's prominence was based on personal qualities that would continue to be apparent even without the social trappings of Lehi-Nephi. Probably the same reasons that led Alma to baptize Helam first led to naming the land for him.

Why wasn't it named for Alma? Perhaps it reflected Alma's abhorrence of kingship. Since it was typical to name the land for the political leader (land of Nephi, land of Zarahemla, land of Mormon, etc.), Alma may have declined to have the land named for him lest it communicate assumptions of kingship.

Variant: The printer's manuscript has "Helaman" here, which was corrected prior to the first printed edition to "Helam." (See commentary accompanying Mosiah 18:12.)

Mosiah 23:20

> 20 And it came to pass that they did multiply and prosper exceedingly in the land of Helam; and they built a city, which they called the city of Helam.

History: Apparently Alma and his people were in Helam long enough to build a city, "multiply," and also "prosper exceedingly." There is no way to know how much time elapsed, but it strongly suggests a minimum of two years, though it could easily have been more. Additionally, a year or two could have passed from the third Lamanite victory over the Limhites to their decision to flee under Ammon's guidance. Since all of these events occurred in Helam prior to the flight of Limhi's people, sufficient time had to have passed for the building, multiplying, and prospering to take place.

---

[10] *Readings in L.D.S. Church History from the Original Manuscripts. A Selection of and Extracts from Letters, Editorials, Private Journals, Records, Periodicals, Histories, Biographies and Other Original Writings Contemporary with and Casting Light upon Early Events in the Church of Jesus Christ of Latter-day Saints,* edited by William E. Berrett and Alma P. Burton, 3 vols. (Salt Lake City: Deseret Book, 1967), 2:417–18.

Variant: The printer's manuscript repeats "Helaman" here, which was corrected prior to the first printed edition to "Helam." (See commentary accompanying Mosiah 18:12.)

Mosiah 23:21–24

> 21 Nevertheless the Lord seeth fit to chasten his people; yea, he trieth their patience and their faith.
> 22 Nevertheless—whosoever putteth his trust in him the same shall be lifted up at the last day. Yea, and thus it was with this people.
> 23 For behold, I will show unto you that they were brought into bondage, and none could deliver them but the Lord their God, yea, even the God of Abraham and Isaac and of Jacob.
> 24 And it came to pass that he did deliver them, and he did show forth his mighty power unto them, and great were their rejoicings.

Redaction: Verses 21–24 are Mormon's sermon. These verses not only introduce the coming text but also explain why Mormon thinks this story is important. To properly understand Mormon's point, we must realize that "nevertheless" (v. 22) is a contrast to "multiply and prosper exceedingly" (v. 21). Mormon has described a righteous people, doing righteous things and prospering as a result. Yet Mormon emphasizes that previous prosperity and righteousness are no protection from chastening and a trial of our faith.

His ultimate message is not that fortune can be quickly reversed but that Yahweh will deliver. While even the righteous suffer tribulations, they will eventually be justified and delivered because of their righteousness.

This introductory part of Alma's story gives us some insight into Mormon's editorial mind. Why does he choose to focus on certain stories but omit other information, particularly information historians might be interested in? Mormon's purpose is a didactic one. He is not *writing* history but *citing* history to demonstrate the interaction between people and the Lord. We are not to learn a few historical facts, but transcendent eternal principles.

Like many in the ancient world, Mormon sees the key to the future in history's moral lessons, because Yahweh is the same being who has ruled throughout history.[11]

Mosiah 23:25–26

> 25 For behold, it came to pass that while they were in the land of Helam, yea, in the city of Helam, while tilling the land round about, behold an army of the Lamanites was in the borders of the land.
> 26 Now it came to pass that the brethren of Alma fled from their fields, and gathered themselves together in the city of Helam; and they were much frightened because of the appearance of the Lamanites.

---

[11]For an interesting discussion of this principle in Judaism, see Joan E. Taylor, *The Immerser: John the Baptist within Second Temple Judaism* (Grand Rapids, Mich.: William B. Eerdmans Publishing, 1997), 225–27.

Redaction: Having introduced the eventual moral, Mormon tells the story. Because it relates the perspective of Alma's people, Mormon obviously had a record created by Alma or under Alma's direction.

Culture: Verses 25 and 26 accurately describe a Mesoamerican village. Verse 25 differentiates the land and the city of Helam. The "land" was the farming area around the central village. Because the people were tilling the "land," they could see a Lamanite army in "the borders of the land," or the area that lay beyond the cultivated area. Quickly they retreat to the more defensible city where resistance can be more easily organized.

This description contrasts with Gideon's and Noah's discovery of Lamanite army from the tower in Lehi-Nephi. They sounded the alarm from the city, not from the "borders of the land." Later, Limhi could see the Lamanite army assembling from this same tower.

In contrast, Alma's people have no warning from a centralized location. Instead, the army comes upon the tillers fairly suddenly, though at a sufficient distance that the people could flee to the city and consult Alma. This scenario suggests that the fields were near the city and that the area between the fields and the "borders" was relatively open. Helam is in a valley whose pass was perhaps an hour or two away from the tilled fields. The image of the valley also fits the description of Helam as a land of "pure water"—possibly a lake, but certainly a river or copious stream.

What size was the city? Not long before Helam is founded, Alma's church numbered 450 members (Mosiah 18:35). Given the comparatively short lapse of time, probably natural increase had not produced a significantly larger population. Possibly Alma's people peacefully incorporated other groups or individuals they encountered, but the record remains silent on this point. As John Sorenson points out, however, that "size had little to do with the use of the label; many a 'town' or even a 'village' could have had more inhabitants than certain cities, but they lacked the crucial criteria to qualify for the name 'city.'" He defines two crucial characteristics: It was "a governmental center (including a temple or cult center as a symbol of royal patronage or presence)," and it was prepared "to be defended militarily."[12]

Apparently, this city did not have a "tower" (Mesoamerican-style stepped pyramid), which would suggest that the Almaites lacked the manpower and time required to construct it. If they had one, perhaps they had no sentry posted. However, since Alma's group had fled from the Lamanites, they presumably would have been wary of an approaching enemy.

Another suggestion that the population is small is that they obviously fear the Lamanites and do not even consider the option of fighting. We do not know the size of the Lamanite army, but it would have been hard to move a large body quickly through mountain passes and to keep it supplied. Therefore, this army was

---

[12]John L. Sorenson, *Nephite Culture and Society*, edited by Matthew R. Sorenson (Salt Lake City: New Sage Books, 1997), 141.

likely a smaller force, but still possibly around a thousand soldiers. A general would be certain to send a force sufficient to outnumber its expected opposition, if possible.

Translation: Verse 25 contains the peculiar phrase: " . . . while they were in the land of Helam, yea, in the city of Helam, while tilling the land round about. . . . " No doubt, these farmers were in the "land of Helam" rather than in the heart of the city, yet the land would have been subject to city's authority.

Variant: The printer's manuscript has "Helaman" here, which was corrected prior to the first printed edition to "Helam." (See commentary accompanying Mosiah 18:12.)

Mosiah 23:27–29

> 27 But Alma went forth and stood among them, and exhorted them that they should not be frightened, but that they should remember the Lord their God and he would deliver them.
> 28 Therefore they hushed their fears, and began to cry unto the Lord that he would soften the hearts of the Lamanites, that they would spare them, and their wives, and their children.
> 29 And it came to pass that the Lord did soften the hearts of the Lamanites. And Alma and his brethren went forth and delivered themselves up into their hands; and the Lamanites took possession of the land of Helam.

Alma promises the people that Yahweh will deliver them if they place their trust in him. The promise is immediately true because the Lamanites spare their lives (v. 29), even though they become a tributary people. The promise is fulfilled in a second sense when Alma and his people escape to Zarahemla, their deliverance complete. This is the story's message. Yahweh will allow his people's patience to be tried but will deliver them (vv. 21–24). For Mormon, this Lamanite domination is not a denial of the people's righteousness or a punishment for unrighteousness, but a trial of that righteousness. These people have already committed to follow Yahweh and, from all we know of them, are faithful to that covenant.

Literature: Mormon turns a parallel phrase in emphasizing the position of Alma's people before the Lamanites: "[They] began to cry unto the Lord that he would soften the hearts of the Lamanites, that they would spare them, and their wives, and their children. And it came to pass that the Lord did soften the hearts of the Lamanites" (Mosiah 23:28–29).

In verse 28 they cry unto the Lord to "soften the hearts of the Lamanites" and "the Lord did soften the hearts of the Lamanites." This repetition of the substance of the prayer ties the request to its granting. They ask God for a certain type of assistance and the repetition of the phrase marks God's direct affirmative response.

Mosiah 23:30

> 30 Now the armies of the Lamanites, which had followed after the people of king Limhi, had been lost in the wilderness for many days.

Geography: This is a new story about the contact between the Lamanites and Almaites from the perspective of the Lamanite army which has been following Limhi's people. They have been "lost in the wilderness for many days." It is not known how this information comes to be on the Nephite plates. It is quite doubtful that a Lamanite army would confess to the Almaites that they had been lost. It is possible that being "lost" is a literary device that allows an army to pursue Limhi and miss them yet find Alma. With the size of Limhi's fleeing population, it is hard to come up with a scenario in which they could disappear without leaving a trace. Perhaps the Lamanite army had simply reached the extent to which it was willing to search for the Limhites. Perhaps this army that discovers the Almaites was not the same one. Because we have the story from Nephite sources, we cannot be certain of the story that Lamanite sources would tell.

Redaction: Mormon uses the word "now" as a verbal marker to begin a new subject, a process we have seen on several other occasions. (See commentary accompanying 1 Nephi 1:19–20.) Mormon is consulting a record that Alma (or his appointee) created. It may have been physically separate from the large plates or it may have been copied into the large plates. It was, however, a record from the perspective of Alma's people and would not have had access to direct information about the Lamanite troop movements or the reasons for them.

Mosiah 23:31–32

> 31 And behold, they had found those priests of king Noah, in a place which they called Amulon; and they had begun to possess the land of Amulon and had begun to till the ground.
> 32 Now the name of the leader of those priests was Amulon.

Culture: The "place," the "land," and the "leader" are all called Amulon, thus confirming the naming pattern of Book of Mormon communities and likewise confirming that the Almaites are an unusual case. While Alma is the de facto leader, the city and land are nevertheless clearly named for Helam, who should also be the political leader. Nevertheless, the people come to Alma for guidance.

Mosiah 23:33

> 33 And it came to pass that Amulon did plead with the Lamanites; and he also sent forth their wives, who were the daughters of the Lamanites, to plead with their brethren, that they should not destroy their husbands.

In sending the Lamanite women to plead for the lives of the renegade Nephite priests, Amulon is repeating the tactic used by Noah's people who fled before the Lamanites. When the men who refused to abandon their wives and children turned to face the Lamanite army, they also had the women plead for them (Mosiah 19:13). It seems likely that this action represented an accepted strategy for negotiating a surrender.

Although these women had been kidnapped and forcibly married to the priests, they were willing to plead for their husbands, instead of demanding rescue and vengeance. Perhaps they had developed some affection for their husbands or, because of the births of children, saw themselves as new families. Perhaps Noah's well-educated priests had managed to persuade their wives to transfer their allegiance to them, even though they were Nephites.

Text: It is unclear what source was used for verses 33–34.

Mosiah 23:34

> 34 And the Lamanites had compassion on Amulon and his brethren, and did not destroy them, because of their wives.

The pleas of the women were effective, as they had been in the Lehi-Nephi example. In Mosiah 19:14 the ostensible reason was the women's beauty, here their identity as Lamanites. In both cases, however, the essentials are the same. Women plead for mercy, and the surrender of their men is accepted, binding the males in a formally subordinate position. Apparently, neither group in either example anticipated bellicose action.

Variant: The initial phrase "It came to pass that" was included in the printer's manuscript and the 1830 edition. It was edited out in making corrections to the printer's manuscript and does not appear in any subsequent printed edition.[13]

Mosiah 23:35

> 35 And Amulon and his brethren did join the Lamanites, and they were traveling in the wilderness in search of the land of Nephi when they discovered the land of Helam, which was possessed by Alma and his brethren.

From Alma's standpoint, this situation could not have been worse. Certainly Noah's priests could no longer be considered his friends. In fact, few are such intense enemies as former comrades.

Geography: The Lamanites' travel from the Amulonites to the land of Helam had to be on a west-east line. The Lamanites would not have gone north; and had they headed directly south, they surely would have missed Helam. Thus, they were traveling through an east-west pass. This is curious as they have departed from the more direct path to their homeland. Being lost might explain their movements, but they were probably capable of discerning the difference between west and south. It would appear that rather than being lost, they were intentionally searching adjoining valley systems.

Mosiah 23:36–37

> 36 And it came to pass that the Lamanites promised unto Alma and his brethren, that if they would show them the way which led to the land of Nephi that they would grant unto them their lives and their liberty.

---

[13] *Book of Mormon Critical Text*, 2:478.

37 But after Alma had shown them the way that led to the land of Nephi the Lamanites would not keep their promise; but they set guards round about the land of Helam, over Alma and his brethren.

A modern reader would find nothing surprising in this treachery, but in the ancient world it is a startling betrayal. Had a promise held only ephemeral value, Alma would not have believed it in the first place and would have sent the army in the wrong direction.

In essence, Mormon describes a promise made and a promise broken. However, it is possible that Mormon misunderstood part of the negotiations between the Lamanite leader army and Alma "and his brethren" (which would have included Helam). Or perhaps Joseph Smith mistook the complexity of the situation. What was promised was *liberty*—which might mean something different to modern readers than it did to the ancient Mesoamericans. The Almaites' lives were spared. Perhaps that was part of the *liberty*.

The Lamanites were setting up a tribute-paying arrangement, as they had done with the Limhites earlier, enforced by surrounding guards. The repetition suggests that such a practice was a standard part of subjugation. Although the translation appears to describe treachery, the actual details suggest that they were merely following the standard procedure in such a situation. It was a procedure that Alma and his brethren would have understood.

Mosiah 23:38

38 And the remainder of them went to the land of Nephi; and a part of them returned to the land of Helam, and also brought with them the wives and the children of the guards who had been left in the land.

Culture: The "guards" constitute a resident garrison, accompanied by families, in a captured city, a situation that occurred in later Mesoamerican city-kingdoms.[14] It is primarily a political move, based on conventions of honor; since, whatever the prowess of the guards, the presence of their women and children makes them more vulnerable and they would still have been outnumbered by the subjugated people. Alma's people might have overwhelmed this "guard" by their numbers, but now the Lamanite army knew where to find them. This is a garrison of deterrence, not domination.

Mosiah 23:39

39 And the king of the Lamanites had granted unto Amulon that he should be a king and a ruler over his people, who were in the land of Helam;

[14]Susan Toby Evans, *Ancient Mexico and Central America: Archaeology and Culture History* (London: Thames & Hudson, 2004), 486, describes an Aztec garrison in a troubled area. In addition to formal garrisons, there was also apparently a practice of establishing a trading presence. Ibid., 489. Another possibility is suggested by T. Patrick Culbert, "Polities in the Northeast Peten, Guatemala," in *Classic Maya Political History*, edited by T. Patrick Culbert (Cambridge, Eng.: Cambridge University Press, 1991), 132, "Several scholars envision local Maya as using Teotihuacanos, perhaps resident in the lowlands as merchant colonies, to gain support in local political maneuvering."

> nevertheless he should have no power to do anything contrary to the will of the king of the Lamanites.

Alma and his people could not have been pleased with Amulon's appointment, but why did the Lamanites find it acceptable? Why would they establish as subject-king a man who had kidnapped Lamanite women and had only recently, perhaps within a matter of days or weeks, joined forces with the Lamanites? Perhaps the Nephites and Lamanites spoke different languages and Amulon, of Nephite descent, could communicate with the subject people. This possibility, however, does not seem likely. Almost certainly, many Nephites remained behind in the city of Nephi when Mosiah led his people away. The Nephite language may well have changed in Zarahemla, as they integrated with the larger Mulekite population, but Zeniff/Noah/Limhi's return to the land of Nephi would have brought them back into contact with people who already spoke the same language—not enough time had elapsed to make their languages mutually exclusive. (See commentary accompanying Mosiah 9:1.)

A more complicated scenario seems more reasonable in explaining Amulon's elevation. His previous power among the Almaites, despite religious and political alienation, would still facilitate a readier acceptance of his authority while a Lamanite appointee would have been seen not only as foreign but as an enemy.

I argue that the Lamanites accepted Amulon's allegiance to them, not only because of the strength of the oath (see commentary accompanying 1 Nephi 2:15, 4:31–35) but also because of the bond of kinship with the Lamanites established by their marriages to Lamanite women. Even though they probably had no direct kin in the army, they were of the same city and therefore considered of the same people, a greater kin group. The combination of their marriages and their oath of fealty would have made the Amulonites into Lamanites. Because they had voluntarily become part of the Lamanite political and cultural system, the Lamanites could trust them to further Lamanite interests.

Text: There is no chapter break at this point in the 1830 edition.

Mosiah 24

Mosiah 24:1

1 And it came to pass that Amulon did gain favor in the eyes of the king of the Lamanites; therefore, the king of the Lamanites granted unto him and his brethren that they should be appointed teachers over his people, yea, even over the people who were in the land of Shemlon, and in the land of Shilom, and in the land of Amulon.

History: Verses 1–7 constitute Mormon's insertion, providing an overview of the Amulonites' influence on the Lamanites. However, this passage poses some problems about their probable historic accuracy:

- Mormon is writing nearly five hundred years after these events.
- It is doubtful that his descriptions of Lamanite policies and tendencies relied on Lamanite records.
- Mormon ascribes most of the eventual Lamanite culture to Nephite culture imported through the Amulonites. This vector of transmission contradicts both the Book of Mormon's internal evidence and the archaeological record.

A more likely explanation is that Mormon is indulging himself in assumptions of his own cultural superiority by attributing to it all of the Lamanite advances that result from this point. This same ethnocentric tendency overshadowed much of the earliest modern research into the history of the New World, since most of the native advances were assumed to be related to the importation of ideas and peoples from the Old World. According to historian Nigel Davis, "Most earlier writers on American origins erred on the side of boldness, claiming that Indian culture derived form such a medley of peoples as Israelites, Egyptians, Assyrians, Koreans, Trojans, Etruscans, Scythians, Greeks, Tartars, Chinese, Irish, Welsh, and Norsemen, to name only a few. Passing references were made to Cretans, less known at the time but perhaps a more obvious choice, in view of the maritime skills."[1]

Mormon writers have been equally assertive in proclaiming the Israelite origins of the American Indian, with equal error in overstepping the Book of Mormon's own claims. Rather than being an explanation of all Amerindian peoples, the Book of Mormon deals with a smaller number of people in a limited geographic area. (See "Excursus: Geography and the Book of Mormon," following 1 Nephi 18.)

---

[1]Nigel Davies, *Voyagers to the New World* (New York: William Morrow and Company, 1979), 6.

However, the question remains open whether there were contacts between the Old World and the New: "The arguments have, in fact, developed into a hundred years' war, with no end in sight," comments Davies. "At the 35th International Congress of Americanists, held in Mexico City in 1962, the experts were once more locked in combat over precisely the same problem, and again tempers became frayed. Since then discussion has continued unabated. . . . Nowadays many anthropologists prefer to keep an open mind about pre-Columbian contacts between the two hemispheres."[2] The result of this more open-minded approach has been the discovery of several indications of ancient contact between the Old and the New Worlds.[3]

For Mormons, the presence of *some* Israelites in the New World is a matter of faith. While the Book of Mormon is quite consistent in describing those Israelites as they participated in a Mesoamerican culture, it says nothing at all about the direction of influence of culture, whether the Israelites provided culture to the Mesoamericans or the Mesoamericans provided it to the Israelites.

Archaeology, on the other hand, is reasonably clear that the greatest transfer of culture was from the Mesoamericans to the Israelites, in that the Mesoamerican culture can be traced to times prior to Book of Mormon contact and there are no obvious Israelite cultural influences in the Mesoamerican culture set. Of course, this finding does not prove that the Israelites were not there, as some archaeologists would propose. It merely states that the material culture of the Book of Mormon participated in that of Mesoamerica, just as modern Mormons in every country participate in the material culture of their own lands, with homes, vehicles, and cooking utensils identical to those of their non-Mormon neighbors. As John E. Clark, LDS archaeologist at Brigham Young University and head of the New World Archaeological Foundation, recently noted: "Book of Mormon cities have been found, they are well known, and their artifacts grace the finest museums. They are merely masked by archaeological labels such as 'Maya,' 'Olmec,' and so on. The problem, then, is not that Book of Mormon artifacts have not been found, only that they have not been recognized for what they are. Again, if we stumbled onto Zarahemla, how would we know? The difficulty is not with evidence but with epistemology."[4]

This tendency to see one's own culture as dominant (and therefore as the source for other cultures) is a very old one. As I read this passage, it was manifesting itself in Mormon's prose when he asserts that most Lamanite advances were due to

---

[2]Ibid., 7. See, for example, Basil Calvin Hedrick, "Quetzalcoatl: European or Indigene?" in *Man across the Sea*, edited by Carroll L. Riley, J. Charles Kelley, Campbell W. Pennington, and Robert L. Rands (Austin: University of Texas Press, 1971).

[3]John L. Sorenson, "Ancient Voyages across the Ocean to America, from 'Impossible' to 'Certain,'" in *Journal of Book of Mormon Studies* 14, no. 1 (2005): 7–16. John L. Sorenson and Carl L. Johannessen, "Biological Evidence for Pre-Columbian Transoceanic Voyages," *Contact and Exchange in the Ancient World*, edited by Victor H. Mair (Honolulu: University of Hawai'i Press, 2006), 238–97.

[4]John E. Clark, "Archaeology, Relics, and Book of Mormon Belief," in *Journal of Book of Mormon Studies* 14, no. 2 (2005): 42.

the Amulonites teaching Nephite ways to the Lamanites. While they may have done so in some cases, the picture Mormon gives of the renaissance of Lamanite culture after contact with a few men overstates the case that can be reconstructed from the Book of Mormon text and the area's archaeology.

Perhaps readers may ask on what basis one questions the accuracy of anything in the Book of Mormon, since Joseph Smith called it the "most correct book."[5] Obviously, "correctness" has much more to do with doctrinal purity than with the absence of error, as the numerous spelling and grammar corrections attest.[6]

Since the "correctness" or the Book of Mormon does not preclude its essential existence as the result of human labor, with the potential imperfections of human nature, we may turn to the Bible as a model for how humans have dealt with information about and from the divine. That text also shows its rootedness in particular places and times and in the culture-bound notions of its writers, inspired though they were. Similarly, we may expect that the Book of Mormon is the result of humans who participate in and express much of their own cultures. In the ancient world, there is a nearly universal tendency to exalt one's own people over any and all others.[7] These touches of ancient values in the Book of Mormon only strengthen our understanding that the book was written by real people, in a real place, during real times.

Mosiah 24:2

> 2 For the Lamanites had taken possession of all these lands; therefore, the king of the Lamanites had appointed kings over all these lands.

History: We should not be surprised that the Lamanites have taken formal possession of these lands which had been abandoned by the Limhites, or the Amulonites. Of more interest is the political system of multiple kings appointed by a superior kings. In ancient Mesoamerica, as elsewhere, the major political unit was the city. Like Greek city-states, each Mesoamerican city was a government unto itself. Nevertheless, the Book of Mormon records an organization involving various kings of the city-states. Later Maya city-states had comparable arrangements, based on intermarriage with other rulers or on the appointment of vassal rulers in conquered lands. Each separate city-state would retain its sovereignty but would acknowledge a loose loyalty to a common benefactor from a larger and more powerful city.

An important historical case of "beholding" relationships between city-states is the relationship between Tikal and Uaxactun in the fourth century A.D. as described by art historian Linda Schele and archaeologist David Freidel:

---

[5]Joseph Smith et al., *History of the Church of Jesus Christ of Latter-day Saints*, edited by B. H. Roberts, 2nd ed. rev. (Vols. 1–6, 1902–12; Vol. 7, 1932; Salt Lake City: Deseret Book, 1973 printing), 4:461.

[6]The *Book of Mormon Critical Text: A Tool for Scholarly Reference*, 3 vols. (Provo, Utah: FARMS, 1987), contains almost all of these alterations over time. Royal Skousen, *Analysis of Textual Variants of the Book of Mormon*, THE CRITICAL TEXT OF THE BOOK OF MORMON (Provo, Utah: Foundation for Ancient Research and Mormon Studies, 2005), is currently being published and is the definitive work.

[7]Donald E. Brown, *Human Universals* (New York: McGraw-Hill, 1991), 138–39.

> In the scenario we have reconstructed, forces from Tikal under the military leadership of Smoking-Frog, the brother of the high king, attacked and defeated the forces of their neighboring kingdom, Uaxactun, on January 16, 378. The victory placed Smoking-Frog on the throne of Uaxactun, where he oversaw the accession of his nephew, Curl-Snout, to Tikal's throne on September 13, A.D. 379. For the next eighteen years, and perhaps as long as twenty-six years, Smoking-Frog ruled Uaxactun, possibly marrying into its ruling family as well. Even though Smoking-Frog ruled Uaxactun, however, he remained extremely important at Tikal. It's possible he was the overall ruler of the new combined kingdom that resulted from his victory in battle.[8]

This arrangement seems similar to that among the Lamanite kings. Each city would have its own king, but there would be a formal relationship with another city, and perhaps an overall "king" who dominated one or more "beholding" cities. Simon Martin, honorary research fellow at the Institute of Archaeology, University College, London, and Nikolai Grube, professor of anthropology and art history at the University of Texas at Austin and the University of Bonn, summarize:

> Over the years scholars have differed both about the size of Maya polities, whether there were just a few regional-scale states or many small statelets; and their corresponding administrations, whether they had strong, centralized governments or weak, decentralized ones. As a result there has been a choice between two contrasting views of Maya society. But the emergence of new information from the inscriptions, in which the Maya directly describe their political world, allows a reassessment of the topic. Our own research . . . points to a pervasive and enduring system of "overkingship" that shaped almost every facet of the Classic landscape. Such a scheme accords closely with wider Mesoamerican practice, while seeming to reconcile the most compelling features of the two existing views, namely the overwhelming evidence for multiple small kingdoms and the great disparities in the size of their capitals.[9]

Mosiah 24:3

> 3 And now the name of the king of the Lamanites was Laman, being called after the name of his father; and therefore he was called king Laman. And he was king over a numerous people.

Culture: The Lamanites may have had a naming convention similar to that of early Nephite kings, in which the king received the throne-name Nephi (Jacob 1:11).[10] This verse documents two subsequent Lamans, but the very fact that the record specifies that "Laman" was a *name* in each case argues against the parallel. (See commentary accompanying Mosiah 9:10.) Indeed, when Mosiah$_1$ left the city of Nephi, he also abandoned the throne-name tradition. Perhaps the Lamanites had also done so or perhaps never adopted the convention. In any event, it is clear that

---

[8]Linda Schele and David Freidel, *A Forest of Kings: The Untold Story of the Ancient Maya* (New York: William Morrow and Company, 1990), 157–58.

[9]Simon Martin and Nikolai Grube, *Chronicle of the Maya Kings and Queens* (London: Thames & Hudson, 2000), 18–19.

[10]John L. Sorenson, *An Ancient American Setting for the Book of Mormon* (Salt Lake City: Deseret Book/Provo, Utah: Foundation for Ancient Research and Mormon Studies, 1985), 240, John L. Sorenson, "Book of Mormon Peoples," in *Encyclopedia of Mormonism*, 4 vols. (New York: Macmillan Publishing, 1992), 1:191.

$Laman_1$ was a venerated ancestor in this royal family. It seems highly doubtful that a Nephite would have been named Laman nor Lemuel or, in parallel fashion, that a Lamanite would have been named Nephi.

Mosiah 24:4

> 4 And he appointed teachers of the brethren of Amulon in every land which was possessed by his people; and thus the language of Nephi began to be taught among all the people of the Lamanites.

Culture: The teaching role of the priests simply recognizes their level of learning. This appointment, therefore, is not necessarily surprising. Why, however, would the Lamanites wish their people to learn the "language of Nephi"? In five hundred years, the two languages would not have moved to complete mutual unintelligibility, except for the proposed cultural milieu in which both groups would be heavily influenced by their absorption into the local population. Even so, that does not explain what is happening here. According to the internal evidence, the "Lamanites" are former "Nephites" who remained behind when $Mosiah_1$ and his people went to Zarahemla. The Zeniffites return to the city of Nephi because Zeniff knows the land and the language. None of the recorded proceedings between Shemlon and Lehi-Nephi indicate any problem in understanding each other. Since the king of the Lamanites referred to here is the king in Shemlon and the priests of Noah were in Lehi-Nephi, then they obviously must have been able to communicate.

The most likely explanation lies in the meaning of "language," not as the spoken word, but as a synonym for "culture." (See commentary accompanying 1 Nephi 1:2–3.) If that is Mormon's meaning here, then the Amulonites are teaching the Lamanites aspects of Nephite culture that would have enhanced their competitive advantage in trading. Verse 7 explicitly links Lamanite wealth to this education and mentions trade (though in a different way than I am suggesting here). However, as suggested in the commentary on verse 1 above, I believe that this is an expression of cultural bias rather than historical accuracy.

Mosiah 24:5

> 5 And they were a people friendly one with another; nevertheless they knew not God; neither did the brethren of Amulon teach them anything concerning the Lord their God, neither the law of Moses; nor did they teach them the words of Abinadi;

History: Modern readers might assume that the priests of Noah were religious teachers, not scientists, but this division of knowledge familiar to a modern reader would have been foreign to the ancient world. The priests would have been learned in all aspects of their culture, both religious and scientific/technological. Thus, their teachings would have been valuable even if they chose to mute religion. For Mormon, however, this was the essential point. Regardless of what advantages the

Lamanites may have gained, they did not learn the really important lessons about Yahweh's relations with man.

Mosiah 24:6

> 6 But they taught them that they should keep their record, and that they might write one to another.

History: Mormon's assumption that the Lamanites learned about writing only from the Nephites is the kind of cultural jingoism we have seen him manifest already. Mesoamerica had already developed writing systems, even though their evolution and distribution are not well understood.[11] Perhaps this particular group of Lamanites did not know how to write, but I find the assertion suspicious because most of the "Lamanites" here are actually former Nephites who had "converted" to Lamanitism. Surely they would have taken their knowledge with them, and they should have been the majority in this area. I see rather that Mormon simply assumed that the Lamanites learned everything of value from the Nephites.

Mosiah 24:7

> 7 And thus the Lamanites began to increase in riches, and began to trade one with another and wax great, and began to be a cunning and a wise people, as to the wisdom of the world, yea, a very cunning people, delighting in all manner of wickedness and plunder, except it were among their own brethren.

Mormon concludes that the Lamanites are cultured and powerful; they have begun to "wax great." Of course they are still "cunning" and delight "in all manner of wickedness," because Mormon sees them only as the enemy, even while he acknowledges, begrudgingly, that they are to be reckoned with.

Mormon incorrectly notes that it is only at this point that they "began to trade." Of course their civilization had developed as described *because* of trade, even if they were focused only on necessities for warfare like obsidian. Anthropologist Donald E. Brown, after an extensive cross-cultural population study, has concluded that trade is so prevalent among virtually all societies that it must be deemed a human universal.[12]

Possibly Lamanite trade skills improved because of Amulonite knowledge and their new skills in keeping records; but it is not possible that they had never traded before. Such an assertion is, however, consistent with Mormon's attitude that anything valuable in Lamanite culture was "stolen" from the Nephites through the Amulonites.

---

[11]Lawrence K. Lo, "Mesoamerican Writing Systems," http://www.ancientscripts.com/ma_ws.html (accessed February 2005). Lo suggests 500 B.C. as an early date for the development of writing systems but shows symbol sets dating as early as 900 B.C. Lo also indicates that there are as many as fifteen different Mesoamerican writing systems, some of which are known only from a single character.

[12]Brown, *Human Universals*, 138.

Mosiah 24:8–9

> 8 And now it came to pass that Amulon began to exercise authority over Alma and his brethren, and began to persecute him, and cause that his children should persecute their children.
> 9 For Amulon knew Alma, that he had been one of the king's priests, and that it was he that believed the words of Abinadi and was driven out before the king, and therefore he was wroth with him; for he was subject to king Laman, yet he exercised authority over them, and put tasks upon them, and put task-masters over them.

Probably the Lamanites did not understand the backlash effect of giving Amulon power over Alma's people. It was in the Lamanites' best interests to have a docile population steadily producing their annual tribute. Amulon's excessive burdens caused such tremendous strain that eventually Alma's people fled, depriving the Lamanites of a tribute-paying, dependent city. It also seems unlikely that the Lamanites would know about the previous history shared by Amulon and Alma and therefore did not see it as enflaming a previous animosity. More likely, they intended this rule to be more compatible than having a Lamanite overseer—enhancing their long-term access to tribute, not potentially disrupting it.

But Amulon is conducting a personal vendetta. While both Alma and Amulon had ended up as leaders of sub-groups, Alma's was larger and more prosperous. Amulon would naturally be jealous, in addition to seeing Alma's rejection of Noah's religious status quo as leading to his (Amulon's) personal downfall. In short, this passage reveals the all-too-human tendency to wreak revenge for imagined wrongs.

Mosiah 24:10

> 10 And it came to pass that so great were their afflictions that they began to cry mightily to God.

Alma's people were not in the usual position of a rebellious people chastened by afflictions until they repent. They were already righteous and surely prayed daily, so why does Mormon say they "*began* to cry mightily to God."

The original tribute status was accepted and acceptable to Alma's people. It was when Amulon increased the burdens upon them that they "began to cry." It is this increased persecution that has pushed them to the limits of their abilities. What "began" was not normal prayers, but specifically prayers for deliverance from what had become an intolerable situation. Of course, in this increased persecution they would increasingly turn to Yahweh for relief, as they could find none in their own powers.

Mosiah 24:11

> 11 And Amulon commanded them that they should stop their cries; and he put guards over them to watch them, that whosoever should be found calling upon God should be put to death.

In addition to Amulon's personal enmity for Alma, their religious differences ran deep. Amulon had to accept at least partial responsibility for Abinadi's death, while Alma had reoriented himself religiously according to Abinadi's teachings. Amulon has already established himself as opposed to Alma's religion; now he uses his power to punish Alma's people for exercising their faith, just as he increased their economic burdens.

Mosiah 24:12

> 12 And Alma and his people did not raise their voices to the Lord their God, but did pour out their hearts to him; and he did know the thoughts of their hearts.

The principle that God knows even the thoughts of our hearts is widespread in the scriptures. In modern days the Lord has said: "Behold, I say unto you, my servants Ezra and Northrop, open ye your ears and hearken to the voice of the Lord your God, whose word is quick and powerful, sharper than a two-edged sword, to the dividing asunder of the joints and marrow, soul and spirit; and is a discerner of the thoughts and intents of the heart" (D&C 33:1).

In the Old Testament, Yahweh assured Solomon, "The Lord searcheth all hearts, and understandeth all the imaginations of the thoughts: if thou seek him, he will be found of thee; but if thou forsake him, he will cast thee off for ever" (1 Chr. 28:9).[13]

In biblical language, the heart is the seat of thought, rather than serving as the seat of emotion as in contemporary Western symbolism.[14] In the heart are "true thoughts" stored; thus, knowing one's "heart" and knowing one's thoughts are the same thing.

Culture: Because the Almaites had to change from vocal prayer to silent prayer, it suggests that they had a practice of praying aloud in a communal setting. It is this communal prayer that Amulon forbids, though it clearly might extend as well to any individual vocal prayer. This ban had more behind it than simple vindictiveness. By forbidding the communal prayer, Amulon also disrupted other possible communal responses, such as organized resistance. By removing an occasion when the people were unitedly lamenting their fate and asking deliverance, Amulon removed a possible threat to his dominance, as he supposed.

As Mormon notes, the prohibition against public communal prayer did nothing to prevent the silent prayers of these righteous people.

Mosiah 24:13–14

> 13 And it came to pass that the voice of the Lord came to them in their afflictions, saying: Lift up your heads and be of good comfort, for I know of the covenant which ye have made unto me; and I will covenant with my people and deliver them out of bondage.

---

[13]See also Ps. 94:11; John 2:24–25; Alma 12:3, 14; Hel. 9:4, 3 Ne. 28:6, D&C 6:16.

[14]Bruce J. Malina, *The New Testament World: Insights from Cultural Anthropology* (Atlanta, Ga.: John Knox Press, 1981), 81. Malina suggests that the heart is one of the loci of "emotion-infused thought."

14 And I will also ease the burdens which are put upon your shoulders, that even you cannot feel them upon your backs, even while you are in bondage; and this will I do that ye may stand as witnesses for me hereafter, and that ye may know of a surety that I, the Lord God, do visit my people in their afflictions.

Redaction: It is not clear what source Mormon was drawing on for this conclusion. It hardly seems likely that each individual received this precise answer. Rather, it seems more likely that Alma have received it as a revelation and that all of his people understood it as the answer to their prayer.

Mosiah 24:15

15 And now it came to pass that the burdens which were laid upon Alma and his brethren were made light; yea, the Lord did strengthen them that they could bear up their burdens with ease, and they did submit cheerfully and with patience to all the will of the Lord.

This verse contains a great lesson about how the Lord assists us. While we might pray for the removal of the burden, the Lord may answer it by increasing our capacity to bear the burden. Bruce Hafen sees this example as part of what he terms "the endowment of hope":

> This is the spiritual endowment of hope—of perspective, of patience, of an inner serenity, a sure inner sight, that is "not weary in well-doing" (D&C 64:33). Such hope is bestowed by the power of the Holy Ghost, "which Comforter filleth with hope" (Moro. 8:26). It is the hope of which Nephi wrote in explaining the process that follows our entry by baptism into the straight and narrow path: "Wherefore, ye must press forward with a steadfastness in Christ, having a perfect brightness of hope and a love of God and of all men" (2 Ne. 31:20).
>
> It is the hope that Mormon recognized as a sustaining, God-given source of strength in the maturing stages of spiritual development: "I would speak unto you that are of the church, that are the peaceable followers of Christ, and that have obtained a sufficient hope by which ye can enter into the rest of the Lord. . . . My brethren, I judge these things of you because of your peaceable walk with the children of men" (Moro. 7:3–4). Not perfect, not frantic; not pessimistic and not artificially cheerful. The walk of those who walk with the endowment of hope is "peaceable."
>
> The practical effect of the endowment of hope is illustrated by the Lord's blessing to Alma and his followers, who were in bondage and were made to carry heavy physical burdens. Alma and his people pleaded with the Lord for help, and he responded: "The burdens which were laid upon Alma and his brethren were made light; yea, the Lord did strengthen them that they could bear up their burdens with ease" (Mosiah 24:15). The Lord intervened in this way, "that they might know of a surety that I, the Lord God, do visit my people in their afflictions" (Mosiah 24:14).
>
> It helps us see the place of hope to know that our development toward spiritual maturity is a process, not an event. It is a distance race, not a sprint. It is thus no race for the short-winded.[15]

---

[15]Bruce C. Hafen, *The Broken Heart: Applying the Atonement to Life's Experiences* (Salt Lake City: Deseret Book, 1989), 183–84.

Mosiah 24:16–17

> 16 And it came to pass that so great was their faith and their patience that the voice of the Lord came unto them again, saying: Be of good comfort, for on the morrow I will deliver you out of bondage.
> 17 And he said unto Alma: Thou shalt go before this people, and I will go with thee and deliver this people out of bondage.

Redaction: The contrast of subject in verses 16 and 17 perhaps tells us a little more of Mormon's source material. In verse 17, the voice of the Lord comes to Alma, suggesting that Alma recorded this information and that Mormon copied it into his own record.

What is less clear is the source of the generalized communication from Yahweh to the people in verse 16. We do not know if it represents Alma's written description or Mormon's assumption. I read it as the communal understanding of Yahweh's answer, which Alma likely wrote and which Mormon copied. When Mormon inserts his opinions (as with King Noah), his interpolations are quite obvious. In this case, the most likely scenario is that Alma was emphasizing his people's spiritual preparation. They understood that Yahweh would deliver them. That it would happen "on the morrow" must be Alma's conclusion after he began to prepare for the journey in accord with his direct revelation. While the people may have understood that deliverance was coming, it is doubtful that they would all have clearly understood that it would occur "on the morrow." Alma appears to be taking a small literary license here as he emphasizes his people's righteousness.

Mosiah 24:18

> 18 Now it came to pass that Alma and his people in the night-time gathered their flocks together, and also of their grain; yea, even all the night-time were they gathering the flocks together.

As with the escape of Limhi's people (Mosiah 22), gathering the flocks might be a nightly task, but gathering supplies for the journey would be a much larger task than normal nightly preparations. As with the Limhites, the fact that they were able to make such preparations without being seen and stopped suggests that the Lamanite/Amulonite presence in the city was limited.

Mosiah 24:19

> 19 And in the morning the Lord caused a deep sleep to come upon the Lamanites, yea, and all their task-masters were in a profound sleep.

Both the Limhites and the Almaites leave with their belongings past sleeping guards. However, Limhi's guards were sleeping because of extra wine while Yahweh himself caused a deeper sleep to come upon the Lamanites guarding Helam. Perhaps this detail suggests that Alma's group had relied almost entirely on their new faith throughout their existence as a people, while the Limhites, who were in the process of repentance, were more used to relying upon themselves than Yahweh. In each case, Yahweh causes a miracle; but perhaps the more active role of the Limhites reflects that, though strong of faith, they still saw themselves as an important part of their own destiny.

Mosiah 24:20

> 20 And Alma and his people departed into the wilderness; and when they had traveled all day they pitched their tents in a valley, and they called the valley Alma, because he led their way in the wilderness.

Given the landscape proposed for Alma's escape route, it is no surprise that they found themselves in a valley. The Cuchumatanes Mountains are a maze of mountains and valleys, which is one explanation for how multiple groups could pass through the same general area but not easily come across each other. (See commentary following Mosiah 23:31–32.)

The naming of the valley Alma is certainly more symbolic, since the Almaites are only a single day away from their oppressors and they certainly would not have considered putting down permanent roots. Nevertheless, the naming reconfirms Alma's leadership. (See commentary accompanying Mosiah 23:19.)

Variant: In the printer's manuscript and the 1830 edition, this verse began: "It came to pass that Alma. . . ." This phrase was removed in the corrections to the printer's manuscript and in subsequent printed editions.[16] The printer's manuscript also had the phrase "and they called *the name of* the valley Alma." Skousen notes that while this is redundant, it is also characteristic of Book of Mormon usage.[17]

Mosiah 24:21–22

> 21 Yea, and in the valley of Alma they poured out their thanks to God because he had been merciful unto them, and eased their burdens, and had delivered them out of bondage; for they were in bondage, and none could deliver them except it were the Lord their God.
> 22 And they gave thanks to God, yea, all their men and all their women and all their children that could speak lifted their voices in the praises of their God.

Alma's community existed because of their religious convictions. They were led out of Helam by a prophet, their escape assured by a miracle. Naturally, they thanked Yahweh for their deliverance. However, there is no mention of sacrifice. When Nephi and his brothers escape Laban's murderous attempts, Lehi offers sacrifices as part of the ceremony of thanksgiving (1 Ne. 5:9). Have the principles of sacrifice changed for the Nephites by this time, or did Mormon simply neglect to include this detail?

Mosiah 24:23

> 23 And now the Lord said unto Alma: Haste thee and get thou and this people out of this land, for the Lamanites have awakened and do pursue thee; therefore get thee out of this land, and I will stop the Lamanites in this valley that they come no further in pursuit of this people.

---

16. *Book of Mormon Critical Text*, 2:482.
17. Skousen, *Analysis of Textual Variants*, 3:1461.

A single day's distance between the Lamanites and Alma's people certainly wasn't enough distance for them to feel safe. Yahweh tells Alma that the Lamanites are in pursuit. A group this size would normally leave clues of their journey that could be followed, at least for a few days, although the army pursuing the Limhites lost their trail after only two days (Mosiah 22:16).

Mosiah 24:24–25

> 24 And it came to pass that they departed out of the valley, and took their journey into the wilderness.
> 25 And after they had been in the wilderness twelve days they arrived in the land of Zarahemla; and king Mosiah did also receive them with joy.

Geography: This verse is important in allowing calculations of the distance between Nephi and Zarahemla.[18] Of course, the Almaites could not take a direct route to Zarahemla but were probably following valleys, both to avoid crossing mountains and to have access to water.

Literature: "Receive them with joy" may have been a set phrase. (See commentary accompanying Mosiah 22:14.)

Variant: In the printer's manuscript, the 1830 and 1840 editions, verse 25 also began with "And it came to pass." This phrase was removed from the corrected printer's manuscript, the 1837 edition, and from all subsequent editions.[19]

Text: There is no break here in the 1830 edition. In fact, this break occurs in the middle of a paragraph in the 1830 edition. Not only was this information not considered the end of a chapter, but it was not even seen as the end of an idea. The following verses deal with Mosiah's reception of the Almaites. Verse 25 is already pointing towards Mosiah, and the earliest verses of chapter 25 pick up at that point.

---

[18]John E. Clark, "A Key for Evaluating Nephite Geographies," Review of Richard Hauck, *Deciphering the Geography of the Book of Mormon*, in *Review of Books on the Book of Mormon* 1 (1989): 54. Sorenson does not explicitly note this verse in either *An Ancient American Setting for the Book of Mormon* or his *The Geography of Book of Mormon Events: A Source Book* (Provo, Utah: FARMS, 1990).

[19]*Book of Mormon Critical Text*, 2:483.

Mosiah 25

Mosiah 25:1–2

1 And now king Mosiah caused that all the people should be gathered together.
2 Now there were not so many of the children of Nephi, or so many of those who were descendants of Nephi, as there were of the people of Zarahemla, who was a descendant of Mulek, and those who came with him into the wilderness.

Verses 1–2 should be read together, principally because they demonstrate the continued conceptual divisions among Mosiah's people. He calls *all* the people, but the chronicle then compares the numbers of Nephites and Mulekites. Even though Benjamin had unified the people, divisions still existed, almost certainly along family lines. This hypothesis reinforces other passages in which kin organizations underlie larger political structures.

Even though we usually understand the Nephites and Lamanites as the two major New World peoples, these definitions are collectives that describe the multiple kin organizations attached to the larger political units. Indeed, "Lamanite" frequently means little more than "not-Nephite." (See commentary accompanying Jacob 1:13.) Within the unit of political Nephites, the lineal Mulekites were the more numerous.

The comparison used here is that there were "not so many" of the Nephites as the Mulekites. Why is that? The Lehites and Mulekites left Jerusalem at almost the same time, the difference between those times too slight to explain a large population difference. We have no information about the size of the Mulekite party, but we may assume that it was a single shipful, obviously consisting of at least some adults of child-bearing age, and perhaps other children besides Mulek himself. In short, there is no reason to suppose that the beginnings of the two peoples would account for the differences, nor is there any reason for believing that one group would have been more successful than another at mixing with local populations. Here are some possible reasons for the population differences:

- The early population split in Lehi's family, resulting in the original Nephite/Lamanite division, obviously decreased the population of Nephites, perhaps leading to a permanently smaller number.
- Simple differences in birth and mortality rates could account for differences in population sizes. Not all lines produce and survive equally.

- I assume, on the basis of the king-name evidence, that Mosiah$_1$ led only a select group of Nephites from the city of Nephi; therefore, his people were a smaller subset of the larger Nephite population (which eventually becomes considered Lamanite on the basis of political differences). This small group of people would clearly have been fewer, and remained fewer, than the descendants of Mulek or Zarahemla.

I favor the third possibility.

Variant: Skousen explains:

> The printer's manuscript in Mosiah 25:2 has the spelling *Muloch,* which the 1830 typesetter changed to *Mulok*. For the 1879 edition, Orson Pratt changed *Mulok* to *Mulek* in the LDS text, under the reasonable assumption that the individual named is the Mulek mentioned in the book of Helaman. This Mulek, the son of king Zedekiah, came to the promised land shortly after Lehi and was the most prominent founder for the people of Zarahemla. . . .
>
> It is, of course theoretically possible that the Book of Mormon is referring to two different individuals: Muloch, an ancestor of Zarahemla, in the book of Mosiah; and Mulek, a son of king Zedekiah, in the book of Helaman. The reference to Muloch in Mosiah 25:2 is rather surprising; Mormon writes here as if he has already mentioned this Muloch and those who came with him. There is a similar example in the book of Alma where Amulek refers to an ancestor of his (namely, Aminadi) that he assumes his listeners are already familiar with [Alma 10:2–3].[1]

Skousen offers this interesting resolution:

> The evidence, taken as a whole, argues that Mosiah 25:2 is referring to the people of Zarahemla and the descent from Muloch and the others who came with him after the fall of the kingdom of Judah. So now the question is: What was the actual name of this son of Zedekiah who survived and was one of the founding fathers for the people of Zarahemla? Based on the manuscript readings there are two possibilities: *Mulock* or *Mulek*. Internal evidence strongly argues that the correct name is *Muloch*. First of all, the earliest extant occurrence of the name in the text is here in Mosiah 25:2. We have only the printer's manuscript for this occurrence, but the same limitation holds for the occurrences of *Mulek* in the book of Helaman. Secondly, the tendency in the transmission of the text has always been to replace the final *ch* spelling in a name with either *ck* or *k:* (1) the 1830 typesetter changed *Muloch* to *Mulok* here in Mosiah 25:2; (2) Oliver Cowdery normally misspelled *Zenoch* as *Zenock,* with the result that the standard text now has only the misspelled *Zenock*. . . .
>
> On the other hand, there are no examples of a name ending in a final *k* ever being misspelled as *ch*.[2]

This particular change is interesting in that we have two important Book of Mormon names that have incorrectly entered our tradition. In this case, we should be speaking of the Mulochites rather than Mulekites. The other instance is the spelling shift from Amlicite to Amalekite. (See commentary accompanying Alma 2:3–4.)

---

[1]Royal Skousen, *Analysis of Textual Variants of the Book of Mormon*, THE CRITICAL TEXT OF THE BOOK OF MORMON (Provo, Utah: Foundation for Ancient Research and Mormon Studies, 2005), Vol. 4, Part 3, 1466.

[2]Ibid., 3:1467.

Chronology: As noted in the chronological discussion accompanying Mosiah 7:1, this reuniting of peoples likely took place after 124 B.C.

Mosiah 25:3

> 3 And there were not so many of the people of Nephi and of the people of Zarahemla as there were of the Lamanites; yea, they were not half so numerous.

Demography: Here is the crux of the demographic problem for the Book of Mormon. If we assume, as has been traditional, that there were no "others" in the land, this statement makes it very difficult to understand the population dynamics of the Lamanites and Nephites. The most traditional interpretation shows Lehi's original colony splitting into two; one group unites with a second set of refugees from Jerusalem. On the Nephite side of the equation, half of the original Lehites would become a minority among a larger population of Mulekites, while the Lamanites would be greater than twice the number of the Nephites and Mulekites together. Thus, the original Lamanite population would have to have a birth and survival rate probably four times higher than that of the Nephites to even come close to making these numbers work.

Complicating this picture even more is the Nephite description of the Lamanites (particularly in early periods) as uncivilized hunter-gatherers. Yet the hunter-gatherer lifestyle cannot sustain large populations.[3] Large populations virtually require agricultural settlements to cultivate, harvest, and store sufficient food. People who rely on hunting and gathering tend to exist in small bands, not large cities.[4] The traditional picture is simply impossible. We must factor in those "others" who were in the New World before the arrival of the Lehites and Mulekites and discount the ethnocentric Nephite portrayal of the Lamanite lifestyle.

Mosiah 25:4

> 4 And now all the people of Nephi were assembled together, and also all the people of Zarahemla, and they were gathered together in two bodies.

---

[3]Susan Toby Evans, *Ancient Mexico and Central America: Archaeology and Culture History* (London: Thames & Hudson, 2004), 24.

[4]Ralph Linton, *The Study of Man: An Introduction* (New York: Appleton-Century-Crofts, 1936, copyright renewed 1964), 215, describes the dynamics of hunting band organization:

> The size of a band is set by the zone of exploitation about its settlement, not by the total territory available to its members. There is always an optimum size for the effective exploitation of this zone. When the band increases very much beyond this point the unit will split if new territory is available for it. When the band falls much below this point, its members must amalgamate with some other band or they will face extinction. If it is impossible for the band to split, the natural forces which deal with overpopulation will come into play to bring its strength back to normal. . . .
>
> Being subject to such a variety of factors, it is natural that the actual size of bands should be highly variable. Where there is no reliance on trade and manufactures, the upper limit for agricultural groups seems to be 350 to 400. Even this requires unusually good soil and well-developed farming techniques, and such a size is rarely reached. Taking the world as a whole the average size of the band for agricultural peoples is probably between 100 and 150. . . . The bands of hunters and food-gatherers are usually much smaller.

Early in the history of the Nephites, Jacob noted that there were still "Nephites; nevertheless, they were called Nephites, Jacobites, Josephites, Zoramites, Lamanites, Lemuelites, and Ishmaelites" (Jacob 1:13). In spite of the availability of tribal/lineage designations, Jacob used only two major categories, Nephite and Lamanite. Now, some five hundred years later, we see two major groups in Zarahemla, which we must assume are descendants of Nephite and Zarahemla/ Mulek. Surely smaller kin organizations existed within each of these larger designations, but the general division between Nephite and Zarahemlaite survived Benjamin's efforts to mold his society into a unified whole. The two groups initially had different religions, cultures, and languages. Those are tremendous obstacles to overcome.

Mosiah 25:5

> 5 And it came to pass that Mosiah did read, and caused to be read, the records of Zeniff to his people; yea, he read the records of the people of Zeniff, from the time they left the land of Zarahemla until they returned again.

The phrase "did read, and caused to be read" is significant. It suggests that large numbers of people were beyond the reach of Mosiah's voice and that messengers had to be sent to read the information to outlying gatherings. Why did Mosiah read the accounts of Limhi and later of Alma? We struggle today with information overload, forgetting that the ancient world was typically bereft of both information and entertainment. Reading these records was not only an important means of communicating important information about the new neighbors but also a form of entertainment. The excuse to gather and to hear something new would have been a popular diversion from the daily tasks of survival.

Furthermore, when Benjamin gathered his people for his great discourse, he had to build a tower, but no tower is mentioned in this description of Mosiah's addressing a larger audience. As was noted in the commentary accompanying Mosiah 2:7, Benjamin may have been speaking in the courtyard of an unfinished temple, so the tower was necessary to lift him higher than the congregation. But in Mosiah's case, the "temple" must have been finished. If it followed the Mesoamerican stepped-style temple, its steps would easily have provided the necessary elevation for Mosiah's public discourse.

Mosiah 25:6

> 6 And he also read the account of Alma and his brethren, and all their afflictions, from the time they left the land of Zarahemla until the time they returned again.

After finishing with Limhi's record, Mosiah reads (or causes to be read) Alma's account. Since our version of these records is abridged, reading the original records aloud may have taken longer than it takes us to read the corresponding versions in the Book of Mormon. Nevertheless, it is not surprising either that the entire account was read or that the people willingly stayed to listen to it. No mention is made of how long it took to finish the reading, but it would not be surprising if the event took place over at least two days, perhaps with the first day devoted to Limhi and the second to Alma.

Skousen sees the ending of this verse as problematic: "This passage presents a difficult reading. Alma and his brethren were probably born in the land of Nephi, not in the land of Zarahemla."[5] His solution to the difficult reading is to suggest that there is a missing line which would have clarified the passage.[6] I see a simpler solution. Verses 5 and 6 appear so directly parallel that they must be intentionally parallel. The similarities between the two groups are being highlighted at the expense of more literally historical information. I believe Mormon saw the parallels as much more important than the clarification of origins. Rather than understand the two groups as identified only by their current leader, Mormon saw them as the remnant of the original Zeniff colony. It was this greater view of the people that allowed him to say that they had left Zarahemla and returned.

Mosiah 25:7–11

> 7 And now, when Mosiah had made an end of reading the records, his people who tarried in the land were struck with wonder and amazement.
> 8 For they knew not what to think; for when they beheld those that had been delivered out of bondage they were filled with exceedingly great joy.
> 9 And again, when they thought of their brethren who had been slain by the Lamanites they were filled with sorrow, and even shed many tears of sorrow.
> 10 And again, when they thought of the immediate goodness of God, and his power in delivering Alma and his brethren out of the hands of the Lamanites and of bondage, they did raise their voices and give thanks to God.
> 11 And again, when they thought upon the Lamanites, who were their brethren, of their sinful and polluted state, they were filled with pain and anguish for the welfare of their souls.

Literature: These verses form a literary set, with each verse consisting of a pair of concepts: The people think about what they have heard, then react to it. This pair is then set into a series of paired contrasts: one positive and one sorrowful. Verse 7 sets up the verses with the "wonder and amazement." The rest of the verses define the nature of that "wonder and amazement."

Verses 8 and 9 create a contrast, as the people contemplate the news, then exhibit opposite reactions (joyful and sorrowful). Verses 10 and 11 form a similar unit: joyful thanks to Yahweh contrasted with pain for those not in Yahweh's favor. These two sets are also in parallel to each other.

---

[5]Skousen, *Analysis of Textual Variants*, 3:1471.

[6]Ibid., 3:1475, "and he also read the account of Alma **and his brethren and all their afflictions and he also read the account** [of] **Ammon** and his brethren and all their afflictions from the time they left the land of Zarahemla until they returned again." This emendation creates a repetition of information in verse 5 without any literary reason for the parallel.

Redaction: This passage is obviously a carefully constructed parallelism. Because it is unusually literary for Mormon's style, it is possible that he is replicating a form that appears in the underlying source, rather than creating it himself.

Mosiah 25:12

> 12 And it came to pass that those who were the children of Amulon and his brethren, who had taken to wife the daughters of the Lamanites, were displeased with the conduct of their fathers, and they would no longer be called by the names of their fathers, therefore they took upon themselves the name of Nephi, that they might be called the children of Nephi and be numbered among those who were called Nephites.

This verse suggests some of the detail missing from our account. Amulon's children have not earlier been mentioned as among those who reached Zarahemla. Furthermore, Mormon neglects to tell us whether they arrived with Limhi or Alma.

If these "children of Amulon" came with Alma they would surely be the children of Amulon's priests and the Lamanite women. However, had Amulon's priests had children in Alma's group before they encountered the priests, surely the reunion would have been sufficiently significant to mention, perhaps with these children playing a mediating role between the two groups. Therefore, it seems more likely that they are the priests' children fathered in Noah's court, then abandoned by their fleeing fathers, and hence cared for (and accompanying) Limhi's people.

But what, exactly, were they doing? Their parents' parents would have been among the Nephites who left Zarahemla to return to the land of Nephi. However, their political allegiance had been to Noah in a different city and cultural location. When the Amulonite children *become* Nephites, they not only proclaim their current political alliance but reject any possible claim to rule based on their fathers' positions. While this point might appear moot since all of Limhi's people were being integrated into Nephite society, retaining hereditary claims of rulership could have created divisiveness. By declaring themselves of Nephi, they wholeheartedly accept integration into their new society.

Mosiah 25:13

> 13 And now all the people of Zarahemla were numbered with the Nephites, and this because the kingdom had been conferred upon none but those who were descendants of Nephi.

This verse logically follows from the allegiances described in verse 12. Just as the sons of Amulon and the priests number themselves with the Nephites and accept dominion by the Nephite rulers, so did the Zarahemlaites. Mormon is reworking original texts dealing with Zarahemla's political structures here, whether he is aware of the reason for including this passage or not. The significance of verses 12–13 is the subordination of potentially legitimate claims of rulership to the superior claim of the Nephite polity/lineage.

This is the context for "Nephite" here, rather than Jacob's more general usage (Jacob 1:13), and it means the ruling lineage of Nephi. Both the children of Amulon and the Zarahemla Mulekites are declaring allegiance to the Nephite dynasty as represented by $Mosiah_1$, Benjamin, and now $Mosiah_2$. They are simultaneously giving up competing claims.

Mosiah 25:14

> 14 And now it came to pass that when Mosiah had made an end of speaking and reading to the people, he desired that Alma should also speak to the people.

Much information that Mormon does not tell us can be surmised from this verse, in which Mosiah publicly introduces Alma to the people. Modern readers of the Book of Mormon are so familiar with Alma that his immediate public role does not seem surprising, but it should be. In contrast to Alma, Limhi apparently moves into a secondary position in his own community (the city and land of Gideon) even though he had been a king. What events precede this discourse that lead to Alma's rapid ascension as Zarahemla's religious leader?

Obviously, Alma and Mosiah held private meetings. Only a poor leader would present a full record of a people about whom he knew nothing. The private meetings would have been held separately, as the two groups arrived separately, with Limhi's group preceding Alma's into the city. Evidence for this sequence is that it was the army pursuing Limhi that stumbled upon Amulon's group and, subsequently, on Alma. The establishment of the Lamanite rule in Helam (Alma's colony) probably became oppressive fairly quickly, but it still would have taken time—say, at least a couple of months—before the situation became intolerable. Thus, Limhi's group had been in Zarahemla for an estimated two months (perhaps more). It is interesting that there is no record of a public reading of their documents until Alma and his people arrive. There is no way to tell if this is an accurate representation of the event of reading records or if Mormon conflated two separate readings for literary convenience.

Nevertheless, this occasion is specifically about Alma. Limhi's record is part of Alma's background, read aloud to justify presenting Alma to the people. In their private meetings, Mosiah had learned of Yahweh's calling of Alma and recognized Alma as a powerful religious leader. As we will shortly see, Alma not only restructures the Nephite religious system, but also their political system. Clearly, Mosiah and Alma almost immediately developed a strong trust and rapport. Not long after his arrival, Alma supplants Mosiah as the religious leader and thereafter supplants the political structure in which Mosiah was king. Either these events occurred with Mosiah's cooperation, or he must be seen as weak and impressionable. There is no indication of the latter, so the former is the better explanation.

For these reasons, Alma addresses the people at Mosiah's behest and with his authorization. Less clear in Mormon's synopsis is the fact that Alma is also being installed as the chief high priest.

Mosiah 25:15

> 15 And Alma did speak unto them, when they were assembled together in large bodies, and he went from one body to another, preaching unto the people repentance and faith on the Lord.

Mormon is describing a process, not a single event. With no clear transition, the action moves from the public reading of records to Alma's ministry as an authorized preacher, circulating among the people. This process suggests some time period after the formal gathering but still during the festival, as the "large bodies" would be gathered only for such a festival. Therefore, what Mosiah has done is bring everyone together and read to them as a whole. He then introduces (and probably explicitly endorses) Alma and sends him to preach to them in groups. These groups consist of at least Nephites, Mulekites, and Limhites (based on Mosiah 25:4 and the specific address to Limhi's people which follows immediately).

It is possible that preaching to these major political groups has more than a simple religious purpose. Since religion and politics were intertwined in the ancient world, Alma is probably establishing his religious authority with the leaders of the individual groups. The multiple kin organizations of Mesoamerica typically had their own hierarchies of leadership, and Alma probably needed to establish his credentials with those leaders as a prerequisite to reforming Nephite religious practices, since reform would be impossible without widespread support from the kin group leaders.

Variant: This verse began "It came to pass that Alma . . . " in the printer's manuscript and the 1830 edition. This phrase was removed from subsequent printed editions.[7]

Mosiah 25:16

> 16 And he did exhort the people of Limhi and his brethren, all those that had been delivered out of bondage, that they should remember that it was the Lord that did deliver them.

The only specifics we have of Alma's teachings to the groups are those presented to Limhi and his followers. It may have been the last or the first presentation, but it was likely the first. The Limhites are the Almaites' family, perhaps even literal kin. They come from the same place, from the same set of experiences. Therefore the empathy between the two groups would have been the highest and it would have been easiest for Alma to establish his innovations first among the Limhites and then among the rest of the people. Perhaps Mormon gives us this one example rather than all of them because the rest were essentially repetitions. In any case, Alma goes to Limhi and his people and preaches the gospel to them as Abinadi and Yahweh had revealed it to him.

Mosiah 25:17

> 17 And it came to pass that after Alma had taught the people many things, and had made an end of speaking to them, that king Limhi was desirous that

[7] *Book of Mormon Critical Text: A Tool for Scholarly Reference*, 3 vols. (Provo, Utah: FARMS, 1987), 2:485.

he might be baptized; and all his people were desirous that they might be baptized also.

Culture: This verse is an important marker in the development of Nephite religion. As background, Limhi is the son of Noah, the son of Zeniff, a Nephite from the city of Nephi who came to Zarahemla with $Mosiah_1$, then led his people back to the land of Nephi. Mormon views Zeniff as a "good" Nephite, which, for Mormon, means someone who follows Yahweh's commandments. Although Noah apostatized, Limhi was apparently faithful. His people, despite a period of apostasy while Noah ruled, had been raised in the Nephite religion and had returned to it by the time they fled to Zarahemla. Thus, Nephites who had known of baptism since the time of $Nephi_1$ (and who had already requested it, Mosiah 21:33) are now being baptized.

According to a modern interpretation, they are being rebaptized after having fallen away. In their own context, however, Alma is introducing baptism with a new meaning. For Alma, baptism (for the first time) symbolizes a covenant rather than a cleansing. Rather than being only an individual action that effects the remission of sins on a personal level, Alma's baptism also introduces the newly baptized person into a congregation. Ancient religion was part of the entire community. Alma's baptism is a way of making a religious covenant distinct from the political covenant that binds them. Alma creates churches.

Mosiah 25:18

> 18 Therefore, Alma did go forth into the water and did baptize them; yea, he did baptize them after the manner he did his brethren in the waters of Mormon; yea, and as many as he did baptize did belong to the church of God; and this because of their belief on the words of Alma.

Culture: Here is the most explicit correlation between Alma's baptism and the entry by covenant into a subset of society—a church. Limhi's people have been with Ammon for some length of time, perhaps a year. They have repented of Noah's apostate ways and returned to a belief in Yahweh as understood and taught by Ammon. Thus, Alma is not baptizing unbelievers, but believers.

While it is tempting to suppose that this baptism is required to return the Limhites to the Nephite religion, clearly Ammon refused to baptize (Mosiah 21:33). This ordinance waited for Alma, just as those who left Lehi-Nephi to go with Alma were baptized in the waters of Mormon.

The mention that those baptized "did belong to the church of God" underscores the concept of a church. For the first time, Nephite society shows an explicit demarcation between a religious congregation and those who were still part of the community but not part of the church.

Mosiah 25:19

> 19 And it came to pass that king Mosiah granted unto Alma that he might establish churches throughout all the land of Zarahemla; and gave him power to ordain priests and teachers over every church.

Culture: Although Limhi's people are members of a church, the rest of the Zarahemlaites are not. Benjamin had placed his people under covenant to become "sons and daughters of God" (Mosiah 5:7). That covenant was to provide the Zarahemlaites with a uniform base of belief, a covenantal means of leveling society. A generation has passed and the assumption of unity has unraveled. There is now an explicit structure separate from the rest of society, something that Benjamin's covenant did not create.

The separation of realms of influence now extends to Mosiah himself. Mosiah grants to Alma the power to ordain priests and teachers over each church. This act effectively diminishes Mosiah's power, as he has bestowed on another an essential role in his society. Mosiah would certainly be the titular head of the church, but he was no longer its effective leader. Alma was.

Alma had tremendous influence. Given the implications of his position in Nephite society and the rapidity with which he acquired that position, we must wonder at the personal charisma he possessed to allow him to so completely imbue Nephite society with his own ideas on religion and government. Government will be discussed later; at this point, it is his religious reforms that are most apparent.

Mosiah 25:20–21

> 20 Now this was done because there were so many people that they could not all be governed by one teacher; neither could they all hear the word of God in one assembly;
> 21 Therefore they did assemble themselves together in different bodies, being called churches; every church having their priests and their teachers, and every priest preaching the word according as it was delivered to him by the mouth of Alma.

Culture: Institutionally, Alma's church has the flexibility to respond to a population increase so large that the people cannot "be governed by one teacher, neither could they all hear the word of God in one assembly." Our modern perspective may conceal how radical this change was—nothing short of a religious revolution. We need to understand what Alma's churches were and the institution they replaced after Alma arrived on the scene.

We really have few details about Alma's churches, but we should not read into it our own concepts of "church." Despite Joseph Smith's use of this term to translate this Book of Mormon organization, it may or may not be accurate.

What do we know about Alma's church from the text alone?

- The church is entered by baptism.
- The church is apparently associated with a small geographic area, allowing for a smaller number of people to view themselves as an associated religious community.
- Each church has local priests and teachers.
- Alma retains a line of control from Alma to each of the priests and teachers, and through them to the congregation.

How do these details contrast with the pre-Alma situation?

- Nephite baptism existed, but there is no indication that it is used as a marker of entrance into a specific covenant that differed from the greater social covenant of Israel. Jacob's doctrinal discussions make it clear that the Nephites considered themselves part of the covenant people. This identity would have continued as a collective covenant up to Alma's time, when his baptism makes an individual covenant. King Benjamin's individually assumed covenants occur in the context and assumption of communal participation in the covenant. Only Alma's baptism denotes a separation in the community rather than a communal action.
- Priests and teachers had been appointed earlier, but were not associated with individual congregations. The original priests and teachers would again have been communal, rather than carrying out the congregation-specific functions Alma assigned them.
- The locus of religious authority resided in the king. Indeed, ancient kingship carried with it the assumption of divine investiture of power, covering all of society. As already remarked numerous times, religion was part and parcel of reality and therefore not seen as something that could be deemed separate. Alma's establishment as an authority separate from the king not only diminishes the king, but establishes the *possibility* of the local "churches" by recognizing that religious authority may be ultimately delegated away from the communal unity embodied by the king.

What then was Alma's church *not*? At least in its inception, it was not a separate religious system among other religious systems. While Alma's reforms ultimately led to the possibility of seeing "church" as synonymous with "sect," in this earliest setting it is much better seen as closer to the original Greek *ekklesia* or "gathering." Alma's church was a congregation geographically separated from other similar congregations for greater ease in instructing the congregation. When the Zarahemla population had grown too large for indoctrination en masse, division into smaller congregations would allow for more effective teaching, and therefore perhaps better understanding, and (one would hope) better daily integration of the correct principles.

Mosiah 25:22

> 22 And thus, notwithstanding there being many churches they were all one church, yea, even the church of God; for there was nothing preached in all the churches except it were repentance and faith in God.

This stress on essential unity of belief underscores that each separate congregation learned the same religion, a unity assured by Alma's position as leader for all of the churches.

Scripture: This verse gives a formulaic definition of what was taught—not "the gospel," or "the commandments of God," or "the law of Moses," but rather: "there was nothing preached in all the churches except it were repentance and faith in God."

Certainly the churches taught much about obedience to Yahweh's will and could not have been limited to sermons about repentance and faith any more than the modern Church could. What is important is the introduction of the phrase with the negative (there was nothing preached . . . except . . .) and the formulaic use of "repentance and faith."

Repentance and faith are keywords that form the basic understanding of the Atoning Messiah. First is the individualized, rather than communal, nature of the religion of the Atoning Messiah; and second is the emphasis on the quartet of doctrines (faith, repentance, atonement, and forgiveness) that form the basis of Christian worship. In contrast is the communal atonement of the law of Moses.

The Old Testament religion is a communal religion. Loyalty to community, king, and God were all one and the same. Christian communities experienced loyalties divided between God and political leaders. Social responsibilities for those who belonged to the Christian community were different for those who belonged to the pagan community. The tacit recognition of at least two religions among the Zarahemlaites (Nephite and anything else, usually Nehorite) provides this same social condition where personal faith is more important than communal loyalty to Yahweh.

These clues suggest that these churches preached the Atoning Messiah, a doctrinal emphasis that would naturally have been consistent with what Alma learned from Abinadi and taught to his first congregation. Thus, the statement deals with the type of gospel being taught—that expounded by Abinadi and other Nephite prophets concerning the Atoning Messiah.

Translation: This verse inserts the denominational meaning of church into the description of Alma's church, which is precisely the definition I have argued against. What is it doing here? I suggest it stems from Mormon's abridgment, made at a much later period when religious divisions have played out very differently from those Alma envisioned when he established the churches/congregations. In other words, this description is Mormon's conclusion based upon his later understanding of the conception, rather than a textually accurate depiction of Alma's churches.

Mosiah 25:23

> 23 And now there were seven churches in the land of Zarahemla. And it came to pass that whosoever were desirous to take upon them the name of Christ, or of God, they did join the churches of God;

Culture: The first organization of congregations has seven separate "churches," each a specific congregation with separate priests and leaders. The text locates them "in the land of Zarahemla," or greater area attached to the city of Zarahemla, not the city proper. Thus, it is probable that the seven represented pre-defined communities structured by the current living arrangements. One congregation would be the city of Zarahemla and the immediately surrounding farming district. The other six were probably dependent towns or hamlets that were some distance from Zarahemla, but which looked to Zarahemla for political/religious leadership. This latter definition is bolstered by the fact that Alma traveled to different cities. These first churches were probably created along the city/town/hamlet boundaries.[8] Since seven is the ancient biblical number of perfection, having seven churches might be predictable regardless of any other organization. However, the number seven does not appear often enough in the Book of Mormon with that meaning to be a sufficient hypothesis. The Mesoamerican use of the number four seems to have replaced the Old World function of "seven." (See commentary accompanying Mosiah 27:1.)

The text indicates that those who wished to take upon themselves the name of Yahweh-Messiah joined these churches. The taking of the name was Benjamin's covenant. While we do not know specifically that Alma also activated the covenant by having his communicants adopt the name of Yahweh-Messiah, it certainly makes sense to continue to promote Benjamin's covenant as well as Alma's baptism.

Translation: The text specifies "the name of Christ, or of God." The Nephite conception of their Atoning Messiah was that he was equivalent to Yahweh and, therefore, the same as their God. (See "Excursus: The Nephite Understanding of God," following 1 Nephi 11.) This passage retains the sense of the original without the alterations that modern Saints would make to communicate distinctions that the Nephites did not understand. Of course we also understand Jesus as incarnate Yahweh, so there is no real difference in our understanding, only the problematic distinctions we make when we use "God" as an exclusive designator of the Father rather than Yahweh.

Mosiah 25:24

> 24 And they were called the people of God. And the Lord did pour out his Spirit upon them, and they were blessed, and prospered in the land.

Text: There is no chapter break here in the 1830 edition. This verse is both a conclusion and a transition for the next verse. While this verse ends part of the story of the establishment of churches, the net social effect of that change comes in the next verse. Whether Mormon explicitly understood the creation of the churches as the enabler for the social divisions he next described we cannot tell. The next chapter, however, focuses on those divisions. Thus, this verse sets up the contrast between the initial outpouring of the Spirit and the religious contentions that will follow.

---

[8]John A. Tvedtnes, "Book of Mormon Tribal Affiliation and Military Castes," in *Warfare in the Book of Mormon*, edited by Stephen D. Ricks and William J. Hamblin (Salt Lake City: Deseret Book/Provo, Utah: Foundation for Ancient Research and Mormon Studies, 1990), 297, suggests an alternate hypothesis, that the seven churches follow the original seven lineages associated with the people of Nephi. While I agree that lineages were still important, the association of a "church" with a lineage either requires that the lineages be distributed separately among cities (for which there is no evidence) or that there be multiple "churches" in a single city. This latter possibility conceives the Nephite "church" as something much closer to our modern idea. Particularly as an innovation, I cannot see more community divisions than just believer/nonbeliever in a single community.

Mosiah 26

Mosiah 26:1

> 1 Now it came to pass that there were many of the rising generation that could not understand the words of king Benjamin, being little children at the time he spake unto his people; and they did not believe the tradition of their fathers.

Mormon describes two characteristics of the nonbelievers. The first is that they "could not understand the words of king Benjamin, being little children at the time he spake." Why did it matter that the small children failed to understand his words? Would their parents not have explained it to them, in terms they could understand, many times as they grew?

The answer might lie in the overwhelming power of Benjamin's setting. The power of Benjamin's speech today is still palpable; but in the context of the time and place, it must have been a unique experience that could not have been replicated. While the adults would have been unable to deny what they felt, the children had no such powerful memory on which to rest their belief. The second answer is more literary. Mormon is contrasting the teaching of past prophets with those of subsequent generations who believe (derivatively) on their words.

Significantly, Mormon's second reason that there were unbelievers was that they "did not believe the tradition of their fathers." Certainly their fathers had attempted to teach the things that they had heard and felt, but with equal certainty some of the rising generation listened to other influences and consequently dismissed some of the teachings of their parents.

Mormon confirms that these children were both too young to have had the personally transforming experience of their parents but had also chosen not to believe in their parents' teachings. He is giving reasons why a particular rising generation is moving away from the traditional Nephite religion. This is essential groundwork for the story of $Alma_2$ and the sons of Mosiah.

Literature: In the original Book of Mormon, this verse followed immediately after our current Mosiah 25:24. It introduces a subject diametrically opposed to the preceding information. The immediately preceding passage established the church with its unity of purpose. Although a division in belief existed before Alma's introduction of a church, the essential tension lay between these non-church Zarahemlaites and the churched Zarahemlaites. By thus presenting the stories, Mormon structurally highlights the social tension by his placement of the literary tension.

Mosiah 26:2–3

> 2 They did not believe what had been said concerning the resurrection of the dead, neither did they believe concerning the coming of Christ.
> 3 And now because of their unbelief they could not understand the word of God; and their hearts were hardened.

Verse 2 highlights the characteristics of the most serious Nephite apostasies. The issue is never over the nature of ritual purity as it is in the New Testament (e.g., Matt. 9:10–11, Luke 6:1–2). While the absolute dividing lines among Sadducees, Pharisees, and Essene are not at all clear, the substance of some issues obviously stem from different interpretations and applications of the law of Moses. None of them deal with the denial of an Atoning Messiah.

The New World was unique both in retaining its belief in the Atoning Messiah (see 1 Nephi, Part 1: Context, Chapter 2, "The Historical Setting of 1 Nephi"), but also in the tremendous religious and social divisions that belief caused. Noah and his priests rejected the Atoning Messiah; affirming the Messiah formed the substance of Abinadi's preaching. (See "Excursus: Religion of the Nehors," following Alma 1.)

Only a short generation after the anti-Messiah apostates had defected to the Lamanites (W of M 1:14–16), the same conflict erupts again in Zarahemla. Thus, even inside Benjamin's society that had been drawn together as one people in a powerful experience, something was still pulling the youngsters away—those children who could not rely on their personal transformation to motivate their adoption of the covenant and name that Benjamin confers upon them.

This situation requires more examination. Cultural change is a complex topic, and multiple factors influence any change. While it is true that the opportunity for innovation exists in any human society, the fact is that change occurs less frequently in self-contained societies. Change typically occurs at the individual level, but the factors that enable individual change eventually spread to the group.[1]

The particular type of change that seems to be described here substantially undermines the common belief structures of an entire community. Surely the adults, with their shared beliefs, are passing them on to their children. In the ancient world, religion's role as the very definition of reality was so strong as to be nearly absolute. This concept of religion's power was so strong that, when one group was defeated by another, the reason for the defeat was often given as the superiority of the winning group's god.

Why, then, are children of very committed parents discarding a fundamental belief so rapidly and in such conspicuously large numbers? That should not happen in a self-contained society. H. G. Barnett, who wrote an early study of innovation, suggests: "Some cultural changes . . . are derived, incidental, unforeseen, and even unwanted. They are in a sense forced as a result of a change in some other part of the cultural nexus. The initial and dominant change is the focus of attention. It

---

[1]H. G. Barnett, *Innovation: The Basis of Cultural Change* (New York: McGraw-Hill Book, 1953), 39.

may have been instituted by some member of the in-group, imposed by a conquering group, or voluntarily adopted from an outside source."[2] The change in Zarahemla would clearly be unwanted change from the parents' perspective. What, then, is its origin? An internal change seems unlikely, since we would have to suppose that an individual in that group of children was a religious innovator and a sufficiently important person for his or her ideas to become popular with peers despite the opposition of their parents.

However, this is the same heresy that occurred in Noah's case and that Sherem suggested even earlier. In other words, this tension has gone on for hundreds of years. The children are not innovating, but copying, which means that they are copying from a group outside their own. In short, this dissension indicates continued contact with a group outside of Zarahemla who had not adopted Benjamin's covenant.

Significantly, because they denied the coming mission of the Atoning Messiah, "they could not understand the word of God; and their hearts were hardened" (v. 3). This rejection of a specific tenet of Nephite religion led them to reject the entire "word of God"—in other words, virtually all of the religious beliefs of their parents and, hence, their parents' view of how the world worked. Almost certainly, they borrowed a competing worldview from another religion. Like other religious conflicts in the Book of Mormon, this one apparently relied on the existence of a competing religion in their immediate vicinity—the same religion that had attacked the Nephite religion in the city of Nephi as well as in Zarahemla.

Threads of Mesoamerican thought can be traced from the Olmec (the earliest high Mesoamerican culture) through the Maya and later to the Aztecs (at the time of the conquest). In a world filled with such a consistent but diametrically opposed worldview, it is not surprising that there are so many apostasies from Nephite religion. While I see the presence of other Mesoamerican cultures as the strong influence in Nephite apostasy, the particular nature of the apostasy suggests that the attraction was to Mesoamerican social institutions, not Mesoamerican religion per se. There is no indication that the Nephites adopted Mesoamerican gods. Rather, they adopted Mesoamerican kingship, its accompanying social hierarchy, and the preeminence it gave wealth. The Nephite apostasy suggests that the changes were adaptations of social hierarchies into a version of the traditional brass-plate religion accompanied by specific denials of the Atoning Messiah. Perhaps Nephite egalitarianism was so tightly bound to the doctrine of the Messiah that rejecting egalitarianism also required rejecting the Messiah. (See "Excursus: The Religion of the Nehors," following Alma 1.)

Mosiah 26:4

4 And they would not be baptized; neither would they join the church. And they were a separate people as to their faith, and remained so ever after, even

---

[2]Ibid., 89.

> in their carnal and sinful state; for they would not call upon the Lord their God.

The dissenters were socially segregated, "a separate people." Ironically, while Alma's churches provided a tighter community of believers inside a larger community, they also allowed for an obvious distinction between church-men and non-church-men. Prior to the institution of the church, religion occurred on a community level, and the individual participation could be overlooked. Once institutions required individual allegiances, dissenters became conspicuous. This polarization would increase cohesiveness among the nonbelievers in almost the same way that membership in the churches increased believers' cohesiveness.

Mormon's conclusion that the dissenters remained separate "ever after" is somewhat problematic since he promptly tells the stories of some who did not. Why would Mormon make a statement of such pessimistic finality, then immediately contradict it? Obviously it is that $Alma_2$ and the sons of Mosiah are the most important exceptions to the rule he has enunciated. Nevertheless, the general trend was the creation of a religious division in Nephite society that afflicted the people "ever after." Indeed, it is quite likely that Mormon was continuing to witness some of the same problems created by the Nephite apostasy.

Mosiah 26:5

> 5 And now in the reign of Mosiah they were not half so numerous as the people of God; but because of the dissensions among the brethren they became more numerous.

Culture: The description "not half so numerous" is the beginnings of the group—or the children (certainly not all of them) who had been too small to retain vivid memories of Benjamin's covenant. However, the movement did not remain small. "Dissensions among the brethren" means internal problems among believers, many of whom began to follow this different religion movement, begun by some among the children's generation.

What, among the beliefs of the children, is so attractive? If this movement is following the traditional historic process, religious apostasy also included wealth, visible trappings, and social distinctions. This division is not a simple ideological difference of opinion, but a foundational struggle over the type of society the Nephites would have with a significant number envying and enjoying the lifestyle of the "others"—those who are generically labeled "Lamanites" in the Book of Mormon even if they were not literal descendants of Laman.

Mosiah 26:6

> 6 For it came to pass that they did deceive many with their flattering words, who were in the church, and did cause them to commit many sins; therefore it became expedient that those who committed sin, that were in the church, should be admonished by the church.

The message of the competing religion contained more than denying the Atoning Messiah. There could not be that many "flattering words" that would deny the Messiah, retain everything else, and still lead people to "commit many sins." This alternate worldview would certainly lead to different practices, which could easily be seen as sin by orthodox believers, requiring them to be "admonished by the church."

The shift to a more Mesoamerican worldview would bring with it a different understanding of God's nature and how the world works and, hence, a significant difference in the doctrine of sacrifices. While the *practice* of sacrifices would remain, the reason for the offering and the being to whom it was offered would all change. For a monotheistic people, offering sacrifices to a different god was clearly sin.

Mosiah 26:7–8

> 7 And it came to pass that they were brought before the priests, and delivered up unto the priests by the teachers; and the priests brought them before Alma, who was the high priest.
> 8 Now king Mosiah had given Alma the authority over the church.

Culture: We have here the growing problem of cultural divisions stemming from doctrinal differences. Because Alma has authority over the churches, a power structure exists that is separate from the rest of the government. Even though Alma operates under Mosiah's direction and authority, his very assignment separates government functions in a way that has never happened before. Because this division of powers is accepted, there is less community weight on dissenters to conform. If the church can be separate from society, that very separation undermines the assumption that the community is a whole, opening the door for social and religious opposition.

Mosiah 26:9–10

> 9 And it came to pass that Alma did not know concerning them; but there were many witnesses against them; yea, the people stood and testified of their iniquity in abundance.
> 10 Now there had not any such thing happened before in the church; therefore Alma was troubled in his spirit, and he caused that they should be brought before the king.

As a newcomer to Zarahemla's society—and furthermore, as one who has spent all his time organizing churches—Alma probably is not well informed about the history of these dissensions, which almost certainly had begun before Alma reached the city.

Alma cannot make a decision, probably because he recognizes that the problem is social as well as religious. He refers the dissenters to the king because they must share responsibility for this social/religious problem.

Variant: The printer's manuscript for verse 9 reads: "And it came to pass that Alma did know concerning them there were many witnesses against them. . . . " At this point, the printer's manuscript is not in Oliver Cowdery's hand, but Oliver did insert *not* into the sentence for some reason. Later, in the 1920 edition, the word *but* was added to help make sense of the sentence. The best sense comes from the version in the uncorrected printer's manuscript.[3]

Mosiah 26:11

> 11 And he said unto the king: Behold, here are many whom we have brought before thee, who are accused of their brethren; yea, and they have been taken in divers iniquities. And they do not repent of their iniquities; therefore we have brought them before thee, that thou mayest judge them according to their crimes.

Of what crimes are the dissenters guilty? And are they really crimes or are they sins? Mormon doesn't say. However, while their faults may have been religious sins, they are brought before the highest social judge because these acts disrupt society and, in that sense, merit the king's judgment.

Mosiah 26:12

> 12 But king Mosiah said unto Alma: Behold, I judge them not; therefore I deliver them into thy hands to be judged.

For an unknown reason, Mosiah declines to judge and returns the problem to Alma. Probably he saw the problem as a religious one which must be handled by the proper religious authority. It seems likely that, understanding the development of diversity within the community, Mosiah understands that he must rule over a kingdom of diverse beliefs without alienating part of the community. For this reason, perhaps, he observes the religious/social distinction by declining to judge.

We know that Mosiah is a believer and therefore in sympathy with Alma's teachings. His action separates religious functions from direct ties to government. By giving the decision to Alma, Mosiah can separate himself from that decision and therefore from its possible social repercussions. Mosiah is thus retaining his ability to govern the entire body, which includes an increasing number of religious dissenters and their sympathizers.

Mosiah 26:13–14

> 13 And now the spirit of Alma was again troubled; and he went and inquired of the Lord what he should do concerning this matter, for he feared that he should do wrong in the sight of God.
> 14 And it came to pass that after he had poured out his whole soul to God, the voice of the Lord came to him, saying:

Alma is in an unprecedented situation here—the first time in Book of Mormon history when there is a division between the government and the official religion.

---

[3]Royal Skousen, *Analysis of Textual Variants of the Book of Mormon*, THE CRITICAL TEXT OF THE BOOK OF MORMON (Provo, Utah: Foundation for Ancient Research and Mormon Studies, 2005), Vol. 4, Part 3, 1483.

Mosiah has reinforced that division by requiring Alma to solve the problem. Baffled, Alma seeks inspiration and receives an answer (vv. 15–32).

Mosiah 26:15

> 15 Blessed art thou, Alma, and blessed are they who were baptized in the waters of Mormon. Thou art blessed because of thy exceeding faith in the words alone of my servant Abinadi.
> 16 And blessed are they because of their exceeding faith in the words alone which thou hast spoken unto them.

Yahweh's first message has little to do with Alma's specific inquiry and instead provides reassurance and support for Alma himself. He nurtures Alma as an individual by telling him he is blessed and that his baptisms are valid.

Literature: Verses 15 and 16 should be read together. The last phrase of 15 is the first part of a parallel that concludes in 16. The text should read:

> Thou art blessed because of thy exceeding faith in the words alone of my servant Abinadi.
>
> And blessed are they because of their exceeding faith in the words alone which thou hast spoken unto them.

Yahweh is identifying the blessings that come from faith, particularly faith in the words of another. The first example is Alma's faith in the words of Abinadi. The second example moves Alma into Abinadi's position and has people believing Alma's words. The parallelism emphasizes that we are blessed by listening to those who speak for Yahweh—that we may gain the full benefit of hearing Yahweh's word through faith in the words of others. In modern revelation we learn:

> For all have not every gift given unto them; for there are many gifts, and to every man is given a gift by the Spirit of God.
>
> To some is given one, and to some is given another, that all may be profited thereby.
>
> To some it is given by the Holy Ghost to know that Jesus Christ is the Son of God, and that he was crucified for the sins of the world.
>
> To others it is given to believe on their words, that they also might have eternal life if they continue faithful. (D&C 46:11–14)

Although there are differing gifts, all gifts of the spirit are gifts nevertheless. They are given to benefit the whole and not to make qualitative differences among the members. This unity of purpose amidst the diversity of gifts was the essence of Paul's message as well:

> Now there are diversities of gifts, but the same Spirit.
>
> And there are differences of administrations, but the same Lord.
>
> And there are diversities of operations, but it is the same God which worketh all in all.
>
> But the manifestation of the Spirit is given to every man to profit withal. (1 Cor. 12:4–7)

The wonderful declaration of the modern revelation in the Doctrine and Covenants is that the ability to believe on the words of others is a gift of the Spirit that places us in the same spiritual category as one who received a direct revelation. Regardless of where our faith comes from, if it transforms us it exalts us.

Mosiah 26:17

> 17 And blessed art thou because thou hast established a church among this people; and they shall be established, and they shall be my people.

Yahweh explicitly accepts Alma's churches. Perhaps the dissent had caused Alma to doubt the wisdom of establishing churches since they seem to have engendered divisions as a side effect. Yahweh may be allaying those fears by telling Alma that he accepts the churches.

The most significant part of this passage is the final statement concerning the church. Yahweh notes: "They shall be my people." This is the ancient Abrahamic covenant. Yahweh is reaffirming the covenant, even though it is no longer a covenant with the community but rather with the church. The covenant now does not reside in lineage, but in the church's authority and ordinances.

Mosiah 26:18

> 18 Yea, blessed is this people who are willing to bear my name; for in my name shall they be called; and they are mine.

After reconfirming and relocating the Abrahamic covenant, Yahweh also reconfirms Benjamin's covenant and relocates it to the church. Where Benjamin's covenant defined a people, this covenant of "bearing my name" will define a segment of the people.

By both acts, Yahweh establishes in the New World what will not become a reality in the Old World for another perhaps 150 to 200 years. The diversity of population and government requires that the covenants become individualized rather than communal, and Yahweh establishes that change here due to the diversity in Zarahemla. That diversity will become more apparent in future chapters.

Mosiah 26:19–20

> 19 And because thou hast inquired of me concerning the transgressor, thou art blessed.
> 20 Thou art my servant; and I covenant with thee that thou shalt have eternal life; and thou shalt serve me and go forth in my name, and shalt gather together my sheep.

Yahweh now makes a third covenant. The first two were communal covenants that were shifted to the church. Now Yahweh makes a specific individual covenant with Alma. He shall have eternal life (Yahweh's promise), and he shall serve Yahweh and "gather together my sheep (Alma's promise).

Mosiah 26:21–22

> 21 And he that will hear my voice shall be my sheep; and him shall ye receive into the church, and him will I also receive.

> 22 For behold, this is my church; whosoever is baptized shall be baptized unto repentance. And whomsoever ye receive shall believe in my name; and him will I freely forgive.

Yahweh then makes a fourth covenant. When Alma gathers Yahweh's "sheep" by preaching and they join the church by baptism, Yahweh will receive them as his people and forgive their sins.

Literature: The text uses the word "sheep" here. In a New World context, this term would be a misnomer since there were no sheep in the New World at this time. However, "sheep" here is clearly a metaphor for "believers." It may or may not have been the precise word Yahweh used with Alma, but it is the term used to mean "believers" in the New Testament and was therefore the appropriate term for Joseph Smith to use in this context.

Mosiah 26:23

> 23 For it is I that taketh upon me the sins of the world; for it is I that hath created them; and it is I that granteth unto him that believeth unto the end a place at my right hand.

How can Yahweh make this covenant of forgiveness of sins through baptism when this event precedes the atonement that creates such forgiveness? Yahweh can make that covenant because he will create the conditions for fulfilling the covenant. In the Book of Mormon, Yahweh-Christ is God. The God who teaches them and communicates with them is the very one who will become incarnate and sacrifice himself for humanity. He has the ability to make this promise because he will fulfill the requirements of this promise.

Text: The first section of this verse may be momentarily confusing: "For it is I that taketh upon me the sins of the world; for it is I that hath created them." The antecedent for "created them" appears to be "sins of the world." Of course, that is not correct. The answer lies in the larger context:

> For behold, this is my church; whosoever is baptized shall be baptized unto repentance. And whomsoever ye receive shall believe in my name; and him will I freely forgive.
>
> For it is I that taketh upon me the sins of the world; for it is I that hath created them [those who believe in his name]; and it is I that granteth unto him that believeth unto the end a place at my right hand.
>
> For behold, in my name are they called; and if they know me they shall come forth, and shall have a place eternally at my right hand. (vv. 22–24)

In both verses 22 and 23, the Lord is speaking of the people of his church. Since the context both before and after is the same people, "them" refers to those people. Part of the problem in reading the verse is the punctuation, which was added by the typesetter. I would suggest this more logical punctuation:

> And whomsoever ye receive shall believe in my name; and him will I freely forgive, for it is I that taketh upon me the sins of the world. For it is I that hath created them [those

who believe in his name] and it is I that granteth unto him that believeth unto the end a place at my right hand.

Mosiah 26:24

24 For behold, in my name are they called; and if they know me they shall come forth, and shall have a place eternally at my right hand.

The blessings promised are not only for this life, but will transcend this life. In verse 23 Yahweh notes that some blessings will be granted "in the end"—meaning the time when the earth's purposes are fulfilled. It will be the time of the Triumphal Messiah. (See commentary accompanying 3 Nephi 12:48.)

Translation: The imagery of the right hand comes from the ancient conceptions of the right hand as good and the left hand as evil. The Latin word for "left" is *sinistra*, which was adopted into English with an obviously pejorative character. Thus, it is a blessing to be on Yahweh's right hand. This conceptual division between the left and the right is well known from the Old World, but less so from the New World.

There is little literature on the meaning of the left hand in Mesoamerica, but there are hints that it was not considered evil, but that it may have been a sign of a connection to the powers of the other world. For example, the left-handed warriors of the Mexica were considered the most fearful, most likely because their left-handedness gave them a military advantage. The name of the Mexica tribal deity was Huitzilopochtli, meaning "hummingbird on/of the left." This context is positive for the Mexica. A fascinating possibility comes from an analysis of the various stelae at the site of Izapa, a much later description of the underworld from the Codices Matritenses, and the Mesoamerican fascination with mirrors.

In Izapa, a preponderance of actions are performed with the left hand.[4] Either the Izapans were statistically left-handed more than any other known population, or the depiction of actions by the left hand had a distinctive significance. The Codices Matritenses describe the underworld as a place of reversals from the real world.[5] And finally, the Mesoamerican mirror of polished obsidian or hematite has symbolic connections to the primordial waters and the underworld. The mirror effect is so well known that we understand a "mirror image" to transform right to left and left to right. In this context, the left hand may be a representation of a connection to the otherworld.

What would these possibilities mean for this passage? I hypothesize that Joseph translated the concept, using an image that was familiar to him, though not necessarily the wording on the plates. Of course, we do not know that wording; but in the social context of Mesoamerica, it seems unlikely that the Old World imagery of "right is good/left is bad" would have survived long enough to be recorded in this time period.

---

[4]I personally examined the photographs of the monuments from Izapa in V. Garth Norman, *Izapa Sculpture, Part 1: Album* (Provo, Utah: BYU New World Archaeological Foundation, , 1976).

[5]Bernardino de Sahagún, "Codices Matritenses," 1540–85, holograph Fol. 84r/v, Library, Royal Palace of the Academy of History, Madrid, Spain. Microfilm in my possession.

Mosiah 26:25–26

> 25 And it shall come to pass that when the second trump shall sound then shall they that never knew me come forth and shall stand before me.
> 26 And then shall they know that I am the Lord their God, that I am their Redeemer; but they would not be redeemed.

Yahweh has described the blessings of those who associate themselves with the church; but Alma's original question was what he should do with the dissenters. Yahweh is preparing that answer. In contrast to the situation of those who are called by his name (and who are numbered with the church) those who "never knew me" will arise at "the end" and will be rejected. They are rejected precisely because this Yahweh who is speaking is the one who redeems them and they have not accepted that redemption (i.e., have not been baptized).

Mosiah 26:27

> 27 And then I will confess unto them that I never knew them; and they shall depart into everlasting fire prepared for the devil and his angels.

Because they never "knew" Yahweh in the sense of accepting him as their redeemer through baptism, Yahweh never "knew" them because they were not called by his name. The fate of those who do not accept Yahweh's redemption is that they are not redeemed.

Mosiah 26:28

> 28 Therefore I say unto you, that he that will not hear my voice, the same shall ye not receive into my church, for him I will not receive at the last day.

Now Yahweh begins to answer Alma's question. The ultimate answer is not part of the immediate world, but of the eternities. That is why Yahweh has explained eternal consequences. Understanding those eternal consequences makes the temporal consequences more clear. Since these dissenters "will not hear my voice," they are not Yahweh's "sheep" and therefore are not part of the church. The Abrahamic and Benjaminic covenants have been relocated to the authority of the church rather than assigned to the entire community, but these dissenters are not part of the covenant and receive none of the covenantal blessings, even though they are part of the community.

Mosiah 26:29–30

> 29 Therefore I say unto you, Go; and whosoever transgresseth against me, him shall ye judge according to the sins which he has committed; and if he confess his sins before thee and me, and repenteth in the sincerity of his heart, him shall ye forgive, and I will forgive him also.
> 30 Yea, and as often as my people repent will I forgive them their trespasses against me.

It is important that Yahweh's first specific instruction involves repentance. Yahweh makes repentance possible and waits to forgive us if we will turn to him. Therefore, he first provides for those whose hearts may be touched and who are able to turn to him. These people will be accepted into the church (and the covenant) and they shall be forgiven (because baptism is part of their covenant upon joining with the church).

Mosiah 26:31

> 31 And ye shall also forgive one another your trespasses; for verily I say unto you, he that forgiveth not his neighbor's trespasses when he says that he repents, the same hath brought himself under condemnation.

This admonition is designed not only to teach individuals what they need to know about forgiveness, but also how to heal a community that could be torn apart by the division between the churched and the unchurched. Yahweh is urging forgiveness, not rancor nor divisiveness.

Mosiah 26:32

> 32 Now I say unto you, Go; and whosoever will not repent of his sins the same shall not be numbered among my people; and this shall be observed from this time forward.

Here is Yahweh's conclusion: Those who will not repent are not numbered with the church and are not part of Yahweh's covenant although they may still be part of the community. With the removal of the covenant from the community, those who do not repent are members of the community only and can no longer inherit the covenant.

Alma learns that there is a real division between the church and the rest of the community. While all may be under Mosiah's rule, only those who accept the Atoning Messiah are part of the church and part of the covenant with Yahweh.

Mosiah 26:33

> 33 And it came to pass when Alma had heard these words he wrote them down that he might have them, and that he might judge the people of that church according to the commandments of God.

Mormon makes note of the fact that Alma wrote down these instructions. Certainly they would be impressed upon Alma's mind, but Alma wanted a more tangible record—part of Alma's "General Handbook" by which "he might judge the people of that church." And of course, writing these words down would make them readily available to future generations.

Mosiah 26:34–36

> 34 And it came to pass that Alma went and judged those that had been taken in iniquity, according to the word of the Lord.
> 35 And whosoever repented of their sins and did confess them, them he did number among the people of the church;

> 36 And those that would not confess their sins and repent of their iniquity, the same were not numbered among the people of the church, and their names were blotted out.

Although it might go without saying that Alma followed Yahweh's instructions, Mormon spells out Alma's obedience for three verses.

Mosiah 26:37–39

> 37 And it came to pass that Alma did regulate all the affairs of the church; and they began again to have peace and to prosper exceedingly in the affairs of the church, walking circumspectly before God, receiving many, and baptizing many.
> 38 And now all these things did Alma and his fellow laborers do who were over the church, walking in all diligence, teaching the word of God in all things, suffering all manner of afflictions, being persecuted by all those who did not belong to the church of God.
> 39 And they did admonish their brethren; and they were also admonished, every one by the word of God, according to his sins, or to the sins which he had committed, being commanded of God to pray without ceasing, and to give thanks in all things.

Mormon summarizes Alma's leadership over the church providing markers of his success: many baptisms. However, verse 38 foreshadows the major conflict to follow. Despite all of the things that are going well inside the church, there are problems outside it. The social division has become so acute that the unchurched have begun persecuting the church members. This situation will be discussed more fully in the next chapter.

Along with the details of the particular story, Dennis L. Largey, professor of ancient scripture at Brigham Young University, identifies several models for the modern church in these chapters:

> Just within Mosiah 25–27 are the following doctrinal truths: (1) Jesus is the head of the Church (Mosiah 26:22); (2) Jesus directs his Church through revelation to his prophet (Mosiah 26:13–32); (3) baptism must be by total immersion (Mosiah 18:14, 25:18); (4) Church members who sin must be admonished by the Church (Mosiah 26:6); (5) the Church may have many congregations, yet there is only one Church—all branches teach the same doctrine as directed by the living prophet (Mosiah 25:21–22); and (6) baptism is necessary to take upon oneself the name of Jesus Christ and to enter into his Church (Mosiah 25:18, 23). The functioning of the Church in Zarahemla is a reflection of the operation of the true Church of Jesus Christ in any age. By having this blueprint, readers are strengthened in their belief that "God is the same yesterday, today, and forever" (Morm. 9:9).[6]

Literature: Mormon is setting up another contrast: the good inside the church with the evil outside it. He will touch on the "good" later but will be concentrating on the "bad" of the persecutions—all of it leading to the good that results from the situation.

---

[6]Dennis L. Largey, "Lessons from the Zarahemla Churches," in *The Book of Mormon: Mosiah, Salvation Only through Christ*, edited by Monte S. Nyman and Charles D. Tate Jr. (Provo, Utah: BYU Religious Studies Center, 1991), 60–61.

Text: There is no break here in the 1830 text. Mormon intended this story to continue without chapter interruption. In fact, there is no paragraph break here in 1830. In the 1830 edition, the paragraph was:

> [not the beginning of the paragraph, it started with verse 34] . . . And they did admonish their brethren; and they were also admonished, every one by the word of God, according to his sins, or to the sins which he had committed, being commanded of God to pray without ceasing, and to give thanks in all things. And now it came to pass that the persecutions which were inflicted on the church by the unbelievers became so great that the church began to murmur, and complain to their leaders concerning the matter; and they did complain to Alma. And Alma laid the case before their king, Mosiah. And Mosiah consulted with his priests.

In that original context, the contrasting of the good and the bad is even clearer.[7]

[7]These passages on Church discipline can be seen as a model for the contemporary LDS Church. H. Donl Peterson, "Church Discipline in the Book of Mosiah," in *The Book of Mormon: Mosiah, Salvation Only through Christ*, edited by Monte S. Nyman and Charles D. Tate Jr. (Provo, Utah: BYU Religious Studies Center, 1991), 211–26.

Mosiah 27

Mosiah 27:1

> 1 And now it came to pass that the persecutions which were inflicted on the church by the unbelievers became so great that the church began to murmur, and complain to their leaders concerning the matter; and they did complain to Alma. And Alma laid the case before their king, Mosiah. And Mosiah consulted with his priests.

Text: The 1830 version of the Book of Mormon has no chapter break at this location. While there is a shift in context, in the original, the literary contrasts were more evident when the contrasting sections followed each other directly. The separation into chapters misses the structure of the original.

History: The separation of church and state in Zarahemla allows for the underlying tensions to become explicit. Once there is a separate entity that is not conterminous with the government, it is easier to disagree with that entity. Resistance flourishes rapidly—so rapidly, in fact, that is suggests that the tensions have never really gone away. Despite Benjamin's attempt to unify his people under Yahweh-Messiah's name, that unity has disappeared only one generation later. The religious tensions that cause the internal strife noted at the end of Words of Mormon have returned with a vengeance.

It is valuable to identify social conditions in Zarahemla as best we can. First, Zarahemla is the chief city, but probably exists in a system with dependent cities. One way of understanding this arrangement is Alma's seven churches. It makes the most sense to have seven churches in seven communities, rather than seven churches within Zarahemla. Mesoamerican cities have ceremonial centers, but the living areas are typically widely dispersed around the ceremonial center. Comparatively few cities from this time period would have been large enough to accommodate seven "churches" in a single ceremonial center. There was also no need for further divisions inside a single community. Everyone was either in or out, a church-man or a non-church-man. (See commentary accompanying Mosiah 25:23.)

Second, we know that the land of Zarahemla is composed of at least four groups: Nephites, Zarahemlaites/Mulekites, the people of Limhi, and the people of Alma. These last two entered Zarahemla as cohesive units. It seems likely that they were larger than could be easily absorbed into Zarahemla. Almost certainly these peoples would have been assigned a separate location. As Alma's group had already created one city (Helam), it would not be surprising if they were to found another city in the land of Zarahemla. The city of Gideon is the most likely candidate (Alma 2:20).

Thus, we have a picture of Zarahemla as the chief of a confederation of cities. Because of travel times, each city would have its own organization and government. This trait will become more obvious in the book of Alma during the section on Alma$_2$'s travels. With all these divisions, it is not surprising that entire city organizations would coalesce as pro- or anti- "church," as happened in Ammonihah and with the Zoramites in Antionum.

Third, a Mesoamerican heritage would have been strong among the Zarahemla-Mulekites and reinforced through trade contacts. Thus, competition between the Mesoamerican culture and the Nephite culture would always be present. The fact that this very conflict resurfaces so frequently in exactly the same form suggests that the Nephite culture and religion was continuously opposed by a competing alternative culture/religion. To some extent, the law of Moses seemed easier for this competing religion to accommodate, as that variation appeared in the city of Lehi-Nephi under Noah. Indeed, some of the intense hostility against the Nephite religion may be explained if the competing religion is a variant of the law of Moses. Typically, it is in religions that are close in beliefs and therefore in direct competition that the gravest and most dangerous feelings arise. (See "Excursus: Religion of the Nehors," following Alma 1.) The persecutions suggest some of this closeness.

Mosiah 27:2–3

> 2 And it came to pass that king Mosiah sent a proclamation throughout the land round about that there should not any unbeliever persecute any of those who belonged to the church of God.
>
> 3 And there was a strict command throughout all the churches that there should be no persecutions among them, that there should be an equality among all men;

Mormon is not completely clear in describing Mosiah's reaction to the problem of the persecutions. Clearly, Mosiah pronounces that such persecutions of believers must stop, but whether he similarly proscribed persecution *by* believers is less clear, though we certainly expect that he did. In any case, these legal restrictions had the purpose of restoring the kingdom's harmony and singleness of purpose.

The last phrase of verse 3 is interesting. There is no reason to believe that it could not have carried the modern understanding of equality before the law. However, Mosiah is describing the people's unity, not their legal rights. Given the social disruptions that continued, even after Benjamin's attempt to unify the people, we would expect Mosiah to make a similar effort. Therefore, I read "equality" not as rights, but social standing. This is a call for social unity rather than fair laws.

Mosiah 27:4

> 4 That they should let no pride nor haughtiness disturb their peace; that every man should esteem his neighbor as himself, laboring with their own hands for their support.

This explanation clarifies Mosiah's meaning of equality. A reconstruction of the original phrasing would be: " . . . that there should be an equality among all men; that they should let no pride nor haughtiness disturb their peace; that every man should esteem his neighbor as himself, laboring with their own hands for their support."

Mormon's "equality" is not as concerned with treatment before the law as it is with leveling social hierarchies. Just as Benjamin had been concerned with his people's social unity, so Mosiah is concerned with maintaining a single society rather than one characterized by divisions. The record does not mention social stratification, but it had been a problem for Benjamin and appears to resurface here as well. Verses 5–6 enjoin the people to "labor with their own hands for their support." The social stratification that commonly occurred in Nephite society stemmed directly from economic pressures that resulted in new social categories of differential status. Like his father, Mosiah is attempting to prevent the rise of elites who lived on the labor of others. In ancient Mesoamerica, such elites would not have been employers who provided jobs in the first place but a group who considered themselves entitled to the fruit of others' labors, a view shared, for a variety of reasons, by the laborers themselves.

In the intercity wars that were a constant threat (or present reality) among the Classic Maya, the conquered presented tribute in regular amounts and at regular intervals to the conquering king. Such wealth moved from the king to the nobility. But in addition to tribute was some version of taxation of the *un*conquered population—an elite population that exacted "tribute" in the form of taxes or donations from a subservient population. While Mosiah's proclamation may have implied a prohibition of intercity warfare, the focus is obviously internal. That threat comes from the creation and maintenance of an elite class. This time period, according to archaeological studies, saw the formation of the hierarchical structures that later flourished as Classic forms of kingship and social hierarchy.[1] Thus, the Book of Mormon shows echoes in Nephite society of the greater social pressures developing in the surrounding world.

Mosiah 27:5

> 5 Yea, and all their priests and teachers should labor with their own hands for their support, in all cases save it were in sickness, or in much want; and doing these things, they did abound in the grace of God.

Culture: These Nephite elites would have been nobles, kinfolk of the king. Others would have been heads of important clans, both Nephite and Mulekite. While the Nephite faction had attained the kingship, the former king had been Mulekite and his clan would have retained considerable social influence. Apparently Mosiah was attempting to "equalize" such kin-based distinctions by requiring that all be treated as equal.

---

[1]Linda Schele and David Freidel, *A Forest of Kings: The Untold Story of the Ancient Maya* (New York: William Morrow and Company, 1990), 97–98.

Another important stratification would have been religious. Those set apart to perform religious rites for the community have prestige, and it is a short step from prestige to privilege. Not only does Mosiah attempt to "equalize" the political-social structure, but he also attempts to "equalize" the social structure stemming from religious roots. However, economic stratification was obviously the strongest, which is why Mosiah so specifically commanded that these potentially privileged people must work with their own hands. Mosiah is reducing economic prestige by reducing access to prestigious items.

Mosiah 27:6

> 6 And there began to be much peace again in the land; and the people began to be very numerous, and began to scatter abroad upon the face of the earth, yea, on the north and on the south, on the east and on the west, building large cities and villages in all quarters of the land.

Culture: Mosiah's attempts to equalize society were effective in holding his kingdom together. Rather than fission, Nephite society actually expanded in all four directions, founding new "cities and villages." This rapid expansion apparently occurred after Alma's arrival. The implication is that this expansion occurred within a brief time period—although it is also possible that Mormon's choice of location for the statement implies stronger chronology than he meant. He may have simply been summarizing a lengthy period of general increase rather than a short-term set of building projects.

Some of the expansion results from the arrival of the peoples of Alma and Limhi, but they do not seem to account for the multiple cities nor the expansion in all compass directions. Zarahemla is experiencing a population explosion that results in the creation of many cities. Building projects are labor-expensive. Being able to build multiple "large cities" simultaneously is an impressive feat.

Where did this population and increase in available labor come from in such a short time? The most reasonable answer is that Zarahemla annexed other communities as part of its expansion, thus accelerating future expansion. Natural increase would have resulted in a time lag before even numerous children were old enough to become productive builders. Large groups must have been added as a unit. With the addition of these communities, probably already at least hamlets, a Zarahemla-centered population was large enough to build new cities, thus furthering the centralizing and unifying trend. The new communities were built up largely from people who were already there but who lacked the more complex city organizations. (See description of the development of Cerros in the commentary accompanying Mosiah 23:13.) The internal descriptions of the Book of Mormon best fit the model of many other peoples in the land who are being variously incorporated into the Nephites rather than the "Nephites/Lamanites were alone" premise.

History: Mormon mentions that cities and villages were built "in all quarters of the land." Mesoamerican cultures bestowed a strong significance on the number four, based upon the four cardinal points. That conceptual division of the world into four quarters carried over into the establishment of other social systems that relied upon four parts: "In an effort to keep the traditions of their fathers alive, the Nahua and Maya nations established four rulers, four governors, or four chiefs, each responsible for one quadrant of land. In Mexico we find that the four executive officers were the chiefs or representatives of the four quarters of the City of Mexico. . . . The entire dominion of Mexico was also divided into four equal quarters, the administration of which was attended to by four lords."[2]

Redaction: See commentary accompanying Helaman 3:8 for a discussion of the use of the cardinal points to indicate "everywhere."

Mosiah 27:7

> 7 And the Lord did visit them and prosper them, and they became a large and wealthy people.

Culture: Mormon credits Yahweh with the prosperity of the Zarahemla kingdom. While this may certainly be true, what cultural and economic factors would predictably create a "large and wealthy" people?

Mormon describes the people as both "very numerous" (v. 6) and also "large" (v. 7). Possibly Mormon simply meant both terms as synonyms; however, it is also possible that the two terms differ in meaning. "Numerous" may refer to the count and "large" to the geographic extent. A "large" people may cover a broad territory and include a large number of affiliated cities, giving the kingdom of Zarahemla a greater and more important presence. With a large kingdom covering multiple city-states, Zarahemla presents a more powerful potential ally and, even more importantly, trading partner. Increase in wealth stems from a people's ability to increase their physical possessions. Internally, all may become wealthy relative to an outside community when the industry of the internal unit produces more of the markings of wealth. Thus, the larger labor base could create more elaborate civil/religious structures, and those visual signs of a people's wealth (measured by their ability to harness labor) become apparent to all.

Here, Mormon appears to describe a society that is growing large and increasing its dependent city-states, allowing a pool of disposable labor that can be used to improve the public architecture ("building large cities," v. 6). This communal use of disposable labor increases community wealth vis-à-vis communities that are not part of Zarahemla. This comparative wealth also provides an incentive for outlying hamlets to join Zarahemla to avail themselves of those same benefits: disposable labor, affluence, and visible public monuments. The communal wealth comes from growth and leads to growth. The peace that Mormon describes comes from either the communal nature of the creation of wealth or, less benevolently, the early stages of internal social stratification by wealth.

---

[2]Diane E. Wirth and Steven L. Olsen, "Four Quarters," in *Reexploring the Book of Mormon*, edited by John W. Welch (Provo, Utah: FARMS, 1992), 145–46.

Literature: Mormon is building his story with a series of contrasts. He gives the good, then the bad in linked sets. In this particular case, it seems likely that balancing this period of peace and prosperity is the upcoming rebellion of the sons of Mosiah and Alma$_2$.

Mosiah 27:8

> 8 Now the sons of Mosiah were numbered among the unbelievers; and also one of the sons of Alma was numbered among them, he being called Alma, after his father; nevertheless, he became a very wicked and an idolatrous man. And he was a man of many words, and did speak much flattery to the people; therefore he led many of the people to do after the manner of his iniquities.

Here Mormon introduces the main characters of this particular story. The sons of Mosiah and one of the sons of Alma$_1$ are "numbered among the unbelievers." The focus is on Alma$_2$ at this point because the story of his conversion will dominate the narrative. Alma$_2$ is not simply an unbeliever. He is a "wicked and an idolatrous man." "Wicked" might describe any number of possible sins, but why "idolatrous"? Clearly he not only disbelieves the Nephite religion but espouses one that views God in some different way—a strong pointer to an "outside" religion. Having adopted that position, he actively encourages others to follow his lead.

The conflict engaged in by the sons of Mosiah and Alma$_2$ is religious, not political. They do not persecute the kingdom of Zarahemla, but rather the "church." They appear to be quite willing to participate in the increased wealth but have rejected Zarahemla's religious component. With what did they replace it? I hypothesize that they replaced it with a religion more compatible with their trading partners[3]—what later became known as the order of the Nehors. Its basic structure is seen in the religion of Noah and his priests: syncretic religion combining aspects of the brass plates with New World social structures. (See "Excursus: Religion of the Nehors," following Alma 1.) Elites who were admired for their wealth and whose displays of wealth were copied also "exported" their belief systems.

From this story, many modern parents take comfort and hope. Mosiah and Alma$_1$ certainly taught their children the gospel. They provided homes that were probably above standard both spiritually and economically, since Mosiah was king and Alma$_1$ the chief priest. Nevertheless, both families had at least one child who rejected parental teachings and followed ideas antithetical to their parents' beliefs. Many modern parents experience the same ordeal. Even when miraculous conversion does not await their children, the parents can at least take some comfort in understanding that even the best parents cannot fully prevent such departures from faith.

---

[3]The Nephite belief in the Messiah, as preached by all of the Nephite prophets, *required* egalitarianism, which preached against the accumulation of goods that would create social hierarchies. Therefore, a religion that denied the Messiah (and therefore the social egalitarianism) would have been much more favorable to trade relations.

Mosiah 27:9

9 And he became a great hinderment to the prosperity of the church of God; stealing away the hearts of the people; causing much dissension among the people; giving a chance for the enemy of God to exercise his power over them.

Alma$_2$ hinders the church's growth, a real possibility because the church and the kingdom of Zarahemla are no longer coterminous. Thus, it is possible that the church might not grow when the city does. Alma$_2$'s actions give "a chance for the enemy of God. . . . " Who is this enemy? Benjamin had used the same language:

> I say unto you, that the man that doeth this, the same cometh out in open rebellion against God; therefore he listeth to obey the evil spirit, and becometh an enemy to all righteousness; therefore, the Lord has no place in him, for he dwelleth not in unholy temples.
>
> Therefore if that man repenteth not, and remaineth and dieth an enemy to God, the demands of divine justice do awaken his immortal soul to a lively sense of his own guilt, which doth cause him to shrink from the presence of the Lord, and doth fill his breast with guilt, and pain, and anguish, which is like an unquenchable fire, whose flame ascendeth up forever and ever. (Mosiah 2:37–38)

The "evil spirit" causes one to become an enemy to Yahweh. Thus, Alma$_2$ is opening doors for the evil spirit by preaching "another" religion, one which denies the Atoning Messiah. No wonder Benjamin could say that, as a result of such actions, "the Lord has no place in him."

Mosiah 27:10–11

10 And now it came to pass that while he was going about to destroy the church of God, for he did go about secretly with the sons of Mosiah seeking to destroy the church, and to lead astray the people of the Lord, contrary to the commandments of God, or even the king—

11 And as I said unto you, as they were going about rebelling against God, behold, the angel of the Lord appeared unto them; and he descended as it were in a cloud; and he spake as it were with a voice of thunder, which caused the earth to shake upon which they stood;

Culture: While the text concentrates primarily on Alma$_2$ and, to a lesser extent on the sons of Mosiah, this group of persecutors traveling together included others (Mosiah 27:33–34).

Reference: Alma$_2$'s story has marked similarities to and differences from the story of Saul/Paul. Both actively work against Christ's gospel. Both men are traveling, engaged in this work, when they see a vision. Saul's story is:

> And Saul, yet breathing out threatenings and slaughter against the disciples of the Lord, went unto the high priest,
>
> And desired of him letters to Damascus to the synagogues, that if he found any of this way, whether they were men or women, he might bring them bound unto Jerusalem.
>
> And as he journeyed, he came near Damascus: and suddenly there shined round about him a light from heaven:
>
> And he fell to the earth, and heard a voice saying unto him, Saul, Saul, why persecutest thou me?

> And he said, Who art thou, Lord? And the Lord said, I am Jesus whom thou persecutest: it is hard for thee to kick against the pricks.
>
> And he trembling and astonished said, Lord, what wilt thou have me to do? And the Lord said unto him, Arise, and go into the city, and it shall be told thee what thou must do.
>
> And the men which journeyed with him stood speechless, hearing a voice, but seeing no man.
>
> And Saul arose from the earth; and when his eyes were opened, he saw no man: but they led him by the hand, and brought him into Damascus.
>
> And he was three days without sight, and neither did eat nor drink. (Acts 9:1–9)

This text will be examined more closely in the verses that follow, but certain differences, more subtle than the similarities, are important to highlight. First is the belief system underlying the persecution. Saul is a Hebrew and a believer in Yahweh. He persecutes because he is part of the established religion that is fending off a dangerous schism. Saul defends the status quo, the mainline religion. In contrast, $Alma_2$ is a member of a minority religion who has rejected his people's primary religion. Thus, Saul begins persecuting Christians with the assumption that he is fighting to preserve Yahweh's religion, while $Alma_2$ has already rejected that religion (and worldview) and espoused a "foreign" religion (and worldview).

The next slight difference comes in the angel's appearance to them. To $Alma_2$ the angel comes in a cloud and to Saul with a bright light from heaven (Acts 9:3). This difference may be more significant than it would first appear. Yahweh appeared to Israel as a pillar of fire, so Saul would be culturally predisposed to recognize deity accompanied by fire and, by extension, light.

The cultural context of Mesoamerica may have been sufficiently different that the cloud was as significant for $Alma_2$ as the light for Saul. While the cultural explication of Mesoamerican clouds comes from a later period than the Book of Mormon, the concept of the sacred appears to have had a long history in Mesoamerica and one cannot discount the possibility that these associations could have been present during Book of Mormon times.

Schele and Mathews describe several Maya structures in *The Code of Kings*. The building known as "the nunnery" in Uxmal (located in the Peten, Yucatan, Mexico) they discuss an S-shape lying on its side with dots around it that appears on the building walls:

> Alternating with the flower lattice are squared, S-shaped scrolls. These scrolls have glyphic counterparts in a sign that reads *muyal*, "cloud. . ."
>
> Maya artists often depicted their visions floating in clouds, sometimes clouds of incense, sometimes the clouds of the sky: these are the *muyal* of the entablature.[4]

I have hypothesized that $Alma_2$ has become a believer in the alternate Mesoamerican religion, countering Nephite Messianism. In that worldview, clouds (whether incense or sky-clouds) would mark the presence of the gods. Thus, the appearance of a being in a cloud would signal communication with the divine for $Alma_2$ in a very powerful way.

---

[4]Linda Schele and Peter Mathews, *The Code of Kings: The Language of Seven Sacred Maya Temples and Tombs* (New York: Scribner, 1998), 270–71.

This detail creates an interesting context for this particular variation from the story of Saul. While the similarities are so obvious as to not require recounting, this particular difference is rather obscure but still possibly deeply significant in the $Alma_2$'s Mesoamerican context.

The next difference is the description of the voice. No description accompanies the voice in Paul's account, but in $Alma_2$'s it is "a voice of thunder" that shakes the earth. Both Saul and $Alma_2$ fall to the ground—Saul/Paul because he appears to recognize majesty, and with $Alma_2$, as a result of the earth's shaking.

Miller and Taube describe the religious connotations of lightning and thunder: "Among the most potent and dramatic natural phenomena of Mexico are lightning storms which light up the sky and shake the earth with thunder."[5] Note that they document thunder-shaking earth, just as $Alma_2$ experienced it. A modern Chamulan (Chamula is a town of the Tzotzil Maya) tale ties thunder to the voice of the gods: "When Our Father still walked the earth, he talked to the earth gods. He told them that they could not make it rain without talking to him first, so that he could punish the people if they did not 'want' the rain enough (if they had not prayed enough). When there are thunderheads, the earth gods are talking to Our Father. Whether rain falls or not depends on him."[6]

Just as with the appearance in a cloud, the thunder and earth-shaking of $Alma_2$'s experience may have Mesoamerican religious significance. As with the cloud imagery, $Alma_2$'s apparent acceptance of the competing Mesoamerican religion would sensitize him to certain modes of divine communication. A being in a cloud accompanied by thunder and shakings would present unmistakable evidence of its divine authenticity and authority.

Text: Verses 10 and 11 are one sentence. Nineteenth-century literature was frequently characterized by lengthy sentences, as we see not only in Joseph's writing but in such fiction as Charles Dickens's novels. What makes this particular sentence difficult is its lengthy, embedded aside. The aside is so long that Mormon has to remind us of the original topic when he picks it up again in verse 11.

Internal Comparison: $Alma_2$ also retells this experience to two of his sons, Helaman and Shiblon. The more extensive account is found in Alma 36:4–26 with a shorter version in Alma 38:6–8. Additionally, S. Kent Brown has examined $Alma_2$'s sermons for indications of this experience's impact on $Alma_2$'s preaching and found that "virtually every one of Alma's recorded sermons, whether they were formal discourses or spontaneous addresses, are characterized by the recollection of one or more features of his three-day conversion experience."[7]

---

[5]Mary Miller and Karl Taube, *An Illustrated Dictionary of the Gods and Symbols of Ancient Mexico and the Maya* (London: Thames & Hudson, 1993), 106.

[6]Quoted in Gary Gossen, *Chamulas in the World of the Sun: Time and Space in a Maya Oral Tradition* (Cambridge, Mass.: Harvard University Press, 1974), 330.

[7]S. Kent Brown, *From Jerusalem to Zarahemla: Literary and Historical Studies of the Book of Mormon* (Provo, Utah: BYU Religious Studies Center, 1998), 126.

The version in Alma 36 is the most extensive. (See commentary accompanying that chapter for a more complete analysis of the three versions.)

Mosiah 27:12

12 And so great was their astonishment, that they fell to the earth, and understood not the words which he spake unto them.

Text: The similarity between this account and that of Saul is that those present fall to the earth and all hear the voice (Acts 9:4, 7). The difference is that, in the Book of Mormon account, all fall and all see the messenger (v. 18). Since $Alma_2$ and the sons of Mosiah have all heard the voice and since I am proceeding on the assumption that they are all adherents of the Mesoamerican religion, they would all have experienced the accompanying divine markers of thunder and earth-tremblings. As a result, all would have fallen before the divine majesty of the appearance. In the Old World example, the companions heard a voice, but the record does not allow us to infer either that they understood it or assumed it to be divine.

Culture: Possibly humility before God in Mesoamerican culture manifested itself as prostration, or possibly they could not keep their feet because of the earth's trembling, but it seems more probable that they fell in response to the event's spiritual power, not its physical power. After King Benjamin's powerful address, the people also prostrated themselves: "And now, it came to pass that when king Benjamin had made an end of speaking the words which had been delivered unto him by the angel of the Lord, that he cast his eyes round about on the multitude, and behold they had fallen to the earth, for the fear of the Lord had come upon them" (Mosiah 4:1). "The fear of the Lord" was the operative factor in Benjamin's case; the "astonishment" of $Alma_2$ and the sons of Mosiah caused them to fall to the earth in the second case. But in both, the spiritual power of the moment and their united action logically reflects a common cultural response to that kind of divine presence.

Mosiah 27:13

13 Nevertheless he cried again, saying: Alma, arise and stand forth, for why persecutest thou the church of God? For the Lord hath said: This is my church, and I will establish it; and nothing shall overthrow it, save it is the transgression of my people.

Text: The similarity to Paul's experience is that "persecution" is part of the divine message in both cases. In Saul's case, however, it is Christ who is persecuted and in $Alma_2$'s it is the church. The fact of persecution exists in both cases; but in the New World, $Alma_2$'s persecution precedes Jesus's coming in the flesh. Thus, in one sense, there was no person with which the church might be directly identified and against whom one might persecute as in the New Testament example.

$Alma_2$'s version of apostasy was almost certainly like that of Noah and his priests in which he accepted much of the competing religion but also held some beliefs of the Mosaic law. In this case, Alma and the sons of Mosiah could not have understood a declaration like that given to Saul because they would not have believed that they were persecuting Yahweh himself, only those who believed in the future Atoning Messiah. Nevertheless, the messenger declares that the church was equated with Yahweh. Alma and the sons of Mosiah were not persecuting people who believed in a nonexistent being, but they were directly persecuting their own God.

Mosiah 27:14

> 14 And again, the angel said: Behold, the Lord hath heard the prayers of his people, and also the prayers of his servant, Alma, who is thy father; for he has prayed with much faith concerning thee that thou mightest be brought to the knowledge of the truth; therefore, for this purpose have I come to convince thee of the power and authority of God, that the prayers of his servants might be answered according to their faith.

This passage is perhaps the Book of Mormon's most emotionally paradoxical. Men who are actively fighting against the church receive a powerful visitation while many men and women who are faithful for a lifetime never receive any manifestation so transcendentally powerful. This comparative approach might easily lead to discouragement, especially since it overlooks the telling fact that the visitation is not a reward, but rather a means of changing the dangerous life-course of these warriors against God. For those who serve faithfully, the ultimate blessing is the same. There is no eternal advantage to $Alma_2$ for having this experience. Faith in this life and following the plan of the gospel, will lead to the same rewards in the next world, with or without a powerful mortal witness. In fact, as the resurrected Christ assured Thomas, "Because thou hast seen me, thou hast believed: blessed are they that have not seen, and yet have believed" (John 20:29).

The opposite pole of this emotional passage is the joy of a parent who learns that his prayers are effective on his child's behalf. The visitation comes at the behest of the people and particularly of $Alma_1$. While not all parental prayers are answered so dramatically, the fervent prayers of parents for their children, both faithful and wayward, are effective in the Lord's time.

Daniel H. Ludlow has commented on this aspect of this verse and the two that follow:

> The Lord has promised that if we ask in faith for that which is right, we shall receive (3 Ne. 18:20). However, he has not promised the manner or the time in which the prayer will be answered. When the angel appeared to Alma the younger and the four sons of Mosiah, the angel made it clear that he had not appeared to them because of their own worthiness. Rather, he said, "For this purpose have I come to convince thee of the power and authority of God, that the prayers of his servants might be answered according to their faith" (Mosiah 27:14). Also the angel pled with them to repent of their sins and "seek to destroy the church no more" that the prayers of the righteous members of the church might be answered (Mosiah 27:16). Evidently it was primarily because of the faithful prayers of Alma the elder and the other members of the church that the angel appeared to Alma the younger and the four sons of Mosiah.[8]

---

[8]Daniel H. Ludlow, *A Companion to Your Study of the Book of Mormon* (Salt Lake City: Deseret Book, 1976), 192.

Mosiah 27:15

> 15 And now behold, can ye dispute the power of God? For behold, doth not my voice shake the earth? And can ye not also behold me before you? And I am sent from God.

The messenger (an angel, as clarified in v. 17) declares his authority—being sent from Yahweh—and also reminds $Alma_2$ of the proof of his power: first, that $Alma_2$ can visually see him, and second, that his voice shook the earth. (See commentary accompanying vv. 10–11.) The angel explicitly cites these two elements as proof of divine origin. The angel does not mention a cloud but the description does (v. 11). Thus, the angel explicitly reminds $Alma_2$ of three indubitable markers of divinity: the cloud, the voice as thunder, and the shaking of the earth. The angel's repetition should confirm that these markers are significant, not simply descriptive.

Mosiah 27:16–17

> 16 Now I say unto thee: Go, and remember the captivity of thy fathers in the land of Helam, and in the land of Nephi; and remember how great things he has done for them; for they were in bondage, and he has delivered them. And now I say unto thee, Alma, go thy way, and seek to destroy the church no more, that their prayers may be answered, and this even if thou wilt of thyself be cast off.
> 17 And now it came to pass that these were the last words which the angel spake unto Alma, and he departed.

The message is directed to $Alma_2$, even though the sons of Mosiah hear it and are also affected by it.

Mosiah 27:18

> 18 And now Alma and those that were with him fell again to the earth, for great was their astonishment; for with their own eyes they had beheld an angel of the Lord; and his voice was as thunder, which shook the earth; and they knew that there was nothing save the power of God that could shake the earth and cause it to tremble as though it would part asunder.

$Alma_2$ and his brethren "fell again" to the earth. Certainly they were capable of rising at some point during this manifestation or they could not have again fallen. Falling to the earth was a physical (literal shaking of the earth) or a cultural response rather than a physical weakness. It may also suggest that they had arisen, not to their feet, but rather to their knees.

Again the specific markers of divinity are repeated: the voice of thunder and the shaking of the earth.

Mosiah 27:19

> 19 And now the astonishment of Alma was so great that he became dumb, that he could not open his mouth; yea, and he became weak, even that he

could not move his hands; therefore he was taken by those that were with him, and carried helpless, even until he was laid before his father.

Reference: Alma$_2$'s similarity to Saul/Paul is clear in the physical incapacity that resulted from the visitation (Acts 9:8). Contrary to Saul, however, Alma$_2$ is completely debilitated. His companions are functional, able to carry him to assistance. Saul was only blind, but Alma$_2$ was dumb and so weak that he was "carried helpless." That he was "laid" before his father indicates that he was too weak even to sit.

This physical weakness apparently resulted from a spiritual struggle, which he recounts later. Perhaps he was so preoccupied with the internal that his body was unable to cope with the external. Whatever the cause, his condition clearly stemmed from his experience with the angel.

Variant: Verse 19 states that "he could not move his *hands*." Ross Geddes suggested to Royal Skousen that this might be a place where "hands" should have been "limbs," as only the inability to move his hands would not require that he be "carried helpless." Skousen examined Mosiah 27:22–23 and Alma 36:23 which reference this event, and both use "limbs," not "hands."[9] There is no textual indication that this is a variant originating in the printer's manuscript because the original is not extant for any of Mosiah. However, it would be a logical emendation as the clear intent is the ineffectiveness of more than just the hands.

Mosiah 27:20

20 And they rehearsed unto his father all that had happened unto them; and his father rejoiced, for he knew that it was the power of God.

Mormon abbreviates the moment of arrival to stress the experience's ultimate import, which is that Alma$_1$ recognized Yahweh's hand and rejoiced. That ultimate rejoicing, however, was probably preceded by anguish when he first saw his son being carried in helpless. If he assumed, as would be natural, that his son was unconscious from an injury or perhaps even dead, much of his joy must have been sheer relief at realizing that his son was not near death—but, in a very real sense, very near true life.

Mosiah 27:21–22

21 And he caused that a multitude should be gathered together that they might witness what the Lord had done for his son, and also for those that were with him.
22 And he caused that the priests should assemble themselves together; and they began to fast, and to pray to the Lord their God that he would open the mouth of Alma, that he might speak, and also that his limbs might receive

[9]Royal Skousen, *Analysis of Textual Variants of the Book of Mormon*, THE CRITICAL TEXT OF THE BOOK OF MORMON (Provo, Utah: Foundation for Ancient Research and Mormon Studies, 2005), Vol. 4, Part 3, 1510–11.

their strength—that the eyes of the people might be opened to see and know of the goodness and glory of God.

$Alma_1$ foresees that his son will make dramatic atonement for his actions against the church. Rather than being the church's persecutor, $Alma_2$ will be its healer and builder. $Alma_1$ therefore assembles a multitude to keep vigil and requests that the priests fast and pray for his son's recovery. That $Alma_1$ assembled the multitude first shows his faith in Yahweh. The people would see the transformation from powerful persecutor to complete invalid, then the transformation back from utter helplessness to restored life.

$Alma_2$ has been fighting against the teaching of the Atoning Messiah who, according to prophecy, will die and be resurrected. Dramatically, $Alma_2$ becomes the visual symbol of (spiritual) death and resurrection. As the Messiah before death was mortal and subject to the world (as $Alma_2$ had proved to be), after resurrection, the Messiah (and $Alma_2$) would belong to Yahweh. While $Alma_2$ was certainly not resurrected as a god, his tremendous transformation revealed him as new person, a powerful advocate for the church he had once persecuted.

This possible resurrection theme provides context for the difference between the experiences of $Alma_2$ and Saul. Where Saul is blinded (perhaps symbolic of his prior refusal to "see" the reality of Jesus as Savior), $Alma_2$ is debilitated. $Alma_2$'s experience symbolizes his particular apostasy.

Culture: The separation of the multitude and the priests demonstrates that the priests were considered a different social group from the "multitude." They were specially appointed to their roles and performed specific functions in behalf of the multitude. Their separate action highlights both their difference, and their function as servants to the multitude in the performance of religious ritual.

Mosiah 27:23

23 And it came to pass after they had fasted and prayed for the space of two days and two nights, the limbs of Alma received their strength, and he stood up and began to speak unto them, bidding them to be of good comfort:

Even after the prayers of the faithful that had brought $Alma_2$ to this experience, additional prayers were offered in his behalf to complete the process and bring him back to strength.

Reference: This experience is both similar to and different from Saul's experience. Like Saul, $Alma_2$ is incapacitated for multiple days. The difference is that Saul was incapacitated for three days (Acts 9:9) and $Alma_2$ for "two days and two nights." Once again, it is possible that the symbolism attached to numbers in the two cultures plays a part in these periods.

For Saul, the three days have at least two references; the days Jonah spent in the belly of the "great fish" (Jonah 1:17) and the days Christ spent in the tomb (Matt. 12:40). In Saul's Old World context and particularly so close to Christ's resurrection, three days of darkness for Saul, like the three days of darkness for

Jonah and Christ, are symbolically symmetrical. When Saul emerged from darkness, he was a new man, one reborn to a new spiritual life.

Alma$_2$ underwent a similar spiritual transformation, but did it in "two days and two nights." This particular construction may be intentional, creating a total "number" of four. In Mesoamerica, four was particularly auspicious, the number of perfection. As a possible parallel, even though the two events are not close in time, Alma$_2$ may also have experienced a "perfect rebirth" after a similar time of "four" periods.

Internal Comparison: Alma is under the Spirit's influence for two days and two nights. Alma 36:10, which also describes this experience, says it lasted three days and three nights: "And it came to pass that I fell to the earth; and it was for the space of three days and three nights that I could not open my mouth, neither had I the use of my limbs."

John W. Welch proposes this explanation: "Even what superficially appears to be a difference is not. Alma 36:16 states that Alma was racked for three days and three nights. Mosiah 27:23, however, says that the priests fasted for two days and two nights. This is because, under Nephite practice, the fast would not have begun until the morning of the next day after the decision to fast (Hel. 9:10)."[10]

Although the single citation does not establish the practice as customary, this explanation is possible. It may well have taken nearly a whole day for the stricken Alma$_2$ to be brought to his father and for the fast to be arranged. Furthermore, Mosiah 27 was recorded by a third party and edited by Mormon while Alma 36 quotes Alma$_2$ directly. Thus, the information comes from two different sources. The amount of time that passed can easily be the very same. The difference lies in how the numbers are selected to describe the event. Alma$_2$ may be more precise in defining the passage of time, while the first scribe may have selected the time covered by the fast *because* it fit into his 2 + 2 = 4 scenario that resulted in the "perfect" number. Alma's number is more significant as a Messianic foreshadowing, the scribes as a "perfect" repentance.

Mosiah 27:24

> 24 For, said he, I have repented of my sins, and have been redeemed of the Lord; behold I am born of the Spirit.

In keeping with the resurrection/new birth theme, Alma$_2$ declares that he is "born of the Spirit" through repentance and redemption from his sins. Redemption is the critical point here. Not only does Alma$_2$'s experience prefigure the Atoning Messiah's death and resurrection but it confirms that mission—the very concepts that Alma$_2$ had denied and argued against. Thus, when Alma$_2$ awakens, his testimony is so completely the reverse of its former trend that he embodies the meaning of the Messiah's future mission.

Redaction: This verse begins a quotation from Alma$_2$ which continues through verse 31. While these are Alma$_2$'s words, it is unlikely that Alma$_2$ recorded them, since he

---

[10]John W. Welch, "Three Accounts of Alma's Conversion," in *Reexploring the Book of Mormon*, edited by John W. Welch (Provo, Utah: FARMS, 1992), 151.

was not yet keeping the records. The text was recorded by a scribe whose words Mormon has been editing.

Mosiah 27:25–26

> 25 And the Lord said unto me: Marvel not that all mankind, yea, men and women, all nations, kindreds, tongues and people, must be born again; yea, born of God, changed from their carnal and fallen state, to a state of righteousness, being redeemed of God, becoming his sons and daughters;
> 26 And thus they become new creatures; and unless they do this, they can in nowise inherit the kingdom of God.

Yahweh assures Alma$_2$, "Marvel not that all mankind, yea, men and women . . . must be born again." Alma$_2$'s terminology is familiar to us, but the language fits Book of Mormon doctrine of the time more closely than contemporary LDS theology.

First, modern Saints typically equate with "being born of the spirit" with baptism and the gift of the Holy Ghost, but neither of these events is part of Alma$_2$'s experience (although he may have received these ordinances earlier). Rather, his particular "birth" is redemption from sin. (See Alma 36:12–21 for the details of his sin/redemption contrast.) Alma$_2$ is born of the Spirit because the atonement of Jesus Christ was applied to his soul (not because of the gift of the Holy Ghost as in modern terminology). It constituted a new birth in that his soul became freed from the bonds of sin—innocent like a newborn child.

This context applies to King Benjamin's admonition: "And now, because of the covenant which ye have made ye shall be called the children of Christ, his sons, and his daughters; for behold, this day he hath spiritually begotten you; for ye say that your hearts are changed through faith on his name; therefore, ye are born of him and have become his sons and his daughters" (Mosiah 5:7).

Benjamin, significantly, also describes this process as being "spiritually begotten." Mormon began this particular discussion of Alma$_2$ with a direct reference to the Benjaminic covenant: "Now it came to pass that there were many of the rising generation that could not understand the words of king Benjamin, being little children at the time he spake unto his people; and they did not believe the tradition of their fathers" (Mosiah 26:1).

Alma$_2$, by accepting the atonement, makes the covenant that he has previously rejected, a point stressed by Mormon, who structured the text so that Benjamin's covenant frames Alma$_2$'s "birth."

Mosiah 27:27

> 27 I say unto you, unless this be the case, they must be cast off; and this I know, because I was like to be cast off.

The experience just prior to Alma$_2$'s transformation showed him the logical extension of his current behavior. He was "like to be cast off," also a parallel with Benjamin's sermon:

> For behold he judgeth, and his judgment is just; and the infant perisheth not that dieth in his infancy; but men drink damnation to their own souls except they humble themselves and become as little children, and believe that salvation was, and is, and is to come, in and through the atoning blood of Christ, the Lord Omnipotent.
>
> For the natural man is an enemy to God, and has been from the fall of Adam, and will be, forever and ever, unless he yields to the enticings of the Holy Spirit, and putteth off the natural man and becometh a saint through the atonement of Christ the Lord, and becometh as a child, submissive, meek, humble, patient, full of love, willing to submit to all things which the Lord seeth fit to inflict upon him, even as a child doth submit to his father. (Mosiah 3:18–19)

Benjamin taught what $Alma_2$ has now so clearly experienced. $Alma_2$ *felt* what it means to be an enemy to Yahweh and to "drink damnation to [his] own soul." Just as Benjamin describes accepting the Messiah as the way of averting damnation, so too will $Alma_2$ be delivered because he accepts Yahweh-Messiah's atonement.

Mosiah 27:28–29

> 28 Nevertheless, after wading through much tribulation, repenting nigh unto death, the Lord in mercy hath seen fit to snatch me out of an everlasting burning, and I am born of God.
>
> 29 My soul hath been redeemed from the gall of bitterness and bonds of iniquity. I was in the darkest abyss; but now I behold the marvelous light of God. My soul was racked with eternal torment; but I am snatched, and my soul is pained no more.

$Alma_2$ contrasts his pre-redemption darkness and tribulation with "an everlasting burning." He clearly (v. 28) contrasts being "nigh unto death" with being "born of God" and, as a result, now being a "son" of the Savior (Mosiah 5:7).

Variant: The printer's manuscript reads: "my soul was *wrecked* with eternal torment." Skousen notes that *wrecked* and *racked* are phonetically similar and that the parallel passages consistently have *racked*. The change to *racked* was first made by Orson Pratt for the 1879 edition and has been retained in the LDS editions of the Book of Mormon.[11]

Mosiah 27:30

> 30 I rejected my Redeemer, and denied that which had been spoken of by our fathers; but now that they may foresee that he will come, and that he remembereth every creature of his creating, he will make himself manifest unto all.

Here $Alma_2$ confesses his sin—not fighting against "the church" but "reject[ing] my Redeemer." $Alma_2$ had fallen into the same religious trap that had snared his father as Noah's priest. His father had broken free of that trap by following a prophet's words, then had gone on to become a powerful voice for the Messiah he had once

---

[11]Skousen, *Analysis of Textual Variants*, 3:1514.

rejected. Now his son treads the same path. Through an angel's intervention, he now understands the Atoning Messiah's mission and will also use this pivotal experience to become Yahweh's mighty servant.

Mosiah 27:31

> 31 Yea, every knee shall bow, and every tongue confess before him. Yea, even at the last day, when all men shall stand to be judged of him, then shall they confess that he is God; then shall they confess, who live without God in the world, that the judgment of an everlasting punishment is just upon them; and they shall quake, and tremble, and shrink beneath the glance of his all-searching eye.

Literature: $Alma_2$ continues with his testimony of the coming Messiah, translating his personal experience into a universal one. Just has he has now confessed the Messiah, so too will "every tongue confess before him." Just as $Alma_2$ has undergone the judgment, so too will all men undergo the judgment. Just as $Alma_2$ quaked and trembled (perhaps an oblique reference to the voice of thunder shaking the ground?) so, too, will all quake and tremble before Yahweh.

Text: The quotation of $Alma_2$'s words ends here, and Mormon returns to summary narration.

Reference: Verse 31 borrows language from Romans 14:11: "For it is written, As I live, saith the Lord, every knee shall bow to me, and every tongue shall confess to God." Paul's language combines phrases from two passages in Isaiah: "As I live" (Isa. 49:18) and "I have sworn by myself, the word is gone out of my mouth in righteousness, and shall not return, That unto me every knee shall bow, every tongue shall swear" (Isa. 45:23). $Alma_2$'s reference was certainly to Isaiah. However, Joseph Smith's translation leans to Paul's recasting.

Mosiah 27:32–33

> 32 And now it came to pass that Alma began from this time forward to teach the people, and those who were with Alma at the time the angel appeared unto them, traveling round about through all the land, publishing to all the people the things which they had heard and seen, and preaching the word of God in much tribulation, being greatly persecuted by those who were unbelievers, being smitten by many of them.
> 33 But notwithstanding all this, they did impart much consolation to the church, confirming their faith, and exhorting them with long-suffering and much travail to keep the commandments of God.

$Alma_2$ and the sons of Mosiah are all converted, although we hear little about the conversion of the sons of Mosiah. Part of their conversion process prompted them to attempt to undo the damage they had done, so they travel through the land "publishing to all the people the things which they had heard and seen." Certainly believers would have accepted their testimony with open arms, but how would they have been received by former co-believers against whom they were now preaching?

It is easy to see that this situation created "much tribulation, being greatly persecuted by those who were unbelievers, being smitten by many of them."

Mosiah 27:34

> 34 And four of them were the sons of Mosiah; and their names were Ammon, and Aaron, and Omner, and Himni; these were the names of the sons of Mosiah.

These four names are given three other times, always in this order (Alma 23:1, 25:17, 31:6). The first three are also mentioned in Alma 31:32. This consistency of name order suggests that it is probably their birth order, making Ammon probably the oldest. However, Daniel Ludlow notes:

> The order of the birth of the four sons of Mosiah is never made clear in the Book of Mormon. The listing in Mosiah 27:34 would indicate that Ammon was the first born followed by Aaron, then Omner, and Himni. Also, the fact that Ammon was the leader on their missionary journey to the Lamanites would seem to indicate that Ammon was the eldest (Alma 17–26). However, when King Mosiah asked his people to select his successor, they first desired that Aaron should be their king and their ruler (Mosiah 29:1–2). In this single instance it appears as though Aaron may have been the eldest son.[12]

Mosiah 27:35–37

> 35 And they traveled throughout all the land of Zarahemla, and among all the people who were under the reign of king Mosiah, zealously striving to repair all the injuries which they had done to the church, confessing all their sins, and publishing all the things which they had seen, and explaining the prophecies and the scriptures to all who desired to hear them.
> 36 And thus they were instruments in the hands of God in bringing many to the knowledge of the truth, yea, to the knowledge of their Redeemer.
> 37 And how blessed are they! For they did publish peace; they did publish good tidings of good; and they did declare unto the people that the Lord reigneth.

These final verses repeat (see v. 32) their efforts to preach their new understanding of the gospel, undoing the damage they had previously caused. The first mention had stressed only $Alma_2$'s preaching, but here the four sons of Mosiah are explicitly included. Their story will be told in detail in Alma 21–26.

Text: These verses conclude a chapter in the 1830 edition and therefore a concept. Mormon closes his record of this transformation by naming the most notable participants: $Alma_2$, Ammon, Aaron, Omner, and Himni all preach the word. The earlier discussion of $Alma_2$'s mission describes the resulting persecution, not mentioned in this recapitulation. Perhaps Mormon is electing to leave the story on the most positive level. These men who began by denying Yahweh, now actively declare him.

---

[12]Ludlow, *A Companion to Your Study of the Book of Mormon*, 192.

Mosiah 28

Mosiah 28:1

> 1 Now it came to pass that after the sons of Mosiah had done all these things, they took a small number with them and returned to their father, the king, and desired of him that he would grant unto them that they might, with these whom they had selected, go up to the land of Nephi that they might preach the things which they had heard, and that they might impart the word of God to their brethren, the Lamanites—

"All these things" that the sons of Mosiah have been doing were attempts to rectify the effects of their preaching against the church in the land of Zarahemla. Because of their privileged position as the sons of the king, they had probably been instrumental in attracting many away from the church in Zarahemla. Therefore, they took their first mission to those whom they had most directly hurt.

This next section describes a secondary "mission." After the sons of Mosiah (and "a small number with them") attempt to rectify the damage they had caused in Zarahemla, they ask to mount a mission to the Lamanites. Why the Lamanites?

The traditional Book of Mormon interpretation would suggest the Lamanites are the only other people around; if all of Zarahemla were converted, there would be nowhere else to go. Even interpreting "Lamanite" as a term for all non-Nephites, as I do, it might still be considered logical to turn to the Lamanites if all of Zarahemla were converted.

However, I find it likely that the sons of Mosiah and $Alma_2$ during their apostate period had been converted to the religion practiced by Noah and his priests. If this is true, it would be natural for the sons of Mosiah to feel concern for those whose incorrect religion they had so recently espoused. This connection to the religion of Noah's priests was likely one of the influencing factors in their choice of returning to the land of Nephi for their mission. (Aaron is specifically in the land of Nephi in Alma 22:1.)

Considering how often the Nephites have pejoratively described the Lamanites (e.g., 2 Ne. 5:21–24; Enos 1:20; Mosiah 9:12, 10:12), we might expect that this cultural preconditioning against anything Lamanite would preclude them as possible missionary targets. Yet like Zeniff (Mosiah 9:1), the sons of Mosiah apparently found much good in the Lamanites and now naturally turn to those people to share with them the same joy they have so recently found.

Mosiah 28:2–4

2 That perhaps they might bring them to the knowledge of the Lord their God, and convince them of the iniquity of their fathers; and that perhaps they might cure them of their hatred towards the Nephites, that they might also be brought to rejoice in the Lord their God, that they might become friendly to one another, and that there should be no more contentions in all the land which the Lord their God had given them.
3 Now they were desirous that salvation should be declared to every creature, for they could not bear that any human soul should perish; yea, even the very thoughts that any soul should endure endless torment did cause them to quake and tremble.
4 And thus did the Spirit of the Lord work upon them, for they were the very vilest of sinners. And the Lord saw fit in his infinite mercy to spare them; nevertheless they suffered much anguish of soul because of their iniquities, suffering much and fearing that they should be cast off forever.

These verses declare the depth of the change experienced by the sons of Mosiah. From being "the vilest of sinners" (v. 4), they have been redeemed, a change so great and soul-transforming that it altered their entire outlook on life. This type of dramatic change is almost the exclusive province of those who have come so far so fast. While all may feel the transforming power of the Spirit, those who have made such a dramatic and drastic change can taste that change more deeply than those for whom the transformation is more incremental. Those who can remember the "taste" of both sides of the judgment are the ones most sensitive to others in the state they have most recently left.

After their redemption, they felt so powerfully Yahweh's joy that they desired to share it with the Lamanites. They could see how this new perspective might completely alter the ages-old conflicts between Lamanite and Nephite (v. 2). This was not a change completely founded in a concern for those who might have been sympathetic to their former life, but a desire for any and all to feel the tremendous joy they felt.

Mosiah 28:5–9

5 And it came to pass that they did plead with their father many days that they might go up to the land of Nephi.
6 And king Mosiah went and inquired of the Lord if he should let his sons go up among the Lamanites to preach the word.
7 And the Lord said unto Mosiah: Let them go up, for many shall believe on their words, and they shall have eternal life; and I will deliver thy sons out of the hands of the Lamanites.
8 And it came to pass that Mosiah granted that they might go and do according to their request.
9 And they took their journey into the wilderness to go up to preach the word among the Lamanites; and I shall give an account of their proceedings hereafter.

The sons of Mosiah address their request to king Mosiah because he is their father, but why do they not address this religious request to $Alma_1$? Zarahemla had a separation between the political and religious. While Mosiah was religious and righteous enough to be use the interpreters (Mosiah 8:13), he is not the head of the church. However, the request had political ramifications. Preaching to the Lamanites could result in the capture of the king's sons, attempts to ransom them, even their execution. The Lamanites might interpret it as a spying mission and the tentative relationships between Zarahemla and the Lamanites might be thrown into disarray. These negative scenarios, of course, all had their positive—and they doubtless hoped more likely—counterparts; but the real risks involved explain why a decision from Mosiah was necessary.

As king, Mosiah took a religious approach to his political action, as shown by his immediate decision to seek Yahweh's will. Once he had reassurance from Yahweh, he knew that the mission would be beneficial.

Variant: Verse 6 began with "It came to pass that King . . . " in the printer's manuscript and the 1830 edition.[1] Joseph Smith crossed it out and it was removed beginning with the 1837 edition.[2]

Verse 6 also saw another change in the 1837 edition that has not been retained. The printer's manuscript reads: "Mosiah went and inquired of the Lord if he *should* let his sons go. . . . " The 1837 edition reads: "Mosiah went and inquired of the Lord if he *would* let his sons go. . . . " This change altered the meaning. In the 1830 reading, Mosiah would be letting the sons go, and in the 1837 reading, it would be the Lord. This was probably an error, and it was returned to the printer's manuscript reading beginning with the 1920 edition. [3]

Mosiah 28:10

> 10 Now king Mosiah had no one to confer the kingdom upon, for there was not any of his sons who would accept of the kingdom.

Why would his sons decline to accept the kingdom? Certainly they would have all been trained from birth in their responsibilities to the kingdom. The one intervening circumstance is their spiritual transformation, which gave them a new priority so intense that they would abandon their inheritance in favor of preaching the gospel. Because any remaining son would have been hard pressed to find a reason to decline the throne, it reinforces the assumption that these four were Mosiah's only sons. It is quite clear from the dynastic histories of virtually all known kingships that competence would be rare as the decisive factor. Their decision to decline the kingship was a direct outcome of their complete change of heart.

---

[1]*Book of Mormon Critical Text: A Tool for Scholarly Reference*, 3 vols. (Provo, Utah: FARMS, 1987), 2:503

[2]Royal Skousen, *Analysis of Textual Variants of the Book of Mormon*, THE CRITICAL TEXT OF THE BOOK OF MORMON (Provo, Utah: Foundation for Ancient Research and Mormon Studies, 2005), Vol. 4, Part 3, 1526.

[3]Ibid., 3:1527.

Nevertheless, something else is going on that Mormon does not tell us. Even if none of Mosiah's sons would accept the throne, royal lines are seldom so narrowly defined. In Mesoamerica such occasions occurred not infrequently among the later Aztecs; in those cases, the throne would pass to the son of a brother, or perhaps to a grandson. Thus, Mosiah's sons had not only declined, but there must have been no other possible heir for this coming change in government, or else Mormon is skipping over some of the details and simply going to the results: the transition from kings to judges among the Nephites.

Mosiah 28:11–12

> 11 Therefore he took the records which were engraven on the plates of brass, and also the plates of Nephi, and all the things which he had kept and preserved according to the commandments of God, after having translated and caused to be written the records which were on the plates of gold which had been found by the people of Limhi, which were delivered to him by the hand of Limhi;
> 12 And this he did because of the great anxiety of his people; for they were desirous beyond measure to know concerning those people who had been destroyed.

Why does Mormon choose to place the translation of the plates found by Limhi's people after the sons of Mosiah decline the kingship? The only indication that Mormon gives is that the people were anxious to know what was on the plates. While this is certainly true, it is not a complete answer.

Unfortunately, Mormon gives us no time frame for any of these events. We have no firm dating until Mosiah 29:45–6 which dates the deaths of both Alma$_1$ and Mosiah 509 years after the departure from Jerusalem. To recount just a few important dates, the deaths of Alma$_1$ and Mosiah would correlate to 92 B.C. Mosiah was crowned in 124 B.C., 462 Nephite years from the departure from Jerusalem. The reunification of the people of Alma$_1$ and Limhi with the people of Zarahemla had to occur after Mosiah was made king—therefore somewhere between 124 B.C. and 92 B.C.

Thus, within this thirty-two-year span the creation of the church in Zarahemla and the conversion of Alma$_2$ and the sons of Mosiah had taken place. Certainly the church would have been established within a year or so after reunification, which would have been a minimum of a year after the Limhites' departure. Adding a couple of years for safety, we might estimate 120 B.C. as a reasonable date for the church's establishment.

It does not appear from Mormon's account that Alma$_1$ and Mosiah died immediately after translating the records. Certainly Mosiah doesn't appear to think that Alma$_1$ is near death. He gave the records to Alma$_1$ without any discussion of Alma$_1$'s possible heirs. Nevertheless, these events had to occur somewhere near the end of his reign or he would not have been considering succession options. Placing the conversion of the sons of Alma$_1$ and Mosiah near the end of this thirty-two-year period provides enough time for the church to be established, for them to decide to oppose it, and to have had some time to be successful.

This situation adds another wrinkle to the sons of Mosiah's request to preach to the Lamanites. The journey would take some time; and no matter how successful or unsuccessful, Mosiah could not be sure that his sons would return speedily. It is perhaps because of their departure that Mosiah begins thinking about transferring the rule.

Mosiah, sons gone and having refused the throne, would know that the transfer of power might involve controversy and contention, a fear he acknowledges (Mosiah 29:7). This mention suggests that Mosiah is preparing for the worst-case scenario. First, he takes care of what he considers most important—the sacred records—by preparing to transfer them to $Alma_1$'s custody for safekeeping. He probably hopes to keep them from becoming an element in a possible power struggle, even war, among the people of Zarahemla. His city suffered from ready-made fault lines along which his people could divide, given a contentious transfer of power.

Apparently one of the preparatory tasks he set himself was translating the record on the gold plates that the Limhites had found and turned over to Mosiah soon after their arrival in Zarahemla, since they were quite interested in their contents (Mosiah 8:9, 11–12). Clearly Mosiah had not translated them during the (as a rough guess) perhaps twenty years they had been in his care. Why he had delayed so long is not explained, but perhaps he understood that the new leader might lack the power to use the two stones. (What we call the Urim and Thummim are never called by that name in the Book of Mormon.)

Mosiah 28:13–16

> 13 And now he translated them by the means of those two stones which were fastened into the two rims of a bow.
> 14 Now these things were prepared from the beginning, and were handed down from generation to generation, for the purpose of interpreting languages;
> 15 And they have been kept and preserved by the hand of the Lord, that he should discover to every creature who should possess the land the iniquities and abominations of his people;
> 16 And whosoever has these things is called seer, after the manner of old times.

Ammon's discussion with Limhi in the city of Lehi-Nephi had provided some details about these stones and the man who could use them:

> Now Ammon said unto him: I can assuredly tell thee, O king, of a man that can translate the records; for he has wherewith that he can look, and translate all records that are of ancient date; and it is a gift from God. And the things are called interpreters, and no man can look in them except he be commanded, lest he should look for that he ought not and he should perish. And whosoever is commanded to look in them, the same is called seer. . . .
>
> But a seer can know of things which are past, and also of things which are to come, and by them shall all things be revealed, or, rather, shall secret things be made manifest,

and hidden things shall come to light, and things which are not known shall be made known by them, and also things shall be made known by them which otherwise could not be known. (Mosiah 8:13, 17)

The current chapter gives a few additional details about the stones, namely their power to facilitate the interpretation of records that cannot otherwise be read. Possession and use of the stones constitutes a seer, who may use the stones to reveal things of the past and future, and make secret things known.

Thus, for Ammon, the stones were more than just a means of reading records. They were a means of seeing the hidden and a way that the knowledge from Yahweh was manifest among men, through the medium of the seer who possessed Yahweh's gift to use those interpreters.

The Old Testament also describes stones called the Urim and Thummim, which appear to function somewhat like Mosiah's in providing divine guidance.[4] This similarity of function might lead readers to assume that the two sets of stones are the same, but such similarities are not required by the text nor the circumstances. It is entirely possible that Yahweh had arranged to provide a second set for the New World Nephites, the essential point of resemblance being that they would work similarly to divine Yahweh's will.

Biblical scholar William Smith suggests their Old World function: "When Joshua is solemnly appointed to succeeded the great hero-lawgiver, he is bidden to stand before Eleazar, the priest, 'who shall ask counsel for him after the judgment of Urim,' and this counsel is to determine the movements of the host of Israel (Num. 27:21). In the blessings of Moses they appear as the crowning glory of the tribe of Levi: 'Thy Thummim and thy Urim are with thy Holy One' (Deut 33:8)."[5] As with the New World interpreters, these Old World stones are not limited in their functions, but rather serve as a means of communicating Yahweh's will. Walther Eichrodt takes a view that is more typical of modern social sciences but which nevertheless captures some of the essential meaning of the stones: "The interpretation of the stones as memorials of Yahweh's self-manifestations was able to subsist side by side with the popular conception that they were receptacles of holy power and signs of God's abiding presence."[6]

One of the stones' functions as presented in the Book of Mormon is to be translators for ancient records, a function they continued to perform as part of the restoration as Joseph began to use them to translate the plates he was given by Moroni.[7] While this particular function is not mentioned in the Old Testament, translation is not the exclusive New World use of these interpreters.

---

[4]Ex. 28:30, Lev. 8:8, Num. 27:21, Deut 33:8, 1 Sam. 28:6, Ezra 2:63, Neh. 7:65. The Urim appears without the accompanying Thummim in the verses that most clearly show the divinatory function (Num. 27:21, 1 Sam. 28:6).

[5]William Smith, *Smith's Bible Dictionary* (Old Tappan, N.J.: Fleming H. Revell, 1970), 719.

[6]Walther Eichrodt, *Theology of the Old Testament*, translated by J. A. Baker (Philadelphia: Westminster Press, 1961), 116.

[7]William E. McLellan wrote that the Book of Mormon interpreters were returned to Moroni after the loss of the 116 manuscript pages. When the translation resumed, it was with a chocolate-colored

> And the Lord said: I will prepare unto my servant Gazelem, a stone, which shall shine forth in darkness unto light, that I may discover unto my people who serve me, that I may discover unto them the works of their brethren, yea, their secret works, their works of darkness, and their wickedness and abominations.
>
> And now, my son, these interpreters were prepared that the word of God might be fulfilled, which he spake, saying:
>
> I will bring forth out of darkness unto light all their secret works and their abominations; and except they repent I will destroy them from off the face of the earth; and I will bring to light all their secrets and abominations, unto every nation that shall hereafter possess the land. (Alma 37:23–25)

While the New World interpreters have similarities to the Old Testament Urim and Thummim, the similarities are in concept and not necessarily in the tasks to which they were applied.

Mosiah 28:17–19

> 17 Now after Mosiah had finished translating these records, behold, it gave an account of the people who were destroyed, from the time that they were destroyed back to the building of the great tower, at the time the Lord confounded the language of the people and they were scattered abroad upon the face of all the earth, yea, and even from that time back until the creation of Adam.
> 18 Now this account did cause the people of Mosiah to mourn exceedingly, yea, they were filled with sorrow; nevertheless it gave them much knowledge, in the which they did rejoice.
> 19 And this account shall be written hereafter; for behold, it is expedient that all people should know the things which are written in this account.

These three verses close the section concerning the translation of the records obtained from the Limhites. As a conclusion, they are quite disappointing. Only verse 17 describes the longed-for content of the record. While Mormon obviously thinks that the content was important, because he will include it later (v. 19, i.e., the book of Ether), he here gives only the barest of synopses. Moroni's later description informs us that Yahweh commanded that a section of the translation be withheld until after the Messiah had been born (Ether 4:5–6). Mormon apparently honored that wish chronologically in his account, even though Mormon was clearly writing after the Messiah's birth.

Text: What is also missing from our current edition of the Book of Mormon is the complete finality of these short verses. These verses end a chapter in the 1830 edition. Thus, original Book of Mormon readers must have felt a great anticipation that Mosiah, the seer-translator, had at last translated the precious record. Then the chapter closes, with only the promise that the text would come later. While it is true that it does come later, it comes only after Mormon had finished absolutely everything else he had to say

---

stone known as the seer stone. Cited in John W. Welch and Tim Rathbone, "The Translation of the Book of Mormon: Preliminary Report on the Basic Historical Information," FARMS Reprint Series (Provo, Utah: FARMS, 1986), 11 note 39.

and given his record to Moroni, who finally included this translated text (Ether 1:1). The implication is that Mormon might have been content to omit this text entirely, despite the obvious significance attached to the translation.

Variant: The 1920 edition added "back" into a phrase in verse 17: "upon the face of the earth yea and even from that time *back* until the creation of Adam." This was probably done to parallel the similar phrase earlier in the verse, but it was a late addition. [8]

Mosiah 28:20

> 20 And now, as I said unto you, that after king Mosiah had done these things, he took the plates of brass, and all the things which he had kept, and conferred them upon Alma, who was the son of Alma; yea, all the records, and also the interpreters, and conferred them upon him, and commanded him that he should keep and preserve them, and also keep a record of the people, handing them down from one generation to another, even as they had been handed down from the time that Lehi left Jerusalem.

As already mentioned, Mosiah appears to prepare for political upheaval, even war, among his people, and transfers into $Alma_1$'s care the records and the interpreters—but not the Liahona or the sword of Laban. Apparently these items were associated with the political, rather than the religious, rule.

The separation of the religious leader from the political leader is mirrored in the separation of sacred artifacts. The Liahona and sword of Laban remain with the political side and the sacred records move to a different lineage as their caretakers. These records will move in and out of the political transmission lines from this point until Mormon himself.

Text: In the 1830 edition the chapter ends with our verse 19. This verse is the beginning of a new chapter, and a new idea for Mormon the editor.

---

[8]Skousen, *Analysis of Textual Variants*, 3:1531.

Mosiah 29

Mosiah 29:1

> 1 Now when Mosiah had done this he sent out throughout all the land, among all the people, desiring to know their will concerning who should be their king.

This passage is problematic because it does not fit the typical king-to-king pattern of power transfer. Nor does this passage describe an election. Indeed, verse 6 suggests that the voice of the people simply confirmed the typical pattern of kingship.

A possible parallel to this situation had occurred in the city of Lehi-Nephi when Limhi and his people are planning an escape: "And now it came to pass that Ammon and king Limhi began to consult with the people how they should deliver themselves out of bondage; and even they did cause that all the people should gather themselves together; and this they did that they might have the voice of the people concerning the matter" (Mosiah 22:1).

This process is known as the "voice of the people." (See Excursus: "The Voice of the People," following Mosiah 29.) At this point, the significant message is that even the Nephite monarchy accommodated communal involvement. Nor is such involvement out of place in a Mesoamerican context, though firm information for it comes, perforce, from a much later period.

Text: As noted in the commentary accompanying Mosiah 28:20, that verse was originally attached to this first verse of our current chapter 29. Here is the reattached paragraph:

> And now, as I said unto you, that after king Mosiah had done these things, he took the plates of brass, and all the things which he had kept, and conferred them upon Alma, who was the son of Alma; yea, all the records, and also the interpreters, and conferred them upon him, and commanded him that he should keep and preserve them, and also keep a record of the people, handing them down from one generation to another, even as they had been handed down from the time that Lehi left Jerusalem.
>
> Now when Mosiah had done this he sent out throughout all the land, among all the people, desiring to know their will concerning who should be their king. (Mosiah 28:20–29:1)

Mosiah 28:20 begins with "and now" which Mormon typically uses to mark a new subject. Mormon has split the power transfer from king to judges into two pieces: preparation, and the creation of the judges (ch. 29).

Variant: The 1830 typesetter changed the printer's manuscript's "*out through* the land" to "*out throughout* the land." It appears that he was attempting to smooth out the phrase, but the result was the somewhat awkward "out throughout."[1]

Mosiah 29:2

> 2 And it came to pass that the voice of the people came, saying: We are desirous that Aaron thy son should be our king and our ruler.

Mosiah's consultation with the voice of the people may not fit cleanly into typical concepts of monarchy, but its importance is that the voice of the people will underpin Mosiah's persuasion about switching to judges (vv. 25–29). The "voice of the people" identified Aaron as the desired next king, highlighting that, although this mechanism would become more important under the system of judges, it already existed (Mosiah 29:26).

Mosiah 29:3

> 3 Now Aaron had gone up to the land of Nephi, therefore the king could not confer the kingdom upon him; neither would Aaron take upon him the kingdom; neither were any of the sons of Mosiah willing to take upon them the kingdom.

Like his father, Mosiah wishes to transfer the kingdom while he is still alive. Obviously, he was still capable of translating the text of our book of Ether. Nevertheless, he may be aware of his approaching death, which Mormon reports in this chapter (v. 46). Obviously, Mosiah was ready to pass on the kingship and the people continued to want a king, but the throne had no heir.

Mosiah 29:4

> 4 Therefore king Mosiah sent again among the people; yea, even a written word sent he among the people. And these were the words that were written, saying:

In contrast to verse 1 where Mosiah simply "sends out" to discover the people, this verse emphasizes that he wrote his second message. While there were clearly literate Nephites, their percentage is less clear. If the messengers were reading the text to illiterate listeners, Mosiah thus ensures its accurate transmission. This particular message was so important to the people that Mosiah wanted it delivered precisely.

It also seems significant that he did not assemble the people but rather sent messengers among them. Those who lived out the ceremonial city-center were probably clustered in kinship groups. The message would be read to these kin groups.

Why is this important? First, the sheer size of the population may have made an assembly problematic, even though Benjamin had done so and Mosiah had

---

[1]Royal Skousen, *Analysis of Textual Variants of the Book of Mormon*, THE CRITICAL TEXT OF THE BOOK OF MORMON (Provo, Utah: Foundation for Ancient Research and Mormon Studies, 2005), Vol. 4, Part 3, 1534.

likewise called an assembly when Limhi's and $Alma_1$'s people arrived. The second reason, I hypothesize, is that Mosiah was consciously keeping the groups small in informing them of his proposed action out of fear that the already tense divisiveness in Zarahemla might be exacerbated by certain kin groups attempting to create a coalition to install their own king and government. Such a real possibility will arise with the kingmen described in the book of Alma (Alma 51:4–5).

Mosiah 29:5

> 5 Behold, O ye my people, or my brethren, for I esteem you as such, I desire that ye should consider the cause which ye are called to consider—for ye are desirous to have a king.

Redaction: Mormon quotes the text of Mosiah's document as it appeared in the official records, thus registering the importance he attached to the exact words.

Mosiah 29:6–9

> 6 Now I declare unto you that he to whom the kingdom doth rightly belong has declined, and will not take upon him the kingdom.
> 7 And now if there should be another appointed in his stead, behold I fear there would rise contentions among you. And who knoweth but what my son, to whom the kingdom doth belong, should turn to be angry and draw away a part of this people after him, which would cause wars and contentions among you, which would be the cause of shedding much blood and perverting the way of the Lord, yea, and destroy the souls of many people.
> 8 Now I say unto you let us be wise and consider these things, for we have no right to destroy my son, neither should we have any right to destroy another if he should be appointed in his stead.
> 9 And if my son should turn again to his pride and vain things he would recall the things which he had said, and claim his right to the kingdom, which would cause him and also this people to commit much sin.

Mosiah describes the classic problem of ambiguous power transfer in a monarchy. Tradition and social conditioning influence the community to accept the "rightful" heir. Everyone knows who that heir will be, thus reducing the probability of conflict in making the transfer. However, history provides ample evidence of troubled succession. The most common cause is the lack of a male heir, which it is also in this case—not because none exists but because no *willing* heir exists.

Contention arises when different factions support candidates who have possible, but not absolute, claims to the throne. In Zarahemla, four known peoples had their own version of a king-tradition: the Nephites, Zarahemlaite/Mulekites, Limhites, and Almaites. Any one of those groups would contain kin networks who knew that they had once been in a royal lineage and might wish to assert that lineage to rulership. Given the religious and kin contentions that we have already seen lying just beneath the surface of Zarahemlaite society, Mosiah's fear of outright civil war over a contested succession seems quite legitimate.

Vocabulary: Verse 9 uses the phrase: " . . . he would recall the things which he had said. . . . " Here "recall" does not mean "remember" but rather "call back" or "retract." The problem will occur if Aaron retracts his renunciation of the throne.

Mosiah 29:10

10 And now let us be wise and look forward to these things, and do that which will make for the peace of this people.

Redaction: This verse is the transition between Mosiah's explanation of the problem and his solution.

Mosiah 29:11

11 Therefore I will be your king the remainder of my days; nevertheless, let us appoint judges, to judge this people according to our law; and we will newly arrange the affairs of this people, for we will appoint wise men to be judges, that will judge this people according to the commandments of God.

Mosiah proposes creating judges rather than kings. Although he offers some reasons for this change, the description is so restrained that it seems likely that the people already had some familiarity with the concept, perhaps because it was an elevation of an existing function. Indeed, Mosiah suggests as much in saying that the judges would "judge this people according to our law."

It is impossible to have judges without law, for there would be no standard for their judgment (except possibly common sense). A king does not need law because the king is the law. Thus, in a kingdom, it is comparatively easy to deal with a novel situation because the king makes a decision (presumably Yahweh's will) which then becomes law for all. The king's removal also removes that personal access to Yahweh's will; therefore, something else must become the basis for ruling. That basis is law.

Zarahemla society had already been transitioning to a concept of law, perhaps supported by the understanding of the rules codified in the law of Moses. When church members are persecuted, the issue comes before Mosiah (Mosiah 27:1–2). The result was the creation of a new law (Mosiah 27:3). The basic mechanisms for law and judgment were already in place for Zarahemla. Mosiah formalized the mechanisms and exalted the position of judge. Without such a foundation, simply declaring a change of government would not be possible. The promotion of judges and the demotion of the king presuppose that something else would take the role of the king as the final judge. Here, it appears to have been the accepted body of law, a concept that was already functioning.

While it has long been understood that kings reigned over the Maya cities, it is now apparent that those kings did not rule autocratically. They ruled with the assistance of a council formed from leaders of important lineages.[2] Political power

---

[2]David Drew, *The Lost Chronicles of the Maya Kings* (Berkeley: University of California Press, 1999), 243.

was held by balancing the tensions among these lineages. This is most dramatically attested in the reign of Yax Pasaj near the final years of Copán where he acts on monumental sculpture in company with important nobles, rather than majestically alone as most kings are represented on the monuments.[3] These lineages or councils operated in buildings designated as *popol nah* or "mat houses." The mat was the symbol of ruling power. The woven mat was a place of honor upon which the ruler sat, and the association of person, place, and thing exalted the simple mat to a symbol. The buildings known as "mat houses" are therefore locations associated with the political system. They might be attached to the state, but also were present in some smaller communities. The various *popol nah* functioned for the debate of policy as well as centers for instruction in ritual dance.[4]

The great houses, or lineages, formed a governmental layer that functioned just below the monarchy and was integral to the political process. Even under the monarchy there were political structures similar to the Nephite judges. In fact, John Pohl notes that in one of the later Mixtec codices: "The four priests . . . specifically conform to descriptions in the *Relación de Tilantongo* and elsewhere of a body of judges who administered the realm for the king."[5]

In the course of history, some Mesoamerican communities appear to have followed the same political path as the Nephites. They disposed of the position of the king. When they did so, these previous structures remained in place but were elevated to perform the centralized ruling function. There is some evidence that this took place at Teotihuacán.[6] It is much more certain that a council of lineage heads ruled in Chichén Itzá.[7] Even though all of these examples post-date the Book

---

[3]Simon Martin and Nikolai Grube, *Chronicle of the Maya Kings and Queens* (London: Thames & Hudson, 2000), 210.

[4]Drew, *The Lost Chronicles of the Maya Kings*, 243. Linda Schele and Peter Mathews, *The Code of Kings: The Language of Seven Sacred Maya Temples and Tombs* (New York: Scribner, 1998), 44.

[5]John M. D. Pohl, "The Four Priests: Political Stability," in *The Ancient Civilizations of Mesoamerica: A Reader*, edited by Michael E. Smith and Marilyn A. Masson (Malden, Mass.: Blackwell Publishers, 2000), 355–56.

[6]George L. Cowgill, "State and Society at Teotihuacan, Mexico," in *The Ancient Civilizations of Mesoamerica: A Reader*, edited by Michael E. Smith and Marilyn A. Masson (Malden, Mass.: Blackwell Publishers, 2000), 315, "Supreme Teo political authority may not always have been strongly concentrated in a single person or lineage. R. Millon suggested that Teo might have been an oligarchic republic. The case now seems stronger, though not yet overwhelming."

[7]Drew, *The Lost Chronicles of the Maya Kings*, 372:

> The inscriptions amongst the buildings to the south of the city centre help to explain how the political system at Chichén Itzá worked. They do not talk of dynastic rulers and their great deeds, as in previous centuries. Instead they mention a number of individuals, with names such as "Kakupakal" or "Kokom," in connection with the dedication of buildings and other ceremonies, often concerned with the maintenance of sacred fires and the drilling of "new fire" on important occasions in the calendar. The glyph for sibling, *y-itah* is used to describe the relationship between these people, suggesting rule by "brothers." Some may indeed have been related in this way and Diego de Landa also talks of the tradition of "brothers" ruling at Chichén Itzá. But the phrase may best be interpreted to mean "companions" or individuals each of roughly equivalent status. They are accorded the title *ahaw*, but significantly none is termed *k'ul ahaw* or supreme, "divine lord." What this would seem to represent is rule by council, by the heads of different lineages. At the time of the Spanish Conquest some small city states still used the term *multepal*, best rendered as "group rule," to describe what was probably a very similar system.

of Mormon, there is no reason to believe that the essential political structures were significantly different in earlier times. (See also commentary accompanying Mosiah 29:45–47 for information on the position of judges in Mesoamerican cultures.)

History: Mosiah's selection of the term "judge" for this new position most likely came from the brass plates record of Israel's judges. It is interesting that Israel moved from judges to a monarchy, while Mosiah reverses that direction.

However, even though the term is the same, significant differences appear between the Israelite judges and the Nephite judges. The Israelite judges seem to arise in response to military crises; they were never true political leaders with ongoing administrative responsibility. In contrast, Nephite judges administered the government with no hint of an overt military function, other than those required of a head of state.[8] Regardless of the differences, however, using a familiar name would tie this new form of government to the sacred past, thus making it easier to accept. (See also commentary accompanying Mosiah 29:45–47.)

Mosiah as Lawgiver: John W. Welch has examined Mosiah as a lawgiver:

> The law of Mosiah primarily made procedural changes and probably did not make radical changes in the substantive rules of the Law of Moses. Mosiah instructed the new Nephite judges to judge "according to the laws . . . given you *by our fathers*" (Mosiah 29:25; italics added), and twenty-two years later the Nephites were still "strict in observing the ordinances of God, according to the law of Moses" (Alma 30:3). . . .
>
> The law of Mosiah . . . prohibited slavery in the land of Zarahemla, for Ammon assured his converts that "it is against the law of our brethren, which was established by my father, that there should be any slaves among them" (Alma 27:9). Previously it had been only by royal benevolence that slavery was not allowed in Zarahemla (Mosiah 2:13). . . .
>
> The law of Mosiah probably also provided that the governor alone had jurisdiction over capital offenses (3 Ne. 6:22), but this regulation may have been introduced a few generations later. . . .
>
> Mosiah's judicial reform remained solid for sixty-two years, but then his laws were "altered and trampled under their feet" (Hel. 4:22). The majority of the people chose evil (Hel. 5:2), Nephi had to deliver the judgment-seat to Cezoram (Hel. 5:1), and judicial corruption soon ensued. (Hel. 8:4, 3 Ne. 6:23).[9]

Mosiah 29:12–13

12 Now it is better that a man should be judged of God than of man, for the judgments of God are always just, but the judgments of man are not always just.
13 Therefore, if it were possible that you could have just men to be your kings, who would establish the laws of God, and judge this people according to his commandments, yea, if ye could have men for your kings who would do even as

---

[8]John A. Tvedtnes, *The Most Correct Book: Insights from a Book of Mormon Scholar* (Salt Lake City: Cornerstone, 1999), 194–97, and Byron R. Merrill, "Government by the Voice of the People: A Witness and a Warning," in *Mosiah, Salvation Only through Christ*, edited by Monte S. Nyman and Charles D. Tate Jr. (Provo, Utah: BYU Religious Studies Center, 1991), 117.

[9]John W. Welch, "The Law of Mosiah," in *Reexploring the Book of Mormon*, edited by John W. Welch (Provo, Utah: FARMS, 1992), 159–61. Welch and I disagree on certain aspects of Mosiah's political reform.

my father Benjamin did for this people—I say unto you, if this could always be the case then it would be expedient that ye should always have kings to rule over you.

How Nephite kingship is conceptualized appears most clearly in verse 12. Right after discussing the potentially revolutionary idea (quite literally revolutionary, given Mosiah's circumstances) of creating judges, Mosiah explains its advantages. However, he prefaces this discussion by acknowledging that a king is also good and perhaps best. The reason that a king is good is that "it is better that a man should be judged of God [acknowledgement that kings had a divine connection to God] than of man."

For Mosiah, the shift from king to judge was a shift in the judgment from Yahweh to man. The judges would judge men according to men—or according to law. The king had judged men according to Yahweh. Modern readers who see in this discussion of judges anti-royalist sentiments characteristic of the early republic miss this extremely important point. Mosiah and kings like him constituted a direct link to Yahweh's will. That connection was unquestionably the best.

The problem in kingship was the occasionally wicked king who was unable to speak for Yahweh and whose judgments would therefore be corrupt. Mosiah juxtaposes his father, Benjamin, a just king, against Noah, a corrupt king (v. 18). Benjamin was the conduit for the Yahweh's law, established Yahweh's will among the people, and judged them by it. The best earthly rule would be an earthly king in communication and conformance with the heavenly king.

Internal Connections: Mosiah is creating an argument that we easily understand but which should have been completely foreign to most of the people of Zarahemla. However, the people of Alma$_1$ were very familiar with it. Alma$_1$ refused his people's offer of the kingship with this argument:

> Behold, it is not expedient that we should have a king; for thus saith the Lord: Ye shall not esteem one flesh above another, or one man shall not think himself above another; therefore I say unto you it is not expedient that ye should have a king.
>
> Nevertheless, if it were possible that ye could always have just men to be your kings it would be well for you to have a king.
>
> But remember the iniquity of king Noah and his priests; and I myself was caught in a snare, and did many things which were abominable in the sight of the Lord, which caused me sore repentance. (Mosiah 23:7–9)

Alma$_1$'s refusal is critical in understanding the transition from king to judges in Zarahemla. Because Mormon quotes this discourse directly from the plates, the textual similarities rightly signal a connection between texts. In this case, Alma$_1$'s refusal closely matches Mosiah's language and argument.

The first important example is Alma$_1$'s declaration, "If it were possible that ye could always have just men to be your kings it would be well for you to have a king"—precisely Mosiah's sentiment in verse 13 though in expanded form: "Therefore, if it were possible that you could have just men to be your kings, who would establish the laws of God, and judge this people according to his commandments, yea, if ye could have men for your kings who would do even as my father Benjamin did for this people—I say unto you, if this could always be the case then it would be expedient that ye should always have kings to rule over you" (Mosiah 29:13).

The basic concept is exactly the same. The first point in Alma$_1$'s refusal is, significantly, the first point in Mosiah's ultimate recommendation against kingship; a king is good if he is a good king. Alma$_1$ uses king Noah as a bad example of a king. In verse 18 Mosiah also uses Noah as his bad example.

The combination of these correspondences with Alma$_1$'s reorganization of Zarahemla's religious structures makes it apparent that Alma$_1$ has had great impact on reconceptualizing its political structures as well. Mosiah clearly esteemed Alma$_1$ very highly and listened to his counsel regarding religion (notably the creation of the churches). Alma$_1$ espouses the very same ideas that Mosiah proclaims here; therefore, it is virtually certain that these are also Alma$_1$'s ideas that Mosiah has adopted.

Even though the current story is about Mosiah, it highlights the tremendous influence of Alma$_1$ on Nephite society. Seldom can one man be credited with altering a people's religious institutions. Seldom can one man be credited with revolutionizing a people's government. Alma did both.

Mosiah 29:14–15

> 14 And even I myself have labored with all the power and faculties which I have possessed, to teach you the commandments of God, and to establish peace throughout the land, that there should be no wars nor contentions, no stealing, nor plundering, nor murdering, nor any manner of iniquity;
> 15 And whosoever has committed iniquity, him have I punished according to the crime which he has committed, according to the law which has been given to us by our fathers.

Mosiah describes Benjamin as the prime example of the just king (v. 13) and proclaims that he has attempted to be the same kind of just king (vv. 14–15). As his father was great in pronouncing Yahweh's commandments, so Mosiah has labored to teach them. Mosiah has also established laws and ruled according to them, not by whim (v. 15). This pattern is an important prelude to elevating the status of law above the throne. It is reinforces the hypothesis that Nephite society was familiar with and accepted the rule of law.

One argument that Alma$_1$ used in refusing the kingship was doctrinal: one man should not be exalted above another (Mosiah 23:7). There is no obvious correlation to this sentiment in Mosiah's declaration, but verse 14 may suggest it and verse 32 makes it explicit. Mosiah used Benjamin as the exemplar of a good king, and one reason for Benjamin's covenant was to eliminate "contentions." These "contentions" were economic, allowing the exaltation of one person over another. Perhaps Mosiah is alluding to this type of "contention," which would provide yet another connection to Alma$_1$'s refusal of the kingship.

Mosiah 29:16–18

> 16 Now I say unto you, that because all men are not just it is not expedient that ye should have a king or kings to rule over you.
> 17 For behold, how much iniquity doth one wicked king cause to be committed, yea, and what great destruction!
> 18 Yea, remember king Noah, his wickedness and his abominations, and also the wickedness and abominations of his people. Behold what great destruction did come upon them; and also because of their iniquities they were brought into bondage.

Mosiah makes a more elaborate statement about his "bad" example. Noah succeeded in leading an entire people astray. Even though Mosiah 25:1–16 gives only an abbreviated version of it, Mosiah had summoned all the people to an assembly in which Alma$_1$ and Limhi recounted their experiences. They would certainly remember Noah's sinister role in his people's enslavement and apostasy.

Mosiah 29:19–20

> 19 And were it not for the interposition of their all-wise Creator, and this because of their sincere repentance, they must unavoidably remain in bondage until now.
> 20 But behold, he did deliver them because they did humble themselves before him; and because they cried mightily unto him he did deliver them out of bondage; and thus doth the Lord work with his power in all cases among the children of men, extending the arm of mercy towards them that put their trust in him.

Rhetoric: The stories of Limhi and Alma$_1$ are both examples of miraculous salvation after tribulation. Noah's wickedness was so great that they could all have been destroyed or at least kept in bondage "were it not for the interposition of their all-wise Creator." Even without a king, Yahweh is still in charge of the universe. In spite of a king, Yahweh can still save his people.

Mosiah's argument here is subtle, but important. He has proclaimed that the ancient connection between Yahweh and king is good. What happens when half of that conduit is severed? Mosiah describes that very event in the story of Noah. Despite Noah's wickedness, Yahweh was able to raise up righteous men to care for his people. Thus, by proclaiming Yahweh's victory, Mosiah affirms Yahweh's continuing importance and, in parallel fashion, the limited effectiveness even of a wicked king.

However, Yahweh could intervene only because of the people's humility (v. 20), a reminder that reestablishing a righteous king (Limhi) did not automatically restore his conduit to Yahweh. It was not the king, but Yahweh, who caused their deliverance. Thus, Yahweh may continue to guide (and save) his people even in the absence of a king.

Mosiah 29:21–24

> 21 And behold, now I say unto you, ye cannot dethrone an iniquitous king save it be through much contention, and the shedding of much blood.

> 22 For behold, he has his friends in iniquity, and he keepeth his guards about him; and he teareth up the laws of those who have reigned in righteousness before him; and he trampleth under his feet the commandments of God;
> 23 And he enacteth laws, and sendeth them forth among his people, yea, laws after the manner of his own wickedness; and whosoever doth not obey his laws he causeth to be destroyed; and whosoever doth rebel against him he will send his armies against them to war, and if he can he will destroy them; and thus an unrighteous king doth pervert the ways of all righteousness.
> 24 And now behold I say unto you, it is not expedient that such abominations should come upon you.

Since law will be elevated in importance, Mosiah distinguishes good laws from bad. Good laws may come from good kings like Benjamin and Mosiah, but bad kings may enact bad laws. Thus, Mosiah will propose more than just the rule of law. He proclaims a new method of creating law, one that acknowledges the reality of both good and bad people but which enhances the opportunity of creating good laws. This method is judging by "the voice of the people" (Mosiah 29:26). Their participation is how the good can be preserved and the bad avoided.

Mosiah 29:25

> 25 Therefore, choose you by the voice of this people, judges, that ye may be judged according to the laws which have been given you by our fathers, which are correct, and which were given them by the hand of the Lord.

The first step is the selection of judges by "the voice of this people" who will judge by law through these judges. The law itself, not the king's person, will constitute a direct connection to Yahweh's will.

Mosiah 29:26

> 26 Now it is not common that the voice of the people desireth anything contrary to that which is right; but it is common for the lesser part of the people to desire that which is not right; therefore this shall ye observe and make it your law—to do your business by the voice of the people.

Kay P. Edwards, professor of family science at Brigham Young University, describes the most common reading of this verse: "King Mosiah proposed to his people the idea that their welfare might be better assured by making a major change in their government structure—from a kingship to a form of democracy. He suggested that this new governmental system be implemented by placing judges chosen by the people at the head of the government."[10]

It is very tempting to equate this passage with an endorsement of democracy, as Edwards does. Without question the principle applies to democratic societies, but this is not the best explanation for what was happening in Mosiah's kingdom. For

---

[10]Kay P. Edwards, "The Kingdom of God and the Kingdoms of Men," in *1 Nephi to Alma 29*, edited by Kent P. Jackson, STUDIES IN SCRIPTURE (Salt Lake City: Deseret Book, 1987), Vol. 7, 277.

Mosiah, the contrast will be between a king supported by God and judges supported by the people. (See "Excursus: The Voice of the People," following this chapter.)

Mosiah 29:27

> 27 And if the time comes that the voice of the people doth choose iniquity, then is the time that the judgments of God will come upon you; yea, then is the time he will visit you with great destruction even as he has hitherto visited this land.

Using the voice of the people as the immediate measure of their actions does not mean that Yahweh no longer has a relationship to the people. Should their collective voice becomes contrary to his will, Yahweh will reassert himself by visiting "great destruction" upon them. The result of that great destruction is not mentioned, but presumably it would remove enough of the people that the righteous might once again dominate.

Mosiah 29:28–29

> 28 And now if ye have judges, and they do not judge you according to the law which has been given, ye can cause that they may be judged of a higher judge.
> 29 If your higher judges do not judge righteous judgments, ye shall cause that a small number of your lower judges should be gathered together, and they shall judge your higher judges, according to the voice of the people.

Mosiah's arrangement of the judges is that they do not constitute the ultimate authority in and of themselves. Using the principle of the voice of the people (where the majority will want the right), he creates judges who also are "the people." By creating higher judges and a court of "peers," Mosiah creates a system in which the judges themselves have a means of becoming the "voice of the people" to make sure that the right thing is done.

From our modern perspective, it would appear that this court of lower judges (v. 29) would somehow poll the "people" or take votes. Were they to do that, the court of judges would not be needed at all. The judges judge by "the voice of the people" because they have sufficient numbers to assure that the right thing will be done. This is not an appeal to a vote that would remove all function from this court. This is best seen as an elevation of the clan heads to a more prominent position. (See commentary accompanying Mosiah 29:39.)

Mosiah 29:30–31

> 30 And I command you to do these things in the fear of the Lord; and I command you to do these things, and that ye have no king; that if these people commit sins and iniquities they shall be answered upon their own heads.
> 31 For behold I say unto you, the sins of many people have been caused by the iniquities of their kings; therefore their iniquities are answered upon the heads of their kings.

Of course, the problem with listening to the voice of the people is that the people might err. Mosiah exhorts his people to choose in accordance with Yahweh's commandments; in so doing, they will always find themselves in the right. Consequences of a wrong choice will be visited upon their heads—a just punishment because they will have made the decision.

Shifting the responsibility from the king to the people might make people long for a king and, hence, for lessened responsibility. Mosiah reminds them that having a king does not insulate them from Yahweh's wrath. They can still suffer even though it will be because of an evil king, not necessarily because of their own choices. Mosiah is showing them a contrast. While it is true that rights engender responsibility, having a king bear that responsibility instead of them personally will not protect them from the evils of the world if the king is not righteous.

Mosiah 29:32

> 32 And now I desire that this inequality should be no more in this land, especially among this my people; but I desire that this land be a land of liberty, and every man may enjoy his rights and privileges alike, so long as the Lord sees fit that we may live and inherit the land, yea, even as long as any of our posterity remains upon the face of the land.

When $Alma_1$ declined kingship in Helam, one of the principles he mentioned was the equality of humankind: "It is not expedient that we should have a king; for thus saith the Lord: Ye shall not esteem one flesh above another, or one man shall not think himself above another; therefore I say unto you it is not expedient that ye should have a king" (Mosiah 23:7).

Mosiah makes this concept explicit in declaring the end to monarchy: "I desire that this inequality should be no more in this land, especially among this my people." What is "this inequality"?

Grammatically, it apparently refers to people who suffer because of the king's sins. That is clearly his primary meaning, but he likely has other meanings associated with this particular image. The social structure of kingdoms virtually requires the exaltation of one man above another, with the king at the top. Mosiah is probably attempting to remedy that inequality as well as the inequality caused when people are punished for the sins of the king.

Culture: It is very interesting that Mosiah denounced "this inequality . . . in this land, especially among this my people." He appears to distinguish between "this land" and "my people." It suggests that he is referring to this mode of kingship in other locations, wishing it were removed from other cities as well as from his own people.

Mosiah 29:33

> 33 And many more things did king Mosiah write unto them, unfolding unto them all the trials and troubles of a righteous king, yea, all the travails of soul for their people, and also all the murmurings of the people to their king; and he explained it all unto them.

Redaction: Curiously, at this point Mormons stops quoting and begins summarizing. He has copied much longer texts before (e.g., Abinadi's defense before the priests). Perhaps Mormon felt that this much of the quotation has established the essential points and that to say more was not essential. Mormon is very interested in people's faith, so he may have included this text because it was clearly important—but not essential to Mormon's main thesis. But he simply does not explain his decision.

Mosiah 29:34–36

> 34 And he told them that these things ought not to be; but that the burden should come upon all the people, that every man might bear his part.
> 35 And he also unfolded unto them all the disadvantages they labored under, by having an unrighteous king to rule over them;
> 36 Yea, all his iniquities and abominations, and all the wars, and contentions, and bloodshed, and the stealing, and the plundering, and the committing of whoredoms, and all manner of iniquities which cannot be enumerated—telling them that these things ought not to be, that they were expressly repugnant to the commandments of God.

Literature: Verses 33–34 form a contrasting pair to verses 35–36. In 33–34 Mosiah discusses the good king who must bear all of the people's burdens. These responsibilities should be returned to their rightful location—to the people themselves.

In contrast to the good king (who still has problems) is the bad king who creates "iniquities and abominations, and all the wars, and contentions, and bloodshed, and the stealing, and the plundering, and the committing of whoredoms, and all manner of iniquities which cannot be enumerated." Mosiah apparently assumes that his people will immediately recognize this list.[11] These very conditions became the norm for the Classic Maya after the close of the Book of Mormon. I hypothesize, therefore, that Mosiah is counseling against some fairly well-known trends.

Mosiah 29:37–38

> 37 And now it came to pass, after king Mosiah had sent these things forth among the people they were convinced of the truth of his words.
> 38 Therefore they relinquished their desires for a king, and became exceedingly anxious that every man should have an equal chance throughout all the land; yea, and every man expressed a willingness to answer for his own sins.

The people accept the rule of judges and, more importantly, accept that they, not the king, bear responsibility for their actions. They are their own measuring stick for right and wrong and must take communal responsibility for the rightness or wrongness of their choices.

---

[11]See similar lists in Alma 16:18, 17:14, 23:3, 37:21, 50:21; Hel. 3:14, 4:12, 6:23, 10:3; Ether 8:16.

Mosiah 29:39

> 39 Therefore, it came to pass that they assembled themselves together in bodies throughout the land, to cast in their voices concerning who should be their judges, to judge them according to the law which had been given them; and they were exceedingly rejoiced because of the liberty which had been granted unto them.

With our understanding of the probable kin-based organization of the Nephites as we have seen throughout their history, we can make some assumptions of how these judges were selected. Since they assembled "in bodies," they were not a single large gathering. All people belonged to kin groups (which would also be geographic groupings), a more logical structure than, say, churches, since not everybody belonged to churches.

If they gathered as kin, then each kin group would recommend a judge who was related to them. As a kinsman, he would protect the interests of his kin against another judge who might favor his own kin but who would, in turn, be checked by equally alert judges. Thus, there would be rough assurance that the common good would be served.

This general structural organization persisted through to Aztec times: "Each district or calpulli in the capital had its own chief, the calpullec, who was elected for life, preferably from the same family, by the inhabitants, and confirmed by the emperor," comments Soustelle. "He had a council of elders, the *ueuetque* [sic, better *heuehuetque*, the 'old ones, elders'] who were probably the oldest and best-known heads of families and he never did anything without taking the opinion of the elders."[12]

While this Aztec chief leader is not necessarily the same as the judges in the Aztec empire, the principle for electing leaders on the basis of kin affiliation closely resembles the same principle that Mosiah's people would have used.

Mosiah 29:40

> 40 And they did wax strong in love towards Mosiah; yea, they did esteem him more than any other man; for they did not look upon him as a tyrant who was seeking for gain, yea, for that lucre which doth corrupt the soul; for he had not exacted riches of them, neither had he delighted in the shedding of blood; but he had established peace in the land, and he had granted unto his people that they should be delivered from all manner of bondage; therefore they did esteem him, yea, exceedingly, beyond measure.

Redaction: This passage appears to be Mormon's eulogy to Mosiah rather than a text from the source plates.

Mosiah 29:41–42

> 41 And it came to pass that they did appoint judges to rule over them, or to judge them according to the law; and this they did throughout all the land.
> 42 And it came to pass that Alma was appointed to be the first chief judge, he being also the high priest, his father having conferred the office upon him, and having given him the charge concerning all the affairs of the church.

---

[12]Soustelle, *The Daily Life of the Aztecs*, 40.

Even though the judges were apparently identified or nominated by popular kin-assemblies, Mosiah appointed them. Thus, the kin-leaders were installed in their new positions by formal action of the outgoing king, the strongest possible conferral of public authority that they could receive.

In the hierarchy of judges, $Alma_2$ is designated as the chief judge. He now has two positions. As high priest, he is the head of the various churches, ordained as such by his father. He is also the chief judge, a position confirmed by Mosiah. It is curious that the *de facto* separation of the religious from the political with Mosiah and $Alma_1$ should be reunited in $Alma_1$'s son. Nevertheless, these positions are not reunited in function. The people would understand that $Alma_2$ bore two official titles, a fact that would become most conspicuous later when $Alma_2$ relinquishes one of them (Alma 5:15–18). Such an action would not have been possible unless the two were still considered separable.

Mosiah 29:43–44

> 43 And now it came to pass that Alma did walk in the ways of the Lord, and he did keep his commandments, and he did judge righteous judgments; and there was continual peace through the land.
> 44 And thus commenced the reign of the judges throughout all the land of Zarahemla, among all the people who were called the Nephites; and Alma was the first and chief judge.

The next major book in the Book of Mormon is the book of Alma. Mormon is preparing us for that development by using $Alma_2$ as one of the terminal points of the $Mosiah_1$ dynasty. Mormon therefore expresses his approval of $Alma_2$—a good man ("walk[s] in the ways of the Lord") who made righteous judgments.

Mosiah 29:45–47

> 45 And now it came to pass that his father died, being eighty and two years old, having lived to fulfil the commandments of God.
> 46 And it came to pass that Mosiah died also, in the thirty and third year of his reign, being sixty and three years old; making in the whole, five hundred and nine years from the time Lehi left Jerusalem.
> 47 And thus ended the reign of the kings over the people of Nephi; and thus ended the days of Alma, who was the founder of their church.

Chronology: Apparently Mosiah and $Alma_1$ died in the same year. Mosiah died at age sixty-three (he began his reign at age thirty; see Mosiah 6:4) and $Alma_1$ at age eighty-two. Five hundred nine Nephite years have passed since the departure from Jerusalem—or 92 B.C. in the correlation used in this commentary.

History: By terminating the monarchy and turning to judges, Mosiah went against the trend in the development of Mesoamerican complex societies but also presaged some governmental forms that would not be clearly apparent for many years after the close of the Book of Mormon.

Archaeologist Robert J. Sharer of the University Museum, University of Pennsylvania, has examined much of the evidence for the development of the concept of the king among the Classic Maya (post-Book of Mormon). He notes that, while the full development of the Classic Maya concept of the god-king was not developed until later, most of the elements were in place by the end of the late Preclassic (which would include Mosiah's time) in places such as El Mirador.[13] The Book of Mormon clearly supports the idea that kings were becoming important in this area long before the Classic period, even if their full cult does not develop until later.

Assuming, as I do in this commentary, that Zarahemla was located in one of the regions that was undergoing this shift to the god-king form, Mosiah was taking action that was dramatically opposed to the general flow of cultural development. Nevertheless, some later examples of judges and rule by special groups are worth our attention. John L. Sorenson notes:

> One of the primary duties of a ruler was to settle disputes among his people, Sometimes that could be done by him personally, but in a population of much size, he would not have time to deal with every conflict. Judges were delegated to carry out that duty.
>
> Cortez, for example, described the situation at the great market in the Aztec capital: "There is in this square a very large building, like a Court of Justice, where there are always ten or twelve persons, sitting as judges, and delivering their decisions upon all cases which arise in the markets."[14]

These judges were appointed by the people and attempted to judge fairly among them. Historian Jacques Soustelle describes these judges:

> The judges were nominated by the sovereign either from the experienced and elderly dignitaries or from among the common people. At Texcoco half the higher judges were of noble family and the other half of plebeian origin. All the chroniclers agree in praising the care with which the emperor and his fellow-kings chose the judges, "taking particular care that they were not drunkards, nor apt to be bribed, nor influenced by personal considerations, or impassioned in their judgments."[15]

The position of judge thus had resurfaced among the Aztecs, if indeed it had ever been gone. Here, however, the judges are arbiters of law and disputes, not leaders of the community.

An example of judges who lead their people occurred in Chichén Itzá (also post-Book of Mormon) which "witnessed the birth of a social and political order based upon a new principle of governance, *mul tepal* 'joint rule.'"[16] Scholars agree that Mesoamerica has had a relatively stable cultural base over time, with much of

---

[13]Robert J. Sharer, "Diversity and Continuity in Maya Civilization," in *Classic Maya Political History*, edited by T. Patrick Culbert (Cambridge, Eng.: Cambridge University Press, 1991), 184.

[14]John L. Sorenson, *Images of Ancient America: Visualizing the Book of Mormon* (Provo, Utah: FARMS, 1998), 116.

[15]Soustelle, *The Daily Life of the Aztecs*, 50. The internal quotation is from Sahagún.

[16]Linda Schele and David Freidel, *A Forest of Kings: The Untold Story of the Ancient Maya* (New York: William Morrow and Company, 1990), 348.

their culture remaining viable today despite the adaptations required by the post-conquest world. While not contemporaneous with Mosiah, these examples nevertheless indicate that Mosiah was not out of place in a Mesoamerican context. The sub-strata institutions that allowed Mosiah to make the change from king to judge enabled those similar changes that we know about in later cultures primarily because we simply have more data for the later peoples. (See also commentary accompanying Mosiah 29:11.)

Text: This is the end of a chapter and of the book of Mosiah.

Excursus: The Voice of the People

The book of Mosiah ends with a dramatic rearrangement in Zarahemla's political landscape. Mosiah not only abdicated his throne; he symbolically destroyed it. He dissolved a monarchy in favor of a government headed by judges. What was this new government? How did it compare to the government by a king?

Mosiah introduces this new political organization with the following injunctions:

> Therefore, choose you by the voice of this people, judges, that ye may be judged according to the laws which have been given you by our fathers, which are correct, and which were given them by the hand of the Lord.
>
> Now it is not common that the voice of the people desireth anything contrary to that which is right, but it is common for the lesser part of the people to desire that which is not right; therefore this shall ye observe and make it your law—to do your business by the voice of the people.
>
> And if the time comes that the voice of the people doth choose iniquity, then is the time that the judgments of God will come upon you; yea, then is the time he will visit you with great destruction even as he has hitherto /visited this land. (Mosiah 29:25–27).

Verse 25 tells us three important things about the new government. First, authority would be vested in several judges rather than a single king. Second, they would judge according to law. Third, an important mechanism of government would be the "voice of the people."

The rule of law is relatively easy to understand as our modern society is also governed by the rule of law. Even the system of judges is not too foreign to us. They formed a governmental hierarchy, with local judges reporting to higher judges:

> And now if ye have judges, and they do not judge you according to the law which has been given, ye can cause that they may be judged of a higher judge.
>
> If your higher judges do not judge righteous judgments, ye shall cause that a small number of your lower judges should be gathered together, and they shall judge your higher judges, according to the voice of the people. (Mosiah 29:28–29)

The third element, "the voice of the people," merits closer examination because we may too easily assume that it is likewise similar to familiar, modern political functions. President Anthony W. Ivins did so in associating it with American democracy: "This book [the Book of Mormon], as has been testified before, is the very embodiment of the spirit of Americanism. We hear a lot about that in these days. In its simplicity it lays down those fundamental principles of democracy upon which every republican form of government must be based and rounded [sic]. It teaches us that there should be no king to dictate upon this land. It teaches us that the will of the people, the voice of the people shall govern."[1] J. Keith Melville, an emeritus professor of political science at Brigham Young University, equates the Nephite judges with democracy:

> The Book of Mormon contains several meaningful discussions of political values. For example, there is the prophet-king Mosiah's comparison of the virtues and vices of monarchy with those of a democratic government. The ideal system, in Mosiah's view, would be to have just kings who would "establish the laws of God" (Mosiah 29:13), but the prospects of wicked kings prompted him to advocate a system of government where judges, chosen by the "voice of the people," would rule within constitutional guidelines and under the laws of God.[2]

However, Richard Lyman Bushman, Gouverneur Morris Professor of History emeritus at Columbia University, counters: "The 'reign of the judges,' as the Book of Mormon calls the period, was a far cry from the republican government Joseph Smith knew."[3] John L. Sorenson notes much continuity between the monarchy and the rule of the judges:

> The discourse on the subject of kingship delivered by King Mosiah II further points up features of the conventional system of kingly rule, with which he saw many problems. He mandated a change in the Nephite system of rule, providing for a chief judge whose powers were more limited than those of a king. However, in many ways the old customs and notions surrounding the king as head of government continued under the "new" system. For instance, judges too were considered "rulers," who not only "reigned" and sat on "thrones" but controlled the distribution of the government's resources obtained by tribute or taxation. The chief judge also led Nephite armies in battle.
>
> Moreover, while the modified system of rule under the judges the people are said to have "cast in their voices" to choose the judges who would "rule" them, this would not have been anything like a "one-man, one-vote" election but probably was an expression of preference by the senior males who led the various kin groups (lineages) who would have arrived at their decision by consultation within their groups and spoke for their unit.[4]

While the voice of the people plays a more prominent role after the establishment of the reign of the judges, it was nevertheless a functioning part of

---

[1]Anthony W. Ivins, *Conference Report*, Sunday afternoon, October 7, 1923, 146, on *GospeLink 2001*, CD-ROM (Salt Lake City: Deseret Book, 2000).

[2]J. Keith Melville, "Joseph Smith, the Constitution, and Individual Liberties," *BYU Studies* 28, no. 2 (Spring 1988): 65.

[3]Richard Lyman Bushman, "The Book of Mormon and the American Revolution," in *Book of Mormon Authorship: New Light on Ancient Origins*, edited by Noel B. Reynolds (Provo, Utah: BYU Religious Studies Center, 1982), 201.

[4]John L. Sorenson, *Nephite Culture and Society*, edited by Matthew R. Sorenson (Salt Lake City: New Sage Books, 1997), 202–3; internal references silently removed. Sorenson provides the following notes on the continuities: "See Alma 12:20 on a judge as 'a chief ruler' in the city of Ammonihah; Alma 35:5, 8, on 'rulers' among the Zoramites; Helaman 7:4–5, judges 'do according to their wills' and enrich themselves; Alma 60:1, 7, 11, 21, rulers 'sit upon your thrones'; Alma 1:2, judges 'reign,' the same term used regarding kings; Alma 2:16, and compare Words of Mormon 1:14, the chief judge leads his forces into battle as had the king; Alma 60:19, 34–35, control of tax resources."

the monarchial system. The earliest mention of the "voice of the people" being used in conjunction with a king is from Zeniff's story. Zeniff was the leader of those who eventually colonized the city of Lehi-Nephi. Limhi, in giving his genealogy, explains: "I am Limhi, the son of Noah, who was the son of Zeniff, who came up out of the land of Zarahemla . . . who was made a king by the *voice of the people*" (Mosiah 7:9; emphasis mine).

It might be possible to read this statement as Zeniff's "election" to kingship, since he apparently did not rule by lineal right, although his son, Noah, and grandson, Limhi, would. However, both Benjamin and Mosiah, who *did* rule by lineal right, also invoke this principle. Benjamin commented in his great public discourse: "But I am like as yourselves, subject to all manner of infirmities in body and mind; *yet I have been chosen by this people*, and consecrated by my father, and was suffered by the . . . Lord that I should be a ruler and a king . . . " (Mosiah 2:11; emphasis mine). Although Benjamin identifies the Lord as the ultimate source of his position, the proximate source is being chosen by the people.

The people's participation in transferring the kingship reappears in Mosiah's attempt to find a successor when his four sons opt for Lamanite missions instead of the throne: "Mosiah . . . sent out throughout all the land, among all the people, desiring to *know their will* concerning who should be their king. And . . . the *voice of the people came*, saying: We are desirous that Aaron thy son should be our king and our ruler" (Mosiah 29:1–2; emphasis mine).

Just as Benjamin was "chosen" by the people, Mosiah solicited the people's preference concerning which son should be the king. In most monarchies, the heir would have been undisputed. While these examples show that the voice of the people functioned in the most important political decision—the change of king—it was not confined to transferring political power. When Ammon and Limhi plan in the land of Lehi-Nephi how to escape Lamanite bondage, they "began to consult with the people . . . ; and even they did cause that all the people should gather themselves together; and this they did that they might have the *voice of the people* concerning the matter" (Mosiah 22:1; emphasis mine). And of course, the voice of the people was presumably mobilized on other decisions that would affect the entire community. The very fact that the voice of the people was functioning under the monarchy should alert us that it was not the same as modern voting or elections.

Just as the voice of the people functioned in installing a king, it was part of installing the judges, and presumably in the same way. During the reign of the judges, an official may have been appointed, or assumed his position by lineal right, but was still confirmed by the voice of the people. For instance, "Helaman, who was the son of Helaman, was appointed to fill the judgment-seat, by the voice of the people" (Hel. 2:2).

Note that $Helaman_2$ was "appointed," but still "inherited" his father's judgment-seat. The father-son lineage gave $Helaman_2$ a presumption of appointment. The people confirmed; they did not appoint. This was not an elected position. Even clearer was the case of Pacumeni: "Pacumeni was appointed, *according to the voice of the people*, to be a chief judge and a governor over the people, to reign in the stead of his brother Pahoran; and it was *according to his right*" (Hel. 1:13; emphasis mine). Thus, Pacumeni became chief judge both by lineal right and by the voice of the people.

A third example of this same conjunction of the voice of the people and an appointment in which they did not make the selection occurred when $Alma_2$ transferred the chief judgeship to Nephihah:

> And he selected a wise man who was among the elders of the church, and gave him power according to the voice of the people, that he might have power to enact laws according to the laws which had been given, and to put them in force according to the wickedness and the crimes of the people.
>
> Now this man's name was Nephihah, and he was appointed chief judge; and he sat in the judgment-seat to judge and to govern the people. (Alma 4:16–17)

In this case, $Alma_2$ apparently had and exercised the prerogative of appointing his successor. His authority to do so was "according to the voice of the people," although this passage contains no specific details of how they communicated that authority. Based on the evidence examined to this point, I suggest that, in transferring political power, the voice of the people functioned as confirmation rather than election.

Nevertheless, in the Book of Mormon record, the voice of the people was active even when there were disputes. Indeed, those disputes are valuable in giving us new insights into how the voice of the people functioned. For example, Pahoran's service as chief judge generated such a dispute:

> And those who were desirous that Pahoran should remain chief judge over the land took upon them the name of freemen; and thus was the division among them, for the freemen had sworn or covenanted to maintain their rights and the privileges of their religion by a free government.
>
> And it came to pass that this matter of their contention was settled by the voice of the people. And it came to pass that the voice of the people came in favor of the freemen, and Pahoran retained the judgment-seat, which caused much rejoicing among the brethren of Pahoran and also many of the people of liberty, who also put the king-men to silence, that they durst not oppose but were obliged to maintain the cause of freedom. (Alma 51:6–7)

Significantly, Pahoran was already sitting as the chief judge. The dispute was whether to retain (confirm) him. In this case, the voice of the people seems to have functioned something like a vote of confidence in a parliamentarian system.[5] If Pahoran had lost, he would have stepped down. Furthermore, the voice of the people had the power to quell (at least in this case) the opposing voice of the king-men.

This incident also reveals that the voice of the people was not only a representation of a statistical community voice; it was invoked in a general assembly. Similarly, Ammon and Limhi "did cause that all the people should gather themselves together; and this that they might have the voice of the people

[5]Donald Arthur Cazier, "A Study of Nephite, Lamanite, and Jaredite Governmental Institutions and Policies as Portrayed in the Book of Mormon" (M.A. thesis, Brigham Young University, 1972), 87, 103, suggests that the voice of the people functioned as a vote of no confidence under the monarchy but was a more democratic institution under the judges.

concerning the matter" (Mosiah 22:1). When it was impractical to physically gather the people together, then the leaders took the question to the people. This approach reaffirms the communal nature of the voice of the people. When possible, they would gather to take the entire community "voice" and when that was not possible, the "voice" of the community was still sought, presumably through representatives of the kin groups (Mosiah 29:1, where Mosiah sent "throughout all the land" for the people's voice on the next king, and Alma 27:21, when the chief judge sent a proclamation "throughout all the land" to obtain the voice of the people about arrangements for the people of Anti-Nephi-Lehi).

One case provides a little more information about how the "voice of the people" might actually function in decision-making:

> Now this was alarming to the people of the church, and also to all those who had not been drawn away after the persuasions of Amlici; for they knew that according to their law that such things must be established by the voice of the people.
>
> Therefore, if it were possible that Amlici should gain the voice of the people, he, being a wicked man, would deprive them of their rights and privileges of the church; for it was his intent to destroy the church of God.
>
> And it came to pass that the people assembled themselves together throughout all the land, every man according to his mind, whether it were for or against Amlici, in separate bodies, having much dispute and wonderful contentions one with another.
>
> And thus they did assemble themselves together to cast in their voices concerning the matter; and they were laid before the judges.
>
> And it came to pass that the voice of the people came against Amlici, that he was not made king over the people. (Alma 2:3–7)

This passage describes the people's assembling in groups, possibly several groups in several locations, and presumably at the village/town/hamlet level along kin-compound lines. The population was already too large to allow for a single assembly split into two. At each location, the two opposing bodies had "much dispute and wonderful contentions." While this division may possibly have been figurative and the debates individual rather than communal, I argue that we should read this verse literally and as collective and organized (though not necessarily orderly) debates. The "voice of the people" appears to quite literally be a group function, not a synonym for ballot-casting. I propose that these groups, probably of men only, created vocal and "wonderful" shouting matches from two points of a public space, then men moving from one group to another as they were persuaded by the arguments. As one group attained the majority, the collective "voice" would be manifest in their increasing numbers, while the opponents' numbers decreased. Therefore, the "vote" was determined for that village/town/hamlet.

Of course, this reconstruction is speculative, but the proposed details fit the descriptions. In some cases, contention may not have been a factor at all, as, for example, in confirming a seated king who already had the weight of lineage behind his selection. Mosiah's succession from Benjamin would be such an example. The process of how the voice of the people functioned, however, is best seen in contested cases. In all cases, it appears to be very different from modern voting.

Bibliography

"The Acoustics of Maya Temples," http://www.luckymojo.com/esoteric/interdisciplinary/architecture/ecclesiastical/mayanacoustics.html (accessed March 2007).

Allen, Joseph L. *Exploring the Lands of the Book of Mormon*. Orem, Utah: SA Publishers, 1989.

"Anales de Cuauhtitlan." In *Codice Chimalpopoca*. Edited by Primo Feliciano Velázquez. Mexico City: Universidad Nacional Autónoma de México, 1975.

Anderson, Arthur J. O., Frances Berdan, and James Lockhart. *Beyond the Codices: The Nahua View of Colonial Mexico*. Berkeley: University of California Press, 1976.

Annals of the Cakchiquels and Title of the Lords of Totonicapan, translated by Dionisio José Chonay and Delia Goetz. Norman: University of Oklahoma Press, 1974.

Barker, Margaret. *The Great Angel: A Study of Israel's Second God*. Louisville, Ky.: Westminster/John Knox, 1992.

"Barnabas." In *The Lost Books of the Bible and the Forgotten Books of Eden*. New York: World Publishing, 1973, 145–65.

Barnett, H. G. *Innovation: The Basis of Cultural Change*. New York: McGraw-Hill Book, 1953.

Barney, Kevin. "Translation Question on Isaiah 53:3." Posted on Scripture-L List, January 16, 2000.

Baron, Dennis. "From Pencils to Pixels: The Stages of Literacy Technology." http://www2.english.uiuc.edu/baron/pencils%20to%20pixels.htm (accessed January 2005).

Bassie, Karen. Unpublished, untitled manuscript 1999. Photocopy in my possession. Used by permission.

Berdan, Frances F., and Patricial Rieff Anawalt, eds. and trans. *The Essential Codex Mendoza*. Volumes 2 and 4 of the full edition, bound together. Berkeley: University of California Press, 1997.

Blenkinsopp, Joseph. *Isaiah 40–55*. THE ANCHOR BIBLE. New York: Doubleday, 2002.

Book of Mormon. 1830; rpt., Independence, Mo.: Herald House, 1970.

Book of Mormon Critical Text: A Tool for Scholarly Reference. 3 vols. Provo, Utah: Foundation for Ancient Research and Mormon Studies, 1987.

Brewster, Quinn. "The Structure of the Book of Mormon: A Theory of Evolutionary Development." *Dialogue: A Journal of Mormon Thought* 29, no. 2 (Summer 1996): 109–40.

Brockington, Donald L. *The Ceramic History of Santa Rosa, Chiapas, Mexico*. PAPERS OF THE NEW WORLD ARCHAEOLOGICAL FOUNDATION, No. 23. Provo, Utah: New World Archaeological Foundation, Brigham Young University, 1967.

Brown, Donald E. *Human Universals*. New York: McGraw-Hill, 1991.

Brown, Raymond E. *An Introduction to the New Testament*. New York: Doubleday, 1997.

Brown, S. Kent. *From Jerusalem to Zarahemla: Literary and Historical Studies of the Book of Mormon*. Provo, Utah: BYU Religious Studies Center, 1998.

Brown, S. Kent. "Nephi's Use of Lehi's Record." In *Rediscovering the Book of Mormon*. Edited by John L. Sorenson and Melvin J. Thorne. Provo, Utah: Foundation for Ancient Research and Mormon Studies, 1991, 3–14.

Bushman, Richard L. "The Book of Mormon and the American Revolution." In *Book of Mormon Authorship: New Light on Ancient Origins*. Edited by Noel B. Reynolds. Provo, Utah: BYU Religious Studies Center, 1982, 189–211.

Brundage, Burr Cartwright. *The Fifth Sun: Aztec Gods, Aztec World*. Austin: University of Texas Press, 1979.

Campbell, Lyle. *The Linguistics of Southeast Chiapas, Mexico*. PAPERS OF THE NEW WORLD ARCHAEOLOGICAL FOUNDATION, No. 50. Provo, Utah: New World Archaeological Foundation, Brigham Young University, 1988.

Campbell, Lyle. "Mesoamerican Linguistics." mimeograph, April 1976.

Campbell, Lyle. *Quichean Linguistic Prehistory*. UNIVERSITY OF CALIFORNIA PUBLICATIONS IN LINGUISTICS, No. 81. Berkeley: University of California Press, 1977.

Campbell, Lyle, and Terrence Kaufman. "A Linguistic Look at the Olmecs." *American Antiquity* 41, no. 1 (January 1976): 80–88.

Card, Orson Scott. "'The Book of Mormon: Artifact or Artifice?' Adapted from a speech given at the BYU Symposium on Life, the Universe, and Everything, February 1993." http://www.nauvoo.com/library/card-bookofmormon.html (accessed June 2004).

Cazier, Donald Arthur. "A Study of Nephite, Lamanite, and Jaredite Governmental Institutions and Policies as Portrayed in the Book of Mormon." M.A. thesis, Brigham Young University, 1972.

Chadwick, Jeffrey R. "Has the Seal of Mulek Been Found?" *Journal of Book of Mormon Studies* 12, no. 2 (2003): 72–83.

Christenson, Allen J. "Maya Harvest Festivals and the Book of Mormon." In *Review of Books on the Book of Mormon* 3 (1991): 1–31.

Clark, John E. "Archaeology, Relics, and Book of Mormon Belief." *Journal of Book of Mormon Studies* 14, no. 2 (2005): 38–49.

Clark, John E. "A Key for Evaluating Nephite Geographies." *Review of Books on the Book of Mormon* 1 (1989): 20–70.

Clifford, Richard J. "The Temple and the Holy Mountain." In *The Temple in Antiquity*. Edited by Truman G. Madsen. Provo, Utah: BYU Religious Studies Center, 1984, 107–24.

Coogan, Michael D. "Wine." In *The Oxford Companion to the Bible*. Edited by Bruce M. Metzger and Michael D. Coogan. New York: Oxford University Press, 1993, 799–800.

Coutts, Alison V. P., et al. "Complete Text of Benjamin's Speech with Notes and Comments." In *King Benjamin's Speech: "That Ye May Learn Wisdom."* Edited by John W. Welch and Stephen D. Ricks. Provo, Utah: FARMS, 1998, 479–623.

Cowgill, George L. "State and Society at Teotihuacan, Mexico." In *The Ancient Civilizations of Mesoamerica: A Reader*. Edited by Michael E. Smith and Marilyn A. Masson. Malden, Mass.: Blackwell Publishers, 2000, 300–323.

Cross, Frank Moore. *Canaanite Myth and Hebrew Epic: Essays in the History of the Religion of Israel*. Cambridge, Mass.: Harvard University Press, 1973.

Crossan, John Dominic. *The Birth of Christianity: Discovering What Happened in the Years Immediately after the Execution of Jesus*. San Francisco: HarperSanFrancisco, 1998.

Crossan, John Dominic. *The Essential Jesus: What Jesus Really Taught*. San Francisco: HarperSanFrancisco, 1995.

Davies, Nigel. *Voyagers to the New World*. New York: William Morrow and Company, 1979.

Delgado, Agustin. *Archaeological Research at Santa Rosa, Chiapas and in the Region of Tehuantepec*. PAPERS OF THE NEW WORLD ARCHAEOLOGICAL FOUNDATION, Nos. 17–18. Provo, Utah: New World Archaeological Foundation, Brigham Young University, 1965.

Dever, William G. *Did God Have a Wife? Archaeology and Folk Religion in Ancient Israel*. Grand Rapids, Mich.: William B. Eerdmans Publishing, 2005.

"Didaché." In *Early Christian Fathers*. Edited by Cyril C. Richardson. New York: Macmillan Publishing, 1970, 171–79.

Diehl, Richard A., and Michael D. Coe. "Olmec Archaeology." In *The Olmec World: Ritual and Rulership*. Princeton, N.J.: Princeton University Art Museum, 1996, 11–25.

Drew, David. *The Lost Chronicles of the Maya Kings*. Berkeley: University of California Press, 1999.

Edwards, Kay P. "The Kingdom of God and the Kingdoms of Men." In *1 Nephi to Alma 29*. Edited by Kent P. Jackson. STUDIES IN SCRIPTURE, Vol. 7. Salt Lake City: Deseret Book, 1987, 270–82.

Ehrman, Bart D. *Lost Christianities: The Battles for Scripture and the Faiths We Never Knew*. New York: Oxford University Press, 2003.

Eichrodt, Walter. *The Theology of the Old Testament*. Translated by J. A. Baker. 2 vols. Philadelphia: Westminster Press, 1967.

Eisenman, Robert, and Michael Wise. *The Dead Sea Scrolls Uncovered: The First Complete Translation and Interpretation of 50 Key Documents Withheld for Over 35 Years*. New York: Barnes and Noble, 1994.

Eliade, Mircea. *Patterns in Comparative Religions*. Translated by Rosemary Sheed. Chicago: Meridian, 1963.

Evans, Susan Toby. *Ancient Mexico and Central America: Archaeology and Culture History*. London: Thames & Hudson, 2004.

Faulring, Scott H., Kent P. Jackson, and Robert J. Matthews, eds. *Joseph Smith's New Translation of the Bible: Original Manuscripts*. Provo, Utah: BYU Religious Studies Center, 2004.

Fissel, Mark Charles. "Tradition and Invention in the Early Stuart Art of War." http://www.aug.edu/mfissel/tradition.htm (accessed January 2005).

Flannery, Kent V. "Two Possible Village Subdivisions: The Courtyard Group and the Residential Ward." In *The Early Mesoamerican Village*. Edited by Kent V. Flannery. New York: Academic Press, 1976, 72–75.

Foster, Lynne V. *Handbook to Life in the Ancient Maya World*. 2002. Rpt. in paperback, New York: Oxford University Press, 2005.

Fox, Everett. *The Five Books of Moses*. Vol. 1 of THE SCHOCKEN BIBLE. Translated by Everett Fox. New York: Schocken Books, 1995.

Frazer, James George. *The Golden Bough: A Study in Magic and Religion*, one-volume abridged edition. New York: Macmillan, 1963.

Freidel, David A. "Preparing the Way." In *The Olmec World. Ritual and Rulership*. Princeton, N.J.: Princeton University Art Museum, 1996, 3–9.

Freidel, David A., and Linda Schele. "Kingship in the Late Preclassic Maya Lowlands." In *The Ancient Civilizations of Mesoamerica*. Edited by Michael E. Smith and Marilyn A. Masson. Malden, Mass.: Blackwell Publishers, 2000, 422–30.

Freidel, David A., Linda Schele, and Joy Parker. *Maya Cosmos: Three Thousand Years on the Shaman's Path*. New York: William Morrow and Company, 1993.

Gardner, Brant A. "Quetzalcoatl and the Myth of the Return." http://frontpage2k.nmia.com/~nahualli/Quetzalcoatl/Elements/Return.htm (accessed March 2007).

Gardner, Brant A. "Reconstructing the Ethnohistory of Myth: A Structural Study of the Aztec 'Legend of the Suns.'" In *Symbol and Meaning beyond the Closed Community: Essays in Mesoamerican Ideas*. Edited by Gary Gossen. Albany: Institute for Mesoamerican Studies, State University of New York at Albany, 1986, 19–34.

Gardner, Brant A. "Scourging with Faggots." *Insights: A Window on the Ancient World* 21, no. 7 (2001): 2–3.

Gardner, Brant A. "A Structural and Semantic Analysis of Classical Nahuatl Kinship Terminology." *Estudios de Cultura Nahuatl* 15 (1982): 110–16.

Garibay K., Ángel María. *Historia de la Literatura Nahuatl*, 2 vols. Mexico City: Editorial Porrúa, S. A., 1971.

Gaskill, Alonzo L. *The Lost Language of Symbolism: An Essential Guide for Recognizing and Interpreting Symbols of the Gospel*. Salt Lake City: Deseret Book, 2003.

Gileadi, Avraham. *The Book of Isaiah: A New Translation with Interpretive Keys from the Book of Mormon*. Salt Lake City: Deseret Book, 1988.

Gillespie, Susan D. *The Aztec Kings: The Construction of Rulership in Mexica History*. Tucson: University of Arizona Press, 1989.

Goff, Alan. "The Stealing of the Daughters of the Lamanites." In *Rediscovering the Book of Mormon*. Edited by John L. Sorenson and Melvin J. Thorne. Provo, Utah: FARMS, 1991, 67–74.

Gossen, Gary. *Chamulas in the World of the Sun: Time and Space in a Maya Oral Tradition*. Cambridge, Mass.: Harvard University Press, 1974.

Gray, John. "The Book of Exodus." In *The Interpreter's One-Volume Commentary on the Bible*. Edited by Charles M. Laymon. Nashville, Tenn.: Abingdon Press, 1971, 33–67.

Grove, David C. *Chalcatzingo: Excavations on the Olmec Frontier*. London: Thames & Hudson, 1984.

Hafen, Bruce C. *The Broken Heart: Applying the Atonement to Life's Experiences*. Salt Lake City: Deseret Book, 1989.

Hamblin, William J. "Armor in the Book of Mormon." In *Warfare in the Book of Mormon*. Edited by Stephen D. Ricks and William J. Hamblin. Salt Lake City: Deseret Book/Provo, Utah: Foundation for Ancient Research and Mormon Studies, 1990, 400–24.

Hamblin, William J. "The Bow and Arrow in the Book of Mormon." In *Warfare in the Book of Mormon*. Edited by Stephen D. Ricks and William J. Hamblin. Salt Lake City: Deseret Book/Provo, Utah: Foundation for Ancient Research and Mormon Studies, 1990, 365–99.

Hamblin, William J. "Sacred Writings on Bronze Plates in the Ancient Mediterranean." FARMS Reprint Series. Provo, Utah: Foundation for Ancient Research and Mormon Studies, 1994.

Hamblin, William J., and A. Brent Merrill. "Notes on the Cimeter Scimitar in the Book of Mormon." In *Warfare in the Book of Mormon*. Edited by Stephen D. Ricks and William J. Hamblin. Salt Lake City: Deseret Book/Provo, Utah: Foundation for Ancient Research and Mormon Studies, 1990, 360–64.

Hammond, Norman. "Inside the Black Box: Defining Maya Polity." In *Classic Maya Political History: Hieroglyphic and Archaeological Evidence*. Edited by T. Patrick Culbert. Cambridge, Eng.: Cambridge University Press, 1991, 253–84.

Hassig, Ross. *Aztec Warfare: Imperial Expansion and Political Control*. Norman: University of Oklahoma Press, 1988.

Hauck, F. Richard. *Deciphering the Geography of the Book of Mormon: Settlements and Routes in Ancient America*. Salt Lake City: Deseret Book, 1988.

Haviland, William A., and Hattula Moholy-Nagy. "Distinguishing the High and Mighty from the Hoi Polloi at Tikal, Guatemala." In *The Ancient Civilizations of Mesoamerica*. Edited by Michael E. Smith and Marilyn A. Masson. Malden, Mass.: Blackwell Publishers, 2000, 39–48.

[No author identified], "Hebrew Tenses." http://www.iclnet.org/pub/resources/text/m.sion/hebrtens.htm (accessed March 2007).

Hedges, Andrew H. "Urim and Thummim." In *Book of Mormon Reference Companion*. Edited by Dennis L. Largey. Salt Lake City: Deseret Book, 2003, 773–74.

Hedrick, Basil Calvin. "Quetzalcoatl: European or Indigene?" In *Man across the Sea: Problems of Pre-Columbian Contacts*. Edited by Carroll L. Riley, J. Charles Kelley, Campbell W. Pennington, and Robert L. Rands. Austin: University of Texas Press, 1971, 255–65.

Henderson, John S. *The World of the Ancient Maya*. 2nd ed. Ithaca, N.Y.: Cornell University Press, 1997.

Holzapfel, Richard Neitzel. "King Herod." In *Masada and the World of the New Testament*. Edited by John F. Hall and John W. Welch. Provo, Utah: BYU Studies, 1997, 35–73.

Horn, Siegfried H. "The Divided Monarchy: The Kingdoms of Judah and Israel." In *Ancient Israel*. Edited by Hershel Shanks, Washington, D.C.: Biblical Archaeology Society, 1998, 109–49.

Horsley, Richard A., and Neil Asher Silberman. *The Message and the Kingdom: How Jesus and Paul Ignited a Revolution and Transformed the Ancient World*. New York: Grosset/Putnam, 1997.

Ivins, Anthony W. *Conference Report,* October 7 1923, 139–48. Retrieved from *GospeLink 2001*. CD-ROM. Salt Lake City: Deseret Book, 2000.

Jackson, Kent P., and Morgan W. Tanner. "Zeniff and Noah." In *1 Nephi to Alma 29*. Edited by Kent P. Jackson. STUDIES IN SCRIPTURE, Vol. 7. Salt Lake City: Deseret Book, 1987, 230–39.

Justeson, John, and Terrence Kaufman. "Un descriframiento de la escritura jeroglifica epi-olmeca: metodos y resultados." *Archaeología* (July–December 1992): 15–25.

Largey, Dennis L. "Lessons from the Zarahemla Churches." In *The Book of Mormon: Mosiah, Salvation Only through Christ*. Edited by Monte S. Nyman and Charles D. Tate Jr. Provo, Utah: BYU Religious Studies Center, 1991, 59–71.

Lederer, Richard. *The Miracle of Language*. New York: Pocket Books, 1991.

Leith, Mary Joan Winn. "Wisdom." In *The Oxford Companion to the Bible*. Edited by Bruce M. Metzger and Michael D. Coogan. New York: Oxford University Press, 1993, 800–801.

Lentz, David L. "Plant Resources of the Ancient Maya: The Paleoethnobotanical Evidence." In *Reconstructing Ancient Maya Diet*. Edited by Christine D. White. Salt Lake City: University of Utah Press, 1999, 3–18.

Ludlow, Victor L. *Isaiah: Prophet, Seer, and Poet*. Salt Lake City: Deseret Book, 1982.

Ludlow, Victor L. "Scribes and Scriptures." In *1 Nephi to Alma 29*. Edited by Kent P. Jackson. STUDIES IN SCRIPTURE, Vol. 7. Salt Lake City: Deseret Book, 1987, 196–204.

Lundquist, John M. "The Common Temple Ideology of the Ancient Near East." In *The Temple in Antiquity*. Edited by Truman G. Madsen. Provo, Utah: BYU Religious Studies Center, 1984, 53–76.

Mackay, Thomas W. "Mormon as Editor: A Study in Colophons, Headers, and Source Indicators." *Journal of Book of Mormon Studies* 2, no. 1 (Fall 1993): 90–109.

Madsen, Truman G. "'Putting On the Names': A Jewish-Christian Legacy." In *By Study and Also by Faith: Essays in Honor of Hugh W. Nibley on the Occasion of His Eightieth Birthday, 27 March 1990*. Edited by John M. Lundquist and Stephen D. Ricks. 2 vols. Salt Lake City: Deseret Book/Provo, Utah: Foundation for Ancient Research and Mormon Studies, 1990, 1:458–81.

Malina, Bruce J. The *New Testament World: Insights from Cultural Anthropology*. Atlanta, Ga.: John Knox Press, 1981.

Malina, Bruce J., and Richard L. Rohrbaugh. *Social-Science Commentary on the Gospel of John*. Minneapolis, Minn.: Fortune Press, 1998.

Marcus, Joyce. *Mesoamerican Writing Systems: Propaganda, Myth, and History in Four Ancient Civilizations*. Princeton, N.J.: Princeton University Press, 1992.

Martin, Simon. "Under a Deadly Star: Warfare among the Classic Maya." In *Maya: Divine Kings of the Rain Forest*. Edited by Nikolai Grube. Cologne, Ger.: Könemann, 2001, 174–85.

Martin, Simon, and Nikolai Grube. *Chronicle of the Maya Kings and Queens*. London: Thames & Hudson, 2000.

Matthews, Robert J. "Abinadi." In *Book of Mormon Reference Companion*. Edited by Dennis L. Largey. Salt Lake City: Deseret Book, 2003, 22–24.

Mauss, Armand L. *All Abraham's Children: Changing Mormon Conceptions of Race and Lineage*. Urbana: University of Illinois Press, 2003.

"Maya Vase Database." http://www.famsi.org/research/kerr/index.html (accessed March 2005).

McAfee, Gene. "Sex." In *The Oxford Companion to the Bible*. Edited by Bruce M. Metzger and Michael D. Coogan. New York: Oxford University Press, 1993, 690–92.

McConkie, Joseph Fielding, and Robert L. Millet. *Doctrinal Commentary on the Book of Mormon*. 4 vols. Salt Lake City: Bookcraft, 1987–92.

McGuire, Benjamin. "Polygamy in the Book of Mormon, Outside Jacob 2." Post to FAIR Message board, August 8, 2005. http://www.mormonapologetics.org/index.php?showtopic=9536&st=15 (accessed August, 2005).

Melville, J. Keith. "Joseph Smith, the Constitution, and Individual Liberties." *BYU Studies* 28, no. 2 (Spring 1988): 65–74.

Merrill, Byron R. "Government by the Voice of the People: A Witness and a Warning." In *The Book of Mormon: Mosiah: Salvation Only through Christ*. Edited by Monte S. Nyman and Charles D. Tate Jr. Provo, Utah: BYU Religious Studies Center, 1991, 113–37.

"Mesoamerican Relic Provides New Clues to Mysterious Ancient Writing System." Press Release, Brigham Young University. http://byunews.byu.edu/release.aspx?story=archive04/Jan/Isthmian (accessed November 2006).

Miller, Arthur G. "Introduction to the Dover Edition." In *Codex Nuttall*. Edited by Zelia Nuttall. New York: Dover Publications, 1975, vii–xviii.

Miller, Mary, and Karl Taube. *An Illustrated Dictionary of the Gods and Symbols of Ancient Mexico and the Maya*. London: Thames and Hudson, 1993.

Montgomery, John. *Dictionary of Maya Hieroglyphs*. New York: Hippocrene Books, 2002.

Morley, Sylvanus G. *The Ancient Maya*. Stanford, Calif.: Stanford University Press, 1956.

Murphy, Thomas W. "Laban's Ghost: On Writing and Transgression." *Dialogue: A Journal of Mormon Thought* 30, no. 2 (Summer 1997): 105–26.

Nibley, Hugh. *An Approach to the Book of Mormon*. Salt Lake City: Church of Jesus Christ of Latter-day Saints, 1957.

Nibley, Hugh. *The Prophetic Book of Mormon*. Vol. 8 of THE COLLECTED WORKS OF HUGH NIBLEY. Salt Lake City: Deseret Book/Provo, Utah: Foundation for Ancient Research and Mormon Studies, 1989.

Nibley, Hugh. *Teachings of the Book of Mormon—Semester 1: Transcripts of Lectures Presented to an Honors Book of Mormon Class at Brigham Young University, 1988–1990*. Provo, Utah: Foundation for Ancient Research and Mormon Studies, 1993.

Nicholson, Henry B. *Topiltzin Quetzalcoatl: The Once and Future Lord of the Toltecs*. Boulder: University Press of Colorado, 2001.

Norman, V. Garth. *Izapa Sculpture. Part 1: Plates*. PAPERS OF THE NEW WORLD ARCHAEOLOGICAL FOUNDATION, No. 30. Provo, Utah: New World Archaeological Foundation, Brigham Young University, 1976.

Norton, Don. "A Reader's Library." *Journal of Book of Mormon Studies* 13, nos. 1–2 (2004): 161–63.

Norwood, L. Ara. "Benjamin or Mosiah? Resolving an Anomaly in Mosiah 21:28." http://www.fairlds.org/FAIR_Conferences/2001_Benjamin_or_Mosiah.html (accessed June 2007).

Palmer, David. *In Search of Cumorah: New Evidences for the Book of Mormon from Ancient Mexico*. Bountiful, Utah: Horizon, 1981.

Parry, Donald W. "Hebraisms and Other Ancient Peculiarities in the Book of Mormon." In *Echoes and Evidences of the Book of Mormon*. Edited by Donald W. Parry, Daniel C. Peterson, and John W. Welch. Provo, Utah: Foundation for Ancient Research and Mormon Studies (FARMS), 2002, 155–89.

Peterson, Daniel C. "Authority in the Book of Mosiah." *FARMS Review* 18, no. 1 (2006): 149–85.

Peterson, Daniel C. "Priesthood in Mosiah." In *The Book of Mormon: Mosiah, Salvation Only through Christ*. Edited by Monte S. Nyman and Charles D. Tate Jr. Provo, Utah: BYU Religious Studies Center, 1991, 187–210.

Peterson, H. Donl. "Church Discipline in the Book of Mosiah." In *The Book of Mormon: Mosiah, Salvation Only through Christ*. Edited by Monte S. Nyman and Charles D. Tate Jr. Provo, Utah: BYU Religious Studies Center, 1991, 211–26.

Phillips, William Revell. "Metals of the Book of Mormon." *Journal of Book of Mormon Studies* 9, no. 2 (2000): 36–43.

Pires-Ferreira, Jane W. "Obsidian Exchange in Formative Mesoamerica." In *The Early American Village*. Edited by Kent V. Flannery. New York: Academic Press, 1976, 292–306.

Pohl, John M. D. "The Four Priests: Political Stability." In *The Ancient Civilizations of Mesoamerica: A Reader*. Edited by Michael E. Smith and Marilyn A. Masson. Malden, Mass.: Blackwell Publishers, 2000, 342–59.

Porter, Bruce H., and Stephen D. Ricks. "Names in Antiquity: Old, New, and Hidden." In *By Study and Also by Faith: Essays in Honor of Hugh W. Nibley on the Occasion of His Eightieth Birthday, 27 March 1990*. Edited by John M. Lundquist and Stephen D. Ricks. 2 vols. Salt Lake City: Deseret Book/Provo, Utah: Foundation for Ancient Research and Mormon Studies, 1990, 1:501–22.

Preface. *Book of Mormon*. 1830 Facsimile Edition. Independence, Mo.: Herald House, 1970.

Radcliffe-Brown, A. R. *Structure and Function in a Primitive Society*. New York: Free Press, 1968.

Readings in L.D.S. Church History from the Original Manuscripts: A Selection of and Extracts from Letters, Editorials, Private Journals, Records, Periodicals, Histories, Biographies and Other Original Writings Contemporary with and Casting Light upon Early Events in the Church of Jesus Christ of Latter-day Saints. Edited by William E. Berrett and Alma P. Burton. 3 vols. Salt Lake City: Deseret Book, 1967.

Reents-Budet, Dorie. *Painting the Maya Universe: Royal Ceramics of the Classic Period*. Durham, N.C.: Duke University Press, 1994.

Reynolds, George, and Janne M. Sjodahl. *Commentary on the Book of Mormon*. Edited and arranged by Philip C. Reynolds. 7 vols. Salt Lake City: Deseret Book, 1955–61.

Ricks, Eldin. "The Small Plates of Nephi and the Words of Mormon." In *The Book of Mormon: Jacob through Words of Mormon, To Learn With Joy*. Edited by Monte S. Nyman and Charles D. Tate Jr. Provo, Utah: BYU Religious Studies Center, 1990, 209–19.

Ricks, Stephen D. "Kingship, Coronation, and Covenant in Mosiah 1–6." In *King Benjamin's Speech*. Edited by John W. Welch and Stephen D. Ricks. Provo, Utah: FARMS, 1998, 233–75.

Roberts, Brigham H. *A Comprehensive History of the Church*. 6 vols. 1930. Rpt., Provo, Utah: Brigham Young University Press, 1965.

Robinson, H. Wheeler. *Inspiration and Revelation in the Old Testament*. Oxford, Eng.: Clarendon Press, 1946.

Rodríguez, Ángel Miguel. "The Place for Applause." http://biblicalresearch.gc.adventist.org/Biblequestions/applause.htm (accessed February 2005).

Sahagún, Bernardino de. *Codices Matritenses*. Holograph Fol. 84r/v. Library of the Royal Palace of the Academy of History, Madrid, Spain. Microfilm in my possession.

Sanders, William T. *Ceramic Stratigraphy at Santa Cruz, Chiapas, Mexico*. PAPERS OF THE NEW WORLD ARCHAEOLOGICAL FOUNDATION, No. 13. Provo, Utah: New World Archaeological Foundation, Brigham Young University, 1961.

Schele, Linda, and David Freidel. *A Forest of Kings: The Untold Story of the Ancient Maya*. New York: William Morrow and Company, 1990.

Schele, Linda, and Peter Mathews. *The Code of Kings: The Language of Seven Sacred Maya Temples and Tombs*. New York: Scribner, 1998.

Schele, Linda, and Mary Ellen Miller. *The Blood of Kings: Dynasty and Ritual in Maya Art*. New York: George Braziller, 1986.

Schiffman, Lawrence H. *From Text to Tradition: A History of Second Temple and Rabbinic Judaism*. Hoboken, N.J.: KTAV Publishing House, 1991.

Schiffman, Lawrence H. *Reclaiming the Dead Sea Scrolls*. New York: Doubleday, 1995.

Schowalter, Daniel N. "Church." In *The Oxford Companion to the Bible*. Edited by Bruce M. Metzger and Michael D. Coogan. New York: Oxford University Press, 1993, 121–22.

"Sefer Torah," *Wikipedia: The Free Encyclopedia*, http://en.wikipedia.org/wiki/Torah_scroll (accessed August 2005).

Sharer, Robert J. "Diversity and Continuity in Maya Civilization." In *Classic Maya Political History: Hieroglyphic and Archaeological Evidence*. Edited by T. Patrick Culbert. Cambridge, Eng.: Cambridge University Press, 1991, 180–98.

Skousen, Royal. *Analysis of Textual Variants of the Book of Mormon*. THE CRITICAL TEXT OF THE BOOK OF MORMON, Vol. 4, 3+ parts. Provo, Utah: Foundation for Ancient Research and Mormon Studies, 2004–06.

Skousen, Royal. "Conjectural Emendation in the Book of Mormon." *FARMS Review* 18, no. 1 (2006): 187–231.

Skousen, Royal. "Critical Methodology and the Text of the Book of Mormon." *Review of Books on the Book of Mormon* 6, no. 1 (1994): 121–44.

Skousen, Royal. "How Joseph Smith Translated the Book of Mormon: Evidence from the Original Manuscript." *Journal of Book of Mormon Studies* 7, no. 1 (1998): 22–31.

Skousen, Royal, ed. *The Original Manuscript of the Book of Mormon*. THE CRITICAL TEXT OF THE BOOK OF MORMON, Vol. 1. Provo, Utah: Foundation for Ancient Research and Mormon Studies, 2001.

Skousen, Royal, ed. *The Printer's Manuscript of the Book of Mormon*. THE CRITICAL TEXT OF THE BOOK OF MORMON, Vol. 2, 2 parts. Provo, Utah: Foundation for Ancient Research and Mormon Studies, 2001.

Skousen, Royal. "'Scourged' vs. 'Scorched' in Mosiah 17:13." *Insights: A Window on the Ancient World* 22, no. 3 (2002): 2–3.

Smith, Joseph, et al., *History of the Church of Jesus Christ of Latter-day Saints*. Edited by B. H. Roberts, 2nd ed. rev. Vols. 1–6, 1902–12; Vol. 7, 1932. Salt Lake City: Deseret Book, 1973 printing.

Smith, Joseph Fielding. *Answers to Gospel Questions*, 5 vols. Salt Lake City: Deseret Book, 1957–66.

Smith, Joseph Fielding. *Doctrines of Salvation*. 3 vols. Salt Lake City: Bookcraft, 1977.

Smith, Joseph Fielding. "Your Question." *Improvement Era* 57, no. 6 (June 1954): page not indicated. Retrieved from *GospeLink 2001*. CD-ROM. Salt Lake City: Deseret Book, 2000.

Smith, William. *Smith's Bible Dictionary*. Old Tappan, N.J.: Fleming H. Revell, 1970.

Snow, Erastus. May 6, 1882. *Journal of Discourses*. 26 vols. Liverpool and London: Latter-day Saints' Book Depot, 1854–86, 23:181–89.

Sorenson, John L. *An Ancient American Setting for the Book of Mormon*. Salt Lake City: Deseret Book/Provo, Utah: Foundation for Ancient Research and Mormon Studies, 1985.

Sorenson, John L. "Ancient Voyages across the Ocean to America, from 'Impossible' to 'Certain.'" *Journal of Book of Mormon Studies* 14, no. 1 (2005): 7–16.

Sorenson, John L. "Fortifications in the Book of Mormon Account Compared with Mesoamerican Fortifications." In *Warfare in the Book of Mormon*. Edited by Stephen D. Ricks and William J. Hamblin. Salt Lake City: Deseret Book/Provo, Utah: Foundation for Ancient Research and Mormon Studies, 1990, 425–44.

Sorenson, John. L. *Images of Ancient America: Visualizing the Book of Mormon*. Provo, Utah: Foundation for Ancient Research and Mormon Studies, 1998.

Sorenson, John L. *Mormon's Map*. Provo, Utah: Foundation for Ancient Research and Mormon Studies, 2000.

Sorenson, John L. *Nephite Culture and Society*. Edited by Matthew R. Sorenson. Salt Lake City: New Sage Books, 1997.

Sorenson, John L. "Was Mulek a 'Blood Son' of King Zedekiah?" *Insights: A Window on the Ancient World* 19, no. 2 (1999): 2.

Sorenson, John L., and Carl L. Johannessen. "Biological Evidence for Pre-Columbian Transoceanic Voyages." In *Contact and Exchange in the Ancient World*. Edited by Victor H. Mair. Honolulu: University of Hawai'i Press, 2006, 238–97.

Soustelle, Jacques. *The Daily Life of the Aztecs on the Eve of the Spanish Conquest*. Stanford, Calif.: Stanford University Press, 1961.

Spackman, Randall P. "Introduction to Book of Mormon Chronology." FARMS Reprint Series. Provo, Utah: Foundation for Ancient Research and Mormon Studies, 1993.

Sperry, Sidney B. *Book of Mormon Compendium*. Salt Lake City: Bookcraft, 1968.

Sperry, Sidney B. *The Problems of the Book of Mormon*. Salt Lake City: Bookcraft, 1964.

Spykerboer, Hendrik C. "Urim and Thummim." In *The Oxford Companion to the Bible*. Edited by Bruce M. Metzger and Michael D. Coogan. New York: Oxford University Press, 1993, 786–87.

Stegemann, Ekkehard W., and Wolfgang Stegemann, *The Jesus Movement: A Social History of Its First Century*. Translated by O. C. Dean Jr. Minneapolis, Minn.: Fortress Press, 1999.

Stuart, David. "'The Arrival of Strangers': Teotihuacan and Tollan in Classic Maya History." In *Mesoamerica's Classic Heritage: From Teotihuacan to the Aztecs*. Edited by David Carrasco, Lindsay Jones, and Scott Sessions. Boulder: University Press of Colorado, 2000, 465–513.

Stuart, George E., and Gene S. Stuart. *The Mysterious Maya*. Washington, D.C.: National Geographic Society, 1977.

Sugiyama, Saburo. "Rulership, Warfare, and Human Sacrifice at the Ciudadela: An Iconographic Study of Feathered Serpent Representations." In *Art, Ideology, and the City of Teotihuacán*. Edited by Janet Catherine Berlo. Washington, D.C.: Dumbarton Oaks Research Library and Collection, 1992, 205–30.

Sugiyama, Saburo. "Teotihuacan as an Origin for Postclassic Feathered Serpent Symbolism." In *Mesoamerica's Classic Heritage: From Teotihuacan to the Aztecs*. Edited by David Carrasco, Lindsay Jones, and Scott Sessions. Boulder: University Press of Colorado, 2000, 117–43.

Tabor, James D. *The Jesus Dynasty: The Hidden History of Jesus, His Royal Family, and the Birth of Christianity*. New York: Simon & Schuster, 2006.

Tanner, John S. "Jacob and His Descendants as Authors." In *Rediscovering the Book of Mormon*. Edited by John L. Sorenson and Melvin J. Thorne. Provo, Utah: Foundation for Ancient Research and Mormon Studies, 1991, 52–66.

Taylor, Joan E. *The Immerser: John the Baptist within Second Temple Judaism*. Grand Rapids, Mich.: William B. Eerdmans Publishing, 1997.

Taube, Karl A. "The Rainmakers: The Olmec and Their Contribution to Mesoamerican Belief and Ritual." In *The Olmec World: Ritual and Rulership*. Princeton, N.J.: Princeton University Art Museum, 1996, 83–103.

Taube, Karl A. "The Turquoise Hearth: Fire, Self Sacrifice, and the Central Mexican Cult of War." In *Mesoamerica's Classic Heritage: From Teotihuacan to the Aztecs*. Edited by David Carrasco, Lindsay Jones, and Scott Sessions. Boulder: University Press of Colorado, 2000. 269–340.

Tedlock, Dennis, trans. *Popol Vuh: The Definitive Edition of the Mayan Book of the Dawn of Life and the Glories of Gods and Kings*. New York: Simon and Schuster, 1985.

"Title of the Lords of Totonicapan." In *Annals of the Cakchiquels and Title of the Lords of Totonicapan*. Translated by Adrian Recinos and Delia Goetz. Norman: University of Oklahoma Press, 1974, 161–96.

Turner, Rodney. "Two Prophets: Abinadi and Alma." In *1 Nephi to Alma 29*. Edited by Kent P. Jackson. STUDIES IN SCRIPTURE, Vol. 7. Salt Lake City: Deseret Book, 1987, 240–59.

Tvedtnes, John A. "As a Garment in a Hot Furnace." In *Pressing Forward with the Book of Mormon*. Edited by John W. Welch and Melvin J. Thorne. Provo, Utah: FARMS, 1999, 127–31.

Tevdtnes, John A. "Book of Mormon Tribal Affiliation and Military Castes." In *Warfare in the Book of Mormon*. Edited by Stephen D. Ricks and William J. Hamblin. Salt Lake City: Deseret Book/Provo, Utah: Foundation for Ancient Research and Mormon Studies, 1990, 296–326.

Tvedtnes, John A. "Isaiah Textual Variants in the Book of Mormon." FARMS Reprint Series, 1981.

Tvedtnes, John A. *The Most Correct Book: Insights from a Book of Mormon Scholar*. Salt Lake City: Cornerstone Publishing, 1999.

Van den Heuvel, Curt. "The Book of Mormon and the King James Version." http://www.infidels.org/library/modern/curt_heuvel/bom_kjv.html (accessed January 2005).

Van Wagoner, Richard S., and Steve Walker. "Joseph Smith: 'The Gift of Seeing.'" *Dialogue: A Journal of Mormon Thought* 15, no. 2 (Summer 1982): 49–68.

Vermes, Geza. *The Dead Sea Scrolls in English*. New York: Penguin Books, 1975.

Washburn, J. N. *Book of Mormon Guidebook and Certain Problems in the Book of Mormon*. Bound in one volume. Self-published, 1968.

Weaver, Muriel Porter. *The Aztecs, Maya, and Their Predecessors: Archaeology of Mesoamerica*. New York: Seminar Press, 1972.

Webster, David. *The Fall of the Ancient Maya: Solving the Mystery of the Maya Collapse*. London: Thames & Hudson, 2002.

Webster, Noah. *An American Dictionary of the English Language*. 1828. *GospeLink 2001*. CD-ROM. Salt Lake City: Deseret Book, 2000.

Welch, John W. "Benjamin, the Man: His Place in Nephite History." In *King Benjamin's Speech*. Edited by John W. Welch and Stephen D. Ricks. Provo, Utah: FARMS, 1998, 23–54.

Welch, John W. "Benjamin's Speech: A Masterful Oration." In *King Benjamin's Speech*. Edited by John W. Welch and Stephen D. Ricks. Provo, Utah: FARMS, 1998, 55–88.

Welch, John W. "Isaiah 53, Mosiah 14, and the Book of Mormon." In *Isaiah in the Book of Mormon*. Edited by Donald W. Parry and John W. Welch. Provo, Utah: FARMS, 1998, 293–312.

Welch, John W. "Parallelism and Chiasmus in Benjamin's Speech." In *King Benjamin's Speech*. Edited by John W. Welch and Stephen D. Ricks. Provo, Utah: FARMS, 1998, 315–410.

Welch, John W. "Three Accounts of Alma's Conversion." In *Reexploring the Book of Mormon*. Edited by John W. Welch. Provo, Utah: FARMS, 1992, 150–53.

Welch, John W., Donald W. Parry, and Stephen D. Ricks. "This Day." In *Reexploring the Book of Mormon*. Edited by John W. Welch. Provo, Utah: FARMS, 1992, 117–19.

Welch, John W., and Tim Rathbone. "The Translation of the Book of Mormon: Preliminary Report on the Basic Historical Information." FARMS Reprint Series. Provo, Utah: Foundation for Ancient Research and Mormon Studies, 1986.

Welch, John W., Robert F. Smith, and Gordon C. Thomasson. "Dancing Maidens and the Fifteenth of Av." In *Reexploring the Book of Mormon*. Edited by John W. Welch. Provo, Utah: FARMS, 1992, 139–41.

Westermann, Claus. *Isaiah 40–66*. Philadelphia: Westminster Press, 1969.

Whiting, Gary R. "The Testimony of Amaleki." In *The Book of Mormon: Jacob through Words of Mormon, To Learn with Joy*. Edited by Monte S. Nyman and Charles D. Tate Jr. Provo, Utah: BYU Religious Studies Center, 1990, 295–306.

Wichmann, Søren. *The Relationship among the Mixe-Zoquean Languages of Mexico*. Salt Lake City: University of Utah Press, 1995.

Widengren, Geo. *The King and the Tree of Life in Ancient Near Eastern Religion*. Uppsala, Sweden: A.-B. Lundequistska Bokhandeln, 1951.

Williams, Clyde James. "Nephi[4]." In *Book of Mormon Reference Companion*. Edited by Dennis L. Largey. Salt Lake City: Deseret Book, 2003, 589.

Wirth, Diane E., and Steven L. Olsen. "Four Quarters." In *Reexploring the Book of Mormon*. Edited by John W. Welch. Provo, Utah: FARMS, 1992, 145–49.

Wise, Michael, Martin Abegg Jr., and Edward Cook. *The Dead Sea Scrolls: A New Translation*. San Francisco: HarperSanFrancisco, 1996.

Zorita, Alonso de. *Life and Labor in Ancient Mexico City: The Brief and Summary Relation of the Lords of New Spain*. Translated by Benjamin Keen. Norman: University of Oklahoma Press, 1963.

Index

See Volume 6 for the series index.

B

C

D

E

I

L

N

O

S

U

V

W

X–Y

Z

Also available from

GREG KOFFORD BOOKS

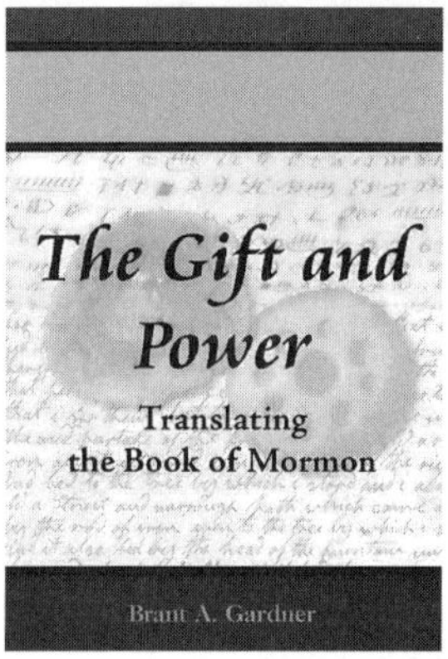

The Gift and Power: Translating the Book of Mormon

Brant A. Gardner

Hardcover, ISBN: 978-1-58958-131-9

From Brant A. Gardner, the author of the highly praised *Second Witness* commentaries on the Book of Mormon, comes *The Gift and Power: Translating the Book of Mormon*. In this first book-length treatment of the translation process, Gardner closely examines the accounts surrounding Joseph Smith's translation of the Book of Mormon to answer a wide spectrum of questions about the process, including: Did the Prophet use seerstones common to folk magicians of his time? How did he use them? And, what is the relationship to the golden plates and the printed text?

Approaching the topic in three sections, part 1 examines the stories told about Joseph, folk magic, and the translation. Part 2 examines the available evidence to determine how closely the English text replicates the original plate text. And part 3 seeks to explain how seer stones worked, why they no longer work, and how Joseph Smith could have produced a translation with them.

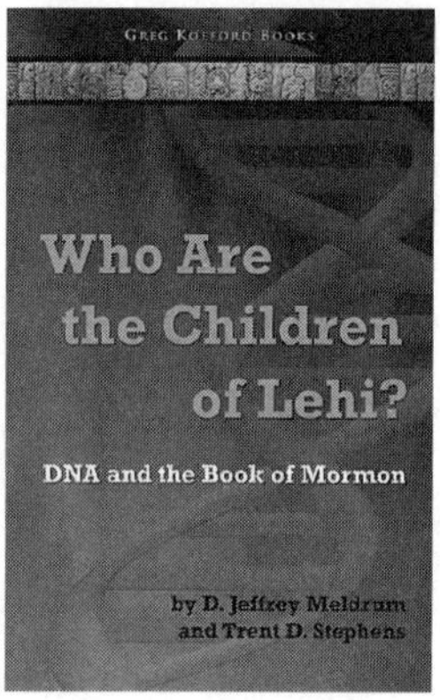

Who Are the Children of Lehi? DNA and the Book of Mormon

D. Jeffrey Meldrum
and Trent D. Stephens

Hardcover, ISBN: 978-1-58958-048-0
Paperback, ISBN: 978-1-58958-129-6

How does the Book of Mormon, keystone of the LDS faith, stand up to data about DNA sequencing that puts the ancestors of modern Native Americans in northeast Asia instead of Palestine?

In *Who Are the Children of Lehi?* Meldrum and Stephens examine the merits and the fallacies of DNA-based interpretations that challenge the Book of Mormon's historicity. They provide clear guides to the science, summarize the studies, illuminate technical points with easy-to-grasp examples, and spell out the data's implications.

The results? There is no straight-line conclusion between DNA evidence and "Lamanites." The Book of Mormon's validity lies beyond the purview of scientific empiricism—as it always has. And finally, inspiringly, they affirm Lehi's kinship as one of covenant, not genes.

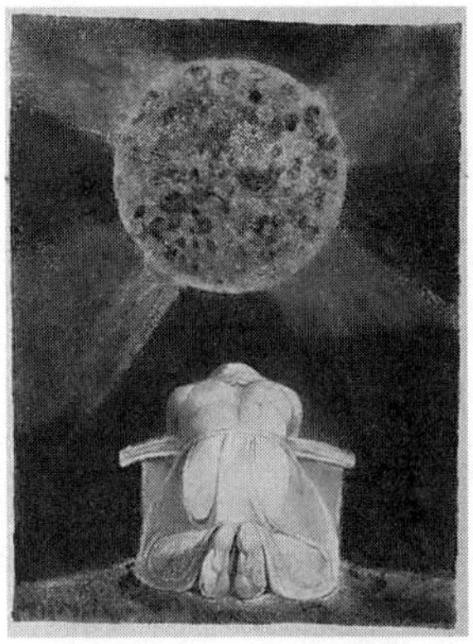

Perspectives on Mormon Theology Series

Brian D. Birch and Loyd Ericson,
series editors

(forthcoming)

This series will feature multiple volumes published on particular theological topics of interest in Latter-day Saint thought. Volumes will be co-edited by leading scholars and graduate students whose interests and knowledge will ensure that the essays in each volume represent quality scholarship and acknowledge the diversity of thought found and expressed in Mormon theological studies. Topics for the first few volumes include: revelation, apostasy, atonement, scripture, and grace.

The *Perspectives on Mormon Theology* series will bring together the best of new and previously published essays on various theological subjects. Each volume will be both a valued resource for academics in Mormon Studies and an illuminating introduction to the broad and sophisticated approaches to Mormon theology.

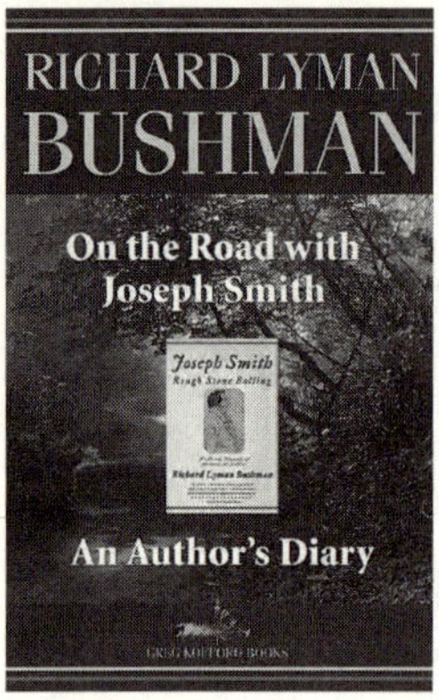

On the Road with Joseph Smith: An Author's Diary

Richard L. Bushman

Paperback, ISBN 978-1-58958-102-9

After living with Joseph Smith for seven years and delivering the final proofs of his landmark study, *Joseph Smith: Rough Stone Rolling* to Knopf in July 2005, biographer Richard Lyman Bushman went "on the road" for a year, crisscrossing the country from coast to coast, delivering addresses on Joseph Smith and attending book-signings for the new biography.

Bushman confesses to hope and humility as he awaits reviews. He frets at the polarization that dismissed the book as either too hard on Joseph Smith or too easy. He yields to a very human compulsion to check sales figures on Amazon.com, but partway through the process stepped back with the recognition, "The book seems to be cutting its own path now, just as [I] hoped."

For readers coming to grips with the ongoing puzzle of the Prophet and the troublesome dimensions of their own faith, Richard Bushman, openly but not insistently presents himself as a believer. "I believe enough to take Joseph Smith seriously," he says. He draws comfort both from what he calls his "mantra" ("Today I will be a follower of Jesus Christ") and also from ongoing engagement with the intellectual challenges of explaining Joseph Smith.

Praise for *On the Road With Joseph Smith*:

"The diary is possibly unparalleled—an author of a recent book candidly dissecting his experiences with both Mormon and non-Mormon audiences . . . certainly deserves wider distribution—in part because it shows a talented historian laying open his vulnerabilities, and also because it shows how much any historian lays on the line when he writes about Joseph Smith."

-Dennis Lythgoe, *Deseret News*

"By turns humorous and poignant, this behind-the-scenes look at Richard Bushman's public and private ruminations about Joseph Smith reveals a great deal—not only about the inner life of one of our greatest scholars, but about Mormonism at the dawn of the 21st century."

-Jana Riess, co-author of *Mormonism for Dummies*

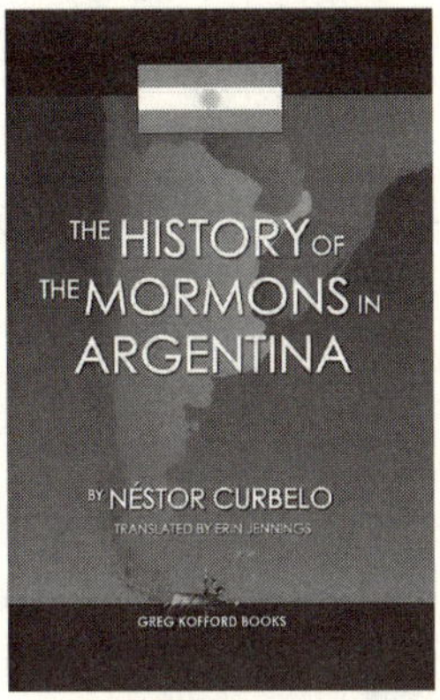

The History of Mormons in Argentina

Néstor Curbelo

English, ISBN: 978-1-58958-052-7
Spanish, ISBN: 978-1-58958-059-6

Originally published in Spanish, Curbelo's The History of the Mormons in Argentina is a groundbreaking book detailing the growth of the Church in this Latin American country.

Through numerous interviews and access to other primary resources, Curbelo has constructed a timeline, and then documents the story of the Church's growth. Starting with a brief discussion of Parley P. Pratt's assignment to preside over the Pacific and South American regions, continuing on with the translation of the scriptures into Spanish, the opening of the first missions in South America, and the building of temples, the book provides a survey history of the Church in Argentina. This book will be of interest not only to history buffs but also to thousands of past, present, and future missionaries.

Translated by Erin Jennings

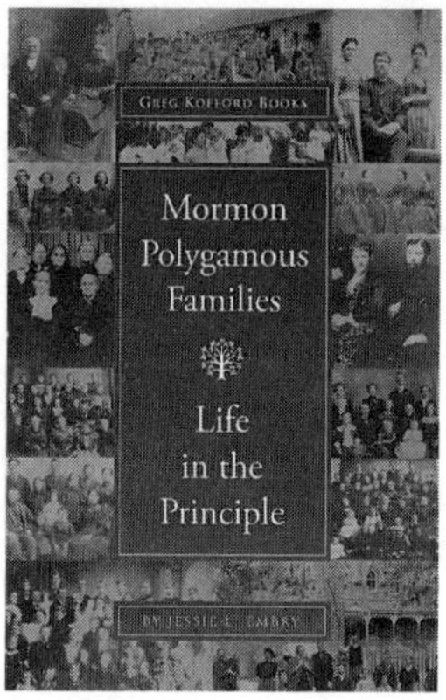

Mormon Polygamous Families: Life in the Principle

Jessie L. Embry

Paperback, ISBN: 978-1-58958-098-5

Mormons and non-Mormons all have their views about how polygamy was practiced in the Church of Jesus Christ of Latter-day Saints during the late nineteenth and early twentieth centuries. Embry has examined the participants themselves in order to understand how men and women living a nineteenth-century Victorian lifestyle adapted to polygamy. Based on records and oral histories with husbands, wives, and children who lived in Mormon polygamous households, this study explores the diverse experiences of individual families and stereotypes about polygamy. The interviews are in some cases the only sources of primary information on how plural families were organized. In addition, children from monogamous families who grew up during the same period were interviewed to form a comparison group. When carefully examined, most of the stereotypes about polygamous marriages do not hold true. In this work it becomes clear that Mormon polygamous families were not much different from Mormon monogamous families and non-Mormon families of the same era. Embry offers a new perspective on the Mormon practice of polygamy that enables readers to gain better understanding of Mormonism historically.

Mormonism and Evolution: The Authoritative LDS Statements

Edited by William E. Evenson and Duane E. Jeffrey

Paperback, ISBN: 978-1-58958-093-0

The Church of Jesus Christ of Latter-day Saints (the Mormon Church) has generally been viewed by the public as anti-evolutionary in its doctrine and teachings. But official statements on the subject by the Church's highest governing quorum and/or president have been considerably more open and diverse than is popularly believed.

This book compiles in full all known authoritative statements (either authored or formally approved for publication) by the Church's highest leaders on the topics of evolution and the origin of human beings. The editors provide historical context for these statements that allows the reader to see what stimulated the issuing of each particular document and how they stand in relation to one another.

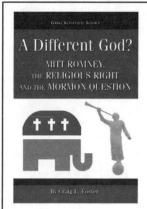

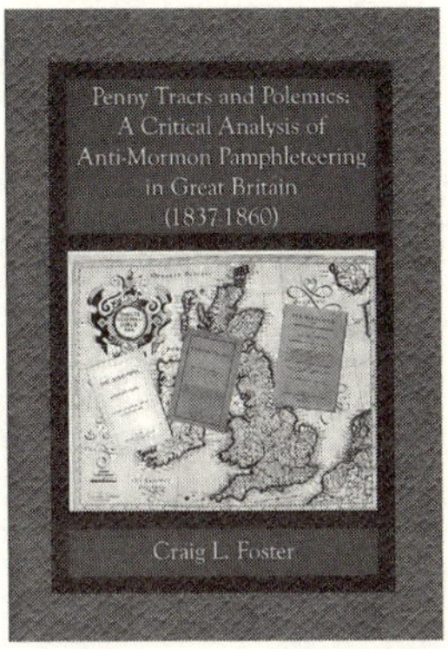

Penny Tracts and Polemics: A Critical Analysis of Anti-Mormon Pamphleteering in Great Britain, 1837–1860

Craig L. Foster

Hardcover, ISBN: 978-1-58958-005-3

By 1860, Mormonism had enjoyed a presence in Great Britain for over twenty years. Mormon missionaries experienced unprecedented success in conversions and many new converts had left Britain's shores for a new life and a new religion in the far western mountains of the American continent.

With the success of the Mormons came tales of duplicity, priestcraft, sexual seduction, and uninhibited depravity among the new religious adherents. Thousands of pamphlets were sold or given to the British populace as a way of discouraging people from joining the Mormon Church. Foster places the creation of these English anti-Mormon pamphlets in their historical context. He discusses the authors, the impact of the publications and the Mormon response. With illustrations and detailed bibliography.

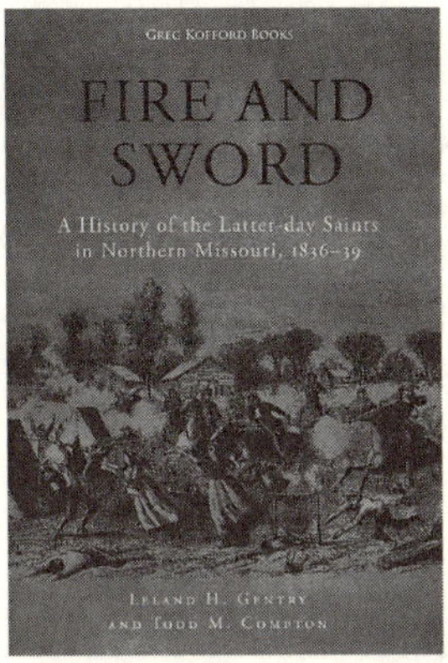

Fire and Sword: A History of the Latter-day Saints in Northern Missouri, 1836-39

Leland Homer Gentry
and Todd M. Compton

Hardcover, ISBN: 978-1-58958-103-6

Many Mormon dreams flourished in Missouri. So did many Mormon nightmares.

The Missouri period—especially from the summer of 1838 when Joseph took over vigorous, personal direction of this new Zion until the spring of 1839 when he escaped after five months of imprisonment—represents a moment of intense crisis in Mormon history. Representing the greatest extremes of devotion and violence, commitment and intolerance, physical suffering and terror—mobbings, battles, massacres, and political "knockdowns"—it shadowed the Mormon psyche for a century.

Leland Gentry was the first to step beyond this disturbing period as a one-sided symbol of religious persecution and move toward understanding it with careful documentation and evenhanded analysis. In Fire and Sword, Todd Compton collaborates with Gentry to update this foundational work with four decades of new scholarship, more insightful critical theory, and the wealth of resources that have become electronically available in the last few years.

Compton gives full credit to Leland Gentry's extraordinary achievement, particularly in documenting the existence of Danites and in attempting to tell the Missourians' side of the story; but he also goes far beyond it, gracefully drawing into the dialogue signal interpretations written since Gentry and introducing the raw urgency of personal writings, eyewitness journalists, and bemused politicians seesawing between human compassion and partisan harshness. In the lush Missouri landscape of the Mormon imagination where Adam and Eve had walked out of the garden and where Adam would return to preside over his posterity, the towering religious creativity of Joseph Smith and clash of religious stereotypes created a swift and traumatic frontier drama that changed the Church.

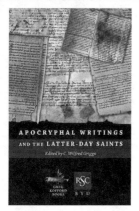

Modern Polygamy and Mormon Fundamentalism: The Generations after the Manifesto

Brian C. Hales

Hardcover, ISBN: 978-1-58958-035-0

Winner of the John Whitmer Historical Association's Smith-Pettit Best Book Award

This fascinating study seeks to trace the historical tapestry that is early Mormon polygamy, details the official discontinuation of the practice by the Church, and, for the first time, describes the many zeal-driven organizations that arose in the wake of that decision. Among the polygamous groups discussed are the LeBaronites, whose "blood atonement" killings sent fear throughout Mormon communities in the late seventies and the eighties; the FLDS Church, which made news recently over its construction of a compound and temple in Texas (Warren Jeffs, the leader of that church, is now standing trial on two felony counts after his being profiled on America's Most Wanted resulted in his capture); and the Allred and Kingston groups, two major factions with substantial membership statistics both in and out of the United States. All these fascinating histories, along with those of the smaller independent groups, are examined and explained in a way that all can appreciate.

Praise for *Modern Polygamy and Mormon Fundamentalism*:

"This book is the most thorough and comprehensive study written on the sugbject to date, providing readers with a clear, candid, and broad sweeping overview of the history, teachings, and practices of modern fundamentalist groups."
—Alexander L. Baugh, Associate Professor of Church History and Doctrine, Brigham Young University

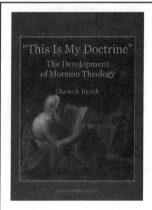

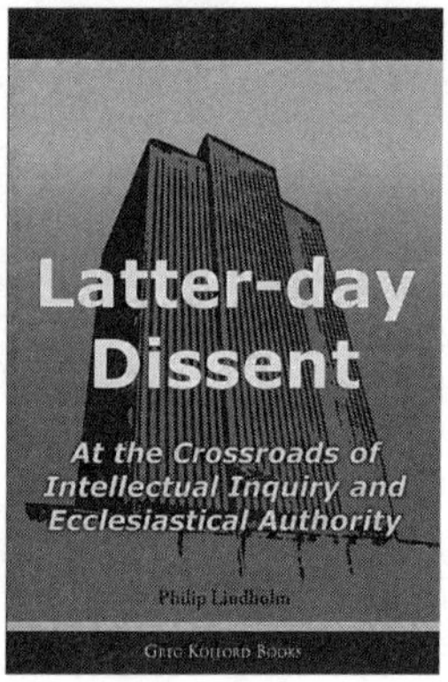

Latter-Day Dissent: At the Crossroads of Intellectual Inquiry and Ecclesiastical Authority

Philip Lindholm

Paperback, ISBN: 978-1-58958-128-9

This volume collects, for the first time in book form, stories from the "September Six," a group of intellectuals officially excommunicated or disfellowshipped from the LDS Church in September of 1993 on charges of "apostasy" or "conduct unbecoming" Church members. Their experiences are significant and yet are largely unknown outside of scholarly or more liberal Mormon circles, which is surprising given that their story was immediately propelled onto screens and cover pages across the Western world.

Interviews by Dr. Philip Lindholm (Ph.D. Theology, University of Oxford) include those of the "September Six," Lynne Kanavel Whitesides, Paul James Toscano, Maxine Hanks, Lavina Fielding Anderson, and D. Michael Quinn; as well as Janice Merrill Allred, Margaret Merrill Toscano, Thomas W. Murphy , and former employee of the LDS Church's Public Affairs Department, Donald B. Jessee.

Each interview illustrates the tension that often exists between the Church and its intellectual critics, and highlights the difficulty of accommodating congregational diversity while maintaining doctrinal unity—a difficulty hearkening back to the very heart of ancient Christianity.

Discourses in Mormon Theology: Philosophical and Theological Possibilities

Edited by
James M. McLachlan and Loyd Ericson

Hardcover, ISBN: 978-1-58958-103-6

A mere two hundred years old, Mormonism is still in its infancy compared to other theological disciplines (Judaism, Catholicism, Buddhism, etc.). This volume will introduce its reader to the rich blend of theological viewpoints that exist within Mormonism. The essays break new ground in Mormon studies by exploring the vast expanse of philosophical territory left largely untouched by traditional approaches to Mormon theology. It presents philosophical and theological essays by many of the finest minds associated with Mormonism in an organized and easy-to-understand manner and provides the reader with a window into the fascinating diversity amongst Mormon philosophers. Open-minded students of pure religion will appreciate this volume's thoughtful inquiries.

These essays were delivered at the first conference of the Society for Mormon Philosophy and Theology. Authors include Grant Underwood, Blake T. Ostler, Dennis Potter, Margaret Merrill Toscano, James E. Faulconer, and Robert L. Millet

Praise for *Discourses in Mormon Theology*:

"In short, *Discourses in Mormon Theology* is an excellent compilation of essays that are sure to feed both the mind and soul. It reminds all of us that beyond the white shirts and ties there exists a universe of theological and moral sensitivity that cries out for study and acclamation."

-Jeff Needle, Association for Mormon Letters

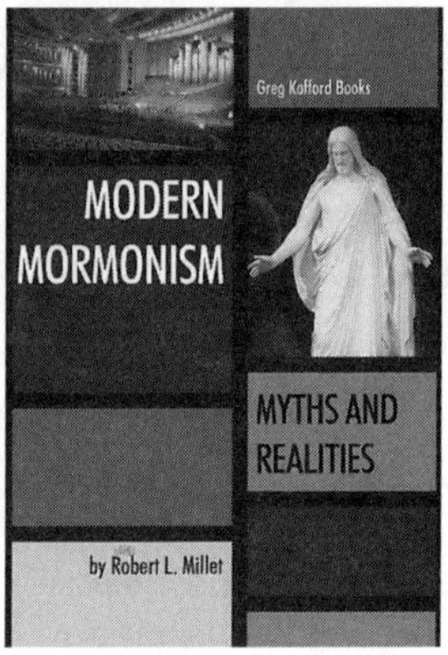

Modern Mormonism: Myths and Realities

Robert L. Millet

Paperback, ISBN: 978-1-58958-127-2

What answer may a Latter-day Saint make to accusations from those of other faiths that "Mormons aren't Christians," or "You think God is a man," and "You worship a different Jesus"? Not only are these charges disconcerting, but the hostility with which they are frequently hurled is equally likely to catch Latter-day Saints off guard.

Now Robert L. Millet, veteran of hundreds of such verbal battles, cogently, helpfully, and scripturally provides important clarifications for Latter-day Saints about eleven of the most frequent myths used to discredit the Church. Along the way, he models how to conduct such a Bible based discussion respectfully, weaving in enlightenment from LDS scriptures and quotations from religious figures in other faiths, ranging from the early church fathers to the archbishop of Canterbury.

Millet enlivens this book with personal experiences as a boy growing up in an area where Mormons were a minuscule and not particularly welcome minority, in one-on-one conversations with men of faith who believed differently, and with his own BYU students who also had lessons to learn about interfaith dialogue. He pleads for greater cooperation in dealing with the genuine moral and social evils afflicting the world, and concludes with his own ardent and reverent testimony of the Savior.

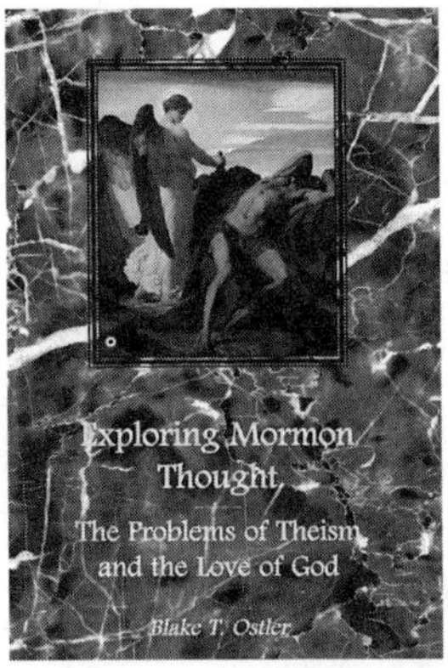

Exploring Mormon Thought Series

Blake T. Ostler

In volume one, *The Attributes of God,* Blake T. Ostler explores Christian and Mormon notions about God. ISBN: 978-1-58958-003-9

In volume two, *The Problems of Theism and the Love of God,* Blake Ostler explores issues related to soteriology, or the theory of salvation. ISBN: 978-1-58958-095-4

In volume three, *Of God and Gods,* Ostler analyzes and responds to the arguments of contemporary international theologians, reconstructs and interprets Joseph Smith's important King Follett Discourse and Sermon in the Grove, and argues persuasively for the Mormon doctrine of "robust deification." ISBN: 978-1-58958-107-4

Praise for the *Exploring Mormon Thought* series:

"These books are the most important works on Mormon theology ever written. There is nothing currently available that is even close to the rigor and sophistication of these volumes. B. H. Roberts and John A. Widtsoe may have had interesting insights in the early part of the twentieth century, but they had neither the temperament nor the training to give a rigorous defense of their views in dialogue with a wider stream of Christian theology. Sterling McMurrin and Truman Madsen had the capacity to engage Mormon theology at this level, but neither one did."

—Neal A. Maxwell Institute, Brigham Young University

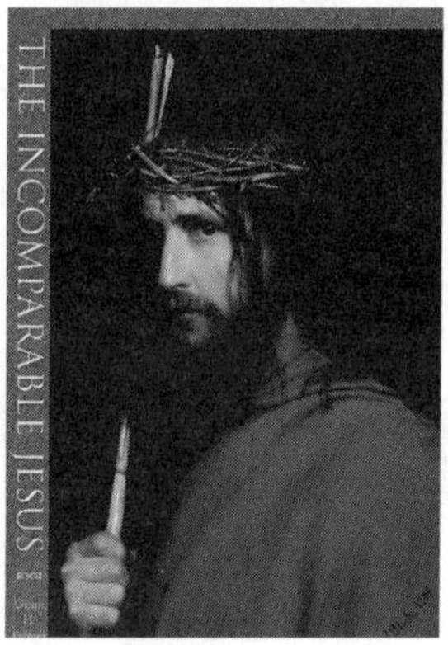

The Incomparable Jesus

Grant H. Palmer

Paperback, ISBN: 978-1-58958-092-3

Distilled from his personal experiences in teaching Jesus to the hard-to-reach, this professional educator has produced a tender testament to the incomparable Jesus. It describes a Savior who walked with him through the halls of the county jail where he served as chaplain, succoring those in need.

In this slim volume, Palmer sensitively shares his understanding of what it means to know Jesus by doing his works. He lists the qualities of divine character attested to by the Apostles Peter and Paul, and also those that Jesus revealed about himself in his masterful Sermon on the Mount, particularly in the beatitudes.

With reverence Palmer shares personal spiritual experiences that were life-changing assurances of Jesus's love for him—a love poured out unstintingly in equally life-changing blessings on prisoners whose crimes had not stopped short of sexual abuse and murder. Reading this book offers a deeper understanding of the Savior's mercy, a stronger sense of his love, and a deeper commitment to follow him.

Hugh Nibley: A Consecrated Life

Boyd Jay Petersen

Hardcover, ISBN: 978-1-58958-019-0

Winner of the Mormon History Association's Best Biography Award

As one of the LDS Church's most widely recognized scholars, Hugh Nibley is both an icon and an enigma. Through complete access to Nibley's correspondence, journals, notes, and papers, Petersen has painted a portrait that reveals the man behind the legend.

Starting with a foreword written by Zina Nibley Petersen and finishing with appendices that include some of the best of Nibley's personal correspondence, the biography reveals aspects of the tapestry of the life of one who has truly consecrated his life to the service of the Lord.

Praise for *A Consecrated Life*:

"Hugh Nibley is generally touted as one of Mormonism's greatest minds and perhaps its most prolific scholarly apologist. Just as hefty as some of Nibley's largest tomes, this authorized biography is delightfully accessible and full of the scholar's delicious wordplay and wit, not to mention some astonishing war stories and insights into Nibley's phenomenal acquisition of languages. Introduced by a personable foreword from the author's wife (who is Nibley's daughter), the book is written with enthusiasm, respect and insight. . . . On the whole, Petersen is a careful scholar who provides helpful historical context. . . . This project is far from hagiography. It fills an important gap in LDS history and will appeal to a wide Mormon audience."

—Publishers Weekly

"Well written and thoroughly researched, Petersen's biography is a must-have for anyone struggling to reconcile faith and reason."

—Greg Taggart, Association for Mormon Letters

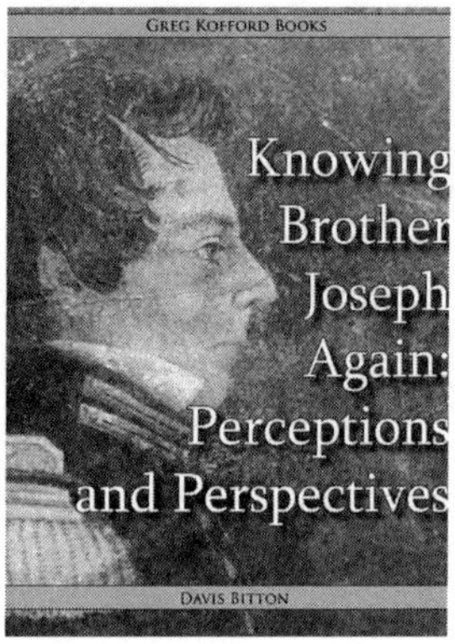

Knowing Brother Joseph Again: Perceptions and Perspectives

Davis Bitton

Hardcover, ISBN: 978-1-58958-123-4

In 1996, Davis Bitton, one of Mormon history's preeminent and much-loved scholars, published a collection of essays on Joseph Smith under the title, *Images of the Prophet Joseph Smith*. A decade later, when the book went out of print, Davis began work on an updated version that would also include some of his other work on the Mormon prophet. The project was only partially finished when his health failed. He died on April 13, 2007, at age seventy-seven. With the aid of additional historians, *Knowing Brother Joseph Again: Perceptions and Perspectives* brings to completion Davis's final work—a testament to his own admiration of the Prophet Joseph Smith.

From Davis Bitton's introducton:

This is not a conventional biography of Joseph Smith, but its intended purpose should not be hard to grasp. That purpose is to trace how Joseph Smith has appeared from different points of view. It is the image of Joseph Smith rather than the man himself that I seek to delineate.

Even when we have cut through the rumor and misinformation that surround all public figures and agree on many details, differences of interpretation remain. We live in an age of relativism. What is beautiful for one is not for another, what is good and moral for one is not for another, and what is true for one is not for another. I shudder at the thought that my presentation here will lead to such soft relativism.

Yet the fact remains that different people saw Joseph Smith in different ways. Even his followers emphasized different facets at different times. From their own perspectives, different people saw him differently or focused on a different facet of his personality at different times. Inescapably, what they observed or found out about him was refracted through the lens of their own experience. Some of the different, flickering, not always compatible views are the subject of this book.

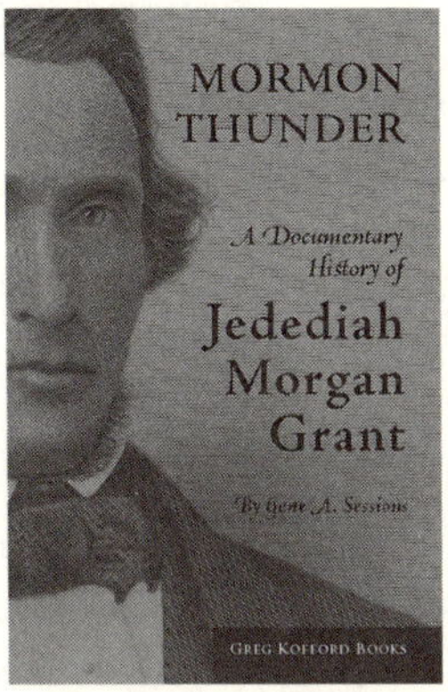

Mormon Thunder: A Documentary History of Jedediah Morgan Grant

Gene A. Sessions

Paperback, ISBN: 978-1-58958-111-1

Jedediah Morgan Grant was a man who knew no compromise when it came to principles—and his principles were clearly representative, argues Gene A. Sessions, of Mormonism's first generation. His life is a glimpse of a Mormon world whose disappearance coincided with the death of this "pious yet rambunctiously radical preacher, flogging away at his people, demanding otherworldliness and constant sacrifice." It was "an eschatological, pre-millennial world in which every individual teetered between salvation and damnation and in which unsanitary privies and appropriating a stray cow held the same potential for eternal doom as blasphemy and adultery."

Updated and newly illustrated with more photographs, this second edition of the award-winning documentary history (first published in 1982) chronicles Grant's ubiquitous role in the Mormon history of the 1840s and '50s. In addition to serving as counselor to Brigham Young during two tumultuous and influential years at the end of his life, he also portentously befriended Thomas L. Kane, worked to temper his unruly brother-in-law William Smith, captained a company of emigrants into the Salt Lake Valley in 1847, and journeyed to the East on several missions to bolster the position of the Mormons during the crises surrounding the runaway judges affair and the public revelation of polygamy.

Jedediah Morgan Grant's voice rises powerfully in these pages, startling in its urgency in summoning his people to sacrifice and moving in its tenderness as he communicated to his family. From hastily scribbled letters to extemporaneous sermons exhorting obedience, and the notations of still stunned listeners, the sound of "Mormon Thunder" rolls again in "a boisterous amplification of what Mormonism really was, and would never be again."

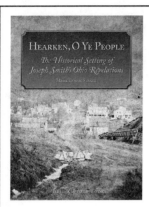

"Let the Earth Bring Forth" Evolution and Scripture

Howard C. Stutz

Paperback, ISBN: 978-1-58958-126-5

A century ago in 1809, Charles Darwin was born. Fifty years later, he published a scientific treatise describing the process of speciation that launched what appeared to be a challenge to the traditional religious interpretation of how life was created on earth. The controversy has erupted anew in the last decade as Creationists and Young Earth adherents challenge school curricula and try to displace "the theory of evolution."

This book is filled with fascinating examples of speciation by the well-known process of mutation but also by the less well-known processes of sexual recombination and polyploidy. In addition to the fossil record, Howard Stutz examines the evidence from the embryo stages of human beings and other creatures to show how selection and differentiation moved development in certain favored directions while leaving behind evidence of earlier, discarded developments. Anatomy, biochemistry, and genetics are all examined in their turn.

With rigorously scientific clarity but in language accessible to a popular audience, the book proceeds to its conclusion, reached after a lifetime of study: the divine map of creation is one supported by both scientific evidence and the scriptures. This is a book to be read, not only for its fascinating scientific insights, but also for a new appreciation of well-known scriptures.

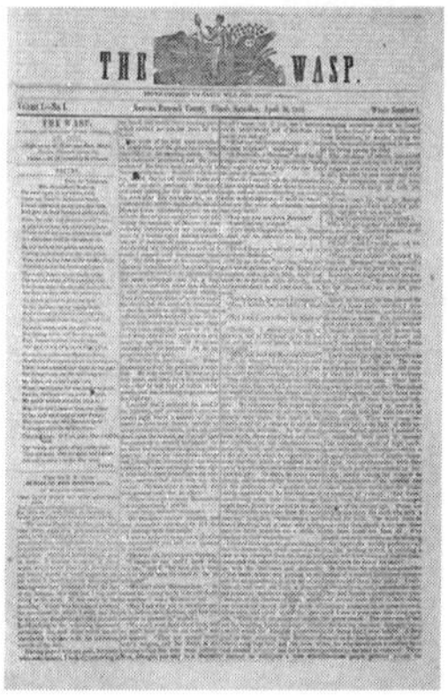
THE WASP.

The Wasp

Hardcover, ISBN: 978-1-58958-050-3

A newspaper published in Nauvoo from April 16, 1842, through April 26, 1843, *The Wasp* provides a crucial window into firsthand accounts of the happenings and concerns of the Saints in Nauvoo. It was initially edited by William Smith, younger brother of Joseph Smith. William was succeeded by John Taylor as editor and Taylor and Wilford Woodruff as printers and publishers. Some of the main stories covered in the newspaper are the August 1842 elections where local candidates endorsed by the Mormons easily won against their opponents, the fall from grace of John C. Bennett, the attempt by the state of Missouri to extradite Joseph Smith as an accessory in the attempted murder of Lilburn W. Boggs, and the Illinois legislature's effort to repeal the Nauvoo charter.

With a foreword by Peter Crawley putting the newspaper in historical context, this first-ever reproduction of the entire run of the *The Wasp* is essential to anyone interested in the Nauvoo period of Mormonism.

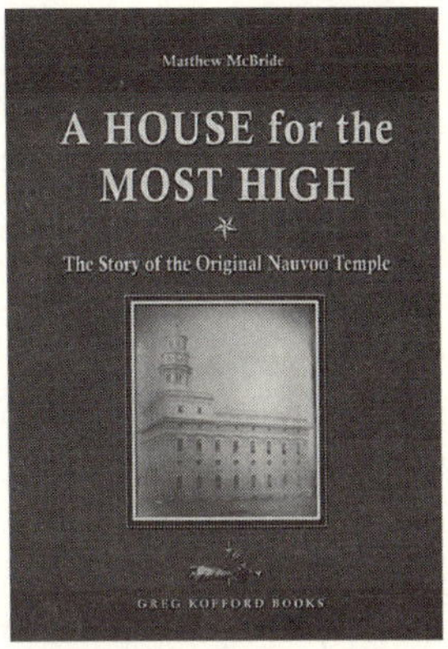

A House for the Most High: The Story of the Original Nauvoo Temple

Matthew McBride

Hardcover, ISBN: 978-1-58958-016-9

This awe-inspiring book is a tribute to the perseverance of the human spirit. *A House for the Most High* is a groundbreaking work from beginning to end with its faithful and comprehensive documentation of the Nauvoo Temple's conception. The behind-the-scenes stories of those determined Saints involved in the great struggle to raise the sacred edifice bring a new appreciation to all readers. McBride's painstaking research now gives us access to valuable first-hand accounts that are drawn straight from the newspaper articles, private diaries, journals, and letters of the steadfast participants.

The opening of this volume gives the reader an extraordinary window into the early temple-building labors of the besieged Church of Jesus Christ of Latter-day Saints, the development of what would become temple-related doctrines in the decade prior to the Nauvoo era, and the 1839 advent of the Saints in Illinois. The main body of this fascinating history covers the significant years, starting from 1840, when this temple was first considered, to the temple's early destruction by a devastating natural disaster. A well-thought-out conclusion completes the epic by telling of the repurchase of the temple lot by the Church in 1937, the lot's excavation in 1962, and the grand announcement in 1999 that the temple would indeed be rebuilt. Also included are an astonishing appendix containing rare and fascinating eyewitness descriptions of the temple and a bibliography of all major source materials. Mormons and non-Mormons alike will discover, within the pages of this book, a true sense of wonder and gratitude for a determined people whose sole desire was to build a sacred and holy temple for the worship of their God.